The Decline of
the Civil Jury

The Decline of
the Civil Jury

Ellen E. Sward
PROFESSOR OF LAW
UNIVERSITY OF KANSAS

CAROLINA ACADEMIC PRESS
Durham, North Carolina

ISBN 0-89089-948-7
LCCN 2001092013

Carolina Academic Press
700 Kent Street
Durham, NC 27701
Telephone (919) 489-7486
Fax (919) 493-5668
www.cap-press.com

Printed in the United States of America

For my parents,
Francis L. and Daisy R. Sword

CONTENTS

PREFACE

This book started out several years ago as an article, but I soon learned that the topic is simply too big to be constrained within the pages of a single article. I also observed that, while much has been written about the civil jury, no one had written a book-length study of it that seeks to bring together all the disparate strands of jury analysis. There are book-length empirical studies of various aspects of the civil jury; there are books that constitute collections of essays or empirical studies on the civil jury; and there are books on the criminal jury, or on "the jury" more generally, with little effort to differentiate the civil from the criminal jury. But there are no recent overviews of the civil jury. Thus, this book fills a niche in jury analysis that is currently unoccupied.

Many people have helped in the production of this book, and I thank all of them for their contributions—which does not make them responsible for any errors I have made. Michael Hoeflich read the book through three times, at various stages of completeness. Other colleagues who read parts of it and offered helpful comments include Bob Casad, David Gottlieb, Rick Levy, Dennis Prater, Paul Schumaker, Sid Shapiro, Jan Sheldon, Tom Stacy, and Larry Wrightsman. I also benefited from comments from participants in a faculty colloquium at the University of Kansas. I had numerous research assistants over the years, including Mike Benkowitz, Suzanne Carey, Brandee Caswell, Amy Fowler, Terri Goodman, Peter Johnston, David McGhee, Jack Mercer, Jason Roth, Nicole Roths, Jan Sandoval, and Rob Vaught. I gratefully acknowledge the support of the University of Kansas General Research Fund and of funding from the University of Kansas School of Law. Finally, I thank my family and friends, who have kept me grounded and helped me become the person I am today.

The Decline of the Civil Jury

INTRODUCTION

Few Americans would question the jury's value in criminal cases, where it serves as an important buffer against governmental power and injects community values into the assessment of culpability. The civil jury is another matter. Alternately glorified and castigated, the civil jury now hangs by a thin, albeit strong, thread—the Seventh Amendment to the United States Constitution.[1] But the civil jury is under attack, and not just by those commentators who make their case aloud. Changes in the civil jury over the last several decades—whether conscious or not—have whittled away at it so that it is but a shell of its former self.[2] There are very good reasons for some of these changes; others are poorly supported either theoretically or empirically. In this book, I will catalogue and analyze the many small changes in the civil jury and show that they add up to a significantly altered civil jury. In this Introduction, I will first outline the differences between civil and criminal juries, then document the decline in the use of the civil jury. I will then describe recent attacks on the civil jury's competence, and finally describe the plan of the book.

I. Civil and Criminal Juries Compared

When Americans think of a jury, they usually think of the criminal jury. Criminal acts are more likely to generate media attention, especially when they concern serious breaches of the public peace or involve celebrities. The trials

---

1. The Seventh Amendment preserves the right to jury trial in civil cases in the federal courts. *See* U.S. CONST., am. VII. Most states also guarantee a right to a civil jury in their constitutions. I will discuss the constitutional right to a civil jury trial in more detail in Chapter 4.

2. *See* Paul D. Carrington, *The Seventh Amendment: Some Bicentennial Reflections*, 1990 U. CHI. LEGAL FORUM 33.

of Timothy McVeigh, Terry Nichols, and O.J. Simpson are good examples. But while civil cases generally are less likely to interest the public, given the right mix of celebrity and subject matter, they, too, can wind up in the public spotlight. The wrongful death case against O.J. Simpson is one example, as is Paula Jones's sexual harassment suit against President Clinton. Civil cases also sometimes generate media attention when they result in huge verdicts for the plaintiff, such as the $144.8 billion verdict in a Florida tobacco class action.[3] Indeed, tobacco and guns have generated a substantial amount of civil litigation recently, including suits by states and municipalities seeking to recover their costs from their citizens' use of such products.[4]

As the O.J. Simpson case shows, the same event can give rise to both civil and criminal cases. There are, of course, some significant differences between civil and criminal matters, reflecting different theoretical bases for the two kinds of cases. The more prominent differences between civil and criminal matters include the societal interest in the matter, the configuration of the parties, the burdens of proof, and the relief granted. Juries in the two kinds of cases also differ in the source of the right to a jury trial, and the powers of the

---

3. *See* Rick Bragg, *Tobacco Lawsuit in Florida Yields Record Damages*, THE NEW YORK TIMES, p. A1 (July 15, 2000). Other recent examples include the multi-billion dollar verdict against Texaco in a suit brought by Pennzoil, *see* Texaco, Inc. v. Pennzoil Co., 729 S.W.2d 768 (Tex. Ct. App. 1987); THOMAS PETZINGER, JR., OIL AND HONOR: THE TEXACO-PENNZOIL WARS (1987); Robert H. Mnookin & Robert B. Wilson, *Rational Bargaining and Market Efficiency: Understanding* Pennzoil v. Texaco, 75 VA. L. REV. 295 (1989); and the case in which a woman who spilled super-heated coffee on herself received a verdict against McDonald's of nearly $3 million, *see* Brad Berliner, *Wrong Message*, CHICAGO TRIBUNE, p. 18 (August 31, 1994); David Rossie, *How About a Hot Cup of Coffee?*, DENVER POST, p. G-05 (August 28, 1994); *Jumpin' Java!*, DALLAS MORNING NEWS, p. 26A (August 25, 1994); *Warning! The Coffee is Hot and Life is Hazardous*, THE COLUMBUS DISPATCH, p. 8A (August 31, 1994). For a discussion of the McDonald's coffee case, see Chapter 1, *infra*, at notes 65–67 and accompanying text.

4. *See* David Segal, *After Tobacco's Success, Lawyers Pick Gun Fight; Same Tactics Aimed at Firearms Industry*, WASHINGTON POST, p. A1 (January 5, 1999), available at 1999 WL 2192231; John Jeter, *Chicago Files Suit Against Gun Makers, Dealers*, WASHINGTON POST, p. A7 (November 13, 1998), available at 1998 WL 22534897; Roberto Suro, *Cities Plan Legal Assault on Makers of Handguns; Tobacco Lawsuits Viewed as Model*, WASHINGTON POST, p. A1 (December 23, 1998), available at 1998 WL 22542661; Joseph P. Fried, *Gun Marketing is Issue in Trial Against Makers*, NEW YORK TIMES, p. A1 (January 6, 1999), available at 1999 WL 9865565; Patrick E. Tyler, *Tobacco Busting Lawyers on New Gold-Dusted Trails*, NEW YORK TIMES, p. A5 (March 10, 1999), available at 1999 WL 9874705; Leslie Wayne, *Gun Makers Learn From Tobacco Fight*, NEW YORK TIMES, p. A4 (December 18, 1997), available at 1997 WL 8017570.

juries. While these differences are important, they are mostly differences of degree.[5]

A. Societal Interest

Crimes are offenses against more than the victims: they offend the public order; they threaten public safety. Crimes violate the fundamental precepts of society—our respect for life, liberty, and property. A criminal tells society that he has no intention of living by its rules. Thus, the whole of society has an interest in bringing criminals to justice. In addition, the community is deeply interested in defining crimes and, in particular, in defining the borders of criminal activity. There are times when justice needs to be tempered with mercy. A criminal trial is, in some sense, a morality play. By contrast, the classic civil case is a relatively simple accident or breach of contract case between two private parties. While such cases are important to the parties and may set precedent that affects others, they are less likely to implicate the fundamental precepts of society.

Nevertheless, some civil cases do have a significant bearing on the fundamental ordering of society. Civil suits have been used to develop civil rights law, from school desegregation[6] to sexual harassment law.[7] I have already noted that civil suits have been used recently to attack the tobacco industry and gun manufacturers. In addition, the government sometimes regulates behavior by giving private parties the right to sue other private parties; antitrust is one example where such private regulatory behavior is common.[8] Even in more mundane matters, civil suits have much to say about societal views of the proper relationships among citizens. For example, civil suits make statements about what is reasonable behavior under a variety of circumstances.[9] Thus,

---

5. *See generally,* Conference Papers, *The Civil-Criminal Distinction,* 7 J. CONTEMP. LEGAL ISSUES 1 (1996) (analyzing the civil-criminal distinction from a variety of perspectives).

6. *See* Brown v. Board of Education of Topeka, 347 U.S. 483 (1954) (holding racial segregation in public schools to be unconstitutional).

7. *See* Meritor Savings Bank FSB v. Vinson, 477 U.S. 57 (1986) (upholding sex discrimination claim based on hostile workplace); Harris v. Forklift Systems, Inc., 114 S. Ct. 367 (1993) (same).

8. *See, e.g.,* 15 U.S.C. § 15 (1997); Brunswick Corp. v. Pueblo Bowl-O-Mat, Inc., 429 U.S. 477 (1977). *See generally,* Louis Michael Seidman, *Points of Intersection: Discontinuities at the Junction of Criminal Law and the Regulatory State,* 7 J. CONTEMP. LEGAL ISSUES 165 (1996) (discussing theoretical difficulties with the overlap of criminal and regulatory law).

9. *See* 1 J.D. LEE AND BARRY LINDAHL, MODERN TORT LAW § 3.04 (rev. ed. 1994).

civil suits can be used to enforce social norms, much as criminal cases do. And civil cases can bring about significant social change, as the school desegregation cases did.

B. The Parties

The government is always the complaining party in criminal cases. Civil cases are usually private disputes between private parties. Nevertheless, the government is often a party to civil litigation as well.[10] Sometimes, rather than relying on private parties, the government brings suit itself to enforce its regulations. At other times, it defends or prosecutes ordinary civil claims like contract or tort actions in its "proprietary" capacity.[11]

C. Burdens of Proof

The burden of proof in a criminal case is proof "beyond a reasonable doubt." It is ultimately up to the jury to decide whether reasonable doubt exists, but the reasonable doubt standard is the highest standard of proof the courts employ, and is, in theory, difficult to meet. Such a high standard is appropriate in criminal cases because the consequences of a conviction are so severe. When we impose a high standard of proof on the government, we are saying, in effect, that we prefer to err on the side of the defendant. In other words, to cite a famous aphorism, we prefer to let ten guilty persons go free rather than convict one innocent one.[12]

By contrast, most civil cases employ the "preponderance of the evidence" standard. Under this standard, if the weight of evidence goes even slightly to the plaintiff's side, the plaintiff should win.[13] This is a much easier burden to

---

10. From October 1, 1995 through September 30, 1996, 269,132 civil cases were commenced in the United States district courts. Of those, 48,755 had the United States as either a plaintiff or a defendant. *See* L. RALPH MECHAM, ADMINISTRATIVE OFFICE OF THE UNITED STATES COURTS, ANNUAL REPORT OF THE DIRECTOR 141 at Table C-3 (1996).

11. *See* Federal Deposit Insurance Corp. v. Harrison, 735 F.2d 408, 411 (11th Cir. 1984) ("Whereas in its sovereign role, the government carries out unique governmental functions for the benefit of the whole public, in its proprietary capacity the government's activities are analogous to those of a private concern."). *See generally,* John F. Conway, Note, *Equitable Estoppel of the Federal Government: An Application of the Proprietary Function Exception to the Traditional Rule,* 55 FORDHAM L. REV. 707 (1987).

12. 4 WILLIAM BLACKSTONE, COMMENTARIES ON THE LAWS OF ENGLAND 352 (Legal Classics Library 1983).

13. The plaintiff should not win if the evidence is evenly balanced.

meet than "beyond a reasonable doubt." This standard allocates the risk of error roughly equally between the parties. The differences in criminal and civil burdens of proof reflect our sense that private civil actions do not normally have consequences as serious as those stemming from a criminal trial.

Some civil cases use an intermediate burden of proof, one that falls somewhere between the preponderance and reasonable doubt standards. Under this standard, the plaintiff must prove her case by "clear and convincing" evidence. This standard is usually employed in cases where public policy suggests that we should be especially cautious in finding liability. An example is fraud, where the consequences of a finding of liability could seriously damage the defendant's reputation.[14] We want, then, to be more certain that fraud exists than we could be under a preponderance standard. The existence of this intermediate burden of proof suggests that some civil cases begin to shade over toward criminal cases.[15]

D. Relief

A criminal defendant who is convicted can be sentenced to prison. He then has a criminal record that can haunt him for the rest of his life. For some categories of murder, he can be sentenced to death. By contrast, civil defendants who are found liable usually have to pay compensatory damages. Civil defendants may also be required to comply with injunctions ordering them to cease doing something damaging, such as polluting a waterway, or to do something for the plaintiff, such as admit her to a school.[16]

Persons convicted of crimes, however, are not always sentenced to prison. Sometimes the punishment is a fine, which can be imposed alone or be accompanied by a prison term. This makes some criminal penalties look much like civil relief, in at least three ways. First, civil liability for compensatory damages

---

14. *See* United States v. American Bell Telephone Co., 167 U.S. 224, 241 (1897); 9 Wigmore on Evidence §2498 (James H. Chadbourn rev. 1981). Of course, if fraud is actually occurring, it is in the public interest to stop it. The use of an intermediate standard of proof in fraud cases could reflect the relative political power of entities that are more likely to be accused of fraud than to be the accuser.

15. The "clear and convincing" standard is also required to establish proof of "actual malice" in libel cases involving a public figure. *See* New York Times v. Sullivan, 367 U.S. 254, 285–86 (1963). This reflects the country's strong support for free expression.

16. *See, e.g.,* Reserve Mining Co. v. Environmental Protection Agency, 514 F.2d 492 (8th Cir. 1975) (upholding injunction against mining company's discharge of carcinogen into Lake Superior); Faulkner v. Jones, 10 F.3d 226 (4th Cir. 1993) (upholding injunction ordering woman admitted to all-male state-supported higher education institution).

can have serious consequences: such damages sometimes amount to a lot of money, and an uninsured or under-insured defendant could be bankrupted by them.[17] While bankruptcy is not the same as a criminal record, it can haunt the debtor for years to come, or even put a corporate debtor out of business. Second, when the government is a party to a civil suit, civil fines or forfeitures may be part of the relief granted.[18] This kind of relief can look much like criminal fines, a point that has led some defendants to claim—usually unsuccessfully, as it turns out—that persons cannot be subjected to both civil fines or forfeitures and criminal proceedings because of the protection against double jeopardy provided for in the Fifth Amendment.[19] Finally, even when both parties are private citizens, punitive damages are sometimes awarded; as the name implies, they are designed to punish—normally a goal of criminal rather than civil law.[20]

---

17. See, e.g., Texaco, Inc. v. Pennzoil Co., 729 S.W.2d 768 (Tex. Ct. App. 1987) (defendant filed for Chapter 11 reorganization in bankruptcy to obtain a stay of execution on a multi-billion-dollar judgment).

18. See Tull v. United States, 481 U.S. 412 (1987) (adjudicating civil fine in Clean Water Act case); Kevin Cole, Civilizing Civil Forfeiture, 7 J. CONTEMP. LEGAL ISSUES 249 (1996) (analyzing relationship between civil forfeiture and crime). Civil forfeiture allows the government to seize property used in criminal activity. See, e.g, Callero-Toledo v. Pearson Yacht Leasing Co., 416 U.S. 663 (1974) (government seized yacht after finding marijuana on board); Goldsmith-Grant Co. v. United States, 254 U.S. 505 (1921) (government seized automobile used in illegal transportation of liquor). See generally, James E. Beaver, Kit G. Navodick & Joseph M. Wallis, Civil Forfeiture and the Eighth Amendment After Austin, 19 SEATTLE U. L. REV. 1 (1995); Monica P. Navarro, Salvaging Civil Forfeiture Under the Drug Abuse and Control Act, 41 WAYNE L. REV. 1609 (1995); Robert Lieske, Civil Forfeiture Law: Replacing the Common Law with the Common Sense Application of the Excessive Fines Clause of the Eighth Amendment, 21 WM. MITCHELL L. REV. 265 (1995). Civil fines may have the same effect as fines in the criminal context, though possibly the stigma is less severe. These procedures suggest substantial blurring of the line between civil and criminal matters.

19. U.S. CONST., am. V. See, e.g., Department of Revenue of Montana v. Kurth Ranch, 114 S. Ct. 1937 (1994) (upholding "tax" of over $200,000 imposed after criminal proceedings on family property on which illegal drugs were found); United States v. One Assortment of 89 Firearms, 465 U.S. 354 (1984) (upholding forfeiture of illegal firearms following criminal proceedings against the owner); One Lot Emerald Cut Stones v. United States, 409 U.S. 232 (1972) (per curiam) (upholding forfeiture of illegally imported gems following criminal proceedings against the owner); United States v. Halper, 490 U.S. 435 (1989) (overturning civil fine of over $130,000 following a criminal conviction when the fine appeared to be punitive rather than remedial). See generally, David S. Rudstein, Civil Penalties and Multiple Punishment Under the Double Jeopardy Clause: Some Unanswered Questions, 46 OKLA. L. REV. 587 (1993).

20. See WILLIAM L. PROSSER, THE LAW OF TORTS 9 (3rd ed. 1964). See generally, Gail Heriot, An Essay on the Civil-Criminal Distinction with Special Reference to Punitive Damages, 7 J. CONTEMP. LEGAL ISSUES 43 (1996).

E. Sources of the Rights to Civil and Criminal Juries

In the federal courts, the rights to criminal and civil juries have different sources. The right to a jury trial in criminal cases is guaranteed in Article III of the Constitution.[21] The Constitution did not initially provide for a civil jury, however, and that was an important reason why some people opposed ratification of the Constitution.[22] By the time the Constitution was ratified, it was widely believed that a Bill of Rights was needed, and the First Congress, in 1789, proposed what are now the first ten amendments to the Constitution.[23] Those ten amendments were ratified in 1791.[24] The Seventh Amendment provides a right to a jury trial in some civil cases,[25] and the Sixth Amendment provides additional rights with respect to criminal jury trials.[26]

---

21. U.S. CONST., art. III, sec. 2, cl. 3. This clause provides:

   The trial of all Crimes, except in Cases of Impeachment, shall be by Jury; and such Trial shall be held in the State where the said Crimes shall have been committed; but when not committed within any State, the Trial shall be at such Place or Places as the Congress may by Law have directed.

22. *See* Charles W. Wolfram, *The Constitutional History of the Seventh Amendment*, 57 MINN. L. REV. 639, 667–73 (1973). Many colonial Americans viewed juries, whether civil or criminal, as essential bulwarks against oppressive power. Some Federalists, however, did not think civil juries were as important under the new government as they had been when colonists were resisting English authority. *See* Chapter 2, *infra*, at note 169 and accompanying text.

23. *See* Resolution of 1789, 1 Stat. 97, 97–98 (Bill of Rights); ROBERT ALLEN RUTLAND, THE BIRTH OF THE BILL OF RIGHTS, 1776–1791, p. 202 (1955).

24. *See id.* at 217.

25. U.S. CONST., am. VII. This Amendment provides:

   In Suits at common law, where the value in controversy shall exceed twenty dollars, the right of trial by jury shall be preserved, and no fact tried by jury, shall be otherwise re-examined in any Court of the United States, than according to the rules of the common law.

For discussions of the interpretation of this Amendment, *see* Chapter 2, *infra*, at notes 171–173 and accompanying text; Chapter 4, *infra*. The second clause of the Amendment, limiting review of jury fact-finding, has been honored more in the breach. *See* Marc E. Sorini, *Factual Malice: Rediscovering the Seventh Amendment in Public Person Libel Cases*, 82 GEO. L.J. 563 (1993); George C. Christie, *Judicial Review of Findings of Fact*, 87 Nw. U.L. REV. 14, 52–53 and n. 156 (1992); Eric Schnapper, *Judges Against Juries—Appellate Review of Federal Civil Jury Verdicts*, 1989 WIS. L. REV. 237. I will be arguing in this book that the first clause has been seriously compromised as well.

26. U.S. CONST., am. VI. This Amendment provides:

   In all criminal prosecutions, the accused shall enjoy the right to a speedy and public trial, by an impartial jury of the State and district wherein the crime shall have been committed, and to be informed of the nature and cause of the accu-

The Supreme Court has held that the Sixth Amendment, which by its terms applies only in federal courts, applies to the states through the due process clause of the Fourteenth Amendment.[27] Thus, criminal defendants have a federal constitutional right to a jury trial in both state and federal courts. The Seventh Amendment, however, has never been held to apply to the states, and so Supreme Court jurisprudence on the right to a civil jury applies only in the federal courts.[28] All of the states, however, provide for both civil and criminal juries either in their constitutions or by statute.

F. Powers of the Civil and Criminal Juries

In most states and the federal system, criminal juries are not responsible for sentencing. In most criminal cases the jury decides guilt or innocence, but does not decide the penalty to be imposed on the guilty. A common, though not universal, exception is the death penalty: juries in many states and the federal system are sometimes asked to decide whether a defendant should be sentenced to death.[29] By contrast, juries in civil cases are responsible not only for deciding liability, but also for deciding on the amount of money damages that a defendant must pay. There are, however, limits to the civil jury's power to decide relief. For example, for historical reasons, civil juries do not decide on equitable relief, such as injunctions.[30] In addition, the Supreme Court has held that civil juries in Clean Water Act cases may decide whether a civil fine is to be imposed, but that the responsibility for determining the amount of the fine rests with the judge.[31] This holding is reminiscent of the allocation of authority between criminal juries and the judge. Even in cases where a civil jury has the

---

sation; to be confronted with the witnesses against him; to have compulsory process for obtaining witnesses in his favor; and to have the Assistance of Counsel for his defence.

The failure of Article III to provide that criminal jury trials would be held in the county in which the alleged crime occurred had also been a source of opposition to the proposed constitution. *See* JEFFREY ABRAMSON, WE, THE JURY: THE JURY SYSTEM AND THE IDEAL OF DEMOCRACY 22–23 (1994).

27. *See* Gideon v. Wainwright, 372 U.S. 335 (1963).

28. *See* Davis v. Edwards, 409 U.S. 1098 (1973) (per curiam).

29. This is illustrated by the Timothy McVeigh and Terry Nichols trials.

30. Injunctions were the province of the English courts of equity, where juries did not operate. For discussions of equity jurisdiction and practice, see Chapter 2, *infra*, at notes 118–145 and accompanying text; Chapter 3, infra, at notes 9–56 and accompanying text; and Chapter 4, *infra*, at notes 4–21 and accompanying text.

31. *See* Tull v. United States, 481 U.S. 412, 425–27 (1987). For a discussion of *Tull*, see Chapter 4, *infra*, at notes 77–94 and accompanying text. The holding in *Tull* is apparently

power to decide the amount of damages, however, the judge has considerable ability to control the ultimate judgment. For example, the judge can use the device of remittitur to lower the amount of the judgment. Remittitur requires a prevailing plaintiff to submit to a new trial unless she is willing to accept an amount less than the jury's verdict.[32] Thus, while civil juries, unlike most criminal juries, have power to determine the relief, they are constrained both by the traditional consignment of the right to determine equitable relief to the judge, and by the power that judges have acquired to control juries' decisions.[33]

Another difference in the powers of the criminal and civil juries is jury nullification, where a jury simply ignores a law it does not like and applies the rule it thinks best.[34] Criminal juries are better able than civil juries to nullify laws because of the constitutional protections afforded to criminal defendants. For example, a defendant could be charged with murder for assisting a suffering relative in suicide, and the jury could acquit out of sympathy for the defendant and his relative, even though the elements of the crime were clearly met. The prosecutor cannot then retry the defendant because of the protection against double jeopardy.[35] Thus, the jury has effectively nullified the law as applied to that defendant. But civil judges have the power to order new trials regardless of which party prevailed in the first trial, and they can do so on the ground, among others, that the verdict was against the great weight of the evidence.[36] In addition, criminal verdicts are always general verdicts: the defendant is either guilty or innocent. Civil verdicts can be broken down so that the jury is required to find specific facts; having found those facts, the jury may or may not be required to apply the law to them.[37] Because they have to

---

limited to fines payable to the government. *See* Feltner v. Columbia Pictures Television, Inc., 523 U.S. 340, 354–55 (1998).

32. For a discussion of remittitur, see Chapter 7, *infra*, at notes 157–161 and accompanying text. Some jurisdictions also permit additur, which is simply the reverse: the judge requires a defendant to submit to a new trial unless he agrees to pay more than the jury's verdict. For a discussion of other ways judges can control juries' decision-making, see Chapter 7, *infra*.

33. For a catalogue of the kinds of control devices judges have at their disposal, see Chapters 6–8, *infra*.

34. *See* Chapter 1, *infra*, at notes 72–108 and accompanying text for a discussion of jury nullification.

35. U.S. CONST., am. V. *See* ABRAMSON, *supra* note 26, at 64.

36. *See, e.g.*, Aetna Casualty & Surety Co. v. Yeatts, 122 F.2d 350 (1941). *See* Chapter 7, *infra*, at notes 154–161 and accompanying text.

37. The devices used are special verdicts and general verdicts with interrogatories. Special verdicts require the jury only to find facts. FED. R. CIV. P. 49(a). The judge then applies the law to the facts. General verdicts with interrogatories ask the jury to apply the law to

find facts specifically, these devices make it more difficult for juries to nullify the law in civil cases, though it is not impossible.

G. Summary

While there are a number of differences between civil and criminal juries, most are a matter of degree rather than of stark contrast. Nevertheless, they provide both theoretical and practical grounds for treating the two kinds of juries differently. Among other things, the scope and depth of control devices that I will describe in this book would be unthinkable for criminal juries, which provide an important buffer between citizens and government authorities — including courts.

II. The Use of the Civil Jury

The use of the civil jury has dropped significantly since 1938, when the Federal Rules of Civil Procedure were promulgated.[38] Indeed, far fewer cases end in trials of any kind. In the two years before promulgation of the Federal Rules, approximately 20% of federal civil cases ended in trials.[39] Table 1 illustrates what has happened since then. By 1995, only 3.2% of civil cases ended in trials. And in most years, fewer than half of all federal civil trials were jury trials. These figures are mirrored in the states, where a 1992 study showed that juries decided about 2% of tort, contract, and real property cases in the state courts

---

the facts it finds, but require it to state what facts it finds. FED. R. CIV. P. 49(b). *See* Chapter 7, *infra*, at notes 172–181 and accompanying text.

38. The Federal Rules of Civil Procedure capped a long reform process in civil procedure, but were nonetheless quite revolutionary in themselves. I discuss some of these revolutionary changes *infra*, at Chapter 3, notes 1–144 and accompanying text; and Chapter 4, notes 22–29 and accompanying text. For general discussions of the revolutionary changes wrought by the Federal Rules, see Douglas Laycock, *Triumph of Equity*, 56 L. & CONTEMP. PROBS. 53 (1993); Stephen F. Subrin, *How Equity Conquered Common Law: The Federal Rules of Civil Procedure in Historical Perspective*, 135 U. PA. L. REV. 909 (1987); Charles E. Clark, *The Federal Rules of Civil Procedure: 1938–1958: Two Decades of the Federal Civil Rules*, 58 COLUM. L. REV. 435 (1958).

39. *See* Stephen C. Yeazell, *The Misunderstood Consequences of Modern Civil Process*, 1994 WIS. L. REV. 631, 633 and n.3. About half of cases in 1938 were "abandoned" — resolved against defendants on default judgments or against plaintiffs for failure to prosecute. *See id.* at 638. That number had dropped to 11% by 1990. *See id.*

Table 1
Use of the Jury in Federal Civil Trials Since 1941
(Five Year Intervals)

Year	Cases Terminated	Total Trials	% of Cases Terminated with Trial	Jury Trials	% of Trials with Jury	% of Terminated Cases Using Jury
1995	229,325	7443	3.2	4126	55.4	1.8
1990	213,429	9263	4.3	4783	51.6	2.2
1985	268,609	12,570	4.7	6278	49.9	2.3
1980	154,985	10,091	6.5	3920	38.8	2.5
1975	103,787	8722	8.4	3512	40.3	3.4
1970	79,466	7975	10.0	3409	42.7	4.3
1965	63,137	7297	11.6	3217	44.1	5.1
1960	61,829	4979	8.1	2479	49.8	4.0
1955	58,974	5239	9.8	2433	46.4	4.1
1950	53,259	5020	9.4	1700	33.9	3.2
1945	52,300	2883	5.5	825	28.6	1.6
1941*	38,561	4524	11.7	2305	32.8	3.8

* First year for which data are available.

Source: Administrative Office of the United States Courts, Annual Reports

of the country's seventy-five most populous counties.[40] A good many of the other 95–98% of cases settle,[41] but more cases are resolved by pre-trial motions today than was the case prior to the Federal Rules.[42] But however the cases are resolved, juries have comparatively less to do now than they did before 1938.

---

40. *See Civil Jury Cases and Verdicts in Large Counties*, Bureau of Justice Statistics Special Report, Civil Justice Survey of State Courts (1992).

41. *See* Marc Galanter and Mia Cahill, *"Most Cases Settle": Judicial Promotion and Regulation of Settlements*, 46 Stan. L. Rev. 1339, 1340 (1994) (saying that two-thirds of civil cases in the federal courts settle). Stephen Yeazell has said that about 34% of cases settle. *See* Yeazell, *supra* note 39, at 638. This disparity could be the result of different methods of counting. A study published in 1986 put the figure closer to two-thirds. *See* Herbert M. Kritzer, *Adjudication to Settlement: Shading in the Gray*, 70 Judicature 161, 164 (1986) (showing that cases "not adjudicated" ranged from 57% to 71% of all state or federal cases).

42. *See* Yeazell, *supra* note 39, at 632–39. *See also* Kritzer, *supra* note 41, at 163 (showing the kinds of motions that must now be considered in order to catalog the kinds of terminations cases can have).

To be sure, most criminal cases are resolved without a trial as well; the plea bargain, the criminal equivalent of a settlement, is the most common kind of resolution.[43] Indeed, if more civil and criminal cases went to trial, our judicial system would be overwhelmed by the workload.[44] Even though only about two per cent of civil cases end in a jury trial, the courts' caseloads have been growing so rapidly that there are still approximately 5000 civil jury trials in the federal courts every year, along with approximately 6000 criminal jury trials.[45] And, as I noted earlier, some of these cases generate considerable media attention. The jury—civil as well as criminal—is more prominent than its relative numbers would suggest.

III. Criticism of the Civil Jury

The jury has had passionate defenders from the earliest days of the republic to the present.[46] More recently, it has had equally vociferous critics. There are two lines to modern criticism of the jury, and both are reflected in the

---

43. *See* L. RALPH MECHAM, ADMINISTRATIVE OFFICE OF THE UNITED STATES COURTS, ANNUAL REPORT OF THE DIRECTOR, 12, T.9 (1990) (showing that approximately 72 per cent of federal criminal cases are resolved by a plea bargain). While 14 per cent of criminal cases are tried, compared to 4–5 percent of civil cases, 78 per cent of criminal trials are jury trials, compared to about 50 per cent of civil cases. *See* Mechem, *supra*, at 155 T.C. 4A.

44. Between 1960 and 1988, civil case filings in federal courts have increased from approximately 51,000 annually to nearly 240,000 annually. Criminal filings have increased from approximately 28,000 to nearly 45,000. *See* 1 FEDERAL COURTS STUDY COMMITTEE: WORKING PAPERS AND SUBCOMMITTEE REPORTS 30, T.5 (1990). *See* Chapter 3, *infra*, at notes 172–180 and accompanying text for a discussion of the "litigation explosion."

45. *See* MECHAM, *supra* note 10, at p. 12, T9, p. 153, T. C4.

46. *See, e.g.,* 15 THOMAS JEFFERSON, THE PAPERS OF THOMAS JEFFERSON 269 (Julian Boyd ed., 1958) ("I consider [the jury] as the only anchor, ever yet imagined by man, by which a government can be held to the principles of it's [sic] constitution."); 1 ALEXIS DeTOCQUEVILLE, DEMOCRACY IN AMERICA 280–87 (New York: Vintage, 1990); LYSANDER SPOONER, AN ESSAY ON THE TRIAL BY JURY (1852); REPORT FROM AN AMERICAN BAR ASSOCIATION/BROOKINGS SYMPOSIUM, CHARTING A FUTURE FOR THE CIVIL JURY SYSTEM (1992) [hereinafter cited as ABA/BROOKINGS REPORT]; various articles collected in VERDICT: ASSESSING THE CIVIL JUSTICE SYSTEM (Robert E. Litan ed., 1993) [hereinafter cited as VERDICT], and in a volume of articles under the heading *The Role of the Jury in Civil Dispute Resolution* at 1990 U. CHI. LEGAL FORUM; STEPHEN J. ADLER, THE JURY: DISORDER IN THE COURT (1994); Hiller B. Zobel, *The Jury on Trial,* 46 AMERICAN HERITAGE 42 (July/August 1995); Irwin A. Horowitz & Thomas E. Willging, *Changing Views of Jury Power: The Nullification Debate, 1787–1988,* 15 L. & HUM. BEHAV. 165 (1991).

work of Jerome Frank, a federal judge and prominent Legal Realist who, in the 1930s and 1940s, wrote extensively on the justice system and expressed dismay at our use of untutored lay decision-makers.[47] One line of criticism simply gives up on the jury, and seeks to minimize its impact; abolition would be preferable for this group of critics, but that would require a Constitutional amendment, considered unlikely.[48] The other line of criticism accepts the jury and sees some value in it, but wants to improve its functioning. This group, therefore, proposes reforms such as allowing jurors to take notes or ask questions; giving juries better instructions and giving those instructions earlier in the process; and making more use of special verdicts, which break down the decision-making task into a series of specific questions.[49] There is considerable overlap in these two groups of critics, as abolitionists would generally favor procedural reforms as a second-best solution. Frank himself appears to overlap the two categories.[50]

Criticism of the civil jury reached a fever pitch during the 1980s, perhaps because opponents of the jury had the ears of the Reagan and Bush Administrations.[51] The criticism, however, was part of a larger "tort reform" movement, pressed most strenuously by the insurance industry, and attacks on the jury itself were often hidden in generic complaints about an alleged radical rise in tort litigation and damage awards.[52] Reformers were especially fond of

---

47. *See* JEROME FRANK, COURTS ON TRIAL 108–25 (1949); JEROME FRANK, LAW AND THE MODERN MIND 170–85 (1930).

48. *See, e.g.,* FRANK, COURTS ON TRIAL, *supra* note 47, at 124–25; Peter Huber, *Junk Science and the Jury,* 1990 U. CHI. LEGAL FORUM 273; Warren E. Burger, *Thinking the Unthinkable,* 31 LOY. L. REV. 205 (1985).

49. *See, e.g.,* Stephen A. Saltzburg, *Improving the Quality of Jury Decisionmaking,* in VERDICT, *supra* note 46; H. Lee Saroking & G. Thomas Munsterman, *Recent Innovations in Civil Jury Trial Procedures,* in VERDICT, *supra* note 46; William W. Schwarzer, *Reforming Jury Trials,* 132 F.R.D. 581 (1991); Saul M. Kassin and Lawrence S. Wrightsman, *On the Requirements of Proof: The Timing of Judicial Instruction and Mock Juror Verdicts,* in IN THE BLACK BOX: CONTROVERSIES IN THE COURTROOM 143 (Lawrence S. Wrightsman, Saul M. Kassin & Cynthia E. Willis eds. 1987).

50. *See* FRANK, COURTS ON TRIAL, *supra* note 47 at 126–45.

51. *See* REPORT OF THE TORT POLICY WORKING GROUP ON THE CAUSES, EXTENT AND POLICY IMPLICATIONS OF THE CURRENT CRISIS IN INSURANCE AVAILABILITY AND AFFORDABILITY (February 1986) [hereinafter cited as REPORT OF THE TORT POLICY WORKING GROUP]; AN UPDATE ON THE LIABILITY CRISIS, TORT POLICY WORKING GROUP (March 1987) [hereinafter cited as UPDATE ON LIABILITY CRISIS]; A REPORT FROM THE PRESIDENT'S COUNCIL ON COMPETITIVENESS, AGENDA FOR CIVIL JUSTICE REFORM IN AMERICA (August 1991).

52. *See, e.g.,* R.H. Malott, *America's Liability Explosion, Can We Afford the Cost?,* 52 VITAL SPEECHES OF THE DAY 180 (1986); William M. McCormick, *The American Tort

telling stories about absurd damage awards by impliedly incompetent juries.[53] The tort reform movement, however, did not focus solely on the rise in damage awards. Reformers, who were most concerned about products liability and medical malpractice, also condemned changes in the substantive law of torts that made it easier for plaintiffs to recover, sometimes urging a return to contract principles under which injured parties could be deemed to have traded away their right to sue.[54]

The tort reform movement generated an equally emphatic response from scholars and from defenders of the system. The more scholarly work shows a tort system that is far more complex and often quite different from the system described by industry spokespersons.[55] The causes of any changes in the tort system are many and varied, and the data themselves need careful evaluation. For example, most scholars argue that reformers have overstated the growth in damage awards by using the mean jury award rather than the median.[56] They argue that most damage awards are quite modest, but that a few extravagant awards skew the mean. Reformers respond that there has been a growth of "million-dollar" awards in recent years, and that those awards affect everything from insurance underwriting to settlement negotiations.[57] There is some truth to both of these positions.

System, A Time to Rebalance the Scales of Justice, 52 VITAL SPEECHES OF THE DAY 267 (1986); JEFFREY O'CONNELL, THE LAWSUIT LOTTERY: ONLY THE LAWYERS WIN (1979); THE LIABILITY MAZE: THE IMPACT OF LIABILITY LAW ON SAFETY AND INNOVATION (Peter W. Huber and Robert E. Litan eds., 1991); WALTER OLSON, THE LITIGATION EXPLOSION: WHAT HAPPENED WHEN AMERICA UNLEASHED THE LAWSUIT (1991); PETER W. HUBER, LIABILITY: THE LEGAL REVOLUTION AND ITS CONSEQUENCES (1988); JEFFREY O'CONNELL AND C. BRIAN KELLY, THE BLAME GAME: INJURIES, INSURANCE, AND INJUSTICE (1987).

53. *See* McCormick, *supra* note 52, at 267; Malott, *supra* note 52, at 180; REPORT OF THE TORT POLICY WORKING GROUP, *supra* note 51, at 32 n.26.

54. *See* HUBER, *supra* note 52 (urging return to contract); O'CONNELL AND KELLY, *supra* note 52; George L. Priest, *The Current Insurance Crisis and Modern Tort Law*, 96 YALE L.J. 1521 (1987).

55. *See, e.g.*, STEPHEN DANIELS AND JOANNE MARTIN, CIVIL JURIES AND THE POLITICS OF REFORM (1995); NEIL VIDMAR, MEDICAL MALPRACTICE AND THE AMERICAN JURY (1995); Michael J. Saks, *Do We Really Know Anything About the Behavior of the Tort Litigation System—And Why Not?*, 140 U. PA. L. REV. 1147 (1992); Joseph Sanders and Craig Joyce, *Off to the Race: The 1980s Tort Crisis and the Law Reform Process*, 27 HOUS. L. REV. 207 (1990).

56. *See, e.g.*, DANIELS AND MARTIN, *supra* note 55, at 51–57 (describing debate over use of mean vs. median).

57. *See* UPDATE ON LIABILITY CRISIS, *supra* note 51, at 32–41.

Some of the critics of tort reform have made quite devastating attacks on the scholarship, and sometimes the industry ties, of the reformers.[58] At the same time, however, some critics of the reformers commit the same sins as the least scholarly of the reformers.[59] Reformers and their critics alike often resort to anecdotal "evidence," sometimes distorting the anecdotes in the process.[60] This horror story approach to the debate is not helpful. It is clear that we need more dispassionate study of the jury if we are to understand it. The jury is not perfect, but neither is it the uncontrolled monster that tort reformers have so often portrayed. Throughout this book, I will discuss in more detail some of the criticisms of the jury that reformers have made, drawing on empirical research where that is available. While the research cannot definitively answer all of the questions that we would like to answer, it should give us pause before we institute "reforms" that undermine the jury.

IV. The Plan of the Book

The plan of the book is as follows. Part I lays the foundation for the portrait of the modern civil jury. I begin with a chapter that explores the reasons for the civil jury. I identify four overlapping roles for the civil jury: a dispute-resolution role; a law-making role; a political role; and a socializing role. Most of these are problematic for one reason or another, but I conclude that they all have a place in our jurisprudence of the jury. In particular, I note that the jury is our only political institution that can require citizens to come together and deliberate about important societal issues. That deliberation touches on all of the jury's roles. Thus, Chapter 1 sets the theme for the book and provides a base against which we can measure the changes that have occurred in the jury's jurisprudence, structure, and operation in the last few decades.

---

58. *See, e.g.,* DANIELS AND MARTIN, *supra* note 55, at ch. 1 (discussing reformers and critics); Mark M. Hager, *Review Essay: Civil Compensation and Its Discontents: A Response to Huber*, 42 STAN. L. REV. 539 (1990) (reviewing HUBER, *supra* note 52); Kenneth J. Chesebro, *Galileo's Retort: Peter Huber's Junk Scholarship*, 42 AM. U. L. REV. 1637 (1993) (reviewing PETER W. HUBER, GALILEO'S REVENGE: JUNK SCIENCE IN THE COURTROOM); Peter A. Bell, *Analyzing Tort Law: The Flawed Premise of NeoContract*, 74 MINN. L. REV. 1177 (1990) (criticizing Huber).

59. *See* HARVEY WACHSMAN, LETHAL MEDICINE: THE EPIDEMIC OF MEDICAL MALPRACTICE IN AMERICA (1993). *See generally,* DANIELS AND MARTIN, *supra* note 55, at 246–48 (criticizing Wachsman).

60. *See* DANIELS AND MARTIN, *supra* note 55, at 4–5, 43–46, 246–48 (discussing use of anecdotes).

To further set the stage, I briefly describe, in Chapter 2, the first nine hundred years or so of the jury's history. In Chapter 3, I then consider a number of changes in the civil jury's milieu that have had a significant impact on its recent development. In civil procedure, our system has come to look more like equitable procedure, where there was no jury trial, than like common law procedure, where there was. The jury also has been associated with the adversary system of adjudication, and the system has become much less adversarial. Our legal system as a whole has become more bureaucratic, with the rise of administrative agencies. Juries do not operate in these agencies. The legal system has also been overwhelmed by a huge increase in litigation in the last few decades, prompting courts to search out ways of expediting the resolution of disputes. Such expedition is not always compatible with a jury trial. In addition, there is simply more knowledge and information afloat today, and thus not only more to litigate about, but more complicated matters that are beyond the ken of the average jury.

Substantive developments in law also have a bearing on the jury's recent development. The complexity of modern society demands more certainty in legal development, so that the various economic actors can plan their activities with some degree of confidence in their legality. But one of the jury's virtues is its flexibility—a virtue sometimes incompatible with certainty. One way the law has become more certain is through codification. The jury is a product of the common law, where law was made by judges and sometimes juries in case-by-case development. Today, however, a large proportion of our law is statutory. Finally, the country is much more diverse than it was, and the modern jury reflects that diversity. While it is undeniably important to have broad representation on juries, that diversity may make it more difficult for juries to reach unanimous decisions.

Part II of the book then describes the recent changes in the civil jury that make it a less significant actor in our judicial system. I begin, in Chapter 4, with the Supreme Court's decisions with respect to the constitutional right to a jury trial. While the Supreme Court's jurisprudence on civil juries suggests at first glance that the jury's role is expanding beyond what it was at common law, a closer look shows that the jury's relative role in American law has shrunk. In particular, the Court has permitted Congress to create whole classes of tribunals where juries do not operate—most notably, administrative agencies. More cases are now adjudicated in federal administrative agencies every year than in the federal courts.

As I show in Chapter 5, the jury has also been signficantly redefined in recent years. The traditional jury trial in both civil and criminal cases required a unanimous verdict by a jury of twelve persons. Until very recently in this country, those twelve persons were almost inevitably white males; early in the country's history, those white males usually had to have a minimum of property. Over the last two decades, however, the Supreme Court has come to permit juries of fewer than twelve persons. Some states allow nonunanimous verdicts in their courts, though the federal courts still require unanimous verdicts unless the parties stipulate to a less than unanimous jury verdict. In addition, several recent Supreme Court decisions help to ensure that juries are broadly reflective of the general population. Women and racial minorities can no longer be systematically excluded from juries. These changes have significantly altered the face of the jury, in both civil and criminal cases. One result is that the jury may be more representative of the general population than are other institutions of government, where there may be subtle but important constraints on the ability of some subgroups of the population to participate, or where apathy keeps some people out of politics. But smaller juries operating with a non-unanimous decision rule could negate those gains.

Perhaps the most important evidence of the civil jury's shrinking role is the growth and refinement, over the last several decades, of numerous ways of controlling the jury. Some of these devices have medieval origins, although control of the jury was not necessarily the reason for their initial development. There are several classes of jury control devices. First, evidentiary controls may limit what evidence the jury can hear, or inject the judge into the jury's decision-making process by requiring her to instruct the jury on the law and allowing her to comment on the evidence. These kinds of controls will be discussed in Chapter 6.

Decision-making controls on the civil jury have an even greater impact on the ability of the jury to exercise independent judgment. These kinds of controls include the assignment of questions of law to the judge for decision, even though the difficulty of distinguishing between fact and law means that the judge may sometimes usurp the jury's fact-finding function; the use of such procedural devices as judgment as a matter of law, summary judgment, special verdicts, and the new trial; developments in the law of preclusion that make it possible for a judge's fact-finding in an equitable case to prevent a jury trial on the same factual issue in a subsequent legal case;[61] and the imposition of caps on the amount of damages that juries can award. These kinds of decision-making controls will be discussed in more detail in Chapter 7.

Finally, judges and litigants have more tools available for avoiding trial altogether, which incidentally reduces the number of jury trials. These include the greater power of the judge to cajole the parties into settlement; and the

---

61. Preclusion prevents the relitigation of cases or issues that have been decided, or should have been decided, in a previous case. *See* Chapter 7, *infra*, at notes 242–263 and accompanying text.

use of alternative dispute resolution, in or out of the courts, sometimes under compulsion. These avoidance methods will be discussed in Chapter 8.

I conclude by arguing that while each of these developments in the law governing civil jury trials is, by itself, not of much consequence, in combination they add up to significant constraints on the jury's functioning. Thus, while we continue to extol the jury's virtues, the jury is but a shadow of its former self. External pressures on the jury, such as I describe in Chapter 3, are probably too great for us to expect, or even to desire, a great resurgence in the civil jury. But the civil jury has virtues that no other political institution in the country has, and we need to understand those virtues and the threats to their realization that come from recent developments in the civil jury. We also need to search for ways to preserve those virtues, whether through the civil jury or through other governmental and societal institutions. I hope that this book will be a step toward those modest goals.

PART I

Theoretical and Historical Frameworks

The civil jury has a nearly thousand year history, and that alone gives it stature: few human institutions have lasted so long. The jury's resilience is all the more remarkable considering that the legal and political systems into which it was born have changed so dramatically in those thousand years. And during those thousand years, the jury has survived numerous attacks, often emerging stronger than it was before. What is it about this institution that gives it such staying power? And, more importantly, can it continue to survive?

Like many political and legal institutions, the jury's very reason for being has changed over the years. While some institutions outlive their usefulness, we can still find good reasons for using a jury in civil cases. Nevertheless, the pace of legal, political, and social change has escalated in the last century, and there are many more pressures on the civil justice system to abandon the jury. That, I think, would be a mistake. In this Part, I will begin to explain that conclusion.

CHAPTER 1

WHY THE CIVIL JURY?

Apologists for the civil jury—and I count myself among the many—must offer justifications for it that make sense in the modern dispute-resolution milieu, but must also suggest ways to preserve the civil jury's valued characteristics. In this Chapter, I will first describe briefly some of the justifications that modern commentators have offered for the civil jury. I will then describe in some detail four roles that I see the civil jury playing in modern society: the dispute-resolution role, the law-making role, the political role, and the socializing role. In Part II of the book, I will assess the changes in the civil jury against these four roles.

I. Modern Justifications for the Civil Jury

In early United States history, the civil jury was just as important a guarantor of freedom as the criminal jury. Both aided resistance to British oppression by refusing to support British authority in colonial matters.[1] The jury as guarantor of freedom continues to be a popular theme, but modern commentators seek other justifications for the civil jury as well. A recent symposium on the civil jury system sponsored by the American Bar Association and the Brookings Institution collected some of the modern justifications and reported them in a booklet that is strongly supportive of the civil jury.[2] The jus-

---

1. For a more detailed account of early American use of the jury, see Chapter 2.

2. *See* REPORT FROM AN AMERICAN BAR ASSOCIATION/BROOKINGS SYMPOSIUM, CHARTING A FUTURE FOR THE CIVIL JURY SYSTEM (1992) [hereinafter cited as ABA/BROOKINGS REPORT]. The Symposium papers are collected in VERDICT: ASSESSING THE CIVIL JURY SYSTEM (Robert E. Litan ed., 1993) [hereinafter cited as VERDICT]. *See also,* Douglas G. Smith, *Structural and Functional Aspects of the Jury: Comparative Analysis and Proposals for Reform,* 48 ALA. L. REV. 441, 469–89 (1997) (describing the advantages of the jury as expressing popular sovereignty, barring governmental abuse and abuse by lawyers, educating the citizenry, legitimating the justice system, injecting common sense into the adjudicatory process, and simplifying the law). Other collections of articles on the civil jury include *The*

tifications are (1) that the jury is a good decision-maker; (2) that the jury offers protection against abuse of power by various governmental entities; (3) that the jury gives voice to community values; (4) that the jury helps check the bureaucratization of the judiciary; (5) that the jury helps to legitimate the official dispute resolution processes by making ordinary citizens a part of them; and (6) that the jury system helps to educate citizens in the workings of the judiciary and the duties of citizenship.[3]

Marc Galanter, a participant in the ABA/Brookings conference, sees the primary role of the jury as regulatory: even though jury verdicts represent only a small proportion of civil case resolutions, litigants are always thinking about what a jury will do, and they negotiate settlements in the shadow of the jury.[4] Galanter calls this "litigotiation."[5] Thus, jury verdicts have effects on the litigation process far beyond the specific cases in which they are rendered. They help parties in other lawsuits make rational settlement decisions.

Of course, this would be true no matter who the decision-maker was. Thus, it is necessary to justify the decision to use a jury rather than a judge. George Priest argues that juries have several characteristics that make them particularly good decision-makers for some kinds of cases. Juries are diverse bodies of lay people, whose ability to represent the sense of the community is high; each jury sits for only one case, and thus is protected from the consequences of a controversial decision; and juries are "aresponsible," in the sense that they do not justify their decision, which is a valuable characteristic when conflict-

---

Role of the Jury in Civil Dispute Resolution, 1990 U. CHI. LEGAL FORUM 1; and *Symposium: The American Civil Jury: Illusion and Reality*, 48 DePAUL L. REV. 197 (1998).

3. *See* ABA/BROOKINGS REPORT, *supra* note 2, at 8–11. George Priest argues that the education function of the civil jury is no longer needed because ours is a mature democracy whose citizens understand the government and their role as citizens. *See* George L. Priest, *Justifying the Civil Jury*, in VERDICT, *supra* note 2, at 126–27 [hereinafter cited as Priest, *Justifying*]; George L. Priest, *The Role of the Civil Jury in a System of Private Litigation*, 1990 U. CHI. LEGAL FORUM 161. But given the apathy that so many citizens display, both as to voting and as to jury service, that assessment seems questionable. *See infra*, Chapter 5, at notes 182–188 for a discussion of citizen avoidance of jury service.

4. *See* Marc Galanter, *The Regulatory Function of the Civil Jury*, in VERDICT, *supra* note 2, at 61–102 [hereinafter cited as Galanter, *Regulatory Function*]; Marc Galanter, *The Civil Jury as Regulator of the Litigation Process*, 1990 U. CHI. LEGAL FORUM 201 [hereinafter cited as Galanter, *Civil Jury as Regulator*]. *See also* Peter H. Schuck, *Mapping the Debate on Jury Reform*, in VERDICT, *supra* note 2, at 307 (saying that an important function of the jury is to shape the parties' predictions about what will happen if the case goes to trial).

5. *See* Galanter, *Regulatory Function*, *supra* note 4, at 61; Galanter, *Civil Jury as Regulator*, *supra* note 4, at 201.

ing social norms are at stake.[6] Priest concludes that juries serve important functions when cases involve "complex or conflicting societal values, political issues, or the government as plaintiff or defendant."[7] He does not see the value of the jury in routine tort cases, such as traffic accident cases.[8] As I will show in Chapter 4, however, it is the routine cases where the right to a civil jury trial seems to have the most protection.

These justifications range from the mundane to the profound. It is one thing to say that the jury should be used because it is a good decision-maker. It is quite another thing to say that the jury should be used because it is the ideal body for sorting out conflicting societal values. The latter gives the jury a role that goes beyond mere dispute-resolution. In the next four sections, I will attempt to sort out the various roles that the civil jury plays.

II. The Dispute-Settling Role of the Civil Jury

The basic purpose of any civil justice system is to resolve private disputes. In the absence of an officially-sanctioned system for civil dispute resolution, disputants may engage in self-help, which could result in a breach of the peace. But this justification for an officially-sanctioned dispute resolution system does not tell us anything about how those disputes should be resolved, or who should resolve them. In this section, I will consider the reasons why we might favor a jury for civil disputes, using the justifications for the jury in criminal "dispute-settling" as a baseline. I will also discuss the inherent limits on the jury's competence in civil matters.

A. Why a Jury for Resolving Civil Cases?

Very few people today would argue that we should abolish the jury in criminal cases. There are those, however, who would abolish or eviscerate the civil

---

6. *See* Priest, *Justifying, supra* note 3, at 124–26. Priest, borrowing from Guido Calabresi and Philip Bobbitt, gives the example of having to choose which of two persons will receive kidney dialysis. Other governmental institutions are ill-suited to making such decisions because they are required to justify the unjustifiable. *See* Priest, *supra*, at 107–08, citing Guido Calabresi and Philip Bobbitt, Tragic Choices 17–19, 186–89, 57–64 (1978).

7. Priest, *Justifying, supra* note 3, at 131.

8. *See id* at 124–26.

jury.[9] The question is whether the differences between civil and criminal juries warrant such different views as to the jury's value. I showed in the Introduction that the line between civil and criminal juries is quite blurred.[10] In this section, I will show that criminal and civil cases are similar in ways that make the jury an appropriate decision-maker in both kinds of cases. I consider two aspects of criminal and civil dispute resolution: the public nature of the dispute, and the need for an equalizing force when the parties are unequal in wealth or power.

1. The Public Nature of Criminal and Civil Dispute Resolution

Crimes are generally regarded as offenses against not only the victim, but the public as a whole. Victims of crimes are witnesses, but they are not re-

---

9. See JEROME FRANK, COURTS ON TRIAL (1949); Peter Huber, *Junk Science and the Jury,* 1990 U. CHI. LEGAL FORUM 273; Warren E. Burger, *Thinking the Unthinkable,* 31 LOY. L. REV. 205 (1985). The distinction between civil and criminal law was some time in the making. See THEODORE F.T. PLUCKNETT, A CONCISE HISTORY OF THE COMMON LAW 421–23 (5th ed. 1956); 2 FREDERICK POLLOCK & FREDERIC WILLIAM MAITLAND, THE HISTORY OF ENGLISH LAW 572-73 ([1968] 1898). Early in English legal history, it probably made more sense than it does now to talk about resolving criminal "disputes." The aggrieved person was responsible for bringing a criminal charge, and was even authorized to avenge the crime by killing the perpetrator. PLUCKNETT, *supra,* at 425. The guilt or innocence of the alleged criminal was then determined when the avenger defended himself in court. *Id.* A crime, then, was seen as a dispute between the alleged criminal and the victim, to be resolved largely as a personal matter. As the law evolved, the Crown took an interest in both civil and criminal matters, and guilt or innocence was established in some sort of trial. Early common law "trials" were often ordeals or battle. See Chapter 2, *infra,* at notes 19–32 and accompanying text. Persons found guilty of crimes would forfeit their property, see PLUCKNETT, *supra,* at 536, but even civil defendants who were found liable might have to pay fines to the king. *Id.* at 455. The distinction between civil and criminal law was not, then, more than a matter of degree. It was particularly difficult in medieval times to distinguish between crimes and torts. *Id.* at 421–23.

10. In addition to the matters described in the Introduction, the lines between criminal and civil cases are being blurred by such developments as the victims' rights movement in criminal law. See generally, JAMES A. RAPP AND FRANK CARRINGTON, VICTIMS' RIGHTS: LAW AND LITIGATION (1991); Ellen Yaroshefsky, *Balancing Victims' Rights and Vigorous Advocacy for the Defendant,* 1989 ANN. SURV. AM. L. 135. The victims' rights movement allows victims of crimes to be involved in the prosecution of the crime in ways not contemplated for many centuries. Some victims' rights provisions allow victims to be informed about and even to participate in decisions about plea agreements. See Sarah N. Welling, *Victim Participation in Plea Bargainings,* 65 WASH. U.L.Q. 301 (1987). Victims also often participate in sentencing hearings by testifying about the impact of the crime on them. See Karen L. Kennard, *The Victim's Veto: A Way to Increase Victim Impact on Criminal Case Dispositions,* 77 CAL. L. REV. 417, 422–37 (1989).

sponsible for bringing charges; the prosecutor makes that decision.[11] Criminal cases generally name either the "people" or the governmental entity whose laws were allegedly violated as the "plaintiff." There are "disputes" to be resolved in criminal cases—whether the accused committed the crime he is charged with, for example—but the premise of criminal law is that the victim is not the only person aggrieved by a criminal act.

There are at least two senses in which a criminal matter can be considered public. First, the public accrues considerable benefit from having a criminal law enforced by the state. Criminal law helps to keep the peace by announcing what conduct is unacceptable in this society, and by deterring conduct deemed unacceptable. In addition, the punishment meted out by the criminal law helps to give people a sense of justice served—those who violate society's fundamental precepts will forfeit some of their rights as citizens. Second, crimes are by their very nature public. As noted, they involve a breach of the fundamental precepts of society: the sanctity of life, the significance of private property, the importance of resolving disputes without resort to violence. A person who commits a crime is telling us that she does not choose to live by the civilizing rules of society. This strikes at the very heart of the polity.

Of course, we must also recognize a significant private element in crimes: private citizens are most often the victims of crimes, and the victims suffer immediate and often severe injuries, whether physical, financial, or psychic. This private element of criminal behavior is what the victims' rights movement, with its increased opportunities for victims to participate in the trial and sentencing of defendants, recognizes.[12] The injuries to the public are more symbolic, but symbolism is an essential part of government, especially democratic government.[13] Moreover, the injuries to the polity could become more concrete if criminal transgressions continually went unpunished, as the fabric of society could well break down.

It is this public character of crime that forms one of the major justifications for using juries in criminal cases. Simply put, the aggrieved public should par-

---

11. As a practical matter, it will be difficult for a prosecutor to bring charges if the victim refuses to cooperate. This is one reason why it has been so difficult to prosecute domestic violence cases. *See* Cheryl Hanna, *No Right to Choose: Mandated Victim Participation in Domestic Violence Prosecutions*, 109 Harv. L. Rev. 1849, 1853 (1996); A.M. Keith, *Domestic Violence and the Court System*, 15 Hamline L. Rev. 105, 108–09 (1991).

12. *See supra*, note 10. There are also some provisions for victims to be compensated, usually out of a public fund established for that purpose. *See, e.g.*, Ala. Code §65-23-16 (1992); Ga. Code Ann. §17-15-1 (1990); Tex. Code Crim. Proc. Ann. art. 56.54 (West 1979) (Supp 1997).

13. *See* Murray Edelman, The Symbolic Uses of Government (1964).

ticipate in the resolution of the charges. If crime is a breach of society's fundamental precepts, members of the public should be well suited to deciding criminal matters. This includes not only whether the accused has committed the crime, but also, if he has, the seriousness of the breach. Whether the accused has committed the crime can be a question of fact, but it can even implicate more fundamental questions, such as whether the act he has been accused of should be a crime.[14] As for the seriousness of the breach, juries can decide how culpable the accused's conduct is by settling on one of several degrees of crime, by finding the accused guilty of a lesser included offense,[15] or by finding the accused guilty of some, but not all, of the crimes he is charged with.[16]

In criminal cases, then, the jury has a role to play because the "dispute" goes beyond resolving what happened. The jury plays a social regulator role by judging the severity of the accused's breach of the public order, or even, on occasion, whether the accused's conduct constitutes a breach of the public order at all. In other words, it is important to have a measure of community values in judging the accused, and the jury provides that. The question for us is whether these factors provide justifications for using juries to resolve civil disputes.

Most civil cases concern private disputes between private parties. The public interest is, arguably at least, less strongly implicated in such disputes. The very fact that the conduct complained of in civil cases has not been criminalized suggests that it does not involve the fundamental precepts of society. One

---

14. Some commentators support the jury's right to "nullify" the law in criminal cases by finding the accused not guilty of a crime he clearly committed but that is excused, in the jury's eyes, on some otherwise unrecognized ground, or by finding the accused not guilty of a crime that the jury thinks should not be a crime. *See, e.g.*, JEFFREY ABRAMSON, WE THE JURY: THE JURY SYSTEM AND THE IDEAL OF DEMOCRACY, ch. 2 (1994). The ground for this is that the people, represented by the jury, are best equipped to decide whether the law should be enforced in a particular case. I will discuss jury nullification in more detail in section II, *infra.*

15. For example, in Kansas, it is error not to instruct the jury on lesser included offenses on which the defendant may be convicted. *See* State v. Cummings, 242 Kan. 84, 91 (1987) (applying KAN. STATE. ANN. § 21-3107(3) (1995), which imposes an affirmative duty on trial judges to instruct the jury as to lesser included offenses). A lesser included offense is a less serious variation of the crime the defendant is charged with. For example, a defendant could be charged with first degree murder, but found guilty of a lesser charge such as second degree murder or manslaughter.

16. The United States Supreme Court has held that a jury can convict on one of three charges even if acquitting on the other two is inconsistent with the conviction. *See* Dunn v. United States, 284 U.S. 390 (1931).

might ask, then, why private citizens should be required to spend time and energy helping other private citizens resolve private disputes. To ask the question that way, however, ignores the very real public interest in having a state-sanctioned system for private dispute resolution. It also draws too stark a line between the public and the private.

Providing a court system for the adjudication of private disputes is one of the functions of government. Having such a system benefits everyone, just as having a system for criminal adjudication benefits everyone. It certainly benefits those citizens who find themselves involved in a dispute that they cannot resolve without authoritative help. But it also benefits those citizens who never make use of the adjudicatory services of the state, because without an authoritative resolution of such disputes, the disputants may well engage in self-help, resulting in a breach of the peace. In addition, the knowledge that the system is in place should they ever need it is a benefit to all citizens, and may even guide them in resolving their disputes outside the system.[17] Thus, there are generalizable public benefits from a system of civil dispute resolution and in this sense civil disputes have much in common with criminal.

In addition to the general public benefit that accrues simply from having a system of civil dispute resolution, civil disputes are similar to criminal because civil disputes are never entirely private. Civil laws order society just as criminal laws do. Furthermore, as I showed in the Introduction, civil disputes sometimes concern matters of substantial public interest. Civil suits have been used to outlaw racial segregation in the public schools and to establish a right to be free from sexual harassment in schools and workplaces. Private citizens and the government alike use civil suits to adjudicate regulatory matters such as responsibility for environmental disasters, alleged antitrust violations, and securities fraud. Civil suits are currently being used to challenge the tobacco industry and gun manufacturers. The importance of such matters extends well beyond individual cases. Even when the issues are more mundane, however, such as a routine traffic accident case, civil disputes between private parties have the potential for helping other private citizens order their lives. Courts decide, for example, how reasonable people are expected to behave under various circumstances, giving guidance to all citizens.[18] They may even impose civil punishment in the form of punitive damages.

---

17. *See* Galanter, *Regulatory Role, supra* note 4. *See also, infra,* notes 109–125 and accompanying text (discussing the regulatory role of the civil jury).

18. *See* 1 J.D. LEE AND BARRY A. LINDAHL, MODERN TORT LAW § 3.04 (rev. ed. 1994). *See also,* Gary Jacobsohn, *Citizen Participation in Policy-Making: The Role of the Jury,* 39 J. POLITICS 73 (1977).

If the public aspects of criminal law are sufficient to justify the use of juries in criminal cases, then, the public aspects of civil law ought to justify juries in civil cases as well. As in criminal cases, the civil jury can express the sense of the community as to matters of public importance by judging whether civil litigants have met community standards of behavior in particular cases.[19] Sometimes, the matters adjudicated in civil cases are every bit as significant for society as criminal matters. The significance of matters adjudicated in civil cases has increased with the rise of public law litigation, such as school desegregation and prison reform litigation, the object of which is to change societal institutions.[20]

2. The Jury as Equalizer

A second reason for the jury in criminal cases is that the jury can help to equalize the parties. When the full power of the state is brought to bear on an individual accused of a crime, that person may well need the mediating influence of a jury of his "peers."[21] The jury will consist of ordinary citizens who have experience with the ordinary events of human existence and can make mitigatory judgments that the law enforcement bureaucracy may be unable to make.[22] Thus, the criminal justice system relies on juries of one's peers to equalize the defendant and the state and to prevent abuses of the government's substantial power.

Unlike criminal cases, civil cases are often between two parties who are roughly equal, so no equalizing force is needed. Disputes between two large corporations or between two individuals are examples, particularly when the

---

19. *See* ABA/BROOKINGS REPORT, *supra* note 2, at 9–10.

20. For general discussions of public law litigation, see Abram Chayes, *The Role of the Judge in Public Law Litigation*, 89 HARV. L. REV. 1281 (1976); Carl Tobias, *Public Law Litigation and the Federal Rules of Civil Procedure*, 74 CORNELL L. REV. 270 (1989). Ironically, however, the jury may not function in such cases because the plaintiffs are often seeking only "equitable" relief. For a discussion of the right to jury trial in legal and equitable matters, *see infra*, Chapter 4. The inability of juries to function in such cases is also inconsistent with Priest's justification for the civil jury as ideal for resolving "complex and conflicting social values," *see supra*, notes 6–8 and accompanying text. *But cf.* John M. Baker, *The Shrinking Role of the Jury in Constitutional Litigation*, 16 WM. MITCHELL L. REV. 697 (1990) (favoring a smaller jury role in litigation over constitutional rights because of the courts' countermajoritarian role in protecting constitutional rights).

21. *See id.* at 9; William W. Schwarzer and Alan Hirsch, *The Modern American Jury: Reflections on Veneration and Distrust*, in VERDICT, *supra* note 2, at 399.

22. *See* ABA/BROOKINGS REPORT, *supra* note 2, at 9 (one of the justifications for the civil jury is that it checks the bureaucratization of the judiciary by bringing amateur decision-makers into the process).

parties have roughly equal resources. There are, nevertheless, two potential sources of inequality in civil law. First, the government is often a party to civil litigation.[23] The government can be a party in its sovereign capacity, using the courts to enforce its regulations. In that capacity, the government/citizen inequality would be similar to the inequality in criminal law, especially when the government seeks some kind of civil penalty—an increasingly common use of the courts.[24] Thus, the government has the capacity to abuse its power in the civil context as well as the criminal, and protection against governmental abuse of power is one of the justifications frequently given for the jury.[25] As a corollary to this, many civil disputes are between manifestly unequal *private* parties: a large corporation and an individual, or a large and a small corporation, for example. The jury can mediate those inequalities as well.[26] The inequality between two private parties does not have the same significance as when the enforcement power of the state is factored into the equation, but the practical effect may be the same.

A related source of inequality in civil law is the presence of "repeat players," sometimes the government, but often corporate or other business entities with considerable money to spend on litigation.[27] The government or business entity generally has not only more resources with which to litigate, but more experience with the system of litigation than do individuals who might be parties against them, and the jury can be seen as moderating that inequality.[28]

---

23. *See* note 10, *supra.*

24. Two recent examples are Tull v. United States, 481 U.S. 412 (1987) (upholding a civil penalty under the Clean Water Act, 33 U.S.C. § 1319(d) (1986)); and United States v. Halper, 490 U.S. 435 (1989) (upholding a civil penalty under the False Claims Act, 31 U.S.C. § 3729(a)(7) (1982 ed. Supp. V)). Civil forfeitures also implicate this inequality. *See supra*, Introduction, at notes 19–22 and accompanying text.

25. *See* ABA/BROOKINGS REPORT, *supra* note 2, at 9.

26. *See* THOMAS CARBONNEAU, ALTERNATIVE DISPUTE RESOLUTION: MELTING THE LANCES AND DISMOUNTING THE STEEDS 208–09 (1989). Many modern tort reformers apparently believe that the jury overcorrects for such inequalities. *See infra*, notes 50–69 and accompanying text. The empirical evidence for such overcorrection is mixed, however, *see id.*

27. *See* Marc Galanter, *Why the "Haves" Come Out Ahead: Speculations on the Limits of Legal Change*, 9 L. & SOC'Y REV. 95, 97 (1974).

28. *See* CARBONNEAU, *supra* note 26, at 208–09. Another device that helps to equalize corporations and individuals, at least when the individuals are tort plaintiffs, is the contingent fee arrangement, which enables injured individuals to sue even when they cannot afford to pay a firm's hourly rates. *See generally,* Lester Buckman, *Contingent Fees Without Contingencies: Hamlet Without the Prince of Denmark?*, 37 U.C.L.A. L. REV. 29, 35–43 (1989).

3. Summary and Conclusion

Civil suits often involve matters of substantial public interest or a serious inequality between the parties. These are the very factors that justify the use of juries in criminal cases. If juries are appropriate for deciding criminal cases, then, they should be equally appropriate for deciding civil disputes, notwithstanding that civil disputes are most often between two private parties. Of course, not all civil cases will involve matters of substantial public interest or unequal parties, and it could be argued that the jury should be limited to those cases that do. But if we were to make such a distinction, we would have to decide on the criteria for allocating cases to judge or jury, which could, itself, lead to increased litigation.[29]

B. Inherent Limits on the Civil Jury's Competence

If the jury is to be accepted as a fact-finder in civil and criminal litigation, it must be competent to handle the tasks assigned to it. That means that it must produce accurate findings untainted by bias or emotion. Accuracy is particularly important in criminal cases, where we strive to avoid punishing the innocent or exonerating the guilty. In civil cases, the jury is simply asked to resolve a dispute that has been framed by the parties. We need for the jury to be accurate within that framework, but as long as the parties are happy with the way the dispute has been framed, we are not as concerned about objective truth.[30] Whether we seek objective truth or the mere settling of a dispute, however, the decision-maker must be capable of understanding the issues and resolving them dispassionately.[31]

---

29. This is reminiscent of George Priest's argument that juries are most appropriate in cases involving conflicting social norms or the government as a party. *See supra*, notes 6–8 and accompanying text. Priest does not discuss the criteria to be used for allocating decisions between judge and jury.

30. For discussions of the difference between finding truth and resolving disputes, see MIRJAN DAMASKA, EVIDENCE LAW ADRIFT 107 (1997); Stephan Landsman, *The Decline of the Adversary System: How the Rhetoric of Swift and Certain Justice Has Affected Adjudication in American Courts*, 29 BUFF. L. REV. 487, 492 (1980); Franklin Strier, *What Can the American Adversary System Learn From an Inquisitorial System of Justice?*, 76 JUDICATURE 109, 161 (1992); Richard D. Friedman, *Anchors and Flotsam: Is Evidence Law Adrift?*, 107 YALE L.J. 1921, 1957–64 (1998) (arguing that the adversary system is supposed to protect individual rights, and that accuracy is important to that goal).

31. For an extensive discussion of jury competence, see *Symposium: Is the Jury Competent?*, 52 L. & CONTEMP. PROB. 1–353 (Autumn 1989).

Most civil and criminal cases are easily accessible to ordinary citizens, in the sense that the facts are relatively straightforward, albeit disputed, and the sense of wrong easily understood. Jurors can call upon their life experiences to judge, for example, whether people could be expected to act as they are alleged to have acted, and for the motives that are attributed to them. About half of all civil jury trials are tort cases,[32] where the issues most often concern what happened and whether the parties behaved reasonably according to community standards. These issues are well within the ken of the average juror.[33]

Most criticism of the jury's competence comes in complex litigation. Both civil and criminal cases can raise scientific, financial, economic, or other substantively difficult issues. Criminal cases, for example, may involve allegedly fraudulent financial transactions[34] or cutting-edge scientific evidence such as DNA matching.[35] Civil cases can concern complex scientific evidence on the causation of disease[36] or the damage from environmental toxins.[37] Juries may well have difficulty with such issues; the typical juror's life experiences do not prepare her to evaluate these complex issues. And if the jury is valued for its injection of community sentiment or common-sense insights into the adjudicative process, these kinds of cases do not play to the jury's strengths.

We would not think of depriving those accused of crime of their right to a jury even in complex cases, but there have been calls for curtailing the civil jury in scientifically or technologically complex cases.[38] Critics invariably claim

32. See Galanter, *Regulatory Function*, *supra* note 4, at 66.

33. There have been criticisms of jury competence even in relatively simple cases, however. The best known is FRANK, *supra* note 9.

34. See STEPHEN J. ADLER, THE JURY: DISORDER IN THE COURTS 67–83 (1994) (discussing the Imelda Marcos trial).

35. See *The Ever-Escalating Evidence Standard*, U.S. NEWS & WORLD REP., p. 17 (May 29, 1995) (discussing the use of D.N.A. evidence at the O.J. Simpson trial).

36. See Brock v. Merrell Dow Pharmaceuticals, Inc., 874 F.2d 307 (5th Cir. 1989); *In re* "Agent Orange" Product Liability Litigation, 611 F. Supp. 1223 (E.D. N.Y. 1985); *In re* Joint Eastern and Southern District Asbestos Litigation, 758 F. Supp. 199 (S.D.N.Y. 1991).

37. An example of this in the popular press is the true story presented in JONATHAN HARR, A CIVIL ACTION (1995). See also, Bean v. Southwestern Waste Management Corp., 482 F. Supp. 673 (S. Tex. 1979); Cunningham v. Anchor Hocking, Corp. 558 So. 2d 93 (Fla. Dist. Ct. App. 1990).

38. See, e.g., PETER W. HUBER, LIABILITY: THE LEGAL REVOLUTION AND ITS CONSEQUENCES (1988). See also, Dan Drazan, *The Case for Special Juries in Toxic Tort Litigation*, 72 JUDICATURE 292 (1989) (arguing for specially qualified juries, such as juries of chemists, in toxic tort litigation). Perhaps because of the Seventh Amendment, many of these commentators do not propose eliminating the jury altogether, but they do propose limiting it in some ways. Drazan and others propose special juries, see *id.* Huber has proposed fur-

that jury incompetence in such cases leads to unfounded or outrageously high awards and leads litigants to sue more frequently because of the chance of winning an undeserved windfall.[39] But the objective evidence suggests that juries generally can handle most complex evidence if it is presented in an accessible manner.[40] Some jury supporters suggest that reforms such as allowing jurors to take notes or ask questions, or instructing them before they hear the evidence, might help them resolve complex issues.[41] Some commentators have argued that many critics of large jury awards tend to focus on the unusual awards and not on statistics that show that most juries make awards that are within a reasonably predictable range,[42] and that most juries handle scientific evidence at least adequately.[43] Indeed, some point out that at least some of the jury's critics are funded largely by corporate interests, including insurance companies, that would prefer to keep jury awards low.[44]

---

ther limiting the evidence that juries see. *See* Huber, *supra* note 9. For general discussions of the jury's role in complex civil litigation, see, *e.g.*, Roger W. Kirst, *The Jury's Historic Domain in Complex Cases*, 58 WASH. L. REV. 1 (1982); Patrick Devlin, *Jury Trial of Complex Cases: English Practice at the Time of the Seventh Amendment*, 80 COLUM. L. REV. 43 (1980); Morris S. Arnold, *A Historical Inquiry Into the Right to Trial by Jury in Complex Civil Litigation*, 128U. PA. L. REV. 829 (1980).

39. *See, e.g.*, Huber, *supra* note 9, at 290–94.

40. *See, e.g.*, Deborah Jones Merritt & Kathryn Barry, *Is the Tort System in Crisis? New Empirical Evidence*, 60 OHIO ST. L.J. 315 (1999); Richard Lempert, *Civil Juries and Complex Cases: Taking Stock After Twelve Years*, in VERDICT, *supra* note 2, at 181 [hereinafter cited as Lempert, *Taking Stock*]; Richard Lempert, *Civil Juries and Complex Cases: Let's Not Rush to Judgment*, 80 MICH. L. REV. 68 (1981) [hereinafter cited as Lempert, *Rush to Judgment*]; Joe S. Cecil, Valerie P. Hans & Elizabeth C. Wiggins, *Citizen Comprehension of Difficult Issues: Lessons From Civil Jury Trials.* 40 AM. U.L. REV. 727, 745 (1991).

41. *See, e.g.*, articles cited in note 40, *supra*; Stephen A. Saltzburg, *Improving the Quality of Jury Decisionmaking*, in VERDICT, *supra* note 2, at 341; H. Lee Sarokin & G. Thomas Munsterman, *Recent Innovations in Civil Jury Trial Procedures*, in VERDICT, *supra* note 2, at 378; William W. Schwarzer, *Reforming Jury Trials*, 132 F.R.D. 581 (1991); Saul M. Kassin and Lawrence S. Wrightsman, *On the Requirements of Proof: The Timing of Judicial Instruction and Mock Juror Verdicts*, in IN THE BLACK BOX: CONTROVERSIES IN THE COURTROOM 143, 154 (Lawrence S. Wrightsman, Saul M. Kassin and Cynthia E. Willis eds. 1987).

42. *See, e.g.*, STEPHEN DANIELS AND JOANNE MARTIN, CIVIL JURIES AND THE POLITICS OF REFORM 238–43 (1994); NEIL VIDMAR, MEDICAL MALPRACTICE AND THE AMERICAN JURY 265–66 (1995).

43. *See* Kenneth J. Chesebro, *Galileo's Retort: Peter Huber's Junk Scholarship*, 42 AM. U.L. REV. 1637, 1699–1702 (1993).

44. This has been said of Peter Huber, for example. *See* DANIELS & MARTIN, *supra* note 42, at 22; Chesebro, *supra* note 43, at 1705–22.

While the empirical evidence that juries cannot handle complex cases is mixed, there is no doubt that some issues are so difficult that it makes little sense for lay decision-makers to resolve them. Indeed, many trial lawyers have stories to tell of juries that were thoroughly confused by complex cases.[45] If nothing else, juries will have very steep learning curves and may still be unable to grasp the issue, especially if it is presented as a disjointed battle of the experts rather than as an organized lesson.[46] On the other hand, judges are often in no better position to decide those issues than juries.[47] Some commentators have suggested specially qualified juries as a solution: juries of persons who know the scientific field in which the dispute arises, for example.[48] Another solution has been the administrative agency, which takes the case away from juries altogether.[49]

Critics of the jury also complain that juries display biases and emotion that undermine their decision-making competence. A common criticism—dating at least to the nineteenth century—is that juries are biased in favor of individual plaintiffs over corporate defendants.[50] Once again, the evidence generally does not support that claim, though the evidence should be interpreted cautiously.[51] Indeed, one study found that judges were more generous than

---

45. An example of the difficulties juries can have with complex data is HARR, *supra* note 37, at 379–92.

46. See DAMASKA, *supra* note 30, at 84–94 (arguing that adversarial presentation of evidence makes it more difficult for juries to understand the issue and its place in the overall field of learning).

47. See Lempert, *Rush to Judgment*, *supra* note 40, at 91.

48. See, e.g., William V. Luneburg & Mark A. Nordenberg, *Specially Qualified Juries and Expert Nonjury Tribunals: Alternatives for Coping with the Complexities of Modern Civil Litigation*, 67 VA. L. REV. 887 (1981); *Developments in the Law—Scientific Evidence: Confronting the New Challenges of Scientific Evidence*, 108 HARV. L. REV. 1481 (1995). For a discussion of specially qualified juries, see *infra*, Chapter 5, at notes 167–175 and accompanying text.

49. See *infra*, Chapter 3, notes 145–171 and accompanying text; Chapter 4, notes 122–215 and accompanying text. For an evaluation of Supreme Court precedent that allows jury-less administrative adjudication, see Ellen E. Sward, *Legislative Courts, Article III, and the Seventh Amendment*, 77 N.C. L. REV. 1037 (1999).

50. See, e.g., HUBER, *supra* note 38, at 11–12; AUDREY CHIN AND MARK A. PETERSON, DEEP POCKETS, EMPTY POCKETS 32 (1985); Stephen Landsman, *The History and Objectives of the Civil Jury System*, in VERDICT, *supra* note 2, at 22, 44–45 (documenting that this perception of bias existed at least by the mid-nineteenth century).

51. See, e.g., Valerie P. Hans, *The Jury's Response to Business and Corporate Wrongdoing*, 52 L. & CONTEMP. PROBS. 177, 190–91 (Autumn 1989); DANIELS AND MARTIN, *supra* note 42, at 173 Chesebro, *supra* note 43, at 1654–56; Landsman, *supra* note 50, at 22, 45 (cit-

juries in tort cases involving corporate defendants.[52] There have also been suggestions in the professional and popular press that juries cannot separate the
facts from the emotion,[53] and that they carry all the biases of the groups to
which they belong and are unable to put aside those biases to engage in rational discourse.[54] But if jurors are irrational, judges must be irrational much
of the time as well, because studies show that judges agree with juries a substantial amount of the time.[55] Indeed, judges tend to believe that juries do a
good job, and to support their continued use.[56] The empirical evidence, too,
fails to show that juries are generally irrational, as they usually return verdicts
that are within expected norms.[57] This is not to deny that there are occasional
irrational verdicts. But critics who think that the jury should be abandoned
because of those occasional irrational verdicts are surely overstating the case.[58]

---

ing study by Lawrence Friedman refuting nineteenth century bias of jurors against corporations).

52. *See* Kevin M. Clermont & Theodore Eisenberg, *Trial by Jury or Judge: Transcending
Empiricism*, 77 CORNELL L. REV. 1124 (1992).

53. *See, e.g.,* Huber, *supra* note 9, at 278–85; FRANK, *supra* note 9, at 114–16. *Doubts
About Juries Don't Come From Jurors*, 16 NATIONAL LAW JOURNAL, Nos. 17–18 (December
27, 1994 to January 3, 1995); *Will Jurors Go With Gut Feeling?*, ORLANDO SENTINEL (October 2, 1995).

54. See, e.g., Jennie Rhine, Note, *The Jury: A Reflection of the Prejudices of the Community*, 20 HASTINGS L.J. 1417 (1969); Sheri Lynn Johnson, *Black Innocence and the White
Jury*, 83 MICH. L. REV. 1611 (1985) (discussing the criminal jury). This view of jurors may
be behind the Supreme Court's requirement that civil and criminal jury panels be representative of the population mix in the community. *See* ABRAMSON, *supra* note 14 (discussing primarily the criminal jury). Some political scientists have disputed assertions that
citizens are generally unable to engage in rational discourse and therefore should not be
trusted with democratic institutions. *See* Donald R. Kinder and Don Herzog, *Democratic
Discussion*, in RECONSIDERING THE DEMOCRATIC PUBLIC 347 (George L. Marcus and Russell L. Hanson eds. 1993).

55. *See, e.g.,* HARRY KALVEN, JR. & HANS ZEISEL, THE AMERICAN JURY 151 (1966); Mark
Curriden, *Putting the Squeeze on Juries*, 86 A.B.A. J. 52, 56 (August 2000) (showing that
96.8% of federal judges agreed with jury verdicts all the time or nearly all the time).

56. *See* Prentice H. Marshall, *A View from the Bench: Practical Perspectives on Juries*,
1990 U. CHI. L. FORUM 147; Valerie Hans, *Attitudes Toward the Civil Jury: A Crisis of Confidence?*, in VERDICT, *supra* note 2, at 248, 23–64 (citing studies); Patrick E. Higginbotham,
Continuing the Dialogue: Civil Juries and the Allocation of Power, 56 TEX. L. REV. 47 (1977);
Curriden, *supra* note 55, at 56 (showing that about 70% of federal judges believe that juries decide about the right number of cases or should decide more).

57. *See* Schuck, *supra* note 4, at 306, 308–312 (criticizing studies, and finding that they
do not support the claim that juries are irrational).

58. As I will show in Chapter 7, the judicial system has found ways to control for juries' occasional irrational excesses.

Some of the most vociferous criticism of jury competence concerns punitive damages.[59] Indeed, there have been numerous calls to take the punitive damage decision away from juries and give it to the judge or to an administrative agency.[60] Punitive damages are, after all, akin to a criminal sentence, which is normally the judge's decision: they are meant to punish and deter.[61] Critics argue that juries are not competent to determine what amount of damages is sufficient to deter conduct that is undesirable. Though there is evidence to suggest that juries are remarkably consistent in their judgments as to the degree of reprehensibility, they have trouble translating those judgments into dollars, resulting in judgments that over- or under-deter (usually over).[62] The evidence as to juries' competence to determine punitive damages is, however, mixed. Some studies show that juries rarely award punitive damages, and that when they do, the awards are generally modest.[63] One commentator has sug-

---

59. *See, e.g., Developments in the Law—The Civil Jury*, 110 HARV. L. REV. 1408, 1519 (1997); Paul Mogin, *Why Judges, Not Juries, Should Set Punitive Damages*, 65 U. CHI. L. REV. 179 (1998); Paul H. Rubin, John E. Calfee, and Mark F. Grady, BMW v. Gore: *Mitigating the Punitive Economics of Punitive Damages*, 5 SUP. CT. ECON. REV. 179 (1997).

60. *See, e.g.,* Mogin, *supra* note 59; Dorsey D. Ellis, Jr., *Punitive Damages, Due Process, and the Jury*, 40 ALA. L. REV. 975, 1005 (1989); W. Kip Viscusi, *Corporate Risk Analysis: A Reckless Act?*, 52 STAN. L. REV. 547 (2000); Cass R. Sunstein, Daniel Kahneman, and David Schkade, *Assessing Punitive Damages (with Notes on Cognition and Valuation in Law)*, 107 YALE L.J. 2071 (1998); David Schkade, Cass R. Sunstein, and Daniel Kahneman, *Are Juries Less Erratic than Individuals? Deliberation, Polarization, and Punitive Damages*, University of Chicago, John M. Olin Law & Economics Working Paper No. 81 (2d Series) (2000).

61. *See* Dorsey D. Ellis, Jr., *Fairness and Efficiency in the Law of Punitive Damages*, 56 So. CAL. L. REV. 1, 3 (1982); Darryl K. Brown, *Structure and Relationship in the Jurisprudence of Juries: Comparing the Capital Sentencing and Punitive Damages Doctrines*, 47 HASTINGS L.J. 1255, 1256 (1996).

62. *See* Sunstein, Kahneman, and Schkade, *supra* note 60; Schkade, Sunstein, and Kahneman, *supra* note 60. *See also,* W. Kip Viscusi, *The Social Costs of Punitive Damages Against Corporations in Environmental and Safety Torts*, 87 GEO. L.J. 285, 314 (1999); Rubin, Calfee, and Grady, *supra* note 59; Viscusi, *supra* note 60.

63. *See* Theodore Eisenberg, John Goerdt, Brian Ostrom, David Rottmann, and Martin T. Wells, *The Predictability of Punitive Damages*, 26 J. LEGAL STUD. 623 (1997); Merritt & Barry, *supra* note 40, at 387–88; Robert MacCoun, *Inside the Black Box: What Empirical Research Tells Us About Decisionmaking by Civil Juries*, in VERDICT, *supra* note 2, at 137, 149–50 (citing studies). Punitive damages are a relatively recent development, having first appeared in the English cases in the middle of the eighteenth century. *See* Wilkes v. Wood, 95 Eng. Rep. 766 (1763); Huckle v. Money, 95 Eng. Rep. 768 (1763) (approving "exemplary damages" for the first time); James B. Sales & Kenneth B. Cole, Jr., *Punitive Damages: A Relic That Has Outlived Its Origins*, 37 VAND. L. REV. 1117, 1120 (1984). Because the right to jury trial is largely historical, *see* Chapters 2 and 4, *infra*, this means that the case for juries' deciding punitive damages is less strong than is the case for their deciding

gested that jury awards have become less consistent as the size of the jury has shrunk.[64] It is the outlandish punitive damage awards that make the news and increase calls for limits on the jury. But even some of the punitive damages awards that have been most ridiculed in the press make more sense when they are examined closely.

For example, the jury that awarded $2.9 million—including $2.7 million in punitive damages—to a McDonald's patron who spilled superheated coffee on herself while driving was castigated in the press.[65] But the evidence presented at trial showed that the victim had obtained her coffee at the drive-through window and was burned when she attempted to remove the lid; that McDonald's coffee was sold at a temperature that causes third-degree burns (the worst kind) in two to seven seconds; that the victim herself suffered third-degree burns requiring skin grafts; that many McDonald's patrons had suffered debilitating and disfiguring third-degree burns over the years from coffee spills; that McDonald's officials admitted at trial that their coffee is not fit for consumption when sold because it is too hot; that McDonald's officials testified that despite this dismal record, the company had no intention of reducing the temperature at which the coffee was sold; and that the $2.7 million punitive damages award represented two days' gross sales of coffee.[66] The jury was clearly trying to send a message, and two days' gross coffee sales appears to be a reasonable way to do it. The judge later reduced the award to $660,000.[67]

This brief review of the literature suggests that juries are generally competent to handle many, if not most, of the cases involving complex facts, punitive damages, and emotional appeal, especially if they are given adequate guidance. There is a good deal of professional literature that offers sug-

---

compensatory damages. It simply does not have the same historical pedigree. Perhaps this is one reason why judges frequently reduce punitive damages. *See* MacCoun, *supra.* For a discussion of the power of judges to reduce jury verdicts, see Chapter 7, *infra,* at notes 157–161 and accompanying text.

64. *See* Michael J. Saks, *The Smaller the Jury, the Greater the Unpredictability,* 79 JUDICATURE 263 (1996). For further discussion of the size of juries, see Chapter 5, *infra.*

65. *See, e.g.,* Brad Berliner, *Wrong Message,* CHICAGO TRIBUNE, p. 18 (August 31, 1994); David Rossie, *How About a Hot Cup of Coffee?,* DENVER POST, p. G-05 (August 28, 1994); *Jumpin' Java!,* DALLAS MORNING NEWS, p. 26A (August 25, 1994); *Warning! The Coffee is Hot and Life is Hazardous,* THE COLUMBUS DISPATCH, p. 8A (August 31, 1994).

66. *See* S. Reed Morgan, *McDonald's Burned Itself,* Legal Times, September 19, 1994, p. 26. Morgan was the plaintiff's lawyer.

67. *See McDonald's Coffee Award Reduced 75% by Judge,* WALL STREET JOURNAL, at A4 (September 15, 1994).

gestions for improving the jury's functioning, and such reforms may be all that is needed to answer the critics in the majority of cases.[68] But the evidence is still coming in, and it is probably premature to leap to a definitive conclusion.

One more observation is worth making. Many of the very kinds of cases where the critics are most vocal are also those where one or both of the justifications for using juries to resolve civil disputes are strongest. For example, a case in which an individual sued a large corporation for an illness due to environmental damage could involve complex scientific data, punitive damages, and alleged anti-corporation bias. But it also involves a matter of considerable public interest—violation of federal and state environmental laws, which are designed to protect the public health and safety—and a serious inequality between the parties. If the comparison to criminal law is valid, this should be precisely the kind of case where juries are most important. At the very least, juries should continue to judge the degree of culpability, even if we leave the translation into dollars to another entity.[69]

---

68. In addition to such reforms as allowing jurors to take notes, *see supra* note 41and accompanying text, some commentators see such procedural devices as the special verdict, in which juries break down the verdict into answers to a series of specific questions, as aiding the jury's decision-making. *See, e.g.,* Lempert, *Taking Stock, supra* note 40, at 201; David C. Brody and John Neiswender, *Judicial Attitudes Toward Jury Reform,* 83 JUDICATURE 298 (2000). For a discussion of special verdicts as a jury control device, *see infra,* Chapter 7, at notes 172–181 and accompanying text. It also has been suggested that adversarial presentation of evidence can make it more difficult for jurors to follow already complex information because the information they need is presented discontinuously: one party presents evidence as to an issue, and the other party does not attempt to refute it until, sometimes, days or weeks later. *See* DAMASKA, *supra* note 30, at 96–103. Because the evidence is not well organized, they may make mistakes in evaluating it. A more rational presentation of the evidence, then, might aid the jury. Rearranging our mode of presenting evidence may be difficult, however, as the adversary system is at the heart of common law adjudication and has been for centuries. There have been significant alterations in the adversary system already, but there may well be limits as to how far we can transform the system. For a discussion of the adversary system and its relation to the jury, see *infra,* Chapter 3, at notes 57–144 and accompanying text.

69. This is the suggestion of Schkade, Sunstein, and Kahneman, *supra* note 60, who propose that juries be asked to make "normative judgments on a bounded numerical scale," which would then be translated into dollars based on expertise or population-wide data on dollar awards. *See id.* at 35. The authors argue that deliberation actually exacerbates problems caused by the jury's having no real boundaries in determining punitive damages.

C. Summary

The civil jury appears to be justified as a settler of disputes on some of the same grounds that justify the use of juries in criminal cases. The primary justification is that there are public aspects of civil cases that are similar in kind, if not degree, to the public aspects of criminal cases. To the extent that the public aspects of civil litigation justify requiring the public to participate in the resolution of private disputes, the jury is an appropriate body for civil decision-making. Similarly, the civil jury can help to equalize unequal parties in civil litigation much as the criminal jury helps to equalize the government and a defendant in criminal adjudication. On the other hand, modern-day criticism of the jury hints that there may be some limits to the jury's competence, particularly when there are substantively complex issues in the case, when punitive damages are involved, or when there is a particularly emotional aspect to the case. The empirical evidence to date provides little support for these criticisms, though they may suggest that we need to reform jury procedures or take a different approach to the presentation of evidence. And even though juries generally do well even in complex cases, they could still encounter cases that are beyond them no matter what we tried to do to make the cases comprehensible. But because the critics attack the jury in precisely the kinds of cases where the justification for civil juries is strongest, we should be cautious about giving in to the criticism.

III. The Law-Making Role of the Civil Jury

It may seem incongruous to speak of the law-making role of the civil jury, because the civil jury today is clearly thought to have a role only in fact-finding.[70] But it is virtually impossible to exclude any actor in the system of civil adjudication from the law-making role completely. Any entity that has decision-making authority within the adjudicatory system may affect, and even decide, legal issues on occasion.[71] There are two aspects of the law-making role of the civil jury that deserve attention: jury nullification and the regulatory role of the jury. Of these, jury nullification has the most immediate effect on

---

70. *See* Chapter 2, *infra*, at notes 188–194 and accompanying text; Chapter 7, *infra*, at notes 1–9 and accompanying text. That was not always the case. Juries around the time of the country's founding were thought to have law-deciding power as well. *See infra*, note 76 and accompanying text.

71. *See* Jonathan D. Casper, *Restructuring the Traditional Civil Jury: The Effects of Changes in Composition and Procedures* 449–50, in Verdict, *supra* note 2.

law, but the regulatory role of the jury may have, in the end, a more profound effect.

A. Jury Nullification

Jury nullification is a highly controversial phenomenon. When it occurs, the jury undertakes to abrogate or modify legal rules, at least as they apply in specific instances. On the one hand, this is thought to give the jury the opportunity to temper justice with mercy, and so to individualize justice.[72] On the other hand, jury nullification has been criticized as inconsistent with our democratic notions of majoritarian politics: a jury that nullifies a duly enacted law is flouting the democratic political process.[73] Even critics, however, usually acknowledge that, in criminal cases at least, jury nullification is sometimes necessary if justice is to be done.[74]

Jury nullification is easier to justify in the criminal context because the public aspects of criminal law are strong and virtually cry out for judgment by the public. The strongest recent defense of jury nullification in criminal cases is Jeffrey Abramson's book, *We, the Jury: The Jury System and the Ideal of Democracy.*[75] As Abramson notes, at the beginning of the country's history, the jury had the power to nullify in both civil and criminal cases.[76] For the most part,

---

72. *See, e.g.,* ABRAMSON, *supra* note 14, at ch. 2; Alan W. Scheflin & Jon M. Van Dyke, *Merciful Juries: The Resilience of Jury Nullification,* 48 WASH. & LEE L. REV. 165 (1991).

73. *See, e.g.,* Martin A. Kotler, *Reappraising the Jury's Role as Finder of Fact,* 20 GA. L. REV. 123 (1985).

74. *See, e.g.,* Andrew D. Leipold, *Rethinking Jury Nullification,* 82 VA. L. REV. 253 (1996) (proposing making jury nullification a formal affirmative defense in criminal cases so as to allow juries to do justice while avoiding collateral costs of jury nullification). There is an enormous literature on jury nullification, especially in criminal cases. Leipold's article is a good source for finding this literature, as is Abramson's book.

75. *See* ABRAMSON, *supra* note 14, at ch. 2.

76. *See* ABRAMSON, *supra* note 14, at 73–77. Indeed, so strong was juries' power over the law that lawyers often argued the law to the juries, and in cases where there was more than one judge presiding, the judges sometimes gave conflicting instructions as to the law, leaving it to the jury to decide what the law was. *See id.* at 30. Two states, Indiana and Maryland, still have constitutional provisions allowing juries to nullify the law. *See id.* at 62 and n. *See also,* Kotler, *supra* note 73, at 159–61. There have been proposals recently in about half the state legislatures to require that juries be instructed on their power to nullify. *See* Joe Lambe, *Bill Would Let Juries Decide Law in Cases,* KANSAS CITY STAR, p. A-1 (April 8, 1996. None has been successful yet. *Id. See also,* Leipold, *supra* note 71, at note 6 and accompanying text. The arrest of abortion protesters has prompted some of this activity, as protesters argue that they should not be guilty of trespass and other crimes if they were acting in good conscience for a "higher" purpose. *See* ABRAMSON, *supra* note 14, at

that power quickly dissipated in civil cases,[77] and by the end of the nineteenth century the Supreme Court had disapproved it in criminal cases as well.[78] Abramson discusses the reasons for this decline, citing the growing complexity of law, the growth of heterogeneous communities, and the shift of power from local to national centers.[79] Nevertheless, Abramson notes that jury nullification has been with us for centuries, and remains a part of criminal adjudication today. He cites as examples the juries that acquitted Dr. Jack Kevorkian of violating a law prohibiting assisted suicide; the jury that found Mayor Marion Barry of Washington D.C. guilty of only minor offenses of the many charged against him; and the jury that returned a split verdict against Oliver North.[80]

While Abramson acknowledges that jury nullification can be very troubling—white juries in the South, for example, often failed to convict persons charged with killing blacks or civil rights workers despite overwhelming evidence[81]— he is a strong supporter of it. He notes, for example, that jury nullification always applies only to give the accused more leniency than might otherwise be expected, and thus "poses no threat to the accused."[82] It is critical, Abramson believes, that juries have this option to "show mercy."[83] Abramson thinks the jury should have this power even though we know that jury nullification will sometimes "go badly."[84]

The question is whether we can justify jury nullification in civil cases. Despite some significant differences between criminal and civil law, some of the same considerations could justify jury nullification in civil cases. As I discussed

---

57–59. Most such arguments are rejected, but in an example of judicial nullification, a federal judge in New York recently accepted such a defense and acquitted anti-abortion defendants of criminal contempt for blocking a clinic. *See* Jan Hoffman, *Judge Acquits Abortion Protesters on Basis of Religious Beliefs*, NEW YORK TIMES, sec. 1, p. 25 (January 19, 1997).

77. *See* MORTON J. HORWITZ, THE TRANSFORMATION OF AMERICAN LAW 1780–1860, pp. 141–43 (1977).

78. *See* ABRAMSON, *supra* note 14, at 85–88, discussing Sparf and Hansen v. United States, 156 U.S. 51 (1895). *See also,* Note, *The Changing Role of the Jury in the Nineteenth Century,* 74 YALE L.J. 170 (1964).

79. ABRAMSON, *supra* note 14, at 88–90. *See also,* Chapter 2, *infra* at notes 180–186 and accompanying text (discussing reasons for decline of civil jury).

80. *See* ABRAMSON, *supra* note 14, at 65–67.

81. *Id.* at 61–62. *See also,* Gerard N. Magliocca, *The Philosopher's Stone: Dualist Democracy and the Jury,* 69 U. COLO. L. REV. 175, 197 (1997).

82. *See* ABRAMSON, *supra* note 14, at 92.

83. *Id.*

84. *Id.*

in Part II of this Chapter, there are substantial public aspects to civil law, including judgments about important legal precepts that govern and guide us as citizens. In addition, governmental regulation can be enforced not only by criminal penalites, but by civil ones as well, such as civil forfeiture or fines.[85] In such contexts, it might be useful to have citizens judging how the law should apply in specific instances, even when their answer is that it should not apply at all. The specific application of civil rules may well be unfair, and juries, which are unaccountable and constituted only for the case at hand, may be better suited to do justice when the strict application of the law would seem to require an unjust result.[86] Judges may well feel more constrained to follow the letter of the law.

Consistent jury nullification in civil cases can be symptomatic of deeper problems with the law itself. An example is the development of comparative negligence law, which allows the fact-finder to weigh the relative negligence of the plaintiff and defendant in deciding on a verdict.[87] In reaction to a perceived pro-plaintiff bias on the part of jurors, common law courts in the nineteenth century had developed the doctrine of contributory negligence.[88] Contributory negligence is the doctrine that if the plaintiff shares in the negligence that caused her injury, she cannot recover anything from the defendant, even if the defendant's negligence was considerably greater than hers.[89] This reduced the number of cases in which plaintiffs could recover from businesses that had injured them, and allowed commerce to develop more freely.[90] The contributory negligence rule was sometimes enforced by the judges' acting to take cases away from the jury when there was clear evidence of the plaintiff's contributory negligence.[91]

Not all cases escaped the jury, however, and cases that did go to the jury often ran into jury nullification. The contributory negligence rule was too harsh for most juries to stomach, and many returned verdicts for plaintiffs de-

85. See supra, Introduction, at notes 18-19 and accompanying text.

86. See Priest, Justifying, in VERDICT, supra note 2. See also, ABA/BROOKINGS REPORT, supra note 2, at 8–11 (justifications for the civil jury include protection against abuse of power and a check on the bureaucratization of the judiciary).

87. For discussions of the development of comparative negligence law, see Stephen C. Yeazell, The New Jury and Ancient Jury Conflict, 1990 U. CHI. L. FORUM 87, 113; Landsman, supra note 49, at 45–47.

88. See Fleming James, Jr., Contributory Negligence, 62 YALE L.J. 691, 695 (1953); 1 LEE & LINDAHL, supra note 18, at § 10.02.

89. See DAN B. DOBBS, TORTS AND COMPENSATION 233 (1985).

90. See id.; James, supra note 88, at 695–96.

91. See 1 LEE & LINDAHL, supra note 18, at § 10.36.

spite strong evidence of contributory negligence.[92] Usually the damages awarded reflected some sense of the comparative negligence of the plaintiff and the defendant.[93] This rebellion by juries eventually contributed to formal changes in the law in most states, so that some form of comparative negligence is now the rule among states rather than the exception.[94] Thus, this kind of systematic jury nullification in civil cases can lead to salutary changes in the law—something that may not occur if we had no juries or did not accept occasional nullification from them. Indeed, one might view this application of jury nullification as a protection against abuse of power by government acting in concert with powerful commercial interests.[95]

Some cautionary notes must be sounded about jury nullification in civil cases, however. First, some civil law is designed not to compensate or punish for past wrongs, but to order people's affairs. This is true, for example, of much of contract law. While contract law is often made, or at least interpreted, in the context of litigated cases—where something has gone wrong—the basic purpose of contract law is to provide a framework in which people can have some confidence that the arrangements they make will be upheld. Jury nullification in that context could cause disruptions and uncertainty in contractual relations, which could have serious consequences for commercial activity. This is true of all kinds of civil law that have this regulatory rather than compensatory purpose.

Second, some civil cases arise out of statutes that are extraordinarily complex and based on considered legislative judgments about economics, sociology, science, or other specialized disciplines.[96] There are two potential problems with jury nullification of such statutes. One is that the jury would then be nullifying the work of a duly constituted institution of representative democracy. To the extent that there is any justification for nullification arising out of principles of democracy,[97] the justification loses some significance from the clash with other democratic decision-making.[98] To be sure, criminal

---

92. *See* Yeazell, *supra* note 87, at 113–14.

93. *See id.*

94. *See* DOBBS, *supra* note 89, at 242–43. Some states have adopted a hybrid of contributory and comparative negligence, allowing the plaintiff to recover a proportionate award if her negligence was responsible for less than 50% of her injuries, but to recover nothing if she were more than 50% responsible for her own injuries. *See id.* at 243.

95. *See* ABA/BROOKINGS REPORT, *supra* note 2, at 9.

96. *See, e.g.,* 15 U.S.C. §1 *et seq.* (1994) (antitrust); 7 U.S.C. §136 (1994) (environmental pesticide control).

97. *See* section III, *infra.*

98. *See* Kotler, *supra* note 73, at 161–66.

law is now reflected in statutes as well, but the basis for the legislative judgment in criminal law is usually easier to grasp and easier to modify in particular instances.

This brings me to the second problem with jury nullification of complex civil statutes: they often are the result of an evaluation of extremely complex information that juries cannot possibly consider, both because they are not equipped with the educational background they would need (or the staffs to pore over the specialized information), and because the information is not available to them. The legislative judgment is reflected in the bottom line civil rule enacted in the statute. The jury has no access to the mounds of information that went into that bottom line rule. Thus, jury nullification in civil law often implicates both clashes among democratic institutions and serious differentials in the access to information. This is not to say these problems never occur in criminal law—only that they are more common and more pronounced in civil law.[99]

Finally, jury nullification in civil cases is not uni-directional, as it is in criminal cases, where nullification always benefits the defendant.[100] Jury nullification in civil cases can benefit either the plaintiff or the defendant. If it favors the plaintiff, it could result in *greater* liability for the defendant than the applicable legal principles would require. Indeed, some corporate defendants complain that this is what juries do in products liability cases, though I have pointed out that the evidence for such bias is mixed.[101] On the other hand, if juries do that, it may reflect a judgment on the part of jurors that the applicable legal principles do not hold manufacturers sufficiently accountable. For example, applicable legal principles could be that punitive damages should be sufficient only to deter the defendant's tortious conduct in the future, but the

---

99. I should also point out, however, that writers in several different contexts have noted that revolutionary change, which is sometimes reflected in statutes, often has unforeseen consequences. *See, e.g.,* Edmund Burke, *Selections From Reflections on the Revolution in France,* in SELECT WORKS OF EDMUND BURKE 371 *et seq.* (Legal Classics Library, E.J. Payne ed. 1990). *Cf.* ANTHONY T. KRONMAN, THE LOST LAWYER: FAILING IDEALS OF THE LEGAL PROFESSION 225–64 (1993) (discussing the effect of modern legal doctrines such as law and economics and critical legal studies on the legal profession). The potential for these unforeseen consequences may suggest a need for jury nullification, so that necessary corrections can be made in specific cases, at least until the legislature responds. *Cf. also,* GUIDO CALABRESI, A COMMON LAW FOR THE AGE OF STATUTES (1982) (arguing that judges should have common law powers to abrogate or alter statutes that have become outdated).

100. *See* ABRAMSON, *supra* note 14, at 67.

101. *See* Neal R. Feigenson, *The Rhetoric of Torts: How Advocates Help Jurors Think About Causation, Reasonableness, and Responsibility,* 47 HASTINGS L.J. 61, 120n.154 (1995).

jury might also wish to punish particularly egregious conduct.[102] As was the case with contributory negligence, consistent jury verdicts that are at odds with legal principles may suggest a need to rethink those principles.

It is hard to say, then, that jury nullification should never take place in civil cases. Indeed, the very existence of the jury implies occasional jury nullification, even if that opportunity for nullification was not the jury's original purpose. As Jeffrey Abramson said, "[o]ne is left to wonder whether the rejection of jury nullification is not a rejection of the idea of the jury altogether."[103] On the other hand, we must be cautious. Civil law is not criminal law, and some of the differences suggest reasons for more concern about jury nullification in civil cases.

One more point needs airing. The concept of jury nullification assumes that the jury is refusing to follow the law and that the rest of the legal system is being faithful to the law. That is not always the case. Judges can also "nullify" the law.[104] Judges tend to come from the ranks of society's elite,[105] and may have a perspective on law that differs from that of the more broadly representative jury. Thus, they may interpret a statute narrowly or in ways that are inconsistent with legislative intent.[106] Sometimes when that happens, the legislature steps in to clarify its intent or correct the court's interpretation, which is what happened in 1991 after the Supreme Court issued a series of decisions interpreting civil rights laws in ways that Congress had not intended.[107] But the jury can also counter the phenomenon of judicial nullification. Sometimes

---

102. *See, e.g.*, Joe Lambe, *Court cuts $89 million from award*, KANSAS CITY STAR, at A-1 (Nov. 26, 1997) (reporting that jurors complained about judge's reduction of award, saying lower amount not enough to punish and to force recall of defective product).

103. ABRAMSON, *supra* note 14, at 93.

104. For an example of judicial nullification, see note 76, *supra*.

105. *See* Sheldon Goldman, *Federal Judicial Recruitment*, in THE AMERICAN COURTS: A CRITICAL ASSESSMENT 195 (John B. Gates & Charles Johnson eds. 1991); JOHN R. SCHMIDHAUSER, JUDGES AND JUSTICES: THE FEDERAL APPELLATE JUDICIARY 49–55 (1979).

106. This is a criticism that has been leveled at some members of the current Supreme Court, most notably Justice Scalia. *See, e.g.*, Bradley C. Karkkainen, *"Plain Meaning": Justice Scalia's Jurisprudence of Strict Statutory Construction*, 17 HARV. J.L. & PUB. POL'Y 401 (1994); William N. Eskridge, Jr., *The New Textualism*, 37 U.C.L.A. L. REV. 621 (1990). The Court has succeeded in nullifying much of the citizen suit legislation in environmental law by narrowly interpreting the doctrine of standing, itself a relatively new doctrine. *See* Lujan v. Defenders of Wildlife, 504 U.S. 555 (1992); Cass R. Sunstein, *What's Standing After Lujan? Of Citizen Suits, "Injuries," and Article III*, 91 MICH. L. REV. 163 (1992). The Court's nullification, unlike the jury's, affects many cases.

107. The corrective legislation was the Civil Rights Act of 1991, Pub. L. 102–66, 105 Stat. 1071, *codified at* 42 U.S.C. § 1981 *et.seq.* (1994). *See generally, The Civil Rights Act of 1991: A Symposium*, 54 LA. L. REV. 1459 (1994); Symposium, *The Civil Rights Act of 1991:*

when a jury fails to follow a judge's instruction as to the law, it may be the jury that is right and the judge who is wrong. Significantly, the Civil Rights Act of 1991 provided, for the first time, for a right to jury trial in Title VII employment discrimination cases.[108]

B. The Regulatory Role of the Civil Jury

In theory, jury decisions should have no precedential value. They are, by definition, decisions on facts, not law, and precedent concerns law. But many issues decided by juries are not pure questions of fact. For example, when a jury decides whether a defendant acted reasonably under the circumstances—a typical jury issue—the question is partly one of fact (was he reasonable or not?) and partly one of law (is this a standard of behavior that we find appropriate for ourselves and our fellow citizens?). It is, in other words, a mixed question of law and fact.[109] Any time the decision mixes law and fact, there is a potential for a precedent-setting decision. Indeed, that is what the common law is: decisions about new mixes of fact and law. Common law precedent consists of neither fact nor law alone, but both in disparate combinations.[110]

Nevertheless, jury verdicts are not considered formally precedential, and there are several good reasons for that. First, juries do not have to justify their decisions. When judges decide cases, they must justify them with written opinions discussing the facts, the law, and the application of law to fact.[111] Juries, more often than not, simply render a general verdict, saying which party prevails and, if relevant, how much compensation the losing party must pay. Without reasons, a jury's decision can have no precedential value because we do not know what it was about the defendant's behavior that was (or was not) culpable.[112] Second, juries are assembled to decide only one case. They must do justice in that one case, but are not expected to consider the broader im-

---

Theory and Practice, 68 NOTRE DAME L. REV. 911 (1993); Symposium, *The Civil Rights Act of 1991: Unraveling the Controversy*, 45 RUTGERS L. REV. 887 (1993).

108. *See* 42 U.S.C. § 1981a (1994).

109. I discuss the variations on law and fact in Chapter 7, *infra*, at notes 1–143 and accompanying text.

110. For an illustration of how common law precedent develops case-by-case and fact-by-fact, see Lon L. Fuller, *The Forms and Limits of Adjudication*, 92 HARV. L. REV. 353, 375–78 (1979).

111. *See, e.g.*, FED. R. CIV. P. 52(a).

112. *See* Fuller, *supra* note 110, at 387–88. *See also*, Priest, *Justifying*, *supra* note 3, at 108 (arguing that the fact that the jury does not justify its decision is one reason why it is ideal for resolving some kinds of conflicts).

pact on society of their decision.[113] Third, if we are to adhere to the dichotomy between juries as fact-finders and judges as law-finders, we cannot afford to think of juries as setting precedent. If juries can set precedent, they have considerable power over the development of law. This would give the jury an even greater power than it has when it nullifies the law, because nullification occurs only in the specific case at hand.[114] Precedent-setting decisions affect other cases well into the future. Not only do we seem uncomfortable about having an unaccountable body of lay persons convened for a single case exercising such power, we do not even place the primary authority for precedent-setting judicial decisions in the trial judges. Rather, that primary authority is allocated to the courts of appeals through standards of review that permit appellate courts to review trial court decisions about law on a non-deferential basis.[115] Thus, there seem to be some very good reasons for not allowing jury verdicts to have formal precedent-setting effects.

Even when the jury does not explicitly set precedent, however, the effects of a jury's decision may extend far beyond the case that jury decided. As Marc Galanter has noted, a jury's decision in one case may well guide other litigants' decisions about whether to sue, where to sue, and whether to settle and for how much.[116] For the most part, however, jury verdicts do not guide other juries, though there have been suggestions that juries should receive information about what other juries have done with similar cases.[117]

Jury verdicts do more, however, than merely guide litigants in their settlement talks. They can also affect the primary behavior of the litigants and of other citizens. This effect could be especially strong with respect to corporate citizens, which are in a better position to evaluate what juries are doing and to adjust their behavior accordingly. Juries that award large damages in product liability litigation, for example, are telling a business—and others similarly situated—that it needs to improve the safety of its product. To avoid large judgments in the future, the theory is that the corporation will make the necessary

---

113. That does not mean that juries ignore the broader impact, of course. When juries award punitive damages, they are generally trying to say something to the defendant about how he should behave in the future, and may well be thinking about how similarly situated defendants will react to the decision as well.

114. *See* ABRAMSON, *supra* note 14, at 61–62.

115. *See* Ellen E. Sward, *Appellate Review of Judicial Fact-finding*, 40 KAN. L. REV. 1, 9 (1991).

116. *See, e.g.*, Galanter, *Regulatory Function*, *supra* note 4; Galanter, *The Civil Jury as Regulator*, *supra* note 4. *See also,* Jacobsohn, *supra* note 18.

117. *See* Galanter, *Regulatory Function*, *supra* note 4, at 91.

changes, leading to greater consumer safety. This regulatory role has long been a part of tort theory,[118] and juries are important actors in that system.

If the regulatory role is to be effective, however, there must be adequate information about jury verdicts. There are at least three sources of information about juries' verdicts. First, there have been several empirical studies on jury behavior that could help guide parties with similar cases.[119] Second, several services have begun reporting on jury verdicts.[120] Finally, lawyers talk among themselves, telling stories about the juries they have seen.

Several empirical studies have demonstrated that lawyers in general are quite poor at predicting jury outcomes.[121] To some extent, this may be because lawyers tend to rely more on anecdotal evidence than on the empirical studies or reporting services that are available.[122] If lawyers do look at studies or services, they often do not know how to use them.[123] A second reason for lawyers' lack of success in predicting jury outcomes may be that juries are too variable for the verdicts to have much to say about the lawyers' own cases. They can be variable because of differences in community sentiment in vari-

---

118. *See* John A. Siliciano, *Corporate Behavior and the Social Efficiency of Tort Law*, 85 MICH. L. REV. 1820, 1820 & n.3 (1987); R. H. Coase, *The Problem of Social Cost*, 3 J. L. & ECON. 1, 1–2 (1960). The alternative to using tort law to fulfill this regulatory function is, of course, direct government regulation of corporate behavior.

119. *See, e.g.,* DANIELS AND MARTIN, *supra* note 42; VIDMAR, *supra* note 42; Michael Saks, *Do We Really Know Anything About the Behavior of the Tort Litigation System—And Why Not?*, 140 U. PA. L. REV. 1147 (1992).

While there is inherent value in knowing the kinds of things these works report on, some of them were written in part to counter propaganda from businesses and their governmental allies that were seeking to generate support for "reform" of the civil justice system. *See* DANIELS AND MARTIN, *supra* note 42, at ch. 1, *citing, e.g.,* PETER HUBER, GALILEO'S REVENGE: JUNK SCIENCE IN THE COURTROOM (1991) and A REPORT FROM THE PRESIDENT'S COUNCIL ON COMPETITIVENESS: AGENDA FOR CIVIL JUSTICE REFORM IN AMERICA (1991).

120. There is even a professional organization for jury verdict publishers, called The National Association of State Jury Verdict Publishers. Some of the publishers also report on federal jury verdicts in their states. See http://www.juryverdicts.com/index.htm. *See also,* Carrie Menkel-Meadow, *Whose Dispute Is It Anyway? A Philosophical and Democratic Defense of Settlement (In Some Cases)*, 83 Geo. L.J. 2663, 2681n.88 (1995) (discussing jury verdict reporters).

121. *See* GERALD R. WILLIAMS, LEGAL NEGOTIATION AND SETTLEMENT 5–7 (1983); PATRICIA M. DANZON, MEDICAL MALPRACTICE: THEORY, EVIDENCE, AND PUBLIC POLICY 50–51 (1985); Philip J. Hermann, *Predicting Verdicts in Personal Injury Cases*, 475 INS. L.J. 505 (1962).

122. *See* Galanter, *Regulatory Function, supra* note 4, at 86.

123. *See id.* at 90.

ous parts of the country, or because the particular jury that decides a case may be a reflection of careful selection procedures, perhaps involving unequal resources that allow one party to have greater success at selecting a favorable jury than the other.[124] Indeed, the lawyer trying to decide whether jury verdicts in other cases can tell her anything about her own case may well think she will have better luck at selecting a jury or presenting her case.

These potential problems can certainly be overcome, however. Jury reporting services break down their reporting by region, to account for regional differences in outcomes. At the same time, lawyers can benefit from studying aggregate figures rather than anecdotes about special cases.[125] Thus juries, at least in the aggregate, can have an effect beyond the specific cases they decide. This is a subtle means of regulating behavior, as lawyers can use information about what juries are likely to do both to assess risks in litigation and to advise clients on how they should conduct themselves.

C. Summary

While the case for jury nullification in civil cases is not as strong as it is for criminal cases, there does seem to be some role for nullification to play. Indeed, it is difficult to contemplate a serious role for the jury unless there is some potential for uncorrected jury nullification. Many of the justifications that are usually offered for jury trials seem to assume the possibility of jury nullification, even in civil cases. Thus, for example, the reliance on community sentiment seems to assume that community sentiment might alter the effect of the law, strictly applied.

The jury also seems to have a regulatory role, and that role might be more defensible than nullification in civil cases. Not only can jury verdicts help litigants in other cases make decisions about the conduct of the litigation, including settlement, but those verdicts can prompt potential defendants to adopt behavioral changes that could lead to greater overall health and

---

124. For a discussion of scientific jury selection, *see infra*, Chapter 5, at notes 145–150 and accompanying text.

125. *See* Introduction, *supra*, at notes 46–60. One commentator argues that lawyers tend to give more credence to the mean jury awards rather than the median, thus giving more weight than is reasonable to outlier awards—awards significantly higher or lower than the usual award. *See* Huber, *supra* note 9, at 280, 290. The problem, if it is one, could presumably be resolved through education. Lawyers generally use data on jury awards, if at all, to help them decide on an appropriate settlement figure. But if the lawyer is using the figures in part to judge the potential risk should the case go to trial, the so-called outlier awards may have some significance.

safety.[126] Conversely, a jury decision not to hold a particular defendant accountable could reflect a community sense that we should accept the risks of the defendant's behavior, perhaps because it leads to greater social good than harm.

IV. The Political Role of the Civil Jury

In the American system of government, the judicial branch is supposed to be the least "political" branch. Federal judges are insulated from political pressure by their lifetime appointments and the constitutional guarantee against diminution in salary.[127] The purpose is to leave judges free to protect the rights of individuals against the "tyranny of the majority."[128] In so doing, judges sometimes render decisions that affect the course of political events in the country.[129] It is the power of judicial review of state and federal legislation that allows the judiciary to play this political role.[130]

Juries are, if anything, less subject to political pressure than judges because they are largely anonymous, assembled for just one case, and not required to justify their decisions.[131] While juries have no formal power of judicial review, they nevertheless have a role to play within the judicial branch, and that role can have political overtones. A part of the jury's political role

---

126. Excessive jury verdicts could result in overregulation, of course, but as I have shown, most jury verdicts are not excessive. *See supra*, notes 42, 57–67 and accompanying text. It is also possible that the potential cost of defending a product against multiple suits could prompt a business to drop the product even when the product was safe. But this is a cost of having a system of civil liability rather than of the jury itself.

127. *See* U.S. CONST. art. III, sec. 1.

128. The phrase "tyranny of the majority" comes from DeTocqueville. *See* 1 ALEXIS DETOCQUEVILLE, DEMOCRACY IN AMERICA 258–62 (Phillips Bradley ed., 1990 [1835]). *See also,* ALEXANDER BICKEL, THE LEAST DANGEROUS BRANCH (1962) (arguing that the countermajoritarian characteristics of the judiciary have positive effects, but urging judicial discretion in exercising judicial review).

129. The most important recent example is the Supreme Court's decision concerning the 2000 presidential election. *See* Bush v. Gore, 531 U.S. ___ , 121 S.Ct. 525, 148 L. Ed. 2d. 388 (2000). *See also, e.g.,* Brown v. Board of Education, 347 U.S. 483 (1954) (school desegregation); Roe v. Wade, 410 U.S. 113 (1973) (abortion); Gomillion v. Lightfoot, 364 U.S. 339 (1960) (voting rights).

130. *See* Marbury v. Madison, 5 U.S. (1 Cranch.) 137 (1803) (asserting the power of judicial review). *See also,* THE FEDERALIST PAPERS, No. 78 (Hamilton) (Isaac Kramnick ed., 1987 [1788]) (discussing the power of judicial review).

131. *See* Priest, *Justifying, supra* note 3, at 105.

is captured in the discussion in the last section on jury nullification (the jury's equivalent of judicial review) and the regulatory role of juries, but that discussion does not fully explain why we might want juries to play such a role. In this section, I will explore the political rationale for the jury. I will ground the rationale in democratic theory, and will focus on two characteristics of democratic government that give the jury a political flavor: participation and deliberation. I conclude that the jury is the only remaining widespread governmental institution that fully reflects these two characteristics.

A. Participation

While democratic theorists rarely talk about the jury at any length, the link between participatory forms of democracy and the jury should be clear: the jury, in fact, is a paradigm of participatory democracy.[132] But one of the most divisive issues among democratic theorists is the scope of direct citizen participation in the institutions of government. While active participation is for many the essence of democratic citizenship,[133] a recurring theme in the history of democratic theory is fear of the common person. Sometimes that fear is expressed directly; sometimes it is disguised. But it always seems to lurk in the background, and it may affect how we view the jury.

1. The Rise and Fall of Participatory Democracy

The earliest democracy was in Athens in about the sixth century B.C. It was a participatory democracy, with all citizens taking part in deliberations about governmental decisions, and with "juries" of several hundred citizens deciding judicial matters, including, for example, the fate of Socrates.[134] Nevertheless, the Athenian democracy was quite limited in scope. Citizenship was strictly

---

132. Democratic theory has taken on many forms over the years, with differing emphases on participation. For a description of some variations on democratic theory, see DAVID HELD, MODELS OF DEMOCRACY (1987). See also, JAMES L. HYLAND, DEMOCRATIC THEORY: THE PHILOSOPHICAL FOUNDATIONS (1995) (describing the philosophical bases for the varieties of democratic theory). For some discussions of the evolution of democratic theory, especially in the twentieth century, see, e.g., PETER BACHRACH, THE THEORY OF DEMOCRATIC ELITISM 1–46 (1980); CAROLE PATEMAN, PARTICIPATION AND DEMOCRATIC THEORY 1–44(1970); ROBERT A. DAHL, DEMOCRACY AND ITS CRITICS 1–36 (1989) (hereinafter cited as DAHL, DEMOCRACY).

133. See Will Kymlicka and Wayne Norman, Return of the Citizen: A Survey of Recent Work on Citizenship Theory, in THEORIZING CITIZENSHIP 284 (Ronald Beiner ed. 1995).

134. See HELD, supra note 132, at 20–22, 28.

and narrowly defined to exclude all women and slaves, as well as other persons whose business kept them close to home, such as farmers.[135] Rome had a similar arrangement, but citizenship there was defined more as including those who had dominion, generally legal in nature, over people and things—in other words, wealthy men.[136] Participation in these ancient democracies was deep but narrow. Athens and Rome were also small enough that widespread participation was possible, especially given the narrow definition of citizenship.

After these democracies passed out of existence, it was some two thousand years before democratic theory again became an important part of political philosophy. Democratic practices continued to develop, however. The Magna Carta, signed by King John in 1215, was an important statement of the rights of English nobility vis-à-vis the king, including the right to a jury of one's peers.[137] And the development of Parliament during the thirteenth century was a step toward more widespread political participation.[138] During this period of democratic growth, the jury came to be the favored method of proof in English courts, though jurors, like members of Parliament, had to be free men, which disqualified most people.[139]

Modern democratic theory has its roots in some of the social contract theorists like Thomas Hobbes[140] and Jean-Jacques Rousseau.[141] They saw gov-

---

135. *See* J.G.A. Pocock, *The Ideal of Citizenship Since Classical Times*, in THEORIZING CITIZENSHIP, *supra* note 130. This public/private dichotomy systematically disfavors women, and is still at work to a considerable extent in modern society. *See* SUSAN MOLLER OKIN, JUSTICE, GENDER, AND THE FAMILY (1989).

136. *See* HELD, *supra* note 132, at 35–36.

137. *See* PLUCKNETT, *supra* note 9, at 22–26. *See generally*, J.C. HOLT, MAGNA CARTA (1965); FAITH THOMPSON, MAGNA CARTA: ITS ROLE IN THE MAKING OF THE ENGLISH CONSTITUTION, 1300–1629 (1948).

138. It is difficult to date the origin of Parliament, as it did not appear fully formed like the American Congress. Parliament originated as counsels called by the King to advise him on matters of the realm. Early Parliaments handled all kinds of matters: executive, legislative, and judicial. On the early Parliament, see generally, HISTORICAL STUDIES OF THE ENGLISH PARLIAMENT (2 vols., E.B. Fryde & Edward Miller eds., 1970)[hereinafter cited as HISTORICAL STUDIES]; PETER SPUFFORD, ORIGINS OF THE ENGLISH PARLIAMENT (1967); ALBERT BEEBE WHITE, THE MAKING OF THE ENGLISH CONSTITUTION, 449–1485, at pp. 298–401 (1908); 1 POLLOCK & MAITLAND, *supra* note 90, at 199–202; FRANKLIN FERRISS RUSSELL, OUTLINE OF LEGAL HISTORY 20–25 (1929).

139. *See* 2 POLLOCK & MAITLAND, *supra* note 9, at 621, 642.

140. *See* THOMAS HOBBES, LEVIATHAN, in 23 GREAT BOOKS OF THE WESTERN WORLD (Robert M. Hutchins ed. 1952).

141. *See* JEAN-JACQUES ROUSSEAU, THE SOCIAL CONTRACT, in 38 GREAT BOOKS OF THE WESTERN WORLD (Robert M. Hutchins ed. 1952).

ernment as a result of an early "agreement" among pre-political persons to give up some of the rights they would have as independent people in the state of nature in exchange for the sovereign's protection of their lives and property. Hobbes and Rousseau, however, had quite different views about the ability of the people to self-govern. Hobbes was quite pessimistic, and preferred that the contract put sovereignty in the hands of a ruler whose power would be absolute.[142] Thus, while the initial contract was democratic, Hobbes did not favor democratic governmental institutions. Rousseau, on the other hand preferred that the power remain in the people, and he favored governmental institutions that facilitated participation.[143]

The reality of democracy in England was somewhere in between. For one thing, England was too big to accommodate full participation in governmental decisions. Thus, representative democracy took hold, with voting as the primary means of participation. For another, the king and the nobility were slow to open participation to the common people, so even the right to vote was limited.[144] The English political theorist John Locke, who influenced the American Revolution, exemplifies this middle ground. His theories were classically liberal and individualistic; he viewed all government as existing only to protect individual initiative and property rights.[145] He had no particular predilection for participatory democracy; rather, his was a theory of representative democracy based on majoritarian principles.[146] The majority, however, was probably a majority of property owners, as Locke considered only those who had property to be full citizens.[147] During Locke's time, juries also were limited to property holders.[148]

These different views of participation are reflected among the founders of the United States. The most aristocratic of the founders was Alexander Hamilton, who distrusted democracy as essentially anarchical.[149] Jefferson, by con-

---

142. *See* HOBBES, *supra* note 140, at 109–112.

143. *See* ROUSSEAU, *supra* note 141, at 392–96.

144. See 2 HISTORICAL STUDIES, *supra* note 138, at 8–9.

145. *See* JOHN LOCKE, SECOND TREATISE OF GOVERNMENT 75–80 (Richard Cox ed., 1982). For a discussion of Locke's theories, see C.B. MACPHERSON, THE POLITICAL THEORY OF POSSESSIVE INDIVIDUALISM 194–262 (1962).

146. *See* LOCKE, *supra* note 145, at 79–80; PATEMAN, *supra* note 132, at 20.

147. *See* MACPHERSON, *supra* note 145, at 221–57. For Locke, only those persons who had, through their labor and ingenuity, given value to property were entitled to full citizenship.

148. *See* LORD PATRICK DEVLIN, TRIAL BY JURY 17 (1966).

149. *See* CLAUDE G. BOWERS, JEFFERSON AND HAMILTON: THE STRUGGLE FOR DEMOCRACY IN AMERICA 28–29 (1925); GERALD STOURZH, ALEXANDER HAMILTON AND THE IDEA

trast, had great faith in ordinary people and favored considerable citizen involvement in public life.[150] Madison, who had the most influence on the shape of the Constitution,[151] occupied a middle ground, though he, like Hamilton, feared and distrusted ordinary citizens, as he believed that they tended to form factions that could trample the rights of the political minority.[152] The distrust of ordinary citizens is reflected, for example, in the sections of the original Constitution that provided for indirect election of the President and the Senate.[153] In addition, many of the checks and balances of American democracy are designed to protect minority views and interests.[154] The judiciary itself is intended to be counter-majoritarian, a fact that disturbs some people, who wonder why a counter-majoritarian institution has a place in a democracy.[155]

The original Constitution, reflecting Madison's views, did not provide for a civil jury in federal courts, though it did guarantee a jury trial in criminal cases.[156] Madison and the other drafters may have thought that there was little need for a civil jury as a buffer against governmental authority once the

---

OF REPUBLICAN GOVERNMENT 44–48 (1970); THE FEDERALIST PAPERS, No. 35 (Hamilton), *supra* note 130 (arguing that landholders can best represent the common people).

150. *See* CALEB PERRY PATTERSON, THE CONSTITUTIONAL PRINCIPLES OF THOMAS JEFFERSON 56–58 (1953). It should be noted that Jefferson did not take part in the drafting of the Constitution, nor did he participate directly in any of the ratification debates. He was in Europe at the time as an emissary of the United States.

151. *See* Charles W. Wolfram, *The Constitutional History of the Seventh Amendment*, 57 MINN. L. REV. 639, 656 (1973). *See generally*, ROBERT J. MORGAN, JAMES MADISON ON THE CONSTITUTION AND THE BILL OF RIGHTS (1988); IRVING BRANT, JAMES MADISON, FATHER OF THE CONSTITUTION 1787–1800 (1950); EDWARD MCNALL BURNS, JAMES MADISON, PHILOSOPHER OF THE CONSTITUTION (1938).

152. *See* THE FEDERALIST PAPERS, No. 10 (Madison), *supra* note 130. Madison remained a lifelong friend of Jefferson's, but he collaborated with Hamilton in writing *The Federalist Papers*, a series of articles offering an extensive defense of the proposed Constitution that appeared during the ratification debates. Jefferson and Hamilton were more antagonistic to one another. *See* CLAUDE G. BOWERS, JEFFERSON AND HAMILTON (1925); DUMAS MALONE, JEFFERSON AND THE RIGHTS OF MAN, Ch. XXVII (1925).

153. U.S. CONST. art I, sec. 3 (senators); *id* at art. II, sec. 1 (president). The Seventeenth Amendment, ratified in 1913, provided for direct election of senators.

154. *See* THE FEDERALIST PAPERS, No. 51 (Madison), *supra* note 130.

155. *See, e.g.*, Eakin v. Raub, 12 Serg. & Rawle 330, 354–55 (Pa. 1825) (Gibson, J., dissenting); James Bradley Thayer, *The Origin and Scope of the American Doctrine of Constitutional Law*, in LEGAL ESSAYS 1 (1908); Learned Hand, *The Contribution of an Independent Judiciary to Civilization*, in THE SPIRIT OF LIBERTY 164–65 (Irving Dilliard ed., 3rd. ed. 1960). Like the Federalists, there are some people who are not troubled by the judiciary's counter-majoritarian position. *See, e.g.,* BICKEL, *supra* note 128, at 28.

156. *See* U.S. CONST. art. III, §2, cl. 3.

colonists had achieved independence from England.[157] But Madison's lack of faith in ordinary citizens may have been part of the reason as well. In any event, the failure of the Constitution to provide a bill of rights, including the right to a civil jury trial, was an important ground of opposition to the proposed Constitution.[158] While Jefferson, observing the debates from France, ultimately supported the Constitution, he, too, was concerned about the lack of a bill of rights.[159] Defenders of the Constitution ultimately prevailed, but it was understood that one of the first things Congress had to do was propose a bill of rights as amendments to the Constitution.[160] The First Congress did so, and the first ten amendments to the Constitution were ratified in 1791.[161] It is the Seventh Amendment that guarantees a right to jury trial in civil cases. The Constitution, then, reflects a mixture of democratic and counter-democratic institutions, with the jury as one of the more democratic ones.

2. Modern Ideas About Participation

The twentieth century saw two developments that had profound effects on democratic theory. One was the collapse of European democracies into totalitarianism in the 1930s,[162] which led many democratic theorists to a renewed distrust of citizen participation.[163] Another was the growth of social science, which revealed a disturbing anti-democratic sentiment among ordinary citizens.[164] One result of these developments was the formation of a theory of democratic elites, in which the role of the people is seen as nothing more than choosing, at periodic elections, between competing elites that wish to govern.[165] Better, theorists thought, to entrust government to the elites, with as

---

157. *See* Landsman, *supra* note 50, at 37; Wolfram, *supra* note 151, at 661.

158. *See* Wolfram, *supra* note 151, at 667–73, 725; ROBERT ALLEN RUTLAND, THE BIRTH OF THE BILL OF RIGHTS, 1776–1791, pp. 106–58 (1955).

159. *See* MALONE, *supra* note 152, at 168. Jefferson's initial reaction to the Constitution was negative. *See id.* at 162–69.

160. *See* RUTLAND, *supra* note 158, at pp. 159–89.

161. *See generally,* RUTLAND, *supra* note 158.

162. *See* DAHL, DEMOCRACY, *supra* note 132, at 235.

163. *See, e.g.,* J.L. TALMON, THE RISE OF TOTALITARIAN DEMOCRACY (1952).

164. *See* EDWARD R. PURCELL, JR., THE CRISIS OF DEMOCRATIC THEORY: SCIENTIFIC NATURALISM AND THE PROBLEM OF VALUE 13–114 (1973) (documenting early social science findings); DAVID M. RICCI, THE TRAGEDY OF POLITICAL SCIENCE 77–96 (1984) (same); SEYMOUR MARTIN LIPSET, POLITICAL MAN (1960) (reporting study of political attitudes).

165. *See,* JOSEPH SCHUMPETER, CAPITALISM, SOCIALISM, AND DEMOCRACY (1950); ROBERT A. DAHL, A PREFACE TO DEMOCRATIC THEORY (1956) (hereinafter cited as DAHL, PREFACE); BACHRACH, *supra* note 132.

little intervention from the anti-democratic public as possible, than to permit any widespread participation in government.[166]

More recently, there has been a revival of support for democratic participation. Critics of the theory of democratic elitism have appeared, arguing for more, rather than less participation.[167] The general thrust of the criticism is that earlier studies of political behavior did not do justice to the quality of citizen participation—that citizens do a much better job, and have more respect for democratic institutions, than appeared from those early studies.[168] In addition, some of these critics point out that participation educates citizens about society's problems and solutions, and so the more participation there is, the better the citizenry will be.[169] Indeed, the educational value of participation in the institutions of government—including the jury—has a long and honored place in democratic theory.[170] Some of the modern theorists, recognizing the difficulty of ensuring widespread political participation in huge modern democracies, argue for democratization of other societal institutions, such as the workplace.[171]

These modern democrats are strongly represented in the civic republican and communitarianism movements. The new civic republicans, calling on Jeffersonian traditions, are found in numerous disciplines, but they share a desire for more emphasis on civic responsibility and participation.[172] A related movement that has gained strength in recent years is communitarianism, which focuses on participation in the institutions of society more generally,

---

166. *See* BACHRACH, *supra* note 132, at 47–64. This is reminiscent of Hamilton's and even Madison's views. *See* James P. Martin, *When Repression is Democratic and Constitutional: The Federalist Theory of Representation and the Sedition Act of 1798*, 66 U. CHI. L. REV. 117 (1999) (showing that Madison and the Federalists thought that once the people had voted, their political role was over).

167. *See, e.g.,* BACHRACH, *supra* note 132; PATEMAN, *supra* note 132; PURCELL, *supra* note 164.

168. *See* Benjamin I. Page and Robert Y. Shapiro, *The Rational Public and Democracy*, in RECONSIDERING THE DEMOCRATIC ᴾUBLIC 37–40 (George E. Marcus and Russell L. Hanson eds. 1993).

169. *See* PATEMAN, *supra* note 132, at 30, 105.

170. *See, e.g.,* JOHN STUART MILL, REPRESENTATIVE GOVERNMENT 380–89, in 43 GREAT BOOKS OF THE WESTERN WORLD (Robert Maynard Hutchins ed. 1952); 15 THOMAS JEFFERSON, THE PAPERS OF THOMAS JEFFERSON 283 (Julian Boyd ed., 1958); 1 DETOCQUEVILLE, *supra* note 128, at 280–87; ABA/BROOKINGS, *supra* note 2, at 11.

171. *See, e.g.,* BACHRACH, *supra* note 132; PATEMAN, *supra* note 132.

172. *See, e.g.,* BENJAMIN BARBER, STRONG DEMOCRACY (1984) (political theorist); Frank Michelman, *Law's Republic*, 97 YALE L.J. 1493 (1988) (legal theorist); Cass R. Sunstein, *Beyond the Republican Revival*, 97 YALE L.J. 1539 (1988) (legal theorist).

including, but not limited to, government.[173] Proponents of these movements share a trust in democratic institutions and in the people who participate in them, and think that society and its members benefit from more widespread participation in governmental and societal decision-making. The views of civic republicans and communitarians are often in sharp contrast to "liberal" democrats, who tend to be more concerned about freedom from too much governmental interference.[174] Civic republicans and communitarians believe in doing one's civic duty; there is more to citizenship, in other words, than the opportunity to participate—there is an *obligation* to do so.[175]

The civic republican and communitarian traditions offer a strong political justification for the civil jury. If, as I have shown, civil adjudication has a public character, the republican and communitarian traditions would suggest not only that it is appropriate for the public to be involved in the process, but that we have obligations, as citizens, to take part. Indeed, the communitarians, especially, would point out that simply knowing that one has civic obligations, such as jury duty, is beneficial.[176] It ties people to other members of the community and to the institutions of government and society, and gives them more of a stake in those institutions.[177] Liberal, and especially elitist, theories of democracy really do not provide strong support for the jury because they lack a strong foundation for required political participation. The libertarian branch of liberal theory is especially hostile to the concept of required political participation, as libertarians tend to think that people should participate

---

173. The unofficial leader of this movement seems to be the sociologist Amitai Etzioni, but it has drawn people from many disciplines and from across the political spectrum. *See, e.g.,* Amitai Etzioni, The Spirit of Community (1993); The New Communitarian Thinking (Amitai Etzioni, ed. 1995); Mary Ann Glendon, Rights Talk (1992); Michael J. Sandel, Democracy's Discontent (1996). Communitarianism differs from civic republicanism primarily in its focus on citizen participation in, and obligations to, the institutions of society as a whole and not merely government. *See* Ronald Beiner, *Introduction,* in Theorizing Citizenship, *supra* note 133.

174. I use "liberal" here to mean the political theory that favors as much freedom from governmental constraints as is possible. This theory gives the government a very small role. This is the classic sense of "liberal," and it is now closer to what we would call the libertarian position. *See generally,* Stephen Mulhall and Adam Swift, Liberals and Communitarians (2d ed. 1996).

175. *See* Thomas A. Spragens, Jr., *Communitarian Liberalism,* in New Communitarian Thinking, *supra* note 173, at 50–51; Etzioni, *supra* note 173 at 247–50.

176. *See* Spragens, *supra* note 175, at 49–50; Etzioni, *supra* note 173, at 159–60.

177. *See also,* ABA/Brookings Report, *supra* note 2, at 10–11 (one justification for the civil jury is that it legitimates the judiciary through citizen participation).

only if they want to.[178] Liberal or libertarian theories tend to value individual autonomy; civic republican and communitarian theories tend to value the connection we have to each other and to the institutions we live within. It seems to me that both autonomy and connectedness have a place.[179] The key is finding the right mix. But the jury is the only civic republican or communitarian governmental institution we have. In part, that is because it is the only one that comes with an enforceable duty to participate. It is also the only one that, in theory at least, enforces that duty across social, political, economic, racial and gender lines. If I am right that liberalism on the one hand and civic republicanism or communitarianism on the other both represent values that we should wish to preserve, we cannot afford to lose the only governmental institution that represents the latter.

B. Deliberation

Participation can range from occasional isolated acts of voting to active engagement in determining and executing public policy. Any level of participation, however, involves some degree of deliberation, by which I mean a coming together of interested persons to discuss a problem or issue and seek solutions. How much deliberation we get depends in part on the decision rule that we use. A majoritarian decision rule is likely to result in less deliberation than a consensus deliberation rule. Consensus requires more discussion and perhaps more compromise.

The American political system as a whole uses a majoritarian decision rule: the majority prevails in elections no matter how slim the margin. Deliberation occurs within the institutions of government but not, for the most part, outside of them. Indeed, there is some evidence that the Federalists believed that once an election produced a winner, it was illegitimate for citizens to criticize those who had been elected; their only recourse was to vote them out of office in the next election.[180] This accounts for Federalist support of laws against "seditious libel."[181] Today, of course, laws against seditious libel are clearly unconstitutional, and we can say just about anything about the government and those who serve in it. But are we deliberating?

---

178. *See* ETZIONI, *supra* note 173, at 15; MULHALL & SWIFT, *supra* note 174, at xv; WILL KYMLICKA, CONTEMPORARY POLITICAL PHILOSOPHY: AN INTRODUCTION 95–159 (1990).

179. *See* MICHAEL WALZER, SPHERES OF JUSTICE: A DEFENSE OF PLURALISM AND EQUALITY 64–94 (1983).

180. *See generally,* Martin, *supra* note 166.

181. *See id.*

It is impossible for 280 million people to deliberate together, and in the era of the sound byte, very little of substance is said in public. It is also unrealistic to expect consensus in a country so large and so diverse. Nevertheless, there have been several recent efforts to encourage more deliberation, though they have met with limited success. Recent national elections have featured "town meetings," in which candidates talk with ordinary citizens. These may be too few and far between to have much of an impact, but they are a start. Citizens have also kept talk radio going for years, though there is some question whether people are really listening—critical if deliberation is to take place— or simply waiting for their own chance to talk. Some people tout the referendum as the epitome of citizen participation, but for most citizens, there is no participation in or deliberation about the proposal itself—only the opportunity to vote for or against it.[182] There have even been some more radical proposals, designed to facilitate deliberation, such as one for a national town meeting, where participants would be randomly selected and required to attend.[183] Indeed, "deliberative democracy"—a form of democracy that would facilitate talk—is being touted as an answer to our national political malaise.[184]

There are limits to our ability to generate true deliberation within the majoritarian election system, however. Majoritarian voting is an example of what Jane Mansbridge calls "adversary democracy," and it is not conducive to much deliberation.[185] Rather, deliberation occurs in what Mansbridge calls "unitary

---

182. *See* Daniel M. Warner, *Direct Democracy: The Right of the People to Make Fools of Themselves; The Use and Abuse of Initiative and Referendum*, 19 SEATTLE U. L. REV. 47, 77–78 (1995); David B. Magleby, *Let the Voters Decide? An Assessment of the Initiative and Referendum Process*, 66 U. COLO. L. REV. 13, 43–44 (1995). *See generally,* Sherman J. Clarke, *A Populist Critique of Direct Democracy*, 112 HARV. L. REV. 434 (1998).

183. *See* JAMES S. FISHKIN, DEMOCRACY AND DELIBERATION: NEW DIRECTIONS FOR DEMOCRATIC REFORM (1991).

184. *See, e.g.,* FISHKIN, *supra* note 183; CASS R. SUNSTEIN, THE PARTIAL CONSTITUTION (1993); Joseph M. Bessette, *Deliberative Democracy: The Majority Principle in Republican Government*, in HOW DEMOCRATIC IS THE CONSTITUTION? (Robert A. Goldwin & William A. Schambra eds., 1980); David M. Estlund, *Who's Afraid of Deliberative Democracy? On the Strategic/Deliberative Dichotomy in Recent Constitutional Jurisprudence*, 71 TEX. L. REV. 1437 (1993). For a criticism of deliberative democracy, see James A. Gardner, *Shut Up and Vote: A Critique of Deliberative Democracy and the Life of Talk*, 63 TENN. L. REV. 421 (1996).

185. *See* JANE MANSBRIDGE, BEYOND ADVERSARY DEMOCRACY (1983). Adversary democracy presumes a clash of interests; equality of power, in the sense of voting power; a majoritarian decision rule; and either no deliberation or deliberation in the form of a public debate among distant participants. *Id.* at 5, T.1. Mansbridge argues that adversary democracy is necessary to protect equality of power when people do not have a commonality of interests. *Id.* at 5–6.

democracies"—small communities, such as workplaces or New England town meetings, where the participants have common interests or goals.[186] The United States is too large and too diverse for much deliberation to occur in the public discourse.

The jury, however, is small enough and focused enough for real deliberation to occur. Jurors have a common goal of reaching the right decision in the case before them, and they must deliberate face-to-face until that unanimous (consensus) decision is reached. None of our other widespread governmental institutions has these characteristics. Only the jury among our governmental institutions requires diverse people to come together and deliberate to a unanimous decision.[187]

Perhaps it is these characteristics of the jury that have prompted so many people to argue that jury duty serves to make citizens better participants in the public discourse. This is one of the justifications for the jury offered by the ABA/Brookings symposium.[188] The observation is of long standing, however, and it is consistent with democratic theory in general.[189] Thomas Jefferson argued that the jury is "the school by which [the] people learn the exer-

---

186. *See id.* at 5. Unitary democracies are characterized by commonality of interests, equality of respect, a consensus decision rule, and face-to-face deliberation. *See id.* at 5, T.1.

187. Some administrative agencies have procedures where interested parties come together to negotiate regulations. *See* Philip J. Harter, *Negotiating Regulations: A Cure for Malaise*, 71 GEO. L.J. 1 (1982); Lawrence Susskind & Gerard McMahon, *The Theory and Practice of Negotiated Rulemaking*, 3 YALE J. REG. 133 (1985); Jody Freeman, *Collaborative Governance in the Administrative State*, 45 U.C.L.A. L. REV. 1 (1997). These procedures do not involve deliberative decision-making, but rather are more akin to mediated settlements among interested parties. There has been some criticism of these procedures. *See* Jim Rossi, *Participation Run Amok: The Costs of Mass Participation for Deliberative Agency Decisionmaking*, 92 NW.U.L. REV. 173 (1997).

188. *See* ABA/BROOKINGS REPORT, *supra* note 2, at 9. One recent study suggests that jury deliberation has a polarizing effect when the decision the jury is called upon to make is relatively unbounded, such as a punitive damages award. *See* Schkade, Sunstein, and Kahneman, *supra* note 60. The polarization is shown by higher or lower punitive damage awards from juries than the individual jurors would have reached. In general, the authors found that if the individuals were already predisposed to a high award, jury deliberation made it higher; the same effect, in the opposite direction, is true when the individuals are predisposed to a low award. The study, however, does not suggest that deliberation would skew a bounded judgment, such as whether or not someone is liable, or what the plaintiff's dollar losses were.

189. *See* PATEMAN, *supra* note 132, at 31–32 (arguing that participation makes people better citizens by educating them as to civic matters); JOHN STUART MILL, ON LIBERTY (Elizabeth Rapaport ed. 1978) (same). *See also*, ABA/BROOKINGS REPORT, *supra* note 2, at 11 (listing educational value as one justification for civil jury).

cise of civic duties as well as rights."[190] De Tocqueville also extolled the jury for its educational benefits, saying that "the jury, which is the most energetic means of making the people rule, is also the most efficacious means of teaching it how to rule well."[191]

There are good reasons for viewing the jury as a training ground for the civic discourse that is so necessary to making a democracy work. Jurors with disparate backgrounds and outlooks must come together and deliberate about what are often some very difficult issues. This deliberation requires that the jurors listen to one another, respect one another's opinions, and try to find some common ground. As citizens succeed at this most difficult task, they should become more adept at the art of political discourse.[192]

C. Summary and Conclusion

The jury is the only one of our widespread public institutions in which ordinary citizens can participate directly in government and deliberate together about important public issues. Indeed, one significant aspect of the jury is

---

190. See ABRAMSON, *supra* note 14, at 31, *quoting* SHANNON C. STIMSON, THE AMERICAN REVOLUTION IN THE LAW: ANGLO AMERICAN JURISPRUDENCE BEFORE JOHN MARSHALL 88 (1990). Jefferson, however, did not believe that juries should have the power to decide law, which suggests that he saw the jury as a political rather than a legal entity. See STIMSON, *supra*. See also, 15 JEFFERSON, *supra* note 170, at 269 ("I consider [the jury] as the only anchor, ever yet imagined by man, by which a government can be held to the principles of it's [sic] constitution.")

191. 1 DeTOCQUEVILLE, *supra* note 128, at 284–85.

192. While I would never attribute a cause-and-effect relationship to it, it is perhaps telling that the civil jury is in something of an eclipse, relatively speaking, at the same time that political discourse in this country has sunk to a depressing low. A wide range of commentators have lamented the breakdown in our ability to talk to each other. See, e.g., David Broder, *Civil Discourse and Values Seldom Go Out of Date*, KANSAS CITY STAR, p. C7 (January 3, 1996); Robert D. Putnam, *The Strange Disappearance of Civic America*, in THE AMERICAN PROSPECT 34 (Winter 1996). The jury requires that citizens talk to each other in exactly the same ways that civic society requires. There is no real way to tell if jurors' experiences make them better citizens in this important sense, though there is certainly some empirical evidence suggesting that jurors both think they have benefited from jury service and generally come away from such service with heightened respect for our system of dispute resolution. See generally, Shari Seidman Diamond, *What Jurors Think: Expectations and Reactions of Citizens Who Serve as Jurors*, in VERDICT, *supra* note 2; Professor Daniel W. Shuman & Dr. Jean A. Hamilton, *Jury Service—It May Change Your Mind: Perceptions of Fairness of Jurors and Nonjurors*, 46 S.M.U. L. REV. 449 (1992). Thus, the jury seems to have a role to play in helping citizens learn about the kinds of discourse that are important to a functioning democracy.

that citizens are *required* to participate. All of our other institutions are voluntary. And when citizens participate directly in deliberations about important governmental decisions, society as a whole benefits from having more informed members who are adept at political discourse and who feel more of a stake in the government. Jefferson thought the judicial branch particularly well suited to citizen participation.[193] Judicial decisions are often easier to understand than legislative or executive ones, and they are certainly more focused, making them ideal for the jury.

While the criminal jury as well as the civil produces these benefits, there are good reasons for believing that the civil jury is at least as important, in this political sense, as the criminal. First, the civil jury increases the opportunities that citizens have to serve. If citizens benefit from jury service, then we should make jury service available to as many as possible. Second, as DeTocqueville said over one hundred and fifty years ago, citizens are more attuned to civil cases than criminal—they are more likely to have experience with the material of civil cases, and so more likely to see its relevance for their own lives.[194]

V. The Socializing Role of the Civil Jury

We live in a complex, multi-cultural society, but often the parts do not talk to one another. Jury duty requires diverse people to work together for a common end. It requires that we respect each other's perspectives. It requires that we try to understand lives that are quite different from our own. And it does all this not in the rarefied atmospheres of speculation or entertainment, but in real cases involving real people. Even apart from political participation and deliberation, then, jury duty can help us to understand and get along with each other.[195]

There are, of course, many other places where diverse people can come together and get to know one another. The military, for example, is now one of the most diverse governmental departments.[196] We might also hope that our schools and colleges would provide opportunities for young people to expand their horizons by seeking out people who are "different," but it is a common-

---

193. *See* ABRAMSON, *supra* note 14, at 30 (quoting *Letter of Jefferson to the Abbe Arnoux* in 15 JEFFERSON *supra* note 170, at 283. Jefferson said that "[t]he execution of the laws is more important than the making [of] them." *Id.*

194. *See* 1 DETOCQUEVILLE, *supra* note 128, at 284–85.

195. *See* ABA/BROOKINGS REPORT, *supra* note 2, at 8–11.

196. *See* MICKEY KAUS, THE END OF EQUALITY, ch. 6 (1992) (describing some public institutions that can bring people together, including the draft and national service).

place that in schools and on college campuses, racial groups often go their separate ways.[197] The workplace is another place where all employees must work together to get the job done, though some jobs require only superficial cooperation; in addition, many workplaces are not themselves very diverse, particularly in the upper levels of management, which are some ninety-five per cent white and male.[198]

These examples show that, for the most part, mingling and cooperation with people whose backgrounds and perspectives differ from one's own is strictly voluntary in this country. People who are already inclined to learn about other cultures are the people most likely to partake of these opportunities. The jury, by contrast, is not only one of the most diverse institutions in America, whether governmental or private;[199] it is also the only one that is obligatory. Even the military is now a voluntary force. This means that the jury has the potential for teaching us all a great deal about the society we live in, the people who comprise it, and our system of authoritative dispute resolution. And it can perform those functions even for people who do not serve, because jurors return to their homes and jobs and talk about their experiences.[200]

VI. Summary and Conclusion

I have identified a number of roles that the civil jury can play, some of which overlap. The first is the dispute-settling role. I asked whether there were good reasons for requiring private citizens to assist other private citizens in resolving private disputes. Because there are significant public aspects of civil disputes, I concluded that there are, though there may be limits to the jury's competence. The jury also plays a law-making role, though the justifications for that role are harder to make. The law-making role includes jury nullification. While jury nullification is more justifiable in criminal cases than in civil, I conclude that jury nullification has played a positive role in civil cases in the past, and that we should be reluctant to try to ban it entirely, even if we could.

197. *See* Shelby Steele, *Rise of "the New Segregation": The "Politics of Difference" Threatens to Produce a Divided Society*, 121 USA TODAY MAGAZINE 53 (March 1993).

198. *See* Francine Knowles, *Opening Up Top Executive Ranks*, CHICAGO SUN-TIMES, FINANCE SECTION, at 45 (July 4, 1996); Robin Abcarian, *Not Too Young to See an Unlevel Playing Field*, LOS ANGELES TIMES, at E1 (June 9, 1996).

199. *See* Laura Gaston Dooley, *Our Juries, Our Selves: The Power, Perception, and Politics of the Civil Jury*, 80 CORNELL L. REV. 325, 359–60 (1995).

200. *See* Priest, *Justifying, supra* note 3, at 123.

The jury's law-making role also includes a regulatory role, as the jury tells us, for example, what is (or is not) reasonable behavior under various circumstances. Jury verdicts can also prompt manufacturers to change their manufacturing designs or practices.

The political role underlies all of this. I have pointed out that the jury is our only widespread political institution that requires private citizens to participate in deliberations about important governmental decisions. Jury service educates citizens about public issues and keeps them involved in, and therefore concerned about, their country's institutions. Similarly, the jury has the potential for playing a significant socializing role because jury service requires diverse people to work together to find common ground and with it a solution to the puzzle placed before them. In so doing, people learn to understand and respect one another, not only for their common humanity, but for their differences as well.

The jury has not always played these roles, however. In the next chapter, I will trace the history of the jury from its English origins through the nineteenth century.

CHAPTER 2

The Early History of
the Civil Jury Trial

The origins of the jury as we know it are lost in the mists of time.[1] While
there is widespread agreement about its most likely precursor, there are significant gaps in its history, and some aspects of that history are almost impossible to tease out of the existing record. Nevertheless, there is much that
we do know about the development of the civil jury in England, and much
that we can be reasonably certain about. That early history reaches out into
modern times and shapes much of the modern jury, so it is important to understand it.

I. The Civil Jury in England

The jury grew up in the common law courts in England and was well-suited
to the structure and procedures of those courts. But the original jury was an
administrative arm of the king, and the king had considerable incentive to
control the jury. In addition, England had a complementary system of jurisprudence known as "equity," where juries did not operate.

---

1. One of the best general histories of the English jury is found in James B. Thayer, A
Preliminary Treatise on Evidence at the Common Law ([1969]1898). Others are
William Forsyth, History of Trial by Jury (1875); Theodore F.T. Plucknett, A Con-
cise History of the Common Law 106–38 (1956); 1 Frederick Pollock and Frederic
William Maitland, The History of English Law 138–46 ([1968]1898); 2 *id.* at
598–674; 1 W.S. Holdsworth, A History Of English Law, 135–69 (1908); Lord
Patrick Devlin, Trial By Jury (1956); Stephen Landsman, *The Civil Jury in America:
Scenes from an Unappreciated History*, 44 Hastings L.J. 579 (1993). *See also,* Leonard W.
Levy, The Palladium of Justice: Origins of Trial by Jury (1999) (discussing, prima-
rily, the criminal jury).

A. The Origins and Growth of the Civil Jury in England

Constitutional and procedural histories of modern England generally begin with the Norman Conquest in 1066. The two centuries after the Conquest saw, among other things, the establishment of the king's common law courts, the growth of the jury, the origins of equity, the definition of the rights of English people in the Magna Carta, and the beginnings of Parliament. In this section, I will discuss the jury's intimate relationship with the king's common law courts.

1. Common Law Courts and the Jury

Litigants in England after the Norman Conquest were faced with a wide array of courts, from local manorial courts to the king's courts.[2] For the most part, civil litigation was conducted locally, with the king becoming involved only if the suit had implications for him, such as revenue.[3] Thus, courts were highly decentralized.[4] Subjects could always appeal to the king,[5] however, and the chief means of doing so in the decades after the Conquest was to appear at an eyre, which was a traveling court that made a complete circuit of the kingdom roughly every seven years.[6] But because the circuit took so long, a litigant could have a long wait for justice. Thus, litigants began going directly to the king or the Chancellor, who was the king's chief administrative officer, and seeking a writ.[7] A writ, which was an order to the sheriff to bring the defendant before the court, gave the court immediate jurisdiction over the matter.[8] Obtaining a writ, then, was initially an exception to the normal proce-

---

2. *See* S.F.C. Milsom, Historical Foundations of the Common Law 13–25 (2nd ed. 1981); John Hudson, The Formation of the English Common Law, Ch. 2 (1996).

3. *See* Milsom, *supra* note 2, at 25–27.

4. This was true of governmental administration as a whole. *See* Thayer, *supra* note 1, at 48–49. One of the difficult tasks that William the Conquerer faced was uniting his new realm. His successors used the courts to achieve significant centralization. *See infra,* notes 43–46 and accompanying text.

5. *See* Hudson, *supra* note 2, at 27–31.

6. *See* Milsom, *supra* note 2, at 33–36. An eyre was more than a court, however. Medieval kings made no distinction between the administration of the government and the court system; an eyre audited the king's realm in addition to hearing pleas. *Id.* at 27–31; Hudson, *supra* note 2, at 123–26.

7. *See* Milsom, *supra* note 2, at 33–35. A writ was not required in all medieval English courts, but was required in the royal common pleas court, which eventually took over most of the business of the other early English courts. *See id.* at 33–36.

8. *See id.* at 33.

dure, though it gradually became the accepted mode of commencing a civil suit, as more and more cases were routed to the king's courts through the writ system.[9]

A writ embodied a form of action, which is akin to a modern cause of action in that it created a legal right for which a remedy could be had.[10] Thus, there was a substantive side to a writ.[11] Writs were quite rigidly defined, and different writs could not be joined in a single lawsuit. If a single set of circumstances suggested that a litigant was entitled to more than one writ, she would have to bring separate lawsuits.[12] This kept lawsuits relatively simple, but it could work an injustice on litigants, who might have to give up some of their claims or undertake the expense of multiple lawsuits.

There was also a procedural side to a writ: it prescribed both the procedures to be followed and the mode of proof.[13] The first stage of any lawsuit, however, was presenting the case to the court. Around the time of the Norman Conquest, English procedure provided for the presentation of the plain-

---

9. *See id.* at 33–36.

10. *See* 1 JOHN NORTON POMEROY, A TREATISE ON EQUITY JURISPRUDENCE §§ 21–22 (5th ed., Spencer W. Symons ed. 1941) [hereinafter cited as POMEROY, TREATISE]. Some modern commentators would prefer to drop the term "cause of action" and simply refer to "claims," which are defined as the set of facts out of which legal rights and remedies arise. *See, e.g.,* American Law Institute, Federal Code Revision Project 21–22 (Tentative Draft No. 1, April 8, 1997); Douglas D. McFarland, *The Unconstitutional Stub of Section 1441(c),* 54 OHIO ST. L.J. 1059, 1066 (1993) (citing Charles E. Clark, *The Code Cause of Action,* 33 YALE L.J. 817, 837 (1924). I think, however, that "cause of action" and "claim" refer to two different things. If a claim is a set of facts—an event—out of which a right to relief arises, a cause of action is the legal theory that gives rise to that right. A single claim could give rise to multiple causes of action. *See* Edward Hartnett, *A New Trick From an Old and Abused Dog: Section 1441(c) Lives and Now Permits the Remand of Federal Question Cases,* 63 FORDHAM L. REV. 1099, 1134–39 (1995) (discussing McFarland and Clark, *supra*; Oliver L. McCaskill, *Actions and Causes of Action,* 34 YALE L.J. 614 (1925); and JOHN N. POMEROY, REMEDIES AND REMEDIAL RIGHTS BY THE CIVIL ACTION ACCORDING TO THE REFORMED AMERICAN PROCEDURE (1876)). *See* Rees v. Heyser, 404 N.E.2d 1183, 1185 (Ind. App. 1980). Practitioners and judges are well aware that in order to state a claim, a plaintiff must plead the elements of a cause of action. *See, e.g.,* Gooley v. Mobil Oil Corp., 851 F.2d 513, 515 (1st Cir. 1988).

11. I discuss the substantive aspects of writs *infra,* Chapter 3, at notes 185–201 and accompanying text.

12. *See* JOSEPH H. KOFFLER & ALISON REPPY, HANDBOOK OF COMMON LAW PLEADING 39 (1969); Stephen N. Subrin, *How Equity Conquered the Common Law: The Federal Rules of Civil Procedure in Historical Perspective,* 135 U.PA. L. REV. 909, 916 (1987).

13. *See* HAROLD GREVILLE HANBURY, MODERN EQUITY 2 (2nd ed. 1937); MILSOM, *supra* note 2, at 34, 36; FLEMING JAMES, CIVIL PROCEDURE § 1.3 (1965).

tiff's case by witnesses, called the *secta*.[14] These were not witnesses in the usual sense, but only helped the plaintiff establish that he had a claim.[15] After the development of the writs, an elaborate system of pleading evolved in which the parties answered each other's claims and defenses orally in open court, in formalized steps designed to narrow the case to a single issue.[16] The issue could be of law or of fact, but there could be only one.[17] Simplicity was the essence of a common law suit. Claims, embodied in the writs, could not be joined and neither, for the most part, could parties.[18] Thus, a common law suit generally involved a single cause of action, a single plaintiff, a single defendant, and a single issue.

Once the issue was defined through the pleading, someone had to prove it. The mode of proof varied from one writ to another, as did the assignment of the burden of proof. Some writs allowed proof by witnesses, in which the par-

---

14. *See* THAYER, *supra* note 1, at 10–16.

15. *Id.*

16. *See generally,* HENRY JOHN STEPHEN, A TREATISE ON THE PRINCIPLES OF PLEADING IN CIVIL ACTIONS 147–56 (Tyler ed. 1882). Eventually, the common law courts began to sanction the general issue plea, which simply allowed the defendant to dispute the plaintiff's claim without specifiying the ground for the dispute. This procedure could allow several issues, both law and fact, to be presented for resolution. *See* David Millon, *Positivism in the Historiography of the Common Law,* 1989 WIS. L. REV. 669, 675–77. While the single-issue pleading rules were difficult to accommodate to an increasingly complex world, the general issue plea may have gone too far in the opposite direction. Among other things, the general issue plea allowed for a fairly free-wheeling jury nullification. When juries are asked to decide cases where the legal issue is disguised by a general issue plea, the jury has considerable *de facto* power to nullify.

17. Common law courts eventually distinguished between law and fact, assigning questions of law to the judge for decision, and questions of fact to the jury. *See infra,* notes 97–103 and accompanying text. Early trials made no such distinction, as the only question was who was right, and God decided that by overseeing the proof. *See infra,* notes 19–33 and accompanying text.

18. *See* Douglas Laycock, *The Triumph of Equity,* 56 L. & CONTEMP. PROBS. 53, 65 (Summer 1993); Subrin, *supra* note 12, at 916–17; F.W. MAITLAND, EQUITY ALSO THE FORMS OF ACTION AT COMMON LAW, TWO COURSES OF LECTURES 298–99 (A.H. Chaytor & W. J. Whittaker eds. 1920); Geoffrey C. Hazard, Jr., *Forms of Action Under the Federal Rules of Civil Procedure,* 63 N. DAK. L. REV. 628, 629–30 (1988). Joinder of claims by the same plaintiff against the same defendant was allowed if both claims fell under the same form of action. 7 CHARLES ALAN WRIGHT, ARTHUR R. MILLER AND MARY KAY KANE, FEDERAL PRACTICE AND PROCEDURE: CIVIL 2d §1651 (1986). No permissive joinder of plaintiffs was available. *Id.* Compulsory joinder of plaintiffs occurred only if the plaintiffs had a joint interest in the matter. *Id.;* 1 POMEROY, TREATISE, *supra* note 10, at §113. Joinder of defendants was mandatory if their potential liability was joint, and permissive if their potential liability was joint and several. WRIGHT, MILLER & KANE, *supra,* at §1651.

ties summoned witnesses who swore to the facts before a judge.[19] Despite some superficial similarity, this procedure is not like a modern trial. One could generally win, apparently, by having more witnesses than one's opponent, and if the witnesses' statements or their number made the result inconclusive, one of the parties would have to prove the matter by one of the other methods available in English courts.[20] Trial by witnesses fell into disuse in all but a handful of cases, but was not formally abolished until 1833.[21]

Better known are the ordeal, battle, and compurgation. Ordeal required the accused or the party with the burden of proof to take an oath and then submit to some dangerous ordeal.[22] If the person emerged from the ordeal unscathed, then he had proved his case. This was the shortest-lived method of proof following the Norman Conquest, however. It was effectively abolished when the Church, in the Lateran Council of 1215, forbade the participation of clergy in the ordeal.[23] Because clergy were necessary to administer the oath, ordeal disappeared from England within a few years of the Lateran Council.[24]

Trial by battle required the parties to engage in a duel of some sort, often a fight to the death. Civil litigants could, eventually, hire champions to do their fighting for them, and a corps of champions grew up—often quite unsavory characters.[25] Battle was a Norman import and was not initially very popular in England.[26] Nevertheless, litigants throughout the centuries occa-

---

19. *See* THAYER, *supra* note 1, at 17–24.
20. *See id.* at 17.
21. *Id.* at 24.
22. *See id.* at 34–39. One example of an ordeal is wrapping the hand in leaves and holding a red-hot iron for a prescribed period of time, after which the hand was inspected. The party was innocent if the hand was unscathed, and guilty if it was burned. Another example, particularly harrowing, is that the party with the burden of proof was thrown into a pool of water. In a perverse twist, the person was guilty if he floated, and innocent if the water swallowed him. In the latter instance, he had to hope he could be fished out of the water in time to save his life. *See id.* at 35n.1. *See also* PLUCKNETT, *supra* note 1, at 113–15. For extensive discussions of trial by ordeal, see Paul R. Hyams, *Trial by Ordeal: The Key to Proof in the Early Common Law*, in ON THE LAWS AND CUSTOMS OF ENGLAND: ESSAYS IN HONOR OF SAMUEL E. THORNE 90 (Morris S. Arnold, Thomas A. Green, Sally A. Scully and Stephen D. White, eds. 1981); Trisha Olson, *Of Enchantment: The Passing of the Ordeals and the Rise of the Jury Trial*, 50 SYRACUSE L. REV. 109 (2000) (arguing that ordeal in criminal cases served "sacramental" functions as well as truth-defining ones).
23. *See* THAYER, *supra* note 1, at 37.
24. *Id.*
25. *See* PLUCKNETT, *supra* note 1, at 117.
26. *See* DEVLIN, *supra* note 1, at 8.

sionally demanded the right to trial by battle, and judges occasionally allowed them to have it.[27] Battle was finally abolished in 1819.[28]

Finally, litigants could sometimes prove their cases by compurgation, also called wager of law.[29] With this method of proof, the party with the burden of proof brought in family and friends who would swear to the truth of his cause. These compurgators, or "oath-helpers," were not necessarily people who knew anything about the case; in effect, they were swearing to their faith in the litigant whose side they supported.[30] The oath could be quite complicated and difficult, and even the smallest error by any one of the compurgators would cause the party to lose.[31] Nevertheless, some litigants were quite fond of this method of proof and, like battle and trial by witnesses, it survived and was occasionally used until its statutory abolition in 1833.[32]

None of these modes of proof involved the rational evaluation of evidence. Most of them had some element of magic in them—God would ensure that the party with right on his side would prevail in battle, or would come through the ordeal unscathed.[33] These modes of proof were unsatisfactory, and litigants and officials alike were eager for more rational approaches. Thus, the way was opened for the development of the jury trial.

Most historians count the jury that prepared the Domesday Book as the major precursor of the modern jury.[34] The Domesday Book was a census of

---

27. *See* THAYER, *supra* note 1, at 43–45; CHARLES REMBAR, THE LAW OF THE LAND: THE EVOLUTION OF OUR LEGAL SYSTEM 18–19 (1980).

28. *Id.* at 45. *See* J.H. BAKER, INTRODUCTION TO ENGLISH LEGAL HISTORY 87n.10 (3d ed. 1990); *see also,* V.G. KIERNAN, THE DUEL IN EUROPEAN HISTORY 204–22 (1988) (noting that the duel remained popular in England despite the ban, and the courts had considerable difficulty enforcing the ban, especially among military officers). Kiernan also suggests that boxing replaced the duel in the nineteenth century as a means of settling grievances. *Id.* at 213–15.

29. *See generally,* THAYER, *supra* note 1, at 24–34.

30. *Id.* at 24–25.

31. *See* PLUCKNETT, *supra* note 1, at 115–16. The risk was sufficiently great that some litigants preferred the ordeal, in which the party undergoing the ordeal often prevailed. 2 POLLOCK & MAITLAND, *supra* note 1, at 601. The ordeal of the hot iron was particularly easy to beat. *Id.* at 598–99.

32. THAYER, *supra* note 1, at 34.

33. Suspicions that God may not have been taking a hand in these matters may have grown when it became obvious that the person undergoing the ordeal usually prevailed, so easy was it to escape unscathed. *See* 2 POLLOCK & MAITLAND, *supra* note 1, at 598–99.

34. *See* PLUCKNETT, *supra* note 1, at 110–12; MELVILLE MADISON BIGELOW, HISTORY OF PROCEDURE IN ENGLAND 334 (1880); 1 POLLOCK & MAITLAND, *supra* note 1, at 139–141; 1 HOLDSWORTH, *supra* note 1, at 145–46; THAYER, *supra* note 1, at 7–8. On the Domes-

landholding prepared shortly after the Norman Conquest by a "jury" of county officials and feudal land-holders.[35] This jury was summoned by William the Conqueror to perform the administrative task, under oath, of surveying his realm. The new king wanted to know who held what land in England, and he used a tool that was familiar to him—the Norman inquest—to find out. The theory behind the inquest was that people in the neighborhood would have more information than the king, and that the most efficient way of getting the necessary information was to summon such people and require them to state under oath the facts that the king desired to know. The Domesday jury was such a group of people. The document it produced is the earliest extant public record in England.[36]

A jury modeled on the Norman inquest began to be offered in the king's courts no later than the twelfth century.[37] The court summoned freemen of the neighborhood, usually knights, and required them to swear as to what had happened.[38] They could answer on their own knowledge, or they could inquire among their neighbors and relatives, but they were supposed to know, or to find out, the answer to the question the court asked.[39] In other words, like the Domesday jurors, they were more like witnesses than neutral fact-find-

---

day Book, see generally, V. H. GALBRAITH, DOMESDAY BOOK: ITS PLACE IN ADMINISTRATIVE HISTORY (1974); FREDERIC W. MAITLAND, DOMESDAY BOOK AND BEYOND (1897); R. WELLDON FINN, THE DOMESDAY INQUEST (1961). There were some other apparent precursors of the jury as it developed in England, and while they helped pave the way for the Norman inquest, none can be traced in a direct line to the modern-day jury. *See* PLUCKNETT, *supra* note 1, at 107–09; FORSYTH, *supra* note 1, at 45–77. *See also,* JOHN P. DAWSON, A HISTORY OF LAY JUDGES 119-20 (1960) (stating that there is "meager evidence" that juries were known in England before 1066). *But see* W.R. CORNISH, THE JURY 11 (1968) (favoring the theory that the Normans inherited the jury from an already existing English jury system). One commentator notes the difference between the way the Normans used the jury, *i.e.*, for commissioned inquests, and the way the English used the jury before the Normans arrived, *i.e.*, for settling disputes. *See* R.C. VAN CAENEGEM, THE BIRTH OF THE ENGLISH COMMON LAW 73–79 (1988). Van Caenegem finds the Norman inquest the more likely ancestor of the modern jury, and given the history traced in this Chapter, that seems correct.

35. *See* THAYER, *supra* note 1, at ch. II; LLOYD E. MOORE, THE JURY: TOOL OF KINGS, PALLADIUM OF LIBERTY 33 (2nd ed. 1988).

36. *See* PLUCKNETT, *supra* note 1, at 11–12.

37. *See* THAYER, *supra* note 1, at 54–67.

38. *See id.* at 62.

39. *Id.* at 63. Jurors who were summoned but who had no information as to the facts were replaced. If the twelve jurors who were summoned disagreed among themselves, jurors were added until there were twelve who agreed with one side or the other. *See id.* at 62–63; FORSYTH, *supra* note 1, at 197.

ers.[40] Development of this new mode of trial was slow at first, as it was a foreign device that displaced familiar modes of trial.[41] But the jury came to be the preferred factfinder in civil and criminal trials because of its superiority over competing methods of proof.[42]

The most significant development of jury trials came in the reign of Henry II, a king with a great love of, and facility for, the law.[43] Henry did two things that made his courts, which competed with the local courts for business, quite popular. First, he allowed new writs to issue, creating new forms of action, and therefore new business for his courts. Second, he made the jury trial the mode of proof prescribed for the new writs he was creating.[44] His successors continued this, so that the older modes of trial eventually were limited to those few writs that had been available before Henry's ascent to the throne. Thus, the creation of these new writs hastened the demise of the older modes of trial. The new writs, combined with the growing popularity of the jury trial, meant that the king's courts eventually became quite popular at the expense of county or manorial courts, where the jury did not operate.[45] That, in turn, helped to centralize the authority of the monarch.[46]

---

40. *See* PLUCKNETT, *supra* note 1, at 120–30; John Marshall Mitnick, *From Neighbor-Witness to Judges of Proofs: The Transformation of the English Civil Juror*, 32 AM. J. LEGAL HIST. 201, 201 (1988).

41. *See* THAYER, *supra* note 1, at 47–65.

42. *See* PLUCKNETT, *supra* note 1, at 110–12.

43. *See id.* at 53–54; PLUCKNETT, *supra* note 1, at 19, 111–12. King Henry II reigned from 1154 to 1189.

44. *See* THAYER, *supra* note 1, at 60. As noted above, the writs specified not only the substantive rights and remedies, but the procedures and the mode of proof. *See* note 13, *supra*, and accompanying text. Ironically, criminal juries were in some ways harder to establish. The mode of trial in criminal cases was thought to require the consent of the accused, at least for methods other than ordeal or battle, which were historically prescribed. *See* THAYER, *supra* note 1, at 74–77. Thus, even when the jury trial became compulsory for "notorious felons" under the Statute of Westminster in 1275, it was thought that the accused either had to voluntarily put himself before the jury or suffer torture until he died. *See* PLUCKNETT, *supra* note 1, at 125–26. Death was sometimes preferable because it preserved the accused's estate for his heirs. A convicted felon's property was forfeited to the crown. *Id.* at 126. The practice of torturing accused criminals who refused to consent to a jury trial continued until it was abolished in 1772, as English lawyers seemed unable to break through the disabling idea that consent was required. *Id.*; THAYER, *supra* note 1, at 74.

45. *See id.* at 48–49. Originally, only the king could require people to appear and take an oath, so the jury could operate only in the king's courts. *Id.* The jury did later spread to local courts. *Id.* at 49–50.

46. *See* Alice Stopford Green, *The Centralization of Norman Justice Under Henry II*, in SELECT ESSAYS IN ANGLO-AMERICAN LEGAL HISTORY 111–38 (Association of American Law

Little detail is known about the beginnings of the transition from this inquest jury, in which the jurors were supposed to know or find out the answer to the question raised by the litigation, to the modern jury, with presentations of evidence by the parties and a decision by a jury that did not necessarily know anything about the case except what was presented in court. There is evidence, however, that jury trials in substantially modern form occurred at the end of the fifteenth century.[47] It is also apparent, however, that there was no clean break from the witness-juror of Norman England. For some time before and after the late fifteenth century, some kinds of witnesses would retire with the jury to reach a decision.[48] Generally, this procedure was limited to witnesses to documents, who could be required to testify.[49] Witnesses to the event did sometimes testify in open court, but because they could not be required to testify, they were open to charges of maintenance if they came to court voluntarily.[50] Needless to say, this discouraged witnesses from coming forward. It was not until about 1562 that the parties could require all witnesses, and not just document witnesses, to testify.[51] Even with the growing use of witnesses, however, jurors were entitled to base their decisions on personal knowledge as late as 1670.[52] But less than one hundred years later, jurors were prohibited from bringing personal knowledge to bear on their decisions.[53]

While the jury remained the only method of trial in civil cases in English common law courts until 1854, that year marked the first movement away

---

Schools, 1907). The administrative and judicial departments were not so neatly separated in Norman England as they are now. THAYER, *supra* note 1, at 48–49. Because the inquest was both an administrative tool, as with the Domesday Book, and a judicial tool, as with the new mode of trial Henry offered, its use helped to centralize both aspects of government.

47. *See* PLUCKNETT, *supra* note 1, at 129–30.

48. *See* Mitnick, *supra* note 40, at 204.

49. *Id.*

50. *See* THAYER, *supra* note 1, at 124–29. Maintenance is defined as "[a]n officious intermeddling in a suit which in no way belongs to one, by maintaining or assisting either party, with money or otherwise, to prosecute or defend it." BLACK's LAW DICTIONARY 860 (5th ed. 1979).

51. *See* THAYER, *supra* note 1, at 102.

52. *See* Bushell's Case, 135 Vaughan, 124 Eng. Rep. 1006 (1670); Mitnick, *supra* note 40, at 203–07.

53. *See* Mitnick, *supra* note 40, at 207, *citing* 3 WILLIAM BLACKSTONE, COMMENTARIES ON THE LAWS OF ENGLAND, at 374–75 (1768). Mitnick suggests that the rule against jurors' using personal knowledge was established no later than the decision of Dormer v. Parkhurst, Andr. 315, 95 Eng. Rep. 414 (K.B. 1738). Mitnick, *supra* note 40, at 226.

from the civil jury, with the enactment of a statute that allowed the parties to agree to trial before a judge.[54] Today, in England, jury trials are available of right in only a handful of civil cases.[55] Jury trials in all other civil cases are a matter of judicial discretion.[56]

2. The Shape of the Jury

Early juries varied in number, but twelve seems to have been the most common size.[57] The reasons for this are not entirely clear.[58] It is possible that the number twelve was simply a way to weigh evidence: the required quantum of proof for important matters was twelve witnesses, and early jurors were witnesses.[59] There is some evidence that the number twelve has roots in the Scandinavian countries and was transmitted to courts in Anglo-Saxon England

---

54. See DEVLIN, *supra* note 1, at 130. At the same time, England was moving toward a merger of law and equity, which had been two separate but complementary legal systems. For a description of equity, see *infra*, notes 118–145 and accompanying text. For a description of the merger of law and equity, see Chapter 3, *infra*, at notes 1–8 and accompanying text.

55. *Id.* at 130–31; James Driscoll, *The Decline of the English Jury*, 17 AM. BUS. L.J. 99, 107n.58 (1979) (listing fraud, libel, slander, malicious prosecution, and false imprisonment as actions triable to a jury, but noting that an English court can deny a party a jury trial even in these actions if the particular case warrants it).

56. *Id.* at 130–33. The decline of the civil jury in England was hastened in the twentieth century. *See* Alexander Holtzoff, *Modern Trends in Trial by Jury*, 16 WASH & LEE L. REV. 27, 38 (1959). Limitations first came about as a temporary wartime measure in 1918. *See* DEVLIN, *supra* note 1, at 131. At that time, civil jury trials were limited to cases concerning libel, slander, malicious prosecution, false imprisonment, seduction, breach of promise of marriage, and fraud. *Id.* These limitations became permanent in 1933 for economic reasons. *See* Edson L. Haines, *The Disappearance of Civil Juries in England, Canada and Australia*, 4 DEF. L.J. 118, 118 (1958). As this last title suggests, civil juries are rare in Canada and Australia as well. While the civil jury was never as vital in continental Europe as it was in common-law countries, it has largely disappeared there as well. *See* CORNISH, *supra* note 34, at 17. Interestingly, the decline of the civil jury in many foreign countries sometimes drives litigants to the United States, hoping to take advantage of the expansive right to a jury trial. *See, e.g.,* Grodinsky v. Fairchild Indus., Inc., 507 F. Supp. 1245, 1250–51 (D. Md. 1981) (suit dismissed on plaintiff's failure to show that the Canadian judicial system, despite the lack of a jury trial, does not provide fair and just compensation to the parties in the suit); Panama Processes v. Cities Service Co., 500 F. Supp. 787, 800 (S.D.N.Y. 1980) (dismissal of suit when plaintiff's preference for common law jury trial was outweighed by defendant's evidence that a Brazilian court could fairly adjudicate the case without a jury).

57. *See* 1 HOLDSWORTH, *supra* note 1, at 153; DEVLIN, *supra* note 1, at 8–9; THAYER, *supra* note 1, at 85–86; FORSYTH, *supra* note 1, at 197–99.

58. *See* DEVLIN, *supra* note 1, at 8; Williams v. Florida, 399 U.S.78, 88–89 (1970).

59. *See* FORSYTH, *supra* note 1, at 198–99.

through Scandinavian colonies.[60] The number also seems to have a mystical side to it, with allusions to "the twelve tribes of Israel, the twelve patriarchs, and the twelve officers of Solomon recorded in the Book of Kings, and the twelve Apostles."[61] That mysticism was perhaps attractive to a profession not far removed from magical forms of "proof."[62] In any event, the number of jurors has been fixed at twelve since the middle of the fourteenth century.[63]

The rule that juries must reach unanimous verdicts was apparently also in place by the mid-fourteenth century, but the reasons for that are not entirely clear either.[64] It has been suggested that when jurors were thought of as witnesses, there could be no disagreement about the facts, because there could be only one "true" verdict.[65] Medieval lawyers were not far removed from reliance on the verdict of God, so the sense that legal truth is absolute and knowable is understandable. It has also been suggested that the unanimity rule was a logical result of requiring twelve witnesses to prove a point. Early common law courts would call twelve jurors, but if the jurors did not agree, the court would add jurors until there were twelve who agreed.[66] When courts stopped the practice of adding jurors, the result was a unanimity requirement.[67] Whatever the reasons for the size and decision rule requirements, they have remained an essential part of the jury's definition until very recently.[68]

There were also limits on who was eligible for jury service. Women could not serve on juries, and there were property qualifications that kept most men off the jury as well.[69] Thus, jurors in medieval England tended to be from the more educated and successful classes. The original reason for property qualifications was that property owners were more susceptible to fines that might be used to control them, and therefore less corruptible.[70] That reason is no

---

60. *See id.* at 198.

61. Williams, 399 U.S. at 88; DEVLIN, *supra* note 1, at 8.

62. See *id.* at 8–9; 1 HOLDSWORTH, *supra* note 1, at 153 n.1.

63. *See* Colgrove v. Battin, 413 U.S. 149, 177 (1973) (Marshall, J., dissenting) (quoting A. SCOTT, FUNDAMENTALS OF PROCEDURE IN ACTIONS AT LAW 75–76 (1922).

64. *See* 1 HOLDSWORTH, *supra* note 1, at 157; THAYER, *supra* note 1, at 86–87; BAKER, *supra* note 28, at 89–90; Apodaca v. Oregon, 406 U.S. 404, 407 n.2 (1972).

65. *See* 1 HOLDSWORTH, *supra* note 1, at 156; Apodaca, 406 U.S. at 407 n.2.

66. *See* FORSYTH, *supra* note 1, at 197; THAYER, *supra* note 1, at 62–63. In the early common law, dissenting jurors could be fined on the ground that they were perjurors. *See* FORSYTH, *supra* note 1, at 199–200.

67. *See* FORSYTH, *supra* note 1, at 197–200.

68. For a discussion of recent changes in the definition of the jury, see Chapter 5, *infra*.

69. *See* THAYER, *supra* note 1, at 90; DEVLIN, *supra* note 1, at 17–18.

70. *See* DEVLIN, *supra* note 1, at 17.

longer viable, if it ever was, and property restrictions on eligibility no longer exist.[71]

3. Summary and Conclusion

This brief history shows that the common law system had three primary characteristics: the writ system, which defined and limited the substantive law and prescribed the procedures the litigants would use to resolve the issue; a system of pleading designed to produce a single issue, whether of law or fact; and a trial by jury. Juries, which were composed of twelve men of means, were to render their decisions by unanimous verdict.

B. Control of the Civil Jury in England

Juries have never had free rein, as judicial control has been part of the jury procedure from the very beginning.[72] The oldest methods of control were attaint and fines, which punished jurors for wrong verdicts.[73] The new trial was a later development, devised to take the place of attaint when that ancient mode of control lost its effectiveness. The assignment of questions of law to judges is another means of controlling the jury, as it takes issues away from the jury altogether. Most commentators say that the law of evidence is also intended to control the jury,[74] but the law of evidence is, like the new trial, a relatively late development.[75]

1. Early Methods: Attaint and Fines

The earliest jury control device in civil cases was the attaint.[76] The idea behind attaint was that jurors were witnesses who rendered judgment based on personal knowledge and swore to the truth of their verdict. Thus, a wrong verdict was perjury, and jurors who rendered a wrong verdict were

---

71. See DEVLIN, *supra* note 1, at 166. In federal courts in the United States, jurors cannot be excluded because of race, color, religion, sex, national origin, or economic status. *See* 28 U.S.C. § 1862 (1994).

72. See THAYER, *supra* note 1, at 155 ("The court always held towards the jury a relation of control, and the books are full of traces of ordinary discipline.")

73. See 1 HOLDSWORTH, *supra* note 1, at 161–66; THAYER, *supra* note 1, at ch. III.

74. See THAYER, *supra* note 1, at 181.

75. See generally, *id.*

76. See PLUCKNETT, *supra* note 1, at 131–34. Plucknett notes that attaint was "the only ancient method" of reviewing verdicts. *Id.* at 131.

punished as perjurors.[77] When the losing party challenged the verdict by attaint, a second jury, generally of twenty-four persons, was empaneled to consider the evidence again.[78] If the second jury disagreed with the first, the first was attainted and the jurors' punishment was severe: the jurors "were imprisoned for a year, forfeited their goods, became infamous, their wives and children were turned out, and their lands laid waste."[79] Usually, the second jury's verdict was substituted for the first, but that did not occur if the party challenging the verdict had voluntarily chosen to have a jury decide the matter.[80] Those who willingly "put themselves on the country" were deemed to suffer the consequences of that choice, even if the verdict was wrong.[81]

The origins of this procedure are somewhat obscure, though there is reference to it as early as the twelfth century.[82] It was enacted by statute in 1360.[83] A mere two centuries later, however, it was rarely used.[84] There are several reasons for this rapid decline. First, the jury, for the most part, had ceased to decide cases based on personal knowledge by the late sixteenth century; rather, the jury based its decision primarily on the evidence presented in court.[85]

---

77. *See* DEVLIN, *supra* note 1, at 67–68; 2 POLLOCK & MAITLAND, *supra* note 1, at 665; BAKER, *supra* note 28, at 156. On attaint generally, see THAYER, *supra* note 1, at ch. IV; 1 HOLDSWORTH, *supra* note 1, at 161–66; 2 POLLOCK & MAITLAND, *supra* note 1, at 665–68.
78. The second jury was limited to the same evidence that the first had considered. The first jury could not be charged with perjury based on evidence it knew nothing about. *See* THAYER, *supra* note 1, at 137–38.
79. 1 HOLDSWORTH, *supra* note 1, at 161–62. *See also* THAYER, *supra* note 1, at 63. Thayer says that while attainted jurors lost their chattels, they did not lose their freeholds. *Id.*
80. THAYER, *supra* note 1, at 140; 2 POLLOCK & MAITLAND, *supra* note 1, at 665. This assumes, of course, that the party had some choice in the mode of trial and chose the jury. If the party sued under a writ that required a jury as the mode of trial, the attaint jury's verdict could substitute for that of the original.
81. THAYER, *supra* note 1, at 140.
82. *Id.* at 141. Thayer cites Glanvill's treatise, which was probably written in the late twelfth century, as referring to the practice of punishing jurors and comparing the practice to that of punishing champions for their "false" oaths. *Id.* at 140–41. The "falsity" of champions' oaths was established when they lost the battle.
83. *Id.* at 148; 1 HOLDSWORTH, *supra* note 1, at 162.
84. 1 HOLDSWORTH, *supra* note 1, at 163.
85. The evolution of the jury from a body of witnesses to triers of fact based on evidence presented in court is described in detail at THAYER, *supra* note 1, at ch. 3; and Mitnick, *supra* note 40. *See also,* Stephen C. Yeazell, *The New Jury and the Ancient Jury Conflict,* 1990 U. CHI. LEGAL F. 87, 93; LEON GREEN, JUDGE AND JURY 203–07 (1930); FORSYTH, *supra* note 1, at 125–38.

Thus, the logic of labeling jurors perjurors had evaporated.[86] Second, attaint was always unpopular with the second jury, as members of that jury did not wish to find their neighbors guilty of perjury.[87] Finally, attaint procedures were cumbersome and so difficult to use that litigants rarely resorted to it.[88]

Fining jurors was also a common practice. In civil cases, from an early time, jurors could be fined for ministerial errors. For example, jurors generally were not allowed food, drink or heat until they rendered a decision.[89] Jurors who violated this stricture could be fined. Generally, the milder punishment of fining jurors was reserved for these ministerial errors, while attaint was used for judicial errors—errors in the decision-making.[90] When, by the late sixteenth century, it became apparent that attaint was ineffective in controlling juries,[91] judges began imposing fines on civil jurors for judicial errors.[92] This practice was not generally approved by appellate courts, however,[93] and the failure of both ancient methods of jury control is the main impetus, in civil cases, for the development of the new trial.[94]

2. The New Trial

With attaint largely abandoned and fines for jurors disapproved, judges began searching in earnest for another method of controlling juries. Attaint had always involved a second trial before a new jury, but the new trial standing alone had been harder to justify, especially while juries were responsible for determining the facts on their own, which they could do as late as 1670.[95]

---

86. *See* THAYER *supra* note 1, at 150–51, 163; PLUCKNETT, *supra* note 1, at 132.

87. *See* 1 HOLDSWORTH, *supra* note 1, at 163; THAYER, *supra* note 1, at 150; Yeazell, *supra* note 85, at 93n.18; Mitnick, *supra* note 40, at 695.

88. *See* Millon, *supra* note 16, at 697–700; THAYER, *supra* note 1, at 149–50.

89. *See* DEVLIN, *supra* note 1, at 50–52; BAKER, *supra* note 28, at 89–90.

90. 1 HOLDSWORTH, *supra* note 1, at 163–64. It is sometimes said that attaint, in fact, lay only for corruption of jurors and not for mere errors. *See* Mitnick, *supra* note 40, at 689–95. In criminal cases, where attaint was unavailable, there was a long history of judges fining jurors, particularly for bribery or perjury. *See* GREEN, *supra* note 85, at 19; THAYER, *supra* note 1, at 156. Sometimes judges even imprisoned jurors for refusing to return the verdict the judge demanded. *See infra*, note 103 and accompanying text.

91. From some accounts, it seemed that most jurors took bribes from the litigants, secure in the knowledge that they would never be punished. *See* THAYER, *supra* note 1, at 149–50.

92. *See* THAYER, *supra* note 1, at 139, 151–52.

93. *See id.* at 139–40, 164–66.

94. *See generally,* Mitnick, *supra* note 40; *see also,* THAYER, *supra* note 1, at 169.

95. *See* Bushell's Case, 135 Vaughan, 124 Eng. Rep. 1006 (1670).

The new trial is premised on the notion that the jury bases its decision only on evidence presented in open court and that, therefore, the judge can legitimately assess whether the jury has reached a correct verdict. If it has not, the judge should vacate the verdict and order a new trial before a new jury. By the late eighteenth century, it was clear that jurors in civil cases were permitted to consider only evidence that was presented in open court, and the new trial, divorced from attaint, was firmly established in England.[96]

3. Law and Fact

Civil juries were officially limited in their powers and duties to fact-finding, while judges decided questions of law. This division of labor was aided and abetted by common law pleading rules, which helped the parties narrow the matter to a single issue of law or fact.[97] Some pleas raised issues of law, and some raised issues of fact.[98] It is not clear, however, when this limitation on the jury's power arose. At least one historian thinks it may be no older than the seventeenth century, when Lord Coke expressed it in his famous maxim on the division of power between judges and juries.[99] Lord Coke, however, seemed to think that he was stating an established principle.[100]

Despite this official prohibition on law-making by civil juries, however, juries had some opportunities to decide questions of law. Such *de facto* law-making was particularly likely when the general issue plea obscured whether the dispute was one of fact or law.[101] The general issue plea, which developed in the late fifteenth century, allowed defendants to deny a plaintiff's allegations

---

96. See THAYER, *supra* note 1, at 136; Mitnick, *supra* note 40, at 233; Stephan A. Landsman, *A Brief Survey of the Development of the Adversary System*, 44 OHIO ST. L.J. 713, 730 (1983).

97. See THAYER, *supra* note 1, at 115–18. On the relationship between pleading and jury control, see MORRIS S. ARNOLD, INTRODUCTION, IN 1 SELECT CASES OF TRESPASS FROM THE KING'S COURTS, 1307–1399, at pp. x–xx (Selden Society, vol. 100, 1985).

98. The demurrer, for example raised a question of law: it said that even if the opposing party is correct on the facts, there is no legal right to recover. The traverse, however raised questions of fact: it denied the opposing party's factual allegations. See JOHN J. COUND, ET AL., CIVIL PROCEDURE: CASES AND MATERIALS 449–50 (7th ed. 1997).

99. See 1 HOLDSWORTH, *supra* note 1, at 135 n.7. Coke spoke his maxim in Latin, but roughly translated, it says that questions of fact are not for judges and questions of law are not for juries. See THAYER, *supra* note 1, at 185.

100. See *id.*, saying that Coke attributed the saying, perhaps erroneously, to Bracton. Bracton wrote a treatise on the English common law in the thirteenth century. See SIR WILLIAM HOLDSWORTH, SOME MAKERS OF ENGLISH LAW 16–24 (1938).

101. Millon, *supra* note 16.

generally instead of specifying the reason for the denial.[102] In addition, there were some statutes that explicitly gave civil juries the power to decide the law.[103]

4. Rules of Evidence

When proof at trial consisted of surviving the ordeal or the battle, or of finding enough compurgators to support you, there was no need for rules of evidence. The early modes of proof depended on divine intervention to ensure that right prevailed. Nor was there a need for rules of evidence when juries consisted of persons from the community who knew about the contested incident or were required to make inquiries about it. Those jurors were expected to arrive at the trial fully apprised of the matter, and no one asked how they discovered their information. Only when juries' decisions came to be based solely on evidence presented at trial did rules begin to develop that governed what evidence could be part of the proof presented.[104] It is this relationship that caused one of the most noted historians of evidence to say that evidence is "the child of the jury system."[105] Indeed, it is significant that rules

---

102. *See id.* at 675–77; BAKER, *supra* note 28, at 84. If the reason was specified, the judge could decide if it raised a question of fact or law, and decide the issue himself if it raised an issue of law. *See generally, id.*; MILSOM, *supra* note 2, at ch. II.

103. *See* PLUCKNETT, *supra* note 1, at 138 (Fox's Libel Act of 1792). Criminal juries in England were thought to have law-making power after *Bushell's Case,* 135 Vaughan, 124 Eng. Rep. 1006 (1670). In that case, William Penn and William Mead were charged with violation of the Conventicles Act, a statute designed to suppress religions other than the Church of England. *See* THAYER, *supra* note 1, at 202. The Act made it a crime to hold assemblies under color of any religion other than the Church of England. *Id.* The jury, though pressured by the court to return a guilty verdict, refused to convict the accused. *Id.* at 224–25. The judge attempted to punish the jurors by fining them and ordering them to jail until they paid. *Id.* at 236. *Bushell's Case,* as a criminal case, did not involve attaint. *See id.* at 211. Four jurors refused to pay, and challenged the fines in court. The Court of Common Pleas eventually held that jurors could not be punished for their verdicts. *See* Bushell's Case, 135 Vaughan, 124 Eng. Rep. 1006. While criminal juries in England were thought, after *Bushell's Case,* to be masters of the law, civil juries were still limited to fact-finding. *See* Edith Guild Henderson, *The Background of the Seventh Amendment,* 80 HARV. L. REV. 289, 290–91 (1966). To be sure, there were some calls for more freedom for civil juries to decide the law, but they did not prevail. *See* Henderson, *supra,* at 291 and n.5. For a detailed discussion of Bushell's Case, see THOMAS ANDREW GREEN, VERDICT ACCORDING TO CONSCIENCE 200–64 (1985). On the relative power of judges and juries, *see generally,* THAYER, *supra* note 1, at ch. V.

104. *See* Yeazell, *supra* note 85, at 93–95; PLUCKNETT, *supra* note 1, at 178. The transformation of the jury from witnesses to judges of the proof took some time. *See supra,* notes 37–53 and accompanying text.

105. THAYER, *supra* note 1, at 266. *See also,* Karl H. Kunert, *Some Observations on the Origin and Structure of Evidence Rules Under the Common Law System and the Civil Law Sys-*

of evidence are far more fully developed in the common law countries, where the jury flourished, than in civil law countries, where it did not.[106] Nor did the rules of evidence operate to any great extent in English courts that did not use the jury, such as courts of equity.[107] Even today, wrongly admitted evidence is far more likely to result in a new trial when the trial was to a jury than when it was to the judge alone.[108]

Commentators have explained this growth of evidence as an attempt to rationalize proof.[109] If we are not to count on divine intervention, then "the jury had to have rational bases for its answer."[110] But the imposition of rules on what evidence a jury may receive, without any corresponding concern for evidence that a judge receives, strongly suggests that judges and litigants did not fully trust the jury to reach rational decisions. The rules of evidence, then, were a means of jury control.[111] They gave the judge discretion to disallow certain evidence, even when the evidence was relevant.[112] By excluding from the jury evidence that is more likely to confuse or prejudice them than to help them resolve the dispute, judges try to prevent wrong verdicts.

With the development of trials based on evidence presented in open court came an expectation that judges would help juries by commenting on the evidence.[113] The practice may have originated when juries were asked to return

---

tem of "Free Proof" in the German Code of Civil Procedure, 16 BUFF. L. REV. 122, 126–31 (1966).

106. *See* THAYER, *supra* note 1, at 270 ("where people did not have the jury,…although they, no less than we, worked out a rational system, they developed under the head of evidence, no separate and systematized branch of the law.").

107. *See* THAYER, *supra* note 1, at 508.

108. 1 JOHN HENRY WIGMORE, EVIDENCE IN TRIALS AT COMMON LAW §4d.1. (Peter Tillers rev. 1983). Wrongly excluded evidence is another matter. If the judge in a bench trial excluded relevant, admissible evidence, it must be presumed that it did not enter his calculations in coming to a decision. If the evidence could have affected his calculus, a new trial would be necessary. *See, e.g.,* Builders Steel Co. v. Commissioner of Internal Revenue, 179 F.2d 377, 379 (8th Cir. 1950); Collins v. Owen, 310 F.2d 884, 885 (8th Cir. 1963).

109. *See, e.g.,* EDMUND MORRIS MORGAN, SOME PROBLEMS OF PROOF UNDER THE ANGLO-AMERICAN SYSTEM OF LITIGATION 1–35 (1956).

110. *Id.* at 16–17.

111. *See e.g.,* THAYER, *supra* note 1, at 180–81; Paul D. Carrington, *The Seventh Amendment: Some Bicentennial Reflections,* 1990 U. CHI. LEGAL FORUM 34, 39–41. *But see* JOHN BALDWIN & MICHAEL MCCONVILLE, JURY TRIALS (1979) (saying that rules of evidence were simply an artifact of a system that allowed presentation of evidence in court and were not meant to control the jury).

112. *See* THAYER, *supra* note 1, at 516–17; DEVLIN, *supra* note 1, at 114.

113. *See* PLUCKNETT, *supra* note 1, at 136–37; Edson R. Sunderland, *The Inefficiency of the Jury,* 13 MICH. L. REV. 302, 311 (1915).

verdicts on a general issue plea, and so needed some guidance on the law.[114] But judges in England did not stop with the law; rather, they also organized the evidence for the jury and advised the jury on the weight and probative value of the evidence.[115] The jury was still considered to be the ultimate factfinder, but, because it consisted of lay persons unfamiliar with legal proof, it was thought to need guidance.[116] The jury has been free to disregard the judge's advice as to facts since 1670.[117]

5. Summary

Early methods of controlling the jury—attaint and fines—were direct and harsh. They treated jurors as recalcitrant obstructionists or even as perjurors. But those methods of control failed both because they lost their rationale and because the participants in the English justice system were reluctant to use them. Later jury control devices were more subtle. The new trial simply allowed the parties to try again with another jury. The law/fact distinction took some decisions out of the jury's hands altogether. And the rules of evidence controlled what the jury heard. As I will show in Part II of this book, this subtle approach to jury control has been quite successful in modern America.

C. Courts of Equity

The common law is one of England's crowning achievements. Today, it represents one of two major systems of law in the western world, the other being statute-based civil law, which developed in Continental Europe from Roman roots. But the common law was incomplete: to do complete justice, England needed the complementary system of equity.[118]

---

114. *See* Plucknett, *supra* note 1, at 136–37.

115. *See* Sir Matthew Hale, The History of the Common Law in England 164–65 (Charles M. Gray ed. 1971); Arthur T. Vanderbilt, *Judges and Jurors: Their Functions, Qualifications, and Selection*, 36 B.U. L. Rev. 1, 6 (1956); Judge Allen Hartman, *The "Whys" and "Whynots" of Judicial Comments on Evidence in Jury Trials*, 23 Loy. U. Chi. L.J. 1, 2–3 (1991).

116. *See* Hale, *supra* note 115, at 165; Robert Wyness Millar, Civil Procedure of the Trial Courts in Historical Perspective 310 (1952); Hartman, *supra* note 115, at 12–13; Vanderbilt, *supra* note 115, at 6.

117. This freedom arises from *Bushell's Case*, 135 Vaughan, 124 Eng. Rep. 1006 (1670), a criminal case described in footnote 103. *Bushell's Case* also allowed the jury to disregard the law. That aspect of the decision was never thought to apply to civil cases. *See supra*, note 103.

118. England also had courts of admiralty, which handled maritime matters. A jury did not operate in admiralty courts. *See generally*, Plucknett, *supra* note 1, at ch. 5.

1. The Need for Equity

After the initial flurry of writs that established the king's courts as the preferred courts for civil litigation, writs came to be quite rigidly defined, probably because they represented an exception to the normal modes of litigation.[119] Thus, litigants sometimes had to strain to find a writ, and with it a form of action, that fit the problem.[120] In addition, though the Chancellor had some continuing power over the creation of common law rights and remedies through his power to issue writs,[121] it was common law judges who took over once the writ was issued,[122] and the early common law judges were slow to adapt the limited number of writs to new situations or changing circumstances.[123] Not even a statute specifically authorizing the Chancery to create new writs could shake these early judges from their rigid application of existing law.[124]

Equity was originally conceived as a means of correcting the injustice that common law courts sometimes did because of their rigid rules.[125] It arose out of the right of litigants to appeal to the king's discretion if they thought they

---

119. See MILSOM, supra note 2, at 35. Writs proliferated under Henry II, but the use of writs to litigate cases was still relatively new in his day. See supra, notes 43–46 and accompanying text.

120. See HANBURY, supra note 13, at 3; H. ROSS PERRY, COMMON-LAW PLEADING 142 (1897).

121. See HANBURY, supra note 13, at 2; PLUCKNETT, supra note 1, at 163–64. Parliament was beginning to assert its authority over the creation of writs at this time, however, so there was competition for the Chancellor's power. See KOFFLER AND REPPY, supra note 12, at 41.

122. See 1 POMEROY, TREATISE, supra note 10, at §§21–22; HANBURY, supra note13, at 2.

123. See 1 POMEROY, TREATISE, supra note 10, at §§22–23.

124. Id. at §§24–28. Pomeroy attributes this, in part, to the common law judges' abhorrence of all things Roman. Rome had a concept of equity, but Roman equity did not need separate courts to manifest itself. See W.W. BUCKLAND, EQUITY IN ROMAN LAW 1 ([1983]1911). Common law judges refused to follow the Roman example. See 1 POMEROY, TREATISE, supra note 10, at §20. Hanbury, describing the foiled attempts of the Chancery to issue new writs, says, "[t]he river of law, whereof the Chancery was the source, flowed into a lock of which the common law judges were the keepers, and only a thin trickle came out on the other side." HANBURY, supra note 13, at 2. See also, PLUCKNETT, supra note 19, at 164. On the other hand, equity borrowed more freely from Roman concepts. See Thomas Edward Scrutton, Roman Law Influence in Chancery, Church Courts, Admiralty, and Law Merchant, in SELECT ESSAYS IN ANGLO-AMERICAN LEGAL HISTORY 208–47 (Association of American Law Schools, 1907).

125. See 1 POMEROY, TREATISE, supra note 10, at §§16–23. For a discussion of the origins and philosophy of equity, see id. at §§1–128; HANBURY, supra note 13, at 1–28.

were suffering an injustice at the hands of the king's common law courts. Eventually, the appeals came to be taken directly to the king's representative, the Chancellor, who began recognizing rights and offering remedies and procedures unavailable in the common law courts.[126] While equity would act only when the petitioner could not obtain justice in a common law court, it had a mandate to do justice, and a wide-ranging authority when it did act.[127]

2. Equitable Rights and Remedies

Equity could recognize rights that did not exist at common law. For example, the early common law courts would enforce a contract that was under seal even if there was evidence that the party resisting enforcement had been fraudulently induced to enter into the contract.[128] The early common law did not recognize the defense of fraud under those circumstances. The aggrieved party, however, could go to equity, which did recognize a defense of fraud, and obtain an injunction against enforcement of the contract.[129]

Similarly, while the common law recognized personal rights, equity might recognize a broader set of rights, and correspondingly broader remedies. For example, if two people had a contract for the sale of a piece of real property, the common law recognized a personal right in the seller to the agreed consideration, as well as a personal duty to transfer title to the property; correspondingly, the buyer had a personal right to have title to the property as well as a personal duty to provide the agreed consideration. If the seller breached, the common law viewed the breach as an irrevocable past event and provided the buyer a remedy of compensatory damages.[130] The buyer, in other words, had a personal right to have the contract honored, but no right in the land itself. Equity, by contrast, recognized that the buyer had a right *in the property*, and gave the buyer an equitable estate in the land. Equity would then provide a remedy of specific performance, and order the seller to transfer title.[131]

---

126. One description of some of the historic differences is found in Laycock, *supra* note 18. *See also* Subrin, *supra* note 12.

127. For a discussion of equity jurisdiction, see Chapter 4, *infra*, at notes 4–21 and accompanying text.

128. *See* COUND, ET AL., *supra* note 98, at 481.

129. *See* 1 POMEROY, TREATISE, *supra* note 10, at § 221.

130. *See id.* at § 105.

131. *See id.* Equity would not order specific performance if compensatory damages were an adequate remedy. But because each piece of real estate is unique, compensatory damages are an inadequate remedy for breach of a contract for the sale of real property. If the contract had been for the sale of wheat, equity would not entertain the action. *See* Chap-

This example illustrates the close relationship between rights and remedies. The rights recognized by the common law and equity may be similar—both recognize a right to have the contract performed—but the common law right is a personal right, whereas the equitable right is a right in the property itself. As a result, the remedies differ—the common law provides compensatory damages to the injured person, and equity requires the seller to transfer the property to the holder of the equitable estate. Indeed, because the common law was seen as a system for enforcing personal rights, an award of money damages was the usual remedy.[132] Equity, which recognized a wider range of rights, allowed for a wider range of remedies—remedies that were unavailable in common law courts—such as injunctions, where the court orders a party to do something or to refrain from doing something;[133] specific performance of contracts;[134] the shareholders' derivative action;[135] the accounting;[136] and the creation of such long-term instruments as mortgages, receiverships, and trusts.[137] Equitable remedies tend to adjust the relationships of the parties, and many of them require continued supervision by the court.[138]

English plaintiffs, then, had to determine what kind of remedy they sought, and that determined whether they would go to a common law court or a court of equity. For example, if someone breached a contract, the aggrieved party could go to a common law court seeking money damages or, if money damages

---

ter 4, *infra*, at notes 9–10 and accompanying text. *See also*, WILLIAM F. WALSH, A TREATISE ON EQUITY § 59 (1930); RESTATEMENT (2ND) OF CONTRACTS § 359 (1979).

132. *See* 1 POMEROY, TREATISE, *supra* note 10, at §§ 22–23. Other legal remedies included recovery of land and recovery of chattels. *Id.*

133. *See generally, id.* at §§ 221–221(a), 221(c).

134. *See* 1 *id.* at § 221(b).

135. *See* 4 *id.* at §§ 1095–1095(c). Shareholders in a corporation generally had no power over the corporation's decision about whether to pursue a claim—that decision was given to the corporation's directors. Thus, common law courts would dismiss a suit brought by a shareholder on behalf of the corporation. But if the directors refused to pursue a claim, shareholders could go into equity, establish the directors' refusal to act, and pursue their claim, on behalf of the corporation, in that court. Often, such claims were against the directors themselves, for example for breach of fiduciary duty, which explains why the directors did not act. *See id.* at § 1095n.15 &16 (citing cases).

136. *See* 1 *id.* at § 112(8); 4 *id.* at §§ 1420–1421. This allowed a litigant to go into equity when, for example, the financial issues between the parties were too complicated for a jury to handle.

137. *See generally,* 3 *id.* at § 910.

138. *See generally,* MAITLAND, *supra* note 18; G.W. KEETON AND L.A. SHERIDAN, EQUITY (2d ed. 1976); 1 DAN B.DOBBS, LAW OF REMEDIES 59–60 (1993).

were inadequate, to a court of equity seeking specific performance of the contract.[139]

3. Equitable Procedures

Equitable procedures were quite different from common law procedures. First, equity judges were not bound by rigid writs; an equity suit was commenced by filing a bill of complaint with the court.[140] An equitable suit was more open-ended than a common law suit, and a petitioner in equity had more freedom to explain the injustice she thought was being done. Second, there was no attempt to isolate a single issue, or to limit the case to a single plaintiff and a single defendant. Equity allowed joinder of claims and parties, and equity procedures even included rudimentary class actions.[141]

Finally, the jury did not function in courts of equity; rather, the judge was the trier of fact. Indeed, while history rather than logic dictates the lack of a jury in equity, the jury may be inconsistent with equity for several reasons. First, in equity, the petitioner is appealing to the king's discretion to suspend the strict application of the common law in order to do justice.[142] Thus, discretion is one of the most important characteristics of equity.[143] If courts of equity were to do justice, their judges had to have some flexibility to decide what justice required—what remedy, if any, to grant. Sometimes this entailed creating remedies that did not exist, though the courts eventually devised a slate of equitable remedies and rules governing when those remedies would be granted.[144] Discretion was not compatible with a jury, which was designed to give a yes or no answer to a single factual question.

Second, many equitable claims were thought to be too complex for a jury of laypersons to handle; they may involve complicated financial transactions,

---

139. *See* 4 POMEROY, TREATISE, *supra* note 10, at §§ 1400–1410. There were other equitable remedies relating to contracts as well, including reformation and rescission. *See generally, id.* at §§ 872, 910.

140. *See* 1 JOSEPH STORY, EQUITY JURISPRUDENCE 22–23 (1886); 1 POMEROY, TREATISE, *supra* note 10, at § 35.

141. *See* 2 *id.* at §§ 113 (joinder of claims), 257 (joinder of parties); 4 *id.* at § 1394 (describing the English Bill of Peace, predecessor to the class action).

142. Interestingly, a sometimes subtle appeal to jurors' supposed powers to nullify "bad" laws is behind some of the modern justifications for the jury, but especially the criminal jury.

143. *See* Laycock, *supra* note 18, at 71–73.

144. *See generally,* 1 STORY, *supra* note 140, at 21; 1 POMEROY, TREATISE, *supra* note 10, at §§ 46–49; 110–112.

for example.[145] They could also be quite complex because of the joinder of claims and parties. Finally, many equitable remedies involved creation of long-term legal instruments like trusts or mortgages, which required continued supervision by the court; such supervision could not be carried out by a jury of lay persons whose connection to the court was of limited duration. These characteristics of equity—discretion, complexity, and continued supervision—thus seem inconsistent with the institution of the jury, at least as that institution existed in medieval England.

4. Summary and Conclusion

The most obvious distinction between common law and equity, considering all three points of comparison—rights, remedies, and procedures—is that the common law is backward-looking while equity is forward-looking. Law seeks to define legal wrongs, decide whether such wrongs were committed in the past, and provide one-time compensation for any such wrongs. Equity seeks to identify problems and find on-going solutions for them. Most jurisdictions no longer operate separate courts of law and equity, but we still distinguish between legal and equitable rights and remedies, and that distinction is nowhere more important than in defining the right to a jury trial in the federal courts, a topic I will address in Chapter 4.

D. Summary

By the time of the American Revolution, the civil jury in England had evolved to its modern form. Jurors were summoned to hear evidence, and were supposed to render a judgment based only upon the evidence presented in open court. Theirs was a fact-finding role, with the job of law-deciding given to the judges. There were twelve jurors, and they were required to render a unanimous verdict. Ancient methods of jury control concentrated on punishing jurors for "wrong" verdicts. But as juries evolved from witnesses to evaluators of evidence presented in court, the logic that allowed judges to punish them began to dissolve. Methods of control became less harsh and more directed toward correcting erroneous verdicts or preventing them in the first place. But there was a significant body of law—equity—in which the jury did not function at all.

---

145. The equitable remedy of an accounting was justified by this concern about complexity. *See* Dairy Queen v. Wood, 369 U.S. 469 (1962) (requiring jury trial despite claim for equitable accounting because modern procedural rules make it easier for juries to handle such issues). *See generally,* KEETON AND SHERIDAN, *supra* note 138, at 417–18.

II. The Civil Jury in the United States

Because the civil jury played a significant role in the struggle leading to the American Revolution, its place in the early American legal universe was different from the role it occupied in England. In particular, the civil jury in early American history had authority to decide the law as well as facts. In addition, the right to a civil jury trial is written into the Constitution, whereas the civil jury in England had no such protection. Despite this exalted position, however, judicial and even legislative control of juries was an important factor in early American history just as it was in England.

A. The Origins of the Civil Jury in the United States

American colonists brought with them from England many English legal practices, including the jury. But jury practice in colonial America varied considerably among the colonies and between the various colonies and England.[146] Despite the differences in jury practice, however, juries—both civil and criminal—were almost uniformly seen as important actors in the American struggle for independence. For example, juries in criminal cases regularly refused to convict persons accused of violating what Americans viewed as politically oppressive laws imposed on them from England.[147] Those oppressive laws often took the form of criminal libel laws, designed to suppress colonial opposition to British rule.[148] But civil juries also played a significant role in colonial America. Civil laws whose intent or effect was to generate revenue for English interests were under attack by juries that refused to enforce them.[149]

---

146. *See generally*, Henderson, *supra* note 103, at 290, 299. There are several possible reasons for this. First, the starting points for jury development in the various colonies were different as the colonies were founded at different times. *See id.* at 299. Thus, as the jury evolved in England, changes in English jury practice could also take hold in America. Second, starting from those different points, the jury could have a separate evolution in the colonies from what was happening in England. Finally, colonies could ignore jury practice in England and devise their own rules.

147. *See* Charles W. Wolfram, *The Constitutional History of the Seventh Amendment*, 57 MINN. L. REV. 639, 653–55 (1973); VINCENT BURANELLI, THE TRIAL OF PETER ZENGER (1957).

148. *See* Henderson, *supra* note 103, at 290–91, 330–33; Wolfram, *supra* note 147, at 654–55; BURANELLI, *supra* note 147.

149. *See* Wolfram, *supra* note 147, at 703–08; WILLIAM E. NELSON, AMERICANIZATION OF THE COMMON LAW 31 (1975) (discussing jury nullification of the Navigation Act).

As a result, British colonial authorities tried to keep controversial civil cases out of the hands of American jurors. They did this by classifying unpopular laws as within the equitable or admiralty jurisdiction—where the jury did not operate—whenever possible.[150]

Perhaps because of this history of independence among civil as well as criminal juries, the value of the civil jury was apparent to citizens of the new country. Nothing happened to change that perception under the short-lived Articles of Confederation. But when the Articles failed and delegates met in 1787 and drafted a new Constitution, the civil jury was not a priority.[151] When the Constitution was drafted with no mention of a civil jury, the omission became a major point of contention in the ratification debates.[152]

Opponents of the Constitution were concerned because Article III of the Constitution guaranteed a right to a jury trial in criminal cases,[153] so they worried that the absence of a similar guarantee for civil juries eliminated the civil jury in federal courts.[154] They were also concerned because the Constitution provided that the Supreme Court's appellate jurisdiction extended to "law and fact," suggesting that even fact-finding by juries could be overturned on appeal.[155] The outcry over the possible elimination of the civil jury is not necessarily as pure as it might seem. One commentator has suggested that a primary motivation for opposition to the Constitution and for the clamor for a guarantee of a civil jury was a desire to protect local debtors.[156] Because the Constitution provided for jurisdiction over actions between citizens of different states and between citizens of states and citizens or subjects of foreign

---

150. *See* Wolfram, *supra* note 147, at 653–56.

151. Indeed, the judiciary article of the Constitution as a whole occupied very little of the delegates' time. *See* Wolfram, *supra* note 147, at 657–58; Henderson, *supra* note 103, at 292. I should note that some people thought that the convention of 1787 was simply going to fix the problems with the Articles, not that it was going to draft a new Constitution. *See* Isaac Kramnick, *Introduction*, in THE FEDERALIST PAPERS 28–29 (Isaac Kramnick ed., 1987 [1788]).

152. *See* Wolfram, *supra* note 147, at 656–730. The absence of a bill of rights as a whole concerned many Americans. *See supra*, Chapter 1, at notes 156–161 and accompanying text.

153. U.S. CONST., art. III, sec. 2.

154. *See* Wolfram, *supra* note 147, at 667–69; Henderson, *supra* note 103, at 297 (quoting "A Democratic Federalist").

155. *See* U.S. CONST., art. III, sec. 2; Henderson, *supra* note 103, at 292–95.

156. *See* Wolfram, *supra* note 147, at 673–705. This has been characterized as a class conflict. *See* Phoebe A. Haddon, *Rethinking the Jury*, 3 WM. & MARY BILL OF RIGHTS J. 29 (1994). Under the Articles of Confederation, the states, which were more powerful than the central government, protected local debtors. Thus, local debtors preferred the Articles over the Constitution. *See* Wolfram, *supra* note 147, at 677.

countries, creditors from other states or even from England could come into the federal courts in the various states and seek to enforce their debts against citizens of those states.[157] Opponents of the Constitution thought that jurors drawn from those states would be less likely to enforce such debts against their fellow citizens than would a judge who was simply applying the law, though they were reluctant to say that explicitly in the ratification debates.[158]

Other arguments advanced in favor of a civil jury trial right were perhaps more genuine. They included a perceived need to protect citizens of the states against corrupt federal judges;[159] "the frustration of unwise legislation; the overturning of the practices of courts of vice-admiralty; the vindication of the interests of private citizens in litigation with the government; and the protection of litigants against overbearing and oppressive judges."[160] The idea that juries could frustrate unwise legislative or administrative action was particularly important because at the time of the ratification debates, Americans widely believed that juries had the right to decide the law even in civil cases.[161] This practice differed substantially from English civil practice, where civil juries were thought to have no formal power over the law.[162] In any event, these justifications include the jury's roles as nullifiers and as equalizers.

---

157. *See* Wolfram, *supra* note 147, at 677. Wolfram says that diversity and alienage jurisdiction were included in the Constitution in part to cope with a lack of debt enforcement under the Articles of Confederation. *Id.* Federalists, who supported the Constitution, were more likely to be creditors; anti-federalists, who opposed the Constitution, were more likely to be debtors. *Id.* at 703–04.

158. *See id.* at 703–05. The United States had agreed to assist the British with debt collection when it made peace with England after the Revolution. *See* Wolfram, *supra* note 147, at 675–76. Thus, there were treaty obligations at stake.

159. *See id.* at 653.

160. *Id.* at 671. *See generally, id.* at 667–710.

161. *See id.* at 705–06n.183. *See generally,* Yeazell, *supra* note 85, at 103–06; Landsman, *supra* note 1, at 600–605; Note, *The Changing Role of the Jury in the Nineteenth Century,* 74 YALE L.J. 170, 172 (1964); NELSON, *supra* note 149, at 3–29 (discussing pre-revolutionary Massachusetts). Some commentators have suggested that juries also checked the power of judges. *See* Carrington, *supra* note 111, at 34–41 (noting that one original mission of the civil jury was to restrain the power of the federal judiciary); NELSON, *supra* note 149, at 16–21 (explaining that colonial courts had broad powers, more so than the executive and legislature, and the jury was a means to check the courts' powers).

162. *See* Henderson, *supra* note 103, at 291; Carrington, *supra* note 111, at 44. In England, a civil jury had no power to decide questions of law except when questions of law and fact were so intermingled that they could not be distinguished. *See* Henderson, *supra* note 103, at 335. Nevertheless, as noted earlier, English civil juries may have had considerable *de facto* law-deciding authority because cases that were sent to them on a general issue often had embedded legal questions. *See supra,* notes 101–102 and accompanying text.

It is not hard to see why Americans would have favored giving juries the power to decide the law. First, as described above, civil juries played an important role in the revolutionary struggle against oppressive British laws enacted without the colonists' representation.[163] Second, many judges in colonial and early United States history did not have legal training, so were not viewed with much respect as law-deciders.[164] Even those who did have legal training were sometimes viewed with distrust.[165] Finally, Americans had considerable "faith in the ability of the common people."[166] Indeed, educated Americans were likely to have at least some formal training in law, as even elementary school readers contained passages on some fairly sophisticated legal concepts.[167]

Arguments in favor of the civil jury were advanced largely by Anti-Federalists, who favored leaving more power in the hands of the states.[168] Federalists, who did not think a civil jury guarantee was necessary, argued (1) by implication, that the civil jury was less important after the revolution, because the English oppressors no longer ruled; indeed, the Federalists argued that the people could trust their elected representatives in Congress to provide a jury where necessary;[169] (2) that in any event the absence of an explicit guarantee of a civil jury did not mean that the civil jury was abolished;[170] and (3) that it was impossible to draft a guarantee of a civil jury right because civil jury practice varied so widely among the states.[171]

---

163. *See supra*, notes 147–150 and accompanying text.

164. This is especially true of frontier judges. *See* Carrington, *supra* note 111, at 44.

165. *See* Note, *supra* note 161, at 172.

166. *Id.*

167. *See generally*, M. H. Hoeflich, *Law in the Republican Classroom*, 43 KAN. L. REV. 711 (1995).

168. *See* Wolfram, *supra* note 147, at 667 and n.77.

169. *See* Henderson, *supra* note 103, at 296, *quoting* James Wilson, in P. FORD, PAMPHLETS ON THE CONSTITUTION, *reprinted at* 3 RECORDS OF THE FEDERAL CONVENTION OF 1787, at 101 (M. Farrand ed. 1937); Wolfram, *supra* note 147, at 664–65; Stephan Landsman, *The History and Objectives of the Civil Jury System*, in VERDICT: ASSESSING THE CIVIL JURY SYSTEM 22, 37 (Robert E. Litan ed., 1993); THE FEDERALIST, No. 83 (Hamilton), *supra* note 151. *Cf.* James P. Martin, *When Repression is Democratic and Constitutional: The Federalist Theory of Representation and the Sedition Act of 1798*, 66 U. CHI. L. REV. 117 (1999) (arguing that Federalists believed that once citizens had elected their representatives, the citizens had no further role in deliberating governmental policies).

170. *See* Henderson, *supra* note 103, at 294; Wolfram, *supra* note 147, at 662–63.

171. *See* Henderson, *supra* note 103, at 294; Wolfram, *supra* note 147, at 663–64. The basic Federalist position is set out in THE FEDERALIST PAPERS, No. 83, (Hamilton), *supra* note 151.

The result of this vigorous debate, carried out largely in the state ratifying conventions and in the press, was the Seventh Amendment. The wording of the Seventh Amendment is deceptively simple. It provides,

> In Suits at common law, where the value in controversy shall exceed twenty dollars, the right of trial by jury shall be preserved, and no fact tried by a jury shall be otherwise re-examined in any Court of the United States, than according to the rules of common law.[172]

Because of the references to the "common law," the Amendment obviously did not apply to cases brought in equity or admiralty, where no jury trial right existed.[173] But beyond that, the meaning of the Amendment was left to judicial interpretation. In particular, the question was what the Amendment meant when it said the right to jury trial was to be "preserved." Given the disparate jury trial practices of the states, if the "preservation" of the right required federal courts to apply the right as it existed in the states, there would have been considerable variation in the practice within the federal court system.[174] This variation was originally given as a reason for the framers' failure to provide for a civil jury in the Constitution.[175] The early federal courts appeared to be seeking a *federal* definition of the right that was to be preserved, often looking to English practice to flesh out that definition.[176] Similarly, the term "preserved" suggests that the right to jury trial is defined as of a particular date, most reasonably 1789 when it was proposed or 1791 when it was ratified.[177] By 1935, these two strands had coalesced into the now-familiar historical test: that the right to jury trial was to be preserved as it existed *in England* in

---

172. U.S. CONST., am. VII.

173. *See* Parsons v. Bedford, 28 U.S. (3 Pet.) 433, 446–47 (1830); Margaret L. Moses, *What the Jury Must Hear: The Supreme Court's Evolving Seventh Amendment Jurisprudence*, 68 GEO. WASH. L. REV. 183, 191 (2000).

174. *See* Wolfram, *supra* note 147, at 712–18; 732–34.

175. *See id.* at 665–66.

176. *See* Parsons, 28 U.S. at 446–47; United States v. Wonson, 28 F. Cas. 745, 751 (No. 16,750) (C.C.D. Mass. 1812). Both *Parsons* and *Wonson* were opinions by Justice Story, the latter in his capacity as circuit justice. According to Wolfram, *Wonson* was the first case to hold that the test for the availability of a jury trial was measured by the practice in England in 1791. *See* Wolfram, *supra* note 147, at 639–41. *But see* Moses, *supra* note 173, at 188–90 (arguing that reference to English practice was not clearly established until 1935).

177. The right could also evolve as the common law evolved, but the right then would be very hard to define. Fixing a date theoretically prevents erosion of the right, though I suggest in this book that the right has eroded nonetheless.

1791.[178] Application of the historical test was greatly complicated, however, by the 1938 merger of law and equity under the Federal Rules of Civil Procedure.[179] The changes in the Court's civil jury jurisprudence brought about by the Federal Rules are described in detail in Chapter 4.

B. The Development of Jury Control

The actual position of the jury—its power in relation to the judge—began to erode almost immediately after the United States Constitution took effect.[180] The trend toward control of the jury began late in the eighteenth century and picked up momentum in the nineteenth.[181] One reason for this may be the idea that jury independence was not as important once the English oppressors were no longer in control. As described above, this argument had been advanced to placate the anti-Federalists over the absence of an explicit right to a civil jury in the Constitution.[182] Thus, while the Constitution was quickly amended to

---

178. *See* Dimick v. Schiedt, 293 U.S. 474, 476 (1935); Baltimore & Carolina Line, Inc. v. Redman, 295 U.S. 654, 657 (1935). The historical test has become well-established and is rarely questioned in the courts. *See generally*, Wolfram, *supra* note 147, at 639–41. Many commentators have criticized it, however, and the criticisms have become more frequent and vociferous recently. *See id.* at 744–47; Carrington, *supra* note 111, at 74–75; Stanton D. Krauss, *The Original Understanding of the Seventh Amendment Right to Jury Trial*, 33 U. RICHMOND L. REV. 407 (1999); Martin Redish, *Seventh Amendment Right to Jury Trial: A Study in the Irrationality of Rational Decision Making*, 70 Nw. U. L. REV. 486 (1975); Rachael E. Schwartz, *"Everything Depends on How You Draw the Lines": An Alternative Interpretation of the Seventh Amendment*, 6 SETON HALL CONST. L.J. 599 (1996); Moses, *supra* note 173. The test does seem to ignore much of the highly relevant commentary over the civil jury that occurred during the ratification debates.

179. The Rules provided simply for "civil actions." FED. R. CIV. P. 2.

180. *See generally*, Note, *supra* note 161; MORTON J. HORWITZ, THE TRANSFORMATION OF AMERICAN LAW 1780–1860, at 28–29, 84–85, 141–43 (1977); Henderson, *supra* note 103, at 299–320. Henderson's article is an attempt to refute the arguments of several twentieth century Supreme Court justices that various control devices provided under the Federal Rules of Civil Procedure are significant departures from jury practice at the time of the ratification and so should be disallowed. *See, e.g.,* Galloway v. United States, 319 U.S. 372, 396 (Black, J., dissenting) (arguing that the directed verdict was unconstitutional as it did not exist in 1791 in the form later prescribed by the Federal Rules). Henderson argues that early jury practice in the federal courts was so varied that "no particular pattern was understood to be prescribed." Henderson, *supra* note 103, at 290. Most of the control devices she describes, however, were not firmly in place in any state until after 1791. *See id.* at 290–320.

181. *See generally*, Henderson, *supra* note 103; Note, *supra* note 161.

182. *See supra*, note 169 and accompanying text.

include a right to a civil jury trial, the resulting civil jury soon lost some of its pre-Revolution power as well as, arguably, some of its reason for being.

An even more powerful incentive for the evisceration of the civil jury, however, was commercial development.[183] In the newly independent and undeveloped United States, commercial development was hampered by existing common law doctrine;[184] by juries that were somewhat unpredictable, undermining the certainty that commercial investors needed to put their money on the line;[185] and by juries that tended to favor the enjoyment of private rights over public projects, for example by awarding significant compensation for property taken by eminent domain.[186] As a result, these commercial interests and their allies in government, including the bench, began to find ways to control the jury.

To some extent, government officials seeking to control the jury took their lessons from the British colonialists: they enacted legislation that took cases away from the jury. For example, many states set up appraisal offices to handle valuation of property taken by eminent domain, thus removing such decisions from jurors altogether.[187] In addition, most state and federal courts soon asserted the power of judges to decide the law, limiting juries to fact-finding.[188] They did this by developing a wide array of jury control devices designed to separate law from fact, including some that allowed judges to find evidence *legally* insufficient to support the verdict. The most exhaustive description of them was done by Edith Guild Henderson.[189] She describes the demurrer, common-law analogue of our modern motion to dismiss for failure to state a claim;[190] directed verdict;[191] demurrer to the ev-

---

183. *See* HORWITZ, *supra* note 180, at 28–29, 84–85, 140–43.

184. *See id.* at 1–4, 253–54.

185. *See id.* at 141–43; NELSON, *supra* note 149, at 8; Carrington, *supra* note 111, at 44–45.

186. HORWITZ, *supra* note 180, at 84. Although there were property qualifications for jurors in the early United States, juries have always been more representative than government officials, including judges. *See* Laura Gaston Dooley, *Our Juries, Our Selves: The Power, Perception, and Politics of the Civil Jury*, 80 CORNELL L. REV. 325, 355–56 and n.153 (1995). Thus, while commercial interests were represented in government, they were likely to be overwhelmed on juries of private citizens who did not appreciate the public benefits those commercial interests claimed to foster.

187. *See* HORWITZ, *supra* note 180, at 29, 67.

188. *See* Henderson, *supra* note 103, at 290–320; Renee B. Lettow, *New Trial for Verdict Against Law: Judge-Jury Relations in Early Nineteenth-Century America*, 71 NOTRE DAME L. REV. 505 (1996).

189. *See* Henderson, *supra* note 103, at 290–320.

190. *Id.* at 300.

191. *Id.* at 302–04. Directed verdict began simply as an instruction to the jury, which

idence;[192] the case reserved;[193] and the judgment notwithstanding the verdict, or j.n.o.v.[194] Two other control devices in the post-colonial arsenal were the special verdict[195]and the new trial,[196] both of which had a long history in England; neither was based on the distinction between law and fact. Another device was the nonsuit, which was initially a voluntary dismissal by a plaintiff, but it became involuntary in some states.[197] Some of these are precursors to modern jury control devices, while others have gone the way of common law pleading.[198] The states varied considerably in their use of these devices, but all were in place somewhere by early in the nineteenth century. Despite these control devices, juries continued, occasionally, to assert their power over the law by nullifying laws they did not agree with. In Chapter 1, I described the jury's rebellion against the doctrine of contributory negligence, which eventually contributed to the development of comparative neg-

---

the jury could ignore, though a new trial might then be in order. It eventually became binding on the jury, probably by the early nineteenth century in most states.

192. *Id.* at 304–05. With this device, a defendant could challenge the plaintiff's evidence, arguing essentially that it was legally insufficient to support the plaintiff's case. This sounds much like the modern directed verdict or judgment as a matter of law. *See infra*, Chapter 7 at notes 87–137 and accompanying text. The significant difference, however, is that a defendant who demurred to the evidence gave up her right to contest the evidence. *See* Henderson, *supra* note 103, at 304–05.

193. *Id.* at 305–07. This device was an argument on a question of law with the jury in reserve in case a question of fact came up.

194. *Id.* at 316–17. Despite the name, the early nineteenth century j.n.o.v. is unlike the modern version, now called judgment as a matter of law. The early nineteenth century version was an attack on the pleadings in cases where a demurrer would have been proper. Henderson, *supra* note 103, at 316–17. The modern version is an attack on the sufficiency of the evidence. *See infra*, Chapter 7, at notes 87–143 and accompanying text.

195. Henderson, *supra* note 103, at 307–10. Originally a jury-initiated device designed to protect jurors from attaint, *see* LEON GREEN, JUDGE AND JURY 353 (1930), the special verdict became compulsory during the early nineteenth century. *See* Henderson, *supra* note 103, at 307–10. The special verdict was fact-finding only, with the ultimate question of who prevailed in the litigation left to the judge, presumably based on the jury's fact-finding. *Id.* *See infra*, Chapter 7, at notes 172–181 and accompanying text.

196. Henderson, *supra* note 103, at 311–16.

197. *Id.* at 300–01.

198. Some of these control devices were justified, at least initially, on grounds other than the need to control juries. *See* Pamela J. Stephens, *Controlling the Civil Jury: Towards a Functional Model of Justification*, 76 KY. L.J. 81, 95–134 (1987) (reviewing the historical development of jury control devices). *See also*, NELSON, *supra* note 131, at 26–27 (explaining that some such devices were used to preserve proper procedures). I will discuss modern versions of these control devices in Chapter 7.

ligence rules in most states.[199] But without formal power over the law, the jury's power waned.

While much of this development took place in the states, where the Seventh Amendment did not apply,[200] the development reflects a change in the philosophy governing judge/jury relations that affected all American courts.[201] Today, there are only two states where juries have formal power over the law,[202] and other decisionmakers play a more significant role in dispute resolution.

III. Summary

The English civil jury's evolution from witnesses to judges is a story that is well known, at least in its broad outlines. But the history of the jury reveals many twists and turns that may belie the reverence in which we hold it today. A significant body of English law—equity—did not use the jury at all. In addition, the distinction between law and fact, with juries precluded, at least formally, from decisions on the law, is several centuries old. Moreover, methods for controlling the civil jury have been a part of the English practice from the beginning, with attaint the most prominent and the most harsh. When attaint could no longer be used, new methods—notably the new trial—had to be developed to fill the vacuum. Today in England, there is little need to control the civil jury, because it is nearly dead. In the country where the jury evolved and rose to glory, most civil litigants cannot choose a jury trial.

The American history is somewhat different. Because the civil jury played a prominent role in the colonists' resistance to British rule, it was thought to be more independent than the English jury. In particular, civil juries in the early United States were widely thought to have law-deciding power, unlike their English counterparts. So critical was this role that the right to a civil jury is enshrined in the Bill of Rights and so is a constitutional right in the United States. But even here, the power of the civil jury waned dramatically in the

---

199. *See supra*, Chapter 1, at notes 87–91 and accompanying text.

200. Indeed, amount in controversy requirements for federal diversity jurisdiction, which were enacted in the Judiciary Act of 1789, probably kept most tort cases out of federal courts altogether. *See* William R. Casto, *The First Congress's Understanding of Its Authority Over the Federal Courts' Jurisdiction*, 26 B.C.L. Rev. 11-1, 1113–14 (1985).

201. *See* Lettow, *supra* note 188.

202. *See* Jeffrey Abramson, We the Jury: The Jury System and the Ideal of Democracy 62 (1994).

early decades of the country's history. Commercial development may well be the most significant cause of this, but the primary method of sapping jury power was to develop jury control devices.

The jury has never regained the position it had in the early years of the country's history. Its decline has been particularly dramatic in the twentieth century. In Chapter 3, I document some of the reasons why.

RECENT CHANGES IN THE CIVIL JURY'S ENVIRONMENT

The pace of the civil jury's evolution has accelerated over the last several decades, as I will show in Part II of this book. But a better word may well be "devolution," as the changes that have occurred recently are not always consistent with a fully functional civil jury. In this Chapter, I will describe a number of factors that may have led to this diminution of the jury.

The Federal Rules of Civil Procedure, promulgated in 1938, are the progenitors of two *procedural changes* that have significantly altered the milieu in which the jury operates: the Rules adopted procedures from the old courts of equity and largely abandoned common law procedures, and they profoundly altered the adversary system that characterizes common law procedure. *Systemic changes* include the rise of administrative agencies, where juries are not used; the litigation explosion, which has overwhelmed the courts and the juries they use; and the explosion of knowledge, which both increases the variety of things we can litigate about and may take the subjects of litigation beyond the ken of ordinary jurors. *Substantive changes* include the increased need for more certainty than common law development, and especially the jury, could provide; and the codification of substantive law. Finally, there is a *political change*: the civil rights movement and shifts in immigration have greatly diversified the participants in the American political process, including the jury; the original jury, however, functioned in a more homogeneous society, where consensus was arguably easier to reach. Together, these factors have had a signficant impact on the jury's functioning and perhaps its continued viability.

I. Procedural Changes

The jury developed hand in glove with the system of common law and with the adversary system of adjudication. Indeed, it is difficult to say which came first; the jury, the common law, and the adversary system developed together in a symbiotic relationship. Recently, however, equity has swallowed up the common law, so that our procedural system looks much more equitable than legal. In addition, we have given the adversary system many of the characteristics of the inquisitorial systems of continental Europe. These changes cannot help but affect the jury's functioning. The event that marks these two developments is the adoption of the Federal Rules of Civil Procedure.

A. Common Law and Equity Under the Federal Rules of Civil Procedure

1. The Path to the Federal Rules

Procedural reform began in both England and the United States during the nineteenth century, largely because the procedural system based on separate courts of law and equity had become too complex and difficult to navigate.[1] The reform movement in the United States was initially a movement of the

---

1. England began tinkering with the system as early as 1813, apparently motivated by problems with the courts of equity, which had become more rule-bound than the common law courts. *See* J.H. BAKER, AN INTRODUCTION TO ENGLISH LEGAL HISTORY 122–30 (3rd ed. 1990). Equity was supposed to function as the king's conscience, and not by such rigid rules. *See id.* at 126–28. The problem was handled, ultimately, by a merger of law and equity, which occurred over a period of approximately twenty years. In 1854, law courts were empowered to employ some equity procedures, and equity courts to grant some legal relief and to use juries. *See id.* at 131. Courts of equity had always had some power to decide legal matters under the so-called "clean-up doctrine." They could decide legal matters that were incidental to some equitable matter that was properly before them. *See* 1 JOHN NORTON POMEROY, A TREATISE ON EQUITY JURISPRUDENCE §§ 181, 231 (5th ed., Symonds ed. 1941). The 19th century reforms went well beyond the clean-up doctrine. For further discussion of equity jurisdiction, see *infra*, Chapter 4, at notes 4–21 and accompanying text. By 1875, a full merger of law and equity had been accomplished, with legal and equitable procedures merged, and with the forms of action abolished. *See id.* at 131–32. For a detailed history of this transformation, see 15 SIR WILLIAM HOLDSWORTH, A HISTORY OF ENGLISH LAW 102–38 (1965). Understandably, the merger was accompanied by some problems of interpretation, as the old common law procedures had differed substantially from the equity procedures. Parliament attempted to resolve these problems with the Judicature Act of 1873, which provided that equity procedures would prevail in most cases. *See id.* at 134–35. As I will soon show, equity was more than a system of procedures, however. There is substantive law in equity as well, and the Judicature Act did not resolve the question whether substantive equity law governed related common law issues. *See id.* at 135–38.

state courts. The progenitor was New York's Field Code of 1848, which, much like the English statutes, merged law and equity, abolished the forms of action, and simplified pleading requirements.[2] The Code itself required that it be construed so as to do "substantial justice between the parties."[3] Many states adopted variations of the Field Code.

The story is different in the federal courts. The First Congress created lower federal courts when it enacted the Judiciary Act of 1789.[4] It did not, however, create separate courts of law and equity. Rather, the same court heard actions in both law and equity, using different procedures for the two kinds of actions. Under the Conformity Act, the federal courts were required to use state rules of procedure for common law actions.[5] There were federal rules of equity procedure, however, dating from 1822.[6] This system meant that, while there was federal procedural uniformity when the court was sitting as a court of equity, there was considerable procedural variation on the common law side of the court, particularly as reform of state procedure proliferated in the nineteenth century. It was not until 1934, however, that Congress enacted the Rules Enabling Act, which authorized the Supreme Court to promulgate uniform rules of procedure for the federal courts, covering both law and equity.[7] The Fed-

---

2. *See* JOHN J. COUND, ET AL., CIVIL PROCEDURE 483–86 (7th ed. 1997). The Field Code was named for its principal drafter, David Dudley Field. *See id.* at 485.

3. *See id.* at 486, *quoting* N.Y. Laws 1849, ch. 438, § 159.

4. *See* Judiciary Act of 1789, 1 Stat. 73, §§ 2–4 (1789). The Constitution itself creates only the Supreme Court. All other federal courts must be authorized by Congress. *See* U.S. CONST. art. III, § 1.

5. *See* Practice Conformity Act, ch. 225, 17 Stat. 197 (1872). *See generally,* ROBERT C. CASAD, HOWARD P. FINK & PETER N. SIMON, CIVIL PROCEDURE 428–29 (2nd ed. 1989). This practice dates to 1789, when the First Congress enacted the Process Act of 1789, ch. 21, § 2, 1 Stat. 93 (1789).

6. *See* Rules of Practice for the Courts of Equity of the United States, 20 U.S. (7 Wheat.) v (1822). The Supreme Court's authority to promulgate the Federal Equity Rules was granted in 1792. See Act of May 8, 1792, ch. 36, § 2, 1 Stat. 275, 276 (1792).

7. *See* Act of June 19, 1934, Pub. L. No. 73-415, 48 Stat. 1064, codified as amended at 28 U.S.C. § 2072 (1994). *See generally,* Carl Tobias, *Public Law Litigation and the Federal Rules of Civil Procedure,* 74 CORNELL L. REV. 270, 271–77 (1989). The Supreme Court does not draft the rules itself. Rather, the Judicial Conference appoints an Advisory Committee of the bench and bar to draft proposed rules and amendments. *See* 28 U.S.C. § 2073(a)(2) (1994). This Advisory Committee transmits its proposed rules or amendments, along with explanatory commentary, to the Judicial Conference and then to the Supreme Court. *See id.* at § 2073(d). If the Court accepts the proposals, it must transmit them to Congress by May 1 of the year in which they are to become effective. *See* 28 U.S.C. § 2074 (1994). The rules take effect on December 1 of that year unless Congress rejects them. *See id.*

eral Rules of Civil Procedure were the result of this authorization, and they took effect on September 16, 1938.[8]

2. The Common Law and the Federal Rules

Like the Field Code and its progeny in the state courts, the Federal Rules merged law and equity procedures and abolished the common law forms of action.[9] The Advisory Committee that drafted these rules had to decide how to merge the old common law and equitable procedures. Almost across the board, the Advisory Committee selected the rules of equity over the common law rules.[10] This is best illustrated by comparing the Federal Rules to the chief characteristics of the common law: the writ system, single-issue pleading, and the jury.

---

8. *See* CHARLES E. CLARK, HANDBOOK OF THE LAW OF CODE PLEADING 37–38 (2nd ed. 1947). *See generally,* 4 CHARLES ALAN WRIGHT AND ARTHUR R. MILLER, FEDERAL PRACTICE AND PROCEDURE § 1004 (1987).

9. *See* FED. R. CIV. P. 2. *See also,* advisory committee notes. Merger of law and equity was also the approach taken in England. *See supra,* note 1. To a modern reader, it may seem odd to talk about the forms of action being abolished in federal courts, because the common law is generally the province of the state, and not the federal government. But at the time the federal rules were being drafted, the federal courts regularly applied their own version of common law rules, disregarding the sometimes conflicting common law rules of the states in which they were sitting. This was the rule of *Swift v. Tyson,* 41 U.S. (16 Pet.) 1 (1842), which had held that federal courts did not need to apply state common law rules, but were free to apply their own. *Swift* was an interpretation of the Rules of Decision Act, now codified at 28 U.S.C. § 1652 (1994), which required federal courts to apply state law in diversity cases. *Swift* had interpreted the Act to refer only to statutory law and not the common law. *Swift* was overruled in *Erie R. Co. v. Tompkins,* 304 U.S. 64 (1938), which was decided the same year that the Federal Rules took effect. Under *Erie,* federal courts are required to apply state common law as well as state statutes.

10. *See* Douglas Laycock, *The Triumph of Equity,* 56 L. & CONTEMP. PROBS. 53, 64 (Summer 1993); Stephen N. Subrin, *How Equity Conquered Common Law: The Federal Rules of Civil Procedure in Historical Perspective,* 135 U. PA. L. REV. 909, 922 (1987); Charles E. Clark and James Wm. Moore, *A New Federal Civil Procedure I: The Background,* 44 YALE L.J. 387, 434–35 (1935); Alexander Holtzoff, *Origin and Sources of the Federal Rules of Civil Procedure,* 30 N.Y.U.L. REV. 1057, 1058 (1955). Laycock's article is part of a symposium on Modern Equity in the Summer 1993 issue of LAW AND CONTEMPORARY PROBLEMS, and other articles address this takeover by equity, though with a more narrow focus. Not all of the conference participants believed that equity had triumphed, however. *See* Thomas D. Rowe, Jr., *No Final Victories: The Incompleteness of Equity's Triumph in Federal Public Law,* 56 L. & CONTEMP. PROBS. 105 (Summer 1993).

a. The Writ System

As I showed in Chapter 2, a writ conferred subject matter jurisdiction on the court to which the writ was addressed.[11] In the United States, the jurisdictional aspects of the writ had long been a nullity, as subject matter jurisdiction in the federal courts has usually been conferred by general statutes and not by particular writs.[12] But the form of action embodied in a writ also defined a legal right and remedy and prescribed procedures for deciding the dispute, including the mode of proof. This function of a form of action, and therefore of a writ, had been eroding for some time, especially in the states, and the Federal Rules further hampered it. To be sure, the legal rights and remedies are still encompassed within a "cause of action," which defines the elements that a plaintiff must establish in order to prevail, but procedures and modes of proof were no longer specific to a particular cause of action.[13] With the Federal Rules, and the Field Code before them, came "trans-substantive procedure"—general procedural rules applicable to all kinds of cases.[14] This looks much more like equity, which had long had trans-substantive procedural rules.[15]

---

11. *See* Chapter 2, *supra*, at note 8 and accompanying text.

12. *See, e.g.,* Judiciary Act of 1789, 1 Stat. 73, § 11 (1789) (diversity). Diversity jurisdiction is now codified at 28 U.S.C. § 1332 (1994). General federal question jurisdiction was not conferred on federal courts until 1875. *See* Act of March 3, 1875, ch. 137, § 1, 18 Stat. 470 (1875). Before that, Congress did frequently confer federal jurisdiction in particular matters. It would, for example, create a right and a remedy, and then confer federal jurisdiction over actions concerning that right and remedy. This is reminiscent of a writ, though the federal statutes did not provide for particularized procedures. General federal question jurisdiction is now codified at 28 U.S.C. § 1331 (1994).

13. For a discussion of the sometimes problematic terminology ("claim" and "cause of action"), see Chapter 2, *supra*, at note 10.

14. *See* Paul D. Carrington, *Making Rules to Dispose of Manifestly Unfounded Assertions: An Exorcism of the Bogy of Non-Trans-Substantive Rules of Civil Procedure*, 137 U. PA. L. REV. 2067, 2079–85 (1989); Geoffrey C. Hazard, Jr., *Discovery Vices and Trans-Substantive Virtues in the Federal Rules of Civil Procedure*, 137 U. PA. L. REV. 2237, 2244–47 (1989); Robert M. Cover, *For James Wm. Moore: Some Reflections on a Reading of the Rules*, 84 YALE L.J. 718, 732–36 (1975). Congress has recently begun enacting some particularized procedural rules. For example, there are now some special pleading rules for securities fraud cases. *See* Private Securities Litigation Reform Act of 1995, Pub. L. No. 104-67, 109 Stat. 737 (codified in scattered sections in 15 U.S.C.). *See also*, Y2K Act, Pub. L. No. 106-37 (106th Cong., 1st Sess. 1999) (enacting particular rules for litigation over the Y2K problem).

15. *See* Rules of Practice for the Courts of Equity of the United States, 20 U.S. (7 Wheat.) v (1822); Laycock, *supra* note 10, at 64; Mark C. Weber, *The Federal Civil Rules*

More importantly, the writ system severely limited joinder of claims and parties, as a plaintiff could sue under only one writ at a time, and parties could rarely join in a single suit.[16] Thus, most common law suits involved a single plaintiff suing a single defendant. The Federal Rules may well take us about as far from this aspect of the writ system as it is possible to get. They allow for a broad joinder of both claims and parties, with the goal of trying all related matters together.[17] Under some circumstances, the Federal Rules even allow unrelated claims to be asserted in a suit.[18] With the permission of the judge, parties can litigate a case as a class action, in which the named parties repre-

---

Amendments of 1993 and Complex Litigation: A Comment on Transsubstantivity and Special Rules for Large and Small Federal Cases, 14 REV. LITIG. 113, 120 (Winter 1994). Because the Conformity Act required federal courts to employ a state's common law procedures in cases arising in that state, and because so many states had adopted trans-substantive procedural rules following the Field Code, the federal courts had been applying trans-substantive procedural rules for several decades before adoption of the Federal Rules.

16. *See supra*, Chapter 2, notes 16–18 and accompanying text.

17. *See* Charles E. Clark, *The Proposed Federal Rules of Civil Procedure*, 22 A.B.A. J. 447, 448–49 (1936). Defendants are required to assert counterclaims against plaintiffs when those counterclaims arise out of the same transaction or occurrence as the plaintiff's claim against the defendant. FED. R. CIV. P. 13(a). The consequence of failing to raise a compulsory counterclaim is that the party loses that claim forever. *See* 6 WRIGHT & MILLER, *supra* note 8, at §1417; Baker v. Gold Seal Liquors, 417 U.S. 467, 469n.1 (1974); Crutcher v. Aetna Life Insurance Co., 746 F.2d 1076, 1080 (5th Cir. 1984). Co-parties can assert cross-claims against one another as long as those claims arise out of the same transaction or occurrence as the original claim or a counterclaim to the original claim. FED. R. CIV. P. 13(b). Defendants can assert third-party claims against persons who were not parties to the original claim, in effect adding parties to the litigation. FED. R. CIV. P. 14. Plaintiffs with related claims can join together to sue a defendant, or a plaintiff can sue multiple defendants who may be jointly liable. FED. R. CIV. P. 20. Non-parties can intervene in a case, either of right or permissively. FED. R. CIV. P. 24. Intervention of right requires either that a statute confers the right to intervene or that the intervenor claims an interest in the action that could be impaired by the suit, and that no one already a party to the suit can adequately represent her interests. FED. R. CIV. P. 24(a). Permissive intervention may be allowed when a statute confers a conditional right to intervene or when the intervenor's claims have a question of law or fact in common with the main claim. FED. R. CIV. P. 24(b).

18. In general, if a party is asserting a claim against another party, he can join with it any other claims that he has against that party, whether or not related. FED. R. CIV. P. 18. Under some circumstances, defendants may also be permitted to assert counterclaims against the plaintiff even if the counterclaim is unrelated to the plaintiff's claim. FED. R. CIV. P. 13(b). The court can, in its discretion, refuse to allow a permissive counterclaim. *See* Globe Indemnity Co. v. Teixeira, 230 F. Supp. 444, 448 (D. Haw. 1963); Aetna Insurance Co. v. Pennsylvania Manufacturers Association, 456 F. Supp. 627, 635 (E.D. Pa. 1978).

sent others similarly situated.[19] These rules can make for some very complicated lawsuits, which can be hard for a jury to sort out; by contrast, the common law writ system guaranteed relatively simple suits.[20]

b. Single-Issue Pleading Rules

The second characteristic of the common law—single-issue pleading
rules—is also missing from the Federal Rules.[21] Under common law pleading
rules, the goal was to identify a single issue of fact or law (not both), and the
remedy was limited, usually, to money damages. But I have just shown that
federal suits can involve multiple causes of action and multiple parties, which
necessarily means multiple issues. Furthermore, federal cases can be compli-
caed even if there is a single plaintiff and a single defendant. Within a single

---

19. FED. R. CIV. P. 23. Most class actions are plaintiff class actions, in which the named
plaintiff represents other claimants against the defendant. Defendant class actions are also
permitted, however, in which a named defendant represents others who are potentially liable to the plaintiff. *See* Note, *Defendant Class Actions*, 91 HARV. L. REV. 630 (1978); Barry
M. Wolfson, *Defendant Class Actions*, 38 OHIO ST. L.J. 459, 460 (1977); Note, *Statutes of
Limitations and Defendant Class Actions*, 82 MICH. L. REV. 347, 348n.12 (1983).

20. There are some jurisdictional limitations on some of this activity, but the rules
themselves are quite free-wheeling. A federal court must have subject matter jurisdiction
over each cause of action in the case. Thus, if there are two persons who are injured in a
single accident, each must satisfy the requirements of diversity jurisdiction. In some cases,
if the causes of action are related, the court can assert supplemental jurisdiction over a
cause of action that is not otherwise within the court's subject matter jurisdiction. *See* 28
U.S.C. § 1367 (1994). At this writing, the meaning and scope of § 1367 is a matter of considerable confusion and debate, and there are efforts underway to redraft § 1367. *See generally*, Rochelle Cooper Dreyfuss, *The Debate Over § 1367: Defining the Power to Define Fed-
eral Judicial Power*, 41 EMORY L.J. 13 (1992); Karen Nelson Moore, *The Supplemental
Jurisdiction Statute: An Important But Controversial Supplement to Federal Jurisdiction*, 41
EMORY L.J. 31 (1992); Thomas C. Arthur & Richard D. Freer, *Grasping at Burnt Straws:
The Disaster of the Supplemental Jurisdiction Statute*, 40 EMORY L.J. 963 (1991); Thomas D.
Rowe, Jr., *et al., Compounding or Creating Confusion About Supplemental Jurisdiction? A
Reply to Professor Freer*, 40 EMORY L.J. 943 (1991); Christopher M. Fairman, *Abdication to
Academia: The Case of the Supplemental Jurisdiction Statute, 28 U.S.C. § 1367*, 19 SETON
HALL LEGIS. J. 157 (1994). An attempt by the Supreme Court to clarify one question about
§ 1367 failed when the Court split 4–4. *See* Free v. Abbott Laboratories, Inc., 529 U.S. 333
(2000).

21. This characteristic had been eroding for some time before adoption of the federal
rules. Recall that the goal of common law pleading was to reduce the matter to a single
issue of either fact or law, but that the parties could sometimes avoid that by a general issue
plea, which obscured what was at issue and left more of the case to the jury. *See supra*,
Chapter 2, at notes 16–18 and accompanying text.

cause of action, there can be issues of fact and law, and requests for multiple remedies, both legal and equitable.[22] The parties can also make inconsistent allegations, as long as they are made in good faith.[23] In short, the Federal Rules are much closer to equity, which allowed joinder of claims and parties, and which often decided multiple issues.[24] The multiplicity of issues in federal litigation greatly complicates cases, making it harder for juries to function.

c. The Jury

The last characteristic feature of common law procedures is the jury, which was virtually the only common law survivor in the Federal Rules, and that may well be because the jury is constitutionally mandated.[25] Many of the members of the first Advisory Committee, which drafted the rules, were hostile to the jury and would have been happy to abolish it.[26] As abolition was not possible,

---

22. Some of these issues may be eliminated during the lengthy pre-trial procedures that the Federal Rules provide for, but the trial could still have to resolve multiple issues.

23. See FED. R. CIV. P. 8(e). A defendant might, for example, deny that he had committed a tort at all, but assert that if he did, it was excused because it was done in self-defense.

24. For example, equity could decide issues that were peculiarly equitable, but it could also decide common law matters that were incidental to the equity issue under the so-called "clean-up doctrine." For a discussion of the clean-up doctrine, see *infra*, Chapter 4, at notes 16–17 and accompanying text.

25. See Laycock, *supra* note 10, at 66; Subrin, *supra* note 10, at 924. Some common-law pleading concepts survived, but with different, and more descriptive, names. Thus, the old common-law demurrer became the defense of failure to state a claim, which could lead to dismissal without trial. For example, the complaint could allege that the defendant called the plaintiff a "jerk," but that is not an actionable offense, so the complaint would be dismissed. The old common-law avoidance became the affirmative defense, which assumes the truth of the complaint's allegations but asserts new information that negates liability. For example, a defendant could admit that he struck the plaintiff, but assert that he did so in self-defense.

26. See Subrin, *supra* note 10, at 999–1000; A. Leo Levin, *Equitable Clean-up and the Jury: A Suggested Orientation*, 100 U. PA. L. REV. 320, 325 (1951). See also, CLARK, *supra* note 8, at 67–69) (advocating presumption in favor of a bench trial). Clark was a principal drafter of the Federal Rules of Civil Procedure. Levin, writing in 1951, noted that the jury trial pendulum was swinging the other way by then, apparently because the democratic value of the jury was thought worth a sacrifice of efficiency. See Levin, *supra*, at 325. While the populist democratic values underlying the jury are evident to many, it is doubtful that the jury's opponents were driven primarily by concerns for efficiency. Some commentators have suggested that juries generally do not favor the kind of interests largely represented by the original Advisory Committee, whose practitioner members came mostly from firms that represented large corporate clients. See, e.g., Subrin, *supra* note 10, at 963

they instead created a presumption in favor of a bench trial. They did this by providing that trial by jury is waived if it is not demanded within a very narrow time frame.[27] While federal litigants had been able to waive their right to a jury trial since at least 1819,[28] the presumption was clearly in favor of a jury trial. Indeed, application of a common law rule preventing appeal by writ of error if a jury did not find the facts may have limited the use of waiver.[29] Even after Congress, in 1865, provided that litigants could waive the right to a jury trial by written stipulation, and that the matter was appealable on the same terms as if the jury had found the facts,[30] the courts continued to apply the common law rule if the parties waived a jury trial orally rather than in writing.[31] In 1930, Congress provided that bench trials were fully appealable even if the waiver was oral, but it maintained the requirement that the parties had to stipulate to a bench trial or the trial would be by jury.[32] The 1938 Federal Rules, thus, turned the long-standing preference for a jury trial on its head by providing that a jury trial would be waived unless specifically demanded.[33]

3. Equity and the Federal Rules

Not only have the characteristic common law procedures largely disappeared under the Federal Rules in favor of quite different equity rules, but

---

n.310; Laura Kalman, Legal Realism at Yale 1927–1960, at p. 21 (1986). As I showed in Chapter 1, however, the empirical evidence on that point does not clearly show systematic anti-corporation bias.

27. *See* Fed. R. Civ. P. 38. A jury trial must be demanded within ten days after service of the last pleading directed to the issue that is subject to a jury trial. According to the advisory committee notes, this procedure was followed in many states and in England, so the idea was not new. Indeed, it suggests that the jury's decline began well before the Federal Rules were promulgated.

28. *See* Bank of Columbia v. Okely, 17 U.S. (4 Wheat.) 235, 244 (1819); Robert Wyness Millar, Civil Procedure of the Trial Court in Historical Perspective 260 (1952).

29. *See* Kelsey v. Forsyth, 62 U.S. (21 How.) 85, 87–88 (1858). The parties could also appeal by writ of error if they stipulated to the facts, but if the facts were found by the judge, the matter was not appealable. *See* Exporters of Manufacturers' Products, Inc. v. Butterworth-Judson Co., 258 U.S. 365, 367 (1922).

30. *See* Act of March 3, 1865, ch. 86, §4, 13 Stat. 501.

31. *See, e.g.*, Bond v. Dustin, 112 U.S. 604 (1884).

32. *See* Act of May 29, 1930, ch. 357, 46 Stat. 486.

33. The 1865 statute, as modified in 1930, was repealed by the Revision Act of 1948, 62 Stat. 869, as the Federal Rules of Civil Procedure made it unnecessary. *See* H. Rep. No. 308 to accompany H. R. 3214 (80th Cong., 1st Sess. 1947, at A239. *See generally*, 8 James Wm. Moore, *et al.*, Moore's Federal Practice 39 App.100 (3rd ed., 1999).

many fundamentals of equity procedure that have no common law counterpart have made their way into the Federal Rules.[34] Indeed, the very premise of Equity—that it was to do justice even when the common law could
not—is unequivocally a part of the Federal Rules. Rule 1 says that the Rules
are to be construed and administered "to secure the just, speedy, and inexpensive determination of every action."[35] While no procedural system can
be legitimate if it is not set up to do justice, common law procedures did
not appeal so bluntly to justice, and often worked injustices because of their
inflexible adherence to the letter of the rules and the law. That is why Equity was needed as a corrective. But equity is now built into the federal
rules.[36]

The general characteristic of equity that is specifically designed to promote justice is discretion.[37] Historically, equity provided for appeals to the
king's conscience—to his sense of justice.[38] The king had the discretion necessary to do justice. In the federal system, many decisions that a judge makes
in the course of the litigation are discretionary, including decisions regarding sanctions for filing unsupported papers;[39] decisions on whether to allow
permissive counterclaims or cross claims;[40] the decision whether to dismiss
or continue a case when a necessary party cannot be joined;[41] the decision

---

34. *See generally,* Subrin, *supra* note 10, at 922.

35. *See* FED. R. CIV. P. 1. Other rules mandate that the judge permit amendments to
pleadings "when justice so requires," *see* FED. R. CIV. P. 15(a), and to hold separate trials
on various claims or issues within the suit if she deems such separate suits necessary "in
furtherance of convenience or to avoid prejudice, *see* FED. R. CIV. P. 42(b).

36. There is nothing unusual about a merged law and equity. Many concepts that we
now call equitable were part of the law of Rome, for example, which did not have separate
courts of equity. *See* W.W. BUCKLAND, EQUITY IN ROMAN LAW ([1983]1911).

37. *See* Laycock, *supra* note 10, at 71–73.

38. *See supra,* Chapter 2, at notes 125–127 and accompanying text. Of course, discretion can lead to abuse as well. If the king has no conscience, he will do justice only by accident. The same can be said of judges, juries, and other decision-makers.

39. FED. R. CIV. P. 11. *See, e.g.,* Witherspoon v. Roadway Express, Inc., 782 F. Supp.
567, 570 (D. Kan. 1992) (judge properly exercised discretion to sanction plaintiff for filing
false *in forma pauperis* petition).

40. FED. R. CIV. P. 13(b), (b) and (g). *See, e.g.,* Rohner, Gehrig & Co. v. Capital City
Bank, 655 F.2d 571, 576 (5th Cir. 1981) (judge properly exercised discretion to refuse permission to add omitted counterclaim).

41. FED. R. CIV. P. 19(b). *See, e.g.,* United States v. Aetna Casualty & Surety Co., 338
U.S. 366, 382 (1949) (courts have discretionary authority to proceed with litigation when
necessary parties cannot be joined); Federated Mutual Implement and Hardware Insurance
Co. v. Zimmerman, 33 F.R.D. 8 (D. Kan. 1963) (judge exercised discretion to allow a sub-
rogation case to continue without a necessary party).

whether to certify a class action;[42] numerous decisions relating to discovery;[43] the decision whether to hold separate trials on some of the claims or issues in the case;[44] and the decision whether to grant a new trial.[45] There are many more examples. The conduct of litigation, in other words, is in the hands of the judge. In addition, judges continue to have discretion over equitable remedies, such as injunctions.[46] Because courts of appeals review discretionary decisions under the highly deferential "abuse of discretion" standard,[47] that means that district judges have considerable latitude under the Federal Rules. Common law procedures generally did not allow this kind of discretion, but kept the judges strictly within the bounds of the writ.[48]

In addition to this general characteristic, a number of equitable devices are found in the Federal Rules. Discovery, for example was an equitable device, though discovery under the equity rules was not as extensive as it is under the Federal Rules.[49] Class actions were also found in equity, though, once again,

---

42. FED. R. CIV. P. 23. *See, e.g.,* Malonas v. Williams, 691 F.2d 931, 938 (10th Cir. 1982) (judge properly exercised discretion to certify a class of former students suing for injunction to prevent mistreatment of students); Mazus v. Department of Transportation, 629 F.2d 870, 876 (3rd Cir. 1980) (judge properly exercised discretion to refuse to certify a class action when plaintiff could not establish the existence of a class).

43. FED. R. CIV. P. 26(b)(2). *See, e.g.,* Naartex Consulting Corp. v. Watt, 722 F.2d 779, 788 (D.C. Cir. 1983) (judge properly exercised discretion to refuse discovery when there was no apparent claim).

44. FED. R. CIV. P. 42(b). *See, e.g.,* Ammesmaki v. Interlake Steamship Co., 342 F.2d 627, 631 (7th Cir. 1965) (judge properly exercised discretion to refuse separate trial when issue was which of two defendants was liable and for how much).

45. FED. R. CIV. P. 59. *See, e.g.,* Allied Chemical Corp. v. Daiflon, Inc., 449 U.S. 33, 36 (1980) (decision whether to grant new trial "is confided almost entirely to the exercise of discretion on the part of the trial court").

46. This discretionary authority over injunctions and other equitable remedies is one factor in the growth of "public law litigation," where the parties and their attorneys litigate against public authorities over matters of public interest, such as school desegregation and institutional reform. *See generally,* Abram Chayes, *The Role of the Judge in Public Law Litigation,* 89 HARV. L. REV. 1281 (1976); Owen M. Fiss, *The Forms of Justice,* 93 HARV. L. REV. 1 (1979); OWEN M. FISS, THE CIVIL RIGHTS INJUNCTION (1978).

47. *See* 1 STEVEN ALAN CHILDRESS AND MARTHA S. DAVIS, FEDERAL STANDARDS OF REVIEW § 4.21 (2d ed. 1992).

48. Nevertheless, common law judges eventually were able to get very creative with causes of action, a development that mitigated the injustice that common law courts sometimes did. I discuss this *infra,* at notes 185–194 and accompanying text.

49. *See* FED. R. CIV. P. 26–37. Equity allowed a party to discover material in the other party's hands that was needed for making the discovering party's own case. It did not allow discovery of the opposing party's materials. *See* 1 POMEROY, *supra* note 1, at § 201.

they were not as broad as they are under the Federal Rules.[50] The federal rules explicitly provide for injunctions,[51] receivers,[52] and specific performance,[53] all equitable remedies. The Rules allow the use of aides to the court, such as masters,[54] who can help interpret complex factual matters such as accounting; this is akin to the equitable remedy of accounting.[55] A cursory review of the first Advisory Committee's notes to the original rules shows that most are drawn from the Federal Equity Rules. In short, equity principles and procedures dominate the Federal Rules of Civil Procedure; once again, the only significant common law survivor is the jury.[56]

4. Summary

Common law procedures were well suited to the jury, as they simplified the litigation process and made the dispute accessible to ordinary citizens. The writ system confined the dispute to a single legal theory, generally involving only one plaintiff and one defendant. The single-issue pleading rules aimed to reduce the dispute to one simple yes-or-no question as to either fact or law, but not both. The jury functioned easily in such a system. By contrast, equity procedures allowed for some quite complicated cases, with multiple parties, multiple claims, and multiple issues. Equity also left considerable room for the exercise of discretion. Significantly, the jury did not operate in equity. The drafters of the Federal Rules rejected the principal characteristics of common law procedures (except for the constitutionally-mandated jury), and adopted those of equity instead. The complexity that results is bound to make it difficult for a jury to

---

50. *See* 1 HERBERT NEWBERG AND ALBA CONTE, NEWBERG ON CLASS ACTIONS, § 1.09 (3rd ed. 1992). Under the Federal Rules of Civil Procedure, there are three kinds of class actions. One allows a class if the absent members of the class or the opposing party would be prejudiced by not having the matter decided once as to all affected parties. *See* FED. R. CIV. P. 23(b)(1). The second allows a class when injunctive relief affecting a large number of people is sought against a defendant. *See* FED. R. CIV. P. 23(b)(2). The third allows a class in mass tort cases if certain requirements are met. *See* FED. R. CIV. P. 23(b)(3).
51. *See* FED. R. CIV. P. 65.
52. *See* FED. R. CIV. P. 66.
53. *See* FED. R. CIV. P. 70.
54. *See* FED. R. CIV. P. 53.
55. The Supreme Court has found that litigants do not need the equitable remedy of accounting in part because masters are available to help sort out the financial transactions. See Dairy Queen v. Wood, 369 U.S. 469, 478 (1962). *See infra*, Chapter 4, at notes 49–54 and accompanying text. As a result, juries are available even when the plaintiff specifically asks for an accounting. *See id.* at 480.
56. *See generally*, Subrin, *supra* note 10.

function. That effect is compounded, however, when we consider another feature of adjudication in common law courts: the adversary system.

B. The Decline of the Adversary System

There are two primary kinds of adjudicatory systems in the western world: adversary and inquisitory.[57] The adversary system is a feature of English common law adjudication, and is used in England and other common law countries.[58] Inquisitorial adjudication is characteristic of continental Europe and is used generally in civil law countries.[59]

1. The Adversary System Defined

a. Characteristics

A pure adversary system has two primary characteristics: (1) party control of the litigation; and (2) a passive decision-maker, who merely listens to arguments and renders a decision.[60] The parties themselves, and not the judge, are responsible for the conduct of the litigation, including investigation of the

---

57. There are, however, other dispute resolution systems, including mediation. *See* THE DISPUTING PROCESS—LAW IN TEN SOCIETIES (Laura Nader & Harry F. Todd eds. 1978); JEROLD S. AUERBACH, JUSTICE WITHOUT LAW? (1983).

58. *See* Ellen E. Sward, *Values, Ideology, and the Evolution of the Adversary System*, 64 IND. L.J. 301, 319–26 (1989).

59. *See* Geoffrey C. Hazard, Jr., *From Whom No Secrets Are Hid*, 76 TEX. L. REV. 1665, 1672–75 (1998). Common law is distinguished from civil law in the source of its laws. Common law is judge-made law; civil law is statutory. *See* Peter G. Stein, *Roman Law, Common Law and Civil Law*, 66 TULANE L. REV. 1591, 1594–98 (1992) Civil law is a descendant of Roman law, which England refused to adopt. *See* BAKER, *supra* note 1, at 33–35. There is also a philosophical distinction between the two systems. Common law is incremental and reactive: it is made in reaction to specific problems that arise involving specific persons. Civil law is comprehensive and proactive: it is created as a whole system, which attempts to foresee problems and provide for them. *See* Peter Strauss, *The Common Law and Statutes*, 70 U.COLO. L. REV. 225 (1999). Despite the different origins and philosophy, the two systems of law often have quite similar legal rules and principles. *See* M.H. HOEFLICH, ROMAN AND CIVIL LAW AND THE DEVELOPMENT OF ANGLO-AMERICAN JURISPRUDENCE IN THE NINETEENTH CENTURY 15–25 (1997). Legal principles are solidified in the common law through precedent, and in civil law by the comprehensive Code. *See* Strauss, *supra*, at 235.

60. *See* Sward, *supra* note 58, at 312–13; Lon L. Fuller, *The Adversary System*, in TALKS ON AMERICAN LAW 45 (Harold J. Berman ed., rev. ed. 1971); STEPHAN LANDSMAN, THE ADVERSARY SYSTEM: A DESCRIPTION AND DEFENSE 1 (1984).

facts and law, and presentation of evidence and argumentation to the judge.[61] Adversarial judges usually do not act unless a party asks them to act.[62] When they do act, the action is generally narrow—responsive to the moving party's request but no more. The decision-maker simply determines which party had the better argument, and a winner and a loser emerge.

Inquisitorial systems, by contrast, have a decision-maker who is more involved in the development of the case, and parties who have concomitantly less control.[63] The inquisitorial judge can pursue avenues of investigation not suggested by the parties, and decline to pursue issues that the parties suggest. The judge has an opportunity to render a verdict that compromises the matter so as to do justice to all.[64]

In addition to these two primary characteristics, adversarial and inquisitorial adjudication are distinguished by the structure of the trial. Adversarial adjudication normally features a continuous trial, or one that continues without significant interruption until it is completed.[65] Inquisitorial adjudication, by contrast, may have many interruptions in the trial, with judges stopping the trial so that more investigation can be done.[66]

These are the most prominent characteristics of "pure" adversarial and inquisitorial systems. Of course, there is no such thing as a pure adversary system or a pure inquisitorial system, and there probably never has been. Each kind of adjudicatory system has both advantages and disadvantages, and each kind of adjudicatory system has taken on some of the characteristics of the other.[67] As I will show momentarily, the American adversary system has moved significantly toward inquisitorial adjudication under the Federal Rules of Civil Procedure, though the American system is still far from the kind of compre-

---

61. See Sward, *supra* note 58, at 312.
62. See Fuller, *supra* note 60, at 45. Judges have always had the power to take some acts *sua sponte*, or without being asked to act, but that power was, until recently, carefully guarded. The most prominent example is probably the court's power to dismiss a case for lack of subject matter jurisdiction without a motion from a party. See FED. R. CIV. P. 12(h)(3).
63. See Sward, *supra* note 58, at 313–15.
64. See id. at 315. The parties can certainly disagree about whether justice was, in fact, done.
65. See id. at 313–14.
66. See id. at 314.
67. See id. at 316; MIRJAN R. DAMASKA, EVIDENCE LAW ADRIFT 7–8 (1997); John H. Langbein, *The German Advantage in Civil Procedure*, 52 U. CHI. L. REV. 823, 855–56 (1985); Richard A. Posner, *An Economic Approach to the Law of Evidence*, 51 STAN. L. REV. 1477, 1487–1502 (1999).

hensive judicial control found in Continental Europe.[68] First, however, it is important to understand the justification for the adversary system, and how that justification evolved over time.

b. Justification

The adversary system took some time to evolve, and the justification for it has evolved as well. While we can certainly see adversary-ness in some early modes of proof, notably battle, the original jury of neighbor-witnesses was anything but adversarial. Early jurors were drawn from the area where the event had occurred so that the jury would comprise people who should know something about the matter. If they did not know, they were required to ask their neighbors about the facts, decide what the truth was, and swear to the facts in court.[69] The parties would have had little to say about the matter, at least in theory. In other words, the early jury was a purely inquisitorial device.[70] Nevertheless, it is easy to see why, once the role of the jury changed and the common law system solidified, the adversary system began to develop.

When jurors were no longer expected to know or discover anything about the matter, but became evaluators of evidence presented in court, the task of investigation and presentation of evidence had to go somewhere. The choices were the judge or the parties. The judge may have been inappropriate because judges were representatives of the king who generally did not live in the region where the dispute arose; rather, they traveled around the country, hearing cases as they went.[71] They were in a given area for only a short time, and it could be as much as seven years before they returned.[72] Judges could not be responsible for the investigation under such a system. By default, the job fell to the parties. The fact that judges traveled also justifies the continuous trial. Judges and parties needed a continuous trial so that the matter could be concluded without undue delay.[73]

---

68. The inquisitorial systems of Continental Europe have also been on the move, with civil adjudication, especially, featuring more party involvement in the development of evidence and argumentation. *See* DAMASKA, *supra* note 67, at 107–08.

69. *See supra*, Chapter 2, at notes 34–42 and accompanying text.

70. The very terminology shows this. The Norman import that was the progenitor of the modern jury was called an "inquest." *See* BAKER, *supra* note 1, at 86–88; JAMES BRADLEY THAYER, A PRELIMINARY TREATISE ON EVIDENCE AT THE COMMON LAW 47–53 (1898).

71. *See* THEODORE F.T. PLUCKNETT, A CONCISE HISTORY OF THE COMMON LAW 234–35 (1956); 1 FREDERICK POLLOCK AND FREDERIC WILLIAM MAITLAND, THE HISTORY OF ENGLISH LAW 153–56 (2d ed. 1968); S.F.C. MILSOM, HISTORICAL FOUNDATIONS OF THE COMMON LAW 27–32 (2nd ed. 1981).

72. *See id.* at 30.

73. It has been suggested that the adversary system developed because of the jury. *See*

The original justification for the adversary system was thus quite practical, but proponents now justify it on very different grounds. They argue that if judges become involved in the adjudicative process too early, they could reach conclusions too early—before the facts and the law in the case are developed and ready for decision.[74] Judges might then make rulings in the case that cut off branches of inquiry, or even that determine the case, without having full information about the case.[75] In addition, the parties themselves have more of a stake in the outcome and are likely to do a better job of investigating the facts and law and crafting legal arguments than would a judge with no personal interest in the case.[76] This ensures that the court will hear the best arguments on both sides of the question, which will aid in decisionmaking. The sharp clash of evidence and argument is needed to frame the issue for the decision-maker, who otherwise knows nothing about the case.[77] Indeed, that sharp clash helps to frame the issue as an either/or question, which is easy for an adjudicatory system to answer—especially an adjudicatory system dependent on lay jurors.[78] The adversary system is also thought to do a good job of legitimating the outcome of the litigation: if the parties themselves are in control of the evidence and argumentation, they are more likely to accept an unfavorable outcome than if they were relatively uninvolved.[79]

It is harder to see a good modern justification for a continuous trial, at least based on adversarial theory. The jury still provides a good justification, of course: it would be logistically difficult to require jurors to return to court again and again, with weeks or even months separating the short bursts of

JOHN BALDWIN AND MICHAEL McCONVILLE, JURY TRIALS 18 (1979). The precise cause and effect, however, is impossible to identify. The jury, the adversary system, and the common law were part of a system that developed together. *See also*, DAMASKA, *supra* note 67, at 128–29 (discussing the effect of the jury, the continuous trial, and the adversary system, all features of common law adjudication, on evidence law).

74. *See* LANDSMAN, *supra* note 60, at 49–50; Stephen A. Saltzburg, *The Unnecessarily Expanding Role of the American Trial Judge*, 64 VA. L. REV. 1, 16–17 (1978); Sward, *supra* note 58, at 313; DAMASKA, *supra* note 67, at 82.

75. *See* Sward, *supra* note 58, at 313; LANDSMAN, *supra* note 60, at 2–3; Fuller, *supra* note 60, at 43.

76. *See* Sward, *supra* note 58, at 313; LANDSMAN, *supra* note 60, at 4; Stephen McG. Bundy, *The Policy in Favor of Settlement in and Adversary System*, 44 HASTINGS L.J. 1, 9 (1992).

77. *See* LANDSMAN, *supra* note 60, at 2; Sward, *supra* note 58, at 312–13.

78. *See* COUND, ET AL., *supra* note 2, at 2–3.

79. *See* STEPHAN LANDSMAN, READINGS ON ADVERSARIAL JUSTICE: THE AMERICAN APPROACH TO LITIGATION 33–34 (1988).

service.[80] But in theory, a bench trial could be discontinuous even in an adversary system. One possible adversarial justification for the continuous trial—not dependent on the existence of a jury—is that it will be harder for a passive decision-maker, whether judge or jury, to keep evidence in mind over long breaks in the proceedings.[81] In inquisitorial systems, where discontinuous trials are the norm, the judge is involved in evidence-gathering during the breaks. The adversarial judge, however, would put the case aside until the next installment of the trial, and the evidence adduced in earlier installments could fade in her memory. Thus, the evidence introduced at the most recent installment might carry more weight than it deserves.

There are problems with pure adversarial adjudication, of course. First, it assumes that the parties have roughly equal skills and resources to devote to the litigation, but that is often not the case. A battle of unequal parties is not a real test of truth.[82] Second, the parties have both more incentive and more opportunity to manipulate the truth, as by withholding evidence or even outright lying. In a pure adversary system, discovery would not be available, so if one party held a damaging piece of evidence, it would be easy to withhold it.[83] In addition, adversarial adjudication may encourage what is sometimes

---

80. *See* DAMASKA, *supra* note 67, at 60. In the criminal system, however, grand juries often take such breaks.

81. *See* MOLLY SELVIN & LARRY PICUS, THE DEBATE OVER JURY PERFORMANCE: OBSERVATIONS FROM A RECENT ASBESTOS CASE 45 (1987) (discussing the jury); Joseph Sanders, *Scientifically Complex Cases, Trial By Jury, and the Erosion of the Adversarial Process*, 48 DEPAUL L. REV. 355, 361 (1998) (same); Thomas O. Nelson, *Savings and Forgetting from Long-term Memory*, 10 J. OF VERBAL LEARNING & VERBAL BEHAV. 571 (1971).

82. The quality of investigation and argument will depend in part on the resources available to the parties and their lawyers' legal skills. *See* Sward, *supra* note 58, at 312. The modern federal rules contain some devices that help to equalize the parties in some respects, such as discovery. *See id.* Contingency fee arrangments might also be seen as helping to equalize resources. *See* Robert S. Thompson, *Decision, Disciplined Inferences and the Adversary Process*, 13 CARDOZO L. REV. 725, 773n.168 (1991); Jeffrey J. Parker, Note, *Contingent Expert Witness Fees: Access and Legitimacy*, 64 S. CAL. L. REV. 1363, 1370 (1991). *But see*, Owen M. Fiss, *Against Settlement*, 93 YALE L.J. 1073, 1077 (1984). As I suggested in Chapter 1, the jury itself helps to equalize unequal parties.

83. Because it constrains party control over the development of evidence, discovery is a nonadversarial element in modern adversarial adjudication. *See* Sward, *supra* note 58, at 328–29. Discovery was available in the courts of equity, and a common law litigant who needed information from the other side could go there seeking discovery of the matter. But equitable discovery was quite limited—a party could get information held by the other side only if it was important to the discoverer's case; no one could discover information relating to his opponent's case. *See* 1 POMEROY, *supra* note 1, at §193; Edson R. Sunderland, *Scope and Method of Discovery Before Trial*, 42 YALE L.J. 863, 866 (1933).

referred to as "Rambo" tactics.[84] Finally, it may be difficult for parties who have been involved in hotly contested adversarial adjudication to maintain a relationship with their opponents.[85]

Inquisitorial adjudication avoids the problems associated with pure adversarial adjudication. The parties do not have to have equal skills or resources, because the judge plays a large role in the investigation, and can help to equalize unequal litigants. It should be harder for the litigants to manipulate the truth, though not impossible. The inquisitorial system is less likely to provoke uncivil behavior among the parties or their attorneys. And the parties are better able to maintain a relationship following the litigation. Proponents believe that inquisitorial adjudication is more likely to uncover the truth.[86] Indeed, it has been said that inquisitorial systems aim to find the objective truth, while adversarial systems are more concerned with resolving the dispute that the parties have framed.[87] There is nothing inherently superior about either goal, however, and inquisitorial adjudication may produce judges who judge too soon, and parties who are less confident in the outcome. On the other hand, adversarial adjudication may favor the wealthy and make it difficult for the parties to mend fences with their opponents.

---

84. *See* Robert N. Sayler, *Rambo Litigation: Why Hardball Tactics Don't Work*, 74 A.B.A.J. 78, 79 (March, 1988); Jean M. Cary, *Rambo Depositions: Controlling an Ethical Cancer in Civil Litigation*, 25 HOFSTRA L. REV. 561, 571 (1996). One example is abuse of discovery, which has led to some modifications of the discovery rules, including limits on the number of interrogatories one may serve, FED. R. CIV. P. 33(a), or depositions one may take, FED. R. CIV. P. 30(a)(2)(A), without leave of court. *See generally,* James Skakalik, *et al., Discovery Management: A Further Analysis of the Civil Justice Reform Act Evaluation Data*, 39 B.C. L. REV. 613, 621–26 (1998); William W. Schwarzer, *The Federal Rules, The Adversary System, and Discovery Reform*, 50 U. PITT. L. REV. 703 (1989); Wayne Brazil, *The Adversary Character of Civil Discovery: A Critique and Proposals for Change*, 31 VAND. L. REV. 1295 (1978).

85. This is one reason why there is so much alternative dispute resolution in family law and other areas where the parties will have to continue dealing with each other when the dispute has been resolved. *See* Dwight Golann, *Making Alternative Dispute Resolution Mandatory: The Constitutional Issues*, 68 OR. L. REV. 487, 490 (1989).

86. *See* Franklin Strier, *Making Jury Trials More Truthful*, 30 U.C. DAVIS L. REV. 95, 142 (1996); E. Allan Lind *et al., Discovery and Presentation of Evidence in Adversary and Nonadversary Proceedings*, 71 MICH. L. REV. 1129, 1130–31 (1973). It is ironic that both systems are sometimes justified as more likely to uncover the truth.

87. *See* Stephan Landsman, *The Decline of the Adversary System: How the Rhetoric of Swift and Certain Justice Has Affected Adjudication in American Courts*, 29 BUFF. L. REV. 487, 492 (1980). *See also,* DAMASKA, *supra* note 67, at 120 (noting that the adversary system aims to resolve disputes rather than to uncover the objective truth, and distinguishing inquisitorial systems on this ground).

Perhaps for these reasons, modern adjudicatory systems, while predominantly either adversarial or inquisitorial, have adopted characteristics of both.[88]

The adversary system and the common law go hand-in-hand: the greatest flowering of adversarial adjudication has occurred in the common law courts. Not only is it not a feature of the civil law courts of continental Europe, but it is not even a significant feature of Equity, which always had more active judges. In Equity, judges might be more closely involved in the production of evidence than would a common law judge.[89] Equity judges also had considerable discretion as to the remedy, and could issue orders that might involve them in continued supervision of the case.[90] Equity judges could answer questions that could not be framed as either/or propositions. Thus, the very fact that equitable procedures dominate the Federal Rules suggests some alteration of the adversary system. As I show in the next section, however, the alteration is much more than a simple byproduct of equitable procedures.

2. The Adversary System Under the Federal Rules

Just as the Federal Rules have profoundly altered common law procedures, so have they profoundly altered the adversary system. This can best be illustrated by describing the effect the Federal Rules have had on the primary characteristics of adversarial adjudication: passive judges and active parties. The Rules also affect the incidental characteristic of the continuous trial.

a. The Role of the Judge

i. The Need for Active Judges. I have already shown that litigation under the Federal Rules can be extraordinarily complex, with multiple claims and mul-

---

88. *See* Sward, *supra* note 58, at 316; Damaska, *supra* note 67, at 106–08; Posner, *supra* note 67, at 1487–1502.

89. An example of this is the equitable device of accounting, where the judge would review a party's accounting records to decipher complicated transactions. 1 Pomeroy, *supra* note 1, at § 112.

90. They could, for example, issue injunctions; create trusts, mortgages, and other long-term instruments; and appoint receivers. This is just a sampling of the range of equitable remedies. For more complete discussions of equity and equitable remedies, *see, e.g.*, 4 Pomeroy, *supra* note 1; Sir Robert Megarry and P.V. Baker, Snell's Principles of Equity (1973); George W. Keeton and L.A. Sheridan, Equity (1976); F. W. Maitland, Equity, Also the Forms of Action at Common Law (1920); J. R. Lewis, Outlines of Equity (1968). *See also,* Chapter 2, *supra* at notes 128–139 and accompanying text.

tiple parties.[91] Under such a system, it is not surprising that the normal party-centered case management sometimes breaks down. A case with multiple parties can have either a leadership vacuum, where no one is managing the overall litigation, or a battle among parties and attorneys for the leadership role, resulting in no effective leadership. In addition, litigation under the Federal Rules goes through more stages than the pleading and proof stages characteristic of common law adversarial adjudication. Most importantly, the Federal Rules provide for a lengthy discovery period sandwiched between pleading and proof. Discovery itself is almost bound to lead to management problems. Discovery is non-adversarial in the sense that it requires adversaries to share information, thereby diminishing party control.[92] Tales of discovery abuse are abundant, and outside management is often necessary to contain it.[93]

There are also many kinds of motions that parties can file, each of which requires a response from the court.[94] Some of them, like the motion to dismiss for failure to state a claim, had common law analogues, but some, like the motion for summary judgment, did not.[95] Discovery itself often necessitates motions. The parties, for example, can use various discovery motions to test the scope of the opponent's case: a party could move that certain discovery not be had on the ground that the claim or defense that the discovery relates to is groundless.[96] It is impossible, however, to catalogue all of the possible motions a trial judge could see. Every time a litigant wants the judge to do something, she files a motion. In a system where available motions seem to be limited only by the imagination of lawyers, there are many opportunities for the parties to delay the proceedings. This may require that judicial personnel step into the management void and keep the case moving forward.

---

91. *See supra*, notes 11–24 and accompanying text.

92. *See* Sward, *supra* note 58, at 327.

93. *See* Note, *Discovery Abuse Under the Federal Rules: Causes and Cures*, 92 Yale L.J. 352, 356–60 (1982); Robert L. Haig and Warren N. Stone, *Litigation Reform*, 67 St. John's L.J. 843, 869, (1993).

94. *See* David F. Herr et al., Motion Practice §8.1 (2nd ed. 1991); The Honorable Margaret B. Seymour, *Dispositive Motions and the Role of the United States Magistrate Judge*, 50 S.C. L. Rev. 639 (1999).

95. The motion to dismiss for failure to state a claim, Fed. R. Civ. P. 12(b)(6), derives from the common law demurrer. A party will usually seek a summary judgment after discovery. There was no analogous stage of litigation under common law procedures, so there was no analogous motion.

96. This would usually be a motion for protective order under Fed. R. Civ. P. 26(c). A recent amendment to Rule 26(c) requires the parties to consult in hopes of working out their disagreement before filing a motion for protective order.

ii. Sources of Judicial Management Authority. Authority for judicial management of litigation has several sources, but the door was opened with the promulgation of Rule 16 in the 1938 Federal Rules of Civil Procedure. Rule 16 allowed judges to hold pre-trial conferences aimed at helping the parties narrow issues for trial.[97] That authority has expanded considerably in the last three decades, spurred in part by the 1969 publication of the Federal Judicial Center's *Manual for Complex Litigation*, a guide for litigators in complex cases that outlined methods for judges to become intensively involved in the day-to-day management of such cases.[98] Taking cues from the Manual, many district courts in the 1970s promulgated local rules that allowed for extensive judicial management.[99]

In 1983, Rule 16 was greatly expanded to allow for more active judicial management.[100] While the goal of the original Rule 16 was to help the parties formulate issues for trial,[101] the 1983 version allowed more and earlier intervention by the trial judge in the day-to-day management of the case. Congress then jumped into the fray, enacting the Civil Justice Reform Act (CJRA) in 1990.[102] The CJRA is a Congressional mandate to judges and judicial districts to institute management procedures. The purposes were "to facilitate deliberate adjudication of civil cases on the merits, monitor discovery, improve litigation management, and ensure just, speedy, and inexpensive resolution of civil disputes."[103] To that end, each District Court was to formulate a plan for reducing expense and delay.[104] The plan may include giving considerable management authority to judges and authorizing referrals to alternative dispute resolution.[105] Some of the activities authorized by the CJRA were incorporated

---

97. *See* Appendix 1, Fed. R. Civ. P. 16—1938 Rule; E. Donald Elliott, *Managerial Judging and the Evolution of Procedure*, 53 U.Chi. L. Rev. 306, 323 (1986).

98. The *Manual* is now in its third edition. *See* Federal Judicial Center, Manual for Complex Litigation Third (1995).

99. *See* Robert F. Peckham, *The Federal Judge as a Case Manager: The New Role in Guiding a Case from Filing to Disposition*, 69 Calif. L. Rev. 770 (1981) (discussing rules in the Northern District of California).

100. *See* Appendix 2, Fed. R. Civ. P. 16—1983 Rule.

101. *See* David L. Shapiro, *Federal Rule 16: A Look at the Theory and Practice of Rulemaking*, 137 U.Pa. L. Rev. 1969, 1978 (1989); Elliott, *supra* note 97, at 318–22.

102. *See* 28 U.S.C. §§471–482 (1994). Relevant portions of the CJRA are reproduced in Appendix 4.

103. 28 U.S.C. §471 (1994).

104. *See id.*

105. *See* 28 U.S.C. §473(a)(2), (3) and (6) (1994). Section 473 of theAct describes the content of a civil justice expense and delay reduction plan. Relevant portions of the Act are reproduced in Appendix 4.

into the Federal Rules in a 1993 amendment to Rule 16.[106] Rule 16 now enables judges to work with the parties, largely through a series of pretrial conferences, to expedite disposition of the case; establish and maintain control so as to prevent protracted litigation; "discourag[e] wasteful pretrial activities"; improve trial preparation; and facilitate settlement.[107]

There are other rules that facilitate judicial management as well. Rule 26 gives judges explicit authority to manage the parties' use of discovery,[108] even allowing the court to act on its own initiative.[109] Rule 23 provides judges with a variety of management tools for class actions.[110] Judges can also manage cases through the use of magistrate judges and masters. Magistrate judges are adjuncts to the district courts, with authority to hear and decide non-dispositive pre-trial motions, such as motions for protective orders or motions to compel discovery;[111] serve as a special master;[112] and even conduct trials with the consent of the parties.[113] In many federal districts, oversight of pre-trial matters is routinely assigned to magistrate judges.[114] Masters are appointed

---

106. *See, e.g.,* FED. R. CIV. P. 16(a)(2) (providing that court should establish early and ongoing control of litigation); 28 U.S.C. §473(a)(2) (1994) (same); FED. R. CIV. P. 16(b)(3) (providing that court is to control the extent and timing of discovery; 28 U.S.C. §473(a)(2)(C) (1994) (same); FED. R. CIV. P. 16(c)(9) (providing that court can require that the parties explore settlement at pretrial conferences); 28 U.S.C. §473(a)(3)(A) (1994) (same). The 1993 version of Rule 16 is reproduced in Appendix 3.

107. *See* Appendix 3, Rule 16(a) (1993 version).

108. For example, judges can limit discovery that is duplicative or burdensome, thus cutting off some avenues of investigation. FED. R. CIV. P. 26(b)(2).

109. *See* FED. R. CIV. P. 26(b) and (g). As we have seen, adversarial judges historically have waited for a motion by a party before acting. *See* notes 60–62 *supra*, and accompanying text.

110. *See* FED. R. CIV. P. 23. These include the power to certify a class, *id.* at 23(a); and the power to approve settlements in class actions, *see id.* at 23(d).

111. *See* 28 U.S.C. §636(b)(1)(A) (1994); Sunview Condominium Association v. Flexo International, Ltd., 116 F.3rd 962, 964 (1st Cir. 1997) (holding that a motion to compel discovery is nondispositive); Hutchinson v. Pfeil, 105 F.3rd 562, 565 (10th Cir. 1997) (holding that motion to disqualify counsel is nondispositive).

112. *See* 28 U.S.C. §636(b)(2) (1994).

113. *See* 28 U.S.C. §636(c) (1994).

114. *See, e.g.,* D. Ariz. Loc. R. 1.17(d)(2) (1994); C.D. Cal. Loc. R. 1.7.19 (1995); D. Del. Loc. R. 72.1(a)(4) (1995); M.D. Fla. Loc. R. 6.01(18) (1995). *See generally,* Philip M. Pro and Thomas C. Hnatowski, *Measured Progress: The Evolution and Administration of the Federal Magistrate Judges System,* 44 AM. U.L. REV. 1503 (1995); Hon. Jacob Hagopian, *United States Magistrate Judges: A Look at the Growth and Development of the Position,* 39 FED. B. NEWS & J. 416 (1992); Magistrate Judge J. Daniel Breen, *Mediation and the Magistrate Judge,* 26 MEMPHIS L. REV. 1007 (1996). On the one hand, this makes judicial man-

most commonly to review specialized evidence and make reports, but the language of the rule is quite broad as to what a judge can appoint a master to do.[115] While the appointment of masters is supposed to "be the exception and not the rule[,]" the use of masters has grown over the years and is especially common in complex cases.[116]

Judges have considerable authority to enforce their managerial decisions through sanctions. Rule 11, which, like Rules 16 and 26, was amended in 1983 and again in 1993,[117] authorizes the imposition of sanctions against parties or, more commonly, their attorneys who, because of a failure to conduct adequate research and investigation, file groundless papers with the court.[118] The purpose of this rule is to deter the filing of frivolous documents.[119] The current version of the rule allows the judge to act on his own initiative, but limits the judge somewhat in imposing sanctions on his own initiative, as he must issue

---

agement somewhat less problematic from the standpoint of adversarial theory: the judge's passive role is preserved. On the other hand, active judicial personnel reduce the role of the parties. Congress provided the authorization for magistrate judges in 1968.

115. Rule 53(c) says, "[t]he order of reference to the master may specify or limit the master's powers." The language is permissive rather than mandatory; it suggests that the judge need not limit the master's powers. Courts, however, are unlikely to approve regular reference to masters to take over all or a major portion of the judge's duties. *See* La Buy v. Howes Leather Co., 352 U.S. 249 (1957) (approving issuance of a writ of mandamus that ordered a district judge to conduct the trial himself rather than refer the trial to a master; the judge had a pattern of referring trials to masters). For examples of how masters are commonly used, see United States v. Conservation Chemical Co., 106 F.R.D. 210, 219 (1985) (master reviewed evidence of environmental contamination); Turner Construction Co. v. First Indemnity of America, 829 F. Supp. 752 (E.D. Pa. 1993) (master appointed to sort out factual issues relating to liability under suretyship agreements).

116. Fed. R. Civ. P. 53(b). *See* Manual for Complex Litigation, *supra* note 98, at §§ 20.14 and 21.52.

117. For a discussion of this amendment, see *Symposium, Amended Rule 11 of the Federal Rules of Civil Procedure*, 54 Fordham L. Rev. 1–33 (1985).

118. Fed. R. Civ. P. 11(c)(1)(B). Unless the 1983 version of the Rule differs significantly from the 1993 version, my citations are to the 1993 version.

119. *See* Fed. R. Civ. P. 11(c)(2) (sanctions limited to amount necessary to deter future conduct by the party or by others similarly situated). The 1983 version of the rule did not clearly state that deterrence was the primary goal of the rule. Other possible goals include compensating the opposing party for expenses incurred in defending against the frivolous submission. Many courts and commentators emphasized deterrence, however, and sanctions were rarely high enough to provide complete compensation. *See*, William W. Schwarzer, *Rule 11 Revisited*, 101 Harv. L. Rev. 1013, 1019–20 (1988); Melissa L. Nelken, *Sanctions Under Federal Rule 11 — Some "Chilling" Problems in the Struggle Between Compensation and Punishment*, 74 Geo. L.J. 1313, 1323–25 (1986).

a show cause order before imposing them,[120] and cannot impose monetary sanctions unless he issues the show cause order before a voluntary dismissal or settlement.[121] The court also has power under Rule 37 to sanction parties for failure to comply with discovery requests.[122] The Rule 37 power is exercised only at the behest of the parties; there is no provision for a judge to act on her own initiative. Nevertheless, judges have a good deal of discretion in deciding whether to impose sanctions and what sanctions to impose.[123] The most severe sanctions will cost the offending party the case.[124]

---

120. FED. R. CIV. P. 11(c)(1)(B).

121. FED. R. CIV. P. 11(c)(2)(B). A show cause order requires the offending party to demonstrate to the judge why the contemplated sanction should not be imposed. A judge could not order sanctions without giving the offending party or lawyer a chance to defend himself, and the show cause order gives him that chance.

The judge can also impose sanctions under Rule 11 at the request of a party. FED. R. CIV. P. 11(c)(1). Indeed, it is rare for a judge to act on his own initiative, in part because litigants have been so eager, since the 1983 amendments, to seek sanctions. See Jeffrey W. Stempel, *Sanctions, Symmetry, and Safe Harbors: Limiting Misapplication of Rule 11 By Harmonizing It With Pre-Verdict Dismissal Devices*, 60 FORDHAM L. REV. 257, 258 (1991). Because that excessive zeal resulted in a great deal of Rule 11 litigation, the Rule was amended again in 1993 to require that a party seeking sanctions give the opposing party 21 days to withdraw offending documents before seeking sanctions from the court. FED. R. CIV. P. 11(c)(1). See generally Byron C. Keeling, *Toward a Balanced Approach to "Frivolous" Litigation: A Critical Review of Federal Rule 11 and State Sanctions Provisions*, 21 PEPPERDINE L. REV. 1067 (1994). Rule 11 has been criticized for its potential effect on the willingness of litigants to test the continued viability of a particular rule of law or to propose new law. See Mark S. Stein, *Rule 11 in the Real World: How the Dynamics of Litigation Defeat the Purpose of Imposing Attorney Fee Sanctions for the Assertion of Frivolous Legal Arguments*, 132 F.R.D. 309, 329 (1990); Lawrence M. Grosberg, *Allusion and Reality in Regulating Lawyer Performance: Rethinking Rule 11*, 32 VILL. L. REV. 575, 598–99 (1987). The drafters attempted to balance the concern for frivolous litigation against the desire to encourage innovative litigation by providing that sanctions are unavailable against a party who makes "a nonfrivolous argument for the extension, modification, or reversal of existing law or the establishment of new law." FED. R. CIV. P. 11(b)(2). Because we can never know how many cases are not brought because of the fear of sanctions, it is impossible to know whether this compromise is effective. Nevertheless, the judge's power to impose sanctions could have such a deterrent effect.

122. FED. R. CIV. P. 37(d).

123. See National Hockey League v. Metropolitan Hockey Club, Inc., 427 U.S. 639, 643 (1976); Rojias v. Stevenson, 31 F.3d 995, 1005 (10th Cir. 1994).

124. The available sanctions include orders that matters be taken as established; that a party be prohibited from introducing evidence on the disputed matter, making it impossible for the party to prove its contentions; and that pleadings or parts of pleadings be stricken, thereby removing issues from the case. See FED. R. CIV. P. 37(b)(2). The most se-

Judges also have inherent power to impose sanctions, and that power seems to be growing. The Supreme Court held more than thirty years ago that a court can dismiss a case when the plaintiff repeatedly delays or misses pretrial conference dates.[125] The Court found that the power, which is "necessary in order to prevent undue delays in the disposition of pending cases and to avoid congestion in the calendars of the District Courts[,]...is of ancient origin,"[126] and needs no statutory authorization. More recently, the Supreme Court held that a party who engaged in fraud and other bad-faith conduct outside of court could be assessed his opponent's attorneys' fees as a sanction for that conduct, even without explicit authorization in a statute or rule.[127]

Judicial management has evoked both enthusiastic advocacy and thoughtful criticism. Advocates tout the cost- and time-saving benefits of having judges more actively involved in management.[128] In other words, the justification for judicial management is efficiency. Critics argue that judicial management removes judges from their traditional roles in an adversary system, and brings about all of the evils that the passive judicial role was meant to avoid.[129] It is the advocates who have prevailed, however. There may well be efficiency gains from having more active judges, but there is no doubt that managerial judges must frequently step out of their passive role.

---

vere sanctions are usually reserved for cases where there have been multiple failures to comply.

125. Link v. Wabash R. Co., 370 U.S. 626 (1962).

126. *Id.* at 629–30.

127. Chambers v. Nasco, Inc., 501 U.S. 32 (1991). In American courts, each party normally pays her own attorneys' fees; there is no fee-shifting in the absence of explicit statutory authorization. This contrasts with the "English rule," which provides that the losing party pay the winning party's attorneys' fees. *See* ROBERT L. ROSSI, ATTORNEYS' FEES §7:4 (2nd ed. 1995). In *Chambers*, there was no other authority for sanctions because the conduct did not involve filing papers with the court, as required by FED. R. CIV. P. 11, or conduct by an attorney, as required by 28 U.S.C. §1927 (1994). *Id.* at 41. Courts have other inherent powers as well. *See infra*, Chapter 8, at note 19 (describing judges' inherent power with respect to settlement).

128. *See, e.g.,* Peckham, *supra* note 99, at 770–71; David S. Clark, *Adjudication to Administration: A Statistical Analysis of Federal District Courts in the Twentieth Century,* 55 S. CAL. L. REV. 65, 77 (1981); Milton Pollack, *Pretrial Procedures More Effectively Handled,* 65 F.R.D. 475, 482–84 (1974); MAURICE ROSENBURG, THE PRETRIAL CONFERENCE AND EFFECTIVE JUSTICE 12–15 (1964).

129. *See, e.g.,* Judith Resnik, *Managerial Judges,* 96 HARV. L. REV. 376, 424–26 (1982); Stephen A. Saltzburg, *The Unnecessarily Expanding Role of the American Trial Judge,* 64 VA. L. REV. 1, 13–19 (1978). *See also* Chayes, *supra* note 46, at 1285–88 (discussing the judge's expanding role in public law litigation).

b. The Role of the Parties

The rules that I have been describing have a flip side as well. Every rule that gives judges or magistrate judges more managerial authority takes an equal amount of managerial authority away from the parties. Under the judicial management rules, parties can be required to adhere to the judge's timetable, attend a series of conferences, and participate in settlement talks. Indeed, the parties can experience considerable judicial pressure to settle their cases.[130] When a judge uses a master to develop and evaluate evidence, she reduces the parties' control over the development and presentation of evidence, which is the hallmark of adversarial adjudication.[131]

But perhaps the most significant means by which the Rules reduce party control is discovery. Discovery gives the parties a variety of tools to obtain information not only about their own cases, but about their opponents' cases.[132] Dis-

---

130. Many of the management tools at the judge's disposal are designed to encourage settlements, and judges are much more likely to raise the possibility of settlement in pretrial conferences, to urge the parties to settle, and even to take an active role in mediating settlements. *See generally,* Marc Galanter,... *A Settlement Judge, Not a Trial Judge: Judicial Mediation in the United States,* 12 J. L. & Soc'y 1 (1985); Resnik, *supra* note 129, at 379; Daisy Hurst Floyd, *Can the Judge Do That? The Need for a Clearer Judicial Role in Settlement,* 26 Ariz. St. L.J. 45, 49 (1994); Peter Schuck, Agent Orange On Trial: Mass Toxic Disasters in the Courts 163–65 (1986).

131. As I noted earlier, while masters can perform a wide range of tasks, the most common is the development and evaluation of evidence. Masters, for example, might be given free rein to examine a party's financial records and make recommendations to the court as to the fact-finding. *See, e.g.,* Beck v. Communications Workers of America, 776 F.2d 1187, 1210 (4th Cir. 1985); Reed v. Cleveland Board of Education, 607 F.2d 737 (6th Cir. 1979). While the master's report is not conclusive, it could have a significant impact on the outcome of the trial because it is likely to be perceived as impartial and therefore more accurate. *See* Damaska, *supra* note 67, at 69–70. When the master's report is presented to the judge, the parties have an opportunity to argue about whether it should be a part of the record. *See* Equal Employment Opportunity Commisssion v. Local 580, International Association of Bridge, Structural, and Ornamental Ironworkers, 133 F.R.D. 445, 448 (S.D.N.Y. 1990); Levin v. Garfinkle, 540 F. Supp. 1228, 1236 (E.D. Pa. 1982). Not only does this far exceed the traditional authority of judges in an adversary system, but it encroaches on party control.

132. Discovery is governed by Rules 26–37 of the Federal Rules of Civil Procedure. The discovery devices available to the parties are depositions, in which parties ask witnesses questions under oath, Fed. R. Civ. P. 30; interrogatories, in which parties ask other parties a series of written questions that must be answered under oath, Fed. R. Civ. P. 33; requests for production of documents and tangible things, in which parties ask other parties for documents or for access to physical evidence, Fed. R. Civ. P. 34; physical and mental examinations, in which parties may seek an order compelling another party whose physical

covery is a non-adversarial element in the adversary system.[133] It requires parties who historically would have prepared their cases in isolation to share information—sometimes damaging information. That is a difficult thing to do, especially for lawyers who are trained in zealous adversarial advocacy. But in recent years, discovery has become even more intrusive. The original rules required parties to produce evidence only if the opponent asked for it.[134] In 1993, however, the discovery rules were amended to provide for mandatory disclosure of certain information, such as names of witnesses and identification of relevant documents. This discovery is required even if the opponent does not request it.[135] In addition, the Federal Rules now contain limits on the number of depositions and interrogatories each side can use; a party who wants to exceed the number must obtain judicial approval.[136] In short, discovery itself limits the con-

---

or mental condition is in controversy to undergo an examination by the requesting party's doctor, FED. R. CIV. P. 35; and requests to admit, in which a party asks another party to admit to certain allegedly undisputed facts, FED. R. CIV. P. 36.

Historically, discovery was not available in the adversarial common law courts; rather, it was an equitable device. See Developments in the Law—Discovery, 74 HARV. L. REV. 940, 946–48 (1961). It enabled a party to obtain information in his opponent's hands that related to his own proof; he could not get information relating to his opponent's proof. See Sarah N. Welling, Discovery of Nonparty's Tangible Things Under the Federal Rules of Civil Procedure, 59 NOTRE DAME L. REV. 110, 133 (1983); Paul R. Sugarman and Marc G. Perlin, Proposed Changes to Discovery Rules in Aid of "Tort Reform": Has the Case Been Made?, 42 AM. U. L. REV. 1465, 1489 (1993). When the Federal Rules were adopted, discovery became a major part of them. Instead of using pleadings to narrow issues and discover the opponent's case, as was done under the common law, see Developments in the Law, supra, at 948; Wolfson, supra note 19, at 21; Welling, supra, at 130, litigants were expected merely to give general notice of claims and defenses in the pleadings, and then use discovery to flesh out the case. See Wolfson, supra note 19, at 34.

133. See Sward, supra note 58, at 328.

134. This approach raised ethical issues as parties attempted to construe discovery requests narrowly to avoid having to turn over damaging information. But it was generally accepted that a party could hide even a smoking gun if the other side's request did not encompass it. See MONROE FREEDMAN, LAWYERS' ETHICS IN AND ADVERSARY SYSTEM 1–8 (1975).

135. See FED. R. CIV. P. 26(a). The scope of this mandatory discovery was narrowed in 2000. Under the current version, for example, litigants are required to produce a copy of or a description of all documents "in the possession, custody, or control of the party that the disclosing party may use to support its claims or defenses, unless solely for impeachment." Id. at 26(a)(1)(B). See generally, Carl Tobias, Civil Justice Reform Sunset, 1998 U. ILL. L. REV. 547 (discussing 1993 version); Griffin B. Bell, et al., Automatic Disclosure in Discovery—The Rush to Reform, 27 GA. L. REV. 1 (1992) (same).

136. See FED. R. CIV. P. 30(a)(2)(A) (depositions); FED. R. CIV. P. 33(a) (interrogatories). Depositions allow a party to question witnesses in person and under oath. Interrogatories are written questions served on an opposing party.

trol that parties exert over the investigation of their cases by requiring the parties to share information, and party control is further eroded as judges and magistrate judges take over so much of discovery management.[137]

I do not wish to overstate the case. The parties still have considerable control over their cases, as they decide what claims to assert, what defenses to raise, what discovery to seek, what motions to file, what arguments to make, and whether to settle, among other things. Nevertheless, the incursions on party control that the Federal Rules sanction are real and important, as judges have considerable authority to influence the parties' decisions on these and other matters. It is the expanding role of the judge that has inevitably led to a contracting role for the parties. Thus, the two primary characteristics of adversarial adjudication—the passive judge and party control of the litigation—are much altered under the Federal Rules.

c. Continuous Trial

Recall that the adversary system developed within common law adjudication, where the two stages of litigation were pleading and proof, both of which usually occurred in a single session.[138] This allowed for rapid resolution of disputes, which was necessary both because traveling judges had limited time to preside over lawsuits at each locale and because jurors were non-professional decision-makers who had to do their jobs quickly and get back to their usual work.[139]

The federal courts still conduct continuous trials. But the *trial* has become much less important as the *litigation* has become quite extended.[140] Pleadings are written, and are designed not to narrow issues, but to give general notice to the opponent of the claims or defenses.[141] Once the pleadings are complete,

---

137. I have already shown that judges or magistrate judges can control the scope, format, and amount of discovery, whether or not a party asks for such limits. *See supra*, notes 97–127 and accompanying text. Parties can request protective orders, and often do; indeed, the parties usually negotiate protective orders and present them to the judge for her signature. *See* FED. R. CIV. P. 26(c); United States v. Microsoft Corp., 165 F.3rd 952 (D.C. Cir. 1999); Bayer Ag and Miles, Inc. v. Barr Labs. Inc., 162 F.R.D. 456, 458 (S.D.N.Y. 1992). But the judge can act on her own initiative as well. *See* FED. R. CIV. P. 26(b)(2).

138. *See* 2 POLLOCK AND MAITLAND, *supra* note 71, at 603–22.

139. *See supra*, at notes 69–73 and accompanying text. *See also*, WILLIAM FORSYTH, HISTORY OF TRIAL BY JURY 201 (1875) (noting that short trials were the norm in the early days of the common law).

140. For a discussion of the effect of extended litigation on common law evidence law, see DAMASKA, *supra* note 67, at 58–69.

141. *See* 5 WRIGHT & MILLER, *supra* note 8, at § 1202.

the parties engage in discovery, which is particularly time-consuming. Pre-trial motions may follow, such as motions for summary judgment.[142] Especially in complex cases, the entire process can take years.[143] There are many decision points in this process—points where all or parts of the case may be resolved, or where the case may change direction. Discovery is particularly apt to lead to changes in strategy or, often, to settlement. The jury, whose sole purpose is to decide disputed issues of fact, appears—if at all—only at the end of this long process; compared to the judge and the parties, it spends relatively little time in the litigation. Modern litigation, then, looks very different from the common law adversarial trial, where the jury was a prominent player.

C. The Effect of These Procedural Changes on the Jury

It is impossible to sort out the historical cause and effect relationships between the jury, the common law, and the adversary system. Rather, the jury, common law procedures, and the adversary system developed together as part of a unified system of dispute resolution. Under the Federal Rules, however, two parts of the system have been profoundly altered in ways that undermine the continued functioning of the remaining part: the jury. We have been attacking the jury from behind: we have replaced common law procedures with more equitable ones, and we have moved the adversary system some distance toward the inquisitorial model. Neither equity nor inquisitorial systems rely on juries.[144] Thus, the symbiotic relationship between the jury and the procedural system has been upset. It is extremely unlikely that we will ever return to either common law procedures or a purer adversary system. The society we live in produces complex issues for litigation, and both the common law and the adversary system are products of a simpler era. To the extent that the jury

---

142. Summary judgment is a procedure for resolving a matter without a trial. It may be granted when a party establishes that there are no genuine issues of material fact, and that he is entitled to judgment as a matter of law. *See* Fed. R. Civ. P. 56. For an extended discussion of summary judgment, see Chapter 7, *infra*, at notes 18–86 and accompanying text.

143. *See Developments: Attorney Fee Awards*, 5 Class Action Reports 470, 472–519 (Nov.–Dec. 1978); Jonathan Harr, A Civil Action (1995).

144. The reasons for this are historical, but one could make good functional arguments for it as well. *See supra*, Chapter 2, at notes 142–145 and accompanying text. Inquisitorial systems generally employ professional judges and use discontinuous trials, neither of which is conducive to the use of juries. *See* Damaska, *supra* note 67, at 60–61.

is tied to its historical roots in common law adversarial adjudication, these procedural changes portend a continually declining role for the jury.

II. Systemic Changes

Certain changes in the larger system of dispute resolution also affect the jury's vitality. First, for a variety of reasons, we have decided to send some kinds of issues to administrative agencies for resolution, and the jury is inconsistent with the requirements of agency adjudication. Second, again for a variety of reasons, we have experienced a litigation explosion that strains the capacity of the system, and especially of the jury system. Finally, there has been an explosion of knowledge in the twentieth century, and the new knowledge can be highly specialized and well beyond the ken of the average juror. All of these developments have resulted in new ways of resolving disputes, without a jury.

A. The Rise of the Administrative State

Courts are not the only governmental institutions that adjudicate disputes. Over the course of the twentieth century, we increasingly have assigned adjudication of regulatory and public benefit matters to administrative agencies, which do not use juries. I discuss the Supreme Court's cases allowing jury-less adjudication in administrative agencies in Chapter 4.[145] In this section, I will briefly document the growth of such adjudication, explain why Congress sometimes prefers agency adjudication to courts, and explain how the growth in such adjudication affects the jury.

1. The Use of Administrative Agencies

The federal government, followed closely by the states, got heavily into the business of regulation beginning with the New Deal, though there has been some government regulation throughout the country's history.[146] Agencies administer regulatory laws and benefit programs by making rules that implement and clarify the statute, and by enforcing the statute and the rules through

---

145. *See supra,* Chapter 4, at notes 118–211 and accompanying text. For a critique of those decisions, see Ellen E. Sward, *Legislative Courts, Article III, and the Seventh Amendment,* 77 N.C.L. Rev. 1037, 1089–98 (1999).
146. *See infra,* Chapter 4, at notes 136–140 and accompanying text.

administrative adjudication.[147] Federal agencies handle some 350,000 adjudications every year,[148] eclipsing the 240,000 cases filed every year in federal courts.[149] When agencies adjudicate matters, they do not employ juries; instead, agency adjudication is conducted by administrative judges, many of whom are employees of the agency.[150]

2. Reasons for Administrative Adjudication[151]

Congress can have many reasons for constituting an administrative agency. Agencies may bring a greater efficiency to the adjudication of certain matters than an ordinary federal court provides, and they allow the use of expert decision-makers, which is thought to increase both efficiency and accuracy. Congress may believe that a greater degree of uniformity can be achieved if the issues are decided by a single agency rather than by many courts. Congress could also create agencies because it desires to keep control over its regulatory programs in one of the political branches.

---

147. See generally, KENNETH CULP DAVIS AND RICHARD J. PIERCE, JR., ADMINISTRATIVE LAW TREATISE (3d ed. 1994); RICHARD J. PIERCE, JR., ET AL., ADMINISTRATIVE LAW AND PROCESS (2d ed. 1992); BERNARD SCHWARTZ, ADMINISTRATIVE LAW (2d ed. 1984). The statement in the text is a gross oversimplification, as agencies are quite varied in the work they do. They are, however, all governed by the Administrative Procedure Act, 5 U.S.C. §§ 551 et seq. (1994), so their basic structure and governance will have some general similarities.

148. See RICHARD H. FALLON, DANIEL J. MELTZER AND DAVID L. SHAPIRO, HART AND WECHSLER'S THE FEDERAL COURTS AND THE FEDERAL SYSTEM 393 (4th ed. 1996).

149. See 1 FEDERAL COURTS STUDY COMMITTEE: WORKING PAPERS AND SUBCOMMITTEE REPORTS 30T.5 (1990).

150. There are two kinds of administrative judges. Administrative law judges (ALJs), numbering about 1000 throughout the federal agencies, are responsible for adjudicating disputes and have certain protections designed to ensure their independence. See John H. Frye, III, Survey of Non-ALJ Hearing Programs in the Federal Government, 44 ADMIN. L. REV. 261, 263 (1992). There are also about 2700 administrative adjudicators, most of whom have duties in addition to adjudication, and whose independence is less protected than that of the ALJs. Id. at 353. Agencies have procedures designed to keep those employees responsible for adjudication separate from those with responsibility for investigation and prosecution. See 5 U.S.C. § 554(d) (1994); PIERCE, ET AL., supra note 147, at § 9.3.5.

151. This subsection appeared in slightly different form in Sward, supra note 145, at 1052–56.

a. Efficiency

Procedures in federal courts are often cumbersome and time-consuming.[152] As I have shown, liberal joinder of claims and parties under the Federal Rules of Civil Procedure allows cases to become quite complex. Discovery, pre-trial motions, and the jury trial can all make federal litigation a prolonged, expensive experience.[153] Administrative agencies can provide important efficiency benefits. They may employ simpler procedures that allow litigation to progress more rapidly and at lower cost, though they are bound by constitutional due process requirements.[154] They may adjudicate matters without juries, thereby saving time and expense.[155] They may use expert decision-makers, who can get to the heart of the issue more quickly. Once an agency has a case, there may be additional efficiency gains from allowing the court to hear related matters.[156]

The very success of agencies has created another efficiency justification: they handle so many cases every year that it would now be impossible to abolish them.[157] The flood of litigation in the federal courts that would result from such abolition would overwhelm the federal courts. Thus, even if there had

---

152. *See generally,* Symposium, *Reducing the Costs of Civil Litigation,* 37 RUTGERS L. REV. 217 (1985).

153. *See* A. Leo Levin and Denise D. Colliers, *Containing the Cost of Litigation,* 37 RUTGERS L. REV. 219, 227–36 (1985).

154. *See* PIERCE, ET AL., *supra* note 147, at §5.1.3; WILLIAM F. FOX, JR., UNDERSTANDING ADMINISTRATIVE LAW, §4 (1986). Due process does not require federal courts to have time-consuming, cumbersome, and expensive procedures. In theory, we could gain efficiency advantages by streamlining judicial procedures, and some of the "reforms" of recent years are intended to do exactly that. It may be easier, however, to set up alternative dispute resolution mechanisms than to make revolutionary changes in existing federal court procedures—especially if those changes are perceived as offering less protection to litigants.

155. *See* RICHARD A. POSNER, THE FEDERAL COURTS: CHALLENGE AND REFORM 193n.1 (1996); Peter H. Schuck, *Mapping the Debate on Jury Reform,* in VERDICT: ASSESSING THE CIVIL JURY SYSTEM 306, 317–18 (Robert E. Litan ed., 1993); HANS ZEISEL, ET AL., DELAY IN THE COURT 71–81 (2d ed. 1978).

156. *See, e.g.,* Commodities Futures Trading Commission v. Schor, 478 U.S. 833, 855–56 (1986). This is much like the efficiency justification under the Federal Rules for the compulsory counterclaim rule, which requires the assertion of counterclaims that arise out of the same transaction or occurrence as the original claim. FED. R. CIV. P. 13(a). Indeed, agencies sometimes have compulsory counterclaim rules of their own, which require litigants to assert claims otherwise cognizable in federal courts. *See, e.g.,* 17 C.F.R. §12.19 (1999) (CFTC counterclaim rule).

157. *See* Richard H. Fallon, Jr., *Legislative Courts, Administrative Agencies, and Article III,* 101 HARV. L. REV. 915, 925 (1988).

been no efficiency issues in the formation of agencies, efficiency concerns weigh heavily in favor of retaining them now.

b. Expertise

One reason why agencies are more efficient is that they employ expert decision-makers, in contrast to federal courts, where the decision-makers are either generalist judges or lay jurors.[158] It may be time-consuming and expensive to try to educate judicial decision-makers on the intricacies of an esoteric field.[159] Efficiency is not the only reason for using expert decision-makers, however. While we value the generalist judge as one who can bring a wide range of experience and knowledge to bear on a problem,[160] the modern world presents us with some issues that can only be understood by persons who are specialists in the field.[161] In such instances, the task of educating lay decision-makers may be nearly impossible. Thus, agencies often are explicitly created to take advantage of the presumed greater accuracy that may be had from decision-makers who are experts in the field.[162]

---

158. The only current Article III courts with specialized subject matter jurisdiction are the United States Court of Appeals for the Federal Circuit and the Court of International Trade. The Federal Circuit has enough specialties that it has some of the benefits of a generalist court. *See* 28 U.S.C. § 1295 (1994) (appeals concerning international trade, patent, and a variety of specialized statutes). The Court of International Trade has a more limited jurisdiction, much of which is jurisdiction to review administrative decisions relating to tariffs and trade. *See* 28 U.S. C. §§ 1581, 1582, 1584 (1994). It can also hear counterclaims relating to such matters, however. *See* 28 U.S.C. § 1583 (1994).

159. The primary means of educating generalist judges and lay decision-makers in federal courts is through expert witnesses. *See* Samuel R. Gross, *Expert Evidence*, 1991 WIS. L. REV. 1113, 1116. Many trials, however, become a battle of experts, making it difficult for persons outside the field to make rational judgments. *See, e.g.,* Ferebee v. Chevron Chemical Co., 736 F.2d. 1529 (D.C. Cir. 1984)(disagreement between experts over how soon a disease would manifest itself after exposure to toxic chemicals). *See* Andrew MacGregor Smith, Note, *Using Impartial Experts in Valuation: A Forum-Specific Approach*, 35 WM. & MARY L. REV. 1241, 1244–45 (1994).

160. *See, e.g.,* Harold H. Bruff, *Specialized Courts in Administrative Law*, 43 ADMIN. L. REV. 329, 331 (1991); Richard A. Posner, *Will the Federal Courts of Appeals Survive Until 1984? An Essay on Delegation and Specialization of the Judicial Function*, 56 S. CAL. L. REV. 761, 779 (1983); Ellen R. Jordan, *Specialized Courts: A Choice?*, 76 Nw. U. L. REV. 745, 745, 748 (1981); Simon Rifkind, *A Special Court for Patent Litigation? The Danger of a Specialized Judiciary*, 37 A.B.A.J. 425, 425 (1951).

161. *See infra*, notes 181–184 and accompanying text for a discussion of the "Knowledge Explosion."

162. *See* LOUIS L. JAFFE, JUDICIAL CONTROL OF ADMINISTRATIVE ACTION 121–32 (1965).

c. Uniformity

If one agency administers an area of law, there will be greater uniformity in interpretation than if dozens of lower courts are making the decisions. When lower federal courts disagree, it can take years to work out their differences; indeed, it may take a trip to the Supreme Court. In complex regulatory schemes that apply throughout the country, Congress may prefer to achieve uniform national enforcement immediately, which it can do with agency rulemaking and adjudication.

d. Control

When Congress creates a regulatory program and provides that adjudication of matters arising under its provisions be done in an agency, it is possible that at least part of Congress's motive is control. Regulatory matters will often have significant political content, and it is understandable that Congress would prefer to maintain political control of all aspects of the regulation, as it helps ensure that the regulatory program will be carried out. Agency adjudicators could be controlled, at least to some degree, by the political appointment power.[163] This is a troubling justification for agency adjudication, however, as it is in direct conflict with the values reflected in our constitutional structure—separation of powers and judicial independence—and with the political ideals behind the Seventh Amendment.[164] Actions that are politically desirable are not necessarily constitutional, and courts are intended to be politically unaccountable so that they can prevent overreaching by the po-

---

163. Some administrative agencies are independent of any branch of government, and they are less susceptible to such political control. See Pierce, et al., supra note 147, at §4.4.1a; Davis & Pierce, supra note 147, at §2.5. Others, however, are controlled, usually by the executive, through the power of appointment: a new President appoints the agency heads and so can set the agency's political agenda. And because some rulemaking occurs in the course of adjudication, that means adjudication is, to some degree, under the control of the political branches. See, e.g., Merton C. Bernstein, The NLRB's Adjudication-Rule Making Dilemma Under the Administrative Procedure Act, 79 Yale L.J. 571 (1970); Cornelius J. Peck, A Critique of the National Labor Relations Board's Performance in Policy Formulation: Adjudication and Rule Making, 117 U. Pa. L. Rev. 254 (1968). See generally, David L. Shapiro, The Choice of Rulemaking or Adjudication in the Development of Administrative Policy, 78 Harv. L. Rev. 921 (1965).

164. See supra, Chapter 1, at notes 127–194 and accompanying text. See also, Sward, supra note 145, at 1049–52.

litical branches.[165] The more an agency is controlled by the political branches, the less it can fulfill that function.

3. Effect on Jury

The jury is inconsistent with all of these justifications for agency adjudication of regulatory disputes. First, the jury is the least efficient decision-maker. Jurors have a steep learning curve because they generally have not made adjudicative decisions before, and have no training to assist them in doing so. Juries are more expensive than adjudicators who are already on the government payroll,[166] and proceedings in which they are involved are more time-consuming than those involving professional adjudicators.[167] Second, by definition, the jury is a body of amateurs, called upon to bring community values into the litigation process. But community values take a back seat to financial or scientific data in some of the work that agencies do. Third, juries produce less uniformity than any other kind of decision-maker. They have less knowledge of prior decisions, and more variability in background and outlook. They also have at least some capacity for nullifying laws they disagree with, which could be particularly problematic in regulatory matters. Finally, the political branches have no control over individual juries.[168]

---

165. *See* ALEXANDER M. BICKEL, THE LEAST DANGEROUS BRANCH (1962); CHRISTOPHER WOLFE, THE RISE OF MODERN JUDICIAL REVIEW 74–75 (1986).

166. Jurors are paid a nominal daily fee for their services. *See, e.g.,* 28 U.S.C. § 1821 (1994) (providing that jurors are paid $40 per day). They may also be paid mileage for travel to the courthouse, especially when they reside some distance from the courthouse. *See, e.g.,* 28 U.S.C. § 1871 (1994) (providing that jurors get same mileage allowance as government officials).

167. *See* George L. Priest, *Justifying the Civil Jury,* in VERDICT, *supra* note 155, at 131–32. When trial will be by jury, the parties must spend some time selecting a jury, and there are likely to be more interruptions for evidentiary rulings. *See* DAMASKA, *supra* note 67, at 60–61.

168. As I will show in this book, judges have quite a lot of control over juries, but Article III judges are not under the control of the political branches either, except through the initial appointment power. Juries, then, are twice removed from control by the political branches. Congress has in recent years tried to constrain jury decision-making through such things as caps on damages, *see infra,* Chapter 7, at notes 188–203 and accompanying text, but such prior constraints on decision-making, whether they apply to judges or juries, are quite different from political interference with specific decisions. I should note that Congress sometimes tries to dictate decisions in pending cases, and the Court has struck down legislation that attempts to do that. *See* United States v. Klein, 80 U.S. (13 Wall.) 128 (1872). There is a fine line, however, between dictating results and changing the

THE DECLINE OF THE CIVIL JURY

The system that we have developed seems quite well-entrenched. A great deal of the country's business is done in agencies, and businesses and individuals alike have adjusted to a regulatory regimen with its administrative adjudication.[169] Indeed, as I will show in the next chapter, the Supreme Court has been quite accommodating in allowing Congress to establish administrative agencies that operate without a jury. Even critics of the Court's jurisprudence allowing agency adjudication concede that overturning it now would be too disruptive.[170] It is virtually impossible then, that we will see a resurgence of the jury in the bureaucratic state.[171]

B. The Litigation Explosion

Over the last few decades, the United States has undergone a litigation explosion, with substantial increases in both civil and criminal litigation.[172] The reasons for the litigation explosion are in some dispute. Some commentators argue that we have become more litigious generally, aided and abetted by juries that habitually grant huge damage awards, both compensatory and punitive.[173] Some implicate changes in substantive law that broaden potential liability.[174] Others argue that Americans have always relied heavily on courts;[175] indeed,

---

law mid-stream, and the Courts permit the latter. See, e.g., Robertson v. Seattle Audubon Society, 503 U.S. 429 (1992).

169. Some of the harshest critics of President Reagan's deregulation plan were the regulated businesses. See Susan Rose-Ackerman, Defending the State: A Skeptical Look at "Regulatory Reform" in the Eighties, 61 COLO. L. REV. 517, 524–25 (1990) (regulated industries wanted competent administration and clarity and certainty in their environment).

170. See, e.g., Fallon, supra note 157, at 916–17; Martin H. Redish, Legislative Courts, Administrative Agencies, and the Northern Pipeline Decision, 1993 DUKE L.J. 197, 199–200; Sward, supra note 145, at 1043.

171. I criticize the supreme Court's jurisprudence and suggest some ways agencies could accommodate the jury in Sward, supra note 145.

172. Between 1960 and 1988, civil case filings in federal courts have increased from approximately 51,000 annually to nearly 240,000 annually. Criminal filings have increased from approximately 28,000 to nearly 45,000. See 1 FEDERAL COURTS STUDY COMMITTEE, supra note 149, at 30, T.5.

173. See, e.g., WALTER K. OLSON, THE LITIGATION EXPLOSION 282–83 (1991); JETHRO K. LIEBERMAN, THE LITIGIOUS SOCIETY 34 (1981). As I showed in Chapter 1, such complaints about the jury have little empirical support. See supra, Chapter 1, at notes 30–69 and accompanying text.

174. See, e.g., George L. Priest, The Invention of Enterprise Liability: A Critical History of the Intellectual Foundations of Modern Tort Law, 14 J. LEGAL STUD. 461 (December 1985).

175. See, e.g., Michael J. Saks, Do We Really Know Anything About the Behavior of the Tort Litigation System—And Why Not?, 140 U. PA. L. REV. 1147, 1151–54 (1992).

DeTocqueville noted the propensity of Americans to take cases to court for resolution as early as the 1830s.[176] On this view, the litigation explosion is simply a natural result of the population explosion[177] and the increase in legal issues about which one can litigate.[178] Congress and the state legislatures, for example, have created hundreds of causes of action over the last few decades.[179]

Whatever the reasons, the fact remains that there are so many cases in the courts today that trials would be impossible in anything close to all of them—much less jury trials. Jury trials take longer than bench trials,[180] and both kinds of trials take longer than settlements or the resolution of cases on motions. There is, then, considerable incentive for actors within the system to resolve cases without juries, or even without trials.

C. The Knowledge Explosion

Another development that affects the jury is the explosion of knowledge in the twentieth century. Research in science, including social science, has vastly increased our store of knowledge, and the technological development that knowledge has spawned has made that knowledge widely available. This affects the jury in at least two ways. First, it may contribute to the litigation explosion in that there are now more things for people to litigate about. We have learned, for example, that some chemicals cause cancer, and people who develop those cancers may now seek to recover from those whose economic activity allegedly caused it.[181]

Second, the knowledge explosion may take more of those litigated matters beyond the realm of jury competence.[182] As information becomes more specialized, jurors are unable to rely on the common sense that was the hallmark

---

176. See 1 ALEXIS DETOCQUEVILLE, DEMOCRACY IN AMERICA 280 (Phillips Bradley ed., 1990 [1835]).

177. In 1940, the population of the United States was approximately 132 million. In 1990, it had jumped to almost 250 million. See U.S. Census Bureau, *Selected Historical Census Data: Population and Housing Counts*, Internet URL: http://www.census.gov/population/censusdata/pop-hc.html (August 13, 1996).

178. See, e.g., Saks, *supra* note 175, at 1209–11.

179. See Carl Tobias, *Silver Linings in Federal Civil Justice Reform*, 59 BROOKLYN L. REV. 857, 867–68 (1993).

180. See ROBERT E. KEETON, TRIAL TACTICS AND METHODS 247 (2d ed. 1973); HANS ZEISEL, ET AL., *supra* note 155, at 8–9.

181. For a popular account of one such case, see HARR, *supra* note 143.

182. For a discussion of the literature on jury competence, which is more optimistic than I suggest in the text, *see supra* Chapter 1, at notes 30–69 and accompanying text.

of the jury, but must struggle through complicated scientific, economic or financial data. The litigant who seeks to prove that a chemical caused his cancer, for example, likely will have to present evidence of the chemical's effects on the human body, as well as epidemiological evidence that relies heavily on statistics.[183] Very few jurors will have had training in such disciplines.[184]

D. Summary

We have developed an administrative state to help govern our complex society. That bureaucracy is both inconsistent with amateur decision-making and so well-entrenched that dismantling it would be seriously disruptive and expensive. In addition, we face a litigation explosion that taxes our judicial system and makes alternatives to full-blown litigation—especially jury trials—essential if the system is to function. Finally, the knowledge explosion means that much of the fodder for modern litigation is arguably beyond the ken of amateur decision-makers. Indeed, agency adjudication may be one result of the litigation explosion and the knowledge explosion—agencies offer efficient, expert adjudication of complex issues. These developments mean that the jury is a less effective decision-maker than it was at the country's founding.

III. Substantive Legal Changes

Developments in substantive law also constrain the use of the jury. Substantive law in England and the United States came primarily from common law development. For a variety of reasons, we need more certainty than this kind of legal development would allow. This may be one reason for the rise of statutes, which present different analytical problems than the common law. The jury is a less comfortable fit with a substantive scheme that needs a substantial degree of certainty and is built around statutes.

---

183. *See* Michael Dore, *A Commentary on the Use of Epidemiological Evidence in Demonstrating Cause in Fact*, 7 HARV. ENV. L. REV. 429, 431 (1983).

184. One way the courts have dealt with the knowledge explosion is the use of expert witnesses. *See infra*, Chapter 6, at notes 91–100 and accompanying text. Administrative agencies are a systemic response to complex data. *See supra*, notes 145–171 and accompanying text. *See infra*, Chapter 4, at notes 128–215 for a discussion of the Supreme Court's jurisprudence on agencies. *See also*, Sward, *supra* note 145, at 1062–1073. The problems with scientifically complex evidence are compounded by adversarial presentation of evidence, which is disjointed and hard to follow. *See* DAMASKA, *supra* note 67, at 60.

A. Background: The Substantive Side of the Common Law

The substance of our common law rules originated in the royal writs, which allowed parties to sue in the royal courts.[185] The writs provided remedies, and thereby created rights.[186] At first, the royal writs were considered extraordinary, as litigants had a variety of other courts available to them.[187] Perhaps for that reason, early common law judges interpreted the writs quite narrowly and refused to recognize new ones.[188] Very few new writs were created after the thirteenth century,[189] and courts of equity began to arise to handle matters not covered by the writs.[190]

Royal justice proved quite popular despite the rigid writ system, however, and as litigants flocked to the royal courts, the writs became regularized.[191] Once the writs became standard fare, the king's judges began to get creative. The writs themselves provided only the bare bones of the right at issue, and the judges fleshed it out by defining terms and filling gaps.[192] Eventually, the judges created legal fictions to make it possible for writs to cover circumstances that were not within the formal terms of the writ.[193] The substance of the common law, as embodied in the forms of action, is what emerged from the writ system and the common law processes that applied to it.[194] It is judge-made law.

---

185. For discussions of the writ system, see R.C. VAN CAENNEGEM, ROYAL WRITS IN ENGLAND FROM THE CONQUEST TO GLANVILL (Selden Society, Vol. 77, 1959); MELVILLE MADISON BIGELOW, HISTORY OF PROCEDURE IN ENGLAND FROM THE NORMAN CONQUEST, ch.IV (1880); MILSOM, *supra* note 71, at 33–38. For a discussion of the procedural aspects of the writs, see *supra*, Chapter 2, at notes 13–18 and accompanying text.

186. See MAITLAND, *supra* note 90, at 372.

187. See MILSOM, *supra* note 71, at 35. For a discussion of the various courts in Norman England, see *id.* at ch. 1.

188. See HAROLD GREVILLE HANBURY, MODERN EQUITY 2 (2nd ed. 1937).

189. See 2 POLLOCK AND MAITLAND, *supra* note 71, at 564.

190. See 1 POMEROY, *supra* note 1, at §§21–29.

191. See BAKER, *supra* note 1, at 70–78.

192. See BAKER, *supra* note 1, at 80.

193. See MAITLAND, *supra* note 90, at 372–73. Legal fictions made it possible for the writ of trespass, once a standard, rather pedestrian writ, to take over a wide range of actions. See 2 POLLOCK AND MAITLAND, *supra* note 71, at 564.

194. See MAITLAND, *supra* note 90, at 372. Maitland quotes Sir Henry Sumner Maine as saying that "[s]ubstantive law is secreted in the interstices of procedure." *Id.* Maitland himself notes that "the great text-books take the form of treatises on procedure." *Id.* See

The substantive common law has several characteristics that distinguish it from the substantive law of Continental Europe. Common law does not start with a comprehensive body of law; rather, common law is incremental. It is built up case by case, from the ground up. The civil law of Continental Europe is based on comprehensive codes, usually derived from the Roman codes.[195] Common law is reactive: it develops in reaction to problems that arise. Civil law is proactive: the drafters of comprehensive codes attempt to anticipate problems and provide for them. Common law is flexible and individualized. When new circumstances arise, common law courts have considerable ability to adapt the law or even make new law. There must be flexibility in code-based law as well, of course, but the code in civil law countries is always the ultimate authority.[196] In addition, there must be some measure of uniformity in the common law; that uniformity is provided by the doctrine of precedent, which demands that like cases be treated alike.[197] Still, there is enough factual variety in the cases that distinctions allow for highly individualized law-making.[198]

The jury fits well in a common law system. Juries are masters of individualized justice, as they sit for only one case and are concerned with doing justice in that case only. They are flexible and reactive. They are not formal lawmakers, of course, which distinguishes their role from that of the common law judge. But the development of the general issue plea in England often allowed them to make law for the case before them,[199] and juries in the United States following the Revolution had formal law-making power, at least for the case before them.[200] In addition, juries have the power, if not the right, to nullify laws, at least in some circumstances.[201] The kind of individualized justice

---

generally, CHARLES M. HEPBURN, THE HISTORICAL DEVELOPMENT OF CODE PLEADING 43–51 (1897).

195. For discussions of Roman and civil (Continental) law, see generally, HOEFLICH, *supra* note 59; REINHARD ZIMMERMAN, THE LAW OF OBLIGATIONS: ROMAN FOUNDATIONS OF THE CIVILIAN TRADITION (1990).

196. For a discussion of the difference between civil law and common law, see Strauss, *supra* note 59; FREDERICK H. LAWSON, A COMMON LAWYER LOOKS AT THE CIVIL LAW (1955).

197. *See* Earl Maltz, *The Nature of Precedent*, 66 N.C. L. REV. 367, 368 (1988). In the United States, there have been attempts to state the general common law rules in several areas of law, though these statements do not have the force of law. *See, e.g.*, RESTATEMENT (2d) of Torts (1965).

198. *See* Strauss, *supra* note 59, at 242–46.

199. On the general issue plea, see *supra*, Chapter 2, at note 16 and accompanying text.

200. *See id.* at note 161 and accompanying text.

201. *See supra*, Chapter 1, at notes 72–108 and accompanying text.

that juries provided was precisely analogous to what common law judges were doing in building the common law.

B. The Need for Certainty

The common law's incremental, individualized approach works best in a society that is relatively small, has a localized economy, and has a homogeneous population.[202] In such circumstances, the contingent nature of the substantive law is not problematic, as there is substantial agreement about what justice is, and mistakes in legal doctrine have limited effects. The conditions necessary for an effective common law have been dissipating for almost the country's entire history, however. The young United States aspired to develop the country and to become a commercial center.[203] Development requires a dependable substantive law, so that the normal business risks would not be exacerbated by an uncertain law.[204] Juries appeared to be the early villains in creating too much uncertainty, largely because they had law-deciding authority. As long as juries had such power, developers could never be certain whether their development projects would find legal support.[205] The result was that the jury's power was curtailed signficantly over the course of the nineteenth century.[206]

Today, of course, the need for a stable substantive law is even greater. The country is large, with commercial enterprises that span the nation and even the globe. The population is quite diverse, representing different cultural traditions and different ways of doing business. The global market is even more diverse. Thus, we have a greater need for rules that govern our interactions, so that we can have some prior understanding of the consequences of our actions. In a common law system, certainty is better served by having judges rather than juries decide all of the issues in a case because judges can be expected to feel more constrained by precedent. The kind of flexible, *ad hoc* justice that juries provide could be too disruptive.

---

202. *See* Melvin Aron Eisenberg, The Nature of the Common Law 14–20 (1988) (discussing need for homogeneous population).
203. *See id.* at 8; Morton J. Horwitz, The Transformation of American Law 1780–1860, p.18 (1977).
204. *See id* at 110–11.
205. *See id.* at 143.
206. *See supra*, Chapter 2, at notes 180–202 and accompanying text. The jury's decline can also be attributed to the fact that juries were quite conservative in their approach to development, and often failed to see the public benefits it provided. *See* Horwitz, *supra* note 203, at ch. II. Thus, if the common law were to grow in ways that allowed such development, the jury's role would have to be curtailed. *Id.* at 28–29.

C. The Rise of Statutes

Another way to enhance certainty in law is through statutes, and the country has seen an enormous growth in statutory law, especially in the last century. Statutes are general rather than individualized, proactive rather than reactive, and comprehensive rather than incremental.[207] The twentieth century saw two kinds of statutory development in the United States. First, there was considerable codification of the common law, some of which simply put existing legal doctrine into statutes, and some of which modified the law to some degree.[208] Second, Congress and the states created whole new categories of law, unheard of at common law.[209] Whether codifications of common law or new categories of law, some of this statutory development consists of complex, comprehensive codes.[210] Indeed, the codification effort has been so successful that many people today are quite distrustful of judicial law-making, notwithstanding our long common law tradition.[211]

There are at least three reasons why this development may hinder the jury's functioning. First, questions of statutory interpretation have come to the forefront: what does the statute mean? Questions of statutory interpretation are considered questions of law, where the jury has no role.[212] Lawyers and judges are steeped in the principles of statutory construction, but juries would have little understanding of those principles and could easily make errors.[213] Such errors could occur even in the course of fact-finding, as questions of fact are

---

207. *But see* Strauss, *supra* note 59, at 231–35 (arguing that statutory law in common law countries tends to be incremental and reactive in that legislatures enact statutes that are narrowly tailored to respond to specific problems but do not attempt to enact comprehensive codes that cover the entire universe of legal matters).

208. *See* Mark D. Rosen, *What Has Happened to the Common Law?—Recent American Codifications and Their Impact on Judicial Practice and the Law's Subsequent Development*, 1994 Wis. L. Rev. 1119, 1123–24.

209. Environmental law and civil rights law are two examples.

210. *See, e.g.,* Internal Revenue Code, 26 U.S.C. §1 et seq. (1994); 11 U.S.C. §101 et seq. (1994) (bankruptcy).

211. *See generally, e.g.,* Robert H. Bork, The Tempting of America: The Political Seduction of the Law (1990); Gary L. McDowell, Curbing the Courts: The Constitution and the Limites of Judicial Power (1988); Edwin Meese III, *A Return to Constitutional Interpretation From Judicial Law-Making*, 40 N.Y.L. Sch. L. Rev. 925 (1996).

212. *See* 2A Norman Singer, Sutherland Statutory Construction §45.02 (5th ed. 1992); Frederick J. de Slovere, *The Functions of Judge and Jury in the Interpretation of Statutes*, 46 Harv. L. Rev. 1086 (1933).

213. *See generally,* Singer, *supra* note 212; Earl T. Crawford, The Construction of Statutes (1940).

not always easily separable from questions of statutory construction.[214] Second, where the statute at issue is part of a comprehensive code, juries may have difficulty seeing the whole that the statute is dealing with, and so be unable to fit the case within that whole. More errors could result.[215] Finally, the power of the jury to nullify laws, which, acknowledged or not, is one of the reasons for a jury, is incongruous in the context of statutes, where a democratically elected and presumably accountable legislative body has considered the issues and enacted the statute. An unaccountable and unelected jury should not presume to overturn the legislature's considered judgments.[216] Statutes may also reflect considerable legislative investigation aimed at finding the best solution for a broad-based problem—a task that juries, which hear information only about the case before them, cannot perform.[217] In short, in a country that relies more heavily on statutes than on the common law to develop legal doctrine, it is easy to see why the jury may be eclipsed by other actors in the judicial system.

D. Summary

The common law foundations of our substantive law have been undermined by twentieth century developments. First, the contingent nature of the common law is not well suited to a human network that is complex, diverse, commercial, and global. More certainty is required than the common law can provide if we are to have confidence in our relationships with one another. Second, and perhaps relatedly, the United States has undergone a widespread and successful codification effort, so that much of our law is now statutory rather than judge-made. Both of these developments affect our use of the jury. Juries, with their ability to nullify law and their narrow focus on

---

214. *See infra,* Chapter 7, at notes 2–9 and accompanying text (describing the difficulty of distinguishing fact from law).

215. The common law has also developed into a comprehensive system of law, so this problem may not be significantly different from the problems juries face in deciding cases under the common law. Common law, however, is based more on common sense ideals, whereas some of the comprehensive codes that now exist are based on scientific or other data that are less accessible to juries. *See supra,* Chapter 1, at note 99 and accompanying text.

216. *See supra,* Chapter 1, at notes 96–98 and accompanying text. *But cf.,* GUIDO CALABRESI, A COMMON LAW FOR THE AGE OF STATUTES (1982) (arguing that judges, under some circumstances, should have the power to nullify statutes that are no longer viable, just as they can nullify common law rules).

217. *See supra,* Chapter 1, at note 99 and accompanying text.

the case before them, are less well suited to decision-making in a society where substantial certainty in economic and other relationships is needed. And juries are less well equipped for decision-making in an age of statutes, especially where the statutes reflect a comprehensive view of an area of law and a considered, democratically derived judgment as to the proper approach.

IV. Political Change: The Diversification of America

The jury evolved in an English society that was quite homogeneous. On top of that, the English imposed property and other qualifications that kept the jury "predominantly male, middle-aged, middle-minded and middle-class" well into the twentieth century.[218] It may well be this very homogeneity that made unanimous jury verdicts possible.[219] The original thirteen colonies were similarly homogeneous. Colonial governments, like England, imposed qualifications on jury service, so that juries generally consisted entirely of free white men of English heritage, usually landowners.[220] Once independence was achieved, state and federal governments continued to restrict eligibility for jury service.[221] Thus, while juries were not particularly representative, they remained sufficiently homogeneous to function effectively.

It goes without saying that the United States is a much more diverse country today than it was at its founding, with many more cultural backgrounds represented among its 280 million people. In addition, we have become more committed to broad-based political representation, no longer accepting the notion that wealth or other characteristics make a person a better voter, officeholder, or juror. Thus, over the country's history, a series of legislative acts and Supreme Court decisions opened jury duty to all, regardless of race, gender, or wealth.[222] Modern juries are more representative of the general population than

---

218. LORD PATRICK DEVLIN, TRIAL BY JURY 20 (1956).

219. *Id.* at 22–23.

220. See William E. Nelson, *The Eighteenth Century Background of John Marshall's Constitutional Jurisprudence*, 76 MICH. L. REV. 893, 919 n.142 (1978).

221. *See* Strauder v. West Virginia, 100 U.S. 303 (1879); Taylor v. Louisiana, 419 U.S. 522 (1975).

222. *See infra*, Chapter 5, at notes 90–115 and accompanying text. Formal restrictions on the racial makeup of juries were eliminated in the nineteenth century, though de facto restrictions continued until well into the twentieth century. Formal restrictions on gender were not eliminated until the middle of the twentieth century. Most states began moving

are either judges or lawyers, with women and minorities found much more often on juries than in the ranks of the bench and bar.[223] This broader representation means that members of a particular jury may differ significantly in background, experiences, and beliefs, and it may be more difficult for them to reach consensus. Men and women could have quite different views on sexual harrassment, for example, with women concerned that their complaints are not taken seriously and men worried about where the line is drawn between innocent flirting and harassment. As consensus (unanimity) is the traditional decision rule for juries, the very diversity of the jury—which gives it important political and socializing roles—may make it harder for the jury to function.

V. Conclusion

The milieu in which the jury operates has changed significantly over the course of the nation's history. The procedure of which it is a part is more equitable and less adversarial than the procedure of its origins. The system of dispute resolution in which it is a player has added an important player, the administrative agency, as an alternative to the jury. In addition, the system must deal with many more cases, and cases with more advanced technical evidence than ever before. We need for our substantive law to be more certain and predictable than the common law—particularly when juries are involved—can be, and, perhaps for that reason, our substantive law has come to rely more on statutes than on common law development. And we are a much more diverse nation than we were at the founding, and much more supportive of broad-based political participation, including participation on juries.

Each of these changes alone affects the ability of the jury to function effectively, but alone, each could probably be weathered. Collectively, however, they so change the environment in which the civil jury operates that we must question whether the jury can survive. The jury is resilient, and it has a proud

---

away from property qualifications early in the country's history. *See* Albert W. Alschuler and Andrew G. Deiss, *A Brief History of the Criminal Jury in the United States,* 61 U. CHI. L. REV. 867, 877–82 (1994).

223. *See, e.g., Report of the Second Circuit Task Force on Gender, Racial, and Ethnic Fairness in the Courts,* 1997 ANN. SURV. OF AM. L. 9. *But see* Laura Gaston Dooley, *Essay, Our Juries, Our Selves: Power, Perception, and Politics of the Civil Jury,* 80 CORNELL L. REV. 325 (1995) (arguing that while women and minorities are well-represented on juries, the increase in their representation coincides with a significant growth in methods designed to allow judges to control the jury). *See infra,* Chapters 6–8 for support for Dooley's argument.

history, but these changes strike at its very foundation. In Part II of this book, I will consider a variety of adaptations we have made to these changed circumstances: doctrines and procedural devices that allow us to keep the jury (as we must, unless the Constitution is to be amended) but to accommodate it to its new environment.

Appendix 1—Rule 16, 1938 Version
Fed. R. Civ. P. 16, 28 U.S.C.A. (1960)

Rule 16. Pre-Trial Procedure; Formulating Issues.

In any action, the court may in its discretion direct the attorneys for the parties to appear before it for a conference to consider

(1) The simplification of the issues;

(2) The necessity or desirability of amendments to the pleadings;

(3) The possibility of obtaining admissions of fact and of documents which will avoid unnecessary proof;

(4) The limitation of the number of expert witnesses;

(5) The advisability of a preliminary reference of issues to a master for findings to be used as evidence when the trial is to be by jury;

(6) Such other matters as may aid in the disposition of the action.

The court shall make an order which recites the action taken at the conference, the amendments allowed to the pleadings, and the agreements made by the parties as to any of the matters considered, and which limits the issues for trial to those not disposed of by admissions or agreements of counsel; and such order when entered controls the subsequent course of the action, unless modified at the trial to prevent manifest injustice. The court in its discretion may establish by rule a pre-trial calendar on which actions may be placed for consideration as above provided and may either confine the calendar to jury actions or to non-jury actions or extend it to all actions.

Appendix 2—Rule 16, 1983 Version
Fed. R. Civ. P. 16, 28 U.S.C.A. (Supp. 1991)

Rule 16. Pretrial Conferences; Scheduling; Management

(a) **Pretrial Conferences; Objectives.** In any action, the court may in its discretion direct the attorneys for the parties and any unrepresented parties to appear before it for a conference or conferences before trial for such purposes as

(1) expediting the disposition of the action;

(2) establishing early and continuing control so that the case will not be protracted because of lack of management;

(3) discouraging wasteful pretrial activities;

(4) improving the quality of the trial through more thorough preparation, and;

(5) facilitating the settlement of the case.

(b) **Scheduling and Planning.** Except in categories of actions exempted by district court rule as inappropriate, the judge, or a magistrate when authorized by district court rule, shall, after consulting with the attorneys for the parties and any unrepresented parties, by a scheduling conference, telephone, mail, or other suitable means, enter a scheduling order that limits the time

(1) to join other parties and to amend the pleadings;

(2) to file and hear motions; and

(3) to complete discovery.

The scheduling order also may include

(4) the date or dates for conferences before trial, a final pretrial conference, and trial; and

(5) any other matters appropriate in the circumstances of the case.

The order shall issue as soon as practicable but in no event more than 120 days after filing of the complaint. A schedule shall not be modified except by leave of the judge or a magistrate when authorized by district court rule upon a showing of good cause.

(c) **Subjects to Be Discussed at Pretrial Conferences.** The participants at any conference under this rule may consider and take action with respect to

(1) the formulation and simplification of the issues, including the elimination of frivolous claims or defenses;

(2) the necessity or desirability of amendments to the pleadings;

(3) the possibility of obtaining admissions of fact and of documents which will avoid unnecessary proof, stipulations regarding the authenticity of documents, and advance rulings from the court on the admissibility of evidence;

(4) the avoidance of unnecessary proof and of cumulative evidence;

(5) the identification of witnesses and documents, the need and schedule for filing and exchanging pretrial briefs, and the date or dates for further conferences and for trial;

(6) the advisability of referring matters to a magistrate or master;

(7) the possibility of settlement or the use of extrajudicial procedures to resolve the dispute;

(8) the form and substance of the pretrial order;

(9) the disposition of pending motions;

(10) the need for adopting special procedures for managing potentially difficult or protracted actions that may involve complex issues, multiple parties, difficult legal questions, or unusual proof problems; and

(11) such other matters as may aid in the disposition of the action.

At least one of the attorneys for each party participating in any conference before trial shall have authority to enter into stipulations and to make admissions regarding all matters that the participants may reasonably anticipate may be discussed.

(d) **Final Pretrial Conference.** Any final pretrial conference shall be held as close to the time of trial as reasonable under the circumstances. The participants at any such conference shall formulate a plan for trial, including a program for facilitating the admission of evidence. The conference shall be attended by at least one of the attorneys who will conduct the trial for each of the parties and by any unrepresented parties.

(e) **Pretrial Orders.** After any conference held pursuant to this rule, an order shall be entered reciting the action taken. This order shall control the subsequent course of the action unless modified by a subsequent order. The order following a final pretrial conference shall be modified only to prevent manifest injustice.

(f) **Sanctions.** If a party or party's attorney fails to obey a scheduling or pretrial order, or if no appearance is made on behalf of a party at a scheduling or pretrial conference, or if a party or party's attorney is substantially unprepared to participate in the conference, or if a party or party's attorney fails to participate in good faith, the judge, upon motion or the judge's own initiative, may make such orders with regard thereto as are just, and among others any of the orders provided in Rule 37(b)(2)(B), (C), (D). In lieu of or in addition to any other sanction, the judge shall require the party or the attorney representing the party or both to pay the reasonable expenses incurred because of any noncompliance with this rule, including attorney's fees, unless the judge finds that the noncompliance was substantially justified or that other circumstances make an award of expenses unjust.

Appendix 3—Rule 16, 1993 Version
Title 28, United States Code (1994)
Appendix—Rules of Civil Procedure, pp. 680-81

Rule 16. Pretrial Conferences; Scheduling; Management

(a) PRETRIAL CONFERENCES; OBJECTIVES. In any action, the court may in its discretion direct the attorneys for the parties and any unrepresented parties to appear before it for a conference or conferences before trial for such purposes as

(1) expediting the disposition of the action;
(2) establishing early and continuing control so that the case will not be protracted because of lack of management;
(3) discouraging wasteful pretrial activities;
(4) improving the quality of the trial through more thorough preparation, and;
(5) facilitating the settlement of the case.

(b) SCHEDULING AND PLANNING. Except in categories of actions exempted by district court rule as inappropriate, the district judge, or a magistrate judge when authorized by district court rule, shall, after receiving the report from the parties under Rule 26(f) or after consulting with the attorneys for the parties and any unrepresented parties by a scheduling conference, telephone, mail, or other suitable means, enter a scheduling order that limits the time

(1) to join other parties and to amend the pleadings;
(2) to file motions; and
(3) to complete discovery.

The scheduling order may also include

(4) modifications of the times for disclosures under Rules 26(a) and 26(e)(1) and of the extent of discovery to be permitted;
(5) the date or dates for conferences before trial, a final pretrial conference, and trial; and
(6) any other matters appropriate in the circumstances of the case.

The order shall issue as soon as practicable but in any event within 90 days after the appearance of a defendant and within 120 days after the complaint has been served on a defendant. A schedule shall not be modified except upon a showing of good cause and by leave of the district judge or, when authorized by local rule, by a magistrate judge.

(c) SUBJECTS FOR CONSIDERATION AT PRETRIAL CONFERENCES. At any conference under this rule consideration may be given, and the court may take appropriate action, with respect to

(1) the formulation and simplification of the issues, including the elimination of frivolous claims or defenses;
(2) the necessity or desirability of amendments to pleadings;
(3) the possibility of obtaining admissions of fact and of documents which will avoid unnecessary proof, stipulations regarding the authenticity of documents, and advance rulings from the court on the admissibility of evidence;
(4) the avoidance of unnecessary proof and of cumulative evidence, and limitations or restrictions on the use of testimony under Rule 702 of the Federal Rules of Evidence;

(5) the appropriateness and timing of summary adjudication under Rule 56;

(6) the control and scheduling of discovery, including orders affecting disclosures and discovery pursuant to Rule 26 and Rules 29 through 37;

(7) the identification of witnesses and documents, the need and schedule for filing and exchanging pretrial briefs, and the date or dates for further conferences and for trial;

(8) the advisability of referring matters to a magistrate judge or master;

(9) settlement and the use of special procedures to assist in resolving the dispute when authorized by statute or local rule;

(10) the form and substance of the pretrial order;

(11) the disposition of pending motions;

(12) the need for adopting special procedures for managing potentially difficult or protracted actions that may involve complex issues, multiple parties, difficult legal questions, or unusual proof problems;

(13) an order for a separate trial pursuant to Rule 42(b) with respect to a claim, counterclaim, cross-claim, or third-party claim, or with respect to any particular issue in the case;

(14) an order directing a party or parties to present evidence early in the trial with respect to a manageable issue that could, on the evidence, be the basis for a judgment as a matter of law under Rule 50(a) or a judgment on partial findings under Rule 52(c);

(15) an order establishing a reasonable limit on the time allowed for presenting evidence; and

(16) such other matters as may facilitate the just, speedy, and inexpensive disposition of the action.

At least one of the attorneys for each party participating in any conference before trial shall have authority to enter into stipulations and to make admissions regarding all matters that the participants may reasonably anticipate may be discussed. If appropriate, the court may require that a party or its representative be present or reasonably available by telephone in order to consider possible settlement of the dispute.

(d) FINAL PRETRIAL CONFERENCE. Any final pretrial conference shall be held as close to the time of trial as reasonable under the circumstances. The participants at any such conference shall formulate a plan for trial, including a program for facilitating the admission of evidence. The conference shall be attended by at least one of the attorneys who will conduct the trial for each of the parties and by any unrepresented parties.

(e) PRETRIAL ORDERS. After any conference held pursuant to this rule, an order shall be entered reciting the action taken. This order shall control the subsequent course of the action unless modified by a subsequent order. The order following a final pretrial conference shall be modified only to prevent manifest injustice.

(f) SANCTIONS. If a party or party's attorney fails to obey a scheduling or pretrial order, or if no appearance is made on behalf of a party at a scheduling or pretrial conference, or if a party or party's attorney is substantially unprepared to participate in the conference, or if a party or party's attorney fails to participate in good faith, the judge, upon motion or the judge's own initiative, may make such orders with regard thereto as are just, and among others any of the orders provided in Rule 37(b)(2)(B), (C), (D). In lieu of or in addition to any other sanction, the judge shall require the party or the attorney representing the party or both to pay the reasonable expenses incurred because of any noncompliance with this rule, including attorney's fees, unless the judge finds that the noncompliance was substantially justified or that other circumstances make an award of expenses unjust.

Appendix 4—Civil Justice Reform Act
(Selected Sections)
Title 28, United states Code (1994)

CHAPTER 23. CIVIL JUSTICE EXPENSE AND DELAY REDUCTION PLANS.

§ 471. Requirement for a district court civil justice expense and delay reduction plan
There shall be implemented by each United States district court, in accordance with this chapter, a civil justice expense and delay reduction plan. The plan may be a plan developed by such district court or a model plan developed by the Judicial Conference of the United States. The purposes of each plan are to facilitate deliberate adjudication of civil cases on the merits, monitor discovery, improve litigation management, and ensure just, speedy, and inexpensive resolution of civil disputes.

§ 473. Content of civil justice expense and delay reduction plans
(a) In formulating the provisions of its civil justice expense and delay reduction plan, each United States district court, in consultation with an advisory group appointed under section 478 of this title, shall consider and may include the following principles and guidelines of litigation management and cost and delay reduction:
(1) systematic, differential treatment of civil cases that tailors the level of individualized and case specific management to such criteria as case complexity, the amount of time reasonably needed to prepare the case for trial,

and the judicial and other resources required and available for the preparation and disposition of the case;

(2) early and ongoing control of the pretrial process through involvement of a judicial officer in–

(A) assessing and planning the progress of a case;

(B) setting early, firm trial dates, such that the trial is scheduled to occur within eighteen months after the filing of the complaint, unless a judicial officer certifies that–

(i) the demands of the case and its complexity make such a trial date incompatible with serving the ends of justice; or

(ii) the trial cannot reasonably be held within such time because of the complexity of the case or the number or complexity of pending criminal cases;

(C) controlling the extent of discovery and the time for completion of discovery, and ensuring compliance with appropriate requested discovery in a timely fashion; and

(D) setting, at the earliest practicable time, deadlines for filling motions and a time framework for their disposition;

(3) for all cases that the court or an individual judicial officer determines are complex and any other appropriate cases, careful and deliberate monitoring through a discovery-case management conference or a series of such conferences at which the presiding judicial officer–

(A) explores the parties' receptivity to, and the propriety of, settlement or proceeding with the litigation;

(B) identifies or formulates the principal issues in contention and, in appropriate cases, provides for the staged resolution or bifurcation of issues for trial consistent with Rule 42(b) of the Federal Rules of Civil Procedure;

(C) prepares a discovery schedule and plan consistent with any presumptive time limits that a district court may set for the completion of discovery and with any procedures a district court may develop to–

(i) identify and limit the volume of discovery available to avoid unnecessary or unduly burdensome or expensive discovery; and

(ii) phase discovery into two or more stages; and

(D) sets, at the earliest practicable time, deadlines for filing motions and a time framework for their disposition;

(4) encouragement of cost-effective discovery through voluntary exchange of information among litigants and their attorneys and through the use of cooperative discovery devices;

(5) conservation of judicial resources by prohibiting the consideration of discovery motions unless accompanied by a certification that the moving party has made a reasonable and good faith effort to reach agreement with opposing counsel on the matters set forth in the motion; and

(6) authorization to refer appropriate cases to alternative dispute resolution programs that—

(A) have been designated for use in a district court; or

(B) the court may make available, including mediation, minitrial, and summary jury trial.

(b) In formulating the provisions of its civil justice expense and delay reduction plan, each United States district court, in consultation with an advisory group appointed under section 478 of this title, shall consider and may include the following litigation management and cost and delay reduction techniques:

(1) a requirement that counsel for each party to a case jointly present a discovery-case management plan for the case at the initial pretrial conference, or explain the reasons for their failure to do so;

(2) a requirement that each party be represented at each pretrial conference by an attorney who has the authority to bind that party regarding all matters previously identified by the court for discussion at the conference and all reasonably related matters;

(3) a requirement that all requests for extensions of deadlines for completion of discovery or for postponement of the trial be signed by the attorney and the party making the request;

(4) a neutral evaluation program for the presentation of the legal and factual basis of a case to a neutral court representative selected by the court at a nonbinding conference conducted early in the litigation;

(5) a requirement that, upon notice by the court, representatives of the parties with authority to bind them in settlement discussions be present or available by telephone during any settlement conference; and

(6) such other features as the district court considers appropriate after considering the recommendations of the advisory group referred to in section 472(a) of this title.

(c) Nothing in a civil justice expense and delay reduction plan relating to the settlement authority provisions of this section shall alter or conflict with the authority of the Attorney General to conduct litigation on behalf of the United States, or any delegation of the Attorney General.

PART II

The Evolving Civil Jury

The Seventh Amendment has two clauses: the first preserves the right to a civil jury in suits at common law, and the second prohibits courts from reexamining facts found by juries other than by the methods of the common law. Of these, the first is the best known. It has been the subject of more cases and more commentary than the second, and most efforts to control the jury have aimed at taking evidence, issues, or cases away from juries altogether. Thus, most of the discussion in this Part relates to the first clause. The second clause is at issue in some of the control devices I discuss in Chapter 7, most notably the post-verdict judgment as a matter of law.

The Supreme Court has repeatedly said that the Seventh Amendment preserves the "fundamental" right to a civil jury trial, but not all of the details that surrounded such a trial at common law. It inevitably makes this statement, however, in the course of approving procedural devices that diminish the right to jury trial. In fact, it has never satisfactorily defined the "fundamental" right to a jury trial; apparently the fundamental right is what is left after various new procedures whittle away at it.

In this Part, I will explore in some detail what the Seventh Amendment means today, looking both at the Court's basic definition of the right and at its statements about various jury control devices. In so doing, I will document the accelerating decline of the jury in the last half of the twentieth century.

CHAPTER 4

The Constitutional Right
to a Civil Jury Trial

In Chapter 3, I suggested that the major restructuring of civil procedure wrought by the Federal Rules of Civil Procedure means that the jury is less well suited to the modern procedural environment than it was to common law procedure. But the Supreme Court has used those same Federal Rules to broaden the right to jury trial. A jury trial is now required under the Seventh Amendment in cases that would have been heard in equity without a jury in eighteenth century England. Also in Chapter 3, I said that it is more difficult for a jury to function when the source of law is statutes rather than the common law. But the Supreme Court has said that the Seventh Amendment requires a jury for actions founded on statutes that did not exist in eighteenth century England, as long as they raise legal (as opposed to equitable) matters and are litigated in the ordinary federal courts. Finally, I noted in Chapter 3 that juries are inconsistent with the rationale behind administrative adjudication. Here, at least, the Supreme Court's jurisprudence is consistent with my observations: the Court has held that a jury is not required in administrative agencies, though its rationale is poorly developed and problematic.[1] In this Chapter, I will describe how the Supreme Court reached those conclusions.

I. Modern Procedural Developments and the Seventh Amendment

Because the Seventh Amendment "preserves" the right to a jury trial as it existed in England in 1791, the Court has long held that there is a right to a

---

1. For a critique of the Court's rationale with respect to administrative agencies, see Ellen E. Sward, *Legislative Courts, Article III, and the Seventh Amendment*, 77 N.C.L. Rev. 1037 (1999).

jury trial for legal, but not equitable, matters.[2] Thus, it is important to understand how equity co-existed with the common law courts in England, and I will begin by describing that relationship, which is defined in jurisdictional terms.[3] I will then show how modern procedural developments have altered the balance between law and equity.

A. The Historic Relationship Between Law and Equity

Equity offered remedies that were unavailable in common law courts, but equity would act only if the common law courts could not provide an adequate remedy.[4] Common law courts were limited to three remedies: recovery of land (such as ejectment); recovery of chattels (such as replevin); and (most commonly) recovery of money, or money damages.[5] If these were inadequate, then the party could be irreparably harmed unless equity intervened. Equitable remedies were quite wide-ranging; indeed, courts of equity were able to create new remedies to meet new conditions—something early common law judges would not do.[6] The best known equitable remedies are injunctions, which are orders to a party to do something or refrain from doing something,[7] and specific performance of contracts, which is an order to a party to perform her obligations under a contract.[8]

The rule that equity would act only to prevent irreparable harm that the common law courts could not redress was one of a set of rules describing the

---

2. See supra, Chapter 2, at notes 173–178 and accompanying text; Parsons v. Bedford, 28 U.S. (3Pet.) 433 (1830); Capital Traction Co. v. Hof, 174 U.S. 1, 10 (1898); United States v. Louisiana, 399 U.S. 699, 706 (1950).

3. In Chapter 2, I described the historical development of equity in relation to the common law. See supra, Chapter 2, at notes 118–145 and accompanying text. In Chapter 3, I described how the Federal Rules of Civil Procedure altered common law procedures and made federal procedure more equitable in character. See supra, Chapter 3, at notes 9–56 and accompanying text. In this Chapter, I describe in more detail the jurisdiction of common law courts and courts of equity.

4. See 1 DAN B. DOBBS, DOBBS LAW OF REMEDIES: DAMAGES - EQUITY - RESTITUTION, §2.1(1) (2nd ed. 1993).

5. See 1 JOHN NORTON POMEROY, A TREATISE ON EQUITY JURISPRUDENCE, §§22–23 (5th ed., Spencer W. Symons ed. 1941); 2 DOBBS, supra note 4, at §§4.2, 5.17.

6. See 1 POMEROY, supra note 5, at §§28–32. Pomeroy's five-volume treatise on equity, from which this discussion is largely drawn, provides the most exhaustive description of equitable remedies available.

7. See 1 DOBBS, supra note 4, at §2.1(2).

8. See 3 id., at §12.8(1).

relationship between law and equity.[9] An example is in order: If a contract were for the purchase of a specific tract of land, courts of equity would generally intervene if the seller breached the contract. Because each piece of real estate is unique, money damages—the only remedy available in the common law courts—were inadequate. Thus, the purchaser's injury would be irreparable unless the court ordered the seller to sell.[10] But if money would adequately compensate the purchaser for any harm he had suffered, he was limited to that legal remedy, available only in a common law court. If, for example, two people had a contract, not for the sale of land but for the sale of 1000 bushels of wheat, equity would not take jurisdiction of a claim for breach because wheat is fungible, and money damages will adequately compensate the purchaser.

As a corollary to this, defending against a legal claim was considered an adequate legal remedy.[11] Thus, for example, a person could not go into a court of equity and get an injunction prohibiting another person from filing a common law action against her.[12] Defending the common law action would be an adequate legal remedy unless the common law courts did not recognize the proffered defense.[13] Having to defend against *multiple* claims arising out of the same circumstance, however, was not an adequate legal remedy. To prevent a multiplicity of suits, a court of equity would enjoin threatened multiple common law proceedings and handle the matter itself.[14]

Once a court of equity had jurisdiction, it guarded that jurisdiction jealously. If a plaintiff came into a court of equity seeking an equitable remedy such as an injunction, and the defendant later filed suit against her on the same matter in a common law court, the court of equity could enjoin the common law proceedings to prevent the irreparable harm of having to litigate

---

9. Equity also developed a set of procedures governing how litigants could invoke its authority and how it would determine their claims. These procedures differed significantly from common law procedures, in part because courts of equity were not constrained by the presence of the jury. *See, e.g.,* 1 POMEROY, *supra* note 5, at §37.

10. *See* HAROLD GREVILLE HANBURY, MODERN EQUITY 518–19 (2nd ed. 1937).

11. *Id.* at 546–47. *See* Grand Chute v. Winegar, 82 U.S. (15 Wall.) 373, 376 (1873); Dohse v. Market Mens Mut. Ins. Co., 115 N.W.2d 844 (Iowa 1962).

12. *See* 4 POMEROY, *supra* note 5, at §§ 1361–1365.

13. If the defense were that the defendant had fraudulently induced the plaintiff to enter into the contract, for example, the courts of equity would act because common law courts did not recognize that defense. *See* Canning v. Star Publishing Co., 138 F. Supp. 843, 845 (D.Del. 1956); 9 CHARLES ALAN WRIGHT AND ARTHUR MILLER, FEDERAL PRACTICE AND PROCEDURE §2311 (2nd ed. 1995). *See generally,* POMEROY, *supra* note 5, at §§ 1361–1365.

14. *See* 1 POMEROY, *supra* note 5, at §§ 181, 231–242, 243.

two suits at once. In other words, if an adequate legal remedy—in this example, defending against a common law claim—came into existence after the equity court had jurisdiction, the court of equity did not lose the jurisdiction it had legitimately acquired before the common law suit was filed.[15] Then, under the so-called "clean-up doctrine," the equity court could decide all incidental legal issues—legal issues that were related to the equitable issue—and award legal remedies.[16] For example, an equity court might have acquired jurisdiction over a dispute when one of the parties sought an accounting. If the defendant in that action later filed a common law action on a debt against the equity plaintiff, the equity court could enjoin the common law proceedings and, once the accounting was complete, decide the claim on the debt.[17] All of this would take place without a jury, because there was no jury in a court of equity.

In summary, then, the following rules governed equity jurisdiction. First, equity would act only if the petitioner did not have an adequate legal remedy and would be irreparably harmed without equity's intervention.[18] Second, once equity had jurisdiction over some portion of the dispute, it could decide the entire dispute—the so-called "clean-up doctrine."[19] Third, equity could enjoin common law proceedings but would do so only to prevent a multiplicity of suits or where the common law remedy was otherwise inadequate. A multiplicity of suits could occur either because the petitioner was threatened by several claims arising out of a single circumstance,[20] or because an equity defendant attempted to prosecute a common law action after the equity court had acquired jurisdiction over the controversy.[21]

---

15. *See id.* at §§ 253–254.
16. *See id.* at §§ 243–245. The clean-up doctrine has often been discussed in American courts. *See* Ross v. Bernhard, 396 U.S. 469 (1970); Dairy Queen v. Wood, 369 U.S. 469 (1962); Byron v. Clay, 867 F.2d 1049, 1052 (1989); Mowbray v. Moseley, Hallgarten, Estabrook & Weeden, Inc., 795 F.2d 1111 (1986); Medtronic, Inc. v. Intermedics, Inc. 725 F.2d 440 (1984).
17. *See* 1 POMEROY, *supra* note 5, at § 261 n.5–6.
18. *See id.* at §§ 216–222.
19. *See id.* at §§ 231–242.
20. *See id.* at §§ 243–271.
21. *See id.* at §§ 276–281a. These limitations on equity's power to act were observed in the American federal system even though that system never had separate courts of law and equity. The federal system merely used separate procedures within the same courts.

B. The Impact of Changing Procedures on the Right to a Jury Trial in Civil Cases

Civil procedure has changed dramatically since 1791, as I demonstrated in Chapter 3. In this section, I will identify the procedural developments that most affect the right to jury trial, and then describe how the Supreme Court has adapted the right to jury trial to the changing procedure.

1. Twentieth Century Procedural Development

Two aspects of the revolution in procedure are important to this analysis. The first is the allowance, under the Federal Rules of Civil Procedure, of suits raising multiple claims, both legal and equitable, in the same suit. The second is the creation of a new remedy, known to neither law nor equity—the declaratory judgment.

a. The Federal Rules of Civil Procedure

I have already described the significant changes that the Federal Rules of Civil Procedure effected.[22] The most important change for Seventh Amendment jurisprudence is that the Rules permit a wide range of claims to be heard together under a single set of procedures.[23] The Rules do not distinguish between legal claims and equitable claims, but apply "in all suits of a civil nature whether cognizable as cases at law or in equity."[24] Thus, a federal lawsuit may contain a mix of legal and equitable claims. But except to state explicitly that the Seventh Amendment right to jury trial "shall be preserved to the parties inviolate,"[25] the Rules give no guidance about the jury's role in cases with mixed legal and equitable claims.

b. The Declaratory Judgment

Another procedural innovation was Congress's creation of the declaratory judgment remedy in 1934.[26] This remedy allows parties who have an active

---

22. See *supra*, Chapter 3, at notes 1–144 and accompanying text.
23. See *supra*, Chapter 3, at notes 16–24 and accompanying text.
24. FED. R. CIV. P. 1.
25. FED. R. CIV. P. 38(a).
26. 28 U.S. C. §2201 (1994). *See* 3 WILLIAM W. BARRON, ALEXANDER HOLTZOFF, FEDERAL PRACTICE AND PROCEDURE §1261 (1958); 10B WRIGHT & MILLER *supra* note 13, at §2752; 12 JAMES WILLIAM MOORE, MOORE'S FEDERAL PRACTICE, §57App.01 (3rd ed. 1999).

controversy to go to the court for a resolution before they risk liability. For example, two persons might have a dispute about the interpretation of a contract to which both are parties, so one of them will seek a declaration from the court about what the contract means. This can be done before anyone breaches the contract, and can enable the parties to avoid a breach. If only a declaratory judgment is sought, all the court does is declare rights: it does not award any relief, either legal or equitable. Presumably, however, the parties will conduct themselves in accordance with the declaration, though the court can provide further relief if necessary.[27]

Rule 57 of the Federal Rules of Civil Procedure relates to declaratory judgments. It says, in part, that "the right to trial by jury may be demanded under the circumstances and in the manner provided [under the Federal Rules]."[28] But the rule goes on to say that "[t]he existence of another adequate remedy does not preclude a judgment for declaratory relief in cases where it is appropriate."[29] These two provisions in the rule seem to refer, respectively, to legal and equitable principles. The nature of the declaratory judgment remedy, then, was unclear; indeed, it seemed to be an entirely new remedy, neither legal nor equitable.

2. The Right to a Jury Trial Under the New Procedures

These new procedures raised serious questions about the right to a jury trial. First, under the Federal Rules, how was the right to jury trial to be treated when a lawsuit raised both legal and equitable issues and the fact-finding overlapped the legal and equitable issues? Prior to the adoption of unitary procedures, the judge would have found facts in equity, and the jury would have found facts in law. Second, how was the declaratory judgment to be classified for purposes of determining the right to a jury trial? Both of these questions arose in *Beacon Theatres, Inc. v. Westover.*[30]

In *Beacon Theatres,* the operator of a theater (Fox) brought a declaratory judgment action against an arguably competing theater (Beacon) seeking approval, under the antitrust laws, of a contract with movie distributors that gave Fox the exclusive right to show first-run movies in the San Bernardino,

---

27. *See* 28 U.S.C. §2202 (1994). *See generally,* 10B WRIGHT & MILLER, *supra* note 13, at §2771; 12 MOORE, *supra* note 26, at §57.65.

28. FED. R. CIV. P. 57.

29. *Id.*

30. 359 U.S. 500 (1959). For a discussion of *Beacon Theatres,* see John C. McCoid, II, *Procedural Reform and the Right to Jury Trial: A Study of* Beacon Theatres, Inc. v. Westover, 116 U. PA. L. REV. 1 (1967).

California, competitive area for a specified period of time.[31] Fox also sought an injunction, the nature of which was in some dispute. The Supreme Court suggested that the injunction might merely have sought to prevent Beacon from bringing suit against Fox for antitrust damages,[32] which is not a viable equitable remedy because defending such a suit would be an adequate legal remedy. The District Court and the Court of Appeals evidently interpreted the injunction as one seeking to prevent Beacon from harming Fox by threatening Fox and its distributors with multiple lawsuits; such threats may have been interfering with Fox's enjoyment of its contract.[33] Beacon responded to the suit by counterclaiming for treble damages under the antitrust laws,[34] and Beacon asked for a jury trial on its counterclaim. The question of fact common to both Fox's claim and Beacon's counterclaim was whether both theaters were, in fact, in the San Bernardino competitive area; in other words, were the theaters in competition?

The trial judge decided that the plaintiff Fox had raised only equitable issues, and opted to try those issues first, without a jury. Beacon objected that this could deprive it of its right to a jury trial because once the judge decided the factual issue of competitiveness, the issue could not be retried before the jury because of the principles of res judicata and collateral estoppel.[35]

The trial judge, and the court of appeals on mandamus,[36] sought to treat the case as it would have been treated prior to the merger of law and equity. Under the traditional equitable principles described above, the court of eq-

---

31. *Id.* at 502.

32. The prayer for relief asked only for this. *Beacon Theatres,* 359 U.S. at 506.

33. There were two paragraphs in the Complaint that could be interpreted this way. These paragraphs are quoted and discussed at some length in the opinion of the Court of Appeals. *See* Beacon Theatres, Inc. v. Westover, 252 F.2d 864, 866–73 (9th Cir. 1958). The Supreme Court accepted the interpretation of the Court of Appeals because "[t]his liberal construction of a pleading is in line with Rule 8 of the Federal Rules of Civil Procedure." Beacon Theatres, 359 U.S. at 506 (citing Conley v. Gibson, 355 U.S. 41, 47–78 (1957)).

34. Beacon Theatres, 359 U.S. at 503.

35. *Id.* at 504. Res judicata and collateral estoppel—now generally called, respectively, claim and issue preclusion, prevent the relitigation of matters once decided or, in the case of claim preclusion, of claims that should have been raised in previous litigation. For a discussion of the effects of claim and issue preclusion on the right to jury trial, see *infra,* Chapter 7, at notes 242–263 and accompanying text.

36. *Id.* at 501. A writ of mandamus is an original action in the court of appeals against the district judge, asking that the court of appeals order the district judge to do something—here, to conduct a jury trial of all common issues of fact. It is considered extraordinary relief, and is rarely sought and even more rarely granted. *See generally,* 16 WRIGHT & MILLER, *supra* note 13, at § 3932.

uity could have taken cognizance of the case if the injunction were being sought to prevent a threat of multiple lawsuits.[37] Once the court of equity had jurisdiction, it could not lose jurisdiction even if an adequate legal remedy— such as defending against a legal counterclaim—later became available,[38] and it could decide any incidental legal issues under the "clean-up" doctrine.[39] The trial judge in fact had planned to give any question of damages to a jury, but because the judge would have decided the competition question in connection with the equitable claim, a critical question of fact relating to liability on the counterclaim would have been decided solely by the judge.

The Supreme Court disapproved of this plan, holding that modern procedural devices had eliminated the need for equity to act in the case as presented by Fox, and that preservation of the right to a jury trial required having the jury decide issues of fact common to the legal and equitable claims regarding liability as well as damages.[40] The Court first questioned the trial and appellate courts' characterization of the relief sought as equitable, raising two issues. First, as to the declaratory judgment, the Court said that declaratory relief is neither legal nor equitable, but takes its character from the underlying claim. In this case, the declaratory judgment action was in essence a pre-emptive strike against the legal claim that Beacon would have filed against Fox if declaratory relief had been unavailable.[41] In other words, the declaratory judgment action was a defense to a legal claim but with the parties juxtaposed. Thus, the declaratory judgment action had to be characterized as legal.[42] Second, the Court questioned whether the request for an injunction constituted a valid request for equitable relief. If, as it appeared from the prayer for relief, Fox merely wanted to prevent Beacon from filing a legal action against it, that was not grounds for equitable intervention.[43] If both of these views were accepted, the only legitimate relief Fox was seeking was legal, and Beacon would have a right to a jury trial.

---

37. *Id.* at 506, 508.

38. *See supra,* note 15 and accompanying text.

39. *See supra,* notes 16–17 and accompanying text.

40. Beacon Theatres, 359 U.S. at 506.

41. Beacon Theatres, 359 U.S. at 504.

42. Beacon Theatres, 359 U.S. at 504. The dissenting justices objected, saying that the presence of a valid claim for an injunction meant that this could not be viewed as a mere juxtaposition of parties case. That claim for equitable relief, the dissenters thought, gave the trial judge the power to proceed as he had intended. *Id.* at 515 (Stewart, J., dissenting). *See also,* Simler v. Conner, 372 U.S. 221, 223 (1963) (holding that a declaratory judgment action seeking a determination of attorneys' fees was essentially legal in nature).

43. *See* Beacon Theatres, 359 U.S. at 506. *See supra* note 12 and accompanying text.

Ultimately, however, the Court did not rest on this classification issue. Rather, the Court thought that even if the relief Fox sought could be characterized as equitable, the trial judge should have ordered a jury trial with respect to all issues of fact common to Fox's and Beacon's claims. The court viewed the trial judge's decision to hear the equitable claims first as the equivalent of a court of equity's enjoining a common law action. Recall that the historic justification for such an injunction was that the plaintiff would suffer irreparable harm from having to litigate two separate suits.[44] But because there was only one suit, and the rules provide for joining all claims and parties in that one suit,[45] there was no longer any threat of irreparable harm from a separate common law claim. Because irreparable harm is a prerequisite for equity to act, there was no longer any justification for such an injunction.[46] Thus, even under traditional equity principles, Beacon would have been entitled to a jury trial on the factual issues raised by its counterclaim. The Court therefore required the trial judge to conduct a jury trial as to all factual issues that were common to the legal and equitable claims.

At a minimum, the Court's decision in *Beacon Theatres* means that a jury trial is required when legal and equitable claims are asserted in the same case and there are issues of fact common to both.[47] In eighteenth century England, these claims could not have been brought together in a common law court, so there would have been no jury trial for any of the facts related to the equitable claims. If a court of equity had jurisdiction of the matter because the plaintiff sought a proper injunction against a threat of multiple suits, then the court of equity could have heard the legal claim under the clean-up doctrine, and there would have been no jury for the legal claims either. Thus, if the characterization of Fox's claim in *Beacon Theatres* as a claim for an injunction against a threat of multiple suits is accepted, the Court apparently mandated a jury trial when the same case prior to the procedural changes made during the last century would not have been before a jury. The Court's characterization is open to some interpretation,[48] however, so some question remained about how far the Court would go toward this apparent expansion of the right to jury trial.

---

44. *See supra* notes 13–14 and accompanying text.

45. Indeed, Beacon's counterclaim was undoubtedly compulsory under FED. R. CIV. P. 13(a).

46. Beacon Theatres, 359 U.S. at 506, 507.

47. The only exception would be where the party seeking equitable relief would be irreparably harmed by that procedure, but it is hard to imagine such a circumstance. *See id.* at 506–07.

48. If the declaratory judgment action were characterized as legal, and if Fox's request was interpreted as a request for injunctive relief against a single lawsuit, it could be argued

A partial answer came three years later in *Dairy Queen v. Wood*,[49] in which Dairy Queen sought an injunction prohibiting its allegedly defaulting franchisee from using its trademark, and an accounting to determine the amount the franchisee owed under the franchise agreement. Both the injunction and the accounting were traditional equitable remedies. There is not much question that under pre-merger custom, this action would have been in equity.[50] But because under the federal rules the complexity that made equitable accounting necessary could easily be alleviated by the use of masters, the Court held that a jury would have to be provided.[51] The underlying claim under the accounting procedure was a claim for money damages, and that was a traditional legal remedy, even if courts of equity did generally provide that remedy under the clean-up doctrine.[52]

If anything, *Dairy Queen* is a clearer case for classifying the remedy sought as equitable than was *Beacon Theatres*. Accounting has a long history as an equitable remedy,[53] as does the injunction.[54] Still, the accounting was always

that this case was never anything but a legal action. Even if this case would have been equitable historically, however, courts of equity could refuse to hear the damage claims, though they rarely did. Because the antitrust damages sought were significant, a court of equity might have found that the legal issues were not merely "incidental" to the equitable issues. See 1 POMEROY, *supra* note 5, at §233. A court of equity had discretion whether to retain jurisdiction when a common law action was later filed or when legal matters were not merely incidental to the equitable claims. *See, e.g.,* Jones v. Amsel, 130 A.2d 119, 123 (Pa. 1957) (finding that after injunction was issued plaintiff had adequate remedy at law and refusing to retain equity jurisdiction); Tucker v. Simmons, 287 S.W.2d 19 (Tenn. 1956) (finding that a tenant's personal injury claim against a landlord based on fraud was not incidental to the fraud, but was the "gravamen" of the claim); May Stores v. Hartz Mountain-Free, 392 A.2d 251, 254 (N.J. 1978) (holding that a judge has discretion to transfer case to law when equitable action is rendered moot by plaintiff's actions); Jacobson v. First Nat. Bank of Bloomingdale, 31 A.2d 406, 409 (N.J. 1943) (holding that unliquidated damages were not incidental to equity proceeding); Shaw v. G.B. Beaumont Co., 102 A. 151, 152 (N.J. 1917) (holding that consideration of legal matters in equity is discretionary).

49. 369 U.S. 469 (1962).

50. *But see* Ross v. Bernhard, 396 U.S. 531, 549 (1970) (Stewart, J., dissenting) (arguing that *Dairy Queen* "involved a combination of historically separable suits, one in law and one in equity.") Stewart may have been referring to the fact that Dairy Queen could have sought a money judgment at law for breach of contract, without asking for an accounting. The accounting, however, was clearly an equitable remedy pre-merger, and the only remedies Dairy Queen sought were injunctions and an accounting.

51. 369 U.S. at 478–79.

52. *Id.* at 477–478.

53. 4 POMEROY, *supra* note 5, at §1420.

54. *Id.* at §1337.

a means to an end rather than an end in itself. The end toward which accounting moved was a money judgment. That is traditionally legal, notwithstanding that courts of equity regularly awarded a decree for the payment of money following an accounting. The Court in *Dairy Queen* chose to ignore the old and arguably outdated equitable forms for the new reality of the merged system.

Even in *Dairy Queen*, however, the issue was more form than substance. A party in Dairy Queen's position prior to the merger could have brought a common law action for money due under the franchise contract. Equity would assist only if the finances were too complicated for a jury to sort out or if the accounting were ancillary to other equitable relief. *Ross v. Bernhard*,[55] went farther still. There, the plaintiffs, shareholders in a corporation, sought to use the traditionally equitable device of a shareholder's derivative suit to press a claim on the corporation's behalf. Prior to the merger of legal and equitable procedures, a shareholder wishing to sue on behalf of the corporation had to go to equity and file a derivative suit because common law courts would not recognize the shareholder's standing to sue.[56] In other words, unlike the parties seeking to invoke equity principles in *Beacon Theatres* and *Dairy Queen*, the plaintiffs in *Ross* would have been unable to bring their claims in a common law action prior to the merger. This was true even if the claim the shareholder wished to assert on behalf of the corporation was a legal claim, in which case the judge sitting in equity could decide all legal issues under the clean-up doctrine. In *Ross*, the Court held that because the underlying cause of action was legal, a jury would have to be provided, notwithstanding the fact that no shareholder's derivative suit could ever have been tried to a jury prior to the merger.[57] *Ross* illustrates the tension between the underlying philoso-

---

55. 396 U.S. 531 (1970).

56. *See* Note, *The Right to a Jury Trial in a Stockholder's Derivative Action*, 74 YALE L.J. 725, 729 (1965). *See generally,* 4 POMEROY, *supra* note 5, at § 1095. Only directors could authorize suits on behalf of a corporation. *See, e.g.,* WIS. STAT. ANN. § 180.0742 (West 1992); ARIZ. REV. STAT. ANN. § 10-742 (West 1996). *See generally,* HARRY G. HENN, LAW OF CORPORATIONS 771 (2nd ed. 1970).

57. Ross, 396 U.S. at 542–543. Most cases and commentators prior to *Ross* had characterized the shareholders' derivative suit as wholly equitable, largely for historical reasons. *See, e.g.,* Cohen v. Beneficial Industrial Loan Corp., 337 U.S. 541, 547–48 (1949); United Copper Co. v. Amalgamated Copper Co., 244 U.S. 261, 264 (1917); Ross, 396 U.S. at 543–51 (Stewart, J., dissenting); Note, *supra* note 56, at 732. The consequence of this is that there would be no right to a jury trial. One Ninth Circuit decision, however, had found a right to jury trial in such cases under the Federal Rules. *See* DePinto v. Provident Security Life Ins. Co., 323 F.2d 826 (9th Cir. 1963).

phies of those who favored the jury and those who opposed it. The majority, discarding equitable forms altogether with the decision, said:

> Where equitable and legal claims are joined in the same action, there is a right to jury trial on the legal claims which must not be infringed either by trying the legal issues as incidental to the equitable ones or by a court trial of a common issue existing between the two claims. The Seventh Amendment question depends on the nature of the issue to be tried rather than the character of the overall action.[58]

This view is probably inconsistent with the intent of the original Advisory Committee, which sought to contain the jury.[59] Indeed, Justice Stewart in dissent reflects a distrust of the jury more in keeping with the original Advisory Committee's views when he argues that the Court should respect such historically equitable forms as the shareholder's derivative suit:

> Certainly there is no consensus among commentators on the desirability of jury trials in civil actions generally. Particularly where the issues in the case are complex...much can be said for allowing the court discretion to try the case itself.[60]

C. Summary

Equity was born of the early common law's refusal to adapt to changing circumstances. Founded on the king's discretion and appealing to his sense of justice, equity sought to achieve fairness when the common law would not. But equity did not act if the petitioner could get justice from the common law

---

58. Ross v. Bernhard, 396 U.S. at 537–38. The notion that it is the particular issue rather than the character of the overall action that determines the right to a jury trial has been controversial, but seems to be established law now. See, e.g., Markman v. Westview Instruments, Inc., 517 U.S. 370 (1996) (holding that interpretation of a patent is for the judge notwithstanding that the overall claim for patent infringement was triable to a jury). *Markman*, however, might be nothing more than an example of the law/fact distinction. Issues of law have historically been taken from juries even in common law actions. See *infra*, notes 114–116 and accompanying text.

59. See 8 Moore, *supra* note 26, at §§38App.01, 38App.102; Douglas Laycock, *Triumph of Equity*, 56 L. & Contemp. Probs. 53, 66 (1993); Stephen N. Subrin, *How Equity Conquered Common Law: The Federal Rules of Civil Procedure in Historical Perspective*, 135 U. Pa. L. Rev. 909, 923–24 (1987).

60. Ross, 396 U.S. at 545n.5 (Stewart, J., dissenting). Of course, whether jury trials are desirable is not the question under the Seventh Amendment. One's answer to that question can certainly color one's interpretation of the Seventh Amendment, however.

courts. Equity's reluctance to act was reflected in numerous rules governing when equity would take jurisdiction of a case, the most important of which was that the petitioner's legal remedy had to be inadequate. The only way legal and equitable claims could be tried together in this system was if equity had jurisdiction of an equitable claim and took cognizance of related legal claims under the clean-up doctrine; if that happened, both legal and equitable claims were tried in equity without a jury. When legal and equitable procedures were merged in the Federal Rules of Civil Procedure, the effect on the right to jury trial was significant, but not, most likely, as anticipated by the drafters of the Rules. Rather, over the course of about eleven years, beginning more than twenty years after the Rules took effect, the Supreme Court has expanded the right to jury trial into areas that would have been dominated by equity prior to 1938. The Court's holdings that these changes in federal procedural rules expand the range of adequate legal remedies and thus contract the operation of equity are certainly reasonable. But so is the argument that the constitutional right to jury trial should be governed by historical forms and need not be expanded.[61] Under this latter view, Congress, if it so desires, can provide for expanded jury trial rights by statute.[62] Which of these positions one adopts is likely to depend on whether one views the jury with favor or disfavor.

II. The Impact of New Statutory Actions

The shift in our substantive law from common law to statutory sources also raises questions about the scope of the Seventh Amendment. Specifically, given the language of the Seventh Amendment that the right to a jury trial is "preserved," does that right attach to new statutory actions that did not exist in 1791? The answer, for the most part, is "yes."[63] The Court's analytical approach, however, has become quite cumbersome.

---

61. For one such argument, see Martin H. Redish, *Seventh Amendment Right to Jury Trial: A Study in the Irrationality of Rational Decision Making*, 70 Nw. U.L. Rev. 486 (1975).

62. *See id.* at 531.

63. As I will show in Part III of this Chapter, if a statute creates rights and remedies, but assigns them to administrative agencies for adjudication, there is no right to a jury trial. *See infra*, notes 136–215 and accompanying text.

A. The Evolution of the Two-Step Approach

As early as 1830, in *Parsons v. Bedford*,[64] the Court ruled that the Seventh Amendment right to a jury trial extended beyond those actions that actually existed at common law, to all actions in which legal rights were adjudicated.[65] The question remained how to define "legal" rights. The Court's modern approach to that definitional issue has come to rely on parts of a fateful footnote from *Ross v. Bernhard*. That footnote, which purports to be describing existing case law, describes three factors that help the Court decide whether an issue is legal or equitable: "first, the pre-merger custom with reference to such questions; second, the remedy sought; and, third, the practical abilities and limitations of juries."[66] The first two factors have become the basis for the Court's two-step jurisprudence, by which the Court seeks to compare modern actions with historical ones. If the modern action is a common law action with a historical counterpart, the process is not difficult.[67] As applied to statutory actions, the process requires the Court to look first for a historical analogue to the statutory action and then at the remedy. If these inquiries point to the common law, then there is a right to a jury trial for the new statutory action. The third *Ross* factor is not generally part of the analysis.[68]

---

64. 28 U.S. (3 Pet.) 433 (1830).

65. *Id.* at 446–47.

66. 396 U.S. at 538 n.10. No cases are cited in the footnote. Rather, the Court cites Fleming James, Jr., *Right to A Jury Trial in Civil Actions*, 72 Yale L.J. 655 (1963).

67. *See* Granfinanciera, S.A. v. Nordberg, 492 U.S. 33, 41 (1989). The two-step process developed in the context of statutory actions, but it applies to common law actions as well.

68. The third factor might be the basis for the so-called public rights doctrine, which allows jury-less adjudication of "public rights" in administrative agencies and other legislative courts. *See* Granfinanciera, S.A. v. Nordberg, 492 U.S. 33, 75n.4 (1989). *See infra*, notes 136–215 and accompanying text for a discussion of the public rights doctrine. *See also*, Sward, *supra* note 1, at 1089–1114 (critiquing the public rights doctrine as applied to the Seventh Amendment). Some litigants had sought to prevent jury trials in complex cases in Article III courts in the late 1970s, sometimes arguing that a jury trial in complex cases deprived them of their due process rights because of the alleged incompetence of the jury. One such effort prevailed, *see* Japanese Electronics Products Antitrust Litigation, 631 F.2d 1069 (3rd Cir. 1980), *aff'd in part and reversed in part on other grounds following summary judgment*, 723 F.2d 238 (3rd Cir. 1983), *reversed on other grounds*, 475 U.S. 574 (1986). Another failed, *see* In re United States Financial Securities Litigation, 609 F. 2d 411 (9th Cir. 1979), *cert. denied*, 446 U.S. 929 (1980). The Supreme Court has never ruled on this issue. *See generally*, Patrick Devlin, *Jury Trial of Complex Cases: English Practice at the Time of the Seventh Amendment*, 80 Colum. L. Rev. 43 (1980); Morris S. Arnold, *A Historical Inquiry Into the Right to Trial by Jury in Complex Civil Litigation*, 128 U. Pa. L. Rev. 829 (1980).

The first case in which the Court directly confronted the question whether litigants suing under new statutory actions were entitled to jury trials was *Curtis v. Loether*.[69] That case concerned Title VIII of the Civil Rights Act of 1968,[70] which authorized private citizens to bring civil actions to enforce their right to non-discrimination in housing. The Court first noted that "it has long been settled that the right [to jury trial in civil cases] extends beyond the common-law forms of action recognized [in 1791]."[71] Agreeing with the lower court that the right to a jury trial in such cases was "'too obvious to be doubted,'"[72] the Court also noted the wide range of cases in which the Court, without extended discussion, had "found the Seventh Amendment applicable to causes of action based on statutes."[73] Seeing no reason to overrule this long and unanimous line of authority, the Court therefore held that, "[t]he Seventh Amendment does apply to actions enforcing statutory rights, and requires a jury trial upon demand, if the statute creates legal rights and remedies, enforceable in an action for damages in the ordinary courts of law."[74] Because Title VIII provided for money damages, and the plaintiff sought those money damages in an ordinary federal district court, either party could demand a jury trial.[75]

Despite its apparent mere recapitulation of existing authority, *Curtis* is interesting on two counts. First, the holding limits the right to jury trial for statutory actions to those cases tried in the ordinary courts. This leaves untouched the authority of administrative agencies to adjudicate matters without a jury. I will discuss this issue in more detail in the next section. Second, while the Court's approach in *Curtis* was not as systematic as it would later become, the germ of its two-step approach is present. The Court in *Curtis* focused on the remedy, which is the second factor listed in the *Ross* footnote. But the Court also took a brief look—confined largely to a footnote—at analogous common-law actions, finding that the right to non-discrimination in housing was similar to "the common-law duty of innkeepers not to refuse temporary lodging to a traveler without justification," or to an action for "defamation or intentional infliction of mental distress," both of which were cogniz-

---

69. 415 U.S. 189 (1974).
70. Section 812 of Civil Right Act of 1968, 82 Stat. 88, 42 U.S.C. §3612.
71. 415 U.S. at 193.
72. 415 U.S. at 193, quoting Rogers v. Loether, 467 F.2d 1110, 1114 (1972).
73. *Id. See id.* at 193–94 for the Court's list of such cases.
74. *Id.* at 198.
75. *Id.* at 192. The plaintiff did not seek a jury trial in *Curtis,* but the defendant did. This is probably because the plaintiff feared that racial bias on the jury might result in her losing her case, and preferred to leave her case in the hands of the judge. *See id.* at 198.

able in common law courts.[76] The Court, however, was not explicit about the two step process that was soon to become part of its jurisprudence.

The two-step process first became explicit in *Tull v. United States*.[77] There, the question was whether a party was entitled to a jury trial on the liability and amount of a civil penalty under the Clean Water Act.[78] The Court, noting that its task was to determine whether the "statutory action is more similar to cases that were tried in courts of law than to suits tried in courts of equity or admiralty,"[79] set out the two steps it had to take to answer the question. The Court's first step was to "compare the statutory action to 18th-century actions brought in the courts of England prior to the merger of courts of law and equity."[80] The second step was to "examine the remedy sought and determine whether it is legal or equitable in nature."[81] Taking the first step, the Court found persuasive analogies in both law and equity. English common law courts had characterized suits seeking civil penalties as "a particular species of an action in debt that was within the jurisdiction of the courts of law."[82] On the other hand, the action brought by the government in *Tull* also closely resembled two varieties of an equitable action to abate a public nuisance.[83] The Court then concluded that both were appropriate analogies and proceeded to the second step—determining the nature of the remedy—which the Court said was more important than the historical analog anyway.[84]

As for the remedy, the Court asserted that, "[a] civil penalty was a type of remedy at common law that could only be enforced in courts of law."[85] The

---

76. 415 U.S. at 192 n.10. This look at historic analogies to pre-merger actions in law and equity was not new in *Curtis*. The process was cited as settled in *Ross v. Bernhard*, 396 U.S. at 543n.1 (Stewart, J., dissenting) (citing authority). *See also*, Luria v. United States, 231 U.S. 9 (1913). *See generally*, James, *supra* note 66.

77. 481 U.S. 412 (1987).

78. *Id.* at 414.

79. *Id.* at 417.

80. *Id.*

81. *Id.* at 417–18.

82. *Id.* at 418, citing Atcheson v. Everitt, 1 Cowper 382, 98 Eng. Rep. 1142 (K.B. 1776); Calcraft v. Gibbs, 5 T.R. 19, 101 Eng. Rep. 11 (K.B. 1792). Neither of these cases concerned a penalty that was sought by the government; rather, both were suits between private parties under quasi-criminal laws.

83. Tull, 481 U.S. at 417–421.

84. *Id.* at 420–21. The Court cited *Curtis v. Loether*, 415 U.S. at 196, for the proposition that the nature of the remedy was more important than the historical analog. Tull, 481 U.S. at 421. Recall that in *Curtis*, the Court's discussion of the historical analog was confined to a footnote, and that the Court spent most of its time on the remedy.

85. *Id.* at 422.

Court, however, did not cite any English authority for this proposition, but relied on *Curtis v. Loether*, where the Court had said that punitive damages was a legal remedy, and *Ross v. Bernhard*, where the Court had characterized the "treble-damages remedy for securities violation" as "a penalty" constituting "legal relief."[86] The Court found that the penalties sought and imposed in *Tull* were legal rather than equitable in nature because they were designed for "retribution and deterrence" rather than equitable "restitution," given that at least some of the fines were unrelated to the amount of profit the violator had earned.[87] Thus, a jury was required to determine the party's liability for penalties under the Clean Water Act.[88] The Court then rejected arguments for equity jurisdiction based on the clean-up doctrine,[89] finding that the legal relief—substantial monetary penalties—could not be characterized as incidental to any equitable relief sought.[90] All of this goes only to the right to a jury trial to determine liablity for a civil penalty. The Court next held that the determination of the *amount* of the civil penalty was a discretionary decision delegated to judges by Congress, and thus could be done without a jury because discretion is inherent in courts of equity.[91] In doing so, it cited authority saying that the Seventh Amendment preserves only the " 'most fundamental elements' " of the jury trial,[92] and found that "determination of a civil penalty is not an essential function of a jury trial."[93] This decision, which has since been

---

86. *Id.* The origins of punitive damages are somewhat obscure, but the concept is a recent development, appearing in English cases in the middle of the eighteenth century. *See* Wilkes v. Wood, 95 Eng. Rep. 766 (1763); Huckle v. Money, 95 Eng. Rep. 768 (1763) (approving "exemplary damages" for the first time); James B. Sales & Kenneth B. Cole, Jr., *Punitive Damages: A Relic That Has Outlived Its Origins*, 37 Vand. L. Rev. 1117, 1120 (1984). Punitive damages, which are awarded in private litigation to punish particularly egregious conduct, are not quite the same as civil penalties sought by the government. *See* Feltner v. Columbia Pictures Television, Inc., 523 U.S. 340, 354–55 (1998).

87. *Id.* The equitable remedy of restitution sought to restore the plaintiff to the position she would have been in had the violation not occurred. *See* 1 Dobbs, *supra* note 4, at §4.1(1). For example, if someone has lost pay because of a discriminatory failure to promote her, providing her with the backpay that she lost would constitute restitution. *See* Curtis, 415 U.S. at 196; Chauffers, Teamsters and Helpers, Local No. 391 v. Terry, 494 U.S. 558, 571 (1990).

88. *See* Tull, 481 U.S. 412, 425 (1987).

89. The government had sought injunctive relief as well as the civil penalties. *See id.* at 414.

90. *Id.* at 424–25.

91. *Id.* at 427.

92. *Id.* at 426, quoting Galloway v. United States, 319 U.S. 372, 392 (1943).

93. *Id.* at 427. In some rather sweeping language, the Court says that the Seventh Amendment "is silent on the question whether a jury must determine the remedy in a trial

limited to civil penalties payable to the government, also reflects the idea expressed in *Ross* that the Seventh Amendment applies to issues in a case and not to the case as a whole.[94]

The Court in *Tull* rejected an argument by the Government that "both the cause of action and the remedy must be legal in nature before the Seventh Amendment right to a jury trial attaches."[95] Rather, the Court said, "[o]ur search is for a single historical analog, taking into consideration the nature of the cause of action and the remedy as two important factors."[96] The difficulty of this task is apparent in *Tull* itself, but three years later the approach sundered the Court in a decision that generated four separate opinions. In *Chauffers, Teamsters and Helpers, Local No. 391 v. Terry*, a Union member sued the Union for breach of the duty of fair representation.[97] To determine whether the Seventh Amendment required a jury trial for such an action, the Court again went through the two-step process, first searching for analogous actions in law or equity, and then looking at the remedy sought. Significantly, however, at least four of the Justices took issue with various parts of the two-step process. Four Justices found that the action against the Union for breach of its duty of fair rep-

---

in which it must determine liability." *Id.* at 425–26. In a footnote to this statement, the Court says,"[w]e have been presented with no evidence that the Framers meant to extend the right to a jury to the remedy phase of a civil trial." *Id.* at 426n.9. Nevertheless, the Court's holding seems limited to the civil penalty remedy. Given the long history of juries deciding on legal remedies such as money damages, it would be difficult to argue that determining legal remedies other than civil penalties is not a "fundamental element" of the right to a jury trial. *See id.* at 427–28 (Scalia, J., concurring in part and dissenting in part). Scalia, who disagreed with the Court's division of responsibilities, referred to the determination of liability by a jury and of the penalty by the judge as unprecedented. *Id.* at 428. If the Court's approach were to be more generally applied, it would constitute a serious attack on the powers of the jury.

94. *See* Ross v. Bernhard, 396 U.S. 531, 537–38 (1970). The relevant passage is quoted *supra*, at note 58. The Court held that statutory punitive damages payable to a party rather than the government are to be decided by the jury in *Feltner v. Columbia Pictures Television, Inc.*, 523 U.S. 340 (1998).

95. *Id.* at 421 n.6.

96. *Id.* at 422 n.6.

97. 494 U.S. 558, 561 (1990). "The duty of fair representation is inferred from unions' exclusive authority under the National Labor Relations Act (NLRA), 49 Stat. 449, 29 U.S.C. § 159(a) (1982 ed.), to represent all employees in a bargaining unit. *Vaca v. Sipes*, 386 U.S. 171, 177 (1967). The duty requires a union 'to serve the interests of all members without hostility or discrimination toward any, to exercise its discretion with complete good faith and honesty, and to avoid arbitrary conduct.'" *Terry*, 494 U.S. at 563, quoting *Vaca v. Sipes*, 386 U.S. at 177.

resentation was analogous to an equitable action for breach of a trustee's fiduciary duty, but that there was a legal issue embedded in that otherwise equitable action.[98] That legal issue was whether the employer had breached the collective bargaining agreement—an ordinary contract—because such a breach was a prerequisite to an action for breach of the union's duty of fair representation.[99] Thus, these Justices' analysis of the historical analog left them "in equipoise as to whether respondents are entitled to a jury trial."[100] They then turned to the second step and found that the remedy was for the Union to pay backpay to the employee, which they characterized as a legal remedy.[101] While backpay is an equitable remedy when it is seen as restitutionary—as giving the employee what he should have had if the employer had been acting legally—it is equitable only when the backpay is to be paid by the person who should have paid it in the first place; here, that is the employer, which was bankrupt at the time of the suit.[102] Backpay paid by the union was more akin to legal damages, because it compensates the employee for damages suffered because of the union's failure to hold the employer to its contract. Therefore, a jury was required.[103]

Justice Brennan agreed that a jury was required, but he suggested that the Court abandon the first step altogether.[104] The Court, he argued, "has repeatedly discounted the significance of the analogous form of action for deciding where the Seventh Amendment applies."[105] The search for a historical analog was, he thought, an impossible and unnecessary task.[106] He proposed basing the decision solely on whether the relief would have been available, his-

---

98. 494 U.S. at 565–70. Justice Marshall wrote the opinion for this group, which also included Chief Justice Rehnquist and Justices White and Blackmun. It was the Opinion of the Court on all except the portion relating to the historical analogue.

99. *Id.* at 568.

100. *Id.* at 570.

101. *Id.*

102. *Id.* at 563.

103. *Id.* at 572.

104. *Id.* at 574 (Brennan, J., concurring in part and concurring in the judgment).

105. *Id.*

106. Justice Brennan's view is borne out to some extent by the very case he is deciding. The parties had suggested three analogies for the duty of fair representation claim, two of which had precedent in the Supreme Court. The Court noted that it had once found the fair representation claim to be analogous to an equitable action to vacate an arbitration award. *Id.* at 566, citing United Parcel Service, Inc. v. Mitchell, 451 U.S. 56 (1981). But the Court also conceded that it had once "noted in dictum that an attorney malpractice action—a legal action—is 'the closest state-law analogy for the claim against the union.'" *Id.* at 568, citing DelCostello v. Teamsters, 462 U.S. 151 (1983). The Court in *Terry* rejected both of these analogies in favor of the breach of fiduciary duty.

torically, from a common law court, and agreed with the opinion of the Court that this relief was legal.

Justice Stevens also agreed that a jury trial was required, but he thought that the best historical analog was the legal malpractice action, which would have been brought in a common law court.[107] He also argued that duty of fair representation issues "require an understanding of the realities of employment relationships" and "are typical grist for the jury's judgment."[108] Because such cases are "ordinary civil actions involving the stuff of contract and malpractice disputes," there is "no ground for excluding these actions from the jury right."[109]

Finally, Justice Kennedy, in dissent, seemed to prefer a return to a more historical law/equity structure. He argued that the analogy to the trust was appropriate, and that the analogy alone should determine the right to a jury trial.[110] He suggested that if the analogous case would have been heard in equity prior to the merger, no jury would have been available to consider either liability or damages. In coming to this conclusion, he considered the relief generally available in a breach of duty of fair representation case rather than the relief actually requested in this case, and found it to be equitable in nature.[111] Because he viewed the analogy as wholly equitable, he thought it unnecessary to consider cases where legal and equitable issues were joined.[112] In particular, he thought it insignificant that breach of the collective bargaining agreement by the employer was an element of a breach of duty of fair representation claim, as he thought the issue was the overall character of the claim and not its constituent elements.[113]

The various opinions in *Terry* demonstrate considerable disagreement on the Court about how to handle statutory actions with both legal and equitable characteristics. Nevertheless, despite the dissent in *Terry*, it seems that the nature of the remedy is the more important inquiry when such issues arise. The Court has never found that the historical analogy resolves the issue, and has explicitly said that the remedy is the more important factor.

---

107. *Id.* at 581–84 (Stevens, J., concurring in part and concurring in the judgment). There was Supreme Court precedent for this position. *See supra*, note 106.

108. *Id.* at 583.

109. *Id.* Justice Marshall characterized Justice Stevens's argument as more appropriate to the public rights debate. *Id.* at 565n.4.

110. *Id.* at 584 (Kennedy, J., dissenting). Justice Kennedy was joined in his dissent by Justices O'Connor and Scalia.

111. *Id.* at 587. *Terry* was peculiar in that the employer, who normally would have paid the backpay as restitution, was bankrupt and had been dropped from the suit.

112. *Id.* at 589–92.

113. *Id.* at 590–91.

The Court has addressed other Seventh Amendment issues recently, but the basic approach outlined here appears to be intact. In *Markman v. Westview Instruments, Inc.*,[114] the Court held that, though patent infringement actions would have been tried to a jury in England in 1791, the judge is to decide the meaning of claims in the patent. The Court's reasoning was (1) that English practice in 1791 was that the interpretation of documents was a question of law for the court; (2) that Supreme Court precedent suggested that patent specifications, the precursor of patent claims, had been interpreted by judges since at least the nineteenth century; (3) that judges were more capable than juries of deciding the meaning of the specialized terms found in patents; and (4) that uniformity would be better served by having judges decide the meaning of patent claims.[115] *Markman* was, essentially, an elaborate example of the law/fact distinction.[116]

Three years later, the Court in *City of Monterey v. Del Monte Dunes at Monterey, Ltd.*,[117] the Court held that an action brought under 42 U.S.C. § 1983, the basic civil rights statute, is essentially a tort action even when it challenges compensation for a regulatory taking, though a just compensation issue would normally be tried to a judge.[118] The Court split 4–4 on whether the nature of the underlying claim should be considered in deciding whether there is a right to a jury trial in a § 1983 action. Because one justice found a statutory right to a jury trial, the jury's verdict was upheld. This case turns largely on the nature and function of a § 1983 action, so it may have little significance outside of that context, though it is significant for the many § 1983 actions heard in the courts every year.

B. Summary

There are two ways in which the Supreme Court's Seventh Amendment jurisprudence on new statutory actions expands the right to a jury trial. First is the Court's decision—first made early in the country's history and left virtually unchallenged since—to extend the jury trial to actions created by statute

---

114. 517 U.S. 370 (1996).

115. *See id.* at 376–91.

116. The Court said that it did not need to decide whether post-1791 decisions classifying an issue as one of fact would trigger the protections of the Seventh Amendment in the absence of a more specific reason for the decision. *Id.* at 384 n.10. For discussions of the law/fact distinction, see Chapter 2, *supra*, at notes 97–103 and accompanying text; Chapter 7, *infra*, at notes 2–9 and accompanying text.

117. 526 U.S. 687 (1999).

118. *See id.* at 708–18; 42 U.S.C. § 1983 (1994).

and unknown to the common law. The Court could very well have interpreted the Seventh Amendment to include only those actions created by the common law and in existence in 1791. Any further development of the right to jury trial would then have to come by statute.[119] The Court's acceptance of the right to jury trial in new statutory actions expands the right to jury trial every time a new statutory action, creating legal rights and remedies and enforceable in the federal courts, is created.

The second way in which the Court's Seventh Amendment jurisprudence expands the right to a jury trial is similar to the way the right expanded into previously equitable actions after the merger of law and equity. The expansion here is somewhat more difficult to see than in those cases that dealt explicitly with common law or equitable actions because analogies are never exact. But, just as ignoring the form and focusing on the remedy meant that a jury was available in shareholder's derivative suits after the merger where it would not have been before,[120] ignoring the form—the analogy to the equitable breach of a trustee's fiduciary duty, for example—may have made a jury trial available for an action that, had it existed in the eighteenth century, would not have had one. Even in areas where there appears to be a common law analogy as to both form and remedy, such as *Tull*, there often is an equitable analogy as well, meaning that at least some analogous cases probably would have been brought in equity without a jury in eighteenth century England. But the Supreme Court's decisions mandate a jury in all such cases.[121] So far, then, it appears that the Supreme Court's Seventh Amendment jurisprudence has resulted in an expansion of the right to jury trial over what it was in England in 1791.

III. Legislative Courts and the Seventh Amendment[122]

In Chapter 3, I described the rise of administrative agencies as one factor that significantly alters the atmosphere in which the jury operates.[123] I noted

---

119. For an argument in favor of this approach, *see* Redish, *supra* note 61.

120. *See* Ross v. Berhnard, 396 U.S. 531 (1970).

121. Given the decision to base the right to jury trial on eighteenth century analogies, this is probably the right approach. If a jury may have been available, the Court should err on the side of the jury to preserve it as required by the Constitution.

122. I have published a much expanded version of this section as an article. *See* Sward, *supra* note 1.

123. *See supra*, Chapter 3, at notes 145–171 and accompanying text.

there that the rationale for administrative agencies is inconsistent with the jury. But administrative agencies can only operate without a jury if the courts decide that the Seventh Amendment does not require that agencies use juries. That is precisely what has happened. What is more, there are other so-called "legislative courts" where the right to a jury trial may be compromised. These include the adjunct magistrate judges and the bankruptcy courts, which are non-Article III judges operating under the general supervision of Article III judges; courts that handle claims against the United States, such as the United States Court of Federal Claims; and territorial courts, which handle local matters in the United States territories. The result is a vast array of civil adjudication that takes place in specialized tribunals, many of which operate without a jury.

A. Administrative Agencies

Administrative agencies are a breed of "legislative" or "non-Article III" courts. That means that they are not created in accordance with Article III, which requires that judges exercising the judicial power of the United States have life tenure and salary protection.[124] Rather, they are created under Congress's Article I authority to make all laws necessary and proper to execution of the powers of the United States.[125] The Court has developed an elaborate but highly confusing justification for Congress's having created such administrative agencies, and then has asserted that the same justification allows trials in administrative agencies to be without a jury. I have criticized that approach elsewhere;[126] in this section I wish to demonstrate its effect on the right to a jury trial. I should note that one complicating factor is that some of the case law concerns bankruptcy courts, which are properly defined as adjuncts rather than administrative agencies.[127]

---

124. *See* U.S. CONST., art. III, sec. 1. This section provides:
The judicial power of the United States, shall be vested in one Supreme Court, and in such inferior Courts as the Congress may from time to time ordain and establish. The Judges, both of the supreme and inferior Courts, shall hold their offices during good Behaviour, and shall, at stated times, receive for their Services a Compensation, which shall not be diminished during their Continuance in Office.
125. *See id.* at art. I, sec. 8, cl. 18.
126. *See* Sward, *supra* note 1, at 1099–1114.
127. For an argument that adjudication before adjuncts should be easier to justify than adjudication before agencies, notwithstanding the case law that seems to go the other way, *see* Sward, *supra* note 1, at 1084–88.

1. Justifying Non-Article III Adjudication

To understand the problems with non-Article III adjudication, it is first necessary to understand the values behind Article III, the judicial article of the Constitution. I begin this section with a brief description of those values, which are quite different from the Seventh Amendment values I articulated in Chapter 1. I then trace how the Supreme Court developed first the public rights doctrine and then the balancing test to justify adjudication in the most prominent of the non-Article III courts, the administrative agencies.

a. Article III Values: Separation of Powers and Judicial Independence

One of this country's founding principles is that the executive, legislative, and judicial powers should be vested in separate entities.[128] This structure stems from a belief among the founders that concentration of all three functions of government in the same hands leads to tyranny.[129] Strict separation of powers, however, is unattainable and may be undesirable because the efficiency costs would be too great. Thus, a better characterization of the constitutional structure is probably "checks and balances," though we tend to use the term "separation of powers." A system of checks and balances tolerates some overlap of function, but provides many ways for each branch to check

---

128. THE FEDERALIST PAPERS, No. 47 (Madison) & No. 51 (Madison) (Isaac Kramnitz ed., 1987). *See generally,* Paul R. Verkuil, *Separation of Powers, the Rule of Law and the Idea of Independence,* 30 WM. & MARY L. REV. 301 (1989); Malcolm P. Sharp, *The Classical American Doctrine of "The Separation of Powers,"* 2 U. CHI. L. REV. 385 (1935); 10 THE PAPERS OF THOMAS JEFFERSON 272, 603 (Julian P. Boyd, ed. 1954); W. B. GWYN, THE MEANING OF THE SEPARATION OF POWERS (1965). For critiques of the separation of powers doctrine under modern American government, see Philip B. Kurland, *The Rise and Fall of the "Doctrine" of Separation of Powers,* 85 MICH. L. REV. 592 (1986); Peter L. Strauss, *The Place of Agencies in Government: Separation of Powers and the Fourth Branch,* 84 COLUM. L. REV. 573 (1984); JAMES O. FREEDMAN, CRISIS AND LEGITIMACY 15–20 (1978). The current Supreme Court seems bent on reviving a stricter and more formalistic ideal of separation of powers. *See, e.g.,* Plaut v. Spendthrift Farms, Inc., 514 U.S. 211 (1995). *See generally,* Autumn Fox and Stephen R. McAllister, *An Eagle Soaring: The Jurisprudence of Justice Antonin Scalia,* 19 CAMPBELL L. REV. 223, 260 (1997); Comment, *The Supreme Court, 1994 Term,* 109 HARV. L. REV. 10, 229 (1995).

129. *See* THE FEDERALIST PAPERS, *supra* note 128, at No. 47 (Madison) ("The accumulation of all power, legislative, executive, and judiciary, in the same hands, whether of one, a few, or many, and whether hereditary, self-appointed, or elective, may justly be pronounced the very definition of tyranny.").

the others.[130] The most important judicial check on the political branches of government is the power of judicial review.[131] The life tenure and salary protections help to reinforce this structure. Judges who need not fear removal from office or loss of salary from opposing the political branches are more likely to be willing to exercise that important power of judicial review. While there has always been some overlap of function among the three branches in the federal government,[132] the Supreme Court has generally tried to monitor encroachments by one branch of government on the others, and to prevent those that are unacceptable.[133]

The judicial independence that results from separation of powers is an *institutional* value—it benefits all of us equally to know that the courts cannot be manipulated by the political branches, even if we never use the courts ourselves. But individual litigants also have a *personal* interest in judicial independence that the life tenure and salary protections help to preserve.[134] An independent judiciary helps to guarantee a fair and impartial assessment of litigants' cases, unaffected by the political pressures of the day.[135] In particular, persons pressing unpopular positions should have a greater confidence that their positions will receive a fair hearing if the judge cannot lose her job or have her salary reduced for siding with them.

b. Origins of the Public Rights Doctrine

The public rights doctrine was originally founded on the notion that if Congress can, consistent with the Constitution, allow the executive or legislative branch to resolve a particular dispute between the government and a private citizen, there is no bar to its giving such dispute for resolution to a body that

---

130. *See* Geoffrey R. Stone, *et al.*, Constitutional Law 387–88 (3rd ed. 1996) (distinguishing between description of federal structure as separation of powers, which suggests autonomous branches, and description as checks and balances, which suggests overlap). *See also*, Forrest McDonald, Novus Ordo Seclorum 258 (1985) (separation of powers had been abandoned in favor of checks and balances by the framers of the Constitution); Isaac Kramrick, *Introduction*, in The Federalist Papers, *supra* note 128, at 51–52.

131. *See* The Federalist Papers, *supra* note 128, at No. 80 (Hamilton); Marbury v. Madison, 5 U.S. (1 Cranch) 137 (1803) (asserting the power of judicial review).

132. *See* Verkuil, *supra* note 128, at 322.

133. *Id.* at 311.

134. Apart from the separation of powers, there might also be a due process right to an independent judiciary. *See* Wiener v. United States, 357 U.S. 349, 355–56 (1958).

135. *See* Commodities Futures Trading Commission v. Schor, 478 U.S. 833, 848, 850–51 (1986) (noting that the tenure and salary provisions of Article III reflect both a structural interest in separation of powers and a personal interest in an independent judiciary). I am suggesting that separation of powers is both an end in itself and a means to achieving an independent judiciary. The latter has both institutional and individual aspects.

looks like a court but does not have the protections required by Article III. There is a historical basis for the view that some matters are inherently "public" and can be resolved by the political branches. At the time of this country's founding, litigation between a citizen and the sovereign, aside from criminal matters, was rare. Citizens could not sue the government because of the doctrine of sovereign immunity,[136] and the government regulation that existed was handled outside the judicial process by the political branches.[137] Disputes between citizens and the government in its proprietary capacity, such as contract disputes, were sometimes handled in the common law courts if the government brought suit,[138] but such claims both by and against the government were often handled in summary proceedings conducted by government auditors.[139]

Because of this background, early Congresses thought nothing of giving executive departments the authority to perform adjudicatory acts with respect to such governmental matters.[140] The power of Congress to confer such adjudicatory authority apparently received no serious challenge until the middle of the nineteenth century.

The public rights doctrine began with *Murray's Lessee*, et al. *v. Hoboken Land and Improvement Co.*[141] That 1855 decision resolved an Article III challenge to an adjudication by the Treasury Department of amounts due from a collector

---

136. For a discussion of sovereign immunity, *see infra,* notes 229–242 and accompanying text.

137. English and early American legal theorists did not consider government administration to relate to "law" at all. *See, e.g.,* FRANK J. GOODNOW, THE PRINCIPLES OF THE ADMINISTRATIVE LAW OF THE UNITED STATES 1–15 (1905); FREEDMAN, *supra* note 128, at 259. Maitland, in a series of lectures in 1887–88, hesitantly refers to English administrative "law," but says it had only developed in the previous fifty years or so. *See* F.W. MAITLAND, THE CONSTITUTIONAL HISTORY OF ENGLAND 505 (1908). There was, however, more regulation than many modern opponents of regulation care to admit. *See Affirmative Government and the American Economy,* in ARTHUR M. SCHLESINGER, CYCLES OF AMERICAN HISTORY 220–56 (1986).

138. *See* United States v. Cooper Corp., 312 U.S. 600, 604 (1941) (suit by United States in its proprietary capacity is a suit at common law); Cotton v. United States, 52 U.S. (1 How.) 229, 231 (1850) (same); United States v. Dugan, 16 U.S. (3 Wheat.) 172, 181 (1818) (same).

139. *See* Murray's Lessee, 59 U.S. at 283. The government's debtors were often collectors of the revenue who had failed to pay to the government the taxes or other revenues that they had collected. Such debts have a public character.

140. *See* 1 KENNETH CULP DAVIS AND RICHARD J. PIERCE, JR., ADMINISTRATIVE LAW TREATISE, § 1.4 (3d ed. 1994); Richard H. Fallon, Jr., *Of Legislative Courts, Administrative Agencies, and Article III,* 101 HARV. L. REV. 915, 919 (1988).

141. 59 U.S. (18 How.) 272 (1855). *See, e.g.,* Gordon G. Young, *Public Rights and the Federal Judicial Power: From* Murray's Lessee *Through* Crowell *to* Schor, 35 BUFF. L. REV. 765, 769, 795 (1986).

of the customs.[142] The Court, citing established practice in England and some of the states,[143] held that such an adjudication did not fall inherently within the judicial power of Article III.[144] Rather, the Court thought that it was a political matter properly assigned to one of the political branches of government. The Court was persuaded in part by the fact that the United States was a party and in part by the fact that the debt sought to be enforced was a "public" debt, owed by a public servant to the government and encompassing money he had collected in connection with his public duties.[145] The Court said,

---

142. Murray's Lessee, 59 U.S. at 275. Authority for the Treasury Department's adjudication of such cases was granted in the First Congress. *See* Fallon, *supra* note 140, at 919.

143. Murray's Lessee, 59 U.S. at 276–80.

144. *Id.* at 281. The Court did say that Congress could give such adjudications to the courts, however. *See id.* It seems clear that the judicial power extends to public as well as private rights matters. *See* Martin H. Redish and Daniel J. LaFave, *Seventh Amendment Right to Jury Trial in Non-Article III Proceedings: A Study in Dysfunctional Constitutional Theory*, 4 Wm. & Mary Bill of Rts. J. 407, 418 (1995) (arguing that the term "suits" in Article III encompasses administrative disputes). Nonetheless, it has been held that the traditional core of the federal judicial power is private disputes. *See* Northern Pipeline Constr. Co. v. Marathon Pipe Line Co., 458 U.S. 50, 68–70 and n.25 (1982) (plurality opinion). Indeed, in the past the Court has suggested that at least some public rights matters may not even be cognizable in an Article III court because they do not fall within the judicial power of the United States. *See* Williams v. United States, 289 U.S. 553, 578 (1933) (interpreting the constitutional grant of jurisdiction over controversies to which the United States is a party to mean controversies to which the United States is a party plaintiff); *cf.* American Ins. Co. V. Canter, 26 U.S. (1Pet.) 522, 546 (1828) (saying that territorial courts are "incapable of receiving" jurisdiction over cases falling within the Article III judicial power). That position has been abandoned, however, in part because it is inconsistent with the language of Article III. *See* Glidden Co. v. Zdanok, 370 U.S. 530, 550–51(1962). The judicial power includes "Controversies to which the United States shall be a Party" and "Cases, in Law and Equity, arising under the Constitution, [and] the Laws of the United States," U.S. Const. art. III, §2, cl. 1, so public rights cases do fall within the literal language of the Constitution. Indeed, if this were not the case, Article III courts would not be able to review public rights matters decided initially in the administrative agencies. *See* Glidden, 370 U.S. at 545 n.13; Fallon, *supra* note 140, at 943–46.

145. Murray's Lessee, 59 U.S. at 283. The Court suggested that ordinary contract actions between the government and a private citizen could also be seen as public rights. *See id.* at 283. The government, however, was free to sue for breach of contract in the ordinary common law courts. That the citizen could not bring suit against the government in a common law court was due to sovereign immunity, and not the public character of the debt. For an argument that the holding in Murray's Lessee should be limited to the specific facts at issue—recovery of funds from defaulting tax collectors—see Roger W. Kirst, *Administrative Penalties and the Civil Jury: The Supreme Court's Assault on the Seventh Amendment*, 126 U. Pa. L. Rev. 1281, 1300–01 (1978).

> [T]here are matters, involving public rights, which may be presented
> in such a form that the judicial power is capable of acting on them,
> and which are susceptible of judicial determination, but which con-
> gress may or may not bring within the cognizance of the courts of the
> United States, as it may deem proper.[146]

In other words, Congress has the power to assign the adjudication of public
rights to non-Article III bodies if it chooses. Congress is still free, however, to
assign adjudication of public rights to the Article III courts.[147] This is consistent with the historical treatment of such rights as described in *Murray's
Lessee*.[148]

In *Murray's Lessee*, the Court used the term "public rights" without providing much of a definition. In a sort of negative definition, the Court suggested
that public rights do not involve cases falling within the common law, equity,
or admiralty jurisdiction, which would concern private rights.[149] Common law,
equity, and admiralty all usually involved disputes between two or more private parties;[150] in *Murray's Lessee*, the government was a party to the dispute.

The Court apparently did not attempt a definition of both public and private rights until *Crowell v. Benson*,[151] almost eighty years later; in that case, the
presence of the government as a party became a more explicit way to distinguish public from private rights.[152] The Court in *Crowell* said that private
rights concern "the liability of one individual to another under the law as de-

---

146. *Id.* at 284.

147. *Id.* at 283. *See also*, U.S. CONST., art. III, sec. 2, cl. 1 (the federal judicial power
extends to "Controversies to which the United States shall be a Party"). In *Murray's Lessee*
itself, government auditors had determined the amount due from the customs collector
and the Court approved of that adjudication as a "public" right. But the suit came before
the Supreme Court because the collector challenged that administrative determination in
an Article III court, relying on Congress's limited waiver of sovereign immunity for that
purpose. Murray's Lessee, 59 U.S. at 284. The waiver did not allow the court to re-deter-
mine the debt found by the government auditors, however. *Id.* at 284–85.

148. *See id.* at 283.

149. *Id. See* Young, *supra* note 141, at 793–94.

150. *But see* note 144, *supra*.

151. 285 U.S. 22 (1932).

152. I have argued elsewhere that there should be four categories of rights: public rights,
which are based on regulatory statutes that the government seeks to enforce as a party;
quasi-public rights, which are based on regulatory statutes but are enforced by private litigation; replacement rights, which are based on regulatory statutes that replace common
law or equitable rights; and private rights, which are based on the common law and involve private parties, or, perhaps, governments acting in their proprietary capacity. *See*
Sward, *supra* note 1, at 1073–83.

fined;"[153] public rights were "those which arise between the Government and persons subject to its authority in connection with the performance of the constitutional functions of the executive or legislative departments."[154] Thus, the presence of the government as a party was an inherent part of the definition of "public rights." But by 1982, when *Northern Pipeline Construction Co. v. Marathon Pipe Line Co.*[155] was decided, a mere plurality of the Court approved of the *Crowell* definitions of public and private rights. Thus, the stage was set for the development of the balancing test.

c. Recent Developments in the Justification for Agency Adjudication: The Balancing Test

Both *Crowell* and *Northern Pipeline* contained the germs of this new way of justifying administrative agency adjudication. In *Crowell*, the Court approved of agency adjudication of federal worker's compensation claims under the Longshoremen's and Harbor Workers' Compensation Act.[156] Claims brought under the Act were claims by workers against their employers—two private parties. Congress had replaced the workers' rights against their employers under admiralty law with the administrative remedy provided by the Act.[157] The Court approved of the administrative remedy, holding that there was no unconstitutional encroachment on the Article III powers of the judiciary because the agency had to enforce its orders in an Article III court.[158] In addition, the Court required that the Article III court review constitutional and jurisdictional facts *de novo*.[159] Indeed, the Court viewed the agency as an adjunct fact-finder, analogizing it to the jury.[160] Thus, while clearly defining pub-

---

153. Crowell, 285 U.S. at 51.

154. *Id.* at 50. It is not clear whether this definition would include proprietary matters. *Crowell* itself involved a regulatory matter.

155. 458 U.S. 50 (1982).

156. *See* Crowell, 285 U.S. at 42–65.

157. *Id.* at 39–40.

158. *Id.* at 45. Voluntary compliance with the Commission's payment orders could be expected in many cases, however, so federal enforcement was likely to be needed only when there was some dispute over the Commission's resolution of the matter. *Id.* at 43–44.

159. *Id.* at 54. De novo review does not defer to the lower tribunal's decision. The appellate court can decide the issue without considering how the trial court decided it. *See* STEVEN ALAN CHILDRESS AND MARTHA S. DAVIS, STANDARDS OF REVIEW § 2.14 (1986). Other standards of review, such as abuse of discretion, are more deferential to the trial court's decision. *See id.* at § 4.1.

160. *See* Crowell, 285 U.S. at 51. It should be clear that the jury has a quite different constitutional position than does an administrative agency: the jury is constitutionally re-

lic rights as including only matters where the government was a party, the Court permitted non-Article III adjudication of an administrative remedy between two private parties, as long as the essential judicial functions of enforcement and jurisdictional and constitutional fact-finding remained with the Article III court.[161]

Northern Pipeline, which concerned the adjunct bankruptcy courts rather than an administrative agency, was a more complicated decision. The plurality found that Congress's grant of jurisdiction to the bankruptcy courts was unconstitutional because it gave the non-Article III bankruptcy courts jurisdiction that was virtually coterminous with that of an Article III court.[162] That included jurisdiction over private common law claims. Justice Rehnquist, joined by Justice O'Connor, concurred, providing the votes for a finding of unconstitutionality. Justice Rehnquist asserted that it was unnecessary to hold the bankruptcy courts generally unconstitutional when the only problem before the Court was the exercise of jurisdiction over a common law claim.[163] He thought that a non-Article III court could not exercise jurisdiction over a common law claim, but would not go so far as to strike down Congress's entire jurisdictional scheme.[164] Nonetheless, because the jurisdiction over common law claims was so enmeshed in the bankruptcy courts' otherwise constitutional jurisdiction, Justice Rehnquist agreed that Congress needed to reconstitute the courts' jurisdiction.[165]

---

quired under some circumstances, while the administrative agency is entirely a discretionary creation of Congress. In my schemata, I distinguish between agencies and adjuncts. *See infra*, note 210 and accompanying text; Sward, *supra* note 1, at 1044–46.

161. The jurisdictional fact doctrine, which required *de novo* review of findings related to the agency's jurisdiction—such as a finding that an applicant for benefits was injured in connection with his employment—appears to have disappeared. *See* RICHARD J. PIERCE, ET AL., ADMINISTRATIVE LAW AND PROCESS (2nd ed. 1992); 5 KENNETH CULP DAVIS, ADMINISTRATIVE LAW TREATISE § 29:23 (2d ed. 1984). The same is largely true of constitutional facts, *see id.*, except that courts still engage in non-deferential review of "constitutional" facts relating to First Amendment issues. *See, e.g.,* Bose Corp. v. Consumers Union of the U.S., 466 U.S. 485, 508–09n. 27 (1984); Time, Inc. v. Pape, 401 U.S. 279 (1971); New York Times Co.v. Sullivan, 376 U.S. 254 (1964). *See generally,* Henry P. Monaghan, *Constitutional Fact Review*, 85 COLUM. L. REV. 229 (1985).

The Seventh Amendment did not pose a problem in *Crowell* because the remedy that the federal statute replaced was a claim in admiralty, where there was historically no right to a jury trial. Crowell, 285 U.S. at 45.

162. *See* Northern Pipeline, 458 U.S. at 87. Justice Brennan wrote the plurality opinion and was joined by Justices Blackmun, Marshall, and Stevens.

163. *Id.* at 89–92 (Rehnquist, J., concurring).

164. *Id.* at 91–92 (Rehnquist, J., concurring).

165. *Id.* at 92.

It is the dissent in *Northern Pipeline* that is most important, however. Justice White did an exhaustive analysis of the Court's past approvals of non-Article III adjudication and argued that the only way to make sense of them was to view them as balancing Article III values against the reasons that led Congress to create a non-Article III body to adjudicate the particular matter before it.[166] Justice White thought that the balance in Northern Pipeline favored the jurisdictional grant that Congress had made.[167]

Justice White's dissent formed the basis for a new majority that began to come together just three years after *Northern Pipeline*. In *Thomas v. Union Carbide Agricultural Products Co.*,[168] the Court upheld a mandatory arbitration provision in the Federal Insecticide, Fungicide and Rodenticide Act (FIFRA).[169] Arbitration, which would be non-Article III adjudication,[170] was required when a second manufacturer wanted to make use of data submitted by an earlier manufacturer and the two manufacturers could not agree on the amount of money that the second manufacturer had to pay the first for the use of the data.[171] In contrast to the relatively searching review of the matters at issue in *Crowell*, judicial review of the arbitrators' award was limited to claims of fraud, misrepresentation, and other misconduct.[172]

The Court approved of this mandatory arbitration, relying on two distinct grounds. First, the Court devised an expanded definition of "public rights." Although the claim was one between private parties and so appeared to concern only private rights under *Crowell* and the *Northern Pipeline* plurality, the Court found that it had the characteristics of a public right because (1) it was created by Congress, and (2) it was invested with a public,

---

166. *Id.* at 92–118 (White, J., dissenting). Justice White was joined by Justices Burger and Powell. Justice Burger also filed a separate dissent to point out that the Court's holding was reflected in the Rehnquist opinion.

167. *Id.* at 116–17 (White, J., dissenting) (balance favored jurisdictional grant because, among other things, there was Article III review of the bankruptcy court decisions, the jurisdictional grant was not a political power grab, and the reasons for the grant were compelling).

168. 473 U.S. 568 (1985).

169. *Id.* at 594. *See* 7 U.S.C. §§ 136 *et seq.* (1994).

170. Arbitration is often undertaken voluntarily by the parties as an alternative to judicial dispute resolution. *See* 1 EDWARD A. DAUER, MANUAL OF DISPUTE RESOLUTION: ADR LAW AND PRACTICE § 2.02 (1994); Dwight Golann, *Making Alternative Dispute Resolution Mandatory: The Constitutional Issues*, 68 ORE. L. REV. 487, 488–91 (1989). When arbitration is mandatory, however, it replaces Article III adjudication and should be viewed as non-Article III adjudication.

171. *Thomas*, 473 U.S. at 573.

172. *Id.* at 573–74.

rather than private, purpose in that the ability of "follow-on registrants" of the pesticide to make use of data submitted by earlier registrants "serves a public purpose as an integral part of a program safeguarding the public health."[173] Thus, rights could be "public" even if they involved claims between private parties as long as they were created by the legislature rather than the common law, and were an integral part of a scheme designed to promote public health and safety.

There was also a second ground for the decision, however. In words reminiscent of Justice White's dissent in *Northern Pipeline*, the Court in *Thomas* considered Article III requirements in light of "the origin of the rights at issue [and] the concerns guiding the selection by Congress of the particular method for resolving disputes."[174] In *Thomas*, the Court found it significant that Congress had created the rights being adjudicated, so that those rights did not fall "within the range of matters reserved to Article III courts."[175] In addition, Congress was searching for a "pragmatic solution to the difficult problem of spreading the costs of generating adequate information regarding the safety, health, and environmental impact of a potentially dangerous product."[176] These factors outweighed any need to preserve what had to be a minimal Article III interest: because the rights at issue could have been determined by Congress or the executive, there is little encroachment on the Article III judiciary.

The Court in *Thomas* apparently had not decided whether to stay with a public rights rationale or adopt the balancing test first articulated by Justice White in *Northern Pipeline*. But a year after *Thomas*, the balancing test got a more explicit articulation in *Commodities Futures Trading Corporation v. Schor*.[177] *Schor* was an Article III challenge to the CFTC's power to hear a com-

---

173. *Id.* at 589.

174. Thomas, 473 U.S. at 587. *See generally,* Young, *supra* note 141, at 853–56; Fallon, *supra* note 140, at 930; Note, Richard M. Thomas, *Formalism and Functionalism: From* Northern Pipeline *to* Thomas v. Union Carbide Agricultural Products Co., 37 SYRACUSE L. REV. 1003 (1986). As Justice White argued in his *Northern Pipeline* dissent, balancing had always been at least an implicit part of the analysis when Congress set up non-Article III courts. *See* Northern Pipeline, 458 U.S. at 92–118 (White, J., dissenting); Ralph U. Whitten, *Consent, Caseload, and other Justifications for Non-Article III Courts and Judges: A Comment on* Commodities Futures Trading commission v. Schor, 20 CREIGHTON L. REV. 11, 12–19 (1986). The balancing test seemed to become more explicit in *Thomas*, however.

175. Thomas, 473 U.S. 587 (contrasting *Crowell,* which adjudicated rights that replaced existing common law rights).

176. Thomas, 473 U.S. at 590.

177. 478 U.S. 833 (1986).

mon law counterclaim to a regulatory dispute that was within its jurisdiction. Like *Northern Pipeline*, *Schor* thus involved a purely private right. But unlike the Court in *Northern Pipeline*, the Court in *Schor* upheld non-Article III adjudication of that right.

Congress had authorized the CFTC to hear claims by traders against brokers that arose under the Commodity Exchange Act in order to provide an expeditious and inexpensive alternative to litigation, though litigation in an Article III court remained open.[178] The CFTC then adopted a rule allowing the agency to hear counterclaims by the brokers against the traders if the counterclaims arose out of the same transaction or occurrence, such as a counterclaim for the debt owed to the brokers; such counterclaims would be compulsory in the federal courts.[179] The question was whether the CFTC's hearing such counterclaims comported with Article III.[180] The Court identified a number of "factors" that it said helped it decide whether non-Article III adjudication was permitted:

> Among the factors upon which we have focused are the extent to which the "essential attributes of judicial power" are reserved to Article III courts, and, conversely, the extent to which the non-Article III forum exercises the range of jurisdiction and powers normally vested only in Article III courts, the origin and importance of the right to be adjudicated, and the concerns that drove Congress to depart from the requirements of Article III.[181]

Applying these factors, the Court found that (1) while the right being adjudicated in the counterclaim was clearly a private right with its source in the common law; (2) the encroachment on the judicial branch was minimal because the power of the agency was quite limited, especially as the parties had to go to an Article III court for enforcement of the agency's orders; and (3) Congress's intent to provide an expeditious and inexpensive alternative to litigation would be thwarted if the brokers could not assert counterclaims in the CFTC proceeding, because the desire for a single forum to resolve the entire dispute would drive the parties into courts.[182]

There are at least two ways to look at these developments. One is that there are now two distinct tests for administrative adjudication: the public rights

---

178. *Id.* at 836.
179. *Id.* at 837; 17 C.F.R. § 12.19 (1997). *See also* FED. R. CIV. P. 13(a).
180. The Court first had found that the CFTC had the statutory power to promulgate such a rule. Schor, 478 U.S. at 842–43. The rule is found at 17 C.F.R. § 12.19 (1996).
181. Schor, 478 U.S. at 851.
182. *Id.* at 848–56.

doctrine, which allows administrative adjudication of public rights, and the balancing test, which must be applied if non-public rights are at issue. Under this view, the balancing test supplements the public rights doctrine. A second way to look at these developments is that the balancing test has supplanted the public rights doctrine altogether, so that all administrative adjudications are tested by its methods.

2. The Public Rights/Balancing Test and the Seventh Amendment

In the cases discussed so far, the Seventh Amendment usually was not explicitly at issue. But because agencies operate without juries, we must ask whether jury-less administrative adjudication comports with the Seventh Amendment. The short answer is yes. Over the years, the Court has upheld jury-less adjudication in administrative agencies on a variety of theories. Within the last twenty years, however, the Court has settled on the public rights/balancing test as the way to justify such adjudication.[183] In this section, I will describe the evolution of the Court's Seventh Amendment jurisprudence as it relates to administrative agencies. Once again, one of the most significant cases involved an adjunct bankruptcy court rather than an agency.

For much of the twentieth century, the Court upheld jury-less adjudication in administrative agencies whenever the issue appeared, but the rationale was hard to pin down. Sometimes, the Court simply assumed that the Seventh Amendment was inapplicable when administrative adjudication was within Congress's power.[184] Another time, the Court said that fact-finding by the National Labor Relations Board did not involve a suit at common law at all, but rather was a "statutory proceeding."[185] Still later, the Court seemed to recognize that jury trials may be incompatible with agency adjudication, which is founded on expert rather than amateur decision-making.[186] The Court had also

---

183. This approach has been criticized. See Kirst, *supra* note 145.

184. *See* Block v. Hirsh, 256 U.S. 135, 158 (1921). In *Block*, the Court upheld Congress's power to establish, temporarily in wartime, a commission to determine fair rents in the District of Columbia. The commission's adjudication of rents replaced landlords' common law actions of ejectment. *See id.* at 153–54.

185. National Labor Relations Board v. Jones & Laughlin Steel Corp., 301 U.S. 1, 48–49 (1937). This rationale is undermined by *Curtis v. Loether*, 415 U.S. 189 (1974), which said that the Seventh Amendment does apply to statutory actions. *Jones & Laughlin*, however, could also be justified under the public rights doctrine.

186. Pernell v. Southall Realty, 416 U.S. 363, 383 (1974) (discussing *Block v. Hirsh*, 256 U.S. 135 (1921)). *See* LOUIS L. JAFFE, JUDICIAL CONTROL OF ADMINISTRATIVE ACTION 90 (1965) (stating that "the concept of expertise on which the administrative agency rests is not consistent with the use by it of a jury as fact finder").

upheld jury-less adjudication in bankruptcy courts by deciding that bankruptcy courts were courts of equity, and that one who had filed a claim against a bankrupt's estate had transformed her claim from a legal one to an equitable one.[187] These analyses are either unsatisfactory or too narrow to be of general use.

In 1977, the Court finally brought these cases together under the rubric of the public rights doctrine in *Atlas Roofing Co. v. Occupational Safety and Health Review Commission*.[188] *Atlas Roofing* was a challenge, on Seventh Amendment grounds, to a fine assessed by the Occupational Safety and Health Review Commission.[189] In *Atlas Roofing*, the Court held that Congress had the power "to create new public rights and remedies by statute and commit their enforcement, if it chose, to a tribunal other than a court of law—such as an administrative agency—in which facts are not found by juries."[190] The Court's language suggests that it thought that the right to jury trial attaches only in Article III courts.[191]

Atlas Roofing, however, must have seemed to be a relatively easy case. It concerned adjudication of a pure public right by an administrative agency. Historically, pure public rights would not have been heard by juries because they would not have been in the courts at all.[192] Since *Atlas Roofing*, however, the Court has applied the public rights doctrine to bankruptcy courts,[193] developed the balancing test,[194] and held that civil penalties like the one at issue in *Atlas Roofing* concern legal rights and remedies.[195] The question is how these

---

187. Katchen v. Landy, 382 U.S. 323 (1966).

188. 430 U.S. 442 (1977). For a critical analysis of Atlas Roofing, see Kirst, *supra* note 145.

189. *See* Atlas Roofing, 430 U.S. at 447–48. The petitioners in Atlas Roofing were each fined for working conditions that had resulted in an employee's death. *See id.* at 447. One petitioner was fined $7500 for willful violation of a safety standard. *See id.* The other was fined $600 for a serious violation of a safety standard. *See id.* Both petitioners were ordered to abate the hazard immediately. *See id.*

190. *Id.* at 460.

191. The Court clearly thought that it was simply following long-standing law, even though the public rights doctrine was a new way of justifying it. *See* Atlas Roofing, 430 U.S. at 450–56, 460 (citing cases).

192. *See supra*, notes 136–139 and accompanying text.

193. *See* Northern Pipeline, 458 U.S. 50 (1982). The Court in *Northern Pipeline* found that only private rights were at stake in that case. It is not clear what the Court would have done if it had found public rights at stake.

194. *See* Thomas v. Union Carbide, 473 U.S.568 (1985); Commodities Futures Trading Commission v. Schor, 478 U.S. 833 (1986); *see also, supra*, notes 156–182 and accompanying text (describing development of the balancing test).

195. *See* Tull v. United States, 481 U.S. 412 (1987).

developments affect the analysis of the right to a jury trial in administrative agencies and bankruptcy courts. The Court istself has suggested that the analysis is exactly the same whether the issue is Article III or the Seventh Amendment. In *Granfinanciera, S.A. v. Nordberg,* the Court said,

> if a statutory cause of action is legal in nature, the question whether the Seventh Amendment permits Congress to assign its adjudication to a tribunal that does not employ juries as factfinders requires the same answer as the question whether Article III allows Congress to assign adjudication of that cause of action to a non-Article III tribunal.... [I]f Congress may assign the adjudication of a statutory cause of action to a non-Article III tribunal, then the Seventh Amendment poses no independent bar to the adjudication of that action by a non-jury factfinder.[196]

The outcome of *Granfinanciera,* however belies this language. *Granfinanciera,* which was decided after the Court had developed the balancing test to assess non-Article III adjudication, was a Seventh Amendment challenge to jury-less adjudication of a *private* right in a *bankruptcy court.* The Court there required a jury trial for a claim by a bankruptcy trustee against a third party to whom estate property allegedly had been fraudulently transferred.[197] The third party had not filed a claim in the bankruptcy proceedings.[198] In reaching its conclusion, the Court first applied the two-part test developed in *Curtis, Tull,* and *Terry,* and found (1) that a fraudulent conveyance action was one that would have been tried to a jury prior to the merger of law and equity, and (2) that the relief sought was legal—money damages.[199] Thus, the action involved legal rights and remedies, but it was not assigned for adjudication to an Article III court.

The Court then considered whether Congress had "permissibly withdrawn jurisdiction over that action by courts of law and assigned it exclusively to non-Article III tribunals sitting without juries."[200] Specifically, the Court said that "[t]he sole issue before us is whether the Seventh Amendment confers on

---

196. 492 U.S. 33, 53–54 (1989).

197. *See id.* at 64.

198. *See id.* This makes *Granfinanciera* consistent with *Katchen,* 382 U.S. 323. The third party in *Granfinanciera* had not filed a claim in the estate, while the third party in *Katchen* had. *See* Granfinanciera, 492 U.S. at 58; Katchen, 382 U.S. at 325. *See also,* Langenkamp v. Culp, 498 U.S. 42, 44–45 (1990) (holding, after *Granfinanciera,* that one who files a claim in bankruptcy waives the right to a jury trial).

199. Granfinanciera, 492 U.S. at 42–49.

200. *Id.* at 49.

petitioners a right to a jury trial in the face of Congress' decision to allow a non-Article III tribunal to adjudicate the claims against them."[201] The answer to this question, the Court thought, depended on whether the legal rights at issue were public or private.

Acknowledging that its conclusion was open to debate, the Court nonetheless found that only private rights were at stake in *Granfinanciera*.[202] The Court apparently found the point debatable because under *Thomas*, Congress could permit non-Article III adjudication of matters between two private parties if the matters were "closely intertwined with a federal regulatory program,"[203] and bankruptcy was arguably a federal regulatory program. But the fraudulent conveyance action in *Granfinanciera* was a private right because it (1) was a dispute between two private parties, (2) that had passed into the bankruptcy context virtually unaltered from its common law roots,[204] and (3) that had not

---

201. *Id.* at 50. The very statement of the issue is odd, given that the Court ultimately said that the Article III and Seventh Amendment analyses are the same. *See* text at note 196, *supra*. If a jury is required, and if the Seventh Amendment and Article III require the same analysis, it would seem that an Article III court is required as well. *See* Redish and LaFave, *supra* note 144, at 431. The Court, however, ultimately concluded that the Seventh Amendment required a jury in the case before it without deciding whether Article III requires a judge with life tenure and salary protections in that case. The Court explicitly said it was not considering the question whether bankruptcy courts could conduct jury trials. Granfinanciera, 492 U.S. at 64. That issue remained open, and generated considerable commentary and a variety of proposals for judicial or legislative action. *See, e.g., Symposium on Jury Trials in Bankruptcy Courts*, 65 AM. BANKR. L.J. 1 (1991); Ned W. Waxman, *Jury Trials After Granfinanciera: Three Proposals for Reform*, 52 OHIO ST. L.J. 705 (1991); Anthony Michael Sabino, Esq., *Jury Trials, Bankruptcy Judges, and Article III: The Constitutional Crisis of the Bankruptcy Court*, 21 SETON HALL L. REV. 258 (1991); Robert G. Skelton & Donald F. Harris, *Bankruptcy Jurisdiction and Jury Trials: The Constitutional Nightmare Continues*, 8 BANKR. DEVS. J. 469 (1991). Congress has since authorized bankruptcy judges to preside over jury trials, but only if the district court has designated the judge to conduct such trials and the parties all expressly consent. *See* 28 U.S.C.A. § 157(e) (Supp. 1995). This is similar to the power of magistrates to conduct jury trials with the consent of the parties. *See* 28 U.S.C. § 636(c) (1994); S. Elizabeth Gibson, *Jury Trials in Bankruptcy: Obeying the Commands of Article III and the Seventh Amendment*, 72 MINN. L. REV. 967, 1045 (1988).

202. *See* Granfinanciera, 492 U.S. at 50, 55. The Court is never very clear about the reasons for its decision, and there were a total of four opinions in the case. The opinion of the Court was by Justice Brennan. Justice Scalia concurred in part and dissented in part, and Justices White and Blackmun each dissented. Justice O'Connor joined Justice Blackmun's dissent.

203. *Id.* at 54.

204. Fraudulent conveyance actions can be brought under either of two provisions in the Bankruptcy Code. The Code itself establishes an action for fraudulent conveyance. *See*

been transformed into an equitable action because the transferee had not filed a claim in the bankruptcy.[205] In other words, the fraudulent conveyance action in *Granfinanciera* could not, on any theory, be called a public right.[206] Thus, a jury was required.

Granfinanciera muddies both the Article III and the Seventh Amendment waters to a considerable degree. This can be seen by comparing the outcome in *Granfinanciera* to that in *Schor*. In both *Schor* and *Granfinanciera*, the issue at stake was a pure private right. Yet the Court allowed non-Article III adjudication of the private right in *Schor*, but did not allow jury-less adjudication of the private right in *Granfinanciera*.[207] This is so even though the Court in *Granfinanciera* asserted that the Article III and Seventh Amendment analyses are the same. There are at least three possible ways to account for these different outcomes. First, the Article III and Seventh Amendment analyses are in fact different, and the Court is more solicitous of the Seventh Amendment than of Article III. There are several problems with this. The first is that it is not what the Court plainly said in *Granfinanciera*.[208] Second, *Granfinanciera* seems consistent with *Northern Pipeline*, which refused to allow a non-Article III court to hear a pure private rights matter.[209] This gives some credence to *Granfinanciera*'s statement that the Article III and Seventh Amendment analyses are the same. *Schor*, however, then remains inconsistent with the cases and the doctrine. Finally, if the considerations are different for Article III and the Seventh Amendment, the Court, having held that they are not different, has given us no hint as to how to analyze those differences.

A second possible explanation for the different outcomes in *Schor* and *Granfinanciera* is that *Schor* involved an administrative agency and *Granfinanciera* an adjunct. This would also account for the outcome in *Northern*

11 U.S.C. §548 (1994). In addition, the bankruptcy trustee may recover fraudulently conveyed property under state law using 11 U.S.C. §544(b) (1994).

205. Granfinanciera, 492 U.S. at 57–58.

206. Because the party to whom the property had been conveyed had not filed a claim in bankruptcy, waiver is not a justification for jury-less non-Article III adjudication either. *See infra*, notes 262–267 and accompanying text for a discussion of waiver.

207. Had the issue arisen, the Court might have found that the customer in *Schor* had waived his right to a jury trial by bringing his claim against the broker in the agency where no jury functioned rather than in an Article III court.

208. *See* text at note 196, *supra*.

209. *See* Northern Pipeline, 458 U.S. at 50–51. The Article III issue was not argued before the Supreme Court in *Granfinanciera*, so the absence of a decision on the matter is not determinative. *See* Petitioner's Brief, Granfinanciera, S.A. v. Nordberg, 492 U.S. 33 (1989) (No. 87-1716).

Pipeline, which, like *Granfinanciera,* involved the adjunct bankruptcy courts. This explanation would mean that the Court is more likely to allow jury-less non-Article III adjudication of pure private rights in an administrative agency than in an adjunct. With regard to the Seventh Amendment, the logic of this could be that if adjuncts are subsidiaries of Article III courts, the right to a jury trial attaches to matters involving legal rights and remedies because they are somehow "really" in an Article III court. The logic fails with respect to the Article III issues, however, because it would suggest that the Court should be less concerned about adjuncts hearing pure private rights matters than administrative agencies, but the cases go the other way.[210] This explanation would, however, account for the Court's statement that the Article III and Seventh Amendment analyses are the same. A major problem with this explanation is that the Court has given no hint that it even considered the difference in the kind of non-Article III court that was used. And, once again, if this difference is signficant, the Court has not told us why or how to analyze the issues.

A third possible explanation is that the party objecting to the mode of adjudication—whether the objection was to the non-Article III status of the court or to the lack of a jury—was voluntarily before a non-Article III court in *Schor,* but was an involuntary defendant in both *Granfinanciera* and *Northern Pipeline.* This, however, sounds more like waiver.[211] And because the Court held in *Schor* that a party cannot waive the institutional interest in the separation of powers reflected in Article III,[212] it cannot really be said that the plaintiff in *Schor* had properly waived his interest in an Article III court by bringing his claim in an administrative agency. In other words, it did not matter that the plaintiff in *Schor* was in the administrative agency voluntarily. Neither the plaintiff in *Schor* nor the defendant in *Granfinanciera* had properly waived any objection to the mode of adjudication.

3. Summary and Conclusion

Parts I and II of this Chapter show that the Court has interpreted the Seventh Amendment broadly in light of procedural changes and the growth in statute-based substantive law. On the other hand, applying the public rights

---

210. *Compare* Northern Pipeline, 458 U.S. at 84 (adjunct cannot hear pure private right), with Schor, 478 U.S. at 857 (agency can hear private right if balance favors it). If an adjunct is "really" an Article III court, then the balancing test should find much less of an encroachment on Article III values when an adjunct is used than when an agency is used.

211. *See infra,* notes 262–267 and accompanying text.

212. *See* Schor, 478 U.S. at 851.

doctrine or the balancing test to the question whether there is a right to a civil jury trial in non-Article III courts is a way of restricting the Seventh Amendment right to jury trial. Given that there are approximately 340,000 administrative adjudications every year compared to 240,000 in the federal courts,[213] this means that a substantial number of civil adjudications are not subject to the Seventh Amendment. Many of those adjudications involve matters that would carry a Seventh Amendment right to a jury trial if they were adjudicated in an Article III court because the Court has said that claims brought in federal courts that are based on statutes are subject to the Seventh Amendment, including civil penalties sought by the government.[214] But the Court permits Congress to assign those very same claims to administrative agencies that do not use juries. The Court, in other words, has given with one hand and taken away with the other.

The problem is compounded by the fact that the balancing test that the Court uses to assess whether agency adjudication comports with Article III and (apparently) the Seventh Amendment does not articulate or weigh any Seventh Amendment values. Indeed, the Court's language in *Granfinanciera* suggests that the Seventh Amendment analysis is entirely derivative of the Article III analysis. The values of community sentiment and of political participation, for example, are not even considered and rejected—they are ignored altogether. And review of agency action by an Article III court, which may help to preserve Article III values, does nothing whatever to preserve Seventh Amendment values.[215]

B. Other Non-Article III Courts

There are a variety of other non-Article III courts, and the Seventh Amendment is at risk in some of them. Non-Article III courts include adjuncts, courts established to handle claims against the government, and territorial courts.[216] The justifications for allowing jury-less adjudication in these courts varies by the type of court.

---

213. *See supra*, Chapter 3, at notes 146–150 and accompanying text.

214. *See* Curtis v. Loether, 415 U.S. 189 (1974); Tull v. United States, 481 U.S. 412 (1987).

215. I expand on these ideas in Sward, *supra* note 1, at 1105–08.

216. Military courts are another breed of non-Article III courts, but they do not handle civil matters, so I will not discuss them here. *See* Sward, *supra* note 1, at 1049 for brief discussions of military courts.

1. Adjuncts

Adjuncts include magistrate judges[217] and bankruptcy courts.[218] Both magistrate judges and bankruptcy courts function within the Article III district courts and are under the general supervision of district court judges. They operate under a reference from the district court, which can withdraw that reference at any time.[219] Although both are considered adjuncts, the Supreme Court has treated magistrates and bankruptcy courts differently for Article III purposes, applying the public rights doctrine or the balancing test to bankruptcy courts[220] but not, so far, to magistrate judges. Rather, the Court has approved some adjudication before magistrate judges, who do not operate within separate courts, on the ground that they are merely a part of and subsidiary to the federal district courts.[221] This difference in the Article III

---

217. *See* 28 U.S.C. §§ 631 *et seq.* (1994).

218. *See* 28 U.S.C. § 151 (1994).

219. *See, e.g.,* 28 U.S.C. § 157(a) (1994) (allowing district courts to refer matters to bankruptcy courts); 28 U.S.C. § 631 (1994) (describing powers and duties of magistrates and the power of judges to refer matters to magistrates). *See generally,* Linda Silberman, *Judicial Adjuncts Revisited: The Proliferation of Ad Hoc Procedure,* 137 U. PA. L. REV. 2131 (1989) (examining modern judicial adjuncts under the Federal Rules of Civil Procedure). Many district courts make blanket references of certain matters to magistrates, and of all bankruptcy matters to the district's bankruptcy court. *See, e.g.,* S.D. FLA. R. 87.2 referring all bankruptcy cases to the bankruptcy courts); S.D. FLA. MAJ. R. 1 (describing the authority of magistrate judges); D. OR. R. 2100–1 (referring all bankruptcy cases to the bankruptcy courts); D. OR. R. 72.1 (describing the authority of magistrate judges).

220. *See* Granfinanciera, S.A. v. Nordberg, 492 U.S. 33, 53–54 (1989).

221. *Id.* at 55 n.10. While magistrate judges take part in cases brought originally in an Article III court and follow the Article III court's rules, bankruptcy judges operate within a separate court. They have their own rules, separate from the Federal Rules of Civil Procedure, and cases can sometimes be commenced directly in bankruptcy courts. *See* FED. R. BANKR. P. 1002. Some districts will have a bankruptcy clerk, and in those districts, cases can be commenced by filing a petition with the bankruptcy clerk. Otherwise, cases must be filed with the district court's clerk. *See id.,* adv. comm. notes (1987 amendments). The bankruptcy courts have a wide-ranging jurisdiction over matters both central to and related to bankruptcies, including the power to enter final judgments. *See* 28 U.S.C. § 157 (1994). They also have considerable independent procedural authority, including the power to conduct trials, *see* 28 U.S.C. § 157(e) (1994), though they remain nominally under the district courts' control. By contrast, magistrate judges operate within the existing district courts, assisting the district judges by managing discovery, hearing pretrial motions, and, if the parties consent, conducting trials. *See, e.g.,* D. COLO. R. 72.2–72.6 (describing the functions of magistrate judges); D. WASH. MAJ. R. 1–13 (same). They follow the same Federal Rules of Civil Procedure that the district judges follow, *see* 28 U.S.C. § 636(a) (1994), though their powers are more restricted than those of district judges. Magistrate judges can

treatment has implications for the Seventh Amendment right to jury trial as well.[222]

Both magistrate judges and bankruptcy judges can conduct jury trials, but only with the consent of the parties;[223] without that consent, the jury trial must be held before a district court judge. But because, under *Granfinanciera*, the parties in a bankruptcy court apparently have a Seventh Amendment right to a jury trial only when pure private rights are at stake,[224] the parties to a bankruptcy proceeding will have fewer opportunities to opt for a jury trial than will litigants in the district courts. In the district courts, public as well as private rights are subject to the Seventh Amendment if the matter concerns legal rights and remedies.[225] In other words, although both magistrate judges and bankruptcy courts are adjuncts and therefore a part of the federal district courts, bankruptcy courts are treated more like administrative agencies than magistrate judges are, and the right to jury trial in bankruptcy courts is correspondingly restricted in bankruptcy courts, but not with respect to magistrates.[226]

One additional justification for jury-less adjudication in bankruptcy courts has also been part of the Supreme Court's jurisprudence. The Court held in *Katchen v. Landy* that when a creditor files a claim with the bankruptcy court,

---

decide "non-dispositive" matters themselves, with only deferential review by the district court. *Id.* at §636(b)(1). They can hear and make recommendations as to dispositive matters, such as summary judgment motions, but the district court must make a *de novo* determination of the matter. *Id.* The Court has held that the district court is not required to conduct a *de novo hearing*. *See* United States v. Raddatz, 447 U.S. 667, 674 (1980). The parties can also consent to a magistrate judge's hearing and deciding dispositive matters. *See id.* at 636(c). Because of these differences, it is easy to see bankruptcy courts as more akin to administrative agencies than to magistrate judges.

222. *See* Raddatz, 447 U.S. at 681.

223. *See* 28 U.S.C. §636(c)(1) (1994) (magistrate judges); 28 U.S.C. §157(e) (1994) (bankruptcy judges).

224. See Owensboro Distilling Co. v. Inter-Trade, Inc., 108 B.R. 572, 574 (1989); G. Eric Brunstad, et. al., *Review of Proposals of the National Bankruptcy Review Commission Pertaining to Business Bankruptcies: Part I*, 53 Bus. Law. 1381, 1439 (1998).

225. *See* Curtis v. Loether, 415 U.S. 189, 194 (1974); Tull v. United States, 481 U.S. 412, 417 (1987).

226. As I have demonstrated, pure private rights can be heard in administrative agencies without a jury under some circumstances. *See supra*, notes 177–182 and accompanying text; Commodities Futures Trading Commission v. Schor, 478 U.S. 833 (1986). Thus, the analogy is not exact, as the Court in *Granfinanciera* required a jury for pure private rights in bankruptcy courts. These holdings are, perhaps, illustrative of the confusion in the Court's Seventh Amendment jurisprudence.

the creditor's legal claim is transformed into an equitable claim for his share of the estate, and that therefore neither the creditor nor the estate has a right to a jury trial as to any claims that the estate might have against the creditor.[227] *Katchen* is apparently still good law despite *Granfinanciera*, as the creditor in *Granfinanciera*, who was held entitled to a jury trial, had not filed a claim in the bankruptcy.[228] Thus, a wide range of matters that would have been subject to the Seventh Amendment in an ordinary federal court in the absence of bankruptcy are determined in the bankruptcy courts without a jury.

2. Courts for Claims Against the Government

Congress has also established some courts that adjudicate claims against the government. These include the Tax Court, which adjudicates claims by taxpayers who dispute deficiency determinations by the Internal Revenue Service;[229] and the United States Court of Federal Claims, which adjudicates a variety of proprietary claims against the United States, such as contract claims.[230] These courts have judges who are appointed for fixed terms,[231] and they operate without juries.[232]

The Supreme Court has held these courts to be constitutional on sovereign immunity grounds: because the sovereign cannot be sued without its consent, the sovereign may give consent but attach conditions.[233] These courts reflect

---

227. *See* Katchen v. Landy, 382 U.S. 323, 338 (1966).

228. *See* Langenkamp v. Culp, 498 U.S. 42, 44–45 (1990).

229. *See* 26 U.S.C. §7441 (1994). *See generally*, HAROLD DUBROFF, THE UNITED STATES TAX COURT: AN HISTORICAL ANALYSIS 395–493 (1979); 15 STAND. FED. TAX REP. (CCH) ¶42, 758 (1996).

230. *See* 28 U.S.C. §1491 (1994). Regulatory matters are those that the government engages in because of its sovereign authority. Proprietary matters are those that the government engages in because it, like any private entity, must contract for services, etc. Proprietary matters are such things as torts, contracts, and leases. *See generally*, 17 CHARLES ALAN WRIGHT, ARTHUR R. MILLER AND EDWARD H. COOPER, FEDERAL PRACTICE AND PROCEDURE, §4101 (1988).

231. *See, e.g.*, 28 U.S.C. §172(a) (1994) (15 year terms for judges in the Court of Federal Claims).

232. *See* United States v. Sherwood, 312 U.S. 584, 587 (1941).

233. *See* McElrath v. United States, 102 U.S. 426, 440 (1880). Although there is no explicit basis for sovereign immunity with respect to the federal government in the United States Constitution, sovereign immunity was invoked early in the country's history through judicial action. *See* Rebecca Heintz, *Sovereign Immunity and Clean Water: A Supreme Misstep*, 24 ENVTL. L.J. 263, 267 (1994). The doctrine had "become so 'entrenched' in the decisions of American courts that by mid-nineteenth century the rule had attained the 'immutability of a maxim.'" THEODORE R. GIUTTARI, THE AMERICAN LAW OF SOVEREIGN

two separate conditions: that the case be heard in a non-Article III court by judges without the tenure and salary protections provided by Article III, and that the case be heard without a jury. At the same time, however, if the government in its proprietary capacity sues a private citizen, it must generally bring the suit in an Article III court, where a jury will be available if the government's claim concerns legal rights and remedies.[234]

The government, of course, can consent to be sued in ordinary federal courts or even state courts; it does not need to set up a specialized court to handle claims against it.[235] Even if the government consents to be sued in an existing Article III court, it can condition the suit on trial without a jury.[236] But the presence of a specialized court does make a difference. If the government sued a citizen in an Article III court and the citizen asserted a compulsory counterclaim, the rule apparently is that a jury trial would be available for the government's claim against the citizen, but not for the citizen's claim against the government.[237] But the specialized courts, which do not use juries,

---

IMMUNITY: AN ANALYSIS OF LEGAL INTERPRETATION 37 (1970). The only reference to sovereign immunity in the Constitution is the Eleventh Amendment, which was added to ensure the sovereign immunity of states. *See* Vicki C. Jackson, *The Supreme Court, the Eleventh Amendment, and State Sovereign Immunity*, 98 YALE L.J. 1, 3 (1988); Herbert Hovenkamp, *Judicial Restraint and Constitutional Federalism: The Supreme Court's Lopez and Seminole Tribe Decisions*, 96 COLUM. L. REV. 2213, 2240 (1996).

234. *See* 28 U.S.C. § 1345 (1994) (district courts have jurisdiction over claims by the United States). The Court has consistently held that suits by the government against a citizen are suits at common law. *See* United States v. Cooper Corp., 312 U.S. 600, 604 (1941); Cotton v. United States, 52 U.S. (11 How.) 229, 231 (1850); Dugan v. United States, 16 U.S. (3 Wheat.) 172, 181 (1818). The United States could also sue in state courts, which are not Article III courts, but it will choose to do so only on rare occasions. *See* United States v. Lee, 106 U.S. 198 (1882) (dicta); United States v. American Ditch Association, 2 F. Supp. 867, 868 (D. Idaho 1933) (dicta).

235. *See, e.g.,* Federal Tort Claims Act, 28 U.S.C. § 267 (1994); McCarran Amendment, 43 U.S.C. § 666 (1994). *Cf.* Kansas Tort Claims Act, KAN. STAT. ANN. § 75-6101 (1994) (state consent to suit).

236. *See* Lehman v. Nakshian, 453 U.S. 156, 160 (1981). The federal government has given a very wide-ranging consent to suit. *See* 14 CHARLES ALAN WRIGHT, ARTHUR R. MILLER AND EDWARD H. COOPER, FEDERAL PREACTICE AND PROCEDURE, § 3656 (1988). Nevertheless, as long as such consent is required, it is likely that the courts will uphold conditions that the government deems proper, including the condition that the suit be tried without a jury.

237. I say "apparently" because the Supreme Court has never decided the issue. The rule stated in the text is widely assumed to be correct, however. *See* United States v. Rosati, 97 F.R.D. 259, 261 (D.N.J. 1951); 8 MOORE, ET AL., *supra* note 26, at § 38.40(2)(d); 9 WRIGHT & MILLER, *supra* note 13, at § 2314.

have compulsory counterclaim rules, too.[238] Thus, if a citizen files suit against the government in the Court of Federal Claims, she will be met with any counterclaim the government has against her that arises out of the same transaction or occurrence as the government's claim against her, and she will not be able to litigate either her claim or the government's counterclaim with a jury.[239] The Court has never found this problematic. As the Court said in 1880 in *McElrath v. United States*:[240]

> Congress, by the act in question, informs the claimant that if he avails himself of the privilege of suing the government in the special court organized for that purpose, he may be met with a set-off, counterclaim, or other demand of the government, upon which judgment may go against him, without the intervention of a jury."[241]

Thus, under some circumstances, the citizen could lose her right to a jury trial for the government's claims against her solely because of the court in which the government's claim is adjudicated.[242]

3. Territorial Courts

There are three kinds of courts in United States Territories: non-Article III local courts, Article III federal courts, and non-Article III federal courts. *Non-Article III local courts* are usually established by Congress, or by territorial governments, with Congressional authorization, to adjudicate matters arising under local law; they are the territorial equivalent of the state courts.[243] Territories under the country's jurisdiction today include Puerto Rico, Guam, the United States Virgin Islands, and various Pacific island territories. The District of Columbia also has local courts, though Congress's authority to govern the

---

238. *See* 28 U.S.C. § 1503 (1994) (Court of Federal Claims); CL. CT. R. 13(a) (same).
239. McElrath, 102 U.S. at 440.
240. 102 S. Ct. 426 (1880).
241. *Id.* at 440. In the absence of the government's consent to be sued, the claimant would have to go to Congress and seek private legislation paying him for his claim. *See* Floyd D. Shimomura, *The History of Claims Against the United States: The Evolution From a Legislative Toward a Judicial Model of Payment*, 45 LA. L. REV. 625, 635 (1985). That procedure obviously gives the claimant neither an Article III court nor a jury. A non-Article III court seems an improvement on that procedure.
242. If the dearth of reported cases is any indication, however, the issue may not arise often. At the least, the private litigants do not seem to be pressing the issue.
243. *See, e.g.,* Guam, 48 U.S.C. § 1424-1 (1994), and the Virgin Islands, 48 U.S.C. § 1611(a) (1994). Congress is authorized to establish territorial governments under Article IV of the Constitution. *See* U.S. CONST., art. IV, § 3.

District of Columbia has a different source in the Constitution, and Congress itself, rather than a local government, established the local courts for the District of Columbia.[244]

Most of the territories also have federal courts of some kind. The United States district courts in Puerto Rico and the District of Columbia are created under *Article III*, so their judges have the tenure and salary protections of other Article III judges.[245] Some territories, however, including Guam and the Virgin Islands, have *non-Article III federal courts* that handle both local matters and matters within the judicial power of the United States.[246]

Whether there is a right to a jury trial in courts in the territories depends on what kind of court it is. There is a right to a jury trial in the Article III federal courts in the territories, which are not territorial courts.[247] On the other hand, It has been held that the Constitution does not require jury trials in the non-Article III federal courts in either criminal or civil cases.[248] The non-Article III federal district courts in those territories, however, are bound by procedures enacted by the local legislatures, and both Guam and the Virgin Islands have provided for jury trials.[249] The right to a jury trial in the local territorial courts depends on whether the territory is integrated into the United

244. *See* U.S. Const., art. IV, §3 (authorizing Congress to make law relative to the territories); U.S. Const. art. I, sec. 8, cl. 17 (authorizing Congress to make laws relative to the District of Columbia). *See* District of Columbia Court Reform and Criminal Procedures Act of 1970, Pub. L. No. 91-358, 84 Stat. 475, *codified at* D.C. Code §11-101 (1995) (creating local courts for the District of Columbia).

245. *See* 28 U.S.C. §88 (1994) (District of Columbia); 28 U.S.C. §119 (1994) (Puerto Rico). *See also,* Laforest v. Autoridad de Las Fuentes Fluviales de Puerto Rico, 536 F.2d 443, 446 (1st Cir. 1976) (saying that the U.S. District Court for the District of Puerto Rico was bound by the Seventh Amendment).

246. *See, e.g.,* 48 U.S.C. §1424(a) (1994) (Guam); 48 U.S.C. §1611(a) (1994) (Virgin Islands); 48 U.S.C. §1694 (1994) (Trust Territory of the Northern Mariana Islands). *See also,* Government of the Virgin Islands v. Bryan, 738 F.2d 946, 948 (D.V.I. 1990) (holding that U.S. District Court in the Virgin Islands is not an Article III court).

247. *See* Marshall v. Perez Arzuaga, 828 F.2d 845, 849 (1st Cir. 1987), cert. denied, 484 U.S. 1065 (1987).

248. *See* Balzac v. The People of Porto Rico, 258 U.S. 298 (1922) (criminal, Puerto Rico); Pugh v. United States, 212 F.2d 761 (9th Cir. 1954) (criminal, Guam); American Pacific Dairy Products v. Siciliano, 235 F.2d 74 (9th Cir. 1956) (civil, Guam). Since the decision in *Balzac,* the district court in Puerto Rico has been made an Article III court.

249. *See, e.g.,* 7 G.C.A. §22104 (1995) (Guam); 5 V.I.C. §321 (1994) (Virgin Islands). This reliance on local legislatures for the jury trial right makes sense if territorial courts are analogized to state courts, because the Seventh Amendment does not apply to state courts. 2 Ronald D. Rotunda, *et al.,*Treatise on Constitutional Law: Substance and Procedure §17.8 n.12 (1986).

States.[250] A non-integrated territory is one that had a well-developed legal system when the United States acquired it, such as Puerto Rico and the Philippines.[251] By contrast, the Court thought that integrated territories were simply territories that offered "opportunity for immigration and settlement by American citizens," who took the full rights of citizenship, including the right to a jury trial, with them into the newly settled territory.[252] Examples include Alaska and the Louisiana Territory.[253]

The rationale for the distinction between integrated and non-integrated territories is quite democratic:

> Congress has thought that a people like the Filipinos or the Porto Ricans, trained to a complete judicial system which knows no juries, living in compact and ancient communities, with definitely formed customs and political conceptions, should be permitted themselves to determine how far they wish to adopt this institution of Anglo-Saxon origin, and when.[254]

Thus, there is no right to a jury trial in non-integrated territories unless the citizens themselves choose one, and then it would exist by virtue of local law rather than the Seventh Amendment.

It appears that the only integrated territory in the United States today is the District of Columbia.[255] There is a Seventh Amendment right to a jury trial in the local courts in the District of Columbia,[256] but it is the only territory where

---

250. *See* Balzac v. People of Porto Rico, 258 U.S. 298, 304–05 (1922).

251. *See id.* at 304–10. Many laws relating to Puerto Rico suggested integration, but the Court rejected that implication in *Balzac. Id.* at 305–13.

252. *Id.* at 309.

253. This rationale completely ignores native populations. The American Indians who occupied the territories into which Americans so freely moved also had well-developed systems for dispute resolution, even if they looked different from the common law system. *See* JEROLD S. AUERBACH, JUSTICE WITHOUT LAW? 128 (1983); James W. Zion & Robert Yazzie, *Indigenous Law in North America in the Wake of the Conquest*, 20 B.C. INT'L & COMP. L.REV. 55, 69–71, 73–75 (1997).

254. *Id.* at 310.

255. In addition to the District of Columbia, American territories today include Puerto Rico, Guam, The United States Virgin Islands, the Northern Mariana Islands in the Pacific, and American Samoa. Statutes related to the territories are found in Title 48 of the United States Code.

256. *See, e.g.,* Pernell v. Southall Realty, 416 U.S. 363, 370 (1974); Capital Traction Company v. Hof, 174 U.S. 1, 5 (1899). This doctrine survived a reorganization of the District's courts that was designed to give the courts a structure similar to that of the states. *See* Pernell, 416 U.S. at 367. Prior to the reorganization, the District had courts with overlapping local and

that is so. Thus, for example, Puerto Rico has a civil law rather than a common law heritage, and its local courts do not use juries.[257] Most of the other territories have chosen, by statute, to use juries for at least some cases in their local courts.[258] Thus, the right to a jury trial in most modern territorial courts is statutory, not constitutional. But because there is usually a statutory right to a jury trial, there is very little litigation over the Seventh Amendment in those courts.

To summarize these principles, there is a constitutional right to a jury trial in all *Article III courts* in the territories. There is no constitutional right to a jury trial in the *local* courts of *non-integrated territories*, such as Puerto Rico, Guam, and the Virgin Islands, but there could be a statutory right. There is, however, a constitutional right to a jury trial in the *local* courts in *integrated* territories, such as the District of Columbia. There is no constitutional right to a jury trial in *non-Article III federal courts* in *non-integrated territories*, but those courts are bound by any local statutes conferring a right to a jury trial.

Whether or not these rules make sense,[259] they mean that persons who litigate in territories that do not have Article III courts have no Seventh Amendment right to a jury trial, whether they are citizens of the territory or of one of the states. This has not been problematic so far, because the right to a jury trial in territorial courts is generally provided by statute. On the other hand, persons litigating in the District of Columbia local courts have a Seventh Amendment right to a jury trial even though persons litigating in the other local territorial courts and in the state courts do not.[260]

---

federal jurisdiction similar to that of the so-called United States District Courts in Guam and the Virgin Islands. *See id.* The old structure, then, consisted of a single court system, in an integrated territory, having both local and Article III jurisdiction. It is understandable that a jury would be required in those courts: in the absence of a right to jury trial in those courts, citizens living in the territory would have no Seventh Amendment right in any court in the territory. Now, however, there is a local court system consisting of the Superior Court and the Court of Appeals, as well as trial and appellate Article III courts. That is much more like the state systems. The Court does not require juries in the state courts, and one wonders why they should be constitutionally required in the analogous courts in the District of Columbia.

257. *See* Marshall v. Perez Arzuaga, 828 F.2d 845, 849 (1st Cir. 1987), cert. denied, 484 U.S. 1065 (1987). The Seventh Amendment is applicable, however, to the Article III federal court in Puerto Rico.

258. *See* note 249, *supra.*

259. I criticize these rules at Sward, *supra* note 1, at 1134–38.

260. The Seventh Amendment does not apply to the states. *See* Minneapolis & St. Louis RR Co. v. Bombolis, 241 U.S. 211, 217 (1916); 2 ROTUNDA ET AL., *supra* note 249, at § 14.2 (1986).

IV. Other Seventh Amendment Interpretations

The Supreme Court has enunciated several other interpretations of the Seventh Amendment that affect its scope. These include the holding that the parties may waive their right to a jury trial; the holding that the Seventh Amendment does not apply to the states; and a wide array of holdings that approve of changes in the jury's structure and of procedural rules that control the jury. The remainder of the book deals with changes in the jury's structure and the various jury control devices.[261] In this section, I will briefly discuss waiver and the applicability of the Seventh Amendment to the states.

A. Waiver

The Supreme Court has recognized litigants' power to waive the right to a jury trial since 1819.[262] Under the current Federal Rules of Civil Procedure, applicable in the ordinary federal courts, parties who do not ask for a jury trial are deemed to have waived it.[263] In some of the non-Article III courts discussed in this Chapter, parties may waive the right to a jury trial merely by bringing suit in the non-Article III court. For example, filing a claim in a bankruptcy court or an administrative agency may constitute a waiver of the right to jury trial, particularly if Article III litigation is a viable alternative.[264]

---

261. See *infra*, Chapter 5 (discussing structure); *id.*, Chapters 6–8 (discussing control devices).

262. See Bank of Columbia v. Okely, 17 U.S. (4 Wheat.) 235, 244 (1819); ROBERT WYNESS MILLAR, CIVIL PROCEDURE OF THE TRIAL COURT IN HISTORICAL PERSPECTIVE 260 (1952). Congress explicitly provided for a power to waive the right to jury trial in 1865. See Act of March 3, 1865, ch. 86, sec. 4, 13 Stat. 501. For a discussion of the development of this right to waive a jury trial, *see supra*, Chapter 3, at notes 25–33 and accompanying text.

263. See FED. R. CIV. P. 38.

264. *Cf.* Commodities Futures Trading Commission v. Schor, 478 U.S. 833, 848–49 (1986) (holding that one waives one's personal interest in an Article III court when one opts for agency adjudication when Article III litigation is an option). One might be tempted to say that by suing the government in the Court of Federal Claims, a party implicitly accepts the conditions on the government's waiver of sovereign immunity, and has thereby waived any right to a jury trial for claims by the government against him. But this is not really a waiver, because the condition of jury-less adjudication can stand alone, without a waiver theory to support it. The government can sometimes condition the provision of governmental benefits (here, the right to sue the government) on waiver of certain constitutional rights. See, e.g., Wyman v. James, 400 U.S. 309, 317 (1971) (holding that govern-

While the general rule is that waiver of any constitutional right must be knowing and voluntary,[265] the government can do things that influence the choice. It can, for example, make the choice to waive a constitutional right more attractive than the choice to assert it.[266] If suing in an administrative agency has significant efficiency advantages over Article III litigation, for example, waiver of the right to a jury trial may be a rational choice for a litigant.[267] Thus, there are two ways Congress and the courts can use waiver to reduce the number of jury trials: making jury trials the exception rather than the rule, as in the Federal Rules of Civil Procedure; and making non-Article III adjudication sufficiently advantageous that waiver of the right to jury trial is attractive to litigants. Of course, litigants may have reasons to waive their right to a jury trial apart from any action by Congress or the courts.

B. Applicability of the Seventh Amendment to the States

Until the ratification of the Fourteenth Amendment, the Bill of Rights applied only to the federal government.[268] Thus, for example, citizens had a federal constitutional right not to be subjected to unreasonable search and seizure by federal officers, but the federal right did not constrain state or local officers.[269] Since ratification of the Fourteenth Amendment, however, most of the

---

ment can condition receipt of welfare benefits on consent to home visits); Red Lion Broadcasting Co. v. FCC, 395 U.S. 367, 389 (1969) (holding that government can condition broadcast licenses on licensees' airing both sides of an issue). There might be an argument that jury-less adjudication is an unconstitutional condition, *see* Sward, *supra* note 1, at 1126–28, but this is not, properly speaking, a waiver.

265. *See, e.g.,* Brookhart v. Janis, 384 U.S. 1, 4 (1966) (discussing waiver of the Sixth Amendment right to confront a witness); Johnson v. Zerbst, 304 U.S. 458, 464 (1938) (discussing the Sixth Amendment right to counsel); Seaboard Lumber Co. v. United States, 903 F.2d 1560, 1563 (D.C. Cir. 1990) (discussing the Seventh Amendment right to jury trial).

266. *See, e. g.,* Austin v. Michigan Chamber of Commerce, 494 U.S. 652, 661 (1990) (First Amendment free speech rights waived to gain advantages of incorporation); Corbitt v. New Jersey, 439 U.S. 212, 219 (1978) (waiver of Fifth Amendment right against self-incrimination in exchange for reduced sentence); Brady v. United States, 397 U.S. 742, 755 (1970) (waiver of Fifth Amendment right against self-incrimination to avoid death sentence).

267. Though the case involved Article III issues rather than the Seventh Amendment, this might have been the case in *Schor. See* Schor, 478 U.S. at 850.

268. *See* Baron v. Baltimore, 32 U.S. (7 Pet.) 243, 249 (1833); 2 ROTUNDA, ET AL., *supra* note 249, at § 14.2.

269. *See* Wolf v. Colorado, 338 U.S. 25, 26 (1949); 2 ROTUNDA, ET AL., *supra* note 249, at § 14.2.

Bill of Rights has been incorporated into the Fourteenth Amendment and applied to the states.[270] The most significant exception is the Seventh Amendment.[271] There is, then, no federal constitutional right to a jury trial in the state courts, though all of the states provide for civil juries either in their own constitutions or by statute or rule.

IV. Summary and Conclusion

The Supreme Court's Seventh Amendment jurisprudence appears, at first, to be quite hospitable to the right to a jury trial in civil cases. The Court has held that twentieth century procedural changes that eliminate the need for equitable procedures mean that the right to a jury trial under the Seventh Amendment is available in cases that would have been tried to a judge prior to those procedural changes. It has also held that newly created statutory rights carry with them a right to a jury trial in the ordinary federal courts if they provide legal rights and remedies. These holdings result in an apparent expansion of the Seventh Amendment right to a jury trial.

There is, however, another body of Supreme Court jurisprudence that seems to overwhelm this modest expansion in the right to a jury trial. First, the Court permits jury-less adjudication in the 340,000 annual administrative adjudications. Thus, while about two per cent of civil cases filed annually in the federal courts are resolved with a jury trial, the figure drops to 0.86 per cent of civil adjudications when administrative adjudications are included. Second, the Court permits jury-less adjudication in several other kinds of non-Article III courts, even when the same matter could be tried to a jury if it were brought in an Article III court. This further erodes the right to a jury trial. Third, Congress and the courts have made waiver of the right to jury trial the exception rather than the rule. Fourth, the Court has refused to apply the Seventh Amendment to the states, though virtually every other provision of the Bill of Rights has been held applicable to the states. If we stopped there, this body of doctrine must be seen as unsupportive of the Seventh Amendment right to a civil jury.[272] But that is not all.

---

270. *See id.*; Duncan v. Louisiana, 391 U.S. 145, 147 (1968).

271. *See* 2 ROTUNDA, *ET AL.*, *supra* note 249, at § 17.8 n.12; Minneapolis & St. Louis RR Co. v. Bombolis, 241 U.S. 211, 217 (1916); Burrell v. Davis, 779 F. Supp. 42, 43 (E.D. Va. 1991).

272. I have criticized the doctrine elsewhere. *See* Sward, *supra* note 1.

In the next four chapters, I will show how Congress and the Supreme Court have aided in the construction of a body of doctrine that changes the jury's structure in fundamental and destructive ways, and that allows the courts to exert substantial control over juries.

CHAPTER 5

DEFINING THE CIVIL JURY

The Supreme Court has said that the Seventh Amendment preserves the fundamental right to a jury trial in civil cases, but not all of its incidental characteristics.[1] The problem is that the Court has never clearly defined the fundamental right to a jury trial. Rather, it has upheld numerous structural and procedural changes relating to the jury on the ground that they are mere incidental characteristics. In addition, it has altered existing procedural devices in ways that make it easier for judges to control juries. In this and the following chapters, I will catalog these developments and demonstrate that they are whittling away at the fundamental right to a jury trial in civil cases, which I began to describe in Chapter 1. In this Chapter, I begin by considering the definition of the civil jury: the number of jurors, the decision rule that they use, and jury selection issues.

I. The Structure of the Civil Jury

The jury has consisted of twelve members since early in its English history.[2] The requirement that jurors reach a unanimous verdict has an equally long and honored pedigree.[3] In the last thirty years, both of those structural characteristics of the civil jury have been challenged, though with varied success. The Supreme Court now permits civil juries as small as six persons in federal courts. It does not allow nonunanimous verdicts in the federal courts, however. In state courts, where the Seventh Amendment does not apply, both six-person juries and nonunanimous verdicts are common.

---

1. *See* Galloway v. United States, 319 U.S. 372, 390 (1943); Colgrove v. Battin, 413 U.S. 149, 152 (1973); Parklane Hosiery Co., Inc. v. Shore, 439 U.S. 322, 336–37 (1979).
2. *See supra,* Chapter 2, at notes 57–63 and accompanying text.
3. *See id.* at notes 64–68 and accompanying text.

A. Number of Jurors

At the time of the Revolution, juries in the United States uniformly consisted of twelve persons.[4] The requirement of a twelve-person jury apparently was not challenged until around the turn of the twentieth century, when the Supreme Court on several occasions upheld the requirement of twelve jurors in both civil and criminal cases in the federal courts.[5] Then, beginning in 1970 with *Williams v. Florida*,[6] came the revolution.

Williams was a state criminal proceeding in which the accused was convicted by a jury of six persons.[7] States are required by the Sixth and Fourteenth Amendments to the United States Constitution to provide juries in criminal cases, but the Court in *Williams* held that the Sixth Amendment did not require a twelve-person jury.[8] The Court based its judgment on two conclusions: first, that nothing in the history of the jury suggested that the framers considered twelve jurors to be a fundamental feature of the right to jury trial;[9] and, second, that social science research indicated that there would be no difference in the quality of judgments that six-person and twelve-person juries rendered.[10] If there is no difference, the Court found, there can be no constitutional significance to the size.

---

4. One writer seeks to show that there were juries of less than twelve in colonial America, but his study does more to establish the significance of the number twelve at the time of the Revolution. *See* H. Richmond Fisher, *The Seventh Amendment and the Common Law: No Magic in Numbers*, 56 F.R.D. 507, 529–31 (1973). Fisher's study shows that some colonies in the seventeenth century provided for six-person juries, but those colonies all eventually adopted rules requiring juries of twelve. The early six-person rules may have been adopted because of the relatively sparse early population of the colonies. Fisher also shows some six-person juries for small claims cases closer to the Revolutionary War, but small claims are a special case. Finally, Fisher shows that juries trying "Slaves and Persons of Color" consisted of two justices and three freeholders in seventeenth century South Carolina. This is a racist historical provision not worthy of any consideration as precedent. *See also* Colgrove, 413 U.S. at 177 n.7 (Marshall, J., dissenting) (criticizing Fisher).

5. *See, e.g.,* American Publishing Co. v. Fisher, 166 U.S. 464 (1897) (civil); Capital Traction Co. v. Hof, 174 U.S. 1 (1899) (civil); Rassmussen v. United States, 197 U.S. 516 (1905) (criminal); Patton v. United States, 281 U.S 276 (1930) (criminal); United States v. Wood, 299 U.S. 123 (1936) (criminal). In one case from 1900, the court held that states could constitute criminal juries of fewer than twelve, at least for non-capital cases. Maxwell v. Dow, 176 U.S. 581, 604–05 (1900).

6. 399 U.S. 78 (1970).

7. *Id.* at 79–80.

8. *Id.* at 86, 91 n.28. The Sixth Amendment was made applicable to the states in Duncan v. Louisiana, 391 U.S. 145, 156 (1967).

9. *See* Williams, 399 U.S. at 92–100.

10. *Id.* at 101–03.

These conclusions are problematic, as I will show momentarily.[11] Nevertheless, three years later, in *Colgrove v. Battin*,[12] the Court relied on substantially similar reasoning to hold that the Seventh Amendment does not require twelve-person juries in civil cases in the federal courts.[13] As a result of *Colgrove* and considerable pressure from judges and judicial administrators, Rule 48 of the Federal Rules of Civil Procedure was amended to explicitly allow six-person juries.[14] Most district courts now provide for juries of fewer than twelve persons by local rule.[15] While *Colgrove* does not apply to state civil adjudications because the Seventh Amendment has never been applied to the states,[16] most states also now allow a jury of fewer than twelve persons in civil cases.[17]

---

11. *See infra,* notes 34–63 and accompanying text.

12. 413 U.S. 149 (1973).

13. *Colgrove* involved a Montana local rule that provided for six-person juries even though Rule 48 of the Federal Rules of Civil Procedure did not explicitly allow six-person juries at the time. The Court found no inconsistency between Rule 48 of the Federal Rules of the Civil Procedure and the local rule. Colgrove, 413 U.S. at 163–64. Rule 48 at the time allowed parties to stipulate to a jury of fewer than twelve persons but made no reference to the power of the local courts to impose a jury of fewer than twelve persons. *Id.* at 151 n.4.

14. *See* FED. R. CIV. P. 48 ("The court shall seat a jury of not fewer than six and not more than twelve members."); Richard S. Arnold, *Trial By Jury: The Constitutional Right to a Jury of Twelve in Civil Trials,* 22 HOFSTRA L. REV. 1, 32–35 (1993); Victor J. Baum, *The Six-Man Jury—The Cross Section Aborted,* 12 JUDGES J. 12, 12–13 (1973). The Court in *Colgrove* left open the question whether juries of fewer than six persons in civil cases would pass constitutional muster. *Id.* at 159–60. The Court later held that juries of fewer than six persons were unconstitutional in criminal cases. *See* Ballew v. Georgia, 435 U.S. 223, 243–45 (1978). Rule 48 does not allow juries of fewer than six in civil cases, so the Court has not had occasion to rule on the constitutionality of such juries in civil cases. *See* FED. R. CIV. P. 48.

15. *See generally,* Fisher, *supra* note 4. As of June, 1996, 84 of the 94 federal district courts had adopted local rules allowing civil juries of fewer than twelve persons. The other ten had no local rule governing jury size, but some of them may have been using juries of fewer than twelve persons by local practice.

16. Charles W. Wolfram, *The Constitutional History of the Seventh Amendment,* 57 MINN. L. REV. 639, 646 n.21 (1973). The Supreme Court held that the Seventh Amendment was not applicable to the states in *Walker v. Souvinet,* 92 U.S. 90, 92 (1875). This principle was affirmed 100 years later in *Davis v. Edwards,* 409 U.S. 1098 (1973) (per curiam).

17. As of June 1996, 45 states allowed civil juries of fewer than twelve persons. Of those 45, nineteen allowed it only by stipulation of the parties. *See also* REID HASTIE, ET AL., INSIDE THE JURY 2 (1983) (noting that the twelve-member unanimous jury was then required in both criminal and civil trials in only seven states).

Although the civil and criminal juries have different origins in the Constitution,[18] the Court's decision in *Colgrove* was largely derivative of *Williams*. In both cases, the Court first concluded that the framers did not necessarily have a twelve-person jury in mind when they provided for the criminal and civil juries.[19] The Court noted that there was considerable variation in the characteristics of the jury trial among the states, and that the framers explicitly meant to respect that variation.[20] The Court in *Colgrove* ruled that the framers only meant to specify that jury trials were required for common law actions, and did not intend to require any particular features of the jury that may have existed at the time of the Seventh Amendment's ratification.[21]

The Court cited *Galloway v. United States*[22] for the proposition that the Seventh Amendment did not " 'bind the federal courts to the exact procedural incidents or details of jury trial according to the common law in 1791.' "[23] *Galloway*, however, concerned the directed verdict, a procedural device that allegedly diminished the jury's fact-finding authority.[24] The number of jurors, by contrast, is a structural feature of the jury. Arguably, the burden ought to be heavier on those who wish to change structural features than on those who seek merely to alter the procedures governing jury trials. There may have been considerable variation in jury procedures in 1791,[25] but the structural requirement of twelve jurors was quite uniform.[26] As Justice Marshall pointed out in a stinging dissent in *Colgrove*, there does not appear to have been any variation among the states in the number of jurors.[27] Marshall argued that if the intent of the framers was not clearly stated, the Court should adhere to

---

18. *See supra*, Introduction, at notes 21–28 and accompanying text.

19. Williams, 399 U.S. at 98; Colgrove, 413 U.S. at 153.

20. Colgrove, 413 U.S. at 153–55.

21. *See id.* at 155.

22. 319 U.S. 372 (1943).

23. Colgrove, 413 U.S. at 156, *quoting* Galloway, 319 U.S. at 390.

24. *See infra*, Chapter 7, at notes 124–134 and accompanying text.

25. *See* Edith Guild Henderson, *The Background of the Seventh Amendment*, 80 HARV. L. REV. 289, 299 (1966). Much of Henderson's evidence relates to the period immediately after 1791.

26. Of course, the practice of including only white men with property was also quite uniform at the time the Constitution was ratified. But the Constitution itself has been amended in ways that make that practice unconstitutional. *See, e.g.,* U.S. CONST. ams. XIV (equal protection), XIX (women's suffrage).

The Court in *Colgrove* also dismissed the long line of precedent requiring twelve-person juries in civil cases as mere dictum. Colgrove, 413 U.S. at 157–58.

27. *Id.* at 176 (Marshall, J., dissenting).

the common practice at the time as indicative of the framers' intent;[28] that was clearly the twelve-person jury.

After concluding that the framers did not necessarily intend for juries to have twelve members, both *Williams* and *Colgrove* then considered whether the jury's size affected any essential function of the jury. The Court in *Colgrove* said that both criminal and civil juries were "to assure a fair and equitable resolution of factual issues."[29] *Williams*, the criminal case, noted that the essential feature of the criminal jury is "in the interposition between the accused and his accuser of the commonsense judgment of a group of laymen, and in the community participation and shared responsibility that results from that group's determination of guilt or innocence."[30] The Court concluded that this essential feature was not a function of the number of jurors.[31] The Court did concede, somewhat grudgingly, that "the number should *probably* be large enough to promote group deliberation, free from outside attempts at intimidation, and to provide a fair possibility for obtaining a representative cross-section of the community."[32] The Court's insertion of the word "probably" is troubling. The features the Court describes are surely essential to the jury's proper functioning. In any event, the Court did not find any reason to think these goals were tied to the number of jurors, "particularly if the requirement of unanimity is retained."[33]

The Court's decision in *Williams* that twelve jurors were not required to preserve the essential features of the jury was based on its understanding of several empirical studies comparing six- and twelve-person juries,[34] as well as its reading of social psychological theory.[35] The Court concluded that these studies showed no difference in outcomes between six- and twelve-person juries. *Colgrove* simply built on that foundation, relying on the studies cited in

---

28. *Id.* at 175 (Marshall, J., dissenting).
29. Colgrove, 413 U.S. at 157, *citing* Gasoline Products Co. V. Champlin Co., 283 U.S. 494, 498 (1931).
30. Williams, 399 U.S. at 100.
31. *Id.*
32. *Id.* (emphasis added).
33. *Id.* The Court noted that it was not expressing an opinion about unanimity, though much of the historical discussion applied to the unanimity requirement as well. It suggested, however, that unanimity may be an essential feature of a criminal jury in order to help insure "that the Government bear the heavier burden of proof." *Id.* at 100n.46. This argument as to unanimity does not apply with the same force, of course, to civil cases. *See infra*, notes 64–87 and accompanying text for a discussion of the unanimity requirement.
34. Williams, 399 U.S. at 101 n.48.
35. *Id.* at 101 n.49.

Williams as well as some subsequent studies, all purporting to show that there was no difference in outcomes between six- and twelve-person juries.[36] Both *Williams* and *Colgrove* then concluded that, given neither a historical nor a functional argument that twelve jurors were required, six-person juries in civil and criminal cases were constitutional. *Colgrove* also noted the expected savings in time and money that could be achieved by reducing the size of the jury,[37] though that is not an argument that ought to rise to constitutional significance. Rather, it is a pragmatic argument: if six-person juries are consitutional, the cost savings may be a good policy reason to adopt them, but that is not a decision for the Supreme Court.

The problem is that none of this is very well-founded. The studies relied upon by the Court in *Williams* and *Colgrove* were flawed,[38] and subsequent studies show, for the most part, that there *are* significant differences between six- and twelve-person juries.[39] Furthermore, any savings in time or money are probably *de minimis*,[40] and are overborne by significant costs in represen-

---

36. Colgrove, 413 U.S. at 158–59 and nn. 13, 15.

37. *See* Colgrove, 413 U.S. at 160 and n.17.

38. *See* Hans Zeisel,... *And Then There Were None: The Diminution of the Federal Jury,* 38 U. CHI. L. REV. 710, 713–15 (1971) [hereinafter cited as Zeisel, *Then There Were None*] (criticizing the studies relied on in *Williams*); Hans Zeisel and Shari Seidman Diamond, *"Convincing Empirical Evidence" on the Six Member Jury,* 41 U. CHI. L. REV. 281, 282–89 (1974) (criticizing the studies relied on in *Colgrove*).

39. *See* MICHAEL J. SAKS, JURY VERDICTS: THE ROLE OF GROUP SIZE AND SOCIAL DECISION RULE 77–104 (1978); HARRY KALVEN, JR. AND HANS ZEISEL, THE AMERICAN JURY 55–103 (1966); JOHN GUINTHER, THE JURY IN AMERICA 75–102 (1988); Robert T. Roper, *Jury Size and Verdict Consistency: "A Line Has to be Drawn Somewhere",* 14 LAW & SOC'Y REV. 977, 992 (1980); Hans Zeisel, *The Waning of the American Jury,* 58 A.B.A. J. 367 (April 1972) [hereinafter cited as Zeisel, *Waning*]. *But see* Alice Padawer-Singer, *Justice or Judgments?,* in THE AMERICAN JURY SYSTEM, FINAL REPORT OF THE ANNUAL CHIEF JUSTICE EARL WARREN CONFERENCE ON ADVOCACY IN THE UNITED STATES (1977); Lawrence R. Mills, *Six-Member and Twelve-Member Juries: An Empirical Study of Trial Results,* 6 MICH. J. OF L. Ref. 671, 710–11 (1973). *See generally,* J. MYRON JACOBSTEIN & ROY M. MERSKY, JURY SIZE: ARTICLES AND BIBLIOGRAPHY FROM THE LITERATURE OF LAW AND THE SOCIAL AND BEHAVIOR SCIENCE (1998) (collecting articles on jury size).

40. *See* William R. Pabst, Jr., *Statistical Studies of the Costs of Six-Man versus Twelve-Man Juries,* 14 WM. & MARY L. REV. 326, 330 (1972) (time savings not realized); Zeisel, *Then There Were None, supra* note 38, at 711 (monetary savings minimal). The authors of one study favor reducing the civil jury to six because of the alleged cost savings, but their own study shows that the annual cost of the jury is only 35¢ per resident of the county. They assert that reducing the jury to six would save half of that. *See* Andrew W. Bogue and Thomas G. Fritz, *The Six-Man Jury,* 17 S. DAK. L. REV. 285, 289 (1972).

tativeness and accuracy, and in flaws in the deliberative process.[41] Some elaboration of these points is in order.

Empirical research on juries is difficult to do because of the secrecy of the jury decision process. Actual deliberations cannot be observed,[42] so substitutes must be developed, and we can never be completely confident of the accuracy of the substitutes. One such substitute is interviewing jurors following real trials, sometimes by asking them to complete questionnaires.[43] The accuracy of such findings, however, depends on the jurors' recall of the deliberations, which no one can confirm.[44] Another substitute is the mock jury.[45] Mock juries, however, have different characteristics than real juries, and that could affect the outcomes.[46] Furthermore, the mock jurors may behave differently than they would if they thought a real case depended on their work.[47]

---

41. See sources cited in note 39, *supra*; Lucy M. Keele, *An Analysis of Six Versus Twelve Person Juries*, 27 TENN. B.J. 32, 35–40 (1991).

42. Kalven and Zeisel, in their famous study of the jury in America, taped several real juries' deliberations, but were stopped after disclosure of the taping drew criticism, including censure by the U.S. Attorney General. They did not report the results because of the controversy. See KALVEN & ZEISEL, *supra* note 39, at pp. xiv–xv; JEFFREY ABRAMSON, WE THE JURY: THE JURY SYSTEM AND THE IDEAL OF DEMOCRACY 196 (1994).

43. See, e.g., KALVEN & ZEISEL, *supra* note 39, at 45–54; GUINTHER, *supra* note 39, at 287–91.

44. There are studies that show that twelve-person juries have better collective recall of evidence presented at trial than six-person juries. See, e.g., SAKS, *supra* note 39, at 265; Padawer-Singer, *supra* note 39 at 54 (finding that six-person juries did not examine evidence as accurately as twelve-person juries and that jurors in six-person juries were much less likely to correct inaccurate recall of other jurors than were jurors in twelve-person juries). This suggests that one person filling out a questionnaire will have imperfect recall of jury deliberations. That imperfect recall will not be corrected by group discussion if the jurors merely fill out questionnaires. Kalven and Zeisel say that questionnaires are better than face-to-face interviews because, being anonymnous, they promote greater honesty. KALVEN & ZEISEL, *supra* note 39, at 46–47.

45. See, e.g., SAKS, *supra* note 39; Roper, *supra* note 39; Alice M. Padawer-Singer, *et al.*, *An Experimental Study of Twelve vs. Six Member Juries Under Unanimous vs. Nonunanimous Decisions*, in PSYCHOLOGY IN THE LEGAL PROCESS 77–86 (Bruce Dennis Sales, ed. 1977).

46. The problems include using only college students, who are not a representative cross section of the community; not using *voir dire;* and not using real judicial personnel to conduct the mock trial. See Padawer-Singer, *et al.*, *supra* note 45, at 78–80 (describing problems with mock jury studies and stating why their mock jury study resolves those problems).

47. Robert MacCoun, *Decisionmaking By Civil Juries*, IN VERDICT: ASSESSING THE CIVIL JURY SYSTEM 145 (Robert E. Litan ed. 1993).

A final problem with empirical research on juries is that it is difficult to identify a benchmark against which to evaluate jury outcomes. It is impossible to determine the accuracy of verdicts; if we knew the correct verdict, we would not need a trial. One way researchers deal with this problem is to compare jury verdicts with the judge's view of the case.[48] The closer the two are, the more likely it is that the jury's verdict is accurate, under this reasoning.[49] Of course, it is not clear why we should assume that the judge is right. Nevertheless, it is important to know the likelihood that results will vary with different decision-makers. Ideally, the result should be the same no matter who is deciding the case. If that were true, however, there would be no arguments about who should decide.

Despite the difficulties with empirical research on juries, there is a considerable body of work, and much of it is quite reliable. While the studies sometimes reach opposite conclusions, the overwhelming body of evidence suggests that larger juries are better than smaller ones on almost any measure. First, most reliable research has shown that there are differences in outcome between large and small juries.[50] In particular, the variation in verdicts in similar cases is likely to be greater with small juries than with large.[51] In addition,

---

48. *See* KALVEN & ZEISEL, *supra* note 39, at 55–117.

49. *Id.* at 57. Kalven & Zeisel found that judge and jury agreed some 75% of the time, which they said would be, to some, "a reassuring sign of the competence and stability of the jury system." *Id.* To others, of course, 25% disagreement could be cause for alarm. *See also*, Mark Curriden, *Putting the Squeeze on Juries*, 86 A.B.A. J. 52 (August 2000) (reporting a Texas study in which over 95% of federal and state judges agreed with the jury either "all the time" or "nearly all the time"). Judicial satisfaction with the jury does not, however, prevent judges from favoring improvements in the jury's functioning. *See* David C. Brody and John Neiswender, *Judicial Attitudes Toward Jury Reform*, 83 JUDICATURE 298 (2000).

50. *See* materials cited at note 39, *supra*. *Cf.* David F. Walbert, *The Effect of Jury Size on the Probability of Conviction: An Evaluation of* Williams v. Florida, 22 CASE W. RES. L. REV. 529, 532 (1971) (criminal jury study). Arguments to the contrary are often based on anecdotal evidence. *See, e.g.,* Anthony T. Augelli, *Six-Member Juries in Civil Actions in the Federal Judicial System*, 3 SETON HALL L. REV. 281, 286 (1972) (noting that the Supreme Court in *Williams* relied on opinion data and its own preception); Edward J. Devitt, *The Six-Man Jury in the Federal Court*, 53 F.R.D 273, 276 (1971). One researcher found that while only a fraction of all jury trials will produce a different verdict with six and twelve person juries, where verdicts of six and twelve person juries do diverge, the verdicts of twelve are likely to be of somewhat higher quality than the verdicts of six and are likely to be superior with respect to other important values, such as quality of deliberation, consistency, community representation, and recall ability. *See* Richard O. Lempert, *Uncovering "Nondiscernible" Differences*, 73 MICH. L. REV. 643, 698–699 (1975).

51. *See* Michael J. Saks, *The Smaller the Jury the Greater the Unpredictability*, 79 JUDICATURE 263, 264 (1996).

small juries are more likely to produce extravagant verdicts.[52] One commentator has noted that complaints about extravagant jury verdicts began surfacing about the same time that juries began shrinking in size.[53]

Second, smaller juries are plagued by problems that arise far less frequently in larger juries. Small juries are likely to be less representative of the community, for example. One critic of small juries showed that if 90% of the people in a community held one view, and the other 10% held the opposite, a member of the community with the minority view is likely to be on a twelve-person jury 72% of the time, but will be on a six-person jury only 47% of the time.[54] This is important because juries are not like ordinary political bodies, where the majority automatically prevails. Juries are supposed to deliberate to a unanimous decision, and minority viewpoints can be critical in fashioning an accurate decision, particularly when those minority viewpoints are grounded in different and relevant perspectives.[55] A jury of insurance executives might have trouble understanding the perspective of consumers, and vice versa.

Studies also show that smaller juries have poorer recall of the evidence and arguments.[56] This is intuitively correct as well: more people will have better collective recall than fewer people. The poorer collective recall in smaller juries may well be related to the finding that there is less discussion of the issues

---

52. *See* Hans Zeisel, *The Debate Over the Civil Jury in Historical Perspective*, 1990 U. CHI. L. FORUM 25, 29; Zeisel, *Then There Were None, supra* note 38, at 717–18.

53. Saks, *supra* note 51, at 264.

54. *See* Zeisel, *Then There Were None, supra* note 38, at 716. One study suggests that a jury must have at least eight persons to be representative. *See* Padawer-Singer, *supra* note 39.

55. Numerous books and articles discuss the very different ways that people can experience things, based on characteristics like race or gender. *See, e.g.,* T. Alexander Aleinikoff, *Race in Constitutional Adjudication*, 63 COLO. L. REV. 325 (1992) (race); CAROL GILLIGAN, IN A DIFFERENT VOICE (1982) (gender); DEBORAH TANNEN, GENDER AND DISCOURSE (1994) (gender); PATRICIA WILLIAMS, THE ALCHEMY OF RACE AND RIGHTS (1991) (race); ELLIS COSE, THE RAGE OF A PRIVILEGED CLASS (1993) (race). Of course, lawyers often want to exclude people from juries whose experience too closely mirrors what is at issue in the case. BNA CIVIL TRIAL MANUAL §71 (1992); AMERICAN BAR ASSOCIATION, THE LITIGATION MANUAL 413 (John G. Koeltl ed., 1989). This is discussed *infra* at notes 151–157 and accompanying text.

56. *See, e.g.,* Saks, *supra* note 51, at 265; Padawer-Singer, *supra* note 39, at 54 (finding that six-person juries did not examine evidence as accurately as twelve-person juries and that jurors in six-person juries were much less likely to correct inaccurate recall of other jurors than were jurors in twelve-person juries).

in smaller juries:[57] if fewer issues are recalled, fewer will be discussed. At the same time, smaller juries are more likely to be dominated by one juror, which can skew the discussion.[58]

While there are studies that call some of these conclusions into question,[59] the bulk of the evidence has become quite convincing. Smaller juries often reach different results than larger ones; they are more likely to award extravagant verdicts; they are less representative; and the quality of their deliberations is likely to be lower than that of a larger jury, for a variety of reasons. Thus, it cannot be said that small juries are just like large ones. In fact, they are not as good.

To compound this conclusion, the savings in time and money that were supposed to be realized from the smaller juries are elusive. One study showed that the savings, *if realized*, amount to four per cent of the judiciary's annual budget and less than one-thousandth of a per cent of the total federal budget,[60] but there is some question whether these savings are being realized.[61] Even if they are, however, they come at the cost of lower quality verdicts, less representation of minority viewpoints, and poorer deliberative processes. Whether or not that raises constitutional concerns, it is certainly poor policy.

There has been at least one proposed amendment to Rule 48 of the Federal Rules of Civil Procedure that would reverse the trend and mandate twelve-person juries in civil cases in the federal courts.[62] The proposal is unpopular in some quarters, however, and it has not been adopted by the advisory committee.[63]

B. The Decision Rule: Unanimity

The Supreme Court has held that unanimous jury verdicts are required in federal courts by both the Sixth and Seventh Amendments.[64] In civil cases, this

---

57. *See id.*

58. John R. Snortum, *The Impact of an Aggressive Juror in Six- and Twelve-Member Juries*, 3 Crim. Just. & Behav. 255, 258 (1976); Baum, *supra* note 14, at 13.

59. *See, e.g.,* Honorable Lloyd L. Wiehl, *The Six-Man Jury*, 4 Gonzaga L. Rev. 35, 40–41 (1968); Edward A. Tamm, *The Five-Man Civil Jury: A Proposed Constitutional Amendment*, 51 Geo. L.J. 120, 134–36 (1962).

60. Hans Zeisel, *Waning, supra* note 39, at 370.

61. *See* Arnold, *supra* note 14, at 25.

62. *See Proposed Amendments to the Federal Rules of Appellate, Bankruptcy, Civil, and Criminal Procedure and Evidence*, 163 F.R.D. 91, 135–38, 147 (1995).

63. *See* Proceedings of the Judicial Conference of the United States 70 (1996) (minutes of meeting of September 17, 1996).

64. *See* Andres v. United States, 333 U.S. 740, 748 (1948) (Seventh Amendment); Duncan v. Louisiana, 391 U.S. 145, 182 (1967) (Sixth Amendment); American Publishing Co. V. Fisher, 166 U.S. 464, 468 (1897) (Seventh Amendment).

decision rule can be modified with the consent of both parties.[65] The rules governing state courts are different. Because the Seventh Amendment does not apply to the states,[66] the states are free to devise their own rules as to both the size of the jury and the decision rule in civil cases. Many of them have moved to a nonunanimous—usually supermajority—decision rule.[67] Most often, five-sixths or three-fourths of the jurors must agree for the verdict to be accepted.[68]

There are two major arguments in favor of nonunanimous verdicts. The first is a multi-faceted efficiency argument. It is likely, proponents of nonunanimous juries say, that such juries will reach the same decisions sooner and fail to reach a decision less often than juries that are required to reach a unanimous verdict.[69] One reason for that is that nonunanimous verdicts prevent juries from failing to reach verdicts because of one or two unreasonable or stubborn jurors.[70] When five of six, or ten of twelve, jurors agree that something happened, proponents argue, it is likely that it did happen.[71] The evidence suggests that nonunanimous juries do indeed reach verdicts faster and

---

65. *See* FED. R. CIV. P. 48. The parties have no power to alter the decision rule in criminal cases.

66. *See* note 16, *supra,* and accompanying text.

67. Forty states allow nonunanimous juries in civil cases, though seventeen of those require the consent of the parties for a nonunanimous jury. Only three states allow nonunanimous juries in criminal cases, and one of those requires the consent of the defendant.

68. *See* Note, *The Erie Doctrine and Nonunanimous Civil Jury Verdicts,* 4 AM. J. TRIAL ADV. 665, 665 and n.2 (1981) (of the thirty-one states that permitted less than unanimous civil jury verdicts at that time, ten required a five-sixths vote, sixteen required a three-fourths vote, two allowed two-thirds concurrence, and three allowed five-sixths verdicts when deliberations go beyond six hours).

Although the Sixth Amendment does apply to the states, the Court, in a pair of decisions in 1972, seems to have held that nonunanimous juries could constitutionally be used in state criminal trials, but not in federal. *See* Apodaca v. Oregon, 406 U.S. 404 (1972); Johnson v. Louisiana, 406 U.S. 356 (1972). *See generally,* LAURENCE H. TRIBE, AMERICAN CONSTITUTIONAL LAW 773 n.25 (2d ed.1988). Due process, however, prohibits nonunanimous verdicts in capital cases. *See* Burch v. Louisiana, 441 U.S. 130, 136 (1978) (citing *Apodaca*).

69. *See, e.g.,* Burch v. Louisiana, 441 U.S. 130, 139 (1979) (citing Brief of the State of Louisiana); Edward P. Schwartz & Warren F. Schwartz, *Decisionmaking by Juries Under Unanimous and Supermajority Voting Rules,* 80 GEO. L. REV. 775, 787 (1992).

70. *See, e.g.,* Thomas F. Croake, *Memorandum on the Advisability and Constitutionality of Six Man Juries and 5/6 Verdicts in Civil Cases,* 44 N.Y. ST. BAR J. 385, 387 (October, 1972).

71. *Id.*

fail to reach verdicts less often, but the studies vary on whether the differences are significant.[72] The savings in time and money, then, may be *de minimis.*[73]

Moreover, the cost to the deliberative ideal may be too great relative to the measured benefits. The assumption that the minority jurors are unreasonable or stubborn, for example, is not proven, and it is particularly problematic at a time when the jury is becoming more diverse. In fact, minority jurors could have a relevant and important perspective that the majority jurors know nothing about or do not understand.[74] They could be right. Abrogating the unanimity rule means that we could lose the benefits of such relevant and important perspectives while we save the costs of a few stubborn jurors. This is a threat to justice.

Furthermore, the ability of minority jurors to correct errors of the majority may depend on maintaining the unanimity rule. Some research suggests that the likelihood that an early minority viewpoint will ultimately prevail depends on the size of the majority.[75] The early majority is more likely to prevail in the end if the vote is 11–1 than if it is 7–5.[76] Other research suggests

---

72. *Compare* Padawer-Singer, *et al.*, *supra* note 45 (concluding that differences in hang rates are not significant); Dale W. Broeder, *The 45 University of Chicago Jury Project*, 38 NEB. L. REV. 744, 746 (1959) (same);. *with* KALVEN & ZEISEL, *supra* note 39, at 461 (documenting 45% reduction in hung juries with a majority decision rule); Robert D. Foss, *Structural Effects in Simulated Jury Decision Making*, 40 JOURNAL OF PERSONALITY AND SOCIAL PSYCHOLOGY 1055, 1058–60 (1981) (showing that juries using nonunanimous decision rules reach decisions somewhat faster and hang significantly less often).

73. *Cf.* ABRAMSON, *supra* note 42, at 201(citing JON M. VAN DYKE, JURY SELECTION PROCEDURES: OUR UNCERTAIN COMMITMENT TO REPRESENTATIVE PANELS 209 (1971)) ("[J]ury trials are such a small percentage of total criminal dispositions in the first place that a small reduction in hung juries would not have much influence on the overall efficiency of the system in resolving cases.").

74. There have been numerous books and articles discussing the different perspectives that people can have based on, for example, race or gender. *See* note 55, *supra*. Lord Devlin, writing in 1956 about English practice, noted that there was a property requirement for jurors in England, a requirement that effectively excluded most women and working class people, though that was changing even as he wrote. *See* LORD PATRICK DEVLIN, TRIAL BY JURY 20–22, 166 (1956). Lord Devlin noted that as long as the unanimity requirement remained in effect, these property requirements were necessary, because otherwise the jury could be so heterogeneous that unanimity might never be achieved. *Id.* at 22–23. Devlin apparently saw no problem with a jury that was "predominantly male, middle-aged, middle-minded and middle-class." *Id.* at 20.

75. Broeder, *supra* note 72, at 748. *See* Norbert L. Kerr and Robert J. MacCoun, *The Effects of Jury Size and Polling Method on the Process and Product of Jury Deliberation*, 48 PERSONALITY & PSYCH. 349, 355–57 & Table 2 (1985).

76. *Id.* at 355 Table 2.

that minorities are more likely to adhere to their positions if they have at least one ally.[77] Thus, 11–1 is significantly different from 10–2. Given that many jurisdictions now have juries of as few as six persons, it is also important that 10–2 is significantly different from 5–1, despite the identical percentage.[78] The presence of the ally in the 10–2 jury could be critical to the outcome, while the lone juror in the 5–1 jury is likely to be overborne by the other jurors, whether or not she is right.[79]

The significance of the ally in the 10–2 jury could become meaningless, however, if the jurisdiction follows a 5/6 verdict rule. The evidence suggests that once a jury has the requisite number of jurors voting one way, the deliberations are likely to end.[80] This could mean that the issues are not considered as fully as if the unanimity requirement were in place.[81] Where community values are at stake in the verdict, it could mean that those values are not thoroughly considered. Where minority perspectives are important to the resolution of the issue, the nonunanimous jury rule could also mean that significant, relevant perspectives are ignored because persons advancing those perspectives cannot hang the jury.[82] These deliberative failures could result in a net cost in accuracy.

The second argument in favor of the nonunanimous jury is that less than unanimous decisions are a part of appellate jurisprudence throughout the United States, where momentous decisions are regularly made by bare ma-

---

77. KALVEN & ZEISEL, *supra* note 39, at 463; GUINTHER, *supra* note 39, at 82.

78. Saks, *supra* note 51, at 265.

79. *See* S.E.Asch, *Effects of Group Pressure Upon the Modification and Distortion of Judgments*, in READINGS IN SOCIAL PSYCHOLOGY 2–11 (Guy E. Swanson, Theodore M. Newcomb, and Eugene L. Hartley eds. 1952). Asch's study showed that unless a person has an ally in a small group, there is a good chance that he will knowingly give a wrong answer so as to conform to the majority position. In this experiment, a series of lateral lines of different lengths was shown to groups of 7–9 persons, all but one of whom were complicit in the experiment. When all of the complicit persons gave false answers as to the length of the lines, the remaining person, who was the subject of the experiment, also gave the incorrect answer 32% of the time, conforming to the majority aligned against him. In a control group, the subjects gave an incorrect answer only 5% of the time.

80. *See* HASTIE, ET AL., *supra* note 17, at 94–98; ABRAMSON, *supra* note 42, at 199 (citing HASTIE, ET AL.; and Charlan Nemeth, *Interactions Between Jurors as a Function of Majority vs. Unanimity Decision Rules*, in IN THE JURY BOX: CONTROVERSIES IN THE COURTROOM 250 (Lawrence S. Wrightsman, Saul M. Kassin and Cynthia E. Willis eds. 1987)).

81. *See* Johnson v. Louisiana, 406 U.S. 356, 388 (1971) (Douglas, J., dissenting).

82. Brief of *Amicus Curiae* American Civil Liberties Union in *Apodaca v. Oregon*, 406 U.S. 404 (1972), in 71 Landmark Briefs and Arguments of the Supreme Court of the United States: Constitutional Law 923, 935 (Philip B. Kurland & Gerhard Casper eds. 1975).

jorities of justices or judges.[83] The two circumstances are quite different, however. Appellate judges, including the justices of the Supreme Court, write lengthy opinions describing the reasons for their decisions. Often there are dissenting and concurring opinions. This occurs after some deliberation among the judges, and the deliberation may continue as they exchange their various written opinions.[84] The written opinions themselves are subject to public commentary, and poorly reasoned opinions may ultimately be overruled or ignored by other courts.[85] The jury, by contrast, does all its deliberation in the jury room, and does not produce a written opinion that can be the subject of reasoned critical analysis.[86] If deliberation is cut off too early, relevant issues may never be raised. The point, then, is not the size of the vote, but the ability of the process that is used to induce high-quality, thorough deliberation. Nonunanimous jury verdicts threaten that deliberative ideal.

Although the Supreme Court has not recently considered whether to maintain the unanimity requirement for civil cases in the federal courts, the reasoning of *Williams* and *Colgrove* may well be applicable. If six hundred years of history were not enough to give the twelve-person jury constitutional stature, neither would a like history save the unanimous verdict. Furthermore, proponents' arguments about the alleged greater efficiency of nonunanimous verdicts and the similar results produced under unanimous and nonunanimous schemes are reminiscent of the arguments made in favor of twelve-person juries. The Court overruled precedent in deciding that six-person juries were constitutional,[87] and it could certainly overrule precedent relating to unanimity if there were good reasons for doing so. The available evidence, however, does not support such a move.

---

83. Croake, *supra* note 70, at 387–88. Five justices on the current court, for example, are redefining federalism by expanding states' rights at the expense of federal power. See, e.g., Alden v. Maine, 527 U.S. 706 (1999); Florida Prepaid Postsecondary Education Expense Board v. College Savings Bank, 527 U.S. 627 (1999); College Savings Bank v. Florida Prepaid Postsecondary Education Expense Board, 527 U.S. 666 (1999). But the most momentous recent decision by a 5–4 vote was Bush v. Gore, 531 U.S. ___, 121 S. Ct. 525, 148 L. Ed. 2d 388 (2000).

84. *See* JOSEPH F. MENEZ, DECISION MAKING IN THE SUPREME COURT OF THE UNITED STATES: A POLITICAL AND BEHAVIORAL VIEW 61–65, 77–81 (1984)

85. *See* GERALD N. ROSENBERG, THE HOLLOW HOPE 72–73 (1991).

86. This is not to say that jury verdicts escape comment and criticism—only that the comment and criticism are no substitute for deliberation.

87. Williams v. Florida, 399 U.S. 78 (1970) (six-person jury approved in state criminal cases), *overruling* Patton v. United States, 281 U.S. 276 (1930) (twelve-person juries required in criminal cases).

C. Summary and Conclusion

The Supreme Court has permitted the use of juries as small as six persons in civil cases in the federal courts. It has not, however, permitted nonunanimous verdicts in the federal courts, though state courts are free to adopt any size or decision rule they desire, consistent with due process.[88] Both small juries and a nonunanimous decision rule are usually justified on pragmatic grounds: such rules mean that juries are less costly; likely to reach the same verdict as a twelve-person unanimous jury, but sooner; and less likely to fail to reach a verdict. These efficiency gains, however, are overborne by serious threats to the quality of verdicts using these rules. Smaller juries may not have adequate minority representation, and so lose valuable perspectives. They have poorer recall of the evidence, and they are more likely to return extravagant and unjustified verdicts. Juries operating under a majority or supermajority decision rule may ignore minority perspectives and fail to deliberate. Moreover, any threats to the deliberative ideal that are posed by either the smaller jury or the nonunanimous jury are compounded when the two are combined. The twelve-person unanimous jury may well be less efficient than its modern counterparts, but the Constitution has some inefficiencies deliberately built into its structure,[89] and the reason is that the cost of efficiency is too great.

II. Composition of the Jury

As America has become more diverse, so has the jury. But for much of the country's history, the drive to diversify the jury has lagged behind the demographics. It is only since the middle of the twentieth century that the Supreme Court has given serious protection to the rights of racial minorities and women to serve on juries and to have racial minorities and women on the juries that hear their cases. The first thing the Court had to do was ensure that racial minorities and women would be included on the venires from which juries are chosen. The second was to protect racial minorities and women from

---

88. The states are not bound by the Seventh Amendment, but they are bound by the Due Process clause of the Fourteenth Amendment. It is possible to imagine a state jury procedure that would run afoul of the Due Process clause, though no state has set up such a procedure so far. Juries of two persons or verdicts based on tie votes, for example, might produce due process challenges.

89. *See* Bowsher v. Synar, 478 U.S. 714, 722 (1985).

race- and gender-based peremptory challenges, by which parties can remove potential jurors without offering an explanation. Today, there are additional pressures on the jury that may reduce its ability to represent a fair cross-section of the community. These include proposals for special juries to hear substantively complex cases; the practice of exempting certain classes of people from jury service; and a growing trend among the populace to ignore jury summonses.

A. The Inclusive Jury

For much of the jury's history, participation was extremely limited. Ownership of property was a prerequisite to jury service in both England and the early United States.[90] Property owners tended to be white men, so even if property were the only criterion, membership on juries would have been quite restricted. But there were also explicit rules in the United States that disallowed all women and black men from serving.[91]

The Fourteenth Amendment, with its clause providing that all citizens enjoy the equal protection of the law, was the catalyst for change.[92] The cases that challenged race-based restrictions on jury service were, at first, all criminal cases, mostly arising in the states. The first case to address the issue of jury composition was *Strauder v. West Virginia*,[93] an 1879 case in which the Court struck down a law that had limited the jury venire to white men.[94] The

---

90. *See* DEVLIN, *supra* note 74, at 17; William E. Nelson, *The Eighteenth Century Background of John Marshall's Constitutional Jurisprudence*, 76 MICH. L. REV. 893, 919n.142 (1978). Devlin says that the original reason for the property qualification was that property owners were more susceptible to punishment by fines and therefore less corruptible. These reasons are no longer viable. There is no property qualification for jury service in the federal courts. *See* 28 U.S.C. § 1865 (1994).

91. *See* Strauder v. West Virginia, 100 U.S. 303, 305 (1879) (striking down the racial restriction in a statute that provided, "All white male persons who are twenty-one years of age and who are citizens of this State shall be liable to serve as jurors.") England also had rules limiting eligibility for jury duty, including gender and property qualifications. *See* DEVLIN, *supra* note 74, at 17.

92. U.S. CONST. am. XIV. The Fourteenth Amendment was ratified in 1868. It was intended to provide freed slaves and other blacks with the same rights as white persons. A thorough history of the Court's jurisprudence on the composition of the jury is found in Raymond J. Broderick, *Why the Peremptory Challenge Should Be Abolished*, 65 TEMPLE L. REV. 369, 374–99 (1992).

93. 100 U.S. 303 at 310 (1879).

94. *Id.* at 305.

Court there held that a person accused of a crime was entitled to a jury "selected without discrimination against his color."[95] Thus the right to be protected was primarily a Fourteenth Amendment right of the accused.[96]

From the beginning, however, the Court distinguished between the composition of the jury venire—the pool from which jurors were selected—and
the individual juries that heard cases, and the Court was more protective of
the venire than the individual juries. On the same day *Strauder* was decided,
the Court held in *Virginia v. Rives* that it would presume state officials' good
faith in selecting the individual jury unless the state had a discriminatory
statute.[97] A year later, in *Neal v. Delaware*, the Court affirmed this hands-off
approach in the course of striking down, on equal protection grounds, a
Delaware law that limited the venire to electors and then limited electors to
whites.[98] The Court there made it clear that *de facto* discrimination in selecting individual juries would be very difficult to prove by holding that such discrimination could be established only by a pattern of exclusion over a long period of time.[99] This approach was reaffirmed as late as 1965 in *Swain v.
Alabama*.[100] In *Swain*, the Court barred prosecutors from using race-based
peremptory challenges, but then made the bar ineffective by maintaining the
defendant's heavy burden of proof, first established in *Neal*.[101] Over the
decades, the Court repeatedly held that the Constitution did not guarantee
that a defendant have a jury with a particular composition; it only guaranteed
that the jury be impartial.[102] But the defendant's burden of proving partiality
was heavy, and could not be discharged just by showing racially specific
peremptory challenges in the defendant's own case.

In the nearly 100 years between *Strauder* and *Swain*, the art of excluding
blacks from juries without running afoul of the Court's pronouncements was
perfected.[103] Even though states could not statutorily exclude blacks from voting lists, for example, they could set eligibility requirements for voting that

95. *Id.* at 309. *Strauder*, however, permitted continued discrimination against women.
See infra, note 107 and accompanying text.
96. *Id.* at 310.
97. 100 U.S. 313, 321 (1879).
98. 103 U.S. 370, 390–91 (1880).
99. *Id.* At 397.
100. 380 U.S. 202 (1965).
101. *Id.* at 227.
102. *See* J.E.B. v. Alabama *ex rel.* T.B., 114 S.Ct. 1419, 1421 (1994); Georga v. McCollum, 505 U.S. 42, 46 (1992); Powers v. Ohio, 499 U.S. 400, 404 (1991); Batson v. Kentucky, 476 U.S. 79, 85–86 (1986).
103. *See* Broderick, *supra* note 92, at 382–89.

virtually guaranteed that no blacks could meet them.[104] When voting lists were then used to prepare the jury venire, the effect was a white jury. Some states used a so-called "key man" method of identifying prospective jurors. Community leaders, who were all white men, were called upon to compile the jury venire, and they generally compiled lists of white men in the community.[105] If any blacks did squeeze through the obstacles, the peremptory challenge generally eliminated them from the actual jury.[106] Thus, the Court's pronouncements about fair selection and an open jury pool were a hollow victory for blacks.

Throughout this period, the Court was completely unconcerned about even statutory discrimination against women. Indeed, the Court in *Strauder* explicitly said that states could "confine the selection [of jurors] to males."[107] The Court's first clear statement of the principle that women could not be systematically excluded from jury service—similar to the 1879 holding in *Strauder* prohibiting systematic discrimination against blacks—did not come until 1975, in *Taylor v. Louisiana,*[108] though there had been hints of such a principle in 1946.[109] In *Taylor,* the Court held unconstitutional a Louisiana statute that allowed women to serve as jurors only if they had registered for service.[110] The result of that statute had been that most juries contained few, if any, women.[111]

As a result of these cases, the states cannot systematically exclude people from jury venires on the basis of race or gender, though there was no real protection against such discrimination until the middle of the twentieth century.[112] Because the federal government is bound by the equal protection clause as well,[113] the federal courts must also produce an inclusive venire.

---

104. *See id.* at 382–83.

105. *Id.* at 382–83.

106. *Id.* at 384.

107. Strauder, 100 U.S. at 310.

108. 419 U.S. 522, 535–36 (1975).

109. *See* Ballard v. U.S., 329 U.S. 187, 195 (1946) (stating that the exclusion of women deprives the jury of the extensive base intended by Congress).

110. Taylor, 419 U.S. at 538.

111. *Id.* at 525.

112. *See* Broderick, *supra* note 92, at 384.

113. While the Fourteenth amendment applies on its face only to the states, the Court has held that the due process clause of the Fifth Amendment, which applies to federal adjudications, incorporates the principles expressed in the Fourteenth Amendment, including the equal protection clause. *See* Bolling v. Sharpe, 347 U.S. 497, 499–500 (1954); JOHN HART ELY, DEMOCRACY AND DISTRUST: A THEORY OF JUDICIAL REVIEW 32 (1980). This principle is commonly referred to as the doctrine of "reverse incorporation." *See* Bradford

These cases, however, did nothing to ensure that a representative jury was selected out of the venire. Congress has gone further by statute, stating that "[i]t
is the policy of the United States that all litigants in Federal courts entitled to
trial by jury shall have the right to grand and petit juries selected at random
from a fair cross section of the community."[114] Congress has also prohibited
courts from excluding citizens from jury service "on account of race, color,
religion, sex, national origin, or economic status."[115] These provisions apply
to both civil and criminal cases,[116] and they apply to individual juries as well
as the venire.

B. The Peremptory Challenge

Congress's words could not be given effect, however, as long as the Court
gave constitutional sanction to the peremptory challenge. The peremptory
challenge is a device that allows parties to strike prospective jurors from the
panel without giving a reason.[117] It thus differs from a challenge for cause,
which requires some clear indication of bias, such as a relationship between a
juror and a witness or a monetary interest in the outcome of the litigation.[118]
The standards for for-cause challenges have become difficult to meet, so they
are not thought to be a very effective means of ensuring an impartial jury.[119]
Peremptory challenges are permitted in the federal courts in both civil and

Russel Clark, Note, *Judicial Review of Congressional Section Five Action: The Fallacy of Reverse Incorporation*, 84 COLUM. L. REV. 1969, 1969 (1984).

114. 28 U.S.C. § 1861 (1994).
115. 28 U.S.C. § 1862 (1994).
116. *See* Minetos v. City University of New York, 925 F. Supp. 177 (S.D.N.Y. 1996)
(civil); Pemberthy v. Beyer, 19 F.3d 857 (3rd. Cir. 1994) (criminal).
117. The peremptory challenge has a long history, at least for criminal cases, dating to
the earliest days of the jury in England. *See* Broderick, *supra* note 92, at 371. Originally a
tool of the Crown meant to secure a jury that would favor the government in criminal prosecutions, *id.*, the peremptory challenge ultimately came to be one of the criminal defendant's most important tools. *Id.* at 372. Parliament attempted to abolish prosecutors' use
of the peremptory challenge as early as 1305. *Id.* at 371. It was abolished in criminal cases
altogether in England in 1988. *Id.* at 373. It does not appear ever to have had much significance in civil cases in England. *See* DEVLIN, *supra* note 74, at 28.
118. *See* Hopt v. Utah, 120 U.S. 430, 433 (1887); ABA PROJECT ON MINIMUM STAN-
DARDS FOR CRIMINAL JUSTICE, STANDARDS RELATING TO TRIAL BY JURY 68–69 (Approved
Draft 1968).
119. Barbara Allen Babcock, *Voir Dire: Preserving Its "Wonderful Powers"*, 27 STAN. L.
REV. 545, 552 (1975).

criminal cases, though there are limits on the number of peremptory challenges each side may use.[120]

The theory behind peremptory challenges is that the jury will be more impartial, and thus more fair, if litigants and their lawyers are able to strike jurors whom they believe are likely to be biased against them, even if they cannot articulate a reason for their beliefs. In other words, litigants and their lawyers should be able to follow their hunches about people.[121] When litigants are comfortable with the jury, it is said, they will be more likely to accept a ruling that goes against them.[122] The peremptory challenge also gives litigants some control over jury selection, in keeping with the theory of the adversary system.[123]

The peremptory challenge plays an important role in our judicial system. It does not further the goals of justice, for example, to seat of jury of racists who are unable to judge African Americans fairly because of their biases. The peremptory challenge is designed to prevent the seating of such persons. Of course, it is impossible to eliminate all biases from the jury simply because everyone is shaped to some extent by his background and perspective.[124] But racism is particularly invidious given this country's history. Sexism is similarly damaging, though some people still refuse to recognize its invidious nature. Peremptory challenges can help eliminate jurors who have racist or sexist biases—or other biases that interfere with their ability to do justice, such as homophobia or xenophobia. For-cause challenges may be undesirable as a device to remove such jurors because the for-cause challenge would require that we label people as racist, sexist, etc. The peremptory challenge can help us avoid such labels and the damage they can do.

---

120. *See* 28 U.S.C. § 1870 (1994) (civil); FED. R. CRIM. P. 24 (criminal). In civil cases, the limit is three per side, but the judge has discretion to increase the number if there are multiple parties on a side. 28 U.S.C. § 1870 (1994). For criminal cases, if the punishment is death, then the limit is twenty per side. If the punishment is greater than one year, then the government is limited to six, and the defendant to ten. If the punishment is less than one year, then the limit is three per side. Fed. R. Crim. P. 24. There is similar variation among the states. California allows twenty peremptory challenges while Arkansas only allows three. *See* Cal. Civ. Proc. Code § 231 (West 1982) (Supp. 1997); Ark. Code Ann. § 16-33-203 (1994).

121. *See* Broderick, *supra* note 92, at 372, 411; Nancy S. Marder, *Beyond Gender: Peremptory Challenges and the Roles of the Jury*, 73 TEX. L. REV. 1041, 1045–46, 1086–92 (1995).

122. Marder, *supra* note 121, at 1045.

123. *Id.* at 1045–46.

124. *See* COSE, *supra* note 55; WILLIAMS, *supra* note 55; GILLIGAN, *supra* note 55; MARTHA MINOW, MAKING ALL THE DIFFERENCE: INCLUSION, EXCLUSION, AND AMERICAN LAW (1990).

Nevertheless, the peremptory challenge itself has generated racism and sexism in jury selection. The primary argument against peremptory challenges is that the hunches that form the basis for peremptory challenges are all too often more reflective of the lawyers' stereotypical views of people than any real sense of a prospective juror's biases in the case before her.[125] Thus, the Supreme Court's refusal to concern itself with the makeup of individual juries may have resulted in some injustice to both litigants and prospective jurors. Finally acknowledging that, the Supreme Court, in a series of recent cases, has prohibited the use of race- and gender-based peremptory challenges by all parties in both civil and criminal cases, though it has declined to bar peremptory challenges altogether.

The first of these cases was *Swain v. Alabama* in 1965,[126] where the Court held that prosecutors could not base peremptory challenges solely on race.[127] But the Court there maintained the nearly impossible evidentiary burdens on a defendant alleging discrimination that it had first articulated in *Neal v. Delaware* in 1880.[128] Neal required the litigant to establish a pattern of race-based exclusion over several years. Thus, *Swain* had little practical effect on the use of the peremptory challenge. Twenty-one years later, the Court in *Batson v. Kentucky* reaffirmed the prohibition on the prosecutor's use of race-based peremptory challenges, while at the same time overruling *Swain* as to the evidentiary burden.[129] The Court held that a defendant could make out a *prima facie* case of discrimination by showing a pattern of exclusion in his own case. The prosecutor then had to articulate a race-neutral reason for excluding specific black jurors or the peremptory challenge would be rejected.[130]

Batson extended the Fourteenth Amendment's equal protection clause to the jury itself, and not just the venire. Building on the jury venire cases, *Batson* held that a black defendant has a Fourteenth Amendment right to a jury from which blacks were not systematically excluded through the discriminatory use of peremptory challenges. Five years later, in *Powers v. Ohio*,[131] the Court found that the excluded juror herself also had a Fourteenth Amendment right not to be excluded from a jury on the basis of race. *Powers* further held that the defendant, who in that case was white, had standing to raise

---

125. *See* Marder, *supra* note 121, at 1087; Broderick, *supra* note 92, at 411–12.
126. 380 U.S. 202 (1965).
127. *Id.* at 203–04.
128. 103 U.S. 370 (1880).
129. 476 U.S. 79 (1986).
130. *Id.* at 84.
131. 499 U.S. 400 (1991).

claims on the excluded black jurors' behalf because the excluded jurors themselves had no opportunity to do so.[132]

This was the rationale that allowed the Court to expand the ban on race-
based peremptory challenges beyond the prosecutor. If the jurors themselves
have a Fourteenth Amendment right not to be discriminatorily excluded from
a jury, no state actor should be able to exclude jurors based on race.[133] Thus,
in the same term as *Powers*, the Court barred litigants in *civil* cases from using
race-based peremptory challenges.[134] Shortly after that, the Court prohibited
defendants from using race-based peremptory challenges in criminal cases.[135]
Finally, in 1994, the Court held that gender-based peremptory challenges were
unconstitutional in civil litigation.[136] The discriminatory use of peremptory
challenges, the Court said, perpetuates negative stereotypes of African-Americans and women.[137] Furthermore, the Court found state action in that the
parties in civil cases and the defendant in criminal cases, in making peremp-

---

132. *Id.* at 411. The general rule is that a party cannot litigate the rights of non-parties. *See* Singleton v. Wulff, 428 U.S. 106, 113–14 (1976).

133. The Fourteenth Amendment bars discrimination only by the government. It does
not prevent discrimination by private parties. *See* NCAA v. Tarkanian, 488 U.S. 179, 191
(1988).

134. Edmonson v. Leesville Concrete Co., 500 U.S. 614 (1991).

135. Georgia v. McCollum, 505 U.S. 42, 48–59 (1992). This ruling was vigorously opposed in briefing before the Court, *see* Brief of Amicus Curiae NAACP Legal Defense and
Educational Fund, Inc. in Georgia v. McCollum, 505 U.S. 42 (1992), in 212 Landmark
Briefs of the Supreme Court of the United States: Constitutional Law 837, 838 (Philip B.
Kurland and Gerhard Casper eds. 1993), and has been the subject of some criticism, largely
on the ground that the prohibition upsets the balance between prosecution and defense
and leaves black defendants without recourse as to potentially racist jurors or jurors who,
while not racist, are not able to understand the black defendant's perspective. *See* McCollum, 505 U.S. at 68 (O'Connor, J., dissenting); *Developments in the Law—Race and the
Criminal Process*, 101 Harv. L. Rev. 1472, 1559–60 (1988). *But see* J. Alexander Tanford,
Racism in the Adversary System: The Defendant's Use of Peremptory Challenges, 63 S. Cal.
L. Rev. 1015 (1990) (arguing, before the *McCollum* decision, that *Batson* should apply to
criminal defendants' use of peremptory challenges in order to combat racism). As this book
concerns civil juries, I will not discuss the potential problems with the *McCollum* ruling.

136. J.E.B. v. Alabama *ex rel.* T.B., 114 S.Ct. 1419 (1994). While the Court has not explicitly banned gender-based peremptory challenges in criminal cases, such challenges do
not survive the rationale of *J.E.B.*

137. Edmonson, 500 U.S. at 630–31; J.E.B., 114 S.Ct. at 1422–27. In *J.E.B.*, the excluded jurors were men, which calls into question the Court's rationale. *See* 114 S. Ct. at
1436–39 (Scalia, J., dissenting). A better rationale may be that persons likely to have relevant perspectives should not be excluded from the jury, but the Fourteenth Amendment
probably does not sustain a challenge on that ground.

tory challenges, use governmental procedures and authority, and the government ratifies these discriminatory decisions by excusing the jurors.[138] The Court has made it clear that it does not intend to ban peremptory challenges altogether.[139] Peremptory challenges are still permitted on race- and gender-neutral grounds, and as long as litigants can articulate a race- or gender-neutral justification for a challenge, they can go on striking African-Americans and women from juries.[140] For creative lawyers, that should not be too difficult a task.[141] It is not clear to what extent other personal characteristics are protected in jury selection, but even if such characteristics as age are covered, they are subject to a much lower level of scrutiny under the Court's Fourteenth Amendment jurisprudence, so neutral reasons should be easy to articulate.[142] But the peremptory challenge is premised on the notion that litigants

---

138. Edmonson, 500 U.S. at 622. This is also why defendants' peremptory challenges in criminal cases involve state action. McCollum, 505 U.S. at 51–53. *See also* Marder, *supra* note 121, at 1075–77.

139. *See* J.E.B., 114 S.Ct. 1429; Marder, *supra* note 121, at 1114.

140. *See id.* at 1115; Broderick, *supra* note 92, at 454–56.

141. *See* Batson, 476 U.S. at 105–06 (Marshall, J., concurring). Not surprisingly, guidance in how to make such challenges is already available. *See* William C. Slusser, *et al.*, *Batson, J.E.B. and Purkett: A Step-by-Step-by-Step Guide to Making and Challenging Peremptory Challenges in Federal Court*, 37 S. TEX. L. REV. 127 (1996). Successful challenges tend to be phrased in subjective terms: the prospective juror did not make eye contact with the lawyer, *see* United States v. Hendrieth, 922 F.2d 748, 749–50 (11th Cir. 1991); or the prospective juror's hair style suggested a belief system that would be prejudicial toward the litigant, *see* Purkett v. Elem, 514 U.S. 765, 769 (1995). *See generally*, State v. Higginbotham, 917 P.2d 545, 548 (Utah 1996) (suggesting race-neutral reasons).

142. Classifications based on race are subject to strict judicial scrutiny under the Court's Fourteenth Amendment jurisprudence. Strict judicial scrutiny governs the Supreme Court's independent review of legislative classifications that implicate fundamental rights or are based on race or national origin. To be upheld under this review, the classification must be necessary to achieve a compelling governmental interest. *See* 2 RONALD D. ROTUNDA, ET AL., TREATISE ON CONSTITUTIONAL LAW: SUBSTANCE AND PROCEDURE § 3.3 (1986). Gender classifications receive heightened scrutiny. Heightened or intermediate scrutiny governs the Supreme Court's review of classifications based on gender, religion, or birth status. The Court gives less deference to legislative judgments under this standard, and will uphold such classifications only if they are "substantially related to a state interest." *See id.*; J.E.B., 114 S.Ct. at 1425. Generally, however, legislatures can classify people without violating the Fourteenth Amendment as long as there is a rational basis for the classification. The rational relationship test governs the Supreme Court's review of classifications not covered by the strict or intermediate scrutiny standards. This standard is highly deferential to the legislative judgment as to the classification. The classification must only bear "a rational relationship to an end of government not prohibited by the Constitution." 2 ROTUNDA, ET AL, *supra*, at § 18.3. An example of a classification subject to rational relationship analysis

can strike some jurors without offering any explanation at all. If litigants are required to articulate even a rational basis—the lowest level of scrutiny—the peremptory challenge may be mortally wounded.

There have been a number of recent calls to finish it off.[143] Opponents of peremptory challenges argue that the biased use of peremptory challenges is a threat to the proper functioning of our judicial system and to our fundamental values.[144] And it is still too easy to evade the prohibitions on biased peremptory challenges. Also troubling is the fact that the peremptory challenge is often used not so much to ensure fairness as to ensure a jury stacked in one's favor. Indeed, a jury consulting industry has recently grown up around the concept of scientific jury selection.[145] Scientific jury selection is designed to identify jurors whose perspectives are such that they are likely to find for the party conducting the study. It uses survey research and other social science sampling techniques to identify the demographic characteristics of persons most likely to side with the consultant's client.[146] It has been used in some

---

is age. Broderick, *supra* note 92, at 400. A rational basis is usually easy to articulate. A court will not invalidate a legislative classification as long as the legislature arguably had a reasonable basis for making the classification. *See* 2 ROTUNDA, ET AL., *supra*, at §18.3. Litigants who employ peremptory challenges against members of groups that are not protected by strict or heightened scrutiny may find it similarly easy to articulate a rational basis for the challenge, if called upon to do so. *See* Barbara D. Underwood, *Ending Race Discrimination in Jury Selection: Whose Right Is It, Anyway?*, 92 COLUM. L. REV. 725, 764–66 (1992) (arguing for a modified peremptory challenge based roughly on the Fourteenth Amendment classifications). *See generally,* Jeffrey J. Rachlinski, *Scientific Jury Selection and the Equal Protection Rights of Venire Persons,* 24 PAC. L.J. 1497 (1993). Indeed, courts have upheld peremptory challenges based on such factors as age and education. *See* Marder, *supra* note 121, at 1066 and notes 101–104. *See also,* Underwood, *supra,* at 765–66 (discussing permissible discrimination against jurors based on such factors as age, disability, occupation, education and wealth). For an attempt to articulate a theory as to exclusion of persons from juries, see Vikram David Amar, *Jury Service as Political Participation Akin to Voting,* 80 CORNELL L. REV. 203 (1995).

143. *See, e.g.,* Broderick, *supra* note 92, at 371, 420–23; Marder, *supra* note 121, at 1046, 1136–38; Batson 476 U.S. at 103 (Marshall, J., concurring); Hon. Theodore McMillan and Christopher J. Petrini, Batson v. Kentucky: *A Promise Unfulfilled,* 58 U.M.K.C. L. REV. 361, 374 (1990).

144. *See, e.g.,* Tanford, *supra* note 135, at 1021–24.

145. *See, e.g.,* Rachlinski, *supra* note 142; Kenneth J. Melilli, Batson *in Practice: What We Have Learned About* Batson *and Peremptory Challenges,* 71 NOTRE DAME L. REV. 447, 501 (1996).

146. *See* Shari Seidman Diamond, *Scientific Jury Selection: What Social Scientists Know and Do Not Know,* 73 JUDICATURE 178 (1990); John H. Kennedy, *Pretrial Standing of Jurors; Becomes Key to the Cases,* BOSTON GLOBE (February 19, 1990), at 1; Gail Appleson,

high-profile criminal cases,[147] and is used in major civil litigation as well, but there is some question about its effectiveness. Some commentators suggest that many of the cases where scientific jury selection is alleged to have been successful were decided as they were because of the evidence or other factors related to the case itself, and not because of who was on the jury.[148] Indeed, there is evidence that who sits on the jury makes little difference in the outcome in most cases.[149] That, in turn, belies the stereotypical views some people have of others, and suggests that most jurors take their responsibilities seriously and try to do a good job.[150]

On the other hand, who sits on the jury could make considerable difference in those cases where varied perspectives are important to a full understanding of the case. For example, men and women likely will have different experiences with sexual harassment, and those experiences may well affect

Corporations Look to Surrogate Juries in Big Cases, REUTERS BUSINESS REPORT (June 5, 1989) (available on Lexis/Nexis Business section); M. Juliet Bonazzoli, Note, *Jury Selection and Bias: Debunking Invidious Stereotypes Through Science*, 18 QLR 247 (1998) (reviewing studies).

147. *See* Mark Davis and Kevin Davis, *Star Rising for Simpson Jury Consultant*, 81 A.B.A. J. 14 (December 1995); ABRAMSON, *supra* note 42, at 155–70 (discussing scientific jury selection in several prominent criminal cases).

148. *See* ABRAMSON, *supra* note 42, at 170; Diamond, *supra* note 146, at 180. Even in the O.J. Simpson trial, where the defense used scientific jury selection but the prosecution did not, factors unrelated to scientific jury selection may have been at play. *See* Davis and Davis, *supra* note 147, at 14 ("It helped that the jury pool was from Los Angeles County, where sentiment was on Simpson's side.").

149. *See* Diamond, *supra* note 146, at 180. Diamond notes that studies show that the evidence presented at trial is the primary determinant of a jury's verdict. Thus, Diamond asserts that scientific jury selection is useful only when the evidence is not weighted strongly in either direction. She further asserts that the best use of social scientists in the trial setting is to aid in preparing the presentation of evidence to the jury, and not in selecting the jury. See also, David Schkade, Cass R. Sunstein, and Daniel Kahneman, *Are Juries Less Erratic than Individuals? Deliberation, Polarization, and Punitive Damages*, University of Chicago, John M. Olin Law & Economics Working Paper No. 81 (2000) (saying that there is substantial agreement across racial, gender, and other lines as to basic norms).

150. It makes sense that it would be difficult to select a perfect jury scientifically. Scientific jury selection is based on social science sampling techniques: people in the community are interviewed to determine what set of demographic characteristics is most likely to favor the party paying for the study. *See* Diamond, *supra* note 146, at 179–80. But the sample of the population that actually sits on the jury is too small to be statistically reliable itself, and social scientists well know that individuals can defy their demographics. *See* ABRAMSON, *supra* note 42, at 171–72. In addition, there is a limited number of peremptory challenges that each party has to shape the jury. *See* note 120, *supra*.

their views on a particular event described at trial.[151] Recent research also shows that men and women often have different styles of discourse[152] and different ways of evaluating moral issues.[153] The different perspectives of blacks and whites stem from their very different experiences with daily living,[154] and those different experiences may well affect their views of the particular practice described at trial.[155] If we recognize that people with different backgrounds may have different perspectives, we must acknowledge that consideration of a variety of perspectives may be critical to a rendering of just decisions.[156] But consultants on scientific jury selection generally aim to seat a jury with only one perspective.[157]

Whether or not scientific jury selection is successful, the concept defies the traditional sense of the jury as the guardian of community values: the very idea behind scientific jury selection is to limit the community from which the jury is drawn to persons pre-disposed toward a particular outcome. The problem is compounded by the fact that wealthy litigants are generally best able to take advantage of the benefits of scientific jury selection. Assuming some effectiveness in scientific jury selection, at least at the margins, the litigation

---

151. *See* Melanie A. Meads, *Applying the Reasonable Woman Standard in Evaluating Sexual Harrassment Claims: Is It Justified?*, 17 L. & PSYCHOL. REV. 209, 211–14 (1993); Joanna L. Grossman, *Note, Women's Jury Service: Right of Citizenship or Privilege of Difference?*, 46 STAN. L. REV. 1115, 1143–46 (1994); Marder, *supra* note 121, at 1063–66.

152. *See* TANNEN, *supra* note 55; DEBORAH TANNEN, TALKING FROM NINE TO FIVE (1994); CATHERINE A. MACKINNON, ONLY WORDS (1993).

153. *See* GILLIGAN, *supra* note 55.

154. *See* COSE, *supra* note 55; WILLIAMS, *supra* note 55.

155. *See* VALERIE P. HANS & NEIL VIDMAR, JUDGING THE JURY 50 (1986); Aleinikoff, *supra* note 55, at 353–55.

156. *See, e.g.*, HANS & VIDMAR, *supra* note 155, at 50, 138–39; Aleinikoff, *supra* note 55. This is not to say that one perspective is more valuable or more correct than another, but only that all relevant perspectives are necessary to just adjudication. But as long as there was a preference on juries for white men, the white male perspective was privileged. The movement away from allowing race– and gender-based peremptory challenges could be viewed as an attempt to correct the inherent bias that existed under prior rules. Not coincidentally, the movement could well result in changes in the outcomes of some cases, as previously unspoken perspectives are heard in the jury room. *But see*, Laura Gaston Dooley, *Essay: Our Juries, Our Selves: Power, Perception, and Politics of the Civil Jury*, 80 CORNELL L. REV. 325 (1995) (arguing that jury control negates the gains in representation on juries for women and African-Americans).

157. Even if the parties have only three peremptory challenges, as is the case in federal civil cases, it should not be difficult to eliminate those with the minority perspective, assuming they can be identified. The very fact that they are in the minority will mean that there are not many in the jury venire.

edge, then, goes to the wealthy, and for reasons having nothing to do with the merits.[158] It is the peremptory challenge that makes this possible.

Critics of the peremptory challenge make some good points. It is true that the peremptory challenge can reflect destructive stereotyping and bias, even under the Court's current rules. It is also true that the peremptory challenge can be used, not to eliminate bias, but to build it into the judicial process by deliberately seating a jury that leans toward one side of the controversy. But eliminating the peremptory challenge, as some commentators have urged, could produce similar damage to the judicial system: litigants may be unable to remove jurors who appear to be biased against them, and the result could be unjust verdicts and less confidence in the judicial system. The question is which approach is more likely to produce just decisions, but the question defies easy answers. It may well be that we do not have enough experience with the Supreme Court's restrictions on the peremptory challenge, as the cases are all relatively recent. Until we have more data, we cannot decide whether it is better to continue with the Court's approach, or to eliminate peremptory challenges altogether. We can, however, identify the issues that we must address in answering that question.

The first issue is how easy it is to articulate race- and gender-neutral reasons for a peremptory challenge. There is some evidence that courts have been quite lenient in accepting reasons.[159] This is not surprising. The peremptory challenge originally required no reason at all, and judges may not wish to probe too deeply even when a reason is required. Such probing could do further damage to the adversary system by requiring a party to give away part of his strategy. The problem is that if it is easy to articulate race- and gender-neutral reasons, real biases in jury selection may simply go underground and be harder to root out. In addition, the requirement that a party articulate race- and gender-neutral reasons for striking jurors may encourage deceit as lawyers who really want to strike all blacks or all women search for other reasons they can give for striking them. If the Supreme Court's requirement that parties articulate race- and gender-neutral reasons for striking jurors is ineffective, or

---

158. The wealthy already have considerable advantages in litigation, particularly if they are repeat participants in the litigation process, as many corporations are. *See* Marc Galanter, *Why the Haves Come Out Ahead: Speculations on the Limits of Legal Change*, 9 L & Soc'y Rev. 95, 97–109 (1974).

159. *See* Purkett v. Elem, 514 U.S. 765, 769 (1995) (accepting explanation that juror had long, unkempt hair); Johnson v. State, 740 S.W.2d 868, 870–71 (Tex. App. 1987) (accepting race-neutral explanations when 9 of prosecutor's 10 strikes were blacks). *See generally*, Richard C. Reuben, *Excuses, Excuses: Any Old Facially Neutral Reason May Be Enough to Defeat an Attack on a Peremptory Challenge*, 82 A.B.A. J. 20 (February 1996).

if it encourages lawyers to lie to the court, some other approach—including, possibly, eliminating peremptory challenges—may have to be considered.

Another issue is whether juries are more fair under the Supreme Court's current doctrine or with no peremptory challenges at all. One role of the jury, identified in Chapter 1, is dispute settling, but the jury can only be successful at that role if it is fair and accurate. This means that jurors must be impartial, suggesting that peremptory challenges may be necessary to eliminate jurors with biases that prevent them from being impartial. It also means that no party should be able to stack the jury in hopes of obtaining a favorable outcome, suggesting that peremptory challenges should not be allowed, because peremptory challenges allow parties to attempt such stacking. Finally, in some cases, fairness and accuracy may require that certain relevant perspectives be represented on the jury.[160] The chances that all relevant perspectives will be heard are enhanced by a random jury selection process, with no peremptory challenges; peremptory challenges allow parties to try to eliminate persons whose perspective differs from their own.[161] Thus, there is no clear answer as to whether the peremptory challenge enhances fairness and accuracy. It may prevent parties from stacking juries and from eliminating relevant perspectives, but it also prevents them from removing genuinely biased jurors. If peremptory challenges were to be eliminated, the challenge for cause would probably have to be strengthened, despite the serious problems that would entail.[162]

---

160. Biased perspectives must be excluded from this statement, however. Fairness and accuracy are not served by having racist jurors who are unable to rule impartially in a case involving African-Americans, even though racists do, unfortunately, represent one perspective in modern America.

161. Some commentators have urged that we deliberately seat juries that reflect all relevant perspectives. See, e.g., Deborah A. Ramirez, The Mixed Jury and the Ancient Custom of Trial by Jury De Medietate Linguae: A History and a Proposal for Change, 74 B.U.L. Rev. 777 (1994); Nancy J. King, Racial Jurymandering: Cancer or Cure? A Contemporary Review of Affirmative Action in Jury Selection, 68 N.Y.U.L. Rev. 808 (1993); Tanya E. Coke, Note, Lady Justice May Be Blind, But Is She a Soul Sister? Race-Neutrality and the Ideal of Representative Juries, 69 N.Y.U.L. Rev. 327, 379–86 (1994); Kim Forde-Mazrui, Jural Districting: Selecting Impartial Juries Through Community Representation, 52 Vand. L. Rev. 353 (1999). There is precedent for this in the so-called mixed jury, which was used by British colonials. When a dispute involved both British citizens and natives of the colonial territory, a jury of six British citizens and six natives was seated. See Ramirez, supra at 783–89; James Bradley Thayer, A Preliminary Treatise on Evidence at the Common Law, 104n.2 (1969 [1898]). One problem with this procedure is identifying the relevant perspectives. Race and gender are obvious, but other characteristics may not be. Furthermore, there is some question how far we may want to carry this as a matter of policy.

162. See supra, notes 119–124 and accompanying text.

Juries also play a political role, as I described in Chapter 1. Juries are the only national governmental body that employs participatory democracy and a consensus decision rule. The jury's political role, centered on participation and deliberation, requires as broad a base of actual jurors as possible, to ensure not only the participation of all citizens, but also meaningful deliberation among those participants. Participation is not, as some suggest, a right;[163] rather, it is an obligation of citizenship.[164] Those who are excluded from jury service, for whatever reason, are denied one of the badges of citizenship.[165] Once again, the question is whether our societal interest in promoting the kind of participation and deliberation that the jury represents is better served by eliminating the peremptory challenge or by continuing to allow it with some restrictions. On the one hand, it appears that we get the broadest base of jurors by eliminating the peremptory challenge. And honest, open-minded deliberations among jurors with different perspectives could do much to educate those jurors not only about different perspectives, but about how much they all have in common. On the other hand, true deliberation could be impossible if some of the jurors are too biased to discuss the case rationally.

In short, there are serious problems with both the peremptory challenge in general and the Supreme Court's current approach to it in particular. But it is not clear that eliminating the peremptory challenge is the answer, because the cost in fairness could be too great. Indeed, the seating of a jury with members who were biased against one of the parties could be a violation of that party's due process rights.[166] Thus, unless clearer evidence materializes that the peremptory challenge does more harm than good, it is not likely to be eliminated. In addition, the peremptory challenge is a means of party control in keeping with the adversary system, and it is unlikely that litigation attorneys would be willing to give it up without a fight.

C. Threats to Jury Diversity

The small jury, the nonunanimous decision rule, and the peremptory challenge all threaten the jury's diversity, or the benefits we hope to obtain from that diversity. There are a number of other threats to jury diversity as well. These include proposals to empanel juries of experts — the so-called "special

---

163. See, e.g., Grossman, *supra* note 151.
164. See 28 U.S.C. § 1870 (1994).
165. See Marder, *supra* note 121, at 1136–38.
166. See Carey v. Piphus, 435 U.S. 247, 259–62 (1978).

juries;" exemptions that allow certain categories of people to avoid jury duty; and, more recently, a trend toward people simply ignoring summonses for jury duty. Each of these deserves brief attention.

1. Special Juries

Some commentators, concerned about the alleged inability of most jurors to deal with the complex cases that form the content of so much modern litigation, have suggested that special, or qualified, juries be empaneled.[167] Such juries would be limited to people with the background necessary to understand the complex material that will be presented at trial. For example, a case involving chemical formulas might be heard by a jury of chemists. They would not, then, be the diverse and generally representative bodies that our ordinary juries are. In the tradeoff between community representation and accuracy, special juries represent a choice for accuracy. That may well be the best choice in a given case, but we need to be aware of what we would be losing.[168]

There is precedent for special juries going back to the earliest days of the jury. In the twelfth century, juries of fishmongers might be empaneled to hear a dispute about spoiled fish, for example.[169] Nevertheless, the special jury is rare in American jurisprudence.[170] While some states have used special juries, with the Supreme Court's approval,[171] there are at least three reasons why the idea has not caught on. First, being of a democratic and egalitarian temperament, Americans have generally thought that the ordinary citizen was capable of sorting out the stuff of most law suits. While the issue is far from settled, there is empirical evidence that bears them out.[172] One study of complex

---

167. *See, e.g.,* William V. Luneburg & Mark A. Nordenberg, *Specially Qualified Juries and Expert Nonjury Tribunals: Alternatives for Coping with the Complexities of Modern Civil Litigation,* 67 Va. L. Rev. 887, 942 (1981); *Developments in the Law— Scientific Evidence: Confronting the New Challenges of Scientific Evidence,* 108 Harv. L. Rev. 1481, 1596 (1995). On the rise of substantively complex cases, see *supra,* Chapter 3, at notes 181–184 and accompanying text.

168. *See supra,* Chapter 1, at note 69 and accompanying text.

169. *See* Luneburg & Nordenberg, *supra* note 167, at 902–03; Thayer, *supra* note 161, at 62–63.

170. *See* Luneburg & Nordenberg, *supra* note 167, at 909.

171. Fay v. New York, 332 U.S. 261, 268–69 (1947); Moore v. New York, 333 U.S. 565, 567 (1948).

172. *See* Richard Lempert, *Civil Juries and Complex Cases: Taking Stock after Twelve Years,* in Verdict: *supra* note 47, at 181; Stephen Daniels and Joanne Martin, Civil Juries and the Politics of Reform (1995); Neil Vidmar, Medical Malpractice and the American Jury (1995); Michael J. Saks, *Do We Really Know Anything About the Be-*

cases found that the most important factor in the jury's ability to decipher the evidence was the quality of the judge's guidance.[173] Apart from judicial guidance, however, ordinary juries could be better equipped to handle such complex matters if peremptory challenges did not so often eliminate those jurors with the most education. Thus, the propriety of special juries may be tied to other aspects of the jury's composition.

A second reason why we have not moved toward the special jury is that we have a variety of other ways of controlling the jury, as I will show in the next three chapters. If judges or even parties can control the flow of information to juries, or the scope and manner of juries' decision-making, special juries may not seem important. A third reason for not using special juries is that we have created another specialized decision-making body outside of the courts that plays the role that special juries might otherwise play: the administrative agency.[174] Administrative adjudication is based on expertise, as would be the special jury.[175]

2. Exemptions

Many jurisdictions have had a practice of exempting whole groups of people from jury duty. Most commonly, exemptions were for doctors, lawyers, teachers, and other professionals.[176] Mothers of small children have also been exempted,[177] and there have been exemptions for people who cannot afford to serve.[178] The reason for these exemptions is that these are people who cannot spare the time from their regular jobs to serve on juries.[179]

---

havior of the Tort Litigation System—And Why Not?, 140 U. PA. L. REV. 1147 (1992); Joe S. Cecil, et al., *Citizen Comprehension of Difficult Issues: Lessons from Civil Jury Trials*, 40 AM. U. L. REV. 727 (1991). *See also, supra* Chapter 1, at notes 30–66 and accompanying text (discussing jury competence).

173. *See* Lempert, *supra* note 172, at 214–15. One of the problems with drawing distinctions between complex and ordinary cases is defining "complex." Cases can be complex because of difficult subject matter or multiple parties, for example. The solutions to any jury problems created by such complexity could depend on the type of complexity.

174. Administrative agencies are discussed *supra*, Chapter 3, at notes 145–171 and accompanying text; and *supra*, Chapter 4, at notes 122–215 and accompanying text.

175. *See supra*, Chapter 3, at notes 158–162 and accompanying text.

176. *See* Joanna Sobol, *Hardship Excuses and Occupational Exemptions: The Impairment of the "Fair Cross-Section of the Community,"* 69 CAL. L. REV. 155, 166 (1995). Persons subject to occupational exemptions may serve if they desire.

177. *See* Grossman, *supra* note 151, at 1138.

178. Sobol, *supra* note 176, at 174.

179. *See id.* at 172.

There are so many problems with the concept of automatic exemptions that many jurisdictions have either scaled them back or eliminated them entirely.[180] First, automatic exemptions eliminate those groups of people from the jury pool altogether, thus undermining the representativeness of the pool. Second, the people eliminated are often the very people who could best help untangle complicated cases, because they are often the best-educated members of the community. Third, such exemptions send some disturbing messages about one's civic responsibilities. It appears that certain people are exempt from those obligations; at the same time, those who remain eligible may feel a certain disrespect, as their jobs are somehow considered expendable. Jury duty seems, then, not a duty of all citizens, but a burden to be avoided if possible. Rather than continue the inequity of granting wholesale exemptions, many jurisdictions now consider requests to be excused on an individual basis.[181] This trend should help to make juries more representative and, perhaps, more capable.

3. Jurors and Civic Responsibility

The move to make the jury pool as large as possible can be foiled, however, by another recent trend: refusal to serve. As I have indicated, jury service is not a right, but a responsibility. The struggle to ensure that all citizens can wear this badge of citizenship has been long and difficult, and is not over yet. It is troubling, then, that many persons called for jury duty today are simply ignoring the summons.[182] This may be part of an overall loss of commitment to the obligations of citizenship, including voting.[183] That in itself

---

180. See id. at 165. See also, Mark Hansen, New York Tackles Jury Standards, 80 A.B.A. J. 22 (January 1994) (noting that 26 states had eliminated all occupational exemptions).

181. See Sobol, supra note 176, at 165.

182. See generally, Susan Carol Losh, Adina W. Wasserman, and Michael A. Wasserman, "Reluctant Jurors:" What Summons Responses Reveal About Jury Duty Attitudes, 83 JUDICATURE 304 (2000). In August 1999, a search of Westlaw's ALLNEWS directory revealed over 100 newspaper articles on this phenomenon in the previous 20 months. See, e.g., Peter Slevin, Many Called, Few Answer for Jury Duty; Report Criticizes System, Suggests Ways to Get People to Serve, WASHINGTON POST (February 19, 1998, at D-4, WL 2468646; Charisse Jones, No Slack for Jury No-Shows; Courts Try to Crack Down on Duty Dodgers, USA TODAY (October 27, 1998, at 3A, WL 5740272. See also, STEPHEN J. ADLER, THE JURY 220 (1994) (saying that the national no-show rate is 55% and that in some jurisdictions as many as two thirds of summonses are ignored).

183. See John R. Petrocik and Daron Shaw, Nonvoting in America: Attitudes and Context, in Political Participation and American Democracy (William Crotty ed., 1991) (noting that with Presidential election turn-out rates at 50–60%, and winners never receiving more than 60% of the votes, American presidents are elected by 25–30% of the citizenry). See generally, RUY A. TEIXEIRA, WHY AMERICANS DON'T VOTE (1988); KEVIN CHEN, PO-

is a serious problem, because the institutions of democracy depend on such commitment. But it also threatens the ideals of participation and deliberation that make the jury work. At least one study showed that people who have served on juries are likely to have more positive views of the system of justice after service than they had before.[184] Another showed a greater willingness to serve again once people have served on a jury.[185] These studies demonstrate the educational value of the jury, over and above its contribution to civic dialogue.

Part of the problem may be that we have done little to make jury service as convenient as possible. Pay for jury service is no more than a token,[186] and some people may lose money by serving on juries. Not all employers continue an employee's salary during jury duty,[187] and some people are self-employed, so that any time away from work means a loss of income. In addition, parents of small children may have nowhere to leave their children; some jurisdictions are beginning to provide day care for jurors.[188] The combination of serious inconvenience or monetary loss and a diminished sense of civic duty may do serious damage to our efforts to secure representative juries. These issues need to be addressed.

III. Summary and Conclusion

There has been considerable experimentation with the structure of the civil jury in recent years. We have seen a movement toward smaller juries, and toward super-majority decision rules. While the Supreme Court has never approved of super-majority decision rules for the federal courts, it permits juries as small as six in the federal courts. Most of the states allow either smaller juries, nonunanimous verdicts, or both. There is substantial evidence, how-

---

LITICAL ALIENATION AND VOTER TURNOUT IN THE UNITED STATES 1960–1988 (1992); BERNARD BARBER, MASS APATHY AND VOLUNTARY SOCIAL PARTICIPATION IN THE UNITED STATES (1980). For figures on voter turnout from 1952–94, see National Election Studies, The NES Guide to Public Opinion and Electoral Behavior, URL:http://www.umich.edu/~nes/resourcs/nesguide/gd-index.htm#6 (May 2, 1996).

184. Diamond, *supra* note 146, at 284–86.

185. *See* GUINTHER, *supra* note 39, at 100.

186. Los Angeles County pays $5 a day. Federal courts pay $40 a day. Sobol, *supra* note 176, at 171.

187. *Id.*

188. *See* Hansen, *supra* note 180, at 22; Editorial, *Commission Takes on Tough Jury Issues*, The San Francisco Chronicle, May 12, 1996, p. 6, 1996 WL 3219711.

ever, that these experiments in jury structure have not been working. Small juries are more likely to reach extravagant verdicts; indeed, one commentator has noted that attacks on jury competence have increased since these changes have taken place.[189] Relevant minority viewpoints are less likely to be represented on smaller juries, and if they are represented, there may not be enough persons on the jury holding that view to affect the course of deliberations, unless the adherent is willing to hang the jury. Similarly, nonunanimous decision rules allow a majority of sufficient size to simply ignore minority viewpoints, and there is evidence that that is exactly what they do. The result is a diminution in deliberation, one of the hallmarks of the jury. And the result of that is likely to be poorer quality verdicts.

It is interesting that the experimentation with small juries and a nonunanimous decision rule has come at the same time that juries are officially opening up to broader participation, with the Supreme Court holding that African-Americans and women cannot be excluded from the jury venire and barring the use of peremptory challenges on the basis of race or gender. The two movements appear to be at odds with each other, because small juries and nonunanimous verdicts tend to silence minority voices. Indeed, it has been suggested that complaints about jury competence may be an excuse to curtail the operation of the most representative and inclusive democratic institution in the country.[190]

The structure and composition of the jury are at a crossroads. Considerable evidence is in about the effect of jury size and the decision rule, and it is not generally favorable to those changes. The question is whether the courts are willing to return to the twelve-person unanimous jury in light if its perceived (but perhaps not proven) inefficiency. Similarly, the Supreme Court's doctrine on peremptory challenges is problematic, and there have been calls for eliminating peremptory challenges altogether. That seems unlikely, so courts and litigants must find some way to make the conditional peremptory challenges work.

---

189. Saks, *supra* note 51, at 264.

190. *See* Dooley, *supra* note 156, at 341. Juries in civil and criminal cases today are easily the most diverse and inclusive of our democratic institutions. *See id.*, 326 and n.5. That may say more about the lack representativeness of our other institutions than about the jury itself, however. There is empirical evidence that juries remain less than representative of the community as a whole, in part because of social factors that make it difficult, for example, to identify and summon eligible blacks, *see* Hiroshi Fukurai, et al., Race and the Jury: Racial Disenfranchisement and the Search for Justice (1993), and in part because the bans on race- and gender-based peremptory challenges are too easy to evade. *See* Jeffrey S. Brand, *The Supreme Court, Equal Protection and Jury Selection: Denying That Race Still Matters*, 1994 Wis. L. Rev. 511.

CHAPTER 6

CONTROLLING THE
EVIDENCE

In Chapter 2, I showed that rules of evidence are a historic means of jury control. In England, rules of evidence allowed judges to exclude evidence deemed unreliable, even if it was relevant and probative. England also expected judges to instruct juries as to the law and to comment on the evidence to the jury, organizing the evidence and giving the jury guidance as to its weight and persuasiveness. In the United States, the approach to evidence is a little different. While exclusion of evidence remains a significant jury control device, American judges rarely comment on evidence. They do, however, instruct juries on the law, and those instructions can exert a subtle influence on the jury's fact-finding. In recent years, the judge's power to control the evidence has taken on added significance as an increase in complex scientific issues has led to a growing professionalization of proof and a stronger gatekeeping role for the judge.

I. Exclusion of Evidence

No country in the world matches the common law countries in the scope of their evidence rules. The common understanding is that the jury is the reason for the rules of evidence. Indeed, the most well-developed rules of evidence today are those in the United States, which is the only country where the jury remains a signficant fact-finding body.[1] In this section, I will show how the power to exclude evidence can control the jury's decision-making. I will then discuss the major modern development in evidence law: the professionalization of proof.

---

1. *See* MIRJAN DAMASKA, EVIDENCE LAW ADRIFT 126 n.4 (1997).

A. The Rules of Evidence and the Jury

The original rules of evidence were common law rules and probably reflect problems that juries had in coping with evidence. As Thayer said, "[t]he law of evidence is the creature of experience rather than logic."[2] Federal courts today are governed by the Federal Rules of Evidence, which build on a base of common law evidence rules.[3] The lofty purpose stated for the Federal Rules is that they should "secure fairness in administration, elimination of unjustifiable expense and delay, and the promotion of growth and development of the law of evidence to the end that the truth may be ascertained and proceedings justly determined."[4] To these ends, the Rules continue the common law practice of placing limits on what a jury will be allowed to hear.

The most fundamental limitation on evidence is relevance.[5] Only relevant evidence is admissible. Relevant evidence is defined as "evidence having any tendency to make the existence of any fact that is of consequence to the determination of the action more probable or less probable than it would be without the evidence."[6] Evidence is not often excluded as irrelevant. Even if evidence is relevant and probative, however, it might not be admissible.[7] The

---

2. JAMES BRADLEY THAYER, A PRELIMINARY TREATISE ON EVIDENCE AT THE COMMON LAW 267 (1969 [1898]). As they originally developed, the rules did three things: (1) prescribed the manner of presenting evidence; (2) fixed the qualifications and privileges of witnesses; and (3) determined what things would not be received in evidence. *Id.* at 264. Of these, Thayer calls the last "the characteristic [function] in our law of evidence." *Id.*

3. Thirty-eight states have followed the federal lead by enacting rules of evidence modeled on the Federal Rules. *See* MICHAEL H. GRAHAM, FEDERAL RULES OF EVIDENCE IN A NUTSHELL, at vi (1996). I will focus on the Federal Rules in this Chapter. The original codification of the Federal Rules of Evidence was done by Congress, but subsequent amendments have been prepared under the authority of the Rules Enabling Act. For a discussion of how the Rules Enabling Act works, see *supra*, Chapter 3, note 11. It is not my purpose here to present a detailed explication of the Rules and how they operate, but merely to show how they constrain what the jury hears. There are several multi-volume treatises on evidence that discuss the rules in more detail. *See, e.g.,* CHRISTOPHER B. MUELLER & LAIRD C. KIRKPATRICK, FEDERAL EVIDENCE (2nd ed. 1994); JACK B. WEINSTEIN AND MARGARET A. BERGER, WEINSTEIN'S FEDERAL EVIDENCE (2nd ed., Joseph M. McLaughlin ed. 1997) [hereinafter cited as WEINSTEIN'S EVIDENCE].

4. FED. R. EVID. 102.

5. THAYER, *supra* note 2, at 264–65. 2 CLIFFORD S. FISHMAN, JONES ON EVIDENCE: CIVIL AND CRIMINAL §11:1 (7th ed. 1994) [hereinafter cited as JONES ON EVIDENCE].

6. FED. R. EVID. 401. Deciding whether evidence is relevant requires reference to the substantive law governing the matter being litigated. *See* THAYER, *supra* note 2, at 468; 2 JONES ON EVIDENCE, *supra* note 5, at §11:2.

7. THAYER, *supra* note 2, at 266; FED. R. EVID. 402. At common law, reasons for re-

Federal Rules of Evidence limit the admission of relevant evidence in two ways. First, some of the rules operate to determine issues without any consideration by the jury. Second, some of the rules allow the judge to exclude evidence from the jury's hearing altogether.

Rules that determine issues include those governing judicial notice and presumptions. Judicial notice allows judges to specify matters that are well known, so that no proof has to be adduced.[8] When judicial notice is taken in a civil trial, the jury is simply told the information and required to accept it as fact.[9] Article II of the Federal Rules of Evidence permits judicial notice of facts that are "either (1) generally known within the territorial jurisdiction of the trial court or (2) capable of accurate and ready determination by resort to sources whose accuracy cannot reasonably be questioned."[10] Judicial notice must be taken if a party requests it and supplies the court "with the necessary information,"[11] but a court may, in its discretion, take judicial notice of facts without being asked.[12] Judicially noticed facts tend to be obvious ones.[13] Judicial notice may be as much a device for saving time as for controlling the jury, as juries would be unlikely to reject obvious facts.

Common law evidence rules also recognized certain presumptions.[14] A presumption is a rule requiring or permitting that the finder of fact draw a particular inference from the evidence even though the evidence does not prove the point directly.[15] For example, it might be presumed that if a person has been absent for seven years, she is dead.[16] Thus, if proof is given that the per-

---

fusing the admission of evidence included that the evidence was too inconsequential; was too remote; had the potential for prejudicing the jury; was capable of being misused or overestimated by the jury; was impolitic or unsafe on public policy grounds; or there was no precedent for admitting such evidence. *See* THAYER, *supra* note 2, at 266.

8. *See id.* at 277–312.

9. *See* EDMUND MORRIS MORGAN, SOME PROBLEMS OF PROOF UNDER THE ANGLO-AMERICAN SYSTEM OF LITIGATION 41 (1956); FED. R. EVID. 201(g). In a criminal case, juries are not required to accept judicially noticed facts as conclusive, but they may do so. *Id.*

10. FED. R. EVID. 201(b).

11. FED. R. EVID. 201(d).

12. FED. R. EVID. 201(c).

13. *See, e.g.,* Transorient Navigators Co. v. M/S Southwind, 788 F.2d 288, 293 (5th Cir. 1986) (judicial notice taken of prevailing interest rates); EEOC v. Delta Air Lines, Inc., 485 F. Supp. 1004, 1008–09 (N.D. Ga. 1980) (judicial notice taken that only females can become pregnant); Lloyd v. Cessna Aircraft Co., 430 F. Supp. 25, 26 (E.D. Tenn. 1976) (judicial notice taken of a national holiday).

14. *See* THAYER, *supra* note 2, at 313–52.

15. 1 JONES ON EVIDENCE, *supra* note 5, at §4:2.

16. *See* THAYER, *supra* note 2, at 319.

son has been absent for seven years, no proof must be adduced of her death. Like the common law rules, the Federal Rules also allow presumptions, though the rules leave it to the courts to specify what presumptions operate in federal courts in federal question cases.[17] State law defines presumptions in federal cases where state law provides the rule of decision.[18]

Rules that allow a judge to exclude evidence from the jury are far more numerous than rules that determine issues. Exclusionary rules fall into three overlapping categories: prejudicial evidence; unreliable evidence; and evidence that we exclude for policy reasons having little to do with the trial process.

Examples of prejudicial evidence include evidence of settlement negotiations,[19] evidence of a party's liability insurance,[20] and evidence of a person's character.[21] Litigants may choose to settle for reasons unrelated to the merits of the case, and offers of settlement should not be held against them in trials. Similarly, the existence of liability insurance does not bear on a person's liability for the acts alleged in the complaint. Finally, a person may be vile, but that is not proof that he committed the particular evil act he is accused of.[22]

Probably the best known example of presumptively unreliable evidence is the hearsay rule, which prevents the introduction of "a statement, other than one made by the declarant while testifying at the trial or hearing, offered in evidence to prove the truth of the matter asserted."[23] Out-of-court statements can be admitted if they are not being used to prove their content. For example, if the issue is whether such a statement was made, but not whether it was true, a witness can testify that she did, indeed, hear it made.[24] The rule ap-

---

17. FED. R. EVID. art. III.

18. FED. R. EVID., art. III. This will be, primarily, cases brought to federal court under the diversity jurisdiction. *See* 28 U.S.C. § 1652 (1994) (state law provides the rule of decision in diversity cases).

19. FED. R. EVID. 408. A related exclusion in the criminal context is the exclusion of evidence of plea bargain discussions. FED. R. EVID. 410. While such discussions can be misleading for the same reasons that settlement discussions in civil cases are misleading, there are more important considerations in the criminal context. Exclusion of such evidence may be necessary to preserve, among other things, a criminal defendant's constitutional right against self-incrimination, U.S. CONST. am. V, and the reasonable doubt standard of proof.

20. FED. R. EVID. 411.

21. FED. R. EVID. 404. *See* EDWARD W. CLEARY, MCCORMICK ON EVIDENCE, § 189 n.2 (3rd ed. 1984) [hereinafter cited as MCCORMICK ON EVIDENCE]

22. *See*, Michelson v. United States, 335 U.S. 467, 475–76 (1948).

23. FED. R. EVID. 801(c). *See also*, THAYER, *supra* note 2, at 499 (describing the common law hearsay rule).

24. *See, e.g.*, M.F. Patterson Dental v. Wadley, 401 F.2d 167 (10th Cir. 1968) (persons who heard allegedly slanderous statement can testify to establish that it was made); Creaghe

plies to documentary evidence as well when the author is absent; a document is hearsay when it is offered to prove the truth of its content because it reflects an out of court statement. The hearsay rule exists because statements that are repeated are notoriously less reliable than the original.[25] This is obvious to anyone who has played the children's game in which a statement is whispered from one to another until the last child says it out loud—and it is gibberish. Similarly, documents can contain errors.

Nevertheless, we also recognize that many statements that are classified as hearsay are, in fact, reliable. Even under the common law, the hearsay rule became subject to exceptions and interpretation,[26] and, if anything, the Federal Rules of Evidence have expanded the exceptions to the point where there are hints in the literature that the hearsay rule should be abolished altogether.[27] An entire article in the Federal Rules is devoted to the hearsay rule and its more than two dozen exceptions.[28] Among others, there are exceptions for various public records, learned treatises, statements about a person's reputation, and statements made while the person was under stress.[29] Out-of-court statements that are excepted from the hearsay rule are deemed more reliable because of the circumstances under which they were made, and thus proper for the jury to consider. The judge in a civil case also has discretion to admit other out-of-court statements if she deems them reliable.[30]

There are several other rules designed to ensure the reliability of evidence. One such common law rule was the "best evidence" rule. Thayer devotes an

---

v. Iowa Home Mutual Casualty Co., 323 F.2d 981 (10th Cir. 1963) (persons who heard terms of oral agreement can testify to establish that the agreement was made). *Cf.* United States v. Jones, 663 F.2d 567 (5th Cir. 1981) (criminal case; defendant's threats against judge admitted to establish that they were made); United States v. Anfield, 539 F.2d 674 (9th Cir. 1976) (prosecutor allowed to testify about what defendant said at a previous trial to show that defendant made inconsistent statements).

25. James Donald Moorehead, *Compromising the Hearsay Rule: The Fallacy of Res Gestae Reliability*, 29 LOY. L.A.L. REV. 203, 205 (1996). *See also*, Laurence H. Tribe, *Triangulating Hearsay*, 87 HARV. L. REV. 957, 958 (1974); Edmund M. Morgan, *Hearsay Dangers and the Application of the Hearsay Concept*, 62 HARV. L. REV. 177, 188 (1948). Indeed, the unreliability of hearsay is so well known, or so intuitive, that jurors apparently ignore it when it does appear in the record. *See* DAMASKA, *supra* note 1, at 31 n.1.

26. *See* THAYER, *supra* note 2, at 520–21.

27. Paul S. Milich, *Hearsay Antinomies: The Case for Abolishing the Rule and Starting Over*, 71 ORE. L. REV. 723 (1992); Paul J. Brysh, Comment, *Abolish the Rule Against Hearsay*, 35 U. PITT. L. REV. 609 (1974).

28. FED. R. EVID., art. VIII.

29. *See* FED. R. EVID. 803, 804.

30. *See* FED. R. EVID. 803(24), 804(b)(5).

entire chapter to the best evidence rule, which required that "the best evidence of which the case, in its nature, is susceptible, must always be produced."[31] Among other things, that generally meant that the original of a document had to be produced, and not mere copies.[32] When the rule first developed, copies were laboriously hand-written and so subject to error.[33] The Federal Rules generally allow the contents of documents to be proved using evidence other than the original.[34] Perhaps we have more faith in photocopy machines than our legal ancestors had in copyists. Another rule designed to ensure reliability is the parol evidence rule, to which Thayer devotes an entire chapter. The parol evidence rule assumed that a written contract contained the parties' entire agreement. The rule then excluded any testimony about additional terms alleged to be part of the contract.[35] Such evidence could be unreliable because a party could be moved by 20/20 hindsight to alter the terms of a contract.[36] The parol evidence rule, however, is not treated at all under the Federal Rules of Evidence; rather, it is considered a principle of contract law.[37]

There are also numerous rules that govern exclusions for public policy reasons. The best known of these is the rule on privileges. Privileges existed at common law,[38] and the Federal Rules continue the practice, but leave the definition of federal privileges to the courts.[39] The Rules also adopt state-defined privileges for cases in federal court where state law provides the rule of decision.[40] Privileges disallow people from testifying about their communications with another person, generally because public policy dictates that there be free and open communication between the two. Common law privileges recognized also by the federal courts and all states include the lawyer/client, hus-

---

31. See THAYER, *supra* note 2, at 486; *see generally, id.* at 484–507.

32. 5 MUELLER & KIRKPATRICK, *supra* note 3, at §556.

33. One can get a flavor for the copyist's work along with a delightful read from CHARLES DICKENS, BLEAK HOUSE (1853).

34. *See* FED. R. EVID. 1003, 1004. There is a provision in the Rules that requires the original, *id.* at 1002, but it is swallowed up by exceptions. *See generally, id.* at art. X.

35. *See generally,* THAYER, *supra* note 2, at 390–483.

36. *See id.* at 396.

37. 2 JONES ON EVIDENCE, *supra* note 5, at §12:21. Both the best evidence rule and the parol evidence rule were subject to numerous exceptions, refinements, and interpretations, so the rules became quite complex. *See* THAYER, *supra* note 2, at 390 ("Few things are darker than [the parol evidence rule], or fuller of subtle difficulties."); *id.* at 488 (describing the best evidence rule as "vague").

38. *See* THAYER, *supra* note 2, at 10; 8 WIGMORE ON EVIDENCE §§2227, 2290, 2380 (McNaughton rev. 1961).

39. FED. R. EVID. 501.

40. FED. R. EVID. 501.

band/wife, and doctor/patient privileges.[41] New privileges may be recognized as well. The Supreme Court recently recognized a psychotherapist/patient privilege, which it held to embrace communications between social workers and patients.[42] The Court there said that all fifty states recognize some form of psychotherapist/patient privilege, though not all states extend it to social workers.[43] Another common privilege is for communications between priest and penitents, which is recognized by all but one state.[44] Less accepted is the privilege for communications between accountants and clients.[45] The purpose of privileges is to encourage the communication that is necessary for these professionals to do their jobs properly, or, in the case of the spousal privilege, to encourage spouses to confide in one another in furtherance of the marital relationship.[46] Thus, even though reports of such communication could be relevant and highly probative, public policy considerations prevent their being introduced at trial unless the client, spouse, or patient waives the privilege.[47]

There are other exclusions based on policy considerations as well. For example, remedial measures taken by a manufacturer after an accident involving its product may be quite relevant, but evidence as to such measures is inadmissible to prove negligence or culpability for the accident.[48] When a product defect allegedly causes an injury, and the manufacturer later changes the product to eliminate the defect, the changes are probative evidence that the defect existed. But if such evidence could be used against the manufacturer at trial, the manufacturer would be less likely to make the changes, thus endangering the public.[49] Similarly, the ban on evidence as to a sexual offense

---

41. McCormick on Evidence, *supra* note 21, at §76.2.

42. Jaffee v. Redmond, 518 U.S. 1, 8 (1996).

43. *Id.* at 12.

44. 8 Wigmore on Evidence, *supra* note 38, at §2395 (1996 supp.). There was no priest/penitent privilege at common law. *See id.* at §2394.

45. Id. at §2286 (1996 supp.) (noting that sixteen states allow an accountant/client privilege).

46. McCormick on Evidence, *supra* note 21, at §72. The spousal privilege is limited to communications relating to the confidential marital relationships. A person can voluntarily testify against his or her spouse as to, for example, the spouse's criminal activity. *See* Travel v. United States, 445 U.S. 40 (1980).

47. 8 Wigmore on Evidence, *supra* note 38, at §§2327, 2340, 2388. The privilege cannot be waived by the professional. *See generally,* George A. Davidson and William H. Voth, *Waiver of the Attorney-Client Privilege,* 64 Ore. L. Rev. 637 (1986).

48. Fed. R. Evid. 407. Such evidence can be admitted to prove "ownership, control, or feasibility of precautionary measures, if controverted," or for impeachment purposes. *Id.*

49. Fed. R. Evid. 407 advisory committee note.

victim's past sexual behavior was instituted because such evidence was all too often used to intimidate victims into not testifying at all.[50]

In addition to these specific rules, the Federal Rules of Evidence contain a catch-all provision that gives the judge a great deal of discretion in deciding whether to admit evidence. Relevant evidence can be excluded "if its probative value is substantially outweighed by the danger of unfair prejudice, confusion of the issues, or misleading the jury, or by considerations of undue delay, waste of time, or needless presentation of cumulative evidence."[51]

The breadth of the judge's power to exclude relevant evidence is enormous. Because judgments about the admission or exclusion of relevant evidence are generally discretionary decisions of the trial judge, such decisions are likely to be reversed on appeal only rarely, as appellate courts review discretionary decisions of the trial judge on an "abuse of discretion" standard.[52] That means that the appellate court will accept even a decision it disagrees with, as long as it was within a wide range of discretion.[53] Furthermore, even if the trial judge or an appeals court decides that evidence was erroneously admitted, it could nonetheless uphold the verdict if it deems the error harmless—that is, if it thinks that the evidence did not af-

---

50. FED. R. EVID. 412 and advisory committee note.

51. FED. R. EVID. 403. See e.g., Carter v. District of Columbia, 795 F.2d 116 (D.C. Cir. 1986) (holding that the reading into evidence of multiple news articles and complaints regarding other officers was prejudicial to police officer defendants); Rozier v. Ford Motor Co., 573 F.2d 1332 (5th Cir. 1978) (holding in a products liability suit that it was error to admit evidence that car's driver had pleaded guilty to voluntary manslaughter); Melton v. Deere & Co., 887 F.2d 1241, (5th Cir. 1989) (holding in products liability suit that judge properly withheld evidence of similar accidents).

52. See, e.g., McGowan v. Cooper Industries, Inc., 863 F.2d 1266, 1271 (6th Cir. 1988). See generally, David P. Leonard, Appellate Review of Evidentiary Rulings, 70 N.C.L. REV. 1155, 1156 (1992). On the discretionary nature of the judge's decision on evidence, see Douglas v. Eaton Corp., 956 F.2d 1339, 1344 (6th Cir. 1992); Jon R. Waltz, Judicial Discretion in the Admission of Evidence Under the Federal Rules of Evidence, 79 N.W.U.L. REV. 1097, 1118 (1984–85); David P. Leonard, Power and Responsibility in Evidence Law, 63 S. CAL. L. REV. 937, 956–57, 974 (1990). Questions as to relevance are not discretionary. A judge could exclude evidence on the ground that it was irrelevant based on her view of the governing legal rules. If her view is mistaken, however, the court of appeals could reverse on a de novo standard of review. See 1 STEVEN ALAN CHILDRESS AND MARTHA S. DAVIS, STANDARDS OF REVIEW §4.2 (1986). Similarly, a judge might refuse to grant a new privilege that a party is arguing for, and the court of appeals will review that decision on a de novo basis. That, indeed, is what happened recently in the lower courts in Jaffee v. Redmond, 518 U.S. 1, 6 (1996).

53. See, e.g., TCP Industries, Inc. v. Uniroyal, Inc. 661 F.2d 542, 550 (6th Cir. 1981). See generally, 1 CHILDRESS & DAVIS, supra note 52, at ch. 4.

fect the jury's verdict.[54] Erroneous exclusion of evidence, by contrast, normally requires a new trial because the evidence was never considered by the jury.[55]

This brief synopsis shows that the rules of evidence define relevance broadly, but impose many restrictions on the admissibility of relevant evidence. Some of these restrictions are based on public policy, such as a desire to encourage people to act in a particular way. Others are designed to prevent what is deemed unreliable evidence from reaching the jury, apparently on the assumption that the jury will be unable to sort out the problem with the evidence. In addition to the specific restrictions, the judge is given considerable latitude to make other evidentiary decisions. Because the judge has considerable discretion as to evidentiary rulings, he has substantial control over the evidence that the jury will hear.

B. The Professionalization of Proof

In Chapter 1, I discussed the difficulties amateur juries might have with complex scientific or technical information, and in Chapter 3, I described how litigation today often encompasses just such issues. While some scientifically complex matters are routed to administrative agencies, as I described in Chapter 4, many remain in the courts, where juries sometimes have to sort them out. We do not yet regularly empanel specialized juries, despite the proposals described in Chapter 5. So the rules of evidence, which developed in a much simpler society, have had to rise to the challenge. There are two problems: deciding what evidence to admit, and making the admitted evidence understandable to lay decision-makers.

1. Admission of Evidence in Complex Cases

There are two issues regarding evidence in complex cases that need consideration. First, while scientific evidence has long been admissible, the

---

54. Errors at trial can be grounds for overturning the judgment, but if the error is harmless, *i.e.*, had no impact on the judgment, the judgment will stand. See FED. R. CIV. P. 61. *See, e.g.,* Conway v. Chemical Leaman Tank Lines, 525 F.2d 927, 929 and n.3 (5th Cir. 1976); Aetna Casualty and Surety Co. v. Gosdin, 803 F.2d 1153, 1159–60 (11th Cir. 1986). This is a somewhat simplistic statement of the harmless error doctrine. In fact, there is considerable disagreement about what constitutes harmless error, in both the civil and the criminal context. *See generally,* Tom Stacy and Kim Dayton, *Rethinking Harmless Constitutional Error,* 88 COLUM. L. REV. 79 (1988) (discussing harmless constitutional error in criminal cases).

55. *See* 21 CHARLES ALAN WRIGHT & KENNETH W. GRAHAM, FEDERAL PRACTICE AND PROCEDURE §5035 (1977). *But see, e.g.,* Wierstak v. Heffernan, 789 F.2d 968, 972 (1st Cir. 1986) (exclusion of evidence offered to impeach ruled harmless error where other evidence to impeach was available).

Supreme Court has recently reformulated the test, arguably altering the roles of judge and jury. Second, some evidence can be expressed only in probabilities, and the courts' methods of dealing with such evidence is the subject of considerable discussion in the academic literature. In this section, I will describe these developments and assess their impact on the jury.

a. Expert Evidence

The long-standing rule for the admissibility of scientific evidence was enunciated in *Frye v. United States*[56] which required that scientific evidence be generally accepted in the scientific community before it could be admitted.[57] In *Frye*, the District of Columbia Circuit refused to sanction admission of evidence from an early form of a lie detector test because the test was not generally accepted as accurate. The general acceptance test became the rule nearly everywhere despite the fact that the Supreme Court, while paying oblique deference to it, never explicitly addressed it.[58] The Supreme Court has finally spoken, however, and it rejected the rule in *Frye* in favor of one that gives the judge a greater gate-keeping role with respect to expert testimony. In *Daubert v. Merrell Dow, Inc.,*[59] the Court held that scientific evidence is admissible when the testimony rests on a reliable foundation and is relevant to the task at hand.[60] Some factors that should be considered in establishing reliability include whether the theory offered is testable; whether it is subject to peer review; what the known or potential rate of error is; and whether the theory has been generally accepted in the scientific community.[61] Thus, general acceptance in the scientific community is merely one factor that the court can consider in determining reliability. The Court has since extended the Daubert test to all expert testimony,[62] and held that the trial judge's decision is to be reviewed on the deferential "abuse of discretion" standard.[63]

---

56. 293 F. 1013 (D.C. Cir. 1923).

57. *Id.* at 1014. *See* 3 WEINSTEIN'S EVIDENCE, *supra* note 3, at ¶702 [03] (1992); Paul C. Gianelli, *The Admissibility of Novel Scientific Evidence: Frye v. United States Half a Century Later*, 80 COLUM. L. REV. 1197, 1204–22 (1980).

58. *See* Laurens Walker & John Monahan, *Daubert and the Reference Manual: An Essay on the Future of Science in Law*, 82 VA. L. REV. 837, 840–41 (1996).

59. 509 U.S. 579 (1993).

60. *Id.* at 589. When the case was returned to the Ninth Circuit, that court held that the challenged expert testimony could not be admitted because it did not meet the relevance prong of *Daubert*. Daubert v. Merrell Dow Pharmaceuticals, Inc., 43 F.3d 1311, 1322 (9th Cir. 1995).

61. Daubert, 509 U.S. at 592–95.

62. *See* Kumho Tire Co., Ltd. v. Carmichael, 526 U.S. 137 (1999).

63. *See* General Electric Co. v. Joiner, 522 U.S. 136 (1997).

Frye required little judgment on the part of the judge, as she could simply defer to the scientific community, though there were sometimes vigorous battles over what was generally accepted. The *Frye* rule routinely kept evidence out of court when it related to new scientific theories that were not fully tested.[64] Such evidence may well have been reliable, but if it had not been verified to the point of general acceptance in the relevant scientific community, the judge was to exclude it.[65] Thus, potentially relevant and probative evidence may have been lost to the trier of fact. On the other hand, Frye could allow the admission of evidence that was generally accepted in a field that had less exacting standards.[66] Such evidence may not be reliable at all.

The *Daubert* rule addresses these problems, but may create some of its own. *Daubert* requires that the judge make decisions about the quality of the proposed expert evidence. Under *Daubert*, the judge may sometimes have to sort out conflicting views within the scientific community about whether a new or experimental process is reliable. She may also have to determine whether an expert's conclusions follow from his data.[67] Of course, the judge may be no more capable of making judgments about scientific or technological reliability than the jury. Like the jurors, the judge is likely to be a lay person with respect to the expert evidence. Yet *Daubert* apparently requires judges to play a gatekeeping role, preventing unreliable scientific evidence from getting to the jury based on their own, possibly limited, understanding of the issues.[68] The *Daubert* rule is thus a double-edged sword: it could result in more unreliable evidence being admitted, but it can also take advantage of developing scientific or technological knowledge.

The judge's gatekeeping role also has mixed implications for the jury. On the one hand, if the judge lets marginal evidence go to the jury, the jury must then sort out the reliability of the evidence, something the scientific commu-

---

64. *See* Gianelli, *supra* note 57, at 1205 and n.46.

65. *See id.*

66. *See* Michael J. Saks, *The Aftermath of* Daubert: *An Evolving Jurisprudence of Expert Evidence*, 40 JURIMETRICS 229, 231 (2000). This could occur in a field where all the research is supported by the industry that is making a particular product. Early research into the safety of tobacco, for example, was supported by the industry rather than by independent entities, so did not flag the threats to health caused by tobacco. I am indebted to my colleague Dennis Prater for this example.

67. *See* Joiner, 522 U.S. at 146. *See generally*, Saks, *supra* note 67.

68. *See* Jay P. Kesan, Ph.D., *A Critical Examination of the Post-*Daubert *Scientific Evidence Landscape*, 52 FOOD & DRUG L.J. 225, 229–30 (1997); Ruth Saunders, Note, *The Circuit Courts' Application of* Daubert v. Merrell Dow Pharmaceuticals, Inc., 46 DRAKE L. REV. 407, 414 (1997).

nity itself has not done. Because the issues are likely to be controversial, there may be, in the end, more opprobrium to be heaped on the jury, and more opportunities for the judge to intervene with such control devices as judgment as a matter of law or the new trial.[69] It is not intuitively obvious that giving the jury such tasks is conducive either to justice or to a strengthening of the jury as a democratic institution. On the other hand, given that many cases raising scientific issues are value-laden, there are good reasons for taking the pulse of the community in at least some cases raising complex scientific issues. If the judge takes too many of those cases away from the jury, the jury will have no opportunity to speak.

b. Probabilistic Evidence

Albert Einstein, who found the probabilistic theories of quantum mechanics deeply troubling, rejected them out of hand with the famous statement that "God does not play dice."[70] It was his most monumental mistake. It is now accepted that the most basic structure of the universe can best be understood in terms of probabilities.[71] Even if God plays dice, however, it is not at all clear that the courts are prepared to. Probabilistic evidence has proved troubling in courts, and there is no real consensus about what role it ought to play.

There are two main problems with probabilistic evidence from the courts' perspective. First, courts are reluctant to hold someone liable if her culpability is defined strictly by probabilities.[72] Second, the adversary system demands a yes or no answer. "Probably" is not easily accommodated in that system. An example will illustrate these problems. If someone is suing a chemical company alleging that his cancer was caused by chemicals that the company disposed of carelessly, the evidence is likely to consist of epidemiological studies.[73] A cer-

---

69. See Chapter 7, *infra*. One possible example of this is the decision granting summary judgment for the defendants in the litigation over the Three Mile Island accident. *In re* TMI Litigation, 927 F. Supp. 834 (M.D. Pa. 1996). Rather than allow the jury to consider the mounds of scientific evidence adduced during discovery, the judge, applying the *Daubert* test, decided for herself that none of the evidence could legally support a verdict for the plaintiffs.

70. NIGEL CALDER, EINSTEIN'S UNIVERSE 141 (1979).

71. See HEINZ R. PAGELS, THE COSMIC CODE (1982).

72. See, e.g., Smith v. Rapid Transit, 58 N.E. 2d 754 (Mass. 1945) (holding that it is not enough that the mathematical chances favor the bus's causing the accident); see also, Guenter v. Armstrong Tire, 406 F.2d 1315 (3rd Cir. 1969) (holding there is no justification for allowing the plaintiff's case to go to the jury based on a probability hypothesis).

73. Epidemiological studies consist of "the statistical study of disease in human populations.... [They] address questions such as 'Does exposure to this chemical increase the in-

tain number of such cancers are going to occur in the population regardless of the chemical company's actions, but some increase in the incidence of such cancers may be attributable to the company.[74] Traditionally, courts are reluctant to allow such probabilistic evidence, because there is no way to establish that the particular plaintiff's cancer is attributable to the company.[75]

Of course, in one sense a trial is always an exercise in probabilistic analysis. The very statement of the burden of proof is probabilistic: in a civil trial, the plaintiff must prove each element of her claim by a preponderance of the evidence.[76] A preponderance of the evidence means greater than a fifty per cent chance—50.1% will do.[77] Thus, the jury has always made probability calculations, though they are generally informed only by their experience. But in a typical trial, the jury does not return a verdict saying that it is 55% sure that the defendant committed (or did not commit) the act complained of. Thus, the probabilistic nature of the analysis is obscured.[78] When overtly probabilistic evidence is introduced, however, the jury is asked to hold someone accountable when a number—sometimes a fairly large number—can be assigned to its risk of error. Not only would the jury be holding someone accountable when there is a good chance he did not cause the injury, but it knows how large a risk it is taking. The jury could be sufficiently uncomfortable with that that it will err on the side of the defendant even when the evi-

---

cidence of cancer in a population?' but not 'Did exposure to this chemical cause a particular person's cancer?'" Michael Dore, *A Commentary on the Use of Epidemiological Evidence in Demonstrating Cause-in-Fact*, 7 HARV. ENVTL. L. REV. 429, 431 (1983). It should be noted that some evidence is both scientific and probabilistic. The example in the text is illustrative.

74. *See, e.g., In re* Agent Orange Product Liability Litigation, 597 F. Supp. 740, 836–37 (E.D.N.Y. 1984); *In re* Joint Eastern and Southern District Asbestos Litigation, 758 F. Supp. 199, 202–03 (S.D.N.Y. 1991).

75. *See* Adrian A.S. Zuckerman, *Law, Fact, or Justice?*, 66 B.U.L. REV. 487, 499–500 (1986); Charles Nesson, *Agent Orange Meets the Blue Bus: Factfinding at the Frontier of Knowledge*, 66 B.U.L. REV. 521, 523–26 (1986).

76. MCCORMICK ON EVIDENCE, *supra* note 21, at §339. The statement in the text oversimplifies the matter. A defendant can have the burden of proof as to some issues in civil trials. One example is an affirmative defense that the defendant raises. *See id* at §337. In addition, some issues in civil trials may require proof by a larger quantum, namely the "clear and convincing" standard. *Id.* at §341.

77. *See* James Brook, *Inevitable Errors: The Preponderance of the Evidence Standard in Civil Litigation*, 18 TULSA L.J. 79, 85 (1982); Ronald J. Allen, *A Reconceptualization of Civil Trials*, 66 B.U.L. REV. 401, 405 (1986).

78. *See* Laurence H. Tribe, *Trial by Mathematics: Precision and Ritual in the Legal Process*, 84 HARV. L. REV. 1372–73 (1971).

dence supports the plaintiff by a preponderance.[79] Alternatively, the judge may be sufficiently uncomfortable with it that she takes the matter out of the jury's hands with one of the control devices I will describe in Chapter 7, such as summary judgment. Some of the debate in the evidence literature concerns the tolerability of overt statements of the risk of error.[80]

Nevertheless, in some cases, probabilistic evidence can establish liability to a fairly high degree of certainty. DNA sampling is one example.[81] In such cases, error is more likely if no liability is found than if it is.[82] Indeed, a jury verdict that found no liability under those circumstances could be set aside under one of the rules I will discuss in Chapter 7.

Another problem occurs when the probabilistic evidence is only a part of the proof offered. There may be some evidence to which a number is assigned, and other evidence to which no number is assigned. When part of the proof has a number attached to it and part does not, critics contend that juries are likely to give too much weight to the number.[83] The jurors' strength is that they call on their experience of human nature and draw an inference. But there is no way they can call on their experience to assess the likelihood that the plaintiff's cancer was caused by the chemical company's product. Lacking that everyday experience, they may be too quick to accept numbers as substitutes. The bottom line, given the discussion so far, is that jurors simply may not know what to do with probabilistic evidence, and so whatever they do, they do badly.[84]

Some commentators have become enthusiastic supporters of the use of Bayes's Theorem to solve problems with the use of probabilistic evidence.[85] Bayes's Theorem is an equation that allows the fact-finder to combine subjective probability figures based on "fuzzy" evidence with an objective probability

---

79. *See id.* at 1349.

80. *See id.* at 1374–75; Allen, *supra* note 78, at 409–15; Zuckerman, *supra* note 76, at 498–502.

81. *See* D.H. Kaye, *The Probability of an Ultimate Issue: The Strange Case of Paternity Testing*, 75 IOWA L. REV. 75, 76 n.2 (1989); Richard D. Friedman, *Generalized Inferences, Individual Merits, and Jury Discretion*, 66 B.U.L. REV. 509, 512–15 (1986).

82. *See* Neil B. Cohen, *The Costs of Acceptability: Blue Buses, Agent Orange, and Aversion to Statistical Evidence*, 66 B.U.L. REV. 563, 568–69 (1986).

83. *See* Tribe, *supra* note 79, at 1361–65.

84. The discussion in the literature on this point is somewhat abstract, however. It seems to consist mostly of what expert commentators think the jury will do rather than what juries actually do.

85. *See, e.g.,* L. JONATHAN COHEN, THE PROBABLE AND THE PROVABLE, (1977); Michael O. Finkelstein and William B. Fairley, *A Bayesian Approach to Identification Evidence*, 83 HARV. L. REV. 489 (1970); Ward Edwards, *Summing Up: The Society of Bayesian Trial Lawyers*, 66 B.U. L. REV. 937 (1986).

figure for more concrete evidence. For example, in a paternity suit, if there is testimonial evidence that one of two men is the father, the initial "fuzzy" probability is 50 per cent that either of them is the father. That is the starting point. The jury would then hear evidence as to the probability that one of the men is the father (or, more particularly, that he is not the father) based on DNA studies of the child, the mother, and the putative father. Bayes's Theorem combines the initial probability—50 per cent—with the more concrete statistical evidence and produces a number.[86] There have been very few attempts to use Bayes's Theorem in actual trials,[87] a fact that proponents in the academic community cheerfully acknowledge.[88] Nevertheless, proponents argue that the accuracy of fact-finding can be enhanced by using tools like Bayes's Theorem.[89]

There are at least two ways in which the use of probabilistic evidence diminishes the role of the jury. First, if probabilistic evidence is given credence, it may substitute for the jury's common sense reading of the matter. But we do not really know whether probabilistic evidence produces greater accuracy than does a jury using common sense or "gut" feelings. Second, if the judge believes that the jury has mishandled the evidence in spite of the guidance it received, she can use one of the control devices described in Chapter 7 to "correct" the verdict. Indeed, the judge may be more willing to step in to tinker with the jury's verdict when the evidence is scientific or probabilistic, on the theory that the jury did not understand it.

2. Expert Witnesses

When scientific or probabilistic evidence is admitted, it is virtually certain that expert witnesses will be needed to explain the evidence to the jury.[90] Intuitively,

---

86. See D.H. Kaye, *What is Bayesianism: A Guide for the Perplexed*, 28 Jurimetrics J. 161, 170–72 (1988); Paul Bergman and Al Moore, *Mistrial by Likelihood Ratio: Bayesian Analysis Meets the F-Word*, 13 Cardozo L. Rev. 589, 596–99 (1991). One could also start with a more subjective probability estimate based on the less concrete factors. See Kaye, *supra*, at 170–72.

87. For some examples of the use of Bayesian analysis, *see, e.g.*, Hartman by Hartman v. Stassis, 504 N.W.2d 129 (Iowa Ct. App. 1993) (paternity); Kammer v. Young, 535 A.2d 936, (Md. Ct. Spec. App. 1988) (paternity); *In re* Paternity of M.J.B., 425 N.W.2d 404 (Wis. 1988) (paternity).

88. See Edwards, *supra* note 85, at 937.

89. See Finkelstein and Fairley, *supra* note 85, at 501–02; Michael O. Finkelstein, *Application of Statistical Decision Theory to the Jury Discrimination Cases*, 80 Harv. L. Rev. 338, 339–40 (1966).

90. See Samuel R. Gross, *Expert Evidence*, 1991 Wis. L. Rev. 1113; Finkelstein and Fairley, *supra* note 85, at 516–17; Jonathan J. Koehler, *Error and Exaggeration in the Presentation of DNA Evidence at Trial*, 34 Jurimetrics J. 21, 36 (1993) (noting a study that found

one might expect that those experts will carry considerable weight with the jury, as juries of lay persons would want to defer to the expert because they have no other basis for a decision.[91] Furthermore, just as probabilistic evidence can cause jurors to ignore the "fuzzy" evidence, the presence of an expert could cause the jury to focus on the matter about which the expert is testifying, and perhaps give less credence to evidence that requires only their own common sense to analyze.

The reality, however, may be somewhat different. Despite the considerable attention that lawyers and academics give to expert witnesses, jurors themselves seem to be less impressed. Some studies have shown that expert testimony has less of an impact on jurors than was once thought.[92] If juries discount experts, it may be because of the adversarial nature of litigation. Most expert witnesses are retained by one of the parties. When the outcome of a case turns on a question that requires expert testimony, the trial may become a "battle of the experts," with the expert witnesses on each side presenting conflicting testimony.[93] There are several problems with this. First, jurors have a hard time knowing which expert to believe, and may be disinclined to believe anyone.[94] In addi-

---

that jurors who received a brief lecture on Bayes's Theorem made better inferential judgments than jurors who received no instruction); David L. Faigman and A.J. Baglioni, Jr., *Bayes's Theorem in the Trial Process: Instructing Jurors on the Value of Statistical Evidence*, 12 L. & Hum. Behavior 1 (1988). Article VII of the Federal Rules of Evidence governs the taking of expert witness testimony.

91. *See* United States v. Brown, 557 F.2d 541, 556 (1977); United States v. Addison, 498 F.2d 741, 744 (D.C. Cir. 1974).

92. *See* Gross, *supra* note 90, at 1178 (citing studies); Joseph Sanders, *Scientifically Complex Cases, Trial by Jury, and the Erosion of Adversarial Processes*, 48 DePaul L. Rev. 355, 364–65 (1998) (citing studies); Wendy S. Neal, Note, General Electric Co. v. Joiner, *118 S.Ct. 512 (1997): The Future of Scientific Evidence in Toxic Tort Litigation*, 67 U. Cin. L. Rev. 881, 883 (1999). Studies do show that experts on eyewitness identification have a substantial impact on the jury, however. *See* Gross, *supra* note 90, at 1178.

93. *See* Andrew MacGregor Smith, Note, *Using Impartial Experts in Valuations: A Forum-Specific Approach*, 35 Wm. & Mary L. Rev. 1241, 1244–45 (1994). For an example of a battle of the experts, see, e.g., Ferebee v. Chevron Chemical Co., 736 F.2d 1529 (D.C. Cir. 1984) (disagreement between experts over how soon a disease would manifest itself after exposure to toxic chemical). *See also*, Veronica Serrato, Note, *Expert Testimony in Child Abuse Prosecutions: The Spectrum of Uses*, 68 B.U. L. Rev. 155, 183 (1988) (discussing disagreements among experts as to the veracity of a child's testimony). In theory, such battles could become less frequent after Daubert v. Merrell Dow, Inc., 509 U.S. 579 (1993), as judges prevent unreliable evidence from being entered. *See supra*, notes 56–69 and accompanying text. But there will still be plenty of issues where there is competent scientific evidence on both sides.

94. *See* Joe S. Cecil, *et al., Citizen Comprehension of Difficult Issues: Lessons from Civil Jury Trials*, 40 Am. U.L. Rev. 727, 754 (1991); Joel Cooper, *et al., Complex Scientific Testimony: How do Jurors Make Decisions?*, 20 L. & Hum. Behav. 379, 390 (1996).

tion, the evidence is sometimes so difficult that jurors have trouble compre-
hending it.[95] This problem is compounded by the fact that the evidence is presented in a disjointed manner, with evidence as to a particular point coming
in seemingly at random.[96] This makes it hard for the jury to organize the evidence. Court-appointed experts could help to organize the evidence and to
mediate the battle of the experts, but court-appointed experts are rare.[97] This
is largely because of a concern that such experts will carry too much weight
with the jury, who will see such experts as neutral and therefore more believable.[98] That could, in effect, take matters out of the hands of the parties, in
violation of the principles of adversary adjudication.[99] The American system
may have become less adversarial under the Federal Rules of Civil Procedure,
as I showed in Chapter 3, but court-appointed experts are too much of a departure from adversarial adjudication for many litigants.

While the effect is not as severe as when expert administrators decide matters, juries may have less influence over decisions where expert witnesses testify.
The advantage of giving experts more influence at the expense of lay juries is
greater accuracy. The advantage is greatest where the science is susceptible of accurate measurement. The disadvantage of giving experts more influence is that
we may lose the benefits of ordinary citizens' common sense judgments. The
disadvantage is greatest where the scientific issue is infused with value choices.

C. Summary and Conclusion

The rules of evidence have long been a device for controlling the jury,
though the control is soft compared to the devices I will discuss in the next
chapter. By excluding evidence from the jury, the court can lead the jury in
what it sees as the correct direction, free from prejudice that can taint its views
of the case. It is the recent trend toward professionalizing proof that is par-

---

95. *See, e.g.*, Sanders, *supra* note 92, at 362–63.
96. *See* DAMASKA, *supra* note 1, at 145; Sanders, *supra* note 92, at 365.
97. Gross, *supra* note 90, at 1190–93. Court-appointed experts are permitted in the
federal courts under FED. R. EVID. 706.
98. *See* Gross, *supra* note 90, at 1190–93.
99. Another possible solution—judges commenting on and organizing the evidence
for the jury—suffers from the same defect. *See infra*, notes 141–157 and accompanying
text. It also would rely on non-expert judges, who may be just as ill-equipped to organize
the evidence. For a discussion of the principles of adversary adjudication, see Ellen E.
Sward, *Values, Ideology, and the Evolution of the Adversary System*, 64 IND. L.J. 301, 312–13
(1989).

ticularly threatening to the jury, however. As issues become more complex, juries have more opportunities to make mistakes. Even if they are corrected by the judge, these mistakes may undermine confidence in the jury. In addition, more scientific and probabilistic evidence means that there is a greater need for expert witnesses, whose views can be quite influential, though the evidence for that is not strong. There are certainly benefits from having experts involved in the decision-making as to complex matters. But few matters are devoid of value choices, and the jury, which reflects the values of the community, may be a necessary part of the equation as well.

II. Instructions to the Jury

The judge decides the law, and the jury decides the facts.[100] A lawsuit, however, determines the entire case. To accommodate the division of responsibility, the judge instructs the jury in the law, usually following pattern jury instructions for the jurisdiction.[101] It is then up to the jury to find the facts and to apply the law, as stated by the judge, to those facts.[102] There are several ways, however, in which the judge's instructions can affect or even guide the jury's fact-finding. First, the distinction between law and fact is sometimes difficult to delineate, so the judge's instructions could spill over into matters of fact. Second, the judge's task includes instruction as to the quantum of proof necessary to find facts, and how she describes that quantum could determine how the jury finds facts. Third, instructions can be easy or hard to follow, and a confused jury may do confusing things. Finally, modern evidence scholars have proposed new ways of structuring legal arguments, which often entail new ways of instructing the jury.

---

100. *See supra*, Chapter 2, at notes 97–103 and accompanying text.

101. *See, e.g.,* FIFTH CIRCUIT CIVIL JURY INSTRUCTIONS (1995); EIGHTH CIRCUIT CIVIL JURY INSTRUCTIONS (1995); NINTH CIRCUIT CIVIL JURY INSTRUCTIONS (1993). Pattern jury instructions will contain instructions that are commonly used in the jurisdiction, and may include instructions for a number of specific kinds of cases. *See, e.g.,* FIFTH CIRCUIT CIVIL JURY INSTRUCTIONS , *supra,* at §6.1 (antitrust); *Id.* at §7.1 (securities violations). There will be times, however, when the judge will not find a pattern instruction for the matter before her. She then will have to compose her own, usually after asking for proposals from the parties.

102. *See* Henk J. Brands, *Qualified Immunity and the Allocation of Decision-Making functions Between Judge and Jury,* 90 COLUM. L. REV. 1045, 1056 (1990); Arthur T. Vanderbilt, *Judges and Jurors: Their Functions, Qualifications and Selection,* 36 B.U.L. REV. 1, 6 (1956).

A. Law and Fact

The distinction between law and fact is one of the most notoriously difficult distinctions in the law.[103] The line between the two is fluid, and the judge, in instructing the jury on the law, may sometimes necessarily cross the line. This is especially true when the judge is instructing the jury as to the rules of evidence. The judge can, for example, tell the jury to ignore evidence that has been placed before it erroneously.[104] She will instruct the jury as to presumptions.[105] She will tell them about matters subject to judicial notice.[106] She may tell them that a party witness's refusal to testify about a particular matter was unfounded and that negative inferences can be drawn from the refusal.[107] In other words, her instructions, while founded on the law of evidence, are really instructions as to fact-finding.

Even when the judge is clearly confining herself to instructions as to the law, the instructions can affect the fact-finding. Instructions, for example, will describe the elements of a cause of action and tell the jury that all elements must be established by a preponderance of the evidence for the plaintiff to recover.[108] This forces the jury to organize the evidence in a particular way, possibly different from its original view of the evidence.[109]

The allocation of questions of law to the judge and fact to the jury also ignores a critically inportant aspect of most cases that touches on both law and fact: value.[110] A jury may come away from a trial with a strong sense of which party should prevail. It may then try to fit the fact-finding to its sense of justice, using the judge's instructions on the law as a guide, but not really caring

---

103. See THAYER, *supra* note 2, at 183–216; Stephen A. Weiner, *The Civil Jury and the Law-Fact Distinction*, 54 CALIF. L. REV. 1867, 1868 (1966). I discuss the law/fact distinction in greater detail in Chapter 7, at notes 2–9 and accompanying text.

104. *See, e.g.,* NINTH CIRCUIT CIVIL JURY INSTRUCTIONS § 3.05 (1993); Holmes v. City of Massillon, 78 F.3rd 1041, 1047 (6th Cir. 1996).

105. *See, e.g.,* 21 WRIGHT AND GRAHAM, *supra* note 55, at § 5127; Gaste v. Kaiserman, 863 F.2d 1061, 1065 (2d Cir. 1988); Ocla Star-Banner Co. v. Damron, 401 U.S. 295, 297–98 (1971).

106. *See, e.g.,* FIFTH CIRCUIT CIVIL JURY INSTRUCTIONS § 2.4 (1995); EIGHTH CIRCUIT CIVIL JURY INSTRUCTIONS § 2.04 (1995). *See also,* cases cited *supra* note 13.

107. *See, e.g.,* Jaffee v. Redmond, 518 U.S. 1, 5–6 (1996).

108. *See, e.g.,* FIFTH CIRCUIT CIVIL JURY INSTRUCTIONS § 2.20 (1995); EIGHTH CIRCUIT CIVIL JURY INSTRUCTIONS § 3.04 (1995).

109. *See* Ronald J. Allen, *The Nature of Juridical Proof,* 13 CARDOZO L. REV. 373, 396–98 (1991).

110. *See* Zuckerman, *supra* note 75, at 494–98.

what the law requires.[111] This is what sometimes happens with jury nullification. Indeed, we like to say that we favor the jury for its ability to introduce common sense community values into litigation, even while we cringe at the thought of nullification.[112]

The judge, then, can influence the jury's fact-finding, wittingly or not, through the instructions he gives. The interplay among law, fact, and value is subtle, but a case is but one entity, composed of all three. It is difficult, if not impossible, to put them into separate cubbyholes.

B. Burdens of Proof

The judge also instructs the jury as to the burden of proof it is to apply. There are just two standard burdens of proof for civil cases: preponderance of the evidence, which is the burden for most civil cases; and clear and convincing evidence, which is used in some jurisdictions for certain disfavored claims, such as fraud[113] or the actual malice element of slander of a public figure.[114] Neither of these standards is normally described in terms of a percentage, though the preponderance standard is commonly understood to require a likelihood of just over fifty per cent.[115] The clear and convincing standard is a heavier burden of proof, but no one knows exactly where it falls, and for the most part we are content to let juries decide.[116] The judge's description of these burdens, however, can affect how the jury weighs the evidence and finds facts.[117]

---

111. See Allen, supra note 109, at 396–401.

112. See Chapter 1, supra, at notes 72–108 and accompanying text for a discussion of jury nullification.

113. See McCormick on Evidence, supra note 21, at § 340.

114. The Supreme Court has held that, under the First Amendment guarantee of free speech, a public figure can only recover for slander if he can establish that the alleged slanderer was motivated by actual malice. See New York Times Co. v. Sullivan, 376 U.S. 254, 279–83 (1964). Mere recklessness as to the facts is not enough. The Court also requires that actual malice be proven by clear and convincing evidence. Id. at 285–86.

115. See Brook, supra note 77, at 85; Allen, supra note 77, at 405.

116. The courts tend to instruct the jury on the clear and convincing standard using language such as "highly probable," but leave it to the jury to decide what that means. See McCormick on Evidence, supra note 21, at § 340; J.P. McBaine, Burden of Proof: Degrees of Belief, 32 Calif. L. Rev. 242, 246–54 (1944).

117. See, e.g., Saul M. Kassin and Lawrence S. Wrightsman, On the Requirements of Proof: The Timing of Judicial Instruction and Mock Juror Verdicts, in In the Jury Box: Controversies in the Courtroom 143, 144 (Lawrence S. Wrightsman, Saul M. Kassin and Cynthia E. Willis eds. 1987) [hereinafter cited as In the Jury Box] (citing N.L. Kerr, et al.,

C. Making Instructions Understandable

Numerous studies have found that instructions may be difficult for the jury to understand, resulting in juror error in the application of law to fact.[118] While there is also some evidence to the contrary,[119] these findings suggest a need for improvement. One of the reasons for pattern jury instructions was a desire to get some consistency in jury instructions.[120] Pattern instructions, however, may have little effect on jury comprehension, even if they reduce the incidence of reversible error in instructing the jury.[121] This may be because the instructions tend to be written in technical legal language.[122] In addition, lawyers and judges may presume that the jurors pay more attention to the instructions than they actually do.[123]

With these findings in mind, researchers have begun to look for better ways to instruct juries. Researchers have studied the psychology of jurors, looking for patterns of thought that might indicate the most effective way of instructing them.[124] Some studies suggest that juries do better when the judge tries to instruct them in plain English rather than legalese.[125] Other

---

Guilt Beyond a Reasonable Doubt: Effects of Concept Definition and Assigned Decision Rule on the Judgments of Mock Jurors, 34 J. PERSONALITY & SOC. PSYCHOL. 282 (1976).

118. *See, e.g.*, Robert MacCoun, *Inside the Black Box: What Empirical Research Tells Us About Decisionmaking By Civil Juries*, in VERDICT: ASSESSING THE CIVIL JURY SYSTEM 137, 152–53 (Robert E. Litan ed. 1993); Robert P. Charrow and Veda R. Charrow, *Making Legal Language Understandable: A Psycholinguistic Study of Jury Instructions*, 79 COLUM. L. REV. 1306, 1358–60 (1979).

119. *See, e.g.*, Joe S. Cecil, *et al.*, *Citizen Comprehension of Difficult Issues: Lessons From Civil Jury Trials*, 40 AM. U.L. REV. 727, 764 (1991); ROBERT L. MCBRIDE, THE ART OF IN-STRUCTING THE JURY §2.11 (1969).

120. *See* Amiram Elwork, *et al.*, *Toward Understandable Jury Instructions*, in IN THE JURY BOX, *supra* note 119, at 161, 162. Pattern instructions are found in every jurisdiction in the United States, though they vary in comprehensiveness.

121. Elwork, *et al.*, *supra* note 120, at 162.

122. *See* Amiram Elwork, *et al.*, *Juridic Decisions: In Ignorance of the Law or In Light of It?*, 1 L. & HUM. BEHAVIOR 163, 164 (1977) [hereinafter cited as Elwork, *Juridic Decisions*].

123. *See* Kassin and Wrightsman, *supra* note 117, at 144.

124. *See, e.g.*, Charrow and Charrow, *supra* note 118, Elwork, *Juridic Decisions*, *supra* note 122.

125. *See, e.g.*, Charrow and Charrow, *supra* note 118, at 1341–58; Elwork, *Juridic Decisions*, *supra* note 122, at 178. The task of reformulating such instructions from legalese to plain English could itself be difficult. Legalese sometimes has concepts and nuances built into it that must be captured in any plain English translation. Pattern plain English instructions would be needed to reduce the incidence of judicial error in instructing juries. Efforts to produce plain English jury instructions are underway in several states. *See, e.g.*,

studies suggest that judges should instruct the jury at the outset of the litigation, before the jury has heard the evidence; instructions at the end may be too late to enable jurors to construct the evidence around the requisite legal framework.[126]

There appear to be two conflicting views at work here, with the concept of jury control at the heart of the matter. On the one hand, if instructions are given in a form more comprehensible to the jurors, the jurors may have more effective control over the outcome. While the goal is helping the jury to reach more legally correct verdicts, jurors who understand the law and the factual requirements for meeting it may be better equipped to nullify the law by structuring their fact-finding to meet the legal requirements, and it may be harder for judges who oversee trials to determine when nullification has occurred. Furthermore, if instructions are given in precise legal language, the judge may be in a better position to control the jury even when the jury did not intend to nullify. If the jury misunderstands instructions and makes fact-finding errors that lead to verdicts inconsistent with what the judge thinks the law requires, the judge can set aside the verdict using his discretionary power to order new trials[127] or even his power to enter judgments contrary to the verdict.[128] Thus, resistance to plain English instructions may occur because of lawyers' and judges' fear of losing control.[129]

D. Structuring the Deliberations

Related to the problem of making jury instructions understandable is the considerable body of scholarship from the last thirty years or so that seeks to understand, and perhaps to structure, the jury's decision-making. The unofficial start to the spate of research is generally thought to be a 1968 article by John Kaplan that discussed decision theory with respect to criminal tri-

---

Mark Curriden, *Jury Reform*, 81 A.B.A. J. 72, 75 (Nov. 1995) (reporting that the Arizona Supreme Court had adopted a rule requiring plain English jury instructions); WILLIAM E. WEGNER, ET AL., CALIFORNIA PRACTICE GUIDE TO CIVIL TRIALS AND EVIDENCE, ch. 14-D (1993–95) (suggesting that jury instructions be written in plain English); George Hathaway, *An Overview of the Plain English Movement for Lawyers... Ten Years Later*, 73 MICH. B.J. 26, 27 (1994) (reporting that Michigan's Plain English Committee had given its Clarity Award to jury instruction committees that had developed plain English instructions).

126. *See, e.g.,* Elwork, *Juridic Decisions, supra* note 122, at 172; E. Barrett Prettyman, *Jury Instructions — First or Last?,* 60 A.B.A. J. 1066 (1960); MCBRIDE, *supra* note 119, at §3.10.

127. *See* Chapter 7, *infra,* notes 144–171 and accompanying text.

128. *See id.* at notes 87–143 and accompanying text.

129. *See* Brenda Danet, *Language in the Legal Process,* 14 L. & SOC. REV. 445, 542 (1980).

als.[130] Decision theory is a means of modeling decision-making processes with a goal of optimizing the quality of the result.[131] There are both descriptive and prescriptive aspects of such research, though most of the research so far is descriptive, seeking to understand how juries go about their task.[132]

Scholars are reluctant, however, to propose using such tools to structure jury decision-making. There are three primary reasons for that reluctance. First, decision theory tends to be rigidly logical or mathematical, but we value the jury for its injection of human sensibility into the decision-making process.[133] Computers can perform the mathematical calculations, but they have no human experience. Second, it would likely be impossible, or nearly so, to train jurors to use such methods. Issues in the case might interact with each other in complex ways, and forcing the thinking into a rigid pattern could cause the jury to miss some opportunities to sort things out in more free-form ways, such as brainstorming. A case might be best analyzed holistically, in other words, rather than atomistically.[134] Another problem is that sometimes the jury is deciding more than what happened. It is also making a value judgment about what happened, and its decision will reflect that.[135] Value judgments are notoriously difficult to measure or to force into equations.[136]

Nevertheless, these studies can provide a valuable aid in helping us develop jury instructions and other techniques that will enable the jury to perform its task optimally. If we understand how jurors go about their decision-making, we can adapt instructions to fit their methods. For example, one scholar has suggested that the traditional jury instruction that tells the jury what the elements of the cause of action are and instructs it that it must find that the plaintiff has proved each by a preponderance of the evidence is incompatible with the jury's mode of

---

130. John Kaplan, *Decision Theory and the Factfinding Process*, 20 Stan. L. Rev. 1065 (1968).

131. *See* Ward Edwards, *Influence Diagrams, Bayesian Imperialism, and the Collins Case: An Appeal to Reason*, 13 Cardozo L. Rev. 1025, 1057 (1991). *See generally*, H. Raiffa, Decision Analysis: Introductory Lectures on Choices Under Uncertainty (1968); W. Feiler, An Introduction to Probability Theory and Its Applications (3d ed. 1968).

132. *See, e.g.*, Reid Hastie, Inside the Juror (1993); Saul M. Kassin & Lawrence S. Wrightsman, The American Jury on Trial: Psychological Perspectives (1988). An early attempt to study jury decision-making was Albert S. Osborn, The Mind of the Juror (1937).

133. *See* Kaplan, *supra* note 130, at 1091.

134. *See* William Twining, *The Boston Symposium: A Comment*, 66 B.U. L. Rev. 391, 399 (1986).

135. *See* Zuckerman, *supra* note 75, at 498–508.

136. *Id.*

thinking and with existing logical and probabilistic constructs.[137] One scholar has proposed a reconceptualization of the trial that would require the jury to fit the parties' stories into a scenario that is more or less believable.[138] And standard probability theory would demonstrate that even if each element of a claim is established by a preponderance, the probability of the whole claim's being true could be less than 50%.[139] One scholar urges, instead, that the parties be required to present full-blown stories to the jury, which will then choose the one it finds most credible.[140] This would capture more of the holistic approach that juries take to such problems anyway.

The scholarship I have described here can be used to help the jury in its decision-making function. If we understand how juries operate, we should be able to find ways to help them do their jobs better. But this scholarship can also be used to better control the jury. There are two ways this could happen. First, if we know how juries operate, instructions can be formulated to get them to do what the judge wants. Second, decision theory could be used to take over the jury's function altogether, on the ground that we can reach better results through such methods than by leaving the decision to the jury. So far, the commentary is concentrated on improving instructions rather than taking over the jury's function, but there is a fine line between helping the jury do its job better and telling the jury what to do. If we are having trouble determining where the line is, it may be because we do not really know where it should be.

---

137. *See* Allen, *supra* note 77, at 404–431.

138. *See id.* at 425–31.

139. *Id.* at 405. For example, if there are two independent elements to the claim, and the jury is satisfied that they are each 60% likely to be true, the chance that *both* are true is only 36%. *Id.* Juries are not generally instructed in such probabilities. Indeed, one of the most spectacular failures of probabilistic evidence involves just such a scenario. In *People v. Collins*, 438 P.2d 33 (1968), the trial court in California permitted an expert witness to testify as to the overall probability that there was another couple with the same characteristics as the accused, based on the probabilities for each of six characteristics. The probability he testified to was one in twelve million. The problem, as the California Supreme Court recognized, was that the six characteristics were not independent, as is required for this technique to be statistically valid. *Id.* at 39.

140. Allen, *supra* note 77, at 426–31. Story-telling, or narrative, is a common theme in modern legal literature, as more lawyers recognize that what they do at trial is tell stories. *See generally, Symposium: Legal Storytelling*, 87 MICH. L. REV. 2073 (1989). In a sense, however, it is nothing new. That is the approach reflected in the ancient methods of proof, such as ordeal, battle, and compurgation, where the parties told their stories and then let God choose between them. *See* S.F.C. Milsom, *Law and Fact in Legal Development*, 17 U. TORONTO L. REV. 1 (1967).

E. Summary

Jury instructions can help to control the jury in a number of ways. First, even though the judge is supposed to instruct the jury as to the law, the instructions can shade over into fact because the line between law and fact is so fluid. Second, instructions regarding the burden of proof give the jury some guidance about how to weigh the evidence. Third, the language used to instruct the jury can confuse or edify, and, ironically, confusing instructions could make it easier to control the jury. Finally, recent application of decision theory to jury deliberations can help us give the jury better guidance, though that may also mean better control; it can also lead to more overt attempts to control the decision process, though no one has suggested such a usurpation of the jury's function yet.

III. Judges Commenting on the Evidence

Related to jury instructions is the power of judges to comment on the weight of the evidence. This power has common law origins, and is uniformly practiced in England, where it is an essential part of any jury trial.[141] The judge's role in England is to summarize, organize and explain the evidence for the jury, and to analyze issues of relevance, credibility, and other matters bearing on the probative value of the evidence.[142] While English authorities are agreed on these responsibilities of the judge, they emphasize that the jury is the ultimate fact-finder, and only needs the judge to guide it on its journey through the evidence—a journey that is unfamiliar to jurors as lay decision-makers.[143] There has always been some concern about judges who go beyond their roles as guides and try, by their commentary, to coerce juries.[144] But by

---

141. Justice Allen Hartman, *The "Whys" and "Whynots" of Judicial Comments on Evidence in Jury Trials*, 23 Loy. U. Chi. L.J. 1, 2–3 (1991); Lord Patrick Devlin, Trial by Jury 116–20 (1956); Robert Wyness Millar, Civil Procedure of the Trial Court in Historical Perspective 310 (1952); Edson R. Sunderland, *The Inefficiency of the Jury*, 13 Mich. L. Rev. 302, 305 (1915).

142. *See* Hartman, *supra* note 141, at 2–3; Vanderbilt, *supra* note 102, at 6; Sir Matthew Hale, The History of the Common Law of England 164–65 (Charles M. Gray ed. 1971).

143. Hartman, *supra* note 141, at 12–13; Vanderbilt, *supra* note 102, at 6; Hale, *supra* note 142, at 165; Millar, *supra* note 141, at 311. The jury has been free to disregard the judge's advice since Bushell's Case, 135 Vaughan, 124 Eng. Rep. 1006 (1670). *See supra*, Chapter 2, note 103.

144. Hartman, *supra* note 141, at 13–14.

and large, a trial in England is considered a joint responsibility of judge and jury, who work together.[145]

The practice of judges commenting on evidence is rare in the United States.[146] Most states forbid a judge's commenting on evidence through their state constitutions, statutes, or decisional rules.[147] While commenting on evidence is permitted in the federal courts under common law rules, it is rare.[148] To some extent, this sentiment against judges commenting on evidence stems from the early history of the country, when judges were deemed either incompetent or in the pockets of the British.[149] Many early judges were lay judges who had no more legal knowledge than did the average juror.[150]

There are occasional calls for an expansion of the power of judges to comment on evidence in American courts as a means of improving jury decision-making.[151] One reason given for allowing judges to comment on the evidence is that the adversarial structure of presentation confuses jurors, as evidence on a particular issue is presented at different times during the trial, making it harder to construct a rational view of the evidence.[152] Judges might be able to assist the jury by commenting on and organizing the evidence. This could be particularly useful if the evidence were complex, such as scientific or probabilistic evidence—at least if the judge herself understood it.

But significant opposition to judges commenting on the evidence keeps the practice from taking root.[153] It is curious that there should be such an aversion to a judge's commenting on the evidence at the same time that other jury

---

145. See DEVLIN, supra note 141, at 120.

146. Id. at 119; Hartman, supra note 141, at 3; MILLAR, supra note 141, at 310.

147. See Hartman, supra note 141, at 17–18; MILLAR, supra note 141, at 310–11; Myron Atkinson, Jr., and LaVern C. Neff, Note, Evidence—Jury Trials—Weight of Evidence—Credibility of Witnesses—Judicial Comment Thereon, 27 N. DAK. L. REV. 199, 205 (1951).

148. See Hartman, supra note 141, at 18–19; 1 WEINSTEIN'S EVIDENCE, supra note 3, at ¶107[01], at 107–10n.8.

149. See Hartman, supra note 141, at 15–16; Vanderbilt, supra note 102, at 56; 1 WEINSTEIN'S EVIDENCE, supra note 3, at ¶107[01]; Austin Wakeman Scott, Trial By Jury and the Reform of Civil Procedure, 31 HARV. L. REV. 669, 677 (1918).

150. See Hartman, supra note 141, at 15–16; Vanderbilt, supra note 102, at 56; 1 WEINSTEIN'S EVIDENCE, supra note 3, at ¶107[01]; Scott, supra note 149, at 677.

151. See MILLAR, supra note 141, at 311–13; Committee of the Section of Judicial Administration of the American Bar Association, Instructions to Jurors, 10 F.R.D. 409, 413 (1949).

152. See DAMASKA, supra note 1, at 51.

153. See Stephen A. Saltzburg, The Unnecessarily Expanding Role of the American Trial Judge, 64 VA. L. REV. 1, 33–43 (1978) (opposing judicial comment on evidence).

control devices seem to be a growth industry. There are at least two possible reasons for this. First, there is a thin line between appropriate commenting on evidence and inappropriate coercive commentary. Some judges may be reluctant to test those limits. Indeed, one commentator suggests education for the judges in how to comment on evidence, in part to overcome judges' reluctance.[154] Second, commenting on the evidence may appear to be a clearer usurpation of the jury's function than most of the other control devices, simply because it can sound like the judge is trying to tell the jury how to find the facts. Other jury control devices may in fact be greater encroachments on the jury's traditional functions, but they can be couched as decisions on questions of law[155] or as devices designed to encourage the parties to settle.[156] Commenting on the evidence, by contrast, looks like judicial interference with the jury's fact-finding role, even when the jury theoretically retains the right to find the facts as it sees them. The jury may well give undue weight to the judge's commentary because members of the jury see her as more experienced, but a single judge may have biases that affect her commentary.[157] Thus, we remain largely content to confine the judge's guidance to the formal instructions.

IV. Summary and Conclusion

The judge has several devices at his disposal to help control how the jury views the evidence. The judge can keep some evidence from the jury altogether, though some exclusions of evidence are done for public policy rather than jury control reasons. The judge can instruct the jury as to the law and the burden of proof, and those instructions can lead the jury toward one view of the evidence rather than another. Indeed, the very formulation of the instructions can affect the jury's deliberations. And as matters that are placed before juries become more technically complex, and our understanding of decision-making processes deepens, there may well be more pressure to give in-

---

154. *See* Hartman, *supra* note 141, at 23–24.

155. For example, decisions on the admission or exclusion of evidence, the legal sufficiency of the evidence, or the preclusive effect of a prior judgment might all be deemed to be questions of law.

156. For example, judicial case management or court-ordered alternative dispute resolution may have this effect. *See* Chapter 8, *infra*.

157. *See* Hartman, *supra* note 141, at 19–20 (summarizing arguments against judges' commenting on the evidence); Saltzburg, *supra* note 153, 35–43.

structions that lead the jury toward a particular outcome. Finally, federal judges can comment on the evidence, but few do so.

These evidentiary controls can have considerable influence on the outcome of the case, but they leave the ultimate decision in the hands of the jury. Thus, they leave open the possibility of jury error or nullification. There are, however, a wide range of control devices by which the judge can take cases away from the jury altogether. I discuss those devices in the next chapter.

CHAPTER 7

Controlling the Jury's Decision-making

A number of jury control devices operate directly on the jury's decision-making, sometimes by taking matters out of the jury's hands, and sometimes by structuring the jury's decision-making. Two of them—the summary judgment and the judgment as a matter of law—depend on the law/fact distinction. Another, the new trial, takes the decision away from one jury and gives it to another. The special verdict requires the jury to break down its decision-making and report specific findings of fact, which makes it easier for the judge to monitor the decision-making. Congress and the courts also have the power to take issues away from the jury by changing jurisdictional or substantive rules; a prominent example is the cap on damages. Finally, changes in the rules governing issue preclusion—the circumstances under which prior litigation will determine issues in a subsequent case—eliminate juries in some cases that otherwise would have had one. Most of these control devices have undergone changes in recent years that make them more effective as jury control devices.

I. Controls Based on the Law/Fact Distinction

The distinction between law and fact existed at common law, but the only way to distinguish them at common law was through pleadings.[1] Thus, if a defendant demurred to the complaint, she was raising a question of law. If she pleaded a traverse, she was attacking the factual allegations of the complaint. Today, there are three jury controls based on the law/fact distinction: the motion to dismiss for failure to state a claim, the summary judgment, and the judgment as a matter of law. Because the law/fact distinction is so important to these control devices, I will first describe it.

---

1. See *supra*, Chapter 2, at notes 97–103 and accompanying text.

A. The Law/Fact Distinction

Distinguishing between questions of fact and questions of law is one of the most difficult things that courts do.[2] The significance of the decision is enormous, however. If the judge decides that an issue poses a question of law, he can decide it himself, taking it from the jury altogether. Some commentators have said that the law/fact distinction is really a euphemism for a policy decision about which questions the judge should decide and which questions the jury should decide.[3]

The law/fact distinction is not a hard and fast line drawn between two clearly defined phenomena. Rather, there are gradations from pure questions of fact to pure questions of law. Pure questions of fact would be questions aimed solely at discovering what happened.[4] Questions of fact are particular to the case before the court. It might be established, for example, that an individual made deliveries for Conglomerate Corporation, that she was paid per

---

2. One indication of this difficulty is the volume of literature that has been produced on the law/fact distinction. It would be impossible to catalog all that has been written on the subject, but a representative sampling includes JAMES BRADLEY THAYER, A PRELIMINARY TREATISE ON EVIDENCE AT THE COMMON LAW 183–262 (1898 [1969]); Stephen A. Weiner, *The Civil Jury and the Law-Fact Distinction*, 54 CALIF. L. REV. 1867 (1966); and Nathan Isaacs, *The Law and the Facts*, 22 COLUM. L. REV. 1 (1922). In addition, the distinction is often discussed in articles dealing with specific subject matter, such as constitutional fact, *see, e.g.*, J. Wilson Parker, *Free Expression and the Function of the Jury*, 65 B.U.L. REV. 483 (1985). Courts also often grapple with the subject. *Compare*, Harvey v. William H. Moore Building Corp., 359 F.2d 649, 654 (2nd Cir. 1966) (holding that whether plaintiff was a "crewman" was a question of fact or mixed question of law/fact for the jury even though facts as to his employment were undisputed); *with* Burriss v. Texaco, Inc., 361 F.2d 169, 174 (4th Cir. 1966) (holding that whether a person was an agent or an independent contractor was to be determined by the judge because there was no dispute as to the basic facts).

3. *See, e.g.*, Weiner, *supra* note 2, at 1868. The issue is complicated by the fact that the law/fact distinction also serves to allocate decision-making responsibility between trial and appellate courts. *See* Ellen E. Sward, *Appellate Review of Judicial Fact-Finding*, 40 KAN. L. REV. 1, 9–12 (1991). The issues in that context are different, but the law/fact distinction drawn in one context can carry over into the other. *See, e.g.*, Parker, *supra* note 2 (discussing the implications for the right to jury trial of *Connick v. Myers*, 461 U.S. 138 (1983), where the Supreme Court held that the question whether a questionnaire distributed by an employee was a matter of public concern and therefore protected by the First Amendment was a question of law for the judge). This is an example of the constitutional fact doctrine, which developed in the context of allocating responsibility between trial and appellate courts. *See generally*, Henry P. Monaghan, *Constitutional Fact Review*, 86 COLUM. L. REV. 229 (1985). As Parker makes clear, however, the implications are broader.

4. *See* Weiner, *supra* note 2, at 1869–71.

delivery, and that she made 85% of her deliveries for Conglomerate. These would be findings of fact. Pure questions of law would be questions going to the existence or meaning of a legal rule, including a statute or a common law rule.[5] Such questions have effects far beyond the immediate case, as they set legal precedent for other litigants.[6] An example of a question of law would be whether, under a statute that required employers to pay unemployment tax on all employees, the tax had to be paid on independent contractors. In other words, was the statute meant to encompass independent contractors as well as more traditional employees?

The real difficulty comes from questions that fall between these two extremes. Two middle categories of questions that frequently appear in the cases and commentary are "ultimate facts" and "mixed" questions of law and fact.[7] In the example described in the previous paragraph, for example, the question whether the delivery person was an independent contractor or an employee would be an "ultimate" fact. It is a conclusion drawn from a number of other facts, and certain legal consequences attach to it. But the question might also have some legal content if, for example, the court found that the statute was meant to cover some independent contractors but not all. The answer would then be dependent upon the mix of characteristics that the delivery person had, and each case will present a slightly different mix. Thus, the legal scope of the statute is defined in terms of the facts presented in individual cases. This is a "mixed" question of law and fact.[8]

As long as the rule about allocating decision-making authority between judge and jury is stated in stark black and white terms, concepts like "ultimate fact" and "mixed" question of law and fact are manipulable. Many questions

5. *Id.* at 1868–69.

6. *See id.* Stare decisis is the doctrine that gives cases precedential value in later cases. It holds that once a court decides a legal issue, lower courts within its jurisdiction are bound by the decision. A Supreme Court decision binds all courts in the United States. A decision by one of the circuit courts of appeals binds all district courts within that circuit, but not district courts in other circuits. For a discussion of the doctrine of *stare decisis*, see, e.g., Earl Maltz, *The Nature of Precedent*, 66 U. N. C. L. Rev. 367 (1988).

7. I have discussed these kinds of issues before. *See* Sward, *supra* note 3, at 31–34. *See also, e.g.,* Frederick Green, *Mixed Questions of Law and Fact*, 15 Harv. L. Rev. 271 (1901); Francis H. Bohlen, *Mixed Questions of Law and Fact*, 72 U. Pa. L. Rev. 111 (1924); Adrian A.S. Zuckerman, *Law, Fact, or Justice?*, 66 B.U.L. Rev. 487, 490–92 (1986); Rosenthal v. Rizzo, 555 F.2d 390, 395 (3rd Cir. 1977) (Aldisert, J. dissenting) (discussing ultimate facts).

8. *See, e.g.,* Frederick J. de Slovere, *The Functions of Judge and Jury in the Interpretation of Statutes*, 46 Harv. L. Rev. 1086 (1933); Fleming James, Jr., *Functions of Judge and Jury in Negligence Cases*, 58 Yale L.J. 667 (1949); Dale W. Broeder, *The Functions of the Jury: Facts or Fictions*, 21 U. Chi. L. Rev. 386 (1954).

in these categories could reasonably be categorized as either fact or law, but there are only two choices, and the choices carry with them polar opposite results as to who decides. It is the judge who determines which category the question falls into.[9] Thus, the judge has considerable control over the jury in that he can keep certain questions out of its hands entirely.

B. Motion to Dismiss for Failure to State a Claim

This motion is the Federal Rules version of the old common law demurrer.[10] Under the common law, the demurrer was used to challenge the legal basis for the plaintiff's claims.[11] For example, if the plaintiff alleged that the defendant had called him a "jerk," the defendant's response would probably have been a demurrer, which admits the allegations of the complaint but asserts that no legal recovery is allowed for the alleged offense. The common law demurrer carried with it some risk. If the court decided that there was a legal basis for the plaintiff's claims, the defendant lost because he had already admitted the allegations of the complaint. By filing the demurrer, he gave up his right to contest those allegations.[12]

The modern rule is much less risky. When a defendant files a motion to dismiss for failure to state a claim, the court will assume *for purposes of the motion only* that the allegations are true.[13] But if the court decides that the plaintiff has stated a claim, that assumption is dropped, and the defendant can contest the factual allegations of the complaint or assert other defenses.[14] Thus, we might expect to see more such motions, and more cases removed from the jury on the basis of the pleadings, than we did at common law. In fact, however, motions to dismiss for failure to state a claim are rarely granted because pleadings under the Federal Rules, which serve only to give notice of

---

9. *See generally,* Monaghan, *supra* note 3, at 234; Parker, *supra* note 2, at 487.

10. Authority for the modern motion to dismiss for failure to state a claim is found at FED. R. CIV. P. 12(b)(6).

11. *See* THEODORE F. T. PLUCKNETT, A CONCISE HISTORY OF THE COMMON LAW 413 (1956).

12. *See* Roger W. Kirst, *The Jury's Historic Domain in Complex Cases,* 58 WASH. L. REV. 1, 15 (1982).

13. *See* N. L. Industries, Inc. v. Kaplan, 792 F.2d 896, 898 (9th Cir. 1986).

14. The defendant could, for example, assert an affirmative defense, which assumes the truth of the allegations but asserts new material, not found in the complaint, as an excuse. *See* FED. R. CIV. P. 8(c). The defendant might, for example, admit striking the plaintiff as alleged in the complaint, but assert that he did so in self-defense and so is not liable.

the claims or defenses, are bare-bones.[15] It is expected that the parties will fill in the details during discovery.[16] Thus, almost any reasonably colorable claim will be accepted.[17] For this reason, the motion to dismiss for failure to state a claim is much less important than summary judgment and judgment as a matter of law for policing the law/fact distinction.

C. Summary Judgment

Summary judgment is a relatively recent addition to the procedural menu. There was no common law rule allowing for summary judgment, and the early varieties of summary proceedings in England and America were limited to specific kinds of cases.[18] In England, summary judgment originated in the mid-nineteenth century, long after the ratification of the Seventh Amendment, with a summary procedure that was available to creditor-plaintiffs who wished to secure a speedy judgment in cases where no apparent defense was available.[19] The purpose of this summary procedure was to prevent debtors from using frivolous defenses to delay collection of debts.[20] Summary proceedings in England have expanded considerably, and are now available in most kinds of cases.[21]

Several varieties of summary proceedings arose in the early history of the United States, mostly in the nineteenth century. All were generally restricted

---

15. This is evident from the forms, which give guidance to litigants about what various litigation documents are supposed to look like. The forms governing complaints are extremely sparse. *See* FED. R. CIV. P., Forms 3–18.

16. *See* Beeman v. Fiester, 852 F.2d 206, 210–11 (7th Cir. 1988).

17. *See* Conley v. Gibson, 355 U.S. 41, 45–46 (1957) (saying that complaints under the Federal Rules "should not be dismissed for failure to state a claim unless it appears beyond doubt that the plaintiff can prove no set of facts in support of his claim which would entitle him to relief."). While Conley may have overstated it, some extremely confusing complaints have been accepted. *See, e.g.,* Dioguardi v. Durning, 139 F.2d 774 (1944).

18. *See* Robert Wyness Millar, *Three American Ventures in Summary Civil Procedure*, 38 YALE L.J. 193, 194–224 (1928).

19. *See* Charles E. Clark and Charles U. Samenow, *The Summary Judgment*, 38 YALE L.J. 423, 424 (1929).

20. *Id.*

21. *See* R.J. WALKER, THE ENGLISH LEGAL SYSTEM 302 (5th ed. 1980). The cases in which summary proceedings are not available are libel, slander, malicious prosecution, false imprisonment, fraud and admiralty actions *in rem. Id.* This list corresponds closely with the list of actions in which civil juries are available in England. *See* Chapter 2, *supra,* at n.56. This may reflect a sense that these are the kinds of cases juries should consider.

to specific kinds of actions, and most were available to plaintiffs only.[22] The justifications for these American summary proceedings varied, but often there was some reason why delay would be costly.[23] By the time the Federal Rules of Civil Procedure were adopted, however, there was considerable support for a summary judgment procedure that applied across the board to all kinds of actions, and that is what the Rules provided for.[24]

The Federal Rules allow either party to move for summary judgment.[25] The motion shall be granted if "there is no genuine issue of material fact and...the moving party is entitled to a judgment as a matter of law."[26] Unlike the motion to dismiss for failure to state a claim, summary judgment motions can be supported with affidavits, depositions, documents, and other material not found in the pleadings.[27] When a motion for summary judgment has been made and properly supported, the party opposing the motion "may not rest upon the mere allegations or denials of [his] pleading, but [his] response, by affidavits or as otherwise provided in this rule, must set forth specific facts showing that there is a genuine issue for trial."[28] The party opposing the motion can, in the alternative, file a cross-motion for summary judgment, conceding that there is no genuine issue of material fact, but contending that he is entitled to judgment as a matter of law. No response is required, however, if the party moving for summary judgment has not established, by her mo-

---

22. *See generally*, Millar, *supra* note 18 at 242. Some kinds of actions in which summary proceedings were available include recovery of liquidated damages on a contract, enforcement of liens and mortgages, and recovery possession of personal property. *Id.* at 242–43.

23. An example is actions against "tenants wrongfully holding over." Millar, *supra* note 18, at 194. Millar also notes that summary proceedings may be allowed for "certain demands against sheriffs and other public officers;... [for] the collection of taxes;... [and for] the non-payment of a debt." *Id.* Summary proceedings were also available for small claims. *See id.* at 196; Clark & Samenow, *supra* note 19, at 425–27.

24. *See* FED. R. CIV. P. 56, advisory committee note to 1937 adoption.

25. FED. R. CIV. P. 56(a) and (b). Summary judgment was thought necessary in part because the "notice pleading" theory of the Federal Rules of Civil Procedure makes pleadings and motions to dismiss less effective as a means of eliminating baseless claims. *See* Jeffrey W. Stempel, *A Distorted Mirror: The Supreme Court's View of Summary Judgment, Directed Verdict, and the Adjudicative Process*, 49 OHIO ST. L.J. 95, 98–99 (1988). I have already noted that the motion to dismiss for failure to state a claim is not very effective at eliminating baseless claims.

26. FED. R. CIV. P. 56(c).

27. *Id.* If a party seeks dismissal for failure to state a claim and supports the motion with material from outside the pleadings, the court is authorized to treat the motion as one for summary judgment. FED. R. CIV. P. 12(b).

28. FED. R. CIV. P. 56(e).

tion and supporting papers, the absence of a genuine issue of material fact.[29] The premise of the summary judgment motion is that because there are no factual issues, there is no need for a trial; the judge is responsible for deciding legal issues, and the motion puts the legal questions to her on allegedly indisputable facts.

Innovative procedures are sometimes slow to take hold, however.[30] Perhaps cognizant of—and wary of—the power the new procedure gave them, judges for much of the history of the Rules have been reluctant to grant motions for summary judgment if there is any hint of a dispute about facts,[31] and that reluctance was often reinforced by appellate courts, which were quick to overturn decisions granting summary judgment.[32]

In 1986, the Supreme Court decided three cases designed to overcome that reluctance. *Celotex Corp. v. Catrett*[33] clarified the test to be applied in considering summary judgment motions and urged lower courts to be more willing to grant them. *Anderson v. Liberty Lobby, Inc.*[34] allows the courts to take account of heightened burdens of proof at trial in deciding whether to grant summary judgments, a result that surely gives the judges greater power to weigh evidence. *Matsushita Electric Industrial Co., Ltd. v. Zenith Radio Corp.*[35] allows a trial judge to grant summary judgment when, despite a voluminous paper record, the judge finds that there is no economically viable motive for the alleged acts, also a result that clearly allows judges to weigh evidence.

In *Celotex*, the widow of a man who had died as a result of inhaling asbestos sued manufacturers of asbestos for wrongful death. One of the manufacturers, Celotex, moved for summary judgment on the ground that the plaintiff had no proof that the decedent had ever come into contact with asbestos that it manufactured. Celotex did not provide affidavits or other proof of its con-

---

29. Adickes v. S.H. Kress & Co., 398 U.S. 144, 184 (1970) ("the party opposing the motion for summary judgment bears the burden of responding only after the moving party has met its burden of coming forward with proof of the absence of any genuine issues of material fact").

30. The law is, by and large, a conservative profession, bound by precedent and reluctant to change rules that its practitioners have grown accustomed to.

31. *See* Martin B. Louis, *Federal Summary Judgment Doctrine: A Critical Analysis*, 83 YALE L.J. 745, 746 and n.7 (1974) (citing cases).

32. *See,* Professional Managers, Inc. v. Fawer, Brian, Hardy and Zatzkis, 799 F.2d 218, 222 (5th Cir. 1986); William W. Schwarzer, *Summary Judgment Under the Federal Rules: Defining Genuine Issues of Material Fact*, 99 F.R.D. 465, 467 (1984).

33. 477 U.S. 317 (1986).

34. 477 U.S. 242 (1986).

35. 475 U.S. 574 (1986).

tention, but merely stated that discovery had produced no evidence of Celotex's liability.[36] The question was whether Celotex had met its burden to produce enough material in support of its motion for summary judgment to require the plaintiff to respond.[37] If it had not, the motion would be denied and the case would go on to trial.

In answering this question, the Court did two things that made it easier for judges to take cases away from the jury. First, it held that Celotex's statement that discovery had failed to support one of the elements of plaintiff's claim was sufficient to require the plaintiff to respond with evidence in support of that element.[38] In other words, Celotex was not required to produce affirmative evidence in support of its motion, but could rely solely on the absence of the plaintiff's evidence. Second, the Court reformulated the standard to be applied in summary judgment motions: a court should not grant a motion for summary judgment if there is evidence that, if believed, could cause a reasonable jury to find for the non-moving party.[39] In making this determination, the courts are to consider all of the evidence presented by both parties and decide if a reasonable jury could find for the non-moving party.[40]

The Court's decision that Celotex could simply state that discovery had failed to produce essential evidence in support of the plaintiff's claim is part of a reformulated methodology for deciding summary judgment. Ironically, Justice Brennan in dissent best explained the majority's methodology.[41] He said that if the party moving for summary judgment has the burden of proof at trial—usually the plaintiff—then that party must produce sufficient credible, admissible evidence to entitle it to a directed verdict at trial if the other party were to make no response.[42] If the moving party produces such evidence, the party opposing the summary judgment will be required to respond; if not,

---

36. 477 U.S. at 321.

37. The plaintiff in *Celotex* argued that Celotex's merely stating that the plaintiff had not produced evidence of an element of her claim is not sufficient to meet this initial burden. She argued that Celotex had to produce affirmative evidence showing no genuine issue of material fact. Celotex, 477 U.S. at 324.

38. *Id.* at 322–26. The Court distinguished *Adickes*, 398 U.S. 144.

39. This is the same standard that is used for judgment as a matter of law, and the Court was explicit about that. See Celotex, 477 U.S. at 321. For a discussion of judgment as a matter of law, see *infra*, notes 87–143 and accompanying text.

40. *See* Celotex, 477 U.S. at 322–23.

41. Justice Brennan agreed with the methodology, but disagreed with the majority in its application of the standard.

42. 477 U.S. at 331. Directed verdicts are now called judgments as a matter of law.

the moving party will be denied summary judgment and the case will proceed. This was not the situation in *Celotex*, where the *non-moving* party had the burden of proof at trial. It will always be difficult for a plaintiff to get a summary judgment because she must establish that there is irrefutable evidence as to every element of her cause of action.

There are two ways a party who does not have the burden of proof at trial— usually the defendant—can produce sufficient evidence to require a response from the non-moving party. First, it can produce affirmative evidence, admissible at trial, negating an element of the opposing party's claim.[43] For example, Celotex could have produced business records showing that it never sold its product to any company that the deceased had worked for. Second, it can demonstrate that the opposing party has failed to adduce any admissible evidence with respect to an element of its claim.[44] Celotex used the second method.[45] It is much easier for defendants to get a summary judgment because they must produce irrefutable evidence negating only one element of the plaintiff's claim.

Thus far, the Court's action probably did not change the law, though it makes the analytical process more explicit and easier to use, and therefore more likely to produce summary judgments.[46] But the Court's statement of the standard for granting a summary judgment probably does change the law.[47] Most judges had been reluctant to grant summary judgment, and there are good reasons for that reluctance. Summary judgment motions are decided on a paper record; the same statement can sound quite different on paper than

---

43. *Id.* at 331.

44. *Id.*

45. The majority and the dissent disagreed over what it meant to demonstrate the absence of evidence, and that is why they ultimately reached opposite conclusions. The majority thought that it was sufficient to claim generally that the depositions and documents produced during discovery did not contain any evidence of one of the elements of plaintiff's claim. *Id.* at 322. The dissent thought that the moving party ought to address any evidence that was produced and demonstrate why it was insufficient or inadmissible. *Id.* at 331. Under the majority's view, the burden of production on the moving party is very small—little more than a requirement that it make a conclusory statement about the absence of evidence.

46. That, in fact, is exactly what has happened. *See* Samuel Issacharoff and George Loewenstein, *Second Thoughts About Summary Judgment,* 100 YALE L.J. 73, 91–93 (1990); Ann C. McGinley, *Credulous Courts and the Tortured Trilogy: The Improper Use of Summary Judgment in Title VII and ADEA Cases,* 34 B.C. L. REV. 203, 228 (1993). The authors cited in this note are discussing the increase in summary judgments favoring defendants as a result of all three of the cases discussed here, and not just *Celotex.*

47. *See* Stempel, *supra* note 25, at 106.

from the mouth of a live witness.[48] Even judges who would be willing to grant a motion for judgment as a matter of law after hearing witnesses were hesitant about using the summary judgment, even though the two motions apparently use the same standard.[49] Thus, if there were any hint of a dispute of fact, the court often denied summary judgment. Most courts looked only at the evidence offered by the non-moving party and made no attempt to weigh the evidence. But *Celotex* allows the judge to consider, and arguably to weigh, all the evidence before her, whether offered by the moving or the non-moving party.[50] After considering all the evidence, the judge is to determine whether a reasonable jury could find for non-moving party. If not, then summary judgment could be granted. The Court then admonished the lower courts to be less reluctant to use summary judgments. The bottom line is that the Court made summary judgments easier to get, especially for defendants, and told the lower courts to start using the tool more freely. But the standard the Court stated seems to allow judges to weigh factual evidence, which is inconsistent with the allocation of fact-finding to juries.[51]

The exhortation to freer use of summary judgments was reinforced in *Anderson v. Liberty Lobby*,[52] decided on the same day as *Celotex*. Liberty Lobby had sued Jack Anderson for libel as a result of a column in which Anderson referred to Liberty Lobby and its founder as right-wing neo-Nazis.[53] Because Liberty Lobby and its founder were considered public figures, an essential element of their libel claim was that Anderson had acted with actual malice.[54] The standard of proof at trial was that actual malice had to be proven by the more difficult "clear and convincing" evidence standard rather than by the

---

48. *See* Coppo v. Van Wieringen, 217 P.2d 294, 297 (1950), *quoting* McLimans v. City of Lancaster, 15 N.W. 194, 195 (Wis. 1883).

49. *See* Stempel, *supra* note 25, at 99; Issacharoff and Loewenstein, *supra* note 46, at 84–87. In *Celotex*, the Court stated quite clearly that the lower courts were to apply the same standard in deciding summary judgments as they would use in deciding whether to grant a judgment as a matter of law. 477 U.S. at 323. The Court cited *Anderson v. Liberty Lobby, Inc.*, 477 U.S. 242, 252 (1986), which was decided on the same day, for this proposition.

50. *See* Stempel, *supra* note 25, at 99, 107; Issacharoff & Loewenstein, *supra* note 46, at 87–91.

51. In those cases where no jury is available or none has been demanded, the problem is less serious, though the difference between a paper record and live witnesses could mean that a judge should still be reluctant to grant summary judgment motions.

52. Anderson v. Liberty Lobby, 477 U.S. 242 (1986).

53. *Id.* at 245.

54. *Id.* at 245.

usual civil standard of a preponderance.[55] Anderson moved for summary judgment, saying that Liberty Lobby had legally insufficient evidence of actual malice. He produced the affidavit of the article's author, which said that the author believed the allegations in the article to be true.[56] Liberty Lobby then presented admissible evidence showing that the sources on which the article was based had been discredited in connection with earlier litigation, and that an editor who worked for Anderson would have had knowledge of that.[57]

The question was whether, in ruling on the motion for summary judgment, the court could take account of the heightened standard of proof for actual malice.[58] The Court said that it could.[59] In other words, after *Anderson*, the question for the lower courts when a defendant moves for summary judgment based on the insufficiency of the plaintiff's evidence is whether a reasonable jury could decide that the plaintiff had proven each element of his claim by whatever quantum of proof is required for that element.[60] The Court, applying this standard, upheld the granting of summary judgment.[61]

There was a vigorous dissent to this holding. Justice Brennan argued that allowing a trial judge on a summary judgment motion to take into account a heightened standard of proof required the judge to weigh the evidence, and thus got the judge into the fact-finding role that is supposed to be reserved to the jury.[62] A standard that asks whether a reasonable jury could reach a decision for one or the other party seems to require some weighing of evidence even if the standard of proof is the preponderance test.[63] If nothing else, the judge must decide how a reasonable jury could view the evidence. But the encroachment on that essential jury function is certainly greater when the reasonableness of the potential jury is measured by a higher standard. This is es-

---

55. Anderson, 477 U.S. at 244. The requirement that a public figure must show actual malice by clear and convincing evidence comes from *New York Times Co. v. Sullivan*, 376 U.S. 254, 279–280 (1964).

56. Anderson, 477 U.S. at 245. Thus, Anderson was presenting affirmative evidence that negated an element of Liberty Lobby's claim. *See supra*, note 43, and accompanying text.

57. Anderson, 477 U.S. at 246.

58. *Id.* at 247.

59. *Id.* at 255.

60. For a discussion of standards of proof, see Introduction, *supra*, at notes 12–15 and accompanying text.

61. Anderson, 477 U.S. at 257.

62. *Id.* at 266–267 (Brennan, J., dissenting). *See* FLEMING JAMES, JR. & GEOFFREY C. HAZARD, JR. CIVIL PROCEDURE §6.18 (2nd ed. 1977).

63. *See* JAMES & HAZARD, *supra* note 62, at §7.13.

282 THE DECLINE OF THE CIVIL JURY

pecially true given that the "clear and convincing" test is fluid and poorly defined, and tends to be determined by the jury in each case.[64] Thus, this rule is likely to result in more summary judgments being granted, some of which will be granted when there is arguably a job for the jury—weighing the evidence.

Matsushita was an antitrust action brought by two American manufacturers of consumer electronic products (CEPs), mostly televisions, against nearly two dozen Japanese manufacturers of CEPs.[65] The plaintiffs claimed a predatory pricing conspiracy, in which the Japanese manufacturers allegedly engaged in a two-decades-long conspiracy to charge below-cost prices in the American market, funded by abnormally high prices in the Japanese market, in order to drive American manufacturers out of business.[66] Following years of discovery, the Japanese manufacturers moved for summary judgment.[67] The district court granted the motion because (1) some aspects of the alleged conspiracy did not cause an antitrust injury to the plaintiffs;[68] and (2) because the evidence adduced in support of the anti-competitive conspiracy was equally susceptible of an inference that the Japanese manufacturers were simply engaging in perfectly legal efforts to compete in the American market.[69] The district court considered this second point a reflection of antitrust case law that held that when evidence can support inferences of both legal and illegal activity, the inference of legal activity must be preferred as a matter of law in the absence of other evidence tending to point unambiguously to the illegal activity.[70]

The court of appeals reversed, holding that a reasonable fact-finder could infer a predatory pricing conspiracy.[71] The Supreme Court, however, in a 5–4

---

64. *See* Chapter 6, *supra*, at notes 112–116 and accompanying text.

65. Matsushita, 475 U.S. at 577–78.

66. *Id.*

67. *Id.* at 578.

68. *Id.* at 579. To recover for violations of antitrust laws, the plaintiffs must have suffered, by virtue of the defendant's act, the kind of injury that the antitrust laws were designed to prevent. *See* Brunswick Corp. v. Pueblo Bowl-O-Mat, Inc., 429 U.S. 477, 489 (1977). A defendant whose acts result in a more competitive environment will not be liable, for example, even if the plaintiff is driven out of business. *See* United States v. Inter-Island Steam Navigation Co., 87 F. Supp. 1010, 1021 (D. Haw. 1950).

69. Matsushita, 475 U.S. at 579.

70. *Id.* at 587–88, citing, *e.g.*, Monsanto Co. v. Spray-Rite Service Corp., 465 U.S. 752 (1984), and First National Bank of Arizona v. Cities service Co., 391 U.S. 253 (1968).

71. Matsushita, 475 U.S. at 580–82. There were also some disagreements between the trial court and the court of appeals about the admissibility of some of the evidence, including expert witness reports. *See id.* at 578–82. The Supreme Court, while agreeing with the court of appeals that some of the evidence had been wrongly excluded, nevertheless found that the excluded evidence would not change the result. *Id.* at 583.

decision, agreed with the district court that the evidence could support an inference of legal competitive activity, and that that inference should be preferred.[72] But the case law on which the district court and the Supreme Court relied for this holding was not clear on that point.[73]

The Court then went on to examine the possible inferences. It found that the Japanese manufacturers had no motive for the alleged conspiracy, as predatory pricing is costly, and produces only speculative advantages.[74] The Court preferred the inference that the Japanese manufacturers were simply using pricing as a legal tool to compete in the American market because the allegations involved a conspiracy among two dozen companies, each of which would benefit financially from cheating on the conspiracy; and that the alleged predatory pricing had produced no apparent anti-competitive effects in its twenty years of existence.[75] The Court said, "[l]ack of motive bears on the range of permissible conclusions that might be drawn from ambiguous evidence: if [the Japanese manufacturers] had no rational economic motive to conspire, and if their conduct is consistent with other, equally plausible explanations, the conduct does not give rise to an inference of conspiracy."[76] The Court remanded the case to the Court of Appeals, saying that that court was "free to consider whether there is other evidence that is sufficiently unambiguous to permit a trier of fact to find that petitioners conspired to price predatorily for two decades despite the absence of any apparent motive to do so."[77]

The Court did two things in *Matsushita* that diminish the role of the jury. First, juries traditionally have the task of drawing reasonable inferences from evidence,[78] but in *Matsushita*, the judges are given authority to draw infer-

---

72. *See id.* at 593–95, 597.

73. *See id.* at 600–01 (White, J., dissenting) (arguing that the Supreme Court majority misinterpreted existing precedent).

74. *Id.* at 588. The Court cited numerous studies suggesting that predatory pricing was rare. But the Court ignored the admissible expert reports suggesting that American business practices were not necessarily an indication of how Japanese business would behave. *See* Stempel, *supra* note 25, at 109. One point that the expert witnesses made was that Japanese businesses are more patient than American businesses, and have a longer-range perspective. These differences might make such a conspiracy more plausible for Japanese businesses. *Id.* at 110.

75. Matsushita, 475 U.S. at 595–97.

76. *Id.* at 596–97.

77. *Id.* at 597. On remand, the court of appeals affirmed the summary judgment as to all the defendants. *In re* Japanese Electronic Products Antitrust Litigation, 807 F.2d 44, 48 (3rd Cir. 1986), *cert. denied sub nom.*, Zenith Radio Corp. v. Matsushita Electric Industrial Co., 481 U.S. 1029 (1987). *See* Stempel, *supra* note 25, at 100.

78. *See* Weiner, *supra* note 2, at 1870.

ences from the evidence and to enter judgments based on those inferences.[79] Second, motive is traditionally a question for juries.[80] In arrogating the evaluation of evidence of motive to the courts, the Supreme Court in *Matsushita* chose to discount expert evidence in the record as to motivation,[81] a clear signal to the lower courts that they may weigh such evidence and decide the issue for themselves. This decision, then, allows trial judges, on motions for summary judgment, to weigh the evidence as to motive and to draw inferences from the evidence, all without the participation of the jury.[82] Indeed, the Court's opinion is replete with examples of its own weighing of the evidence.[83]

These three cases taken together expand the judge's authority to grant summary judgment motions at the expense of the jury's fact-finding role. They have produced considerable commentary, much of it unfavorable,[84] and some of it arguing that the Court's rulings violate the Seventh Amendment guarantee of a right to a civil jury trial.[85] These rulings have also produced significantly more summary judgments, and those summary judgments overwhelmingly favor defendants.[86]

---

79. Matsushita, 475 U.S. at 587. *See* McGinley, *supra* note 46, at 227; Issacharoff & Loewenstein, *supra* note 46, at 87–89.

80. *See* THAYER, *supra* note 2, at 184; Weiner, *supra* note 2, at 1870–71.

81. Matsushita, 475 U.S. at 595–97. *See* Stempel, *supra* note 25, at 112.

82. *See* McGinley, *supra* note 46, at 236–37. The Court's approach also seems to be contrary to the usual practice of drawing all inferences in favor of the *non-moving* party, though that may be a quirk of antitrust law and not a generalizable statement about how courts should view the evidence.

83. Matsushita, 475 U.S. at 592 (concluding that there was no conspiracy because the intended result of such a conspiracy had not occurred); *id.* at 593, 595 (inferring no motive because the alleged conspiracy was unreasonable).

84. Marcy J. Levine, *Summary Judgment: The Majority View Undergoes A Complete Reversal in the 1986 Supreme Court*, 37 EMORY L.J. 171, 172 (1988); D. Michael Risinger, *Another Step in the Counter-Revolution: A Summary Judgment on the Supreme Court's New Approach to Summary Judgment*, 54 BROOKLYN L. REV. 35 (1988); Stempel, *supra* note 25; McGinley, *supra* note 46; Issacharoff & Loewenstein, *supra* note 46.

85. U.S. CONST. am. VII. *See* Stempel, *supra* note 25, at 162–64. *But see,* Lawrence W. Pierce, *Summary Judgment: A Favored Means of Summarily Resolving Disputes*, 53 BROOKLYN L. REV. 279, 280–81 (1987); Kent Sinclair & Patrick Hanes, *Summary Judgment: A Proposal for Procedural Reform in a Core Motion Context*, 36 WM. & MARY L. REV. 1633, 1643 and n.36 (1995).

86. Issacharoff & Loewenstein, *supra* note 46. *See also,* McGinley, *supra* note 46 (arguing that *Celotex, Anderson* and *Matsushita* make it harder for civil rights plaintiffs to survive summary judgment). This is ironic given that the origins of summary proceedings was in devices designed to favor plaintiffs. *See supra,* notes 18–24, and accompanying text. Per-

D. Judgment as a Matter of Law

The term "judgment as a matter of law" was coined in the 1991 amendments to the Federal Rules of Civil Procedure to encompass both directed verdict and judgment notwithstanding the verdict (j.n.o.v.). Like the summary judgment, both of these procedures test the legal sufficiency of the evidence, though at different stages of the trial.[87] The old directed verdict was sought after the evidence was presented but before the jury retired to consider the verdict. The motion for j.n.o.v., by contrast, was not sought until after the jury had returned a verdict and judgment had been entered.[88] Summary judgment, by contrast, is sought before the jury is empaneled. The new unitary "judgment as a matter of law" reflects the fact that all three motions are grounded on the alleged failure of the party opposing the motion to produce legally sufficient evidence to support a verdict in his favor.[89] The language was chosen in part to reflect the close relationship the motion has to the summary judgment. But the concept of legally insufficient evidence is itself of somewhat recent origin, and the standards are still evolving. This motion, then, is a relatively new jury control device. In this section, I will first discuss the origins of the motion, and then the standard for granting it.

1. Origins of the Judgment as a Matter of Law

The history of judgment as a matter of law is somewhat tortured, as the modern procedure has several common law antecedents, none of which is a precise analogue. Indeed, the history reflects different origins, and different standards, for the directed verdict and the j.n.o.v. The directed verdict originated as nothing more than a jury instruction: the defendant could request a directed verdict after the plaintiff had presented her evidence, and if the judge

---

haps it is explainable by the fact that commercial interests tended to benefit both from the early summary proceedings and the recent changes in the summary judgment procedures.

87. *See* Fed. R. Civ. P. 50. The advisory committee notes to the 1991 amendments state that the term "direction of verdict" has been abandoned because the term is misleading as a description of the relationship between judge and jury. "Judgment as a matter of law" applies to both the pre-verdict and the post-verdict motions and thus reflects the identity of the two motions.

88. For a discussion of directed verdict and j.n.o.v., see generally, Edward H. Cooper, *Directions for Directed Verdicts: A Compass for Federal Courts*, 55 Minn. L. Rev. 903 (1971); William Wirt Blume, *Origin and Development of the Directed Verdict*, 48 Mich. L. Rev. 555 (1950) [hereinafter cited as Blume, *Origin*]; John E. Bagalay, Jr., Comment: *Directed Verdicts and the Right to Trial by Jury in the Federal Courts*, 42 Tex. L. Rev. 1053 (1964).

89. Fed. R. Civ. P. 50 advisory committee notes to 1991 amendments.

believed that there was no evidence to support the plaintiff's case, he so instructed the jury.[90] The jury could disregard the judge's instructions, however, and if it did, the judge's only means of control was to grant a new trial.[91]

Judgment n.o.v. appears to be an amalgam of several procedures. One is a device known to common law as a motion in arrest of judgment, which was a motion that attacked the judgment because of an error on the face of the record—most often the alleged insufficiency of the pleadings.[92] This motion was available to *defendants* who lost a jury verdict when the pleadings themselves were defective.[93] *Plaintiffs* who lost a jury verdict, by contrast, used the judgment *non obstante verdicto*, which gave its name to the modern procedure. This device was available when the defendant admitted his wrong-doing, but raised a defense that was invalid on the face of the pleadings.[94] It is significant that both of these motions were available when a party lost a jury verdict but the opposing party's case was defective because of errors in the pleadings. Neither motion attacked the sufficiency of the evidence. Indeed, both were similar to the common law demurrer, which occurred at the pleading stage and attacked the sufficiency of the complaint.[95] All three devices challenged the legal sufficiency of the plaintiff's statement of the case, without regard for any evidence that might be offered.[96] But unlike the demurrer, the motion in arrest of judgment and the motion for j.n.o.v. could be raised after a jury had returned a verdict on the defective pleadings.

One device that did challenge the evidence itself was the demurrer to the evidence.[97] Under this procedure, a defendant would wait until the plaintiff

---

90. *See* Galloway v. United States, 319 U.S. 372, 402 (1943) (Black, J., dissenting); Blume, *Origin, supra* note 88, at 570–74.

91. *See* Cooper, *supra* note 88, at 910; Blume, *Origin, supra* note 88, at 560–61.

92. *See* ROBERT WYNESS MILLAR, CIVIL PROCEDURE OF THE TRIAL COURT IN HISTORICAL PERSPECTIVE 324 (1952); United States v. Sisson, 399 U.S. 267, 280–81 (1970) ("An arrest of judgment [was] the technical term describing the act of a trial judge refusing to enter judgment on the verdict because of an error appearing on the face of the record that rendered the judgment invalid") (citing treatises).

93. Slocum v. New York Life Insurance Co., 228 U.S. 364, 381 (1913).

94. *Id.*

95. *See* William Wirt Blume, *Theory Pleading: A Survey Including the Federal Rules*, 47 MICH. L. REV. 297, 301 (1949) [hereinafter cited as Blume, *Theory Pleading*]; Stempel, *supra* note 25, at 98 n.11; BENJAMIN J. SHIPMAN, HANDBOOK OF COMMON LAW PLEADING 156 (2d Ed. 1895).

96. *See* SHIPMAN, *supra* note 95, at 156–57; Blume, *Theory Pleading, supra* note 95, at 301.

97. *See* MILLAR, *supra* note 92, at 298; Blume, *Origin, supra* note 88, at 561–62; THAYER, *supra* note 2, at 234–39.

had completed her presentation of evidence, then admit the facts that the evidence reflected as well as all inferences that could be drawn from the facts, but argue that the evidence did not permit the plaintiff's recovery as a matter of law.[98] If the judge ruled against the defendant, however, the defendant was not permitted to present any evidence of his own, as he had admitted plaintiff's evidence, and he then lost.[99] This device has not been used in the federal courts since 1826.[100]

Each of these procedures had problems. The demurrer to the evidence allowed the defendant to challenge the sufficiency of the plaintiff's evidence, but required him to forgo the right to present his own evidence. Thus, just as a demurrer to the complaint constituted an admission of the facts the plaintiff has alleged, a demurrer to the evidence constituted an admission of the facts established by the plaintiff's evidence. In both cases, the defendant could present no further defense.[101] The motions in arrest of judgment and for j.n.o.v. were, like the demurrer to the complaint, challenges to the pleadings and not to the evidence. Nevertheless, these last two motions were an improvement over the other procedures because they allowed the parties to challenge the pleadings while also testing the evidence before a jury.[102] For example, a defendant seeking to test both the legal sufficiency of the pleadings and the strength of the evidence would forgo a demurrer, and allow the case to go to the jury. If he lost at trial, he had a jury's verdict as to the evidence, but he could then file a motion in arrest of judgment and challenge the pleadings. By contrast, if he won at trial, he had no need to challenge the pleadings. This was an improvement over the other procedures for testing the law because the others did not allow any evidence to be considered.[103] Thus, these devices seem to have developed, not as a device for controlling the jury, but as a procedural mechanism for allowing a party to contest more than one issue—something not permitted under historic common law procedures.[104]

---

98. *See* Galloway v. United States, 319 U.S. 372, 399–400 (1943) (Black, J., dissenting); Blume, *Origin, supra* note 88, at 561–62; THAYER, *supra* note 2, at 234–39.

99. *See* Galloway, 319 U.S. at 402–03 (Black, J., dissenting); Colleen P. Murphy, *Integrating the Constitutional Authority of Civil and Criminal Juries*, 61 GEO. WASH. L. REV. 723, 764 (1993).

100. Galloway, 319 U.S. at 400 (Black, J., dissenting).

101. *See* Stempel, *supra* note 25, at 98 n.11; Murphy, *supra* note 99, at 764.

102. *See* S.F.C. MILSOM, HISTORICAL FOUNDATIONS OF THE COMMON LAW 73–74 (2d ed. 1981).

103. *See id.*; Galloway, 319 U.S. at 403 (Black, J., dissenting).

104. *See* SHIPMAN, *supra* note 95, at 349–50; Charles H. King, Comment, *Trial Practice—Demurrer Upon Evidence as a Device For Taking a Case From the Jury*, 44 MICH. L. REV. 468, 470 (1945).

2. Modern Developments

a. Seventh Amendment Issues

Eventually, these various procedures merged into the modern directed verdict and judgment notwithstanding the verdict, which came to be primarily attacks on the legal sufficiency of the evidence. This happened first with the development, beginning in 1850, of a directed verdict procedure that allowed the judge to grant a directed verdict when there was " 'no evidence whatever' on the critical issue in the case."[105] This was a combination of the original directed verdict, which was just a jury instruction, and the demurrer to the evidence, which had more teeth.[106] But while the directed verdict evolved over the next few decades, the Court steadfastly resisted a post-verdict procedure that would substitute a judge's judgment for that of the jury. The basis for this refusal was the second clause of the Seventh Amendment, which prohibits judges from reexamining facts found by a jury except in accordance with the common law.[107] A new trial was the only way jury verdicts could be reviewed at common law.[108] This approach was modified somewhat in 1935 when the Court, in *Baltimore and Carolina Line, Inc. v. Redman*[109] approved a procedure where the lower court had reserved decision on a directed verdict, and granted it only after the jury returned a verdict for the non-moving party. Thus, the judge technically was not reviewing the jury's fact-finding, but was granting a delayed motion for directed verdict.

When the Federal Rules of Civil Procedure were promulgated in 1938, they contained a procedure for both directed verdict and post-verdict review. The latter was denominated judgment notwithstanding the verdict, or j.n.o.v, and j.n.o.v. could be sought only if the moving party had first sought a directed

---

105. Galloway, 319 U.S. at 402 (Black, J., dissenting) (quoting Parks v. Ross, 52 U.S. (11 How.) 362 (1850).

106. *See* Galloway, 319 U.S. at 402 (Black, J., dissenting).

107. *See* U.S. Const. am. VII; Slocum v. New York Life Insurance Co., 228 U.S. 364 (1913).

108. *Id.* at 399. *But see*, George C. Christie, *Judicial Review of Findings of Fact*, 87 Nw. U.L. Rev. 14, 52–53 and n.156 (1992) (suggesting that the Seventh Amendment is not much of an impediment to judicial review of fact-finding because the Court is the arbiter of what the evolving common law requires). Christie's article raises the issue of whether the Seventh Amendment preserves the right to a jury trial as it existed at a specific point in time, or whether the right evolves along with the common law. While the Court looks to the law of England in 1791 to define the basic right, it also allows evolving procedure to affect the right.

109. 295 U.S. 654 (1935).

verdict before the jury retired.[110] The rule adopted the approach of *Redman* in providing that an unsuccessful motion for directed verdict was deemed reserved so that the moving party could renew the motion following the jury's verdict, but the Rule made the reservation automatic.[111] This preserved the *Redman* fiction that the decision was not really reviewing a jury's verdict, but was simply a delayed ruling on the motion for directed verdict.[112] The reformulated j.n.o.v. is, nonetheless, a more significant departure from common law practice than the reformulated directed verdict. The new directed verdict removes the disability of the defendant's forgoing the right to defend, and it requires a verdict in accordance with its direction. The new j.n.o.v., however, allows an independent jury verdict to be returned and then sets it aside in favor of the judge's view of the facts.[113] While the Court calls this a decision on the law because it determines the *legal* sufficiency of the evidence, the Court's early discomfort with the procedure and its maintenance of the fiction that the post-verdict judgment as a matter of law is really just a delayed decision on the pre-verdict motion both suggest that the post-verdict judgment as a matter of law is, at the least, very close to a decision on the facts.[114]

The first clause of the Seventh Amendment is also implicated in judgments as a matter of law, at whatever stage of the proceedings they arise. The question is whether judgments as a matter of law, by taking the matter out of the

---

110. *See* 9A Charles Alan Wright and Arthur R. Miller, Federal Practice and Procedure, § 2521 (1995).

111. *See* Blume, *Origin, supra* note 88, at 588–89.

112. *See* 9A Wright and Miller, *supra* note 110, at § 2522; Neely v. Martin K. Eby Construction Co., 386 U.S. 317 (1967).

113. Judges generally prefer the post-verdict j.n.o.v. for efficiency reasons. If the judge grants a directed verdict motion, the jury is dismissed before rendering a verdict. If the court of appeals then overturns the directed verdict, a new jury will have to be empaneled, and the evidence presented again. But if the judge allows the jury to return a verdict and then grants a j.n.o.v., an appellate reversal of his decision would simply reinstate the jury verdict already rendered.

114. The current rule also allows the court of appeals to order a j.n.o.v. *See* Fed R. Civ. P. 50(c). The Supreme Court approved of such appellate oversight in Neely v. Martin K. Eby Construction Co., 386 U.S. 317 (1967). The Court cautioned, however, that courts of appeals should exercise their discretion with care, as it will sometimes be preferable for the court of appeals to remand the case to the trial court for consideration of a new trial motion. *Id.* at 325. The Court recently confirmed these rules and held that courts of appeals can order entry of judgment for the verdict loser even when the reason for the insufficiency of the evidence is that the court of appeals holds expert testimony to have been inadmissible under *Daubert v. Merrell Dow Pharmaceuticals, Inc.*, 509 U.S. 579 (1993). *See* Weisgram v. Marley Co., ___ U.S. ___, 120 S. Ct. 1011 (2000).

hands of the jury, deprive litigants of their Seventh Amendment right to a jury trial. Of course, the law/fact distinction existed at common law, so allocation of legal decisions to the judge seems historically unarguable. But as I have shown, there was no precise historical analog to the modern directed verdict or j.n.o.v. The closest—the demurrer to the evidence—required a litigant to give up an opportunity to challenge the facts if he lost on the law. It was a considerable gamble. That was the basis for the challenge to a directed verdict that had been granted in *Galloway v. United States*.[115] The Court's short answer to the challenge was that by that time, directed verdict practice was well-established in a long line of Supreme Court precedent, and that it was too late to object.[116] But the Court also held that the Seventh Amendment "was designed to preserve the basic institution of jury trials in only its most fundamental elements, not the great mass of procedural forms and details."[117] According to the Court, the reformulated directed verdict was simply a procedural detail, and did not affect the fundamental elements of the jury trial.

b. The Standard for a Granting a Judgment as a Matter of Law

When the directed verdict first came to be used to challenge the sufficiency of the evidence in 1850, the standard was quite strict: the motion could not be granted if there was *any* evidence in support of the party opposing the verdict.[118] This came to be known as the "scintilla" test, because the directed verdict should be refused if there was even a scintilla of evidence in support of the non-moving party.[119] It is not clear that judges in practice ever applied this test in its extreme, which would have precluded directed verdict or j.n.o.v. in almost every instance.[120] In any event, the strict standard lasted for just over

---

115. 319 U.S. 372 (1943).

116. *Id.* at 389. *See also,* Barry Friedman, *The Sedimentary Constitution,* 147 U. PA. L. REV. 1 (1998) (arguing that the Constitution consists not only of the written words, but the historic development as well).

117. Galloway, 319 U.S. at 392.

118. *See id.* at 404 (Black, J. dissenting); Parks v. Ross, 52 U.S. (11 How.) 362, 373 (1850); Richardson v. City of Boston, 60 U.S. (19 How.) 263, 268–69 (1856); Pamela J. Stephens, *Controlling the Civil Jury: Towards a Functional Model of Justification,* 76 KY. L.J. 81, 114 (1987).

119. *See, e.g.,* Stephens, *supra* note 118, at 114, *quoting* Improvement Co. v. Munson, 81 U.S. (14 Wall.) 442, 448 (1871).

120. *See* JAMES, & HAZARD, *supra* note 62, at §7.11 (disputing whether the scintilla rule ever prevailed as a practical matter). Some formulations of the scintilla test incorporate a reasonable jury standard. *See, e.g.,* Thompson, 56 Ky. (17 B. Mon.), at 29. Courts adopt-

twenty years. The first formulation of what has come to be described as the "substantial evidence" test occurred in 1871 in *Improvement Co. v. Munson*,[121] which held that the evidence in favor of the non-moving party must be sufficiently persuasive before the jury will be allowed to proceed. The "substantial evidence" test today is generally described as requiring that if there is evidence that a reasonable jury could believe and, if believed, would result in a verdict for the non-moving party, the court may not grant a motion for directed verdict or j.n.o.v.[122] Another way to put it is that the judge will grant a judgment as a matter of law only if no reasonable jury could decide for the non-moving party.[123] What this means in practice, however, has been open to debate.

The leading United States Supreme Court case on the standard for directed verdict is *Galloway v. United States*,[124] where the Court refused to allow a jury to infer the plaintiff's permanent and continuous mental disability when there was a gap of as much as eight years for which no evidence of disability had been presented, especially as Galloway had married during the eight year gap and his wife presumably could have testified as to his condition.[125] Galloway, who was concededly mentally disabled by 1930, sought to prove that he had been disabled prior to May, 1919, when his military insurance lapsed. He had to prove continuous disability from before that date in order to collect on the insurance. In fact, Galloway had presented some evidence of continuous disability. It was generally circumstantial evidence covering the period from 1918 to about 1922, and it tended to show some instability,[126] but it included a doctor's opinion that Galloway had been disabled prior to 1919. The doctor, however, had not met Galloway until just before the trial.[127] The Court held that

---

ing the substantial evidence test apparently thought they were changing the rule. *See, e.g.*, Galloway, 319 U.S. at 403–04 (Black, J., dissenting).

121. 81 U.S. (14 Wall.) 442, 447–48 (1871). *See also,* Galloway, 319 U.S. at 404 (Black, J., dissenting).

122. *See, e.g.*, Galloway v. United States, 319 U.S. 372, 403 (1943); Boutros v. Canton Regional Transit Authority, 997 F.2d 198, 205 (6th Cir. 1993) (Batchelder, J., concurring).

123. *See, e.g.*, Cannon v. Macon Cty., 1 F.3d 1558, 1562 (11th Cir. 1993); Boeing Co. v. Shipman, 411 F.2d 365, 374 (5th Cir. 1969).

124. 319 U.S. 372 (1943).

125. *Id.* at 386–88.

126. Galloway presented evidence of two incidents of bizarre behavior during the war; testimony from a childhood friend about his condition before and after his service in France; and testimony from a commanding officer about his mood swings. He also presented expert testimony from a psychiatrist who examined Galloway for the first time shortly before the trial and thought Galloway had been insane from July 1918 onward. *See id.* at 381–82.

127. *See id.* at 381–82.

no reasonable jury could infer continuous disability when an eight year period (1922–1930) was unaccounted for.

A vigorous dissent argued that the evidence met the substantial evidence test and that the decision should therefore have been left to the jury. Indeed, the dissent pointed out that the very fact that there was disagreement about whether a reasonable jury could find for Galloway was enough to establish a jury question.[128] Inferences, of course, are usually for the jury to draw.[129] The *Galloway* court nevertheless held that some inferences are improper as a matter of law. As the dissent suggested, this seems to involve at least some weighing of the evidence.

While *Galloway* confirmed the substantial evidence test as the standard for directed verdicts, it did not settle the question how that standard is to be defined. The cases reflect that there are several different views as to what it means for the non-moving party's evidence to be "substantial."[130] The majority of courts have held that the court, in deciding motions for directed verdict and j.n.o.v., now collectively judgment as a matter of law, should consider "all uncontradicted evidence,...but...when there [is] conflicting evidence, the non-movant's version of the evidence should be accepted as true and...all reasonable inferences from the record should be drawn in favor of the nonmovant."[131] This has included inferences of credibility.[132] There are also two extremes, however, each held by a minority of courts. At one extreme, some courts will consider only the nonmoving party's evidence in evaluating a directed verdict motion.[133] At the other, some courts will consider all of the evidence and evaluate how a reasonable jury will view it.[134] This latter approach brings the court closest to weighing the evidence. Arguably, what the Court did in *Galloway* was at least clo e to this latter approach, though most courts have held to the middle ground.

In its October 1999 term the Supreme Court attempted to clarify the standard. In *Reeves v. Sanderson Plumbing Products, Inc.*,[135] the Court held that a

128. *Id.* at 407 (Black, J., dissenting).

129. *See id.* at 396; Anderson v. Liberty Lobby, 477 U.S. 242, 255 (1986); Myers v. Reading Co., 331 U.S. 477, 484 (1947).

130. *See* Stempel, *supra* note 25, at 157–59; CHARLES ALAN WRIGHT, LAW OF FEDERAL COURTS 683–85 (5th ed. 1994); Cooper, *supra* note 88, at 948–53.

131. Stempel, *supra* note 25, at 158. *See also,* Reeves v. Sanderson Plumbing Products, Inc., ___ U.S. ___, 120 S. Ct. 2097 (2000) (discussing standard for granting judgment as a matter of law).

132. *See* Stempel, *supra* note 25, at 158.

133. *Id.*

134. *Id.*

135. ___ U.S. ___, 120 S. Ct. 2097 (2000).

court, in deciding a motion for judgment as a matter of law, should not weigh evidence or make credibility determinations, but "should review the record as a whole," disregarding "all evidence favorable to the moving party that the jury is not required to believe."[136] This sounds like the standard followed by the majority of courts. The Court in *Reeves* refused to allow judgment as a matter of law when the court of appeals had found that the defendant's evidence in an age discrimination case "so overwhelmed the evidence favoring [the plaintiff] that no rational trier of fact could have found that [the plaintiff] was fired because of his age."[137] The Court held that the court of appeals had "impermissibly substituted its judgment concerning the weight of the evidence for the jury's."[138]

Reeves appears to be good news for the vitality of the civil jury, but it leaves some questions unresolved. One commentator had suggested that the three summary judgment cases I discussed in the last section have by implication established that the substantial evidence test will allow judges to evaluate the reasonableness of a jury's view of the evidence, which is the version of the substantial evidence test that is the least protective of the right to jury trial.[139] The Court in the summary judgment cases explicitly said that the standard for granting a summary judgment was the same as the standard for granting a judgment as a matter of law, and its own approach in those cases appeared to allow judges to draw inferences and to weigh evidence.[140]

Reeves suggests either that the Court's words are more cautious than its deeds or that the standard is not, in fact, the same for summary judgment and for judgment as a matter of law. If the standards are not the same, it appears that it is easier for courts to weigh evidence on a summary judgment motion than on a judgment as a matter of law. This is perverse, as the evidence is less developed on summary judgment than on judgment as a matter of law. On the other hand, the post-verdict judgment as a matter of law, which was the circumstance in *Reeves*, is governed by the second clause of the Seventh Amendment, which bars judicial reexamination of facts found by a jury except in accordance with the common law.[141] Summary judgment and pre-verdict judgment as a matter of law are governed only by the first clause, which preserves the right to jury trial, and the Court has said that the

---

136. *Id.* at 2110.
137. *Id.* at 2111.
138. *Id.* at 2111.
139. *See* Stempel, *supra* note 25, at 157–59.
140. *See supra*, notes 33–86 and accompanying text.
141. *See supra*, notes 105–114 and accompanying text.

first clause does not freeze jury procedures in their 1791 form.[142] It could be that the Court is more cautious where the second clause of the Seventh Amendment is at stake, though it has not been clear about drawing such a distinction in the past. In short, some further clarification of the standards for granting summary judgment and judgment as a matter of law would be helpful.

E. Summary

The evolution of summary judgment and judgment as a matter of law has resulted in a greater opportunity for judges to use these devices to take cases away from juries and to weigh evidence themselves, though *Reeves* strikes a cautionary note as to that conclusion.[143] Proponents of freer use of summary judgments and judgments as a matter of law will argue that the plaintiffs in these cases had no legal right to prevail anyway, so that these decisions are having the salutary effect of allowing quick decisions in cases that the plaintiffs cannot win. Thus, summary judgments and judgments as a matter of law are an efficient way of resolving lawsuits in a system that is overwhelmed with litigation. There is some truth to this. But the line between law and fact is tenuous, and when the definition of "law" expands, the definition of "fact" must necessarily contract. Some of what judges do when they decide these motions looks a lot like weighing evidence. And when judges weigh evidence, they are usurping the jury's function, and we are deprived of the community's view of the issues. In some cases, that could be a significant loss.

II. New Trial: Shades of the Common Law

The new trial is a common law method of jury control, and as such would seem to present no constitutional issue.[144] It is also less intrusive on the jury's duties than judgment as a matter of law or summary judgment because, while the matter is taken out of the hands of one jury, it is given to another

---

142. *See* Galloway v. United States, 319 U.S. 372 (1943).

143. *See also* Neely v. Martin K. Eby Construction Co., 386 U.S. 317 (1967); Daniel J. Hartwig Associates, Inc. v. Kanner, 913 F.2d 1213 (1990); Pennsylvania R.R. Co. v. Chamberlain, 288 U.S. 333 (1933).

144. The Seventh Amendment preserves the common law right to a jury trial and allows review of jury verdicts in accordance with common law practices. *See* Chapter 2, *supra*, at notes 95–96, 172–179 and accompanying text.

jury for decision. But the modern new trial gives judges more opportunity to inject themselves into the fact-finding, especially through such devices as remittitur.[145]

New trials are granted when there has been some kind of error during the trial and the error is likely to have affected the outcome.[146] The judge can make errors in admitting or excluding evidence or in instructing the jury.[147] The parties or their attorneys can err in the manner of their argument to the jury,[148] in the way they question witnesses,[149] or in withholding discoverable documents or information from the opposing party.[150] Judges sometimes try to correct their own or the parties' errors mid-trial, by instructing jurors to ignore evidence that should not have been introduced,[151] though there is evidence suggesting that juries have trouble following an instruction to ignore evidence once they have heard it.[152] If an error is sufficiently egregious, a court may declare a mistrial, which means that the trial will have to start over with a new jury.[153] If the error is not corrected before the jury returns a verdict, a new trial may be necessary. Errors by juries can only be corrected by a new trial, or at least the threat of one. There are two primary kinds of jury error, and they shade into one another. The first is an error in weighing the evidence. The second is jury misconduct.

Because weighing the evidence is clearly a traditional function of the jury, granting new trials for errors in weighing the evidence should be problematic. But there is little criticism of it, perhaps because the remedy is a new trial be-

---

145. *See infra* notes 157–161 and accompanying text. The new trial in federal courts is governed by Fed. R. Civ. P. 59.

146. *See* Fed. R. Civ. P. 59 (new trials), 61 (harmless error).

147. *See generally,* Chapter 5, *supra.*

148. *See, e.g.,* Hamilton Copper & Steel Corp. v. Primary Steel, Inc., 898 F.2d 1428, 1430 (9th Cir. 1990) (case dismissed as sanction where plaintiff's counsel repeatedly called documents "contracts" in a case where the existence of a contract was at issue).

149. *See, e.g.,* Sanders v. Wencewicz, 978 F.2d 483, 485 (8th Cir. 1993) (in civil rights action alleging excessive force by police, counsel for police dramatically dropped plaintiff's "rap sheet" in front of jury).

150. *See, e.g.,* Greyhound Lines, Inc. v. Miller, 402 F.2d 134, 144 (8th Cir. 1968) (new trial required when plaintiff withheld relevant medical records).

151. *See, e.g.,* Draper v. Airco, Inc., 580 F.2d 91, 96 and n.9 (3rd Cir. 1978) (jury in wrongful death action instructed to ignore inflammatory statements made during closing argument about alleged conspiracy when no evidence of conspiracy had been introduced).

152. *See, e.g.,* Harold M. Hoffman & Joseph Brodey, *Jurors on Trial,* 17 Mo. L. Rev. 235, 243–45 (1952) (finding that there was only one juror in three cases they studied who was able to follow an instruction to disregard.).

153. *See, e.g.,* O'Rear v. Fruehauf Distributing Co., 554 F.2d 1304 (5th Cir. 1977) (mistrial ordered for prejudicial remarks by counsel).

fore a new jury.[154] Indeed, one court said that a judge's failure to order a new trial when the weight of the evidence demanded it is to allow tyranny to reign.[155] Verdicts that are wholly inconsistent with the evidence may be the result of passion or prejudice, and not a rational or fair evaluation of the evidence.[156] A court must be able to correct the jury's injustices, but if there is legally sufficient evidence to support the verdict, however weak the evidence might be, the judge's only recourse is the new trial. A judge must decide if the jury's verdict is based on legally insufficient evidence, thus permitting a judgment as a matter of law, or merely wrong, permitting only a new trial. The line is a difficult one to draw, but because the judge's power to grant judgments as a matter of law has grown, we are likely to see more cases where the judge substitutes her own view of the evidence for that of the jury, and fewer where she gives the case to a new jury.

Sometimes the jury's error affects the amount of damages but not the liability. The remittitur allows a judge who thinks a jury verdict is excessive to order that a new trial be held *unless* the plaintiff agrees to accept less than the jury's verdict.[157] Usually, the judge selects a damage figure he believes to be correct.[158] And because a second trial will be costly and comes with the risk of an adverse outcome, the threat of a new trial may be enough to persuade a plaintiff to accept the remitted award.[159] This means that the judge, not the

---

154. *See* Robert G. Johnston, *Jury Subornation Through Judicial Control*, 43 L. & CONTEMP. PROBS. 24, 48 (Autumn 1980).

155. See Aetna Casualty & Sureto Co. v. Yeatts, 122 F.2d 350, 353 (4th Cir. 1941). The court describes the new trial as "...a result, not merely legal, but also not manifestly against justice,—a power exercised in pursuance of a sound judicial discretion, without which the jury system would be a capricious and intolerable tyranny, which no people could long endure." *Id.*

156. Of course, they could also be the result of jury nullification, and we need to pay attention to that. Jury nullification can sometimes tell us something about the state of the law. *See supra*, Chapter 1, at notes 72–108 and accompanying text.

157. *See* 11 CHARLES ALAN WRIGHT, ARTHUR R. MILLER & MARY KAY KANE, FEDERAL PRACTICE AND PROCEDURE §2807 (2d ed. 1995).

158. The courts disagree on whether this is the correct approach, or whether the judge should select the highest reasonable figure, even if he would have awarded less if the decision were his alone. For a discussion of the different approaches to setting the figure for remittitur, see Powers v. Allstate Insurance Co., 102 N.W.2d 393, 398–99 (Wis. 1960).

159. The converse of remittitur is additur, where the judge orders that a new trial be held unless the defendant agrees to pay more than the jury's verdict. The last time the Supreme Court discussed additur, it held the procedure to violate the Seventh Amendment because, unlike the remittitur, the additur imposes an award that is beyond what the jury had found to be proper. *See* Dimick v. Schiedt, 293 U.S. 474, 487 (1935). Some states, how-

jury, is determining the amount of damages. Indeed, recent precedent allows appellate courts to order remittitur, which is apparently inconsistent with common law practice.[160] The Supreme Court has recently put some limits on this practice by holding that a court cannot order a remittitur without allowing the plaintiff the option of a new trial.[161]

Jury misconduct can also result in a new trial. Jury misconduct includes such things as visiting the site of an accident[162] or allowing outside information or events to influence the outcome.[163] Juries are supposed to base their decisions solely on evidence presented by the parties in court. Another example of jury misconduct is the quotient verdict, where the jurors add up the amounts that each juror thinks the plaintiff should get, then divide by the number of jurors to determine the award.[164] Juries are supposed to do a rational evaluation of the evidence and ground their decision in that evaluation. These kinds of "misconduct" may be inadvertent: the jury may simply misunderstand its role. But jury nullification could be deliberate misconduct. A jury could understand precisely what result the evidence demands, but choose to disregard the law. As I showed in Chapter 1, however, there may be benefits to jury nullification, and we must be careful about condemning it across the board.

Jury misconduct, including jury nullification, may be difficult to establish because of the rule, in effect in some form in most jurisdictions, that testimony from jurors about their deliberations is inadmissible to impeach their

---

ever, approve of additur under their constitutions. *See, e.g.,* Fisch v. Manger, 130 A.2d 815, 822 (N.J. 1957); Rogers v. City of Loving, 573 P.2d 240, 248 (New Mexico, 1977); Drummond v. Mid-West Growers Cooperative Corp., 542 P.2d 198, 205 (Nev. 1975).

160. *See* Eric Schnapper, *Judges Against Juries—Appellate Review of Federal Civil Jury Verdicts,* 1989 Wis. L. Rev. 237, 344–47.

161. *See* Hetzel v. Prince William County, Virginia, 523 U.S. 208 (1998).

162. *See, e.g.,* Stotts v. Meyer, 822 S.W.2d 887 (Mo. App. 1991). Not all courts will overturn verdicts for such misconduct because of the prohibition on jurors' impeaching their own verdicts. *See, e.g.,* Wilson v. Oklahoma Ry. Co., 248 P.2d 1014 (Okla. 1952) (juror testimony relating to jury's unauthorized view of motorcycle accident scene during trial not admitted). The prohibition on jurors' impeaching their own verdicts is discussed in more detail at notes 165–168, *infra.*

163. *See, e.g.,* Alejo Jiminez v. Heyliger, 792 F. Supp. 910, 916 (D.P.R. 1992) (holding that jury's communication with security officer who supplied them with defendant's exhibits but not plaintiff's was misconduct); Neal v. John, 110 F.R.D. 187, 189 (D.V.I. 1986) (misconduct when juror overheard third party remarks and repeated them to other jurors).

164. *See* McDonald v. Pless, 238 U.S. 264, 265 (1915); Hukle v. Kimble, 243 P.2d 225, 230 (Kan. 1952). If the quotient is used as the starting point for discussion, courts are more likely to uphold its use. *See* Scoggin v. Century Fitness, Inc., 780 F.2d 1316, 1318–20 (8th Cir. 1985).

verdicts.[165] Those jurisdictions that do admit juror testimony usually do so only for evidence of extrinsic misconduct, such as an unauthorized visit to the scene of an accident.[166] Jury deliberations are almost universally beyond inquiry.[167] This protects free and open jury deliberation and enables juries to return politically unpopular verdicts.[168] It also makes jury nullification almost impossible to establish with certainty.

Appellate review of the trial judge's decisions on new trial motions is very deferential.[169] This is largely because the trial judge was there, and has a better sense of the weight of the evidence and of whether an error affected the outcome than does an appellate court that must rely on a written record.[170] Nevertheless, appellate courts seem to have become more aggressive in reviewing new trial motions, especially as to damages.[171]

In short, while the new trial is a relatively old form of jury control and is less intrusive than the judgment as a matter of law, the use of the new trial may be contracting as the judgment as a matter of law expands. More ag-

---

165. *See* Fed. R. Evid. 606(b). *See also* Mark Cammack, *The Jurisprudence of Jury Trials: The No Impeachment Rule and the Conditions for Legitimate Legal Decisionmaking*, 64 U. Colo. L. Rev. 57, 64–68 (1993); David A. Christman, Note, *Federal Rule of Evidence 606(b) and the Problem of "Differential" Jury Error*, 67 N.Y.U.L. Rev. 802, 815–19 (1992).

166. *See* Cammack, *supra* note 165, at 64–68; Christman, *supra* note 165, at 815–19.

167. In Katz v. Eli Lilly & Co., 84 F.R.D. 378 (E.D.N.Y. 1979), the court accepted juror testimony about their deliberations in a *previous* case. The testimony was used to establish that the earlier verdict was a compromise verdict and so should not preclude relitigation of issues decided in that case under the doctrine of issue preclusion. *See* Ina Ruth Bigham, Note, *Use of Juror Depositions to Bar Collateral Estoppel: A Necessary Safeguard or a Dangerous Precedent?*, 34 Vand. L. Rev. 143 (1981). For a discussion of issue preclusion, see *infra*, notes 239–256 and accompanying text. *See* Abraham S. Goldstein, *Jury Secrecy and the Media: The Problem of Postverdict Interviews*, 1993 U. Ill. L. Rev. 295, 304 (1993).

168. *See* Timothy C. Rank, Note, *Federal Rule of Evidence 606(b) and the Post-Trial Reformation of Civil Jury Verdicts*, 76 Minn. L. Rev. 1421, 1443–1444 (1992); Note, *Public Disclosures of Jury Deliberations*, 96 Harv. L. Rev. 886 (1983).

169. *See* 2 Steven Alan Childress and Martha S. Davis, Standards of Review § 11.2 (1986).

170. *See* 1 Childress & Davis, *supra* note 169, at § 4.3.

171. *See generally,* Schnapper, *supra* note 160. Schnapper also criticizes the growing willingness of appellate courts to label juries "irrational," a trend that the Supreme Court has clearly approved with its 1986 summary judgment decisions. *See supra* notes 33–86 and accompanying text. *See also, infra* notes 204–231 and accompanying text (discussing Supreme Court decisions on limiting damages). *But see* Reeves v. Sanderson Plumbing Products, Inc., ___ U.S. ___, 120 S.Ct. 2097 (2000) (stating that judges are not to weigh evidence or make credibility determinations). *See also, supra* notes 135–142 and accompanying text (discussing *Reeves* and the summary judgment cases).

gressive review of jury verdicts by both trial and appellate courts can also result in judges substituting their verdicts for the jury's, especially as to the quantum of damages. The remittitur—the usual means of altering the quantum of damages—technically offers the plaintiff a choice, but it may be an offer he cannot refuse. The new trial, then, sometimes obscures what is really a decision on the facts by a judge. The ban on using juror testimony to impeach a jury verdict offers some protection, but the new trial can be based on the judge's inference of juror misconduct, so the protection is weak.

III. Structuring Jury Decision-Making: Special Verdicts

The traditional jury verdict is a general verdict, in which the jury simply finds for one party and determines applicable damages. The jury reports only the bottom line, but in the privacy of the jury room, it finds facts and applies the law to the facts it finds.[172] The special verdict, on the other hand, is a decision on facts only, with no application of law to fact and no finding for one party or the other.[173] Special verdicts require the judge to take the final step of applying the law to the facts found by the jury. There is also a hybrid, the general verdict with interrogatories, which requires the jury to report both its specific fact-finding and a finding for one party or the other.[174]

The special verdict has ancient origins. It began as a defensive mechanism invented by jurors themselves when they were subject to attaint.[175] The problem was that jurors who made a mistake in applying the law to the facts might be found guilty of perjury in an attaint proceeding.[176] Thus, juries re-

---

172. Martin A. Kotler, *Reappraising the Jury's Role as Finder of Fact*, 20 GA. L. REV. 123, 133 (1985); Stephens, *supra* note 44, at 140–41; Edson R. Sunderland, *Verdicts: General and Special*, 29 YALE L.J. 253, 259 (1920). The judge instructs the jury in the law, but a general verdict requires the jury to apply the law to the facts. When a judge is the fact-finder, she must specify her findings of fact and conclusions of law. FED. R. CIV. P. 52(a).

173. FED. R. CIV. P. 49(a).

174. FED. R. CIV. P. 49(b).

175. *See* THAYER, *supra* note 2, at 154; Fleming James, Jr., *Sufficiency of the Evidence and Jury-Control Devices Available Before Verdict*, 47 VA. L. REV. 218, 242 (1961); Stephens, *supra* note 44, at 95; LEON GREEN, JUDGE AND JURY 353 (1930); Edith Guild Henderson, *The Background of the Seventh Amendment*, 80 HARV. L. REV. 289, 307 (1966).

176. *See* James, *supra* note 175, at 242; Krist, *supra* note 12, at 14; THAYER, *supra* note 2, at 140; Edmund M. Morgan, *A Brief History of Special Verdicts and Special Interrogatories*, 32 YALE L.J. 575, 576–77 and n.3 (1923).

fused to take the final step, instead reporting their fact-finding to the judge and letting him render the verdict.[177] Gradually, however, judges began requiring juries to return special verdicts.[178] One reason for this is that special verdicts aid the jury in its decision-making by breaking the case down into more easily digested issues.[179] But the special vedict and the general verdict with interrogatories also make it easier for judges to control the jury.[180] Using these devices, a judge can prevent both jury nullification and simple errors in the application of law to fact. The special verdict is the more direct route, as it eliminates the jury's ability to say which party should prevail. The general verdict with interrogatories gives the judge the opportunity to decide whether the jury's specific fact-finding is consistent with the general verdict; if it is not, the judge can order a verdict in conformity with the fact-finding, require the jury to consider the matter further, or order a new trial.[181]

---

177. *See* Stephens, *supra* note 118, at 96; Morgan, *supra* note 176, at 577; PLUCKNETT, *supra* note 11, at 417.

178. The decision to use special verdicts or interrogatories is discretionary with the trial judge. *See* Floyd v. Laws, 929 F.2d 1390, 1395 (9th Cir. 1991); Mateyko v. Felix, 924 F.2d 824, 827 (9th Cir. 1991); James, *supra* note 175, at 243–44; Stephens, *supra* note 44, at 108–09.

179. *See* Sunderland, *supra* note 172, at 261; James, *supra* note 175, at 245; Stephens, *supra* note 118, at 161–62.

180. *See* James, *supra* note 175, at 242.

181. *See* James, *supra* note 175, at 243, 244; FED. R. CIV. P. 49(b). In practice, a clever jury could anticipate the result of its fact-finding and simply find the facts consistent with its desired outcome. Juries, however, cannot always anticipate the results of their fact-finding. *See* David E. Pierce, Note, *Informing the Jury of the Legal Effect of Its Answers to Special Verdict Questions Under Kansas Comparative Negligence Law—A Reply to the Masses; A Case for the Minority View*, 16 WASHBURN. L.J. 114, 118 (1976); Stuart F. Schaffer, Comment, *Informing the Jury of the Legal Effect of Special Verdict Answers in Comparative Negligence Actions*, 1981 DUKE L.J. 824, 841; Elizabeth Faulkner, Comment, *Using the Special Verdict to Manage Complex Cases and Avoid Compromise Verdicts*, 21 ARIZ. ST. L.J. 297, 313–14 (1989). Indeed, there is some discussion in the literature about whether juries should be told about how the law applies to the facts that they may find. *See, e.g.*, Stephens, *supra* note 118 at 107–08; Kotler, *supra* note 172, at 134–38; Schaffer, *supra*, at 839–49; Comment, *Informing the Jury of the Legal Effects of Its Answers to Special Verdicts*, 43 MINN. L. REV. 823, 826 (1959). At the root of any such debate is an ambivalence about jury nullification. *See supra* Chapter 1, notes 72–108 and accompanying text.

IV. Removing Cases and Issues from the Jury

There are a number of other ways of keeping cases or issues out of the jury's hands, though that is not always the stated reason for these practices. These include assigning matters to adjudicative bodies that do not use the jury; changing substantive law to eliminate issues for the jury; and limiting the jury's traditional discretion as to some issues.

A. Jurisdictional and Substantive Legislation

Jurisdictional legislation can remove whole classes of cases from the jury by assigning them to another adjudicatory body that does not use juries, usually an administrative agency.[182] One well-known example of states removing a whole class of cases from judicial adjudication is worker's compensation.[183] Workers' compensation schemes abolish the employee's right to sue employers for on-the-job injuries and replace it with a claim on a fund. The fund is administered by a governmental commission and funded through insurance that employers are required to purchase.[184] In the federal system, jurisdictional legislation of this sort usually involves newly created rights, though federal workers' compensation schemes also exist and have been upheld as constitutional under the broad rubric of the public rights doctrine and the balancing test, which I discussed at length in Chapter 4.[185]

Substantive legislation changes the law in a way that removes issues from the jury. An example of this is the enactment of no-fault automobile insurance laws.[186] Issues concerning fault are the usual reason automobile accident cases go to trial, so if fault is removed, fewer cases will be tried to a jury. There is no question that Congress and the state legislatures have the power to change both statutory and common law. Thus, there is no Seventh Amend-

---

182. For a discussion of the constitutionality of assigning federal cases to administrative agencies, see *supra*, Chapter 4, at notes 136–215 and accompanying text.

183. All of the states have worker's compensation programs. *See* 1 ARTHUR LARSON, THE LAW OF WORKMEN'S COMPENSATION, § 5.30 (1993).

184. *See* ARTHUR LARSON, WORKERS' COMPENSATION LAW: CASES, MATERIALS AND TEXT 1–2 (2d ed. 1992).

185. *See* Crowell v. Benson, 285 U.S. 22 (1932); *supra*, Chapter 4, at notes 136–215 and accompanying text.

186. *See generally,* WILLIS PARK ROKES, NO-FAULT INSURANCE (1971); PAUL GILLESPIE & MIRIAM KLIPPER, NO FAULT: WHAT YOU SAVE, GAIN AND LOSE WITH THE NEW AUTO INSURANCE (1972).

ment problem with such substantive legislation.[187] Nevertheless, it is perhaps telling that the English in the colonial period also used jurisdictional and substantive laws to remove cases from colonial juries. Such choices reflect a policy to contain the jury, even if they do not raise constitutional issues.

B. Limiting Jury Discretion: Damage Caps

Both jurisdictional and substantive legislation affecting the right to jury trial have long histories. More recently, Congress and state legislatures have enacted caps on damages, which limit the jury's discretion. In addition to this legislative action, the Supreme Court has recently attempted to clarify the circumstances under which "grossly excessive" jury awards can be a violation of the due process clause. These cases can also effectively limit damages, though judicial decisions leave a little more play in the line.

1. Legislative Caps

Juries can award compensatory damages, which compensate the plaintiff for actual injuries sustained, and, in some cases, punitive damages, which are designed to punish the wrongdoer and deter similar conduct by both the wrongdoer and others who may be tempted to do something similar.[188] There are two kinds of compensatory damages. First, a damage award can compensate for actual out-of-pocket losses, such as medical expenses, cost of repairing property, or cost of future care following a catastrophic injury.[189] Second, a damage award can compensate for less tangible losses, such as pain and suffering, mental anguish, or invasion of privacy.[190] Compensation for out-of-

---

187. Both worker's compensation and no-fault insurance are matters of state law, so such laws primarily affect litigation in state courts. Cases with diverse parties, however, could be tried in federal courts in the absence of such legislation. Thus, such legislation has some effect on the use of juries in federal courts.

188. *See* 1 DAN B. DOBBS, LAW OF REMEDIES §3.11(1) (1993). The circumstances under which punitive damages may be awarded are limited. They are generally available for intentional torts and for gross negligence, but are unavailable for breach of contract. *See* RICHARD L. BLATT, ET AL., PUNITIVE DAMAGES §1.3 (1991); GERALD W. BOSTON, PUNITIVE DAMAGES IN TORT LAW §§2.6–2.8 (1993).

189. *See* 4 FOWLER V. HARPER, FLEMING JAMES, JR. & OSCAR S. GRAY, THE LAW OF TORTS §25.8 (2d ed. 1986); DuPree v. Louisiana Transit Management, 441 So.2d 436, 442 (La. Ct. App. 1983) (damages awarded equal to cost of medical care); Saide v. Stanton, 659 P.2d 35, 37 (Ariz. 1983) (person suffering dental injury awarded future medical expenses).

190. *See* 4 HARPER, JAMES & GRAY, *supra* note 189, at §25.10; Ferrara v. Gallucho, 152 N.E.2d 249, 253 (N.Y. 1958) (upholding award for mental anguish); Alabam Freight Lines v. Thevenot, 204 P.2d 1050, 1053 (Ariz. 1949) (upholding award for pain and suffering).

pocket losses are sometimes called "economic" damages, while compensation for intangible losses are often called "non-economic" damages.[191] Legislative caps on damages almost always relate to either punitive damages or non-economic damages.[192] Compensation for out-of-pocket losses is rarely capped.[193] More than forty state legislatures have enacted caps on damages of one kind or another. Many of these damage caps are limited to medical malpractice cases or product liability claims.[194] Congress has enacted federal damage cap laws as well. Most of these relate to specific kinds of cases, including employment discrimination cases and Y2K litigation.[195] Damage-capping legislation is controversial, however. In 1996, Congress passed The Common Sense Product Liability Legal Reform Act of 1996, which capped punitive damages in product liability cases at two times the sum of economic and non-economic damages or $250,000, whichever was greater, but it was vetoed by President Clinton in May of 1996.[196] Whether or not it is wise, it is generally agreed that legislation capping punitive damages would pass constitutional muster.[197] The

---

191. *See* Colleen P. Murphy, *Determining Compensation: The Tension Between Legislative Power and Jury Authority*, 74 TEX. L. REV. 345, 346 n.4 (1995); 1 MARILYN MINZER, ET AL., DAMAGES IN TORT ACTIONS §§ 3.40–3.41 (1995).

192. *See* 1 MINZER, ET AL., *supra* note 191, § 3.51; Murphy, *supra* note 191, at 346; Charles Jared Knight, Note, *State-Law Punitive Damage Schemes and the Seventh Amendment Right to Jury Trial in the Federal Courts*, 14 REV. LIT. 657, 659–60 (1995).

193. *See* 1 MINZER, ET AL., *supra* note 191, at § 3.52. A few states have capped total damages in medical malpractice actions, which can effectively cap economic damages. *See, e.g.,* COLO. REV. STAT. ANN. § 13-64-302 (1995 Supp.) ($1 million cap); ALA. CODE § 6-5-547 (1987) (same); S.D. CODIFIED LAWS ANN. § 21-3-11 (1977) (same). Many of these codes provide that the cap can be exceeded under specified conditions.

194. *See* Murphy, *supra* note 191, at 377 n.140; 1 MINZER, ET AL., *supra* note 191, at § 3.52; John F. Vargo, *The Emperor's New Clothes: The American Law Institute Adorns a "New Cloth" for Section 402A Products Liability Design Defects—A Survey of the States Reveals a Different Weave*, 26 U. MEM. L. REV. 493 (1996). Some of the legislation provides that juries are not told of the cap before retiring to deliberate, perhaps to prevent them from inflating the economic damage figure to make up for their inability to award higher non-economic or punitive damages. *See* Murphy, *supra* note 191, at 347 and n.8.

195. *See* Murphy, *supra* note 191, at 375; 42 U.S.C. § 1981a(b)(3) (1994) (capping damages in employment discrimination cases); Y2K Act, Pub. L. 106-37, Sec. 5 (July 20, 1999) (capping punitive damages in Y2K litigation).

196. H.R. 956, 104th Cong., 2nd Sess. (1996). *See* Neila Lewis, *President Vetoes Limits on Liability*, N.Y. TIMES, May 3, 1996, at A1. The federal legislation is enacted under the aegis of the Commerce Clause, because the huge damage awards that fuel it are alleged to have an impact on interstate commerce. *See* H.R. 956, 104th Cong., 2nd Sess., at § 2(b) (1996).

197. *See, e.g.,* Murphy, *supra* note 191, at 348–49; Janet V. Hallahan, *Social Interests Versus Plaintiffs' Rights: The Constitutional Battle Over Statutory Limitations on Punitive*

lower federal courts that have considered the constitutionality of caps on compensatory damages have so far upheld them, but the Supreme Court has not ruled on this question.[198]

The asserted justification for these legislative caps is the alleged crisis caused by outrageously high jury verdicts, particularly in some areas of tort law.[199] Evidently of a mind that remittitur and other traditional control devices are not sufficient to stem the tide, legislatures are choosing to limit the damages that juries can award. As I showed in the Introduction and in Chapter 1, however, whether the "crisis" that precipitated the legislation is real is open to debate.[200] There is evidence that the vast majority of jury verdicts are quite reasonable,[201] especially when the juries awarding them consist of twelve persons.[202] The occasional outlying verdict is what gets the attention, but such verdicts are not only rare, but are usually reduced by the trial judge.[203] Regardless of the soundness

---

Damages, 26 LOY U.-CHI. L.J. 405, 435 (1995) (noting a consensus among state and federal courts that there are no constitutional problems with capping punitive damage awards). *But see* Knight, *supra* note 192. The Seventh Amendment is not the only potential constitutional problem. Damage caps could also violate substantive due process rights. *See* Robert E. Riggs, *Constitutionalizing Punitive Damages: The Limits of Due Process*, 52 OHIO ST. L.J. 859, 885 (1991); Jane C. Arancibia, Note, *Statutory Caps on Damage Awards in Medical Malpractice Cases*, 13 OKLA. CITY U.L. REV. 135, 145 (1988).

198. *See, e.g.,* Davis v. Omitowoju, 883 F.2d 1155, 1165 (3rd Cir. 1989); Boyd v. Bulala, 877 F.2d 1191, 1196 (4th Cir. 1989). The argument in these cases was that reduction of the jury's award under the terms of the statute constituted a reexamination of facts found by the jury, but the courts thought that reduction simply reflected the legislative judgment as to the size of damage awards—a judgment that the legislature is authorized to make. *See generally,* Murphy, supra note 191, at 379–81. A forceful argument has recently been put forth that caps on any kind of compensatory damages, including non-economic damages, are unconstitutional under the Seventh Amendment. *See* Murphy, *supra* note 191.

199. *See* Introduction, *supra*, at notes 46–60 and accompanying text.

200. *See id.;* Chapter 1, *supra*, at notes 30–69 and accompanying text. Those arguing that a crisis does exist include, PETER W. HUBER, LIABILITY: THE LEGAL REVOLUTION AND ITS CONSEQUENCES 10 (1988); Charles D. Stewart and Philip G. Piggott, *Punitive Damages Since* Pacific Mutual Life Insurance Co. v. Haslip, 16 AM. J. TRIAL AD. 693, 697 (1993); *Quayle: Are There Too Many Lawyers in America?*, NEW JERSEY L.J. (August 29, 1991). Those arguing that the alleged crisis does not exist include STEPHEN DANIELS AND JOANNE MARTIN, CIVIL JURIES AND THE POLITICS OF REFORM (1995); and NEIL VIDMAR, MEDICAL MALPRACTICE AND THE AMERICAN JURY (1995).

201. *See, e.g.,* DANIELS & MARTIN, *supra* note 200, at 238–39; VIDMAR, *supra* note 200, at 259–61; Michael J. Saks, *Malpractice Misconceptions and Other Lessons About the Litigation System*, 16 JUSTICE SYS. J. 7, 16 (1993).

202. *See* Saks, *supra* note 201, at 17.

203. *See* Robert MacCoun, *Inside the Black Box: What Empirical Research Tells Us About Decisionmaking by Civil Juries*, in VERDICT: ASSESSING THE CIVIL JURY SYSTEM 149–50

of the underlying complaint, however, the legislative cap on damages appears well-ensconced, and so it will continue to control the jury's decision-making.

2. Supreme Court Action

Due process challenges to allegedly excessive punitive damages have been raised occasionally throughout the country's history.[204] In the earliest cases, the Supreme Court, while implicitly acknowledging its authority to consider such challenges, was very deferential to the jury's right to set punitive damages.[205] In the last several years, a new wave of such challenges has been raised in the Supreme Court—all arising in state courts where the Seventh Amendment does not apply—and the Court has obliged with guidelines for reviewing such awards.[206] In *Pacific Mutual Life Insurance Co. v. Haslip*, the Court upheld an award of punitive damages that was more than five times the compensatory damages.[207] The Court found that Alabama, where the case originated, had "established post-trial procedures for scrutinizing punitive awards,"[208] and that those procedures adequately protected defendants from excessive punitive damage awards. In particular, the Court approved Alabama's list of factors to consider: whether the punitive damages were related to the compensatory damages; the degree of reprehensibility; the profit the defendant earned from his wrongdoing; the defendant's financial position; litigation costs; and the availability of criminal or other civil penalties.[209]

(Robert E. Litan ed. 1993). Some verdicts that seem wrong at first glance appear more reasonable upon closer investigation. For a discussion of one such case involving superheated McDonald's coffee, see *supra*, Chapter 1, at notes 65–67 and accompanying text.

204. *See* Pacific Mutual Life Insurance Co. v. Haslip, 499 U.S. 1, 9–12 (1991) (listing cases).

205. *See id.* at 15–18.

206. The Court at first found ways to avoid the issue, *id.* at 12. For example, in two cases the due process challenge was not timely. *See* Browning-Ferris Industries of Vermont, Inc. v. Kelco Disposal, Inc., 492 U.S. 257 (1989); Bankers Life & Casualty Co. v. Crenshaw, 486 U.S. 71 (1988).

207. 499 U.S. 1, 23 (1991). Economic damages were less than $4000, but there is some indication that total compensatory damages awarded were about $200,000. The total award was $1,040,000. *Id* at 6–8 and n.2. There were several other plaintiffs in the case, but they all received smaller total awards. *Id.*

208. *Id.* at 20.

209. *Id.* at 21–22. In *Haslip*, the defendant's agent had defrauded plaintiffs by collecting their employer's health insurance premiums and then pocketing them, resulting in cancellation of the policies. *Id.* at 4–5. That conduct was sufficiently reprehensible and the damage to plaintiffs sufficiently serious that the Court thought the award was appropriate, though close to the line. *Id.* at 23–24.

Two years later, the Court upheld an award of punitive damages that was 526 times the actual damages sustained. In *TXO Production Corp. v. Allied Resources Corp.*,[210] the defendant, TXO, had entered into a royalty agreement with Allied, which owned the oil and gas rights to a tract of land. TXO, however, later manufactured an issue as to Allied's title to the property, apparently with the purpose of renegotiating the royalty agreement.[211] The Court was persuaded to uphold the award because (1) TXO's conduct was particularly egregious; (2) TXO had apparently engaged in this tactic before and was likely to do so again in the absence of a strong message; and (3) TXO was sufficiently wealthy that a smaller award may not have had the desired deterrent effect.[212]

Three years after *TXO*, the Court finally overturned a punitive damage award. In *BMW of North America, Inc. v. Gore*,[213] the punitive damage award was 500 times the actual damages. BMW had a policy of making repairs to new cars for minor damage sustained during shipping and storage, and then selling the cars as new without disclosing the damage. Minor damages were defined as less than three per cent of the car's value.[214] The jury in *BMW* found actual damages to the value of plaintiff's car of $4000, but awarded $4 million in punitive damages, which was apparently reached by multiplying $4000 by the number of people nationwide who had incurred similar damage.[215] That award was remitted by the Alabama Supreme Court to $2 million.[216] But the U.S. Supreme Court rejected even the remitted award. It found none of the circumstances that had permitted large punitive damage awards in past cases: the conduct was not particularly reprehensible;[217] the ratio between the actual and the punitive damages was much larger than most punitive damage awards;[218] and any criminal sanctions that might be available were much smaller.[219] The Court also held that damage to cars in other jurisdictions

---

210. 509 U.S. 443 (1993). This case originated in a West Virginia state court.
211. *See id.* at 448–49.
212. *Id* at 453–62.
213. 517 U.S. 559 (1996).
214. *Id.* at 564.
215. *Id.* at 565.
216. *Id.* at 267
217. *Id.* at 576.
218. *Id.* at 582. The ratio in *TXO* was even larger: 526:1. TXO's conduct, however, was particularly reprehensible, and the potential damage from its activity was very high. TXO, 509 U.S. at 460–62. The Court in BMW also noted that the actual ratio in TXO could be interpreted as only about 10:1 because TXO's tortious plan did not succeed there, but if it had, the actual damages would have been substantial. BMW, 517 U.S. at 582.
219. BMW, 517 U.S. at 584.

should not be a factor in the award, particularly as BMW's actions were not clearly illegal in some of those jurisdictions.[220]

At the same time that it was clarifying the scope of review of punitive damages awards, the Court was ensuring that such review would be available. In *Honda Motor Co., Ltd. v. Oberg*,[221] the Court struck down a provision of the Oregon constitution that prohibited judicial review of a jury's punitive damage awards unless there is "no evidence" to support the verdict.[222] The Court there held that such review was essential to protect defendants' due process rights, even if reversals were relatively rare.[223]

While only one of these cases resulted in a jury verdict's being held excessive, the cases collectively have served to give state courts some guidance as to when a jury's punitive damages award might be unconstitutionally high.[224] The most important factor seems to be the degree of reprehensibility. That seems to be precisely the kind of issue where we want to have a sense of the community, which the jury is designed to provide. But the Court has made it clear that the courts have oversight responsibility that cannot be taken away from them.

The cases discussed so far were all tried in state courts, where the Seventh Amendment does not apply. The interaction between the requirements of due process and those of the Seventh Amendment was not addressed in any of them. But the Court may have given us a hint how it will view that interaction in *Gasperini v. Center for Humanities, Inc.*[225] There, the Court held that federal courts sitting in diversity must comply with a New York statute that requires appellate courts in New York to review juries' compensatory damage awards to determine whether they " 'deviate[] materially from what would be reasonable compensation.' "[226] The defendant's argument had been

---

220. *Id.* at 579.
221. 512 U.S. 415 (1994).
222. *Id.* at 418.
223. *Id.* at 426–27.
224. For a discussion of *Haslip, TXO* and *Honda* and some history relating to punitive damage awards, *see* Hallahan, *supra* note 191; Matthew J. Macario, Note, *Constitutional Law—Punitive Damage Awards and Procedural Due Process in Products Liability Cases—Honda Motor Co., Ltd. v. Oberg*, 114 S. Ct. 2331 (1994), 68 TEMPLE L. REV. 409 (1995); Sandra L. Nunn, Note, *The Due Process Ramifications of Punitive Damages, Continued*: TXO Production Corp. v. Alliance Resources Corp., 113 S.Ct. 2711 (1993), 63 U. CIN. L. REV. 1029 (1995).
225. 518 U.S. 415 (1996).
226. *See* Gasperini v. Center for Humanities, Inc., 518 U.S. 415, 418 (1996), quoting N.Y. Civ. Prac. Law and Rules (CPLR) §5501(c) (McKinney 1995). The standard requires courts, including trial courts, to compare damage awards in similar cases.

that while trial judges historically could reduce jury awards through remittitur and their power to order new trials, appellate oversight of juries' damage awards did not occur under the common law, and so would violate the Reexamination Clause of the Seventh Amendment.[227] But the Supreme Court determined that New York's standard is substantive and so, under the *Erie* doctrine, must be applied in federal diversity actions.[228] In *Gasperini*, the Court held for the first time that the Seventh Amendment does not preclude " 'appellate review of a trial judge's denial of a motion to set aside [a jury verdict] as excessive.' "[229] But to accommodate Seventh Amendment concerns, the Court required that in the federal courts, the trial courts apply New York's "materially deviates" standard in the first instance, and courts of appeals review that determination for abuse of discretion, a highly deferential standard of review.[230]

The *Erie* doctrine requires that federal courts sitting in diversity apply state substantive law, including case law. If the state courts, following *Haslip, TXO, Gore,* and *BMW,* develop standards for reviewing punitive damage awards that are designed to protect the parties' due process rights, those standards would seem to be substantive under the reasoning of *Gasperini*. Thus, federal trial courts would have to apply them, and federal courts of appeals would have to review the trial judges' decisions on an abuse of discretion standard. And if jury awards based on state law can violate the Due Process Clause, it would seem that jury awards based on federal law could also violate it, so that a similar procedure might be required for federal question cases. At the same time, however, federal courts cannot simply remit awards that they find are grossly excessive. The Court has held that to comply with the Seventh Amendment, federal courts must give plaintiffs the option to reject the remitted award and have a new trial.[231]

227. *See* Gasperini, 518 U.S. at 434–36. The Reexamination Clause says that "no fact tried by a jury, shall be otherwise reexamined in any Court of the United States, than according to the rules of the common law." U.S. CONST., Am. VII. *See* Gasperini, 518 U.S. at 431–39.

228. *See id.* at 427–31. The *Erie* doctrine, named for *Erie R Co. v. Tompkins,* 304 U.S. 64 (1938), requires that federal courts sitting in diversity apply state substantive law.

229. Gasperini, 518 U.S. at 436, quoting Grunenthal v. Long Island R. Co., 393 U.S. 156, 164 (1968) (Stewart, J., dissenting).

230. *See* Gasperini, 518 U.S. at 436–39.

231. *See* Hetzel v. Prince William County, Virginia, 523 U.S. 208 (1998) (per curiam).

3. Damage Caps and the Right to a Jury Trial

If there is a problem with excessive damage awards, whether compensatory or punitive, a judicial solution seems preferable to a legislative one. A legislative solution reduces the jury's ability to express the community's sentiment as to non-economic damages and punishment (though it does not eliminate it), and may set damages too low in some cases.[232] Legislative caps set damage limits without benefit of hearing the facts of particular cases. A judicial solution allows free expression of community sentiment but permits the court to intervene when damages are excessive. Judicial review allows the court to consider all the evidence in a particular case before deciding whether the jury's award is within reasonable bounds.[233]

But there are potential problems with judicial review as well. In the federal courts, the Seventh Amendment bars courts from reexamining jury fact-finding except in accordance with the common law.[234] Jury decisions as to economic damages clearly involve fact-finding, as the jury must determine what the out-of-pocket losses are. Non-economic and punitive damages are more fluid. How does one determine the value of pain, the non-economic worth of a lifelong disability, or the non-economic value of a lost loved one? These decisions are less fact-based and more common sensical. That may make them both more appropriate for the jury's determination (because they call for common sense determinations) and more vulnerable to judicial control (because judges arguably would not be reviewing jury fact-finding). Punitive damages are different. Because they are a relatively recent development, they do not have the strong common law tradition that compensatory damages have.[235] In addition, with the exception of the death penalty, we generally leave criminal sentencing—punishment—to the judge rather than the jury, and this suggests leaving punitive damages to the judge as well. But punitive damages give

---

232. Some legislative caps allow damages to exceed the cap in exceptional circumstances. *See, e.g.,* COLO. REV. STAT. ANN. §33-44-113. Juries often are not informed of the caps, so return a verdict for the sum they believe proper without regard to the legislative cap. Thus, they may be able to express their sense of outrage, but because awards in excess of the cap are remitted, the jury's expression has little effect.

233. Such judicial review includes remittitur. *See supra,* notes 157–161 and accompanying text.

234. *See* U.S. CONST. am. VII.

235. For a discussion of the origins of punitive damages, *see supra,* Chapter 1, at notes 59–64 and accompanying text.

the jury an opportunity to express its outrage at a party's behavior, and we should be reluctant to eliminate that valuable gauge of community sentiment.

Balanced against all of this is the parties' right to due process. An excessive damage award violates a party's substantive due process rights.[236] But the evidence is that excessive awards are rare, and that the courts are capable of policing them when they do occur.[237] Thus, a solution such as that suggested by *Gasperini* and the due process cases has some appeal—it allows the jury to express its views fully as to the reprehensibility of the conduct, but provides that truly excessive awards are subject to remittitur or a new trial, and it does so on a case-by-case basis. And because new trials for excessive verdicts were known to the common law, such a procedure seems to be no offense to the Reexamination Clause of the Seventh Amendment.[238]

C. Conclusion

When the legislature removes cases or issues from the courts, or limits the actions that juries can take, it is eliminating any possibility of the jury's having a significant voice in the matter. In cases where the sense of the community is important, that is a significant loss. Unfortunately, the very matters that are being removed from the juries are often those most in need of community assessment. They may involve unequal parties—corporations and consumers, for example; or assessments of the degree of culpability—punitive damages, for example.[239] Thus, even if we concede that juries can sometimes get it wrong, removing the jury's voice is too extreme a solution.

More generally, the effect of removing cases or issues from adjudication in the courts extends far beyond the particular case or parties. The decisions that parties and their lawyers make, from the decision whether to assert a claim to the decision whether to settle and for what, are made against the background

---

236. See BMW of North America, Inc. v. Gore, 517 U.S. 559 (1996); TXO Production Corp. v. Alliance Resources Corp., 509 U.S. 443 (1993); Pacific Mutual Life Insurance Co. v. Haslip, 499 U.S. 1 (1991).

237. See *supra*, Chapter 1, at notes 30–69 and accompanying text.

238. Another suggestion is that juries be asked to rate the reprehensibility of the defendant's conduct on a closed scale, and that experts, such as judges or administrative agencies, translate that judgment into dollars using an appropriate formula. See David Schkade, Cass R. Sunstein, and Daniel Kahneman, *Are Juries Less Erratic Than Individuals? Deliberation, Polarization, and Punitive Damages*, University of Chicago, John M. Olin Law and Economics Working Paper No. 81 (2nd Series) (2000).

239. For a discussion of the jury's role in resolving disputes, see *supra*, Chapter 1, at notes 9–69 and accompanying text.

of the jury trial.[240] When the alternative to settlement is trial by jury, the incentives are different than when the alternative to settlement is an administrative adjudication or a trial before a judge. When damages are capped at the outset, the incentives are different than when the defendant's potential exposure is higher. The removal of a case or issue from the jury, then, alters the balance of power between the parties to the dispute. This alteration in the balance of power almost always favors potential defendants over potential plaintiffs. It is impossible to know, without further study, whether limiting the jury's voice in these ways results in a net increase in justice. But it certainly reduces the jury's ability to speak out on matters of public importance, as well as its role as equalizer—its dispute-settling role.[241]

V. Preclusion

Once known by the cumbersome terms "res judicata" and "collateral estoppel," preclusion prevents relitigation of claims or issues that have once been decided. The doctrine has common law origins and is designed to give litigants some repose and to prevent overburdening the courts with matters that have already been decided.[242] These are important goals in any adjudicatory system, but the question is whether rules of preclusion should be applied so as to prevent a jury trial. The Supreme Court has recently made it easier for preclusion to have just that effect.

There are two kinds of preclusion. Claim preclusion applies when two parties have already litigated a matter to a conclusion on the merits.[243] In subsequent litigation between the two, they will not be able to relitigate matters that were litigated or should have been litigated in the previous suit. In other words, relitigation of the claim is precluded, with "claim" defined in terms of the transaction that gave rise to the suit and not to any particular cause of ac-

---

240. *See, e.g.,* Marc Galanter, *The Regulatory Function of the Civil Jury,* in VERDICT, *supra* note 196. This has been termed "bargaining in the shadow of the jury." *See* MacCoun, *supra* note 196, at 139, citing Marc Galanter, *Jury Shadows: Reflections on the Civil Jury and the "Litigation Explosion,"* in MORRIS S. ARNOLD, ET AL., THE AMERICAN CIVIL JURY 15 (Roscoe Pound—American Trial Lawyers Foundation 1987).

241. For a discussion of the jury's dispute-settling role, see *supra,* Chapter 1, at notes 9–69 and accompanying text.

242. *See* Federated Department Stores, Inc. v. Moitie, 452 U.S. 394, 401 (1981).

243. *See* 18 CHARLES ALAN WRIGHT, ARTHUR R. MILLER AND EDWARD H. COOPER, FEDERAL PRACTICE AND PROCEDURE, § 4402 (1981).

tion.[244] For example, if A and B have a contract under which A lends goods to B with the understanding that B will return the goods at a later date, then upon B's failure to return the goods, A cannot first sue for negligent loss of goods and then later sue for breach of contract.[245] The two suits, while asserting separate causes of action, are transactionally identical and so are part of the same claim.

Issue preclusion, by contrast, concerns separate claims with common issues.[246] Issue preclusion prevents relitigation of issues that have once been decided on the merits, but only if the issue was actually litigated, and the decision was necessary to the outcome of the first case.[247] For example, suppose A sues B for patent infringement, and the court decides that A's patent is valid and has been infringed. If B then continues to infringe, A can file a subsequent suit seeking recovery on the new infringement, but may be able to preclude relitigation of the issue of the patent's validity.[248] Claim preclusion would be unavailable because the new infringement is not the same transaction as the original infringement—it is a new claim.[249]

The original common law rule was that issue preclusion could be invoked only by persons who were bound by the original judgment—parties to the original case or those in privity with a party.[250] This is the doctrine of mutuality. Most jurisdictions have relaxed or abrogated the mutuality doctrine, allowing persons who were not bound by the original suit to assert issue preclusion against the party who lost the original case.[251] Preclusion can be

---

244. See, e.g., Nilsen v. City of Moss Point, 701 F.2d 556, 560n.4 (5th Cir. 1983); Kilgoar v. Colbert County Board of Education, 578 F.2d 1033, 1035 (5th Cir. 1978). See generally, RESTATEMENT (SECOND) OF JUDGMENTS §24 comment A (1982).

245. See id. at illustration 2.

246. See 18 WRIGHT, MILLER & COOPER, supra note 243, at §4402.

247. See Cromwell v. County of Sac, 94 U.S. (4 Otto) 351, 353 (1876) (actually litigated); Block v. Commissioners, 99 U.S. 686, 693 (1878) (necessarily decided). See also, 18 WRIGHT, MILLER & COOPER, supra note 243, at §§4416, 4419, 4421.

248. The example in the text is a modification of Russell v. Place, 94 U.S. (4 Otto) 606 (1876). In that case, preclusion was not applicable because the patent contained two claims, and it was not possible to determine which of claims had been found to be valid and infringed in the earlier litigation.

249. See 18 WRIGHT, MILLER & COOPER, supra note 243, at §4402.

250. See, e.g., Ralph Wolff & Sons v. New Zealand Ins. Co., 248 Ky. 304, 58 S.W.2d 623, 624 (1933). For general discussions of mutuality, see Herbert Semmel, Collateral Estoppel, Mutuality, and Joinder of Parties, 68 COLUM. L. REV. 1457 (1968); Alan N. Polasky, Collateral Estoppel—Effects of Prior Litigation, 39 IOWA L. REV. 217 (1954).

251. Preclusion can prevent someone who was a party to the first case from relitigating a claim or an issue. Neither claim nor issue preclusion can normally be invoked against

defensive—asserted against a plaintiff who had already litigated and lost the matter—or offensive—asserted against a defendant who had already litigated and lost the matter.[252]

Until 1979, preclusion could not be invoked to deprive the parties of their right to a jury trial.[253] Thus, if the prior adjudication was equitable, the mat-

---

someone who was *not* a party to the first suit. A non-party to the first suit can invoke issue preclusion, but cannot have it invoked against him. *See* 18 WRIGHT, MILLER & COOPER, *supra* note 243, at §4449. *But see* Montana v. United States, 440 U.S. 147, 154–55 (1979) (holding that issue preclusion was available against a non-party to the first action who had financed and overseen the litigation in the first action). In *Martin v. Wilks*, 490 U.S. 755, 761–62 (1989), the Supreme Court held that white firefighters who had known of prior litigation by black firefighters that resulted in a consent decree setting goals for the hiring and promotion of black firefighters could not be precluded from a later challenge, on reverse discrimination grounds, to the consent decree. That holding was overturned by the Civil Rights Act of 1991, which provides that persons who have actual notice of such a discrimination suit and a reasonable opportunity to intervene or who are adequately represented by existing parties cannot later challenge a consent decree arising out of the litigation. Pub. L. No. 102-166, tit. I, §108, 105 Stat. 1071, 1076, codified at 42 U.S.C. §§1981 *et seq.* (1994). For a brief history of the abrogation of mutuality, see Michael J. Waggoner, *Fifty Years of Bernhard v. Bank of America is Enough: Collateral Estoppel Should Require Mutuality, But Res Judicata Should Not;* 12 REV. LIT. 391, 429–39 (1993).

252. *See* Parklane, 439 U.S. at 339–40; Waggoner, *supra* note 251, at 403–04; John Bernard Corr, *Supreme Court Doctrine in the Trenches: The Case of Collateral Estoppel,* 27 WM. & MARY L. REV. 35, 38n.16 (1985). Abrogation of mutuality occurred first with defensive issue preclusion. Courts generally approve of non-mutual defensive issue preclusion because it gives plaintiffs an incentive to join all defendants in the original action: if they win the original action, they will have won against all possible defendants, saving them litigation costs, but if they lose against the original defendant, subsequent defendants will be able to use preclusion against them, giving them no reason not to join all defendants. *See* Parklane, 439 U.S. at 329–30. Non-mutual defensive issue preclusion was approved for federal courts in *Blonder-Tongue Laboratories, Inc. v. University of Illinois Foundation,* 402 U.S. 313 (1971).

Non-mutual *offensive* issue preclusion is more problematic. The defendant did not choose the forum and may not have had an adequate opportunity to defend the first case. *See* Parklane, 439 U.S. at 330–31 and n.15. More importantly, non-mutual offensive issue preclusion offers an incentive for the plaintiffs not to join: if the first plaintiff wins, the next can take advantage of that victory, but if the first plaintiff loses, the next cannot be bound because she was not a party to the first case. *Id.* at 329. If preclusion is not allowed, the advantages of judicial economy may result in more joinder of plaintiffs in the first case. *See id.* at 329–30; Jack Ratliff, *Offensive Collateral Estoppel and the Option Effect,* 67 TEX. L. REV. 63, 98 (1988); Corr, *supra,* at 55n.18.

253. *See, e.g.,* Rachal v. Hill, 435 F.2d 59, 64 (5th Cir. 1970), *cert. denied,* 403 U.S. 904 (1971). This decision was criticized in David L. Shapiro and Daniel R. Coquillette, *The Fetish of Jury Trial in Civil Cases: A Comment on Rachal v. Hill,* 85 HARV. L. REV. 442 (1971).

ter would have to be retried to a jury in a subsequent legal action. That rule was changed in *Parklane Hosiery Co. v. Shore*,[254] which was a shareholders' derivative suit charging that the corporation had issued a false and misleading financial statement. The shareholders sought damages and Parklane demanded a jury trial. Prior to the trial in the shareholders' case, a separate equitable action brought against Parklane by the Securities Exchange Commission was decided in the SEC's favor. Because it was an equitable action, no jury was empaneled in that case. The shareholders, who were not parties to the SEC's suit or in privity with the SEC, sought to preclude relitigation of the finding that the financial statement was false and misleading. Parklane objected, arguing, among other things, that because mutuality applied in 1791 when the Seventh Amendment was ratified, the abrogation of mutuality could not constitutionally be used to deprive it of its right to a jury trial.

The Supreme Court rejected this argument, holding that changes in procedures can affect availability of a jury trial without violating the Seventh Amendment.[255] It allowed the use of non-mutual offensive issue preclusion under circumstances where it was fair to do so, and it found it fair in *Parklane*.[256] The one-two punch of *Parklane*—approving of non-mutual offensive issue preclusion for the federal courts in some cases and allowing preclusion even when the effect was to eliminate a jury trial—extends the reach of the preclusion doctrine considerably.[257]

Other extensions of the preclusion rules also affect the right to a jury trial. Some courts allow preclusion based on decisions by administrative agencies,

---

254. 439 U.S. 322, 337 (1979).

255. The Court has taken this approach in other contexts as well. *See, e.g.,* Galloway v. United States, 319 U.S. 372, 388–93 (1943) (holding that directed verdict does not violate the Seventh Amendment); Fidelity & Deposit Co. v. United States, 187 U.S. 315, 319–21 (1902) (holding that summary judgment does not violate the Seventh Amendment); Gasoline Products Co. v. Champlin Refining Co., 283 U.S. 494, 497–98 (1931) (holding that retrial limited to damages does not violate Seventh Amendment even though there was no practice at common law for setting aside a verdict in part).

256. Specifically, if the party who was to be precluded had a full and fair opportunity to litigate in the first action, and if there was no incentive or opportunity to join in the previous suit, non-mutual offensive issue preclusion was approved. *Id.* at 331–33. In *Parklane*, the shareholders could not have joined in the SEC action, and Parklane had both the incentive to litigate the SEC action vigorously and the opportunity to do so in federal court. Thus, the Court upheld the use of non-mutual offensive issue preclusion in that case.

257. Preclusion can be used to prevent a jury trial even where there is no mutuality issue, that is, when the parties are identical in the two lawsuits.

where there is no jury.[258] This is also a relatively recent phenomenon,[259] and the Supreme Court has not ruled on it, but it helps to reinforce the application of the public rights doctrine and the balancing test, which allow litigation of some matters in administrative agencies, where there is no jury, when those issues would otherwise have carried the right to a jury trial.[260] In addition, some courts permit arbitration decisions to preclude subsequent relitigation of issues determined in the arbitration.[261] Arbitration does not use juries, so if issues decided in arbitration are precluded from relitigation before a jury, the right to jury trial is diminished. In that sense, preclusion also helps to reinforce the jury-control aspects of arbitration.[262] Again, the Supreme Court has not ruled on this use of preclusion.

The result of these recent developments in preclusion doctrine is that, in some cases, fact-finding will be transferred from juries to other decision-makers. If an equitable action is decided prior to a related legal action, the judge's fact-finding can be preclusive in the legal action, even if a jury would otherwise have found those facts in the legal action. Similarly, administrative adjudications and arbitrations can preclude subsequent fact-finding by juries, though those doctrines are less well-established. The only constraint on the application of preclusion is the doctrine of mutuality, which, in the federal courts, is largely abrogated.[263] Non-mutual offensive issue preclusion is sub-

---

258. *See* Gear v. City of Des Moines, 514 F. Supp. 1218 (S.D. Iowa 1981); Frye v. United Steelworkers of America, 767 F.2d 1216 (7th Cir. 1985); United States v. Jan Hardware Manufacturing Co., 463 F. Supp. 732 (E.D.N.Y. 1979). *See generally,* Rex R. Perschbacher, *Rethinking Collateral Estoppel: Limiting the Preclusive Effect of Administrative Determinations in Judicial Proceedings,* 35 U. FLA. L. REV. 422 (1983); David A. Brown, Note, *Collateral Estoppel Effects of Administrative Agency Determinations: Where Should Federal Courts Draw the Line,* 73 CORNELL L. REV. 817 (1988).

259. *See* Perschbacher, *supra* note 258, at 423. It is understandable that preclusion based on agency decisions would be of recent development, because agencies themselves have existed in large numbers only since the 1930's.

260. *See* Chapter 4, *supra,* at notes 136–215 and accompanying text.

261. *See* Ritchie v. Landau, 475 F.2d 151 (2nd Cir. 1973); Goldstein v. Doft, 236 F. Supp. 730 (S.D.N.Y. 1964); Sports Factory, Inc. v. Charoff, 586 F. Supp. 342 (E.D. Pa. 1984). *See generally,* G. Richard Shell, *Res Judicata and Collateral Estoppel Effects of Commerical Arbitration,* 35 U.C.L.A. L. REV. 623 (1988); Hiroshi Motomura, *Arbitration and Collateral Estoppel: Using Preclusion to Shape Procedural Choices,* 63 TULANE L. REV. 29 (1988).

262. For a discussion of arbitration as a jury-control device, see Chapter 8, *infra,* at notes 42–63 and accompanying text.

263. In the common law, a court of equity's decision on legal matters under the clean-up doctrine could deprive a party of a jury trial, but only in matters between the same par-

ject to a fairness analysis, and that may provide some constraint, but if mutuality does not apply by its terms, the deprivation of a right to jury trial is not grounds for reviving it.

VI. Summary and Conclusion

While many of the jury control devices described in this Chapter have ancient origins, most have been strengthened in recent years, making it easier for judges to control juries. The standards for awarding judgment as a matter of law and summary judgment have eased, so that judges can become more involved in weighing facts—traditionally the jury's job. These control devices thus begin to encroach on the traditional common law control—the new trial: they allow the judge to decide a case rather than give it to a new jury. The doctrine of preclusion has expanded to allow prior litigation before judges, administrative agencies, and arbitrators to preclude subsequent litigation before a jury, even when invoked by someone who was not a party to the first action. The special verdict has not changed much recently, but its evolution from a protective device favored by jurors to a control mechanism in the hands of the judge illustrates the long road to jury control that all of these mechanisms are on. Both legislatures and courts are finding new ways to limit damage awards. The most troubling is the legislative cap, because it removes from the jury the very kinds of issues that juries are best suited to decide, and it does so without regard for the circumstances of individual cases. A judicially enforced due process limit on punitive damages is probably a better approach to curbing excessive awards, especially as excessive awards are rare. Nevertheless, the Seventh Amendment apparently poses no impediment to legislative caps because Congress and the state legislatures have the power to change the law, even if their premises are wrong.

Some of these changes may well have beneficial effects. They certainly increase the efficiency of the judicial system. Whether they enhance justice is open to some debate. They certainly make it harder to gauge community sentiment about matters of public importance, and they minimize the jury's equalizing effects. They also increase the professionalization of decision-making, which may mean we sacrifice common sense.[264] The Court has said that

---

ties. Non-mutual preclusion did not exist and could not have prevented relitigation with a jury.

264. I do not mean to suggest that judges lack common sense—only that juries are better able, sometimes, to express it. Common sense may also emerge more concretely from

the Seventh Amendment protects the "fundamental" right to a jury trial, and not specific procedural aspects of that right. The question is whether these enhancements of jury control compromise the fundamental right to a jury trial beyond what the Seventh Amendment permits. It seems to me we should be wary of procedural changes whose effect is to remove cases or issues from juries altogether.

---

having numerous citizens deliberate together than from the deliberation—however keen— of one judge.

CHAPTER 8

AVOIDANCE OF TRIAL

Litigants have always had the opportunity to avoid trial altogether, usually by settling, but avoidance has increased dramatically in the last few decades. At the time the Federal Rules of Civil Procedure were adopted, some twenty per cent of civil cases went to trial.[1] That figure has dropped to less than five per cent, about half of which are jury trials. Some of the cases that do not go to trial are resolved through the devices described in Chapter 7, most notably summary judgment. Many, however, are settled voluntarily by the parties or resolved through alternative dispute resolution (ADR). In this Chapter, I will explore the changing incentives to settle that have contributed to this drop in trials, and will then discuss ADR. Finally, I will assess the impact of increased settlements on the jury.

I. Incentives to Settle

There have always been inherent incentives to settle, such as a desire to avoid the cost of litigation, but those incentives are stronger under modern procedural rules. In addition, the judicial management authority in the Federal Rules is now much more focused on encouraging the parties to settle. The result of these developments is more settlements.

A. Inherent Incentives

Inherent incentives to settle include avoiding the cost of litigation; uncertainty as to the outcome if the case goes to trial; concerns that a trial will take too long to resolve; and a variety of individual factors that might encourage the parties to settle.

---

1. *See* Stephen C. Yeazell, *The Misunderstood Consequences of Modern Civil Process*, 1994 WIS. L. REV. 631, 633 and n.3. The figures cited in this paragraph are discussed in the Introduction, *supra*, at notes 38–45 and accompanying text.

1. Cost of Litigation

Sometimes the cost of litigation is not worth the recovery that a plaintiff could expect following a trial. Settling for less saves the cost of litigation, and the plaintiff may well come out ahead. The defendant benefits as well, saving both the cost of litigation and, possibly, a larger judgment at trial.[2] The Federal Rules of Civil Procedure have increased the costs of litigation, so the incentive to settle is greater than it was under other procedural schemes. First, it is very difficult, under the Federal Rules, to have a case dismissed on the pleadings alone.[3] Normally, at least some discovery will be necessary before a court will be willing to rule on the merits. Second, discovery itself can be very expensive, especially if numerous depositions are required.[4] Third, cases with multiple parties and multiple issues are costly because there are more things happening in the litigation, and the lawyers must monitor them all, and respond to many of them.[5] Class actions, though comparatively rare, are notoriously expensive.[6]

The knowledge explosion has also contributed to the cost of litigation, as tech-

---

2. Plaintiffs sometimes sue largely for the settlement value of the case, never intending to take the case to trial. See Samuel R. Gross & Kent D. Syverud, *Getting to No: A Study of Settlement Negotiations and the Selection of Cases for Trial*, 90 MICH. L. REV. 319, 320 (1991). The courts and Congress sometimes try to rein this activity in, sometimes by requiring more detailed pleading than the federal rules normally require. For example, some courts imposed a heightened pleading requirement in civil rights cases until the Supreme Court put a stop to it in *Leatherman v. Tarrant County Narcotics Intelligence & Coordination Unit*, 507 U.S. 163 (1993). Congress has recently required heightened pleading in federal securities fraud cases and Y2K cases. See *Private Securities Litigation Reform Act of 1995*, Pub. L. No. 104-67, 109 Stat. 737 (codified in scattered sections of 15 U.S.C.); *Y2K Act*, Pub. L. No. 106-37 (106th Cong., 1st Sess. 1999).

3. Rule 12(b)(6) allows a defendant to move to dismiss for failure to state a claim. But the Court has held that dismissal under Rule 12(b)(6) is improper unless it is clear that the plaintiff can prove no set of facts that would allow recovery. See *Conley v. Gibson*, 355 U.S. 41, 45–46 (1957). The theory is that the pleadings are to be used only to give general notice to the opposing party of the nature of the party's case, and that the case is fleshed out, and issues narrowed, through discovery. See Richard L. Marcus, *The Revival of Fact Pleading Under the Federal Rules of Civil Procedure*, 86 COLUM. L. REV. 433, 450 (1986).

4. See Thomas E. Willging, et al., *An Empirical Study of Discovery and Disclosure Practice Under the 1993 Federal Rules Amendments*, 39 B.C.L. REV. 525, 537 (1998).

5. See Robert A. Jones & John Meredith, *Management of Complex Mult-Party Litigation*, 31 HOUSTON LAWYER 16, 17 (1994).

6. See Charles Silver, *A Restitutionary Theory of Attorney's Fees in Class Actions*, 76 CORNELL L. REV. 656, 679 (1991); Kenneth S. Abraham, *Individual Action and Collective Responsibility: The Dilemma of Mass Tort Reform*, 73 VA. L. REV. 845, 876 (1987).

nically complex cases may require expert witnesses.[7] Expert witnesses are paid for their time in investigating the matter, and for their time as witnesses.[8] The appearance of expert witnesses at trial may be just the tip of the iceberg, as a party may hire expert witnesses who will not, ultimately, be called at trial. The more technical or scientific issues there are, the more the litigation is likely to cost.

Some of these costs may have to be borne even if the case ultimately settles. For example, the information that a party gleans during discovery, including information from expert witnesses, may help her make an intelligent decision about settlement. Sometimes the trial itself would be almost anticlimactic, both in drama and in cost. But a party who learns, during discovery, that her case is weak is more likely to want to settle rather than risk incurring the additional cost of a trial and having nothing to show for it.

2. Uncertainty

Uncertainty is inherent in litigation: if we knew the outcome, we would not need a trial, and the parties could presumably reach an agreement. Thus, reducing uncertainty could lead to more settlements. This is one reason why many cases settle after discovery, which gives both sides a better basis for estimating the likely outcome at trial.[9] The jury itself is a significant uncertainty factor. While empirical evidence shows that most jury verdicts are within a predictable range and not far off from what the judges think are reasonable,[10] there are rogue juries that reach extravagant verdicts on questionable evidence.[11] This is especially true now that most federal and state juries have fewer than twelve members.[12] And it may be especially true when the evidence

---

7. *See* Samuel R. Gross, *Expert Evidence*, 1991 WIS. L. REV. 1113.

8. *See* FED. R. CIV. P. 26(a)(2); Gross, *supra* note 7, at 1148.

9. *See* Bruce L. Hay, *Civil Discovery: Its Effects and Optimal Scope*, 23 J. LEG. STUD. 481, 513 (1994). Of course, two parties or even two lawyers can look at the same evidence and reach different conclusions. Even if the parties or their lawyers agree about the facts, they can disagree about their legal significance, or about how a jury or a judge is likely to view them.

10. *See* Neil Vidmar, *The Performance of the American Civil Jury: An Empirical Perspective*, 40 ARIZ. L. REV. 849, 853 (1998). *See also, supra* Chapter 1, at notes 30–69 and accompanying text.

11. *See, e.g.,* PETER W. HUBER, GALILEO'S REVENGE: JUNK SCIENCE IN THE COURTROOM 218, 228 (1991).

12. *See* Hans Zeisel, *The Debate Over the Civil Jury in Historical Perspective*, 1990 U. CHI. L. FORUM 25, 29; Hans Zeisel,...*And Then There Were None: The Diminution of the Federal Jury*, 38 U. CHI. L. REV. 710, 717–18 (1971); Michael J. Saks, *The Smaller the Jury the Greater the Unpredictability*, 79 JUDICATURE 263, 264 (1996). As I showed in Chapter 7, judges have considerable power to modify jury verdicts, as through remittitur, or to order

concerns complex scientific or technical data and the parties fail to present the data in an understandable form.[13] Thus, some litigants settle to avoid the uncertainty of a jury verdict.

3. Time

Litigation can be costly, but it can also take a very long time. The Federal Rules have contributed to an increase in the time required to litigate a case. The parties can file numerous motions that the judge must decide, and discovery can, in some cases, go on for years.[14] The explosion in knowledge may also contribute to lengthening trials, as it can take time to hire expert witnesses and have them perform their analyses. Some litigants will settle to avoid a long wait, though defendants—especially those that are likely to be found liable— might prefer to put off the day of reckoning as long as possible. In some jurisdictions, there is a longer wait for a jury trial than a bench trial, so if time is a factor, settlement could be more likely if the case will be tried to a jury rather than a judge.

4. Individual Factors

There are always going to be individual factors in the decision to settle a lawsuit. Some are exacerbated by developments in the Federal Rules, but some are entirely independent. For example, some plaintiffs may need money im-

---

a new trial because the verdict is against the great weight of the evidence. Many extravagant verdicts do not survive these control devices.

13. *See* Vidmar, *supra* note 10, at 855; Neil Vidmar, *Are Juries Competent to Decide Liability in Tort Cases Involving Scientific/Medical Issues: Some Data From Medical Malpractice*, 43 EMORY L.J. 885, 885–95 (1994); Michael S. Jacobs, *Testing the Assumptions Underlying the Debate About Scientific Evidence: A Closer Look at Juror "Incompetence" and Scientific "Objectivity,"* 25 CONN. L. REV. 1083, 1093 (1993); Joe S. Cecil, *et al., Citizen Comprehension of Difficult Issues: Lessons from Civil Jury Trials*, 40 AM. U. L. REV. 717 (1991).

14. *See, e.g.,* JONATHAN HARR, A CIVIL ACTION (1995); Earl C. Dudley, Jr., *Discovery Abuse Revisited: Some Specific Proposals to Amend the Federal Rules of Civil Procedure*, 26 U. SAN FRAN. L. REV. 189, 200 (1992). There are now many judicial management tools that help to speed the litigation along. For example, judges can set time limits on discovery. *See Report on Discovery Under Rule 26(b)(1)*, 127 F.R.D. 625, 629 (1989); Charles W. Sorenson, Jr., *Disclosure Under Federal Rule of Civil Procedure 26(a): Much Ado About Nothing?*, 46 HASTINGS L.J. 679, 697 (1995). Judges can also set an early trial date, which forces the parties to complete discovery and pretrial motions within a narrow time frame. *See* John Burritt McArthur, *The Strange Case of American Civil Procedure and the Missing Uniform Discovery Time Limits*, 24 HOFSTRA L. REV. 865 (1996).

mediately, and so be more willing to settle for less than they might hope to get at trial. Some may settle even before discovery is complete to avoid the cost and delay of discovery. Sometimes the parties expect to have a continuing relationship after the litigation is over, so settlement on mutually agreed terms is better than an adversarial trial.[15] And, of course, the litigants' outlooks toward risk will affect how they assess factors such as uncertainty. For risk-averse litigants, substantial uncertainty about the outcome will increase the desire to settle. Risk-loving litigants might prefer to test the case before a jury. The list of individual factors that could affect settlement is endless, and they can work in both directions: some will encourage settlement, and some will encourage trial.

5. Summary and Conclusion

There are many factors that enter into the parties' decision to settle a case, some of them peculiar to the particular litigants before the court. But changes in the Federal Rules of Civil Procedure and in the subject matter of litigation—detailed in Chapter 3—make it more likely that litigants will settle. Litigation under the Federal Rules is costly and time-consuming, and the parties might choose to avoid it by settling. In addition, discovery reduces uncertainty to a degree that common ground is easier to find, making settlement more likely.

B. Judicial Management and Settlement

I showed in Chapter 3 that when the Federal Rules of Civil Procedure were first adopted, they provided for some judicial management of litigation, but that judicial management has grown phenomenally in the last thirty years or so. It has also changed its focus. Judicial management is now aimed more at encouraging settlement than at more traditional management techniques.[16] Recent amendments to the Federal Rules of Civil Procedure make it clear that encouraging the parties to settle is a fundamental goal of the courts. The parties themselves are now required to meet within a short time after the pleadings are complete to discuss a plan for the litigation, and one of the required

---

15. *See* JAY FOLBERG & ALISON TAYLOR, MEDIATION: A COMPREHENSIVE GUIDE TO RESOLVING CONFLICTS WITHOUT LITIGATION §§ 4–5 (1984).

16. *See* E. Donald Elliott, *Managerial Judging and the Evolution of Procedure*, 53 U. CHI. L. REV. 306, 323–24 (1986).

topics of conversation is the likelihood of settlement.[17] Judges can make settlement a topic of conversation during pretrial conferences,[18] and judges can require that the parties be present or otherwise available to discuss possible settlement during the final pretrial conference.[19]

These rules have emboldened many federal judges to the extent that some of them have become quite persuasive in encouraging the parties to settle.[20] Proponents of such judicial activism point out that a voluntary settlement can be an efficient and mutually satisfactory resolution of a case, and if the judge can help the parties reach an agreement, it could make everyone happy with a minimal drain on the resources of the courts. But there are many critics. Some argue that judges are doing more than facilitating settlement: they are coercing it.[21] If the judge crosses the line into coercion, the parties could leave

---

17. *See* FED. R. CIV. P. 26(f); Leslie M. Kelleher, *The December 1993 Amendments to the Federal Rules of Civil Procedure—A Critical Analysis*, 12 TOURO L. REV. 7, 82 (1995).

18. *See* FED. R. CIV. P. 16 (c).

19. *See* FED. R. CIV. P. 16(c). Judges can require that representatives of party corporations who are present at conferences have authority to make a decision about settlement. This authority was added in the 1993 amendments to Rule 16, and reflects the holding in *G. Heileman Brewing Co. v. Joseph Oat Corp.*, 871 F.2d 648 (7th Cir. 1989). In that case, the Seventh Circuit held that a judge has inherent power—power inherent in all courts regardless of statutory or rule authority—to require a party to be present at a pretrial conference with authority to decide on settlement. *See id.* at 652. With the amendment to Rule 16, it is no longer necessary for the court to invoke its inherent power. Nevertheless, the decision still stands for a potentially significant expansion of the inherent power of the courts because it demonstrates that courts can apply some pressure on the parties to settle even without explicit authorization. The decision in *Heileman Brewing* would be more significant if it were a Supreme Court decision, of course, but an appellate decision can serve as authority for other courts to take similar action. See In re Novak, 932 F.2d 1397, 1405 (11th Cir. 1991) (applying *Heileman*); Local 715, United Rubber, Cork, Linoleum, and Plastics Workers of America v. Michelin American Small Tire, 840 F. Supp. 595, 596 (N.D. Ind. 1993) (following *Heileman*).

20. *See, e.g.,* PETER H. SCHUCK, AGENT ORANGE ON TRIAL 111–67 (1986); Judith Resnik, *Managerial Judging*, 96 HARV. L. REV. 376, 379 (1982); Ruggero J. Aldisert, *A Metropolitan Court Conquers Its Backlog*, 51 JUDICATURE 247 (1968). *See also,* Leandra Lederman, *Which Cases Go to Trial?: An Empirical Study of Predictors of Failure to Settle*, 49 CASE WEST. RES. L. REV. 315, 337–338 (1999) (showing that judges affected which cases settled in the Tax Court). This is not necessarily new. *See* Harry M. Fisher, *Judicial Mediation: How It Works Through Pretrial Conference*, 10 U. CHI. L. REV. 453, 456 (1943). It is more widespread, however.

21. *See* Resnik, *supra* note 20, at 426–31. *But see* Steven Flanders, *Blind Umpires—A Response to Professor Resnik*, 35 HASTINGS L.J. 505 (1984) (supporting the management role of judges).

the court feeling that they were treated unjustly and were denied their day in court. Mediation is also a decidedly non-adversarial role for a judge, and if the case does not settle, the judge's impartiality may be affected. This would be especially true if the judge believed that one of the parties was recalcitrant and had caused the settlement talks to fail.[22]

But there are broader problems with the drive to settle cases as well. Some commentators have suggested that having too many settlements undermines the important law-making role of the courts: any case that is settled cannot make law.[23] In a common law country, the courts' failure to make law would undermine the rule of law. Even when the law is statutory, we need the courts to interpret the statutes.[24] Not all cases raise issues where such a statement is required, of course.[25] But when parties settle, they are not likely to concern themselves with the need for an authoritative statement in an unsettled area of law, or with providing guidance for others. Indeed, it is not uncommon for settlement agreements to be held confidential.[26] A relentless and single-minded drive to settlement, then, may well make it more difficult for society to order itself.[27] Of course, we do not need every case to go to trial in order for the

---

22. See Resnik, supra note 20, at 427; Honorable Peter W. Agnes, Jr., Some Observations and Suggestions Regarding the Settlement Activities of Massachusetts Trial Judges, 31 SUFFOLK U. L. REV. 263, 291 (1997). Of course, magistrates could be given the task of facilitating settlement talks, but often it is the judge who jumps into the middle of it. See, e.g., SCHUCK, supra note 20, at 111–67 (describing the judge's hands-on approach in the Agent Orange litigation settlement). But I leave it to others to debate the propriety of judges facilitating settlement talks. My concern is with the effect of the Federal Rules' strong encouragement of settlement on the jury.

23. See, e.g., Owen Fiss, Against Settlement, 93 YALE L.J. 1073, 1085 (1984); David Luban, Settlements and the Erosion of the Public Realm, 83 GEO. L.J. 2619, 2622–23 (1995). But see, Carrie Menkel-Meadow, Whose Dispute Is It, Anyway?: A Philosophical and Democratic Defense of Settlement (In Some Cases), 83 GEO. L.J. 2663 (1995) [hereinafter cited as Menkel-Meadow, Whose Dispute?] (arguing that the parties to a dispute should be able to settle their disputes in most cases without regard for the needs of the public).

24. See Peter Strauss, The Common Law and Statutes, 70 U. COLO. L. REV. 225, 236–40 (1999) (observing that the courts in common law countries provide authoritative interpretations of statutes, to which the rules of precedent apply, unlike the courts in civil law countries).

25. Sometimes a case will arise in reasonably well-settled areas of law, or it may raise extremely narrow issues unlikely to recur often, if at all. Some cases, by contrast, arise in unsettled areas of law, or raise issues about which many people need guidance.

26. See Luban, supra note 23, at 2648–58; Menkel-Meadow, Whose Dispute?, supra note 23, at 2682–86.

27. See generally Fiss, supra note 23; Luban, supra note 23. There are those, of course, who would say that the best way for society to order itself is by mutual agreement, and a

courts to fulfill their law-making and regulatory functions, but it is possible to drop below the optimum.

C. Summary and Conclusion

The Federal Rules of Civil Procedure have altered incentives to settle so that parties are more likely to settle than to go to trial. The Rules have also been amended recently to allow judges to become more involved in helping the parties to settle their cases, and some have been quite active, even, critics charge, to the point of coercing settlements. The result of this is fewer trials overall, and concomitantly fewer jury trials. While parties should not be required to go to trial, whether before judge or jury, if they do not want to, the relentless drive to settle cases has consequences, perhaps unintended, that undermine both court and jury. We need to temper it.

II. Alternative Dispute Resolution

The drive to settle cases is aided greatly by the growing use of alternative dispute resolution (ADR). ADR is the generic name given to a number of devices for securing resolution of cases without going through the entire litigation process.[28] It includes procedures that have been quite well-established for

---

settlement of a lawsuit is an excellent example of such an arrangement. *See* Melvin Aron Eisenberg, *Private Ordering Through Negotiation: Dispute Settlement and Rulemaking*, 89 HARV. L. REV. 637, 638–39 (1976). *See also*, Avery Katz, *Taking Private Ordering Seriously*, 144 U. PA. L. REV. 1745 (1996); J. Mark Ramsmeyer, *Products Liability Through Private Ordering: Notes on a Japanese Experiment*, 144 U. PA. L. REV. 1823 (1996). Any assistance the courts can provide to enable parties to settle must therefore be good. Litigation, in this view, must be no more than a method for resolving private disputes. *See* Fiss, *supra* note239, at 1075; Menkel-Meadow, *Whose Dispute?*, *supra* note 23, at 2677 and 2682. *See supra*, Chapter 1, at notes 9–69 and accompanying text (discussing the dispute-settling role of the civil jury). Certainly, some cases that are litigated are simply private disputes. But some are much more than that. And as I suggested in Chapter 1, it is appropriate for private citizens to be involved in resolving at least those civil cases that implicate questions about the society we live in. Perhaps, in assessing judicial management techniques designed to encourage settlement, some consideration needs to be given to the needs of the judicial system as a whole, or of society in general.

28. *See generally* STEPHEN B. GOLDBERG, ERIC D. GREEN AND FRANK E. SANDER, DISPUTE RESOLUTION (1985).

some time, such as mediation[29] and arbitration,[30] as well as relatively new devices, such as mini-trials[31] and summary jury trials.[32] Volumes have been written about ADR, some highly positive,[33] others cautionary.[34] The commentators generally identify two purposes to ADR: to make the administration of

---

29. Mediation is probably the oldest form of dispute resolution, as it is the form most likely to be used by "primitive" societies. *See* JEROLD AUERBACH, JUSTICE WITHOUT LAW? (1985). Formal mediation, using trained mediators, is a more recent innovation. *See* FOLBERG AND TAYLOR, *supra* note 15, at 4–5.

30. Arbitration dates back many centuries. *See* Julius Henry Cohen & Kenneth Dayton, *The New Federal Arbitration Law*, 12 VA. L. REV. 265, 266 (1926) (arbitration constituted "almost exclusively the tribunals for the settlement of business disputes in the medieval period."); Edward Powell, *Settlement of Disputes by Arbitration in Fifteenth-Century England*, 2 LAW & HIST. REV. 21, 21–24 (1984); Leo Kanowitz, *Alternative Dispute Resolution and the Public Interest: The Arbitration Experience*, 38 HASTINGS L.J. 239, 239 (1987); Edward Brunet, *Questioning the Quality of Alternate Dispute Resolution*, 62 TUL. L. REV. 1, 10 (1987).

31. *See generally*, Eric D. Green, Jonathan B. Marks & Ronald L. Olsen, *Settling Large Case Litigation: An Alternative Approach*, 11 LOYOLA L.A.L. REV. 493 (1978); Eric D. Green, *The Mini-trial Approach to Dispute Resolution*, CENTER FOR PUBLIC RESOURCES, CORPORATE DISPUTE MANAGEMENT: A MANUAL OF INNOVATIVE CORPORATE STRATEGIES FOR THE AVOIDANCE AND RESOLUTION OF LEGAL DISPUTES 7–12 (1982); Eric D. Green, *Growth of the Mini-Trial*, 9 LITIGATION 12 (Fall 1982); GOLDBERG, GREEN & SANDER, *supra* note 28, at 271–78.

32. *See, generally*, Thomas D. Lambros, *The Summary Jury Trial—An Alternative Method of Resolving Disputes*, 69 JUDICATURE 286 (1986); Thomas D. Lambros and Thomas H. Shunk, *The Summary Jury Trial*, 29 CLEVE. ST. L. REV. 43 (1980); Neil Vidmar and Jeffrey Rice, *Jury-Determined Settlements and Summary Jury Trials: Observations About Alternative Dispute Resolution in an Adversary Culture*, 19 FLA. ST. U.L. REV. 89 (1991); Shirley A. Wiegand, *A New Light Bulb for the Work of the Devil? A Current Assessment of Summary Jury Trials*, 69 ORE. L. REV. 87 (1990); GOLDBERG, GREEN & SANDER, *supra* note 28, at 282–83.

33. *See generally, e.g.*, THOMAS CARBONNEAU, ALTERNATIVE DISPUTE RESOLUTION: MELTING THE LANCES AND DISMOUNTING THE STEEDS (1989); Robert B. McKay, *Rule 16 and Alternative Dispute Resolution*, 63 NOTRE DAME L. REV. 818 (1988); Carrie Menkel-Meadow, *Pursuing Settlement in an Adversary Culture: A Tale of Innovation Co-opted or "The Law of ADR"*, 19 FLA. ST. L. REV. 1 (1991) [hereinafter cited as Menkel-Meadow, *Pursuing Settlement*]; Campbell C. Hutchinson, *The Case for Mandatory Mediation*, 42 LOY. L. REV. 85 (1996); Menkel-Meadow, *Whose Dispute?*, *supra* note 23.

34. *See generally, e.g.*, Harry T. Edwards, *Alternative Dispute Resolution: Panacea or Anathema?* 99 HARV. L. REV. 575 (1987); Richard A. Posner, *The Summary Jury Trial and Other Methods of Alternative Dispute Resolution: Some Cautionary Observations*, 53 U. CHI. L. REV. 366 (1986); Timothy P. Terrell, *Rights and Wrongs in the Rush to Repose: On the Jurisprudential Dangers of Alternative Dispute Resolution*, 36 EMORY L.J. 541 (1987); Kim Dayton, *The Myth of Alternative Dispute Resolution in the Federal Courts*, 68 IOWA L. REV. 889 (1991); Brunet, supra note 30.

justice more efficient, and to enhance the quality of justice.[35] Both of these
goals are usually achieved by making the parties more likely to settle.[36] ADR
can be private—engaged in voluntarily by parties who are looking for a better way to resolve their disputes[37]—or, increasingly, public—imposed as an
official adjunct to adjudication.[38] Even when it is private, however, it is becoming increasingly coercive. In this section, I will describe developments in
both private and public ADR and assess their impact on the right to a jury
trial.

A. "Voluntary" ADR

Litigation is such a ubiquitous phenomenon in modern America—and, indeed, much of the world—that it is hard for us to imagine a time when litigation was unheard of. But early human communities depended on elders or
others selected for their wisdom to help members of the community resolve
their disputes through procedures akin to modern mediation.[39] Many of the
world's communities still rely heavily on such procedures today.[40] The opera-
tive word here is "community." For less formal dispute-resolution structures
to work well, it appears that there must be a strong sense of community.[41]
When community breaks down, or when society is too large and diverse to
constitute a single community, formal, law-based dispute resolution mechanisms like adjudication before courts become more common.

---

35. *See, e.g.*, Menkel-Meadow, *Pursuing Settlement, supra* note 33, at 6–13.

36. *See, e.g.*, Menkel-Meadow, *Pursuing Settlement, supra* note 33, at 14; Goldberg,
Green & Sander, *supra* note 28, at 1–7. Arbitration is an exception. It generally results in
a binding decision. *See* Sarah Rudolph Cole, *Incentives in Arbitration: The Case Against Enforcement of Executory Arbitration Agreements Between Employers and Employees*, 64
U.M.K.C. L. Rev. 449, 454 (1996); Goldberg, Green & Sander, *supra* note 28, at 8;
Michael F. Hoellering, *Continuing Adaptation and Growth, in* Wide World of Arbitration 5 (Charlotte Gold and Susan MacKenzie eds., 1978).

37. *See* Dwight Golann, *Making Alternative Dispute Resolution Mandatory: The Consti-
tutional Issues*, 68 Ore. L. Rev. 487, 488–91 (1989); Maurice Rosenberg, *Resolving Disputes
Differently: Adieu to Adversary Justice?*, 21 Creighton L. Rev. 801, 816 (1988); 1 Edward
A. Dauer, Manual of Dispute Resolution: ADR Law and Practice § 2.02 (1994).

38. Congress authorized federal district courts to set up programs of voluntary or
mandatory ADR as part of the Civil Justice Reform Act of 1990. 28 U.S.C. § 473 (1994).
The 1993 amendments to Fed. R. Civ. P. 16 also allow courts to make use of ADR.

39. *See, e.g.*, Folberg & Taylor, *supra* note 15, at 1–3.

40. *See* The Disputing Process—Law in Ten Societies (Laura Nader and Henry F.
Todd, Jr. eds. (1978).

41. *See* Auerbach, *supra* note 29, at 4.

It should not be surprising, then, that some of the earliest forms of ADR in this country arose in smaller communities within the larger society. Arbitration, for example, developed in large part as an alternative that members of the business community sometimes favored for the resolution of disputes among themselves.[42] Arbitration is a mechanism for submitting a dispute to an individual or a panel, whose decision is binding.[43] While some arbitration has been in use for several centuries at least,[44] the business community's push for arbitration in the United States came in the early part of the twentieth century. Business persons began to find adjudication of their disputes to be less than satisfactory, largely because the decision-makers in the courts, whether judge or jury, often had little understanding of the realities of business and would therefore reach what the litigants viewed as irrational decisions.[45] Arbitrators selected by the disputants themselves were thought to be better decision-makers for such disputes, and clauses requiring the parties to arbitrate began appearing in commercial contracts.[46] In 1926, the American Arbitration Association was founded, dedicated to assisting businesses in the resolution of their disputes.[47]

---

42. See AUERBACH, supra note 29, at 43–44; Cohen & Dayton, supra note 30, at 266; GOLDBERG, GREEN & SANDER, supra note 28, at 189; FRANK ELKOURI AND EDNA ASPER ELKOURI, HOW ARBITRATION WORKS 3 (4th ed. 1985).

43. See ELKOURI & ELKOURI, supra note 42, at 118; WIDE WORLD OF ARBITRATION, supra note 36, at xiii; GOLDBERG, GREEN & SANDER, supra note 28, at 189. If one arbitrator is used, the parties must agree on the arbitrator. See ELKOURI & ELKOURI, supra note 42, at 118; James R. Deye & Lesly L. Britton, Arbitration by the American Arbitration Association, 70 N.D. L. REV. 281, 284 (1994). When a panel is used, the usual process is for each disputant to select an arbitrator from a list of persons who have made themselves available for the purpose, and the two arbitrators thus selected appoint a third. See ELKOURI & ELKOURI, supra note 42, at 129. The parties present evidence to the arbitrators, who render a decision based on that evidence. See id. at 237; GOLDBERG, GREEN & SANDER, supra note 28, at 189.

44. See, e.g., Edward Purcell, Settlement of Disputes by Arbitration in Fifteenth-Century England, 2 L. & HISTORY REV. 21 (1984). See also, materials cited at note 30, supra.

45. See AUERBACH, supra note 29, at 103–04; Overview of the American Arbitration Association, URL: http://www.adr.org/overview.html (May 17, 1996) [hereinafter cited as Overview].

46. See AUERBACH, supra note 29, at 104; FRANCES KELLOR, AMERICAN ARBITRATION: ITS HISTORY, FUNCTIONS AND ACHIEVEMENTS 11 (1948); IAN R. MACNEIL, AMERICAN ARBITRATION LAW: REFORMATION, NATIONALIZATION, INTERNATIONALIZATION 35 (1992).

47. See Overview, supra note 45. The American Arbitration Association was formed by a merger of the Arbitration Society of America and the Arbitration Foundation, both of which had been created within the previous five years. Id.

At about the same time, the Federal Arbitration Act was enacted to encourage voluntary arbitration of commercial disputes.[48] The Act provided that agreements to arbitrate would be enforceable in federal courts and that litigation instituted by one party to an arbitration agreement could be stayed.[49] This encouraged businesses entering into contracts to include arbitration clauses, and the practice grew.[50] Many of these contractual arbitration agreements provide that the parties will use the services of the American Arbitration Association. Today, the American Arbitration Association handles approximately 62,000 matters annually.[51] Judicial review of arbitration awards is generally limited to claims that the required procedures were not followed.[52]

In recent years, the courts have begun interpreting the Federal Arbitration Act to require enforcement of arbitration clauses in contracts between manifestly unequal parties, and that trend has drawn considerable commentary.[53] In particular, arbitration clauses between stockbrokers and investors are being enforced,[54] as are arbitration clauses between employers and employees[55] and

48. See Ellwood F. Oakley, III and Donald O. Mayer, *Arbitration of Employment Discrimination Claims and the Challenge of Contemporary Federalism*, 47 S.C. L. Rev. 475, 480 (1996); Anne Brafford, Note, *Arbitration Clauses in Consumer Contracts of Adhesion: Fair Play or Trap for the Weak and Unwary?*, 21 J. Corp. L. 331, 334–35 (1996). The Federal Arbitration Act is codified at 9 U.S.C. §§1–16 (1994).

49. 9 U.S.C. §§2–3 (1994). See Oakley & Mayer, *supra* note 48, at 481.

50. See Kellor, *supra* note 46, at 167–71.

51. *Overview, supra* note 45.

52. See 9 U.S.C. §§10–11. See also, Heidi M. Hellekson, Note, *Taking the "Alternative" Out of the Dispute Resolution of Title VII Claims: The Implications of a Mandatory Enforcement Scheme of Arbitration Agreements Arising Out of Employment Contracts*, 70 N.D. L. Rev. 435, 441–42 (1994).

53. See, e.g., Christine Godsil Cooper, *Where Are We Going With Gilmer?—Some Ruminations on the Arbitration of Discrimination Claims*, 11 St. Louis U. Pub. L. Rev. 203 (1992); John A. Gray, *Have the Foxes Become the Guardians of the Chickens? The Post-Gilmer Legal Status of Predispute Mandatory Arbitration as a Condition of Employment*, 37 Vill. L. Rev. 113 (1992); Oakley & Mayer, *supra* note 48; Hellekson, *supra* note 52; Brafford, *supra* note 48; Shelly R. James, *Arbitration in the Securities Field: Does the Present System of Arbitration Between Small Investors and Brokerage Firms Really Protect Anyone?*, 21 J. Corp. L. 363 (1996).

54. See Shearson/American Express, Inc. v. McMahon, 482 U.S. 220 (1987); Rodriguez de Quijas v. Shearson/American Express, Inc., 490 U.S. 477 (1989). See generally, James, *supra* note 53; William A. Gregory & William J. Schneider, *Securities Arbitration: A Need for Continued Reform*, 17 Nova L. Rev. 1223 (1993).

55. See Circuit City Stores, Inc. v. Adams, 2001 U.S. LEXIS 2459 (March 21, 2001); Gilmer v. Interstate/Johnson Lane Corp., 500 U.S. 20 (1991); Perry v. Thomas, 482 U.S. 483 (1987); Bayma v. Smith, Barney, Harris Upham & Co., 784 F.2d 1023 (9th Cir. 1986). See generally, Oakley & Mayer, *supra* note 48; Hellekson, *supra* note 52.

between consumers and merchants.[56] In these contexts, the arbitration clause sometimes is enforced even when it was the result of unequal bargaining power, and was included in a contract that the weaker party had no opportunity to negotiate.[57] Sometimes the weaker party seeks to enforce statutory civil rights, such as the federal Age Discrimination in Employment Act,[58] and finds that those statutory claims are also subject to arbitration.[59] Some efforts to curb these trends have been made in Congress, but so far without success.[60]

These developments make it clear that "voluntary" arbitration is not always truly voluntary. It is apparent that some people can be required, for example, to (in effect) waive their right to a jury trial with respect to potential civil rights claims as a condition of employment or other benefits, and the courts will enforce the waiver.[61] To compound the problem, arbitrators are often people with business backgrounds, who we may expect to find it easier to see the business's perspective.[62] Thus, an employee's loss of the jury trial could mean that he will be faced with a decision-making body that is far less representative of the community than a jury would be, and more likely to favor his employer. In other words, arbitration under such circumstances negates the jury's role as equalizer.[63]

Similar problems have cropped up in mediation, which is the other long-standing ADR tool. Mediation is a common alternative to adjudication in do-

---

56. *See* Mitsubishi Motors Corp. v. Soler Chrysler-Plymouth, Inc., 473 U.S. 614 (1985); Allied-Bruce Terminix Cos., Inc. v. Dobson, 115 S.Ct. 834 (1995). *See generally,* Brafford, *supra* note 48.

57. *See, e.g.,* Gilmer, 500 U.S. at 23–24 (employment contract; employee's claim under the Age Discrimination in Employment Act subject to arbitration clause in the contract even though plaintiff had no choice about its inclusion). *See generally,* Brian K. Van Engen, *Post-*Gilmer *Developments in Mandatory Arbitration: The Expansion of Mandatory Arbitration for Statutory Claims and the Congressional Effort to Reverse the Trend,* 21 J. Corp. L. 391 (1996).

58. 29 U.S.C. §§ 621–633 (1994).

59. This was the situation in *Gilmer,* 500 U.S. at 35. *See generally,* Van Engen, *supra* note 57.

60. *See* Van Engen, *supra* note 57, at 410–12.

61. *See* Gilmer, 500 U.S. at 35. *See generally,* Oakley & Mayer, *supra* note 48; Cooper, *supra* note 53; Hellekson, *supra* note 171.

62. *See* Gregory & Schneider, *supra* note 54, at 1240–44; Margaret A. Jacobs, *Men's Club—Riding Crop and Slurs: How Wall Street Dealt With a Sex Bias Case,* Wall Street Journal, at A1 (June 9, 1994).

63. *See* Carbonneau, *supra* note 33, at 208–09. On the role of the jury as equalizer, see Chapter 1, *supra,* at notes 21–28 and accompanying text.

mestic disputes such as divorce, custody, and child support.[64] Often, it enables the parties to the dispute to maintain a continuing relationship, which is especially important when children are involved. Litigation is more likely to disrupt such relationships.[65] One common criticism of mediation, however, is that it tends to confirm relationships of dominance and control that existed prior to the mediation.[66] If this criticism is correct, the wealthier or more powerful party will do better in mediation than the poorer or less powerful.[67] Mediation, then, might work best when the parties are relatively equal or when the mediator is specially trained to mediate unequal parties.

More recently, potential litigants have been experimenting with a variety of new forms of ADR.[68] While governmental agencies are often involved in setting up ADR,[69] much of it is facilitated by private organizations that bill themselves as alternatives to the courts.[70] Alternatives usually focused on mediation and other devices designed to assist the parties with settlement nego-

---

64. *See* Golann, *supra* note 37, at 497; LINDA R. SINGER, SETTLING DISPUTES: CONFLICT RESOLUTION IN BUSINESS, FAMILIES, AND THE LEGAL SYSTEM 31–56 (1990); GOLDBERG, GREEN & SANDER, *supra* note 28, at 313–14.

65. Over the years, meditation has also been attempted in such areas as juvenile proceedings and racial disputes, though with less success. *See* AUERBACH, *supra* note 29, at 117–18, 126, 134–36.

66. *See* Fiss, *supra* note 23, at 1076; AUERBACH, *supra* note 29, at 120, 145.

67. *See* Fiss, *supra* note 23, at 1076; AUERBACH, *supra* note 29, at 120.

68. Some early advocates of the modern ADR movement included Frank E. Sander of Harvard, *see Varieties of Dispute Processing*, address by Frank E. Sander to the Pound Conference, *reprinted in* 70 F.R.D. 111 (1976), and Eric Green of Boston University, *see, e.g., Settling Large Case Litigation: An Alternate Approach*, 11 LOYOLA OF L.A. L. REV. 493 (1978). *See also* EARL JOHNSON, JR., VALERIE KANTOR AND ELIZABETH SCHWARTZ, OUTSIDE THE COURTS: A SURVEY OF DIVERSION ALTERNATIVES IN CIVIL CASES (1977); John J. McGonagle, Jr., *Arbitration of Consumer Disputes*, 27 ARB. J. 65 (1972); Janet Mateson Spencer and Joseph M. Zammit, *Mediation-Arbitration: A Proposal for Private Resolution of Disputes Between Divorced or Separated Parents*, 1976 DUKE L.J. 911; *Symposium, The Value of Arbitration and Mediation in Resolving Community and Racial Disputes Affecting Business*, 29 BUS. L. 1005 (1974).

69. The government often set up Neighborhood Justice Centers, for example, to mediate neighborhood disputes. *See* ROMAN TOMASIC & MALCOLM M. FEELEY, NEIGHBORHOOD JUSTICE: ASSESSMENT OF AN EMERGING IDEA (1980); Richard Danzig, *Toward the Creation of a Complementary, Decentralized System of Criminal Justice*, 26 STAN. L. REV. 1, 41–48 (1973); ROYER F. COOK, JANICE A. ROEHL & DAVID I. SHEPPARD, NEIGHBORHOOD JUSTICE CENTERS FIELD TEST: FINAL EVALUATION REPORT (1980); DANIEL McGILLIS & JOAN MULLEN, NEIGHBORHOOD JUSTICE CENTERS: AN ANALYSIS OF POTENTIAL MODELS (1977); GOLDBERG, GREEN & SANDER, *supra* note 28, at 347–69.

70. These organizations include the Institute for Mediation and Conflict Resolution, the Institute for Collective Bargaining and Group Relations, the Center for Public Resources and PUSH (a group founded by Jesse Jackson).

tiations, but the parties could voluntarily submit to arbitration as well. The difference between this kind of arbitration and the contractual arbitration discussed above is that there is no previously-existing contract binding the parties to arbitration.[71]

The mini-trial is the best known of the innovations in ADR that this movement spawned.[72] Often used in business disputes, the mini-trial is a truncated presentation of each party's case before representatives of the parties "who have not been involved in creating or trying to resolve the underlying dispute, but who have authority or at least persuasive power over the decision of whether to settle."[73] A neutral third party usually presides—often a former judge—and that neutral third party sometimes provides advice about how he thinks the case would fare in litigation.[74] The purpose of the mini-trial is to get realistic information before the parties' decision-makers, who then attempt to settle the case. The parties view it as a possible means to a less expensive and more satisfactory resolution of their dispute.[75]

While mediation and the mini-trial are designed to facilitate negotiated settlements, other ADR innovations are designed to set limits on risk. For example, parties may contract for the defendant to pay specified damages depending on how a jury or an arbitrator rules on liability: if the ruling is for the plaintiff, damages will be one figure; if the ruling is for the defendant, damages will be a different, lower figure.[76]

This is just a sampling of the variety of ADR mechanisms that have been developed since the 1970's.[77] The key to this movement is that it is voluntary, with the parties turning to it not because a contract or a judge told them that they had to, but because they were searching for new and better ways to resolve their disputes. The movement has produced some creative methods for facilitating settlements or otherwise helping the parties make decisions about the litigation they face. But while ADR was becoming popular with litigants,

---

71. *See* GOLDBERG, GREEN, & SANDER, *supra* note 28, at 280–82.

72. For a description of the mini-trial, see *id.* at 271–78.

73. *Id.* at 274.

74. *Id.*

75. Some commentators suggest that getting information to parties about the alternatives to adjudication that are available may be difficult. Lawyers, who are the primary source of information about such alternatives, are so wedded to the adversarial culture of adjudication that they may be uninterested in alternatives, or they may not view them as realistic alternatives. *See, e.g.,* Carrie Menkel-Meadow, *Pursuing Settlement, supra* note 33, at 34–36.

76. *See* GOLDBERG, GREEN & SANDER, *supra* note 28, at 281–82.

77. For descriptions of other ADR devices, see *id.* at 281–85.

it was also catching the attention of judges and legislators, many of whom thought it was worth trying on a more formal basis. Thus, the era of court-annexed ADR was born.

B. Court-Annexed ADR: The Newest Manifestation

While the early modern ADR movement was generally a search by private parties for faster, less costly, and more accurate decision-making, ADR has recently become an adjunct to litigation in the courts. In some sense, it is not truly "alternative," but another tool the courts have to resolve disputes. Indeed, it is often another judicial management tool, as judges now have the authority in most districts to refer cases for alternative dispute resolution.[78] It is no coincidence that court-annexed ADR grew in importance along with judicial management techniques. For the most part, ADR and management share a common purpose: to reduce delay and expense in litigation by providing mechanisms that encourage the parties to settle.[79]

1. Forms

The principal forms of court-annexed alternative dispute resolution in use in the United States today are arbitration, mediation, and summary jury trials. Of these, only arbitration results in a binding decision; the other devices are designed to lead the parties to settlement. Because it is binding, courts that have considered the matter have held that mandatory arbitration would be unconstitutional as a violation of the Seventh Amendment.[80] Thus, while some federal district courts can make referrals to arbitration under their delay and expense reduction plans, such referrals must be with the consent of the parties.[81]

---

78. See 28 U.S.C. § 473 (1994); FED. R. CIV. P. 16. For a description of ADR programs in the federal district courts, see THE FEDERAL JUDICIAL CENTER, THE CIVIL JUSTICE REFORM ACT EXPENSE AND DELAY REDUCTION PLANS: A SOURCEBOOK 269–358 (1995). See also, Menkel-Meadow, Pursuing Settlement, supra note 33, at 15.

79. See Dayton, supra note 34, at 894; GOLDBERG, GREEN & SANDER, supra note 28, at 5; Hutchinson, supra note 33, at 86; Green, Marks & Olsen, supra note 31 at 493; Golann, supra note 37, at 487.

80. See Golann, supra note 37, at 493. Other challenges to mandatory arbitration are based on due process, access to courts, equal protection, separation of powers, and principles of federalism. Id.

81. See, e.g., D. Conn. Loc. R., Add. I, No. 7; D. Mass Loc. R., App. D, R. 4.03; E.D. Mich. Loc. R., Add. I, sec. VI.B.

Judges can also refer cases to mandatory mediation under many local court rules.[82] Like arbitration, mediation generally relies on the participation of outsiders other than judges to assist in the resolution of the dispute, though the judge's presence may be felt in court-annexed mediation.[83] Unlike arbitration, however, the recommendations of mediators are not binding on the parties.[84] Rather, the mediators attempt to work with the parties to achieve a mutually satisfactory resolution of the dispute. Of course, while the judge can order the parties to try to settle their dispute through mediation, she cannot order them to settle. It is possible, however, that the problems I discussed earlier that the weaker party usually has in mediation could be exacerbated when it is the court that orders mediation, as the weaker party then may be overborne by *both* his opponent and the judge, and agree to something neither a judge nor a jury would have ordered. Once again, this is a device that may work best when the parties are relatively equal.

The newest and most innovative court-annexed ADR technique is the summary jury trial, which involves presentation of evidence to a jury in open court, though the presentation is in abbreviated form.[85] The parties can, in fact, summarize for the jury what the evidence would show.[86] This device employs the services of jurors; actual jurors may be called and sworn in as if a real trial were being held.[87] After the evidence is presented, the jurors retire and reach a decision. Their decision, however, is not binding; it is merely another factor that the parties can consider in their settlement talks.[88] The advantage over the mini-trial is that the parties get the reaction of a real jury of lay people instead of a single observer with legal training.[89] One problem that

---

82. *See* Dayton, *supra* note 34, at 891; *see, e.g.*, W.D. Mich. Loc. R. 42; E.D. Wash. Loc. R. 39.1; W.D. Wash Loc. R. 39.1.

83. *See* SCHUCK, *supra* note 20, at 143–67 (describing how the judge appointed two mediators to help the parties reach a settlement and then took a more active role when the parties got close to an agreement).

84. *See* NANCY H. ROGERS & RICHARD A. SALEM, A STUDENT'S GUIDE TO MEDIATION AND THE LAW 3–5 (1987); GOLDBERG, GREEN & SANDER, *supra* note 28, at 91; Hutchinson, *supra* note 33, at 86.

85. *See generally*, Lambros, *supra* note 32; Posner, *supra* note 34; GOLDBERG, GREEN & SANDER, *supra* note 28, at 282–83; Wiegand, *supra* note 32; Vidmar & Rice, *supra* note 32.

86. *See* Posner, *supra* note 34, at 369; Lambros, *supra* note 32, at 288–89.

87. *See* Posner, *supra* note 34, at 369; Lambros, *supra* note 32, at 289.

88. *See id.*; Lambros, *supra* note 32, at 290.

89. Private parties using the mini-trial can use jurors, too, but if the court is not involved in the process, they must, in effect, hire their jurors. The court-annexed summary jury trial makes use of real jurors, chosen from the actual juror pool. *See* Posner, *supra* note 34, at 369. This is obviously a form of alternative dispute resolution that will only be valu-

the participants face, however, is whether to tell the jurors that their decision is only advisory. If they are told, they may take the task less seriously and may well resent the intrusion on their time.[90] On the other hand, not telling them strikes many people as unfair to the jurors and potentially damaging to the political process.[91]

2. Effectiveness of Court-Annexed Alternative Dispute Resolution

There has been very little empirical research as to the effectiveness of alternative dispute resolution in achieving the goals of faster and less expensive resolution of disputes, or of just settlements of disputes. What little there is suggests that ADR has little or no effect on adjudicative efficiency. One study comparing districts where ADR was mandatory and those where it was not showed no difference between the two in the time it took to resolve cases.[92] Indeed, the author notes that for cases that ultimately go to trial, mandatory ADR simply adds another step to the adjudicative process, possibly delaying the resort to a jury.[93] Another study focusing on summary jury trials also showed no effect on judicial efficiency.[94]

It is difficult, at best, to do empirical research into the effect of ADR on the justice of outcomes. One can only speculate. Where ADR fails entirely—that is, where ADR is attempted but the parties still go to trial—the outcome will, of course, be unaffected by the attempt at ADR.[95] Only where ADR leads to settlement, then, do we need to be concerned about the justice of the different outcomes: is the settlement reached because of ADR more just than a judicial outcome would have been? It is impossible to answer such a question

---

able if the ultimate trial is to be a jury trial. Even then, however, the losing party may well think that the jury involved in the summary jury trial was unrepresentative or that full-blown presentation of the evidence would have been more effective for him, and may refuse to be swayed by the jury's advisory decision.

90. *See* Posner, *supra* note 34, at 386; Wiegand, *supra* note 32, at 113–14. Jurors are rarely told beforehand that their decision will not be binding. Learning of that after they have worked hard to reach a decision may undermine their sense of participation in an important governmental process. I identified participation as an important role for the civil jury. *See supra,* Chapter 1, at notes 129–176 and accompanying text.

91. *See* Posner, *supra* note 34, at 386; Wiegand, *supra* note 32, at 113–14.

92. *See* Dayton, *supra* note 34.

93. *Id.* at 930, 943.

94. Posner, *supra* note 34, at 380–85. Judge Posner described his study as "crude" as it was based on relatively little data.

95. This statement must be qualified. The parties could learn things in ADR that cause them to present their cases differently at trial, and that could affect the outcome.

because we do not know what the judicial outcome would have been, nor do we have any infallible way to assess the justice of any outcome.

3. Constitutional Issues

When courts order the use of ADR, as they are now authorized to do under the Civil Justice Reform Act and Rule 16, there is considerable potential for a deprivation of the right to a jury trial.[96] The most serious deprivation of the right to a jury trial comes when ADR is mandatory and has a binding effect.[97] Indeed, courts that have considered the constitutionality of such processes have uniformly found them to violate the Seventh Amendment.[98] There are also several devices that courts use to coerce the use of ADR. These include cost-shifting, where a party that insists on trial after a session of ADR will have to pay the costs of ADR;[99] the requirement that a party seeking a trial after ADR post a bond securing an ultimate judgment, which can be prohibitively expensive;[100] and a provision that the results of any ADR be admissible as evidence at a subsequent trial.[101] These procedures can be constitutional, depending on the court's view of the extent of coercion.[102] Even when it is neither mandatory nor binding, however, ADR has an effect on the right to jury trial much like that of judicial management: to the extent that parties feel pressured by these techniques to settle, there is less likelihood that the issues, some of considerable national importance, will be presented to a jury.

C. Summary

Often, the use of alternative dispute resolution is sought by the parties or their attorneys, who value the opportunity to get a neutral person's view of

---

96. 28 U.S.C. §§473(a)(6)(B) (1994); FED. R. CIV. P. 16 (c)(9). *See generally,* Golann, *supra* note 37, at 502.

97. *See id.* at 504.

98. *See id.*; Menkel-Meadow, *Pursuing Settlement, supra* note 33, at 30; Rhea v. Ferguson, 767 F.2d 266 (6th Cir. 1985) (holding that referral to mediation did not violate party's rights when jury ultimately found facts).

99. *See* Golann, *supra* note 37, at 510–11.

100. *See id.* at 511–13.

101. *See id.* at 513–15.

102. *See id.* at 512–15; Menkel-Meadow, *Pursuing Settlement, supra* note 33, at 18–19; Strandell v. Jackson County, 838 F.2d 884 (7th Cir. 1988) (holding that courts can urge parties to settle, but cannot require them to settle or to participate in a mandatory summary jury trial).

their cases and perhaps save some of the costs of litigation.[103] Except in arbitration, where the arbitrators' decision is binding, the usual resolution is a settlement, guided by the professionals who are assisting with the ADR. Two recent developments in ADR are troubling for those who value jury trials. First, courts have recently begun upholding arbitration agreements between manifestly unequal parties. This deprives the weaker party, who may have had little choice as to whether to agree to arbitration, of his right to the protections of the courts, including jury trials. Second, the federal courts have begun experimenting with court-ordered ADR. In some sense, this is closely related to judicial case management, and some of the same problems may result. In particular, the views of some professional or bureaucratic person or body may prevail in the parties' settlement, and the community sentiment represented by the jury may never be known.

III. Summary and Conclusion

In this Chapter, I have described growing pressure within the civil justice system to get the parties to settle. Some of the pressure is the natural result of changes we have made in our rules of procedure. Some is the result of our deliberately empowering judges to encourage settlements. Settlement may well be the best result, if it means that the parties have worked out a mutually satisfactory solution to their differences. But settlement has its pitfalls as well. The primary concerns are that settlement means that the court will have no opportunity to make an authoritative statement on the law, and that the weaker party may feel more coercion to settle than the stronger.

These are potential problems whether the decision-maker is the judge or the jury. Settlements produce particularly troubling effects on the jury trial, however. Having too many settlements undermines all of the roles that I identified for juries in Chapter 1. If a case settles, no jury will have the opportunity to reflect community sentiment on important issues. No jury can equalize unequal parties. No jury can nullify laws that the community finds unacceptable, or provide information that can regulate litigants' behavior or the primary activities of other citizens. No citizens will have the opportunity to participate in an important governmental decision, and to deliberate to a

---

103. *See* Thomas D. Rowe, Jr., *American Law Institute Study on Paths to a "Better Way": Litigation, Alternatives, and Accommodation: Background Paper,* 1989 Duke L.J. 824, 898 (1989); Margaret Pedrick Sullivan, Comment: *The Scope of Modern Arbitral Awards,* 62 Tul. L. Rev. 1113, 1114 (1988).

consensus decision. No citizens will have the opportunity to work with others who have different backgrounds and perspectives. If we can agree that these are important roles for the jury, then we must find ways to ensure that enough cases go to the jury to make them meaningful, without going to the opposite extreme of coercing unwilling litigants into trial. It is a delicate balance.

CONCLUSION

This book has demonstrated the decline of the civil jury over the course of United States history, and the accelerating rate of that decline in the last half of the twentieth century. There are understandable reasons for this decline, as changes in legal procedure, the dispute processing system, substantive law, and society in general have made it more difficult for the jury to function. Perhaps for these reasons, the Supreme Court has acquiesced in doctrines and procedures that diminish the jury's role. Yet there are still very good reasons for having a civil jury. Civil justice has substantial public elements even in disputes between two private citizens, and the parties to civil disputes are often unequal in power and resources. Occasional jury nullification has been beneficial even in civil cases, though jury nullification is undoubtedly more important in criminal cases. The jury plays a regulatory role, allowing citizens to make private choices based on their knowledge of how juries—representing community sentiment—are likely to view their behavior. The jury is the only national governmental institution where diverse citizens participate directly in important governmental decisions, and where citizens deliberate to a consensus decision. As such, the jury helps citizens learn about public discourse, about their role in society, and about people whose backgrounds and perspectives differ from their own. It helps to give citizens a stake in their government and in society as a whole.

The problem is how to reconcile changing conditions that make it harder for juries to function with strong reasons for maintaining a vital civil jury. There are no simple answers, and I certainly have no magic formula. What follow, instead, are a few thoughts that I hope will focus further thinking and discussion. I arrange these thoughts in order of the steps that we should take if we are to preserve the essence of the civil jury.

Step 1: Understanding What Has Happened

Before we can take any steps toward reconciling changing conditions with strong reasons for a civil jury, we must understand what has happened to the

341

civil jury. I hope that this book is a substantial contribution toward that end. Table 2 helps to illustrate my thesis. The first column lists the roles of the civil jury that I described in Chapter 1. The second column lists the changes in the civil jury's environment that I identified in Chapter 3, all of which make it more difficult for the jury to function. Finally, column 3 lists the various control devices that exist today, and identifies with an asterisk those that have clear roots in English practice. Column 3 also evaluates the effect these controls have had on the civil jury. A plus sign indicates a positive impact; a minus sign indicates a negative impact; and an equal sign indicates that changes in the control device have not had an appreciable effect on the jury. Of all the developments listed in column 3, only the Supreme Court's jurisprudence on two aspects of the constitutional right to a civil jury trial—the law/equity merger and the jury trial for new statutory actions—has had a positive impact.[1]

It is not hard to see what has happened. As environmental changes occur that make it more difficult for the civil jury to function, we respond with new and improved jury control devices, and with a jurisprudence that allows those control devices to flourish. What has been missing in the analysis, with few exceptions, is an examination of the roles we expect the jury to play in modern America. Some examples will illustrate the problem. First, the public rights doctrine/balancing test is a response to the growth of administrative agencies: it allows agencies to function without juries. The public rights/balancing test gives effect to the premise of expertise that is behind administrative agency adjudication. But matters adjudicated in administrative agencies are often, by their very nature, matters where the public interest is high. One important role for the jury is to provide a sense of the community in matters of public importance. The rise of administrative agencies, and the complicity of the Court in banishing the jury from agency adjudication, undermines that role.[2]

---

1. Some might argue that "Composition" should also be treated as a plus, as the jury is clearly more diverse than it was in 1791. I give this category an equal sign, however, because of uncertainty over the effect of peremptory challenges, which can negate formal gains in inclusiveness. See Purkett v. Elem 514 U.S. 765 (1995) (accepting race-neutral explanations for a prosecutor's using nine of ten challenges to strike blacks). It is possible that the net effect is positive even with peremptory challenges, but I am not yet prepared to give this category an unqualified plus. In addition, the decision rule for federal courts should be rated an equal, because federal juries still must reach unanimous verdicts. But the nonunanimous verdict is sufficiently common in the states that this category rates a net minus.

2. I have argued elsewhere that the Seventh Amendment should apply regardless of the kind of tribunal in which adjudication takes place. See Ellen E. Sward, *Legislative Courts, Article III, and the Seventh Amendment*, 77 N. C. L. Rev. 1037 (1999).

Table 2. Overview of the Civil Jury

Roles	Environmental Changes	Controls	Effect on Jury
Dispute Settling	Procedural	Jurisprudence	
• Matters where public interest is high	• Growth of equitable procedures	• Law/equity merger	+
• Matters where parties are unequal	• Decline of adversary system	• Jury trial for new statutory actions	+
		• Public rights/balancing test	−
		• Sovereign immunity*	=
Lawmaking	Systemic	Structure	
• Jury nullification	• Rise of Administrative agencies	• Size*	−
• Regulation	• Litigation explosion	• Decision rule*	−
	• Knowledge explosion	• Composition*	=
Political	Substantive	Evidence	
• Participation	• Need for certainty	• Basic rules*	=
• Deliberation	• Codification	• Expert evidence	−
		• Instructions*	=
Socializing	Political: Diversification of Population	Decision-making	
		• Law/fact distinction*	=
		• Judgment as a matter of law	−
		• Summary judgment	=
		• New Trial*	−
		• Special verdict*	−
		• Damage caps	−
		• Preclusion*	−
		Alternatives	
		• Judicial management	−
		• Alternative Dispute Resolution	−

*Existed in some form in England in 1791. Effect on Jury: + positive impact, − negative impact, = same effect

Second, the shrinking jury and changes in the decision rule are responses to the litigation explosion and to the diversification of the population: they make juries more efficient and more likely to reach agreement. But these changes in the jury's structure also make it less likely that the jury will reflect the balance of community views and less likely that minority views, even if relevant to the matter before the jury, are heard. Thus, they make it harder for the jury to play its political and socializing roles. These changes also make it harder for the jury to reflect accurate community sentiment as to matters of public importance.

Third, judicial management and alternative dispute resolution (ADR) are responses to the growth in equitable procedures, the decline of the adversary system, and the litigation explosion: they make complex cases manageable, and take many cases out of the hands of overburdened courts. Both judicial management and ADR function primarily by facilitating settlement. There is nothing wrong with settlement. If the judicial system can help the parties reach mutually satisfactory resolutions of their disputes, that is undoubtedly a good thing. But the jury has a regulatory role. Settlements take place in the shadow of the jury.[3] If there are insufficient jury verdicts to guide litigants in their settlement negotiations, settlements may be harder to reach and be less fair.

Fourth, the growth of scientific evidence and the experts needed to explain it are a response to the explosion in knowledge. The knowledge explosion may also contribute to the use of administrative agencies, where expertise is the operational premise. But some cases involving scientific evidence also implicate the jury's role in deciding matters of public importance. This is particularly true when the science raises ethical issues: genetic engineering, for example.

Finally, the expanded use of summary judgment and judgment as a matter of law may be a response to the increased need for certainty and to the codification movement. Both the need for certainty and codification have pushed the law/fact dividing line farther along the spectrum, so that it is now easier for a judge to classify an issue as one of law, and to decide it herself. This implicates most of the roles that the jury plays. Summary judgments favor defendants, who are often the more powerful party of the two. Thus, the jury is unable to play an equalizing role. If the jury never gets a chance to render a verdict, it cannot make a statement about matters of public importance, nullify an unpopular law, or set standards for settlements in subsequent cases. If

---

3. See Marc Galanter, *The Regulatory Function of the Civil Jury*, in VERDICT: ASSESSING THE CIVIL JURY SYSTEM 61 (Robert E. Litan ed., 1993).

judgment is rendered before the jury deliberates, we also lose the jury's political and socializing roles.

In short, developments in jury control are understandable responses to concrete problems that have faced the civil justice system, especially in the last half of the twentieth century. It is harder to see, let alone accommodate, the more abstract roles that the jury plays. But our failure to see and accommodate those roles has resulted in a less effective civil jury.

Step 2: Defining the Essence of the Right to a Civil Jury Trial

What I have said so far has begged a very important question: what characteristics are fundamental to the civil jury? The jury can only be "less effective" if these changes have altered those fundamental characteristics negatively. The Supreme Court itself has said that the Seventh Amendment preserves only the essence of the civil jury, and not all of the procedural characteristics that existed in 1791.[4] But the Court has never defined the essence of the civil jury. Indeed, the Court is ill-equipped to provide an overview of the fundamental right to a civil jury because each case it decides presents only a small part of the puzzle: the size of the jury or the constitutionality of a particular procedure, for example. For this reason, the Court tends to say not what *is* fundamental to the civil jury, but only what is *not*. The result is a series of uncoordinated changes in civil jury procedures, none of which is of overriding importance in isolation, but that cumulatively threaten the jury's viability.[5] It is imperative that we define what is fundamental to the civil jury so that we can determine accurately the present state of the civil jury, and, if appropriate, prevent further erosion of the right.

There are at least two possible approaches to defining the essence, or the fundamental characteristics of, the civil jury. The first—and the one that the Court says it favors—is the historical approach. In *Markman v. Westview In-*

---

4. *See* Galloway v. United States, 319 U.S. 372, 390 (1943); Colgrove v. Battin, 413 U.S. 149, 154 (1973); Parklane Hosiery Co. v. Shore, 439 U.S. 322, 336–37 (1979).

5. At the same time, I must acknowledge that the civil jury has a greater impact than its numbers suggest. A jury decides about two per cent of federal civil cases, and a mere eight-tenths of a per cent of federal civil adjudications if agency adjudications are counted. The numbers are similar in the states. But the prospect of a jury trial colors litigation even if the case ultimately settles. Settlement negotiations take place in the shadow of the jury. *See* Marc Galanter, *The Regulatory Function of the Civil Jury*, in VERDICT, *supra* note 3, at 61, 62. What a jury is likely to do thus shapes the ultimate settlement.

struments, Inc., the Court said that while it has attempted to define the "substance of the common-law right" by distinguishing between substance and procedure or between law and fact, the best approach is the "historical method."[6] By this, the Court meant determining whether the issue historically was tried to a jury or, if the issue is of recent vintage, finding a historical analogy. I described the basic historical approach in Chapter 4, but it also appears in the analysis of some features of the jury, such as the size of the jury or the decision rule, and in the analysis of some control devices, such as the judgment as a matter of law or the rules of preclusion. Indeed, the Court usually invokes history even when it decides to ignore it.[7] This approach usually relies on the language of the Seventh Amendment, which "preserves" the right to a jury trial.

There are several problems with the Court's historical approach, however. First, the Court's historical benchmark—English practice in 1791—completely ignores the history surrounding the Seventh Amendment itself, which is what the Court is supposed to be interpreting. As I showed in Chapter 2, the American practice at the time the Seventh Amendment was ratified was different from the English practice in important ways. For example, American civil juries were considered an important buffer between citizen and government. If the Court had heeded this history, some of its Seventh Amendment doctrine might look very different; for example, it arguably could not have devised the public rights doctrine. By now, however, the Court's jurisprudence is so entrenched that even if it is wrong, it would be difficult to change. The 1791 English benchmark and the public rights doctrine are now as much a part of the Constitution as if they were written into it.[8]

---

6. 517 U.S. 370, 378 (1996) (citing cases).

7. *See* Williams v. Florida, 399 U.S. 78, 92–100 (1970) (discussing the history of jury size, but deciding that a twelve-person jury is not fundamental).

8. *See generally,* Barry Friedman & Scott B. Smith, *The Sedimentary Constitution,* 147 U. PA. L. REV. 1 (1998) (describing how the Constitution grows and changes over the years). Nevertheless, there has been a spate of recent articles criticizing the Court's historical approach, many of them arguing that Congress should have more power to determine when juries are used. *See, e.g.,* Stanton D. Krauss, *The Original Understanding of the Seventh Amendment Right to a Jury Trial,* 33 U. RICH. L. REV. 407 (1999) (arguing that the original understanding of the Seventh Amendment was that Congress had full discretion to determine the scope of the civil jury trial right); Martin Redish, *Seventh Amendment Right to a Jury Trial: A Study in the Irrationality of Rational Decision Making,* 70 NW. U. L. REV. 486 (1975) (arguing that the Seventh Amendment should be interpreted to apply to only those precise cases that were tried in common law courts in England); Paul D. Carrington, *The Seventh Amendment: Some Bicentennial Reflections,* 1990 U. CHI. L. FORUM 33, 74–75 (suggesting abandonment of the law/equity distinction in Seventh Amendment jurisprudence);

CONCLUSION 347

Another problem with the Court's approach is that it is inconsistent. The Court has held that unanimous verdicts are required because of history, but that a twelve-person jury is not, though both have long and similar historical pedigrees.[9] The Court has used changes in procedure to justify both expanding the right to jury trial—by requiring juries when related law and equity claims are heard in the same case, for example[10]—and contracting it—by allowing non-mutual issue preclusion to block a jury, for example.[11] Some of these changes have had positive effects and some have not, but they do not reflect a consistent approach to history.

Finally, history is often hard to determine. Analogies between modern statutory actions and common law actions are particularly difficult to draw.[12] Thus, the Court may get its history wrong, or there may be enough choices that the Court can decide whether there will be a jury by manipulating the historical record.

The second approach to defining the essence of the civil jury—favored by several commentators and occasionally used by the Court—is the functional approach. This approach would hold that what the Seventh Amendment preserves is the basic functions of the civil jury. A functional approach allows us to use the jury in those cases where it is most valuable, and to abandon it when it is less useful. George Priest, for example, has suggested that juries are particularly useful for deciding cases involving "complex or conflicting societal values" or "governmental power."[13] Priest does not think juries are particularly

---

Charles W. Wolfram, *The Constitutional History of the Seventh Amendment*, 57 MINN. L. REV. 639 (1973) (arguing that the Seventh Amendment refers to a dynamic common law process and not to a specific point in history); Rachael E. Schwartz, *"Everything Depends on How You Draw the Lines": An Alternative Interpretation of the Seventh Amendment*, 6 SETON HALL CONST. L.J. 599 (1996) (arguing that the Seventh Amendment leaves the scope of the jury trial right to Congress); Kenneth S. Klein, *The Myth of How to Interpret the Seventh Amendment Right to a Civil Jury Trial*, 53 OHIO ST. L.J. 1005 (1992) (arguing that the reference to common law in the Seventh Amendment excludes statutory actions); Margaret L. Moses, *What the Jury Must Hear: The Supreme Court's Evolving Seventh Amendment Jurisprudence*, 68 GEO. WASH. L. REV. 183 (2000) (arguing that the historical test is of recent vintage and does not reflect eighteenth century practice). I have argued that the Seventh Amendment should be interpreted more, not less, expansively. *See* Sward, *supra* note 2.

9. *See supra*, Chapter 5, at notes 4–89 and accompanying text.

10. *See supra*, Chapter 4, at notes 30–62 and accompanying text.

11. *See supra*, Chapter 7, at notes 242–263 and accompanying text.

12. *See, e.g.*, Chauffeurs, Teamsters and Helpers, Local No. 391 v. Terry, 494 U.S. 558 (1990) (generating four separate opinions on the meaning of history).

13. *See* George L. Priest, *Justifying the Civil Jury*, in VERDICT, *supra* note 3, at 103, 112–20.

useful for routine matters that do not involve value judgments or the government as a party. Pamela Stephens argues that juries are most valuable when they are deciding factual questions involving everyday matters (unlike Priest), when public acceptance is important, and when there are special "equity" concerns.[14] The latter include making what appear to be arbitrary value judgments (much like Priest's "complex or conflicting societal values") and nullifying law, though Stephens acknowledges that jury nullification is problematic.[15] The Supreme Court, too, has sometimes taken a functional approach, though it is harder to discern what the Court sees as the primary functions of the jury. Again, the Court's approval of six-person juries is an example, as the Court apparently decided that the function of the jury was to decide facts accurately, and then found—probably erroneously—that small juries were just as good as twelve-person juries at deciding facts accurately and reaching just decisions.[16]

But there are problems with the functional approach as well. First, as the proposals by Priest and Stephens indicate, identifying the appropriate jury functions is difficult. Priest and Stephens seem to agree about some fundamental functions and disagree about others. Second, even if we could decide what functions the jury should serve, it would be hard to decide whether a particular issue fit within the definition. When are we faced with "complex or conflicting societal values," for example? When should we allow jury nullification? Third, the functional approach might be difficult to square with the Constitution. The Seventh Amendment speaks of preserving the right to jury trial, but a functional approach could result in a right to jury trial for equitable claims or for claims against the government if Priest's proposal is accepted, and that would mean an expansion of the right to jury trial beyond anything seen at the common law.

Despite these problems, my own approach is obviously functional. In Chapter 1, I identified several roles that I suggest are fundamental to a vital civil jury. In describing what has happened to the civil jury in the last several decades, I have used those roles as a set point. My suggestions, along with those of Priest, Stephens, and other commentators, provide a basis for further discussion as to what the essence of the civil jury is.[17] I would hope, how-

---

14. See Pamela J. Stephens, *Controlling the Civil Jury: Towards a Functional Model of Justification*, 76 Ky. L.J. 81, 154–59 (1987).

15. See id. Stephens also identifies the functions of judges as deciding legal questions such as the interpretation of statutes, and supervising the litigation process. See id. at 159–61.

16. See supra, Chapter 5, at notes 4–63 and accompanying text.

17. There is also a fairly standard set of justifications for the civil jury that appear in the literature. See, e.g., AMERICAN BAR ASSOCIATION/BROOKINGS SYMPOSIUM, CHARTING

ever, that we can, at some point, suspend discussion and take some action.[18] Thus, I turn to Step 3.

Step 3: Accomplishing Real Jury Reform

Once we understand what has happened and have reached some agreement on what is fundamental to the Seventh Amendment right to a civil jury trial, we must decide how to reform the present system. There have been numerous proposals for jury reform in recent years. Aimed at making the jury work better, these proposals are usually for changes in the way the jury operates, such as allowing jurors to take notes, instructing them on the law before they begin hearing evidence, and allowing them to ask questions.[19] These are important reforms, and we need to continue to experiment with them and to identify what works and what does not. But I suggest that we need more fundamental jury reform if we are to preserve the essence of the civil jury trial. We need jury reform that makes it possible for the jury to play the roles we have assigned to it.

That kind of jury reform is much more difficult to accomplish, largely because we face two hundred years of Supreme Court precedent, some of which undermines those roles. For example, the decision allowing six-person juries seems to have been a serious error, whether one takes a historical or a functional approach to defining the fundamental right. The Court's decisions on

---

A FUTURE FOR THE CIVIL JURY SYSTEM 8–11 (1992) (listing quality of jury decision-making, protecting against abuse of governmental power, stating of community values, checking the bureaucracy, legitimating judicial decisions and educating citizens as virtues of the jury); Douglas G. Smith, *Structural and Functional Aspects of the Jury: Comparative Analysis and Proposals for Reform*, 48 ALA. L. REV. 441, 469–88 (1997) (listing expression of popular sovereignty, protection against abuse by government and lawyers, educating citizens, legitimating judicial decisions, injecting common sense into the adjudicatory process, and simplifying the law as advantages of the jury). I prefer to use the term "roles" because it is more positive. "Justification" is too defensive. The jury is a vital part of our civil justice system and we should treat it as such.

18. I say "suspend" because I do not think we should ever become complacent about the jury's fundamental characteristics, especially if we take a functional approach. At some point, we must act, but we must continue to study the jury and to work on improving its function.

19. *See, e.g.*, Stephen A. Saltzburg, *Improving the Quality of Jury Decisionmaking*, in VERDICT, *supra* note 3, at 341; H. Lee Sarokin & G. Thomas Munsterman, *Recent Innovations in Civil Jury Trial Procedures*, in VERDICT, *supra* note 3, at 378; Ronald S. Longhofer, *Jury Trial Techniques in Complex Civil Litigation*, 32 U. MICH. J. L. REFORM 335 (1999).

public rights and sovereign immunity mean that many cases that are appropriate for jury decision-making under the kind of functional approach I have suggested will never see a jury. The same is true of the Court's decisions that make summary judgment easier to obtain. This precedent needs to be rethought, and in some instances modified or overruled. But such a fundamental overhaul of the Court's thinking in an area is rare, and it is especially difficult when the problem has so many disparate pieces.

Of course, the Court's precedent sets the constitutional limits of the Seventh Amendment, but courts and legislatures can provide for a more extensive civil jury. States are not bound by the Seventh Amendment at all, and could adopt rules that allow their civil juries to function more effectively without regard for the Supreme Court's doctrine. Congress has the power to allow jury trials even in cases where the Seventh Amendment does not require them. Thus, even if Supreme Court precedent stands, Congress could protect and even expand the right to a jury trial, though the protection would be at the mercy of later Congresses.[20] Congress also has considerable power to shape the use of juries through the kind of rights and remedies it creates and the tribunal it assigns to adjudicate those rights. Congress could, for example, require juries in equitable actions.[21] Congress also has the power to waive sovereign immunity and to give cases where the government is the defendant to a jury. Thus, Congress could ensure the right to jury trial even for cases involving the government as a party. Even federal trial courts can do some things to restore the civil jury. For example, they could provide by local rule for twelve-person juries. The Court did not mandate six-person juries, after all; it merely allowed them.

The task before us is a formidable one. We have no generally agreed definition of the fundamental characteristics of the civil jury. We face changes in the jury's environment that make it easy to diminish or even abandon the civil jury. We have well-entrenched Supreme Court precedent that has contributed significantly to the decline of the civil jury. We have a Congress that has made some contributions of its own toward that decline, such as caps on damages. But in spite of all of this, the jury continues to have an impact greater than its

---

20. The problem with this is that Congress has shown little recent inclination to protect the right to jury trial. Indeed, Congress is responsible for imposing caps on damages in a number of recent laws. This could be because potential defendants, which are often well-organized business interests, have more effective lobbyists than potential plaintiffs, who are diffuse and impossible to identify. Potential plaintiffs, however, can be represented in the lobbying game by surrogates, such as trial lawyers.

21. Judges are authorized to empanel advisory juries in equitable matters, and sometimes do. See FED. R. CIV. P. 39(c).

numbers would suggest. Even though juries decide very few civil cases, the jury still influences not only the course of litigation and settlement, but the primary behavior of citizens. The civil jury is down, but it is not out. In this book, I have tried to move us toward a greater understanding of what has happened to the jury, and to suggest, in brief outline form, a strategy for real reform.

BIBLIOGRAPHY

ABA Project on Minimum Standards for Criminal Justice, Standards Relating to Trial by Jury (1986).

Abraham, Kenneth S., *Individual Action and Collective Responsibility: The Dilemma of Mass Tort Reform,* 73 Virginia Law Review 845 (1987).

Abramson, Jeffrey, *We the Jury: The Jury System and the Ideal of Democracy* (1994).

Adler, Stephen J., *The Jury: Disorder in the Court* (1994).

Agnes, Peter W., Jr., Honorable, *Some Observations and Suggestions Regarding the Settlement Activities of Massachusetts Trial Judges,* 31 Suffolk University Law Review 263 (1997).

Aldisert, Ruggero J., *A Metropolitan Court Conquers Its Backlog,* 51 Judicature 247 (1968).

Aleinikoff, T. Alexander, *Race in Constitutional Adjudication,* 63 Colorado Law Review 325 (1992).

Allen, Ronald J., *The Nature of Juridical Proof,* 13 Cardozo Law Review 373 (1991).

———— *A Reconceptualization of Civil Trials,* 66 Boston University Law Review 401 (1986).

Alschuler, Albert W. and Andrew G. Deiss, *A Brief History of the Criminal Jury in the United States* (1994).

Amar, Vikram David, *Jury Service as Political Participation Akin to Voting,* 80 Cornell Law Review 203 (1995).

American Bar Association, *The Litigation Manual* (1989).

American Bar Association/Brooking Symposium, Report, *Charting a Future for the Civil Jury System* (1992).

Appleson, Gail, *Corporations Look to Surrogate Juries in Big Cases,* Reuters Business Report (June 5, 1989).

Arancibia, Jane C., *Statutory Caps on Damage Awards in Medical Malpractice Cases,* 13 Oklahoma City University Law Review 135 (1988).

Arnold, Morris S., *A Historical Inquiry Into the Right to Trial by Jury in Complex Civil Litigation,* 128 University of Pennsylvania Law Review 829 (1980).

———— *"Introduction"* in Select Cases of Trespass From the King's Court (Selden Society, 1985).

Arnold, Richard S., *Trial by Jury: The Constitutional Right to a Jury of Twelve in Civil Trials,* 22 Hofstra Law Review 1 (1993).

Arthur, Thomas C. and Richard D. Freer, *Grasping at Burnt Straws: The Disaster of the Supplemental Jurisdiction Statute,* 40 Emory Law Journal 963 (1991).

Asch, S.E., *"Effects of Group Pressure Upon the Modification and Distortion of Judgments"* in Readings in Social Psychology, (Guy E. Swanson, Theodore M. Newcomb and Eugene L. Hartley eds.,1952).

Atkinson, Myron, Jr., and LaVern C. Neff, *Evidence—Jury Trials—Weight of Evidence—Credibility of Witnesses—Judicial Comment Thereon,* 27 North Dakota Law Review 199 (1951).

Auerbach, Jerold S., *Justice Without Law* (1983).

Augelli, Anthony T., *Six-Member Juries in Civil Actions in the Federal Judicial System,* 3 Seton Hall Law Review 281 (1972).

Babcock, Barbara Allen, *Voir Dire: Preserving Its "Wonderful Powers",* 27 Stanford Law Review 545 (1975).

Bachrach, Peter, *The Theory of Democratic Elitism* (1980).

Bagalay, John E., Jr., *Directed Verdicts and the Right to Trial by Jury in the Federal Courts,* 42 Texas Law Review 1053 (1964).

Baker, J.H., *Introduction to English Legal History* (1990).

Baker, John M., *The Shrinking Role of the Jury in Constitutional Litigation,* 16 William Mitchell Law Review 697 (1990).

Baldwin, John and Michael McConville, *Jury Trials* (1979).

Barber, Bernard, *Mass Apathy and Voluntary Social Participation in the United States* (1980).

Barber, Benjamin, *Strong Democracy* (1984).

Barron, William W. and Alexander Holtzoff, *Federal Practice and Procedure* (1958).

Baum, Victor J., *The Six-Man Jury—The Cross-Section Aborted,* 12 Judges 12 (1973).

Beaver, James E., Kit G. Navodick and Joseph M.Wallis, *Civil Forfeiture and the Eighth Amendment After Austin,* 19 Seattle University Law Review 1 (1995).

Bell, Griffin B., et al., *Automatic Disclosure in Discovery-The Rush to Reform,* 27 Georgia Law Review 1 (1992).

Bell, Peter A., *Analyzing Tort Law: The Flawed Premise of NeoContract,* 74 Minnesota Law Review 1177 (1990).

Bergman, Paul and Al Moore, *Mistrial by Likelihood Ratio: Bayesian Analysis Meets the F- Word,* 13 Cardozo Law Review 589 (1991).

Bernstein, Merton C., *The NLRB's Adjudication-Rule Making Dilemma Under the Administrative Procedure Act,* 79 Yale Law Journal 571 (1970).

Bessette, Joseph M., *"Deliberative Democracy: The Majority Principle in Republican Government"* in How Democratic is the Constitution (Robert A. Goldwin and William A.Schambra eds., 1980).

Bickel, Alexander M., *The Least Dangerous Branch* (1962).

Bigelow, Melville Madison, *History of Procedure in England from the Norman Conquest* (1880).

Bigham, Ina Ruth, *Use of Juror Depositions to Bar Collateral Estoppel: A Necessary Safeguard or a Dangerous Precedent? Note,* 34 Vanderbilt Law Review 143 (1981).

Blackstone, William, *Commentaries on the Laws of England* (1768).

Blatt, Richard L., et al., *Punitive Damages* (1991).

Blume, William Wirt, *Origin and Development of the Directed Verdict,* 48 Michigan Law Review 555 (1950).

———— *Theory Pleading: A Survey Including the Federal Rules*, 47 Michigan Law Review 297 (1949).

Bogue, Andrew W. and Thomas G. Fritz, *The Six-Man Jury*, 17 South Dakota Law Review 285 (1972).

Bohlen, Francis H., *Mixed Questions of Law and Fact*, 77 University of Pennsylvania Law Review 111 (1924).

Bonazzoli, M. Juliet, *Jury Selection and Bias: Debunking Invidious Stereotypes Through Science*, 18 Quinnipiac Law Review 247 (1998).

Bork, Robert H., *The Tempting of America: The Political Seduction of the Law* (1990).

Boston, Gerald W., *Punitive Damages in Tort Law* (1993).

Bowers, Claude G., *Jefferson and Hamilton: The Struggle of Democracy in America* (1925).

Brafford, Anne, *Arbitration Clauses in Consumer Contracts of Adhesion: Fair Play or Trap for the Weak and Unwary?*, 21 Journal of Corporation Law 331 (1996).

Brand, Jeffrey S., *The Supreme Court, Equal Protection and Jury Selection: Denying That Race Still Matters*, 1994 Wisconsin Law Review 511 (1994).

Brands, Henk J., *Qualified Immunity and the Allocation of Decision-Making Functions Between Judge and Jury*, 90 Columbia Law Review 1045 (1990).

Brant, Irving, *James Madison, Father of the Constitution* (1950).

Brazil, Wayne, *The Adversary Character of Civil Discovery: A Critique and Proposals for Change*, 31 Vanderbilt Law Review 1295 (1978).

Breen, J. Daniel, *Magistrate Judge, Mediation and the Magistrate Judge*, 26 Memphis Law Review 100 (1996)

Broderick, Raymond J., *Why the Peremptory Challenge Should be Abolished*, 65 Temple Law Review 369 (1992).

Brody, David C. and John Neiswender, *Judicial Attitudes Toward Jury Reform*, 83 Judicature 298 (2000).

Broeder, Dale W., *The Functions of the Jury: Facts or Fictions*, 21 University of Chicago Law Review 386 (1954).

———— *The University of Chicago Jury Project*, 38 Nebraska Law Review 744 (1959).

Brook, James, *Inevitable Errors: The Preponderance of the Evidence Standard in Civil Litigation*, 18 Tulsa Law Journal 79 (1982).

Brown, Darryl K., *Structure and Relationship in the Jurisprudence of Juries: Comparing the Capital Sentencing and Punitive Damages Doctrines*, 47 Hastings Law Journal 1255 (1996).

Brown, David A., Note, *Collateral Estoppel of Administrative Agency Determinations: Where Should Federal Courts Draw the Line?* 73 Cornell Law Review 817 (1988).

Bruff, Harold H., *Specialized Courts in Administrative Law*, 43 Administrative Law Review 329 (1991).

Brunet, Edward, *Questioning the Quality of Alternate Dispute Resolution*, 62 Tulane Law Review 1 (1987).

Brunstad, Eric, et al., *Review of Proposals of the National Bankruptcy Review Commission Pertaining to Business Bankruptcies: Part 1*, 53 Business Law 1381 (1998).

Brysh, Paul J., *Abolish the Rule Against Hearsay*, 35 University of Pittsburgh Law Review 609 (1974).

Buckland, W.W., *Equity in Roman Law* ([1983]1911).

Buckman, Lester, *Contingent Fees Without Contingencies: Hamlet Without the Prince of Denmark?*, 37 University of California at Los Angeles Law Review 29 (1989).

Bundy, Stephen McG., *The Policy in Favor of Settlement in an Adversary System*, 44 Hastings Law Journal 1 (1992).

Buranelli, Vincent, *The Trial of Peter Zenger* (1957).

Burger, Warren E., *Thinking the Unthinkable*, 31 Loyola Law Review 205 (1985).

Burke, Edmund, *"Selections From Reflections on the Revolution in France"* in Select Works of Edmund Burke (1990).

Burns, Edward McNall, *James Madison, Philosopher of the Constitution* (1938).

Calabresi, Guido, *A Common Law for the Age of Statutes* (1982).

Calabresi, Guido and Philip Bobbitt, *Tragic Choices* (1978).

Calder, Nigel, *Einstein's Universe* (1979).

Cammack, Mark, *The Jurisprudence of Jury Trials: The No Impeachment Rule and the Conditions for Legitimate Legal Decisionmaking*, 64 University of Colorado Law Review 57 (1993).

Carbonneau, Thomas, *Alternative Dispute Resolution: Melting the Lances and Dismounting the Steeds* (1989).

Carrington, Paul D., *Making Rules to Dispose of Manifestly Unfounded Assertions: An Exorcism of the Bogy of Non-Trans-Substantive Rules of Civil Procedure*, 137 University of Pennsylvania Law Review 2067 (1989).

——— *The Seventh Amendment: Some Bicentennial Reflections*, 1990 University of Chicago Legal Forum 33 (1990).

Cary, Jean M., *Rambo Depositions: Controlling an Ethical Cancer in Civil Litigation*, 25 Hofstra Law Review 561 (1996).

Casad, Robert C.,Howard P. Fink and Peter N. Simon, *Civil Procedure* (1989).

Casper, Jonathan D., *"Restructuring the Traditional Civil Jury: The Effects of Changes in Composition and Procedures,"* in Verdict: Assessing the Civil Justice System (Robert E. Litan ed., 1993).

Castro, William R., *The First Congress's Understanding of Its Authority Over the Federal Court's Jurisdiction*, 26 Boston College Law Review 11 (1985).

Cecil, Joe S., Valerie P. Hans and Elizabeth C. Wiggins, *Citizen Comprehension of Difficult Issues: Lessons From Civil Jury Trials*, 40 American University Law Review 727 (1991).

Charrow, Robert P., and Veda R. Charrow, *Making Legal Language Understandable: A Psycholinguistic Study of Jury Instructions*, 79 Columbia Law Review 1306 (1970).

Chayes, Abram, *The Role of the Judge in Public Law Litigation*, 89 Harvard Law Review 1281 (1976).

Chen, Kevin, *Political Alienation and Voter Turnout in the United States* (1992).

Chesebro, Kenneth J., *Galileo's Retort: Peter Huber's Junk Scholarship*, 42 American University Law Review 1637 (1993).

Childress, Steven Alan and Martha S. Davis, *Federal Standards of Review* (1992).

——— *Standards of Review* (1986).

Chin, Audrey and Mark A. Peterson, *Deep Pockets, Empty Pockets* (1985).

Christie, George C., *Judicial Review of Findings of Fact*, 87 Northwestern University Law Review 52 (1992).

Christman, David A., *Federal rule of Evidence 606(b) and the Problem of "Differential" Jury Error*, 67 New York University Law Review 802 (1992).

Clark, Bradford Russell, Note, *Judicial Review of Congressional Section Five Action: The Fallacy of Reverse Incorporation*, 84 Columbia Law Review 1969 (1984).

Clark, Charles E., *The Code Cause of Action*, 33 Yale Law Journal 817 (1924).

—— *Handbook of the Law of Code Pleading* (1947).

—— *The Federal Rules of Civil Procedure: 1938-1958: Two Decades of the Federal Civil Rules*, 58 Columbia Law Review 435 (1958).

—— *The Proposed Federal Rules of Civil Procedure*, 22 American Bar Association Journal 447 (1936).

Clark, Charles E., and Charles U. Samenow, *The Summary Judgment*, 38 Yale Law Journal 423 (1928).

Clark, Charles E., and James Wm. Moore, *A New Federal Civil Procedure: The Background*, 44 Yale Law Journal 387 (1935).

Clark, David S., *Adjudication to Administration: A Statistical Analysis of Federal District Courts in the Twentieth Century*, 55 Southern California Law Review 65 (1981).

Clarke, Sherman J., *A Populist Critique of Direct Democracy*, 112 Harvard Law Review 434 (1998).

Cleary, Edward W., *McCormick on Evidence* (1894).

Clermont, Kevin M., and Theodore Eisenberg, *Trial by Jury or Judge: Transcending Empiricism*, 77 Cornell Law Review 1124 (1992).

Coase, R.H., *The Problem of Social Cost*, 3 Journal of Law & Economics 1 (1960).

Cohen, L. Jonathan, *The Probable and the Provable* (1977).

Cohen, Neil B., *The Costs of Acceptability: Blue Buses, Agent Orange, and Aversion to Statistical Evidence*, 66 Buffalo University Law Review 563 (1986).

Cohen, Julius Henry and Kenneth Dayton, *The New Federal Arbitration Law*, 12 Virginia Law Review 265 (1926).

Coke, Tanya E., Note, *Lady Justice May be Blind, But is She a Soul Sister? Race-Neutrality and the Ideal of Representative Juries*, 69 New York University Law Review 327 (1994).

Cole, Kevin, *Civilizing Civil Forfeiture*, 7 Journal of Contemporary Legal Issues 249 (1996).

Cole, Sarah Rudolph, *Incentives in Arbitration: The Case Against Enforcement of Executory Arbitration Agreements Between Employers and Employees*, 64 University of Missouri at Kansas City Law Review 449 (1996).

Conference Papers, *The Civil-Criminal Distinction*, 7 Journal of Contemporary Legal Issues 1 (1996).

Conway, John F., *Equitable Estoppel of the Federal Government: An Application of the Proprietary Function Exception to the Traditional Rule*, 55 Fordham Law Review 707 (1987).

Cook, Royer F., Janice A. Roehl and David I. Sheppard, *Neighborhood Justice Centers Field Test: Final Evaluation Report* (1980).

Cooper, Christine Godsil, *Where Are We Going With Gilmer?—Some Ruminations on the Arbitration of Discrimination Claims*, 11 St. Louis University Public Law Review 203 (1992).

Cooper, Edward H., *Directions for Directed Verdicts: A Compass for Federal Courts*, 55 Minnesota Law Review 903 (1971).

Cooper, Joel, et al., *Complex Scientific Testimony: How do Jurors Make Decisions*, 20 Law & Human Behavior 379 (1996).

Cornish, W.R., *The Jury* (1968).

Corr, John Bernard, *Supreme Court Doctrine in the Trenches: The Case of Collateral Estoppel*, 27 William & Mary Law Review 35 (1985).

Cound, John H., et al., *Civil Procedure: Cases and Materials* (1997).

Cover, Robert M., *For James Wm. Moore: Some Reflections on a Reading of the Rules*, 84 Yale Law Journal 718 (1975).

Crawford, Earl T., *The Construction of Statutes* (1940).

Croake, Thomas F., *Memorandum on the Advisability and Constitutionality of Six Man Juries and 5/6 Verdicts in Civil Cases*, 44 New York Bar Journal 385 (1972).

Curriden, Mark, *Jury Reform*, 81 American Bar Association Journal 72 (1995).

——— *Putting the Squeeze on Juries*, 86 American Bar Association Journal 52 (2000).

Dahl, Robert A., *A Preface to Democratic Theory* (1956).

——— *Democracy and Its Critics* (1989).

Damaska, Mirjan, *Evidence Law Adrift* (1997).

Danet, Brenda, *Language in the Legal Process*, 14 Law & Society Review 445 (1980).

Daniels, Stephen, and Joanne Martin, *Civil Juries and the Politics of Reform* (1995).

Danson, Patricia M., *Medical Malpractice: Theory, Evidence, and Public Policy* (1985).

Danzig, Richard, *Toward the Creation of a Complementary, Decentralized System of Criminal Justice*, 26 Stanford Law Review 1 (1973).

Dauer, Edward A., *Manual of Dispute Resolution: ADR Law and Practice* (1994).

Davidson, George A., and William H. Voth, *Waiver of the Attorney-Client Privilege*, 64 Oregon Law Review 63 (1986).

Davis, Kenneth Culp, *Administrative Law Treatise* (1984).

Davis, Kenneth Culp and Richard J. Pierce, Jr., *Administrative Law Treatise* (1994).

Davis, Mark and Kevin Davis, *Star Rising for Simpson Jury Consultant*, 81 American Bar Association Journal 14 (1995).

Dayton, Kim, *The Myth of Alternative Dispute Resolution in the Federal Courts*, 68 Iowa Law Review 889 (1991).

DeSlovere, Frederick J., *The Functions of Judge and Jury in the Interpretation of Statutes*, 46 Harvard Law Review 1086 (1933).

DeTocqueville, Alexis, *Democracy in America* (1990[1835]).

Developments: Attorney Fee Awards, 5 Class Action Reports 470 (1978).

Developments in the Law—Discovery, 74 Harvard Law Review 940 (1961).

Developments in the Law—Race and the Criminal Process, 101 Harvard Law Review 1472 (1988).

Developments in the Law—Scientific Evidence: Confronting the New challenges of Scientific Evidence, 108 Harvard Law Review 1481 (1995).

Devitt, Edward J., *The Six-Man Jury in Federal Court*, 53 Federal Rules Digest 273 (1971).

Devlin, Patrick, *The Jury Trial of Complex Cases: English Practice at the Time of the Seventh Amendment*, 80 Columbia Law Review 43 (1980).

——— *Trial by Jury* (1956).

Deye, James R., and Lesly L. Britton, *Arbitration by the American Arbitration Association*, 70 North Dakota Law Review 281 (1994).

Diamond, Shari Seidman, *Scientific Jury Selection: What Social Scientists Know and Do Not Know*, 73 Judicature 178 (1990).

——— *"What Jurors Think: Expectations and Reactions of Citizens Who Serve As Jurors,"* in Verdict: Assessing the Civil Justice System (Robert E. Litan ed., 1993).

Dickens, Charles, *Bleak House* (1853).

Dobbs, Dan B., *Dobbs Law of Remedies* (2nd ed. 1993).

——— *Torts and Compensation* (1985).

Dooley, Laura Gaston, *Essay, Our Juries, Our Selves: Power, Perception, and Politics of the Civil Jury*, 80 Cornell Law Review 325 (1995).

Dore, Michael, *A Commentary on the Use of Epidemiological Evidence in Demonstrating Cause-in-Fact*, 7 Harvard Environmental Law Review 429 (1938).

Doubts About Juries Don't Come From Jurors, 16 National Law Journal, p. S4 (December 27,1994).

Drazan, Dan, *The Case for Special Juries in Toxic Tort Litigation*, 72 Judicature 292 (1989).

Dreyfuss, Rochelle Cooper, *The Debate Over sec. 1367: Defining the Power to Define Federal Judicial Power*, 41 Emory Law Journal 13 (1992).

Driscoll, James, *The Decline of the English Jury* (1979).

Dubroff, Harold, *The United States Tax Court: An Historical Analysis* (1979).

Dudley, Earl C., Jr., *Discovery Abuse Revisited: Some Specific Proposals to Amend the Federal Rules of Civil Procedure*, 26 University of San Francisco Law Review 189 (1992).

Edelman, Murray, *The Symbolic Uses of Government* (1964).

Edwards, Harry T., *Alternative Dispute Resolution: Panacea or Anathema?*, 99 Harvard Law Review 575 (1987).

Edwards, Ward, *Influence Diagrams, Bayesian Imperialism, and the Collins Case: An Appeal to Reason*, 13 Cardozo Law Review 1025 (1991).

——— *Summing Up: The Society of Bayesian Trial Lawyers*, 66 Boston University Law Review 937 (1986)

Eisenberg, Melvin Aron, *The Nature of the Common Law* (1988).

——— *Private Ordering Through Negotiation: Dispute Settlement and Rulemaking*, 89 Harvard Law Review 63 (1976).

Eisenberg, Theodore, John Goerdt, Brian Ostrom, David Rottmann, and Martin T. Wells, *The Predictability of Punitive Damages*, 26 Journal of Legal Studies 623 (1997).

Elkouri, Frank and Edna Asper Elkouri, *How Arbitration Works* (1985).

Elliott, E. Donald, *Managerial Judging and the Evolution of Procedure*, 53 University of Chicago Law Review 306 (1986).

Ellis, Dorsey E., Jr., *Fairness and Efficiency in the Law of Punitive Damages*, 56 Southern California Law Review 1 (1982).
—— *Punitive Damages, Due Process, and the Jury*, 40 Alabama Law Review 975 (1989).
Elwork, Amiram, *et al.*, *Juridic Decisions: In Ignorance of the Law or In Light of the Law?*, 1 Law & Human Behavior 163 (1977).
—— *"Toward Understandable Jury Instructions"* in In the Jury Box: Controversies in the Courtroom (Lawrence S. Wrightsman, Saul M. Kassin & Cynthia E. Willis eds., 1987).
Ely, John Hart, *Democracy and Distrust: A Theory of Judicial Review* (1980).
Eskridge, William N., *The New Textualism*, 37 University of California at Los Angeles Law Review 621 (1990).
Estlund, David M., *Who's Afraid of Deliberative Democracy? On the Strategic/Deliberative Dichotomy in Recent Constitutional Jurisprudence*, 71 Texas Law Review 1437 (1993).
Etzioni, Amitai, ed., *The New Communitarian Thinking* (1995).
—— *The Spirit of Community* (1993).
Faigman, David L.,and A.J. Baglioni, Jr., *Bayes's Theorem in the Trial Process: Instructing Jurors on the Value of Statistical Evidence*, 12 Law & Human Behavior 1 (1988).
Fairman, Christopher M., *Abdication to Academia: The Case of the Supplemental Jurisdiction Statute, 28 U.S.C., sec.1367*, 19 Seton Hall Legislative Journal 157 (1994).
Fallon, Richard H.,Jr., *Of legislative courts, Administrative Agencies, and Article III*, 10 Harvard Law Review 915 (1988).
Fallon, Richard H., Daniel J. Meltzer and David L. Shapiro, *Hart and Wechsler's The Federal Courts and the Federal System* (4th ed. 1996).
Faulkner, Elizabeth, *Using the Special Verdict to Manage Complex Cases and Avoid Compromise Verdicts*, 21 Arizona State Law Journal 61 (1989).
Feigenson, Neal R., *The Rhetoric of Torts: How Advocates Help Jurors Think About Causation, Reasonableness, and Responsibility*, 47 Hastings Law Journal 61 (1995).
Feiler, W., *An Introduction to Probability Theory and Its Applications* (1968).
Finkelstein, Michael O., *Application of Statistical Decision Theory to the Jury Discrimination Cases*, 80 Harvard Law Review 338 (1966).
Finkelstein, Michael O., and William B. Fairley, *A Bayesian Approach to Identification Evidence*, 83 Harvard Law Review 489 (1970).
Finn, Welldon, *The Domesday Inquest* (1961).
Fisher, Harry M., *Judicial Mediation: How It Works Through Pretrial Conference*, 10 University of Chicago Law Review 452 (1943).
Fisher, H. Richmond, *The Seventh Amendment and the Common Law: No Magic in Numbers*, 56 Federal Rules Decisions 507 (1973).
Fishkin, James S., *Democrary and Deliberation: New Directions for Democratic Reform* (1991).
Fishman, Clifford S., *Jones on Evidence: Civil and Criminal* (1994).
Fiss, Owen M., *The Civil Rights Injunction* (1978).

—— The Forms of Justice, 93 Harvard Law Review 1 (1979).

—— Against Settlement, 93 Yale Law Journal 1073 (1984)

Flanders, Steven, Blind Umpires—A Response to Professor Resnik, 35 Hastings Law Journal 505 (1984).

Floyd, Daisy Hurst, Can the Judge Do That? The Need for a Clearer Judicial Role in Settlement, 26 Arizona State Law Journal 45 (1994).

Folberg, Jay and Allison Taylor, Mediation: A Comprehensive Guide to Resolving Conflicts Without Litigation (1984).

Forde-Mazrui, Kim, Jural Districting: Selecting Impartial Juries Through Community Representation, 52 Vanderbilt Law Review 353 (1999).

Forsyth, William, History of Trial by Jury (1875).

Foss, Robert D., Structural Effects in Simulated Jury Decision Making, 40 Journal of Personality and Social Psychology 1055 (1981).

Fox, Autumn and Stephen R. McAllister, An Eagle Soaring: The Jurisprudence of Justice Antonin Scalia, 19 Campbell Law Review 223 (1997).

Fox, William F., Jr., Understanding Administrative Law (1986).

Frank, Jerome, Courts on Trial (1949).

—— Law and the Modern Mind (1930).

Freedman, Monroe, Lawyers' Ethics in an Adversary System (1975).

Freedman, James O., Crisis and Legitimacy (1978).

Freeman, Jody, Collaborative Governance in the Administrative State, 45 University of California at Los Angeles Law Review 1 (1997).

Friedman, Barry, The Sedimentary Constitution, 147 University of Pennsylvania Law Review 1 (1998).

Friedman, Richard D., Anchors and Flotsam: Is Evidence Law Adrift?, 107 Yale Law Journal 1921 (1998).

—— Generalized Inferences, Individual Merits, and Jury Discretion, 66 Boston University Law Review 509 (1986).

Frye, John H., III, Survey of Non-ALJ Hearing Programs in the Federal Government, 44 Administrative Law Review 261 (1992).

Fukurai, Hiroshi, et al., Race and the Jury: Racial Disenfranchisement and the Search for Justice (1993).

Fuller, Lon L., "The Adversary System" in Talks on American Law (Harold J. Berman ed., 1971).

—— The Forms and Limits of Adjudication, 92 Harvard Law Review 353 (1979).

Galanter, Marc, The Civil Jury as Regulator of the Litigation Process, 1990 University of Chicago Legal Forum 201.

—— "Jury Shadows: Reflections on the Civil Jury and the "Litigation Explosion" in The American Civil Jury (1987).

—— "The Regulatory Function of the Civil Jury" in Verdict: Assessing the Civil Jury System, (1993).

—— A Settlement Judge, Not a Trial Judge: Judicial Mediation in the United States, 12 Journal of Law & Society (1985).

—— Why the "Haves" Come Out Ahead: Speculations on the Limits of Legal Change, 9 Law & Society Review 95 (1974).

Galanter, Marc and Mia Cahill, *"Most Cases Settle": Judicial Promotion and Regulation of Settlements,* 46 Stanford Law Review 1339 (1994).

Galbraith, V.H., *Domesday Book: Its Place in Administrative History* (1974).

Gardner, James A., *Shut Up and Vote: A Critique of Deliberative Democracy and the Life of Talk,* 63 Tennessee Law Review 421 (1996).

Gianelly, Paul C., *The Admissibility of Novel Scientific Evidence: Frye v. United States Half a Century Later,* 80 Columbia Law Review 1197 (1980).

Gibson, E. Elizabeth, *Jury Trials in Bankruptcy: Obeying the Commands of Article III and the Seventh Amendment,* 72 Minnesota Law Review 967 (1988).

Gillespie, Paul and Miriam Klipper, *No Fault: What you Save, Gain and Lose With the New Auto Insurance* (1972).

Gilligan, Carol, *In a Different Voice* (1982).

Giuttari, Theodore R., *The American Law of Sovereign Immunity: An Analysis of Legal Interpretation* (1970).

Glendon, Mary Ann, *Rights Talk* (1992).

Golann, Dwight, *Making Alternative Dispute Resolution Mandatory: The Constitutional Issues,* 68 Oregon Law Review 487 (1989).

Goldberg, Stephen B., Eric D. Green and Frank E. Sander, *Dispute Resolution* (1985).

Goldman, Sheldon, *"Federal Judicial Recruitment"* in The American Courts: A Critical Assessment (John B. Gates and Charles A. Johnson, eds., 1991).

Goldstein, Abraham S., *Jury Secrecy and the Media: The Problem of Postverdict Interviews,* 1993 University of Missouri Law Review 295 (1993).

Goodnow, Frank J., *The Principles of the Administrative Law of the United States* (1905).

Graham, Michael H., *Federal Rules of Evidence in a Nutshell* (1996).

Gray, John A., *Have the Foxes Become the Guardians of the Chickens? The Post-Gilmer Legal Status of Predispute Mandatory Arbitration as a Condition of Employment,* 37 Villanova Law Review 113 (1992).

Green, Alice Stopford, *"The Centralization of Norman Justice under Henry II"* in Select Essays in Anglo-American Legal History (1907).

Green, Eric D., *Growth of the Mini-Trial,* 9 Litigation 12 (1982).

——— *"The Mini-Trial Approach to Dispute Resolution,"* in Center for Public Resources, Corporate Dispute Management: A Manual of Innovative Corporate Strategies for the Avoidance and Resolution of Legal Disputes (1982).

Green, Eric D., Jonathan B. Marks and Ronald L. Olsen, *Settling Large Case Litigation: An Alternative Approach,* 11 Loyola at Los Angeles Law Review 493 (1978).

Green, Frederick, *Mixed Questions of Law and Fact,* 15 Harvard Law Review 271 (1901).

Green, Leon, *Judge and Jury* (1930).

Green, Thomas Andrew, *Verdict According to Conscience* (1985).

Gregory, William A., and William J. Schneider, *Securities Arbitration: A Need for Continued Reform,* 17 Nova Law Review 1223 (1993).

Grosberg, Lawrence M., *Illusion and Reality in Regulating Lawyer Performance: Rethinking Rule 11,* 32 Villanova Law Review 575 (1987).

Gross, Samuel R., *Expert Evidence*, 1991 Wisconsin Law Review 1113.

Gross, Samuel R., and Kent D. Syverud, *Getting to No: A Study of Settlement Negotiations and the Selection of Cases for Trial*, 90 Michigan Law Review 319 (1991).

Grossman, Joanna L., *Women's Jury Service: Right of citizenship of Privilege of Difference?*, 46 Stanford Law Review 1115 (1994).

Guinther, John, *The Jury in America* (1988).

Gwyn, W.B., *The Meaning of the Separation of Powers* (1986).

Haddon, Phoebe A., *Rethinking the Jury*, 3 William & Mary Bill of Rights Journal 29 (1994).

Hager, Mark M., *Review Essay: Civil Compensation and Its Discontents: A Response to Huber*, 42 Stanford Law Review 539 (1990).

Hagopian, Jacob, Honorable, *United States Magistrate Judges: A Look at the Growth and Development of the Position*, 39 Federal Bar News & Journal 416 (1992).

Haig, Robert L., and Warren N. Stone, *Litigation Reform*, 67 St. John's Law Journal 843 (1993).

Haines, Edson L., *The Disappearance of Civil Juries in England, Canada, Australia*, 4 Defense Law Journal 118 (1958).

Hale, Matthew, Sir, *The History of the Common Law in England* (1971).

Hallahan, Janet V., *Social Interests Versus Plaintiffs' Rights: The Constitutional Battle Over Statutory Limitations on Punitive Damages*, 26 Loyola University at Chicago Law Journal 405 (1995).

Hanbury, Harold Greville, *Modern Equity* (1937).

Hand, Learned, *"The Contribution of an Independent Judiciary to Civilization"* in The Spirit of Liberty (3rd ed. 1960).

Hanna, Cheryl, *No Right to Choose: Mandated Victim Participation in Domestic Violence Prosecutions*, 109 Harvard Law Review 1849 (1996).

Hans, Valerie P.,*"Attitudes Toward the Civil Jury: A Crisis of Confidence?"* in Verdict: Assessing the Civil Justice System, (Robert E. Litan ed., 1993).

——— *The Jury's Response to Business and Corporate Wrongdoing*, 52 Law & Contemporary Problems 177 (1989).

Hansen, Mark, *New York Tackles Jury Standards*, 80 American Bar Association Journal 22 (1994).

Harr, Johathan, *A Civil Action* (1995).

Harter, Philip J. *Negotiating Regulations: A Cure for Malaise*, 71 Georgetown Law Journal 1 (1982).

Hartman, Allen, Judge, *The "Whys" and "Whynots" of Judicial Comments on Evidence in Jury Trials*, 23 Loyola at Chicago Law Journal 1 (1991).

Hartnett, Edward, *A New Trick From an Old and Abused Dog: Section 1441(c) Lives and Now Permits the Remand of Federal Question Cases*, 63 Fordham Law Review 1099 (1995).

Hastie, Reid, *Inside the Juror* (1993).

Hathaway, George, *An Overview of the Plain English Movement for Lawyers...Ten Years Later*, 73 Michigan Bar Journal 26 (1994).

Hay, Bruce L., *Civil Discovery: Its Effects and Optimal Scope,* 23 Journal of Legal Studies 481 (1994).

Hazard, Geoffrey C., Jr., *Discovery Vices and Trans-Substantive Virtues in the Federal Rules of Civil Procedure,* 137 University of Pennsylvania Law Review 2237 (1989).

——— *Forms of Action under the Federal Rules of Civil Procedure,* 63 North Dakota Law Review 628 (1988).

——— *From Whom No Secrets are Hid,* 76 Texas Law Review 1665 (1998).

Heintz, Rebecca, *Sovereign Immunity and Clean Water: A Supreme Mis-step,* 24 Environmental Law Journal 263 (1994).

Held, David, *Models of Democracy* (1987).

Hellekson, Heidi M., *Taking the "Alternative" Out of the Dispute Resolution of Title VII Claims: The Implications of a Mandatory Enforcement Scheme of Arbitration Agreements Arising Out of Employment Contracts,* 70 North Dakota Law Review 435 (1994).

Henderson, Edith Guild, *The Background of the Seventh Amendment,* 80 Harvard Law Review 289 (1966).

Henn, Harry G., *Law of Corporations* (1970).

Hepburn, Charles M., *The Historical Development of Code Pleading* (1897).

Heriot, Gail, *An Essay on the Civil-Criminal Distinction with Special Reference to Punitive Damages,* 7 J. Contemporary Legal Issues 43 (1996).

Hermann, Phillip J., *Predicting Verdicts in Personal Injury Cases,* 475 Insurance Law Journal 505 (1962).

Herr, David F., *et al., Motion Practice* (1991).

Higginbotham, Patrick E., *Continuing the Dialogue: Civil Juries and the Allocation of Power,* 56 Texas Law Review 47 (1977).

Hoeflich, M.H., *Law in the Republican Classroom,* 43 Kansas Law Review 711 (1995).

——— *Roman and Civil Law and the Development of Anglo-American Jurisprudence in the Nineteenth Century* (1997).

Hoellering, Michael F., *Continuing Adaptation and Growth* in Wide World of Arbitration (Charlotte Gold & Susan Mackenzie eds., 1978).

Hoffman, Harold M., and Joseph Brodey, *Jurors on Trial,* 17 Missouri Law Review 235 (1952).

Holdworth, William, *A History of English Law* (1965).

——— *Some Makers of English Law* (1938).

Holt, J.C., *Magna Carta* (1965).

Holtzoff, Alexander, *Modern Trends in Trial by Jury,* 16 Washington & Lee Law Review 27 (1959).

——— *Origin and Sources of the Federal Rules of Civil Procedure,* 30 New York University Law Review 105 (1955).

Horowitz, Irwin A., and Thomas E. Willging, *Changing Views of Jury Power: The Nullification Debate, 1787-1988,* 15 Law & Human Behavior 165 (1991).

Horwitz, Morton J., *The Transformation of American Law, 1780-1860* (1977).

Hovenkamp, Herbert, *Judicial Restraint and Constitutional Federalism: The Supreme Court's Lopez and Seminole Tribe Decisions,* 96 Columbia Law Review 2213 (1996).

Huber, Peter W., *Galileo's Revenge: Junk Science in the Courtroom* (1991)

—— *Liability: The Legal Revolution and Its Consequences* (1988).

Hutchinson, Campbell, C., *The Case for Mandatory Mediation,* 42 Loyola Law Review 85 (1996).

Hyams, Paul R., *"Trial by Ordeal: The Key to Proof in the Early Common Law"* in On the Laws and Customs of England: Essays in Honor of Samuel E. Thorne (Morris S. Arnold, *et al.* eds., 1981).

Hyland, James J., *Democratic Theory: The Philosophical Foundations* (1995).

Informing the Jury of the Legal Effects of Its Answers to Special Verdicts, 43 Minnesota Law Review 823 (1959).

Isaacs, Nathan, *The Law and the Facts,* 22 Columbia Law Review 1 (1922).

Issacharoff, Samuel, and George Loewenstein, *Second Thoughts About Summary Judgment,* 100 Yale Law Journal 73 (1990).

Jackson, Vicki C., *The Supreme Court, the Eleventh Amendment, and State Sovereign Immunity,* 98 Yale Law Journal 1 (1988).

Jacobs, Michael S., *Testing the Assumption Underlying the Debate About Scientific Evidence: A Closer Look at Juror "Incompetence" and Scientific "Objectivity,"* 25 Connecticut Law Review 1083 (1993).

Jacobsohn, Gary, *Citizen Participation in Policy-Making: The Role of the Jury,* 39 Journal of Politics 73 (1977).

Jacobstein, J. Myron and Roy M. Mersky, *Jury Size: Articles and Bibliography from the Literature of Law and the Social and Behavior Science* (1998).

Jaffe, Louis L., *Judicial Control of Administrative Action* (1965).

James, Fleming, Jr., *Civil Procedure* (1965)

—— *Contributory Negligence,* 62 Yale Law Journal 691 (1953).

—— *Functions of Judge and Jury in Negligence Cases,* 58 Yale Law Journal 667 (1949).

—— *Right to a Jury Trial in Civil Actions,* 72 Yale Law Journal 655 (1963).

—— *Sufficiency of the Evidence and Jury-Control Devices Available Before Verdict,* 47 Virginia L. Review 218 (1961).

James, Fleming Jr. and Geoffrey C. Hazard, Jr., *Civil Procedure* (1977).

James, Shelly R., *Arbitration in the Securities Field: Does the Present System of Arbitration Between Small Investors and Brokerage Firms Really Protect Anyone?,* 21 Journal of Corporate Law 363 (1996).

Jefferson, Thomas, *The Papers of Thomas Jefferson* (Julian Boyd ed, 1958).

Johnson, Earl, Jr., Valerie Kantor and Elizabeth Schwartz, *Outside the Courts: A Survey of Diversion Alternatives in Civil Cases* (1977).

Johnson, Sheri Lynn, *Black Innocence and the White Jury,* 83 Michigan Law Review 1611 (1985).

Johnston, Robert G., *Jury Subornation Through Judicial Control,* 43 Law & Contemporary Problems 24 (1980).

Jones, Robert A. and John Meredith, *Management of Complex Multi-Party Litigation,* 31 Houston Lawyer 16 (1994).

Jordan, Ellen R., *Specialized Courts: A Choice?*, 76 Northwestern University Law Review 745 (1981).

Kalman, Laura, *Legal Realism at Yale* (1986).

Kalven, Harry Jr., and Hans Zeisel, *The American Jury* (1966).

Kanowitz, Leo, *Alternative Dispute Resolution and the Public Interest: The Arbitration Experience*, 38 Hastings Law Journal 239 (1987).

Kaplan, John, *Decision Theory and the Factfinding Process*, 20 Stanford Law Review 1065 (1968).

Karkkainen, Bradley C., *"Plain Meaning": Justice Scalia's Jurisprudence of Strict Statutory Construction*, 17 Harvard Journal of Law & Public Policy 401 (1994).

Kassin, Saul M, and Lawrence S. Wrightsman, *The American Jury on Trial: Psychological Perspectives*, (1988).

———— *"On the Requirements of Proof: The Timing of Judicial Instruction and Mock Juror Verdicts"* in In the Black Box: Controversies in the Courtroom (Lawrence S. Wrightsman, Saul M. Kassin & Cynthia E. Willis eds., 1987).

Katz, Avery, *Taking Private Ordering Seriously*, 144 University of Pennsylvania Law Review 1745 (1996).

Kaus, Mickey, *The End of Equality* (1992).

Kaye, D.H., *The Probability of an Ultimate Issue: The Strange Case of Paternity Testing*, 75 Iowa Law Review 75 (1989).

———— *What is Bayesianism: A Guide for the Perplexed*, 28 Jurimetrics Journal 161 (1988).

Keele, Lucy M., *An Analysis of Six Versus Twelve Person Juries*, 27 Tennessee Bar Journal 32 (1991).

Keeling, Byron C., *Toward a Balanced Approach to "Frivolous" Litigation: A Critical Review of Federal Rule 11 and State Sanctions Provisions*, 21 Pepperdine Law Review 1067 (1994).

Keeton, George W., and L.A. Sheridan, *Equity* (1976).

Keeton, Robert E., *Trial Tactics and Methods* (1973).

Keith, A.M., *Domestic Violence and the Court System*, 15 Hamline Law Review 105 (1991).

Kelleher, Leslie M., *The December 1993 Amendments to the Federal Rules of Civil Procedure—A Critical Analysis,* 12 Touro Law Review 7 (1995).

Kellor, Frances, *American Arbitration: Its History, Functions and Achievements* (1984).

Kennard, Karen L., *The Victim's Veto: A Way to Increase Victim Impact on Criminal Case Dispositions*, 77 California Law Review 417 (1989).

Kerr, Norbert L. and Robert J. MacCoun, *The Effects of Jury Size and Polling Method on the Process and Product of Jury Deliberation*, 48 Personality & Psychology 349 (1985).

Kesan, Jay P., *A Critical Examination of the Post-Daubert Scientific Evidence Landscape*, 52 Food & Drug Law Journal 225 (1997).

Kiernan, V.G., *The Duel in European History* (1988).

Kinder, Donald R., and Don Herzog, *"Democratic Discussion"* in Reconsidering the Democratic Public (George E. Marcus & Russell L. Hanson eds., 1993).

King, Charles H., Comment, *Trial Practice—Demurrer Upon Evidence as a Device for Taking a Case From the Jury*, 44 Michigan Law Review 468 (1945).

King, Nancy J., *Racial Jurymandering: Cancer or Cure? A Contemporary Review of Affirmative Action in Jury Selection*, 68 New York University Law Review 808 (1993).

Kirst, Roger W., *Administrative Penalties and the Civil Jury: The Supreme Court's Assault on the Seventh Amendment*, 126 University of Pennsylvania Law Review 1281 (1978).

——— *The Jury's Historic Domain in Complex Cases*, 58 Washington Law Review 1 (1982).

Klein, Kenneth S., *The Myth of How to Interpret the Seventh Amendment Right to a Civil Jury Trial*, 53 Ohio State Law Journal 1005 (1992).

Knight, Charles Jared, *State-Law Punitive Damage Schemes and the Seventh Amendment Right to Jury Trial in the Federal Courts*, 14 Review of Litigation 657 (1995).

Koehler, Jonathan J., *Error and Exaggeration in the Presentation of DNA Evidence at Trial*, 34 Jurimetrics Journal 21 (1993).

Koffler, Joseph H., and Allison Reppy, *Handbook of Common Law Pleading* (1969).

Kotler Martin A., *Reappraising the Jury's Role as Finder of Fact*, 20 Georgia Law Review 123 (1985).

Kramrick, Isaac, ed., *The Federalist Papers* (1987[1788]).

Krauss, Stanton D., *The Original Understanding of the Seventh Amendment Right to Jury Trial*, 33 University of Richmond Law Review 407 (1999).

Kritzer, Herbert M., *Adjudication to Settlement: Shading in the Gray*, 70 Judicature 161 (1986).

Kronman, Anthony T., *The Lost Lawyer: Failing Ideals of the Legal Profession* (1993).

Kunert, Karl H., *Some Observations on the Origin and Structure of Evidence Rules Under the Common Law System and the Civil Law System of "Free Proof" in the German Code of Civil Procedure*, 16 Buffalo Law Review 122 (1966).

Kurland, Philip B., *The Rise and Fall of the "Doctrine" of Separation of Powers*, 85 Michigan Law Review 592 (1986).

Kymlicka, Wayne and Wayne Norman, *Return of the Citizen: A Survey of Recent Work on Citizenship Theory* in Theorizing Citizenship (Ronald Beiner ed., 1995).

Kymlicka, Will, *Contemporary Political Philosophy: An Introduction* (1990).

Lambros, Thomas, The Summary Jury Trial—An Alternative Method of Resolvingbisputes, 69 Judicature 286 (1986).

Lambros, Thomas D., and Thomas H. Shunk, *The Summary Jury Trial*, 29 Cleveland State Law Review 43 (1980).

Landsman, Stephan A., *The Adversary System: A Description and Defense* (1984).

——— *A Brief Survey of the Development of the Adversary System*, 44 Ohio State Law Journal 713 (1983).

——— *The Civil Jury in America: Scenes from an Unappreciated History*, 44 Hastings Law Journal 574 (1993).

——— *The Decline of the Adversary System: How the Rhetoric of Swift and Certain Justice has Affected Adjudication in American Courts*, 29 Buffalo Law Review 487 (1980).

———— *Readings on Adversarial Justice: The American Approach to Litigation* (1988).

Langbein, John H., *The German Advantage in Civil Procedure*, 52 University of Chicago Law Review 823 (1985).

Larson, Arthur, *Workers' Compensation Law: Cases, Materials and Text* (1992).

Lawson, Frederick, H., *A Common Lawyer Looks at the Civil Law* (1955).

Laycock, Douglas, *The Triumph of Equity*, 56 Law & Contemporary Problems 53 (1993).

Lederman, Leandra, *Which Cases Go to Trial?: An Empirical Study of Predictors of Failure to Settle*, 49 Case Western Reserve Law Review 315 (1999).

Lee, J.D., and Barry Lindahl, *Modern Tort Law* (1994).

Leipold, Andrew D., *Rethinking Jury Nullification*, 82 Virginia Law Review 253 (1996).

Lempert, Richard, *"Civil Juries and Complex Cases: Taking Stock After Twelve Years"* in Verdict: Assessing the Civil Jury System (Robert E. Litan ed., 1993).

———— *Civil Juries and Complex Cases Let's Not Rush to Judgment*, 80 Michigan Law Review 68 (1981).

———— *Uncovering "Nondiscernible" Differences*, 73 Michigan Law Review 643 (1975).

Leonard, David P., *Appellate Review of Evidentiary Rulings*, 70 North Carolina Law Review 1155 (1992).

———— *Power and Responsibility in Evidence Law*, 63 Southern California Law Review 937 (1990).

Lettow, Renee B., *New Trial for Verdict Against Law: Judge-Jury Relations in Early Nineteenth-Century America*, 71 Notre Dame Law Review 505 (1996).

Levin, A. Leo, *Equitable Clean-up and the Jury: A Suggested Orientation*, 100 University of Pennsylvania Law Review 320 (1951).

Levin, A. Leo, and Denise D. Colliers, *Containing the Cost of Litigation*, 37 Rutgers Law Review 219 (1985).

Levine, Marcy J., *Summary Judgment: The Majority View Undergoes a Complete Reversal in the 1986 Supreme Court*, 37 Emory Law Journal 171 (1988).

Levy, Leonard W., *The Palladium Justice: Origins of Trial by Jury* (1999).

Lewis, J.R., *Outlines of Equity* (1968).

Lieberman, Jethro K., *The Litigious Society* (1981).

Lieske, Robert, *Civil Forfeiture Law: Replacing the Common Law with the Common Sense Application of the Excessive Fines Clause of the Eighth Amendment*, 21 William Mitchell Law Review 265 (1995).

Lind, E.Allan. *et al.*, *Discovery and Presentation of Evidence in Adversary and Nonadversary Proceedings*, 71 Michigan Law Review 1129 (1973).

Lipset, Seymour Martin, *Political Man* (1960).

Locke, John, *Second Treatise of Government* (1982).

Longhofer, Ronald S., *Jury Trial Techniques in Complex Civil Litigation*, 32 University of Michigan Journal of Law Reform 335 (1999).

Losh, Susan Carol, Adina W. Wasserman and Michael A. Wasserman, *"Reluctant Jurors:" What Summons Responses Reveal About Jury Duty Attitudes*, 83 Judicature 304 (2000).

Louis, Martin B., *Federal Summary Judgment Doctrine: A Critical Analysis*, 83 Yale Law Journal 745 (1974).

Luban, David, *Settlements and the Erosion of the Public Realm*, 83 Georgia Law Journal 2619 (1995).

Luneburg, William V., and Mark A. Nordenberg, *Specially Qualified Juries and Expert Nonjury Tribunals: Alternatives for Coping with the Complexities of Modern Civil Litigation*, 67 Virginia Law Review 887 (1981).

Macario, Matthew J., *Constitutional Law—Punitive Damage Awards and Procedural Due Process in Products Liability Cases—Honda Motor Co., Ltd. v. Oberg, 114 Supreme Court 2711 (1994)*, 68 Temple Law Review 409 (1995).

MacCoun, Robert, *Decisionmaking by Civil Juries*, in Verdict: Assessing the Civil Jury System, (Robert E. Litan ed., 1993).

——— *Inside the Black Box: What Empirical Research Tells Us About Decisionmaking by Civil Juries*, in Verdict: Assessing the Civil Justice System (Robert E. Litan ed., 1993).

Magleby, David B., *Let the Voters Decide? An Assessment of the Initiative and Referendum Process*, 66 University of Colorado Law Review 13 (1995).

Magliocca, Gerard N., The Philosopher's Stone: Dualist Democracy and the Jury, 69 University of Colorado Law Review 175 (1977).

Maitland, F.W., *The Constitutional History of England* (1908).

——— *Equity, Also the Forms of Action at Common Law* (1920).

Malott, R.H., *America's Liability Explosion, Can We Afford the Cost?*, 52 Vital Speeches of the Day 80 (1986).

Maltz, Earl, *The Nature of Precedent*, 66 University of North Carolina Law Review 367 (1988).

Mansbridge, Jane, *Beyond Adversary Democracy* (1983).

Marcus, Richard L., *The Revival of Fact Pleading Under the Federal Rules of Civil Procedure*, 86 Columbia Law Review 433 (1998).

Marder, Nancy S., *Beyond Gender: Peremptory Challenges and the Roles of the Jury*, 73 Texas Law Review 1041 (1995).

Marshall, Prentice H., *A View from the Bench: Practical Perspectives on Juries*, 1990 University of Chicago Law Forum 147.

Martin, James P., *When Repression is Democratic and Constitutional: The Federalist Theory of Representation and the Sedition Act of 1789*, 66 University of Chicago Law Review 117 (1999).

McArthur, John Burritt, *The Strange Case of American Civil Procedure and the Missing Uniform Discovery Time Limits*, 24 Hofstra Law Review 865 (1996).

McBaine, J.P., *Burden of Proof: Degrees of Belief*, 32 California Law Review 242 (1944).

McBride, Robert L., *The Art of Instructing the Jury*, (1969).

McCaskill, Oliver L., *Actions and Causes of Action*, 34 Yale Law Journal 614 (1925).

McCoid John C., II, *Procedural Reform and the Right to Jury Trial: A Study of Beacon Theatre, Inc. v. Westover*, 116 University of Pennsylvania Law Review 1 (1967).

McCormick, William N., *The American Tort System, A Time to Rebalance the Scales of Justice*, 52 Vital Speeches of the Day 267 (1986).

McDonald, Forrest, *Novus Ordo Seclorum* (1985).

McDonald's Coffee Award Reduced 75% by Judge, Wall Street Journal, at A4, (September 15, 1994).

McDowell, Gary L., *Curbing the Courts: The Constitution and the Limits of Judicial Power* (1988).

McFarland, Douglas D., *The Unconstitutional Stub of Section 1441(c)*, 54 Ohio State Law Journal 1059 (1993).

McGillis, Daniel and Joan Mullen, *Neighborhood Justice Centers: An Analysis of Potential Models* (1977).

McGinley, Ann C., *Credulous Courts and the Tortured Trilogy: he Improper Use of Summary Judgment in Title VII and ADEA Cases*, 34 Boston College Law Review 203 (1993).

McGonagle, John H., Jr., *Arbitration of Consumer Disputes*, 27 Arbitration Journal 65 (1972).

McKay, Robert B.,*Rule 16 and Alternative Dispute Resolution*, 63 Notre Dame Law Review 818 (1988).

McMillan, Theodore, Honorable, and Christopher J. Petrini, Batson v. Kentucky: *A Promise Unfilled*, 58 University of Missouri at Kansas City Law Review 361 (1990).

Meads, Melanie A., *Applying the Resonable Woman Standard in Evaluating Sexual Harrassment Claims: Is It Justified?*, 17 Law & Psychology Review 209 (1993).

Mecham, L.Ralph, *Administrative Office of the United States Courts, Annual Report of the Director* (1996).

Meese, Edwin, III, *A Return to Constitutional Interpretation From Judicial Law-Making*, 40 New York Law School Review 925 (1996).

Megarry, Robert and P. V. Baker, *Snell's Principles of Equity* (1973).

Melilli, Kenneth J., Batson *in Practice: What We Have Learned About* Batson *and Peremptory Challenges*, 71 Notre Dame Law Review 447 (1996).

Menez, Joseph F., *Decision Making in the Supreme Court of the United States: A Political and Behaviorial View* (1984).

Menkel-Meadow, Carrie, *Pursuing Settlement in an Adversary Culture: A Tale of Innovation Co-opted of "The Law of ADR"*, 19 Florida State Law Review 1 (1991).

———— *Whose Dispute Is It anyway?: A Philosophical and Democratic Defense of Settlement (In Some Cases)*, 83 Georgia Law Journal 2663 (1995).

Merritt, Deborah Jones and Kathryn Barry, *Is the Tort System in Crisis? New Empirical Evidence*, 60 Ohio State Law Journal 315 (1988).

Michelman, Frank, *Law's Republic*, 97 Yale Law Journal 1493 (1988).

Milich, Paul S., *Hearsay Antinomies: The Case for Abolishing the Rule and Starting Over*, 71 Oregon Law Review 723 (1992).

Mill, John Stuart, *On Liberty* (1978).

———— *"Representing Government"* in 43 Great Books of the Western World (1952).

Millar, Robert Wyness, *Civil Procedure of the Trial Court in Historical Perspective* (1952).

Three American Ventures in Summary Civil Procedure, 38 Yale Law Journal 193 (1928).

Millon, David, *Positivism in the Historiography of the Common Law*, 1989 Wisconsin Law Review 669 (1989).

Mills, Lawrence R., *Six-Member and Twelve-Member Juries: An Empirical Study of Trial Results*, 6 Michigan Journal of Legal Reference 671 (1973).
Milsom, S.F.C., *Historical Foundations of the Common Law* (1981).
——— *Law and Fact in Legal Development*, 17 Toronto Law Review 1 (1967).
Minow, Martha, *Making All the Difference: Inclusion, Exclusion, and American Law* (1990).
Mitnick, John Marshall, *From Neighbor-Witness to Judges of Proofs: Transformation of the English Civil Juror*, 32 American Journal of Legal History 201 (1998).
Mnookin, Robert H., and Robert B., Wilson, *Rational Bargaining and Market Efficiency: Understanding Pennzoil v. Texaco*, 75 Virginia Law Review 295 (1989).
Mogin, Paul, *Why Judges, Not Juries, Should Set Punitive Damages*, 65 University of Chicago Law Review 179 (1998).
Monaghan, Henry P., *Constitutional Fact Review*, 85 Columbia Law Review 229 (1985).
Moore, Karen Nelson, *The Supplemental Jurisdiction Statute: An Important But Controversial Supplement to Federal Jurisdiction*, 41 Emory Law Journal 31 (1992).
Moore, Lloyd E., *The Jury: Tool of Kings, Palladium of Liberty* (1988).
Moore, James Wm., *et al.*, *Moore's Federal Practice* (1999).
Moorehead, James Donald, *Compromising the Hearsay Rule: The Fallacy of Res Gestae Reliability*, 19 Loyola of Los Angeles Law Review 203 (1996).
Morgan, Edmund M., *A Brief History of Special Verdicts and Special Interrogatories*, 32 Yale Law Journal 575 (1923).
——— *Hearsay Dangers and the Application of the Hearsay Concept*, 62 Harvard Law Review 177 (1948).
——— *Some Problems of Proof Under the Anglo-American System of Litigation* (1956).
Morgan, Robert J., *James Madison on the Constitution and the Bill of Rights* (1988).
Morgan, S. Reed, *McDonald's Burned Itself*, Legal Times, p. 26 (September 19,1994).
Moses, Margaret L., *What the Jury Must Hear: The Supreme Court's Evolving Seventh Amendment Jurisprudence*, 68 George Washington Law Review 29 (2000).
Motomura, Hiroshi, *Arbitration and Collateral Estoppel: Using Preclusion to Shape Procedural Choices*, 62 Tulane Law Review 29 (1988).
Mueller, Christopher B. and Laird C. Kirkpatrick, *Federal Evidence* (1994).
Mulhall, Stephen and Adam Swift, *Liberals and Communitarians* (1996).
Murphy, Colleen P., *Determining Compensation: The Tension Between Legislative Power and Jury Authority*, 74 Texas Law Review 345 (1995).
——— *Integrating the Constitutional Authority of Civil and Criminal Juries*, 61 George Washington Law Review 723 (1993).
Nader, Laura, and Harry F. Todd, Jr., eds., *The Disputing Process: Law in Ten Societies* (1978).
Navarro, Monica P., *Salvaging Civil Forfeiture Under the Drug Abuse and Control Act*, 41 Wayne Law Review 1609 (1995).
Neal, Wendy S., *The Future of Scientific Evidence in Toxic Tort Litigation*, 67 University of Cincinnati Law Review 881 (1999).

Nelken, Melissa L., *Sanctions Under Federal Rule 11-Some "Chilling" Problems in the Struggle Between Compensation and Punishment,* 74 Georgetown Law Journal 1313 (1986).

Nelson, Thomas O., *Savings and Forgetting from Long-term Memory,* 10 Journal of Verbal Learning & Verbal Behavior 571 (1971).

Nelson, William E., *The Americanization of the Common Law* (1975)

――― *The Eighteenth Century Background of John Marshall's Constitutional Jurisprudence,* 76 Michigan Law Review 893 (1978).

Nemeth, Charlan, *Interactions Between Jurors as a Function of Majority vs. Unanimity Decision Rules* in In the Jury Box: Controversies in the Court Room (Lawrence S. Wrightsman, Saul M. Kassin & Cynthia E. Willis eds., 1987).

Nesson, Charles, *Agent Orange Meets the Blue Bus: Factfinding at the Frontier of Knowledge,* 66 Boston University Law Review 521 (1986).

Newberg, Herbert and Alba Conter, *Newberg on Class Actions* (1992).

Note, *The Changing Role of the Jury in the Nineteenth Century,* 74 Yale Law Journal 170 (1964).

Note, *Discovery Abuse Under the Federal Rules: Causes and Cures,* 92 Yale Law Journal 352 (1982).

Note, *The Erie Doctrine and Nonunanimous Civil Jury Verdicts,* 4 American Journal of Trial Advocacy 665 (1981).

Note, *Public Disclosures of Jury Deliberations,* 96 Harvard Law Review 886 (1983).

Nunn, Sandra L., *The Due Process Ramifications of Punitive Damages, Continued: TXO Production Corp. v. Alliance Resources Corp.,* 63 University of Cincinnati Law Review 1029 (1995).

Oakley, Ellwood F., III and Donald O. Mayer, *Arbitration of Employment Discrimination Claims and the Challenge of Contemporary Federalism,* 47 South Carolina Law Review 475 (1996).

Okin, Susan Miller, *Justice, Gender, and the Family* (1989).

Olson, Trisha, *Of Enchantment: Passing of the Ordeals and the Rise of the Jury Trial,* 50 Syracuse Law Review 109 (2000).

Olson, Walter, *The Litigation Explosion: What Happened When America Unleashed the   Lawsuit* (1991).

Osborn, Albert S., *The Mind of the Juror* (1937).

O'Connell, Jeffrey, *The Lawsuit Lottery: Only the Lawyers Win* (1979).

――― *The Liability Maze: The Impact of Liability Law on Safety and Innovation* (1991).

O'Connell, Jeffrey and C. Brian Kelly, *The Blame Game: Injuries, Insurance, and Injustice,* (1987).

Pabst, William R., Jr., *Statistical Studies of the Costs of Six-Man Versus Twelve-Man Juries,* 14 William & Mary Law Review 326 (1972).

Padawer-Singer, Alice M., *et al., "An Experimental Study of Twelve vs. Six Member Juries Under Unanimous vs. Nonunanimous Decisions"* in Psychology in the Legal Process (Bruce Dennis Sales ed., 1977).

――― *"Justice or Judgments"* in The American Jury System, Final Report of the Annual Chief Justice Earl Warren Conference on Advocacy in the United States (1977).

Page, Benjamin I. and Robert Y. Shapiro, *The Rational Public and Democracy* in Reconsidering the Democratic Public (George E. Marcus & Russell L. Hanson eds., 1993).

Pagels, Heinz R., *The Cosmic Code* (1982).

Parker, J. Wilson, *Free Expression and the Function of the Jury*, 65 Boston University Law Review 483 (1989).

Parker, Jeffrey J., *Contingent Expert Witness Fees: Access and Legitimacy*, note, 64 California Law Review 1363 (1991).

Pateman, Carole, *Participation and Democratic Theory* (1970).

Patterson, Caleb Perry, *The Constitutional Principles of Thomas Jefferson* (1953).

Peck, Cornelius J., *A Critique of the National Labor Relations Board's Performance in Policy Formulation: Adjudication and Rule Making*, 117 University of Pennsylvania Law Review 254 (1968).

Peckham, Robert F.,*The Federal Judge as a Case Manager: The New Role in Guiding a Case from Filing to Disposition*, 69 California Law Review 770 (1981).

Perry, H. Ross, *Common-Law Pleading* (1897).

Perschbacher, Rex R.,*Rethinking Collateral Estoppel: Limiting the Preclusive Effect of Administrative Determinations in Judicial Proceedings*, 35 University of Florida Law Review 422 (1983).

Petrocik, John R., and Daron Shaw, *"Nonvoting in America: Attitudes and Context"* in Political Participation and American Democracy (William Crotty ed., 1991).

Petzinger, Thomas, Jr., *Oil and Honor: The Texaco-Pennzoil Wars* (1987).

Pierce, David E., Note, *Informing the Jury of the Legal Effect of Its Answers to Special Verdict Questions Under Kansas Comparative Negligence Law—A Reply to the Masses; A Case for the Minority View*, 16 Washburn Law Journal 114 (1976).

Pierce, Lawrence W., *Summary Judgment: A Favored Means of Summarily Resolving Disputes*, 53 Brooklyn Law Review 279 (1987).

Pierce, Richard J., Jr., *et al.*, *Administrative Law and Process* (1992).

Plucknett, Theodore F. T., *A Concise History of the Common Law* (1956).

Pocock, J. G. A., *"The Ideal of Citizenship Since Classical Times"* in Theorizing Citizenship (Ronald Beiner ed., 1995).

Polasky, Alan N., *Collateral Estoppel-Effects of Prior Litigation*, 39 Iowa Law Review 217 1954).

Pollack, Milton, *Pretrial Procedures More Effectively Handled*, 65 Federal Rules Decisions 475 (1974).

Pollock, Frederick and Frederic William Maitland, *The History of English Law* ([1968]1898).

Pomeroy, John N., *Remedies and Remedial Rights by the Civil Action According to the Reformed American Procedure* (1876).

Pomeroy, John Norton, *A Treatise on Equity Jurisprudence* (1941).

Posner, Richard A., *An Economic Approach to the Law of Evidence*, 51 Stanford Law Review 1477 (1999).

——— *The Federal Courts: Challenge and Reform* (1996).

———— *The Summary Jury Trial and Other Methods of Alternative Dispute Resolution: Some Cautionary Observations*, 53 University of Chicago Law Review 366 (1986).

———— *Will the Federal Courts of Appeals Survive Until 1984? An Essay on Delegation and Specialization of the Judicial Function*, 56 Southern California Law Review 761 (1983).

Powell, Edward, *Settlement of Disputes by Arbitration in Fifteenth-Century England*, 2 Law & History Review 21 (1984).

Prettyman, E. Barrett, *Jury Instructions-First or Last?*, 60 American Bar Association Journal 1066 (1960).

Priest, George L., *The Current Insurance Crisis and Modern Tort Law*, 96 Yale Law Journal 1521 (1987).

———— *The Invention of Enterprise Liability: A Critical History of the Intellectual Foundations of Modern Tort Law*, 14 Journal of Legal Studies 461 (1985).

———— *"Justifying the Civil Jury"* in Verdict: Assessing the Civil Justice System (Robert E. Litan ed., 1993).

———— *The Role of the Civil Jury in a System of Private Litigation*, 1990 University of Chicago Legal Forum 161.

Pro, Philip M. and Thomas C. Hnatowski, *Measured Progress: The Evolution and Administration of the Federal Magistrate Judges System*, 44 American University Law Review 1503 (1995).

Proposed Amendments to the Federal Rules of Appellate, Bankruptcy, Civil, and Criminal Procedure and Evidence, 163 Federal Rules Decisions 91 (1995).

Prosser, William L., *The Law of Torts* (1964).

Purcell, Edward R., *The Crisis of Democratic Theory: Scientific Naturalism and the Problem of Value* (1973).

———— *Settlement of Disputes by Arbitration in Fifteenth-Century England*, 2 Law & History Review 21 (1984).

Putnam, Robert D., *"The Strange Disappearance of Civic America"* in The American Prospect, No. 24, p. 34 (1996).

Quayle: Are There Too Many Lawyers in America?, New Jersey Law Journal (August 29, 1991).

Rachlinski, Jeffrey J., *Scientific Jury Selection and the Equal Protection Rights of Venire Persons*, 24 Pacific Law Journal 1497 (1993).

Raiffa, J., *Decision Analysis: Introductory Lectures on Choices Under Uncertainty* (1968).

Ramirez, Deborah A., *The Mixed Jury and the Ancient Custom of Trial by Jury De Medietate Linguae: A History and a Proposal for Change*, 74 Boston University Law Review 777 1994).

Ramsmeyer, Mark, *Products Liability Through Private Ordering: Notes on a Japanese Experiment*, 144 University of Pennsylvania Law Review 1823 (1996).

Rank, Timothy C., Note, *Federal Rule of Evidence 606(b) and the Post-Trial Reformation of Civil Jury Verdicts*, 76 Minnesota Law Review 142 (1992).

Rapp, James A. and Frank Carrington, *Victims' Rights: Law and Litigation* (1991).

Ratliff, Jack, *Offensive Collateral Estoppel and the Option Effect*, 67 Texas Law Review 63 (1988).

Redish, Martin H., *Legislative Courts Administrative Agencies, and the Northern Pipeline Decision,* 1993 Duke Law Journal 197.

——— *Seventh Amendment Right to Jury Trial: A Study in the Irrationality of Rational Decision Making,* 70 Northwestern University Law Review 486 (1975).

Redish, Martin H. and Daniel J. LaFave, *Seventh Amendment Right to Jury Trial in Non-Article- III Proceedings: A Study in Dysfunctional Constitutional Theory,* 4 William & Mary Bill of Rights Journal 407 (1995).

Rembar, Charles, *The Law of the Land: The Evolution of Our Legal System* (1980).

Resnik, Judith, *Managerial Judges,* 96 Harvard Law Review 376 (1982).

Reuben, Richard C., *Excuses, Excuses: Any Old Facially Neutral Reason May Be Enough to Defeat an Attack on a Peremptory Challenge,* 82 American Bar Association Journal 20 (1996).

Rhine, Jennie, *The Jury: A Reflection of the Prejudices of the Community,* 20 Hastings Law Journal 1417 (1969).

Ricci, David M., *The Tragedy of Political Science* (1984).

Rifkind, Simon, *A Special Court for Patent Litigation? The Danger of a Specialized Judiciary,* 37 American Bar Association Journal 425 (1951).

Riggs, Robert, *Constitutionalizing Punitive Damages: The Limits of Due Process,* 52 Ohio State Law Journal 859 (1991).

Risinger, D.Michael, *Another Step in the Counter-Revolution: A Summary Judgment on the Supreme Court's New Approach to Summary Judgment,* 54 Brooklyn Law Review 35 (1988).

Rogers, Nancy H., and Richard A. Salem, *A Student's Guide to Mediation and the Law* (1987).

Rokes, Willis Park, *No-Fault Insurance* (1971).

Roper, Robert T., *Jury Size and Verdict Consistency: "A Line Has to be Drawn Somewhere",* 14 Law & Society Review 977 (1980).

Rose-Ackerman, Susan, *Defending the State: A Skeptical Look at "Regulatory Reform" in the Eighties,* 61 Colorado Law Review 517 (1990).

Rosen, Mark D., *What Has Happened to the Common Law?-Recent American Codifications and Their Impact on Judicial Practice and the Law's Subsequent Development,* 1994 Wisconsin Law Review 1119.

Rosenberg, Gerald N., *The Hollow Hope* (1991).

Rosenburg, Maurice, *The Pretrial Conference and Effective Justice* (1964).

——— *Resolving Disputes Differently: Adieu to Adversary Justice?,* 21 Creighton Law Review 801 (1988).

Rossi, Jim, *Participation Run Amok: The Costs of Mass Participation for Deliberative Agency Decisionmaking,* 92 Northwestern University Law Review 173 (1997).

Rotunda, Ronald., *et al., Treatise on Constitutional Law: Substance and Procedure* (1986).

Rousseau, Jean-Jacques, *The Social Contract* in 38 Great Books of the Western World (1952).

Rowe, Thomas D., Jr., *American Law Institute Study on Paths to a "Better Way": Litigation, Alternatives and Accommodation: Background Paper,* 1989 Duke Law Journal 824 (1989).

———— *Compounding or Creating Confusion About Supplemental Jurisdiction? A Reply to Professor Freer*, 40 Emory Law Journal 943 (1991).

———— *No Final Victories: The Incompleteness of Equity's Triumph in Federal Public Law*, 56 Law & Contemporary Problems 105 (1993).

Rubin, Paul H., John E. Calfee and Mark F. Grady, *B.M.W v. Gore: Mitigating the Punitive Economics of Punitive Damages*, 5 Supreme Court Economic Review 179 (1997).

Rudstein, David S., *Civil Penalties and Multiple Punishment Under the Double Jeopardy Clause: Some Unanswered Questions*, 46 Oklahoma Law Review 587 (1993).

Russell, Franklin Ferriss, *Outline of Legal History* (1929).

Rutland, Robert Allen, *The Birth of the Bill of Rights* (1955).

Sabino, Anthony Michael, Esq., *Jury Trials, Bankruptcy Judges, and Article III: The Constitutional Crisis of the Bankruptcy Court*, 21 Seton Hall Law Review 258 (1991).

Saks, Michael J., *The Aftermath of Daubert: An Evolving Jurisprudence Expert Evidence*, 40 Jurimetrics 229 (2000).

———— *Do We Really Know Anything About the Behavior of the Tort Litigation System- And Why Not?*, 140 University of Pennsylvania Law Review 1147 (1992).

———— *Jury Verdicts: The Role of Group Size and Social Decision Rule* (1978).

———— *Malpractice Misconceptions and Other Lessons About the Litigation System*, 16 The Justice System Journal 7 (1993).

———— *The Smaller the Jury, the Greater the Unpredictability*, 79 Judicature 263 (1996).

Sales, James B., & Kenneth B. Cole, Jr., *Punitive Damages: A Relic That Has Outlived Its Origins*, 37 Vanderbilt Law Review 1117 (1984).

Saltzburg, Stephen A.,*"Improving the Quality of Jury Decisionmaking,"* in Verdict: Assessing the Civil Justice System (Robert E. Litan ed., 1993).

———— *The Unnecessarily Expanding Role of the American Trial Judge*, 64 Virginia Law Review 1 (1978).

Sandel, Michael J., *Democracy's Discontent* (1996).

Sanders, Joseph, *Scientifically Complex Cases, Trial by Jury, and the Erosion of Adversarial Processes*, 48 DePaul Law Review 355 (1988).

Sanders, Joseph and Craig Joyce, *Off to the Race: The 1980s Tort Crisis and the Law Reform Process*, 27 Houston Law Review 207 (1990).

Sarokin, H. Lee and G. Thomas Munsterman, *"Recent Innovations in Civil Jury Trial Procedures,"* in Verdict: Assessing the Civil Justice System (Robert E. Litan ed., 1993).

Saunders, Ruth, *The Circuit Courts' Application of Daubert v. Merrell Dow Pharmaceuticals, Inc.*, 46 Drake Law Review 407 (1997).

Sayler, Robert N., *Rambo Litigation: Why Hardball Tactics Don't Work*, 74 American Bar Association Journal 78 (1988).

Schaffer, Stuart F., *Informing the Jury of the Legal Effect of Special Verdict Answers in Comparative Negligence Actions*, 1981 Duke Law Journal 824 (1981).

Scheflin, Alan W. And John M. VanDyke, *Merciful Juries: The Resilience of Jury Nullification*, 48 Washington & Lee Law Review 165 (1991).

Schkade, David, Cass R. Sunstein and Daniel Kahneman, *Are Juries Less Erratic Than Individuals? Deliberation, Polarization, and Punitive Damages*, John M. Olin Law & Economics Working Paper No. 81, (2000).

Schmidhauser, John R., *Judges and Justices: The Federal Appellate Judiciary* (1979).

Schnapper, Eric, *Judges Against Juries-Appellate Review of Federal Civil Jury Verdicts*, 1989 Wisconsin Law Review 237 (1989).

Schuck, Peter, *Agent Orange on Trial: Mass Toxic Disasters in the Courts* (1986).

———— *"Mapping the Debate on Jury Reform"* in Verdict: Assessing the Civil Justice System (Robert E. Litan ed., 1993).

Schumpeter, Joseph, *Capitalism, Socialism, and Democracy* (1950).

Schwartz, Bernard, *Administrative Law* (1984).

Schwartz, Edward P. and Warren F. Schwartz, *Decisionmaking by Juries Under Unanimous and Supermajority Voting Rules*, 80 Georgetown Law Review 775 (1992).

Schwartz, Rachael E., *"Everything Depends on How You Draw the Lines": An Alternative Interpretation of the Seventh Amendment*, 6 Seton Hall Constitution Law Journal 599 (1996).

Schwarzer, William W., *The Federal Rules, The Adversary System, and Discovery Reform*, 50 University of Pittsburgh Law Review 703 (1989).

———— *Reforming Jury Trials*, 132 Federal Rules Decisions 581 (1991).

———— *Rule 11 Revisited*, 101 Harvard Law Review 1013 (1988).

———— *Summary Judgment Under the Federal Rules: Defining Genuine Issues of Material Fact*, 99 Federal Rules Decisions 465 (1984).

Schwarzer, William W., and Alan Hirsch, *"The Modern American Jury: Reflections on Veneration and Distrust,"* in Verdict: Assessing the Civil Justice System (Robert E. Litan ed., 1993).

Scott, Austin Wakeman, *Fundamentals of Procedure in Actions at Law* (1922).

———— *Trial by Jury and the Reform of Civil Procedure*, 31 Harvard Law Review 669 (1918).

Seidman, Louis Michael, *Points of Intersection: Discontinuities at the Junction of Criminal Law and the Regulatory State*, 7 Journal of Contemporary Legal Issues 165 (1996).

Selvin, Molly and Larry Picus, *The Debate Over Jury Performance: Observations from a Recent Asbestos Case* (1987).

Semmel, Herbert, *Collateral Estoppel, Mutuality, Joinder of Parties*, 68 Columbia Law Review 1457 (1968).

Serrato, Veronica, *Expert Testimony in Child Abuse Prosecutions: The Spectrum of Uses, Note*, 68 Boston University Law Review 155 (1988).

Seymour, Margaret B., Honorable, *Dispositive Motions and the Role of the United States Magistrate Judge*, 50 South Carolina Law Review 639 (1999).

Shapiro, David L., *The Choice of Rulemaking or Adjudication in the Development of Administrative Policy*, 78 Harvard Law Review 921 (1965).

———— *Federal Rule 16: A Look at the Theory and Practice of Rulemaking*, 137 University of Pennsylvania Law Review 1969 (1989).

Shapiro, David L., and Daniel R. Coquillette, *The Fetish of Jury Trial in Civil Cases: A Comment on* Rachal v. Hill, 85 Harvard Law Review 442 (1971).

Sharp, Malcolm P., *The Classical American Doctrine of "The Separation of Powers,"* 2 University of Chicago Law Review 385 (1935).

Shell, G. Richard, *Res Judicata and Collateral Estoppel Effects of Commercial Arbitration*, 35 University of California at Los Angeles Law Review 623 (1988).

Shimomura, Floyd D., *The History of Claims Against the United States: The Evolution From a Legislative Toward a Judicial Model of Payment*, 45 Louisiana Law Review 625 (1985).

Shipman, Benjamin J., *Handbook of Common Law Pleading*, (1895).

Shuman, Daniel W., Prof. and Dr. Jean A. Hamilton, *Jury Service-It May Change Your Mind Perceptions of Fairness of Jurors and Nonjurors*, 46 Southern Methodist University Law Review 449 (1992).

Silberman, Linda, *Judicial Adjuncts Revisited: The Proliferation of Ad Hoc Procedure*, 137 University of Pennsylvania Law Review 2131 (1989).

Siciliano, John A., *Corporate Behavior and the Social Efficiency of Tort Law*, 85 Michigan Law Review 1820 (1987).

Silver, Charles, *A Restitutionary Theory of Attorney's Fees in Class Actions*, 76 Cornell Law Review 656 (1991).

Sinclair, Kent and Patrick Hanes, *Summary Judgment: A Proposal for Procedural Reform in a Core Motion Context*, 36 William & Mary Law Review 1633 (1995).

Singer, Linda R., *Settling Disputes: Conflict Resolution in Business, Families, and the Legal System* (1990).

Singer, Norman, *Sutherland on Statutory Construction* (1992).

Skakalik, James, et al., *Discovery Management: A Further Analysis of the Civil Justice Reform Act Evaluation Data*, 39 British Columbia Law Review 613 (1998).

Skelton, Robert G., and Donald F. Harris, *Bankruptcy Jurisdiction and the Jury Trials: The Constitutional Nightmare Continues*, 8 Bankruptcy Developments Journal 469 (1991).

Slusser, William C., et al., *A Step-by-Step guide to Making and Challenging Peremptory Challenges in Federal Courts*, 37 South Texas Law Review 127 (1996).

Smith, Andrew MacGregor, *Using Impartial Experts in Valuation: A Forum-Specific Approach*, 35 William & Mary Law Review 1241 (1994).

Smith, Douglas G., *Structural and Functional Aspects of the Jury: Comparative Analysis and Proposals for Reform*, 48 Alabama Law Review 441 (1997).

Snortum, John R., *The Impact of an Aggressive Juror in Six-and Twelve-Member Juries*, 3 Criminal Justice & Behavior 255 (1976).

Sobol, Joanna, *Hardship Excuses and Occupational Exemptions: The Impairment of the "Fair Cross-Section of the Community,"* 69 California Law Review 155 (1995).

Sorenson, Charles W., *Disclosure Under Federal Rule of Civil Procedure 2(a): Much Ado About Nothing?*, 46 Hastings Law Journal 679 (1995).

Sorini, Marc E., *Factual Malice: Rediscovering the Seventh Amendment in Public Person Libel Cases*, 82 Georgetown Law Journal 563 (1993).

Spencer, Janet Mateson, and Joseph M. Zammit, *Mediation-Arbitration: A Proposal for Private Resolution of Disputes Between Divorced or Separated Parents*, 1976 Duke Law Journal 911 (1976).

Spooner, Lysander, *An Essay on the Trial by Jury* (1852).

Spragens, Thomas A., Jr., *"Communitarian Liberalism"* in New Communitarian Thinking (Amitai Etzioni ed., 1996).

Spufford, Peter, *Origins of the English Parliament* (1967).

Stacy, Tom and Kim Dayton, *Rethinking Harmless Constitutional Error*, 88 Columbia Law Review 79 (1988).

Stein, Mark S., *Rule 11 in the Real World: How the Dynamics of Litigation Defeat the Purpose of Imposing Attorney Fee Sanctions for the Assertion of Frivolous Legal Arguments*, 132 Federal Rules Decisions 309 (1990).

Stein, Peter G., *Roman Law, Common Law and Civil Law*, 66 Tulane Law Review 1591 (1992).

Stempel, Jeffrey W., *Sanctions, Symmetry, and Safe Harbors: Limiting Misapplication of Rule 11 by Harmonizing It With Pre-Verdict Dismissal Devices*, 60 Fordham Law Review 257 (1991).

————— *A Distorted Mirror: The Supreme Court's View of Summary Judgment, Directed Verdict, and the Adjudicative Process*, 49 Ohio State Law Journal 95 (1988).

Stephen, Henry John, *A Treatise on the Principles of Pleading in Civil Actions* (1882).

Stephens, Pamela J., *Controlling the Civil Jury: Towards a Functional Model of Justification:* 76 Kentucky Law Journal 81 (1987).

Stewart, Charles D., and Philip G. Piggott, *Punitive Damages Since* Pacific Mutual Life Insurance Co. v. Haslip, 16 American Journal of Trial Advocacy 693 (1993).

Stimson, Shannon C., *The American Revolution in the Law: Anglo-American Jurisprudence Before John Marshall* (1990).

Stone, Geoffrey, *et al.*, *Constitutional Law* (1996).

Story, Joseph, *Equity Jurisprudence* (1886).

Stourzh, Gerald, *Alexander Hamilton and the Idea of Republican Government* (1970).

Strauss, Peter L., *The Common Law and Statutes*, 70 University of Colorado Law Review 225 (1999).

————— The Place of Agencies in Government: Separation of Powers and the Fourth Branch, 84 Columbia Law Review 573 (1984).

Strier, Franklin, *Making Jury Trials More Truthful*, 30 University of California at Davis Law Review 95 (1996).

————— *What Can the American Adversary System Learn From an Inquisitorial System of Justice*, 76 Judicature 109 (1992).

Subrin, Stephen N., How Equity Conquered Common Law: The Federal Rules of Civil Procedure in *Historical Perspective*, 135 University of Pennsylvania Law Review 909 (1987).

Sugarman, Paul R., and Marc G. Perlin, *Proposed Changes to Discovery Rules in Aid of "Tort Reform": Has the Case Been Made?*, 42 American University Law Review 1465 (1993).

Sullivan, Margaret Pedrick, Comment, *The Scope of Modern Arbitral Awards*, 62 Tulane Law Review 1113 (1988).

Sunderland, Edson R., *The Inefficiency of the Jury*, 13 Michigan Law Review 302 (1915).

—— *Scope and Method of Discovery Before Trial*, 42 Yale Law Journal 863 (1933).

—— *Verdicts: General and Special*, 29 Yale Law Journal 253 (1920).

Sunstein, Cass R., *Beyond the Republican Revival*, 97 Yale Law Journal 1539 (1988).

—— *The Partial Constitution* (1993).

—— *What's Standing After Lujan? Of Citizen Suits, "Injuries", and Article III*, 91 Michigan Law Review 163 (1992).

Sunstein, Cass R., Daniel Kahnman and David Schkade, *Assessing Punitive Damages*, 107 Yale Law Journal 2071 (1988).

The Supreme Court, 1994 Term, 109 Harvard Law Review 10 (1995).

Susskind, Lawrence and Gerard McMahon, *The Theory and Practice of Negotiated Rulemaking*, 3 Yale Journal of Regulation 133 (1985).

Sward, Ellen E., *Appellate Review of Judicial Fact-finding*, 40 Kansas Law Review 1 (1991).

—— *Legislative Courts, Article III, and the Seventh Amendment*, 77 North Carolina law Review 1037 (1999).

—— *Values, Ideology, and the Evolution of the Adversary System*, 64 Indiana Law Journal Law Journal 301 (1989).

Symposium, Amended Rule 11 of the Federal Rules of Civil Procedure, 54 Fordham Law Review 1 (1985).

Symposium: Legal Storytelling, 87 Michigan Law Review 2073 (1989).

Symposium: The Civil Rights Act of 1991: Theory and Practice, 68 Notre Dame Law Review 911 (1993).

Symposium: The Civil Rights Acts of 1991: Unraveling the Controversy, 45 Rutgers Law Review 887 (1993).

Symposium: Is the Jury Competent?, 52 Law & Contemporary Problems 1 (1989).

Tamm, Edward A., *The Five-Man Civil Jury: A Proposed Constitutional Amendment*, 51 Georgetown Law Journal 120 (1962).

Tanford, Alexander, *Racism in the Adversary System: The Defendant's Use of Peremptory Challenges*, 63 Southern California Law Review 1015 (1990).

Tannen, Deborah, *Gender and Discourse*, (1994).

Teixeira, Ruy A., *Why Americans Don't Vote*, (1988).

Terrell, Timothy P., *Rights and Wrongs in the Rush to Repose: On the Jurisprudential Dangers of Alternative Dispute Resolution in the Federal Courts*, 36 Emory Law Journal 541 (1987).

Thayer, James Bradley, *The Origin and Scope of the American Doctrine of Constitutional Law* (1908).

—— *A Preliminary Treatise on Evidence at the Common Law* (1898).

Thomas, Richard M., *Formalism and Functionalism: From* Northern Pipeline *to* Thomas v. Union Carbide Agricultural Products Co., 37 Syracuse Law Review 1003 (1986).

Thompson, Faith, *Magna Carta: Its Role in the Making of the English Constitution* (1948).

Thompson, Robert S., *Decision, Disciplined Inferences and the Adversary Process*, 13 Cardozo Law Review 725 (1991).

Tobias, Carl, *Civil Justice Reform Sunset*, 1998 University of Illinois Law Review 547 (1998).

——— *Public Law Litigation and the Federal Rules of Civil Procedure*, 74 Cornell Law Review 270 (1989).

——— *Silver Linings in Federal Civil Justice Reform*, 50 Brooklyn Law Review 857 (1993).

Tomasic, Roman and Malcolm N. Feeley, *Neighborhood Justice: Assessment of an Emerging Idea* (1980).

Tribe, Laurence H., *American Constitutional Law* (1988).

——— *Trial by Mathematics: Precision and Ritual in the Legal Process*, 84 Harvard Law Review 1372 (1971).

———*Triangulating Hearsay*, 87 Harvard Law Review 957 (1974).

Twining, William, *The Boston Symposium: A Comment.*, 66 Boston University Law Review 391 (1986).

Underwood, Barbara D., *Ending Race Discrimination in Jury Selection: Whose Right Is It, Anyway?*, 92 Columbia Law Review 725 (1992).

Van Caenegem, R.C., *The Birth of the English Common Law* (1988).

——— *Royal Writs in England from the Conquest to Glanvill* (1959).

Vanderbilt, Arthur T., *Judges and Jurors: Their Function, Qualifications, and Selection*, 36 Boston University Law Review 1 (1956).

VanDyke, Jon M., *Jury Selection Procedures: Our Uncertain Commitment to a Representative Panels* (1971).

VanEngen, Brian K., *Post-Gilmer Developments in Mandatory Arbitration: The Expansion of Mandatory Arbitration for Statutory Claims and the Congressional Effort to Reverse the Trend*, 21 Journal of Corporation Law 391 (1996).

Vargo, John F., *The Emperor's New Clothes: The American Law Institute Adorns a "New Cloth" for Section 402A Products Liability Design Defects—A Survey of the States Reveals a Different Weave*, 26 University of Memhis Law Review 492 (1996).

Verkuil, Paul R., *Separation of Powers, the Rule of Law and the Idea of Independence*, 30 William & Mary Law Review 301 (1989).

Vidmar, Neil, *Are Juries Competent to Decide Liability in Tort Cases Involving Scientific/Medical Issues: Some Data From Medical Malpractice*, 43 Emory Law Journal 885 (1994).

——— *Medical Malpractice and The American Jury* (1995).

——— *The Performance of the American Civil Jury: An Empirical Perspective*, 40 Arizona Law Review 849 (1998).

Vidmar, Neil and Jeffrey Rice, *Jury-Determined Settlements and Summary Jury Trials: Observation About Alternative Dispute Resolution in an Adversary Culture*, 19 Florida State University Law Review 89 (1991).

Viscusi, W. Kip, *Corporate Risk Analysis: A Reckless Act?*, 52 Stanford Law Review 547 (2000).

———— *The Social Costs of Punitive Damages Against Corporations in Environmental and Safety Torts*, 87 Georgetown Law Journal 285 (1999).

Waggoner, Michael J., *Fifty Years of Bernhard v. Bank of America is Enough: Collateral Estoppel Should Require Mutuality, But Res Judicata Should Not*, 12 Review of Litigation 391 (1993).

Walbert, David F., *The Effect of Jury Size on the Probability of Conviction: An Evaluation of* Williams v. Florida, 22 Case Western Reserve Law Review 1529 (1971).

Walker, Laurens and John Monahan, *Daubert and the Reference Manual: An Essay on the Future of Science in Law*, 82 Virginia Law Review 837 (1996).

Walker, R.J., *The English Legal System* (1980).

Waltz, Jon R., *Judicial Discretion in the Admission of Evidence Under the Federal Rules of Evidence*, 79 Northwestern University Law Review 1097 (1984-85).

Walzer, Michael, *Spheres of Justice: A Defense of Pluralism and Equality* (1983).

Warner, Daniel M., *Direct Democracy: The Right of the People to Make Fools of Themselves; The Use and Abuse of Initiative and Referendum*, 19 Seattle University Law Review 47 (1995).

Waxman, Ned W., *Jury Trials After Granfinanciera: Three Proposals for Reform*, 52 Ohio State Law Journal 705 (1991).

Weber, Mark C., *The Federal Civil Rules Amendments of 1993 and Complex Litigation: A Comment on Transsubstantivity and Special Rules for Large and Small Federal Cases*, 14 Review of Litigation 113 (1994).

Wegner, William, *et al.*, *California Practice Guide to Civil Trials and Evidence* (1993-95).

Weiner, Stephen A., *The Civil Jury and the Law-Fact Distinction*, 54 California Law Review 1867 (1966).

Weinstein, Jack B., and Margaret A. Berger, *Weinstein's Federal Evidence*, (1997).

Welling, Sarah N., *Discovery of Nonparty's Tangible Things Under the Federal Rules of Civil Procedure*, 59 Notre Dame Law Review 110 (1983).

———— *Victim Participation in Plea Bargainings*, 65 Washington University Law Quarterly 301 (1987).

White, Albert Beebe, *The Making of the English Constitution* (1908).

Whitten, Ralph U., *Consent, Caseload, and other Justifications for Non-Article III Courts and Judges: A Comment on* Commodities Futures Trading Commission v. Schor, 20 Creighton Law Review 11 (1986).

Wiegand, Shirley A., *A New Light Bulb for the Work of the Devil? A Current Assessment of Summary Jury Trials*, 69 Oregon Law Review 87 (1990).

Wiehl, Lloyd L., *The Six-Man Jury*, 4 Gonzaga Law Review 35 (1986).

Wigmore, John Henry, *Evidence in Trials at Common Law* (1983).

Willging, Thomas E., *et al.*, *An Empirical Study of Discovery and Disclosure Practice Under the 1993 Federal Rules Amendments*, 39 Boston College Law Review 525 (1986).

Williams, Gerald R., *Legal Negotiation and Settlement* (1983).

Williams, Patricia,*The Alchemy of Race and Rights* (1991).

Wolfe, Christopher, *The Rise of Modern Judicial Review* (1986).

Wolfram, Charles W., *The Constitutional History of the Seventh Amendment*, 57 Minnesota Law Review 639 (1973).

Wolfson, Barry M., *Defendant Class Actions*, 38 Ohio State Law Journal 459 (1977).

———— *Statutes of Limitations and Defendant Class Actions*, 82 Michigan Law Review 347 (1983).

Wright, Charles Alan, *Law of Federal Courts* (1994).

Wright, Charles Alan and Arthur Miller, *Federal Practice and Procedure* (1995).

Wright, Charles Alan and Arthur R.Miller and Mary Kay Kane, *Federal Practice and Procedure* (1995).

Wright, Charles Alan, Arthur R. Miller and Edward H. Cooper, *Federal Practice and Procedure*, (1988).

Wright, Charles Alan and Kenneth W. Graham, *Federal Pratice and Procedure* (1977).

Yaroshefsky, Ellen, *Balancing Victims' Rights and Vigorous Advocacy for the Defendant*, 1989 Annual Survey of American Law 135.

Yeazell, Stephen C., *The Misunderstood Consequences of Modern Civil Process*, 1994 Wisconsin Law Review 631.

———— *The New Jury and the Ancient Jury Conflict*, 1990 University of Chicago Legal Forum 87.

Young, Gordon G., *Public Rights and the Federal Judicial Power: From* Murray's Lessee *Through* Crowell *to* Schor, 35 Buffalo Law Review 765 (1986).

Zeisel, Hans, *...And Then There Were None: The Diminution of the Federal Jury*, 38 University of Chicago Law Review 710 (1971).

———— *The Debate Over the Civil Jury in Historical Perspective*, 1990 University of Chicago Law Forum 25.

———— *The Waning of the American Jury*, 58 American Bar Association Journal 367 (1972).

Zeisel, Hans *et al.*, *Delay in the Court*, (1978).

Zeisel, Hans and Shari Seidman Diamond, *"Convincing Empirical Evidence" on the Six Member Jury*, 41 University of Chicago Law Review 281 (1974).

Zimmerman, Reinhard, *The Law of Obligations: Roman Foundations of the Civilian Tradition*, (1990).

Zion, James W., and Robert Yazzie, *Indigenous Law in North America in the Wake of the Conquest*, 20 Boston College International & Comparative Law Review 55 (1997).

Zobel, Hiller B., *The Jury on Trial*, 46 American Heritage 42 (1995).

Zuckerman, Adrian, *Law, Fact, or Justice?*, 66 Boston University Law Review 487 (1986).

INDEX

Refusal to serve on juries, 240
Remittitur, 304, 308, 310, 297, 299 definition, 11n
Replacement rights, 184n
Representative democracy, 54
Res judicata, 163, 311
Reasonable behavior, 5
Reasonable doubt, 6, 7
Restitution, 173
Revision Act of 1948, 109n
Right to due process, 310
Right to a jury trial, 177, 178, 193, 288n, 290, deprivation of, 337, waive, 205
Right to jury trial in territories, 202, 204
Rights, 87
Roman codes, 140
Roman law, 113n
Rome, 53, 85n
Ross v. Bernhard, 170, 173, 174
Rousseau, Jean-Jacques, 53, 54
Royal justice, 139
Rule of decision, 248
Rules Enabling act, 244n
Rules of Decision Act, 104
Rules of evidence, 82, 83, 251, 261, England, 243
Rules of Practice for the Courts of Equity of the United States, 105n

Sanctions, 123, 124, 125
Scandinavian countries, 76
Schools and colleges, 63
School desegregation, 5, 6, 30
Scientific evidence, 33, 344, rules for, 252, factors for reliability, 252
Scintilla test, 290
Secta, definition, 70
Securities Exchange Commission, 314
Securities fraud, 29
Seditious libel, 59
Self-defense, 108n
Sense of community, 307, 310
Separation of powers, 134, 180

Settlement negotiations, 16, 324, lawsuit, 322
Seventh Amendment, 3, 9, 18, 33n, 56, 98, 134, 155, 157, 161, 168, 170, 173, 174, 175, 177, 178, 180, 190, 192, 194, 196, 198, 203, 204, 209, 211, 218, 275, 284, 289, 290, 293, 294, 301, 309, 317, 334, 337, 345, 347, 348, 349
Sexism, 228
Sexual harassment, 4, 5, 29, 145, 233
Show cause order, 124
Simpson, O.J., 4, 233n
Single-issue pleading rules, 104, 107, 112
Social regulator role of jury, 28
Social science, 56, 137
Social workers, 249
Societal values, conflicting, 25
Society, civilizing rules of, 27
Socrates, 52
Solomon, 77
South Carolina, 210
Sovereign immunity, 182, 199, 350
Special juries, 238
Specific performance, 112, 158
Special verdict, 19, 39n, 97, 299, origins, 299
Standard of proof, heightened, 281
Stare decisis, 273n
Statutes, jury nullification of, 44
Statutory civil rights, 331
Statutory law, 142
Stephens, Pamela, 348
Strauder v. West Virginia, 224
Substantial evidence, 291, test, 293
Substantive law, 138
Substantive legislation, 301
Summary judgment, 19, 129n, 256, 271, 274, 276, 277, 279, 280, 281, 284, 293, 294, 319, 327, 344, 350, origins in U.S., 275
Summary jury trial, 334, 335, 336
Super-majority decision rules, 241
Swain v. Alabama, 225, 229
Symbolism, 27